VERSION 3.1

MW00636778

EXPLORING *the* BODY MACHINE

a Laboratory Manual for Exploring Human Anatomy & Physiology

Daniel Howell, Ph.D.

EXPLORING THE BODY MACHINE, version 3.1
A Laboratory Manual for Exploring Human Anatomy & Physiology
Copyright © 2014 L. Daniel Howell, Ph.D.

All rights reserved. No part of this publication may be used or reproduced in any manner whatsoever without written permission from the copyright holder with the exception of brief quotations for articles and reviews.

Scripture verses are taken from the HOLY BIBLE, NEW INTERNATIONAL VERSION. Copyright © 1973, 1978, 1984 International Bible Society. Used by permission of Zondervan Bible Publishers.

No part of this work may be copied or reprinted without express consent from the author.

Printed in the United States of America.

ISBN: 978-1-4951-1283-6

There are four profits or conditions of Anatomy:
The first forsooth and most, to the might of God to be marveled.
The second, to be knowledgeable of the patient's parts.
The third, to prognosticate of the dispositions to come of the body.
But the fourth is to the curation of sickness.

Guy de Chauliac, *Sermon Universal of Anatomy* (1363)

About the Cover

Did you know that shoes are a primary cause of athlete's foot, toenail fungus, ingrown toenails, hammer toes, fallen arches, bunions, Hallux valgus, blisters, corns, plantar fasciitis and a host of other foot problems? Shoes are even a leading cause of osteoarthritis in the knee and lower back pain.

Most of us think we wear shoes to protect our feet, but the evidence indicates footwear is often more harmful than helpful. We now know that footwear changes the natural human gait when walking and running, and they even change the way we stand. Those changes are negative and result in many of the problems described above. This is mainly because shoe design is dictated by fashion, not function (despite what that shoe company tells you!). A shoe is a tool, like a helmet, and it's prudent to wear shoes under some circumstances, but in our culture we wear them almost all the time, everywhere, and it's this over-use of (poorly designed) footwear that is harming our feet.

Although it is almost universally accepted that shoes are the leading cause of our foot ailments, many podiatrists still insist that we need shoes, especially shoes with "proper support." Indeed, podiatry is the only branch of medicine in which a normal, healthy body part is usually considered insufficient for its function without assistance from a man-made device.

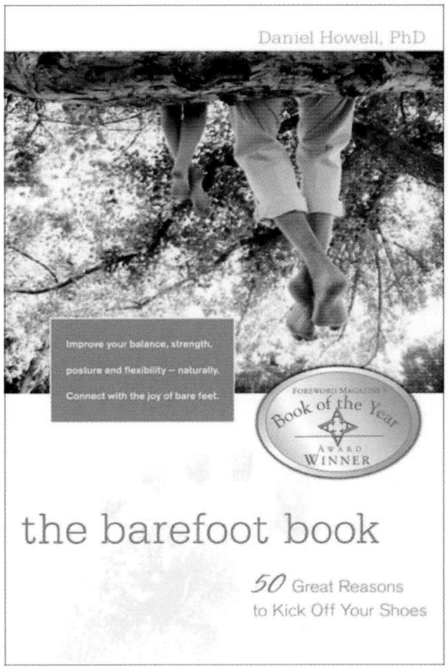

I think differently.

I believe the foot works best when unencumbered by footwear. Like every other part of the body, the foot is perfectly designed for its functions. Very likely, the single best thing you can do for your feet (and knees, hips, and back) is simply *walk barefoot*. In addition, walking barefoot in nature has numerous benefits, including exposure to beneficial bacteria in dirt, tannins in leaves (that toughen your skin), and a delightfully uneven terrain of rocks, roots, and vegetation that stimulates the muscles and reflexes of the lower body. Finally, walking barefoot in nature awakens your senses to your surroundings like nothing else!

Of course, walking barefoot does have risks. Your feet may get bruised and scratched and banged up a little, but those injuries are usually quite minor compared to the long-term effects of shoes. And the more you walk barefoot, the less likely you are to experience injuries. So, do yourself a favor… take a walk. Barefoot!

For more information, check out my website: www.BarefootProfessor.com

TABLE *of* CONTENTS

PREFACE

Human anatomy is a fascinating subject because the subject is *us* – and we humans tend to be fascinated with ourselves. However, learning human anatomy can be a daunting task. When you undertake the study of human anatomy you'll quickly find that there's an enormous amount of cold, hard factual information to memorize. The approach taken by most college textbooks and lab manuals doesn't help the matter. To be fair, those books cram a lot of information into their 1000 or so pages and present the material in a logical and standard format building in complexity. However, they also tend to quickly strip the subject of the fascination that draws many students to it in the first place. By reducing the body to a mountain of bland facts the body becomes less human, less alive. The book you're holding in your hands is meant to be more than a lab manual, it's my attempt to keep the *human* in human anatomy – to bring anatomy back to life and maintain the fascination that can so easily be lost in the details. I've attempted to do this through the liberal use of photography, a casual, conversational writing style and interactive, participatory lab exercises.

My desire for this manual is that it be more than just a treatise on anatomy with the customary exercises, but a *celebration of the human machine*. Many students of anatomy are wanting to enter the medical profession and many of them see their career choice as a "calling." I want to honor that calling by making the study of anatomy as exciting and engaging as possible.

The approach I've taken with respect to illustrations in this manual is considerably more artistic than you'll find in most other anatomy laboratory manuals. First, I prefer photographs of models and actual specimens. Many of the live models pictured in this manual were my own students photographed while performing their lab exercises. I'd like to thank them for their patience as I snapped pictures of their fingers and toes and tongues and other body parts! I also make use of computer renderings from state-of-the-art programs like BioDigital® and the Visible Human Project. Please see the *Note on Anatomical Illustrations* (next page) for more information on these resources.

Finally, this lab manual contains words of wisdom from the greatest Teacher of all. Scripture verses at the beginning of each exercise remind us that the human body is more than physical – we are spiritual beings, too; an important point to remember for many of my students who have a passion for medical missions to impoverished peoples.

Enjoy this manual. May it help you to learn and live better!

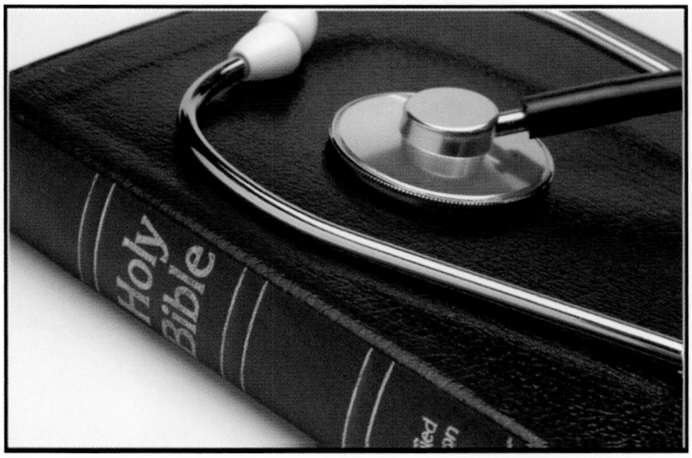

"For you created my inmost being; you knit me together in my mother's womb.

I praise you because I am fearfully and wonderfully made; your works are wonderful, I know that full well."

Psalm 139:13-14

A Note on Anatomical Illustrations

Many of the illustrations in this manual were created using state-of-the-art computer applications, such as The Visible Human Dataset or BioDigital.

The Visible Human database was constructed as part of the Visible Human Project (VHP). The VHP was conceived in 1986 by the National Library of Medicine and brought to fruition over the following 10 years. The datasets (male & female) were produced by transecting frozen male and female cadavers into thin slices and then obtaining high-resolution digital photographs and NMR and CT scans of each slice. The male was transected into 1 mm slices and the female transected into 0.33 mm slices. The datasets, obtained using federal government money, are freely available on the internet through the National Library of Medicine. Most programs for manipulating and viewing the data (e.g., VH Dissector) have been developed by private businesses for purchase, but a few free ones can be found on the internet. Students are encouraged to investigate the Visible Human Project for themselves.

http://www.nlm.nih.gov/research/visible/

BioDigital Human is a virtual human, web-based, interactive application that allows users to visualize the human body in a web browser. The bodies (male and female) are created by 3D artists and computer programmers, not from actual cadavers. Consequently, the product continues to improve as more anatomical details are added regularly. Students are encouraged to explore BioDigital Human for free at *www.biodigital.com.*

exercise 1

anatomical TERMINOLOGY

- introduction to the organ systems -

Now the whole world had one language and a common speech.

Genesis 11:1

Every academic discipline has its own "language" and *Human A & P* is no exception. Before embarking on a study of anatomy, therefore, we must become familiar with the jargon. Many of the names we use in anatomy seem long and strange at first, but they are usually packed with information. This is not the case with people's names. For example, "John" and "Mary" tell us little about those individuals beyond their gender. By contrast, "adductor pollicis brevis muscle" is a very informative name once you learn the meanings of the words. *Pollicis* refers to the thumb, *brevis* means short, and *adductor* specifies a distinct type of motion. Thus, from this muscle's name we can conclude that it's short and moves the thumb in a particular direction (adduction).

Directional References & Planes of Section

Terms that provide directional references and describe planes of section are among the most important to master. The human body is a 3-dimensional object and those terms help orient us when discussing body parts. Pay extra close attention to Figure 1-1 and commit those terms to memory.

Directional references tell us the relative positions of different body parts. We use special terms with exact definitions to describe these positions because words like "above", "behind" or "in front of" can often be ambiguous when describing parts of the body. The terms we use always describe positions with respect to the *anatomical position*, which is standing upright with legs slightly apart, hands by your side with palms facing forward (as shown in Figure 1-1). In that position we would say the hand is **distal** to the elbow, and the head is **superior** to the chest. Even if a person is hanging upside-down, however, we would still describe the head as being superior to the chest because "superior" is in reference to the anatomical position.

Observing the body surface (i.e., surface anatomy) can be very informative, but often we'll want to look inside the body. To do this, we cut the body (figuratively or literally) into slices called planes of section. Sections in the x, y and z planes are particularly useful in the study of anatomy. Cutting the body in the x plane produces a **transverse section**, cutting the body in the z plane

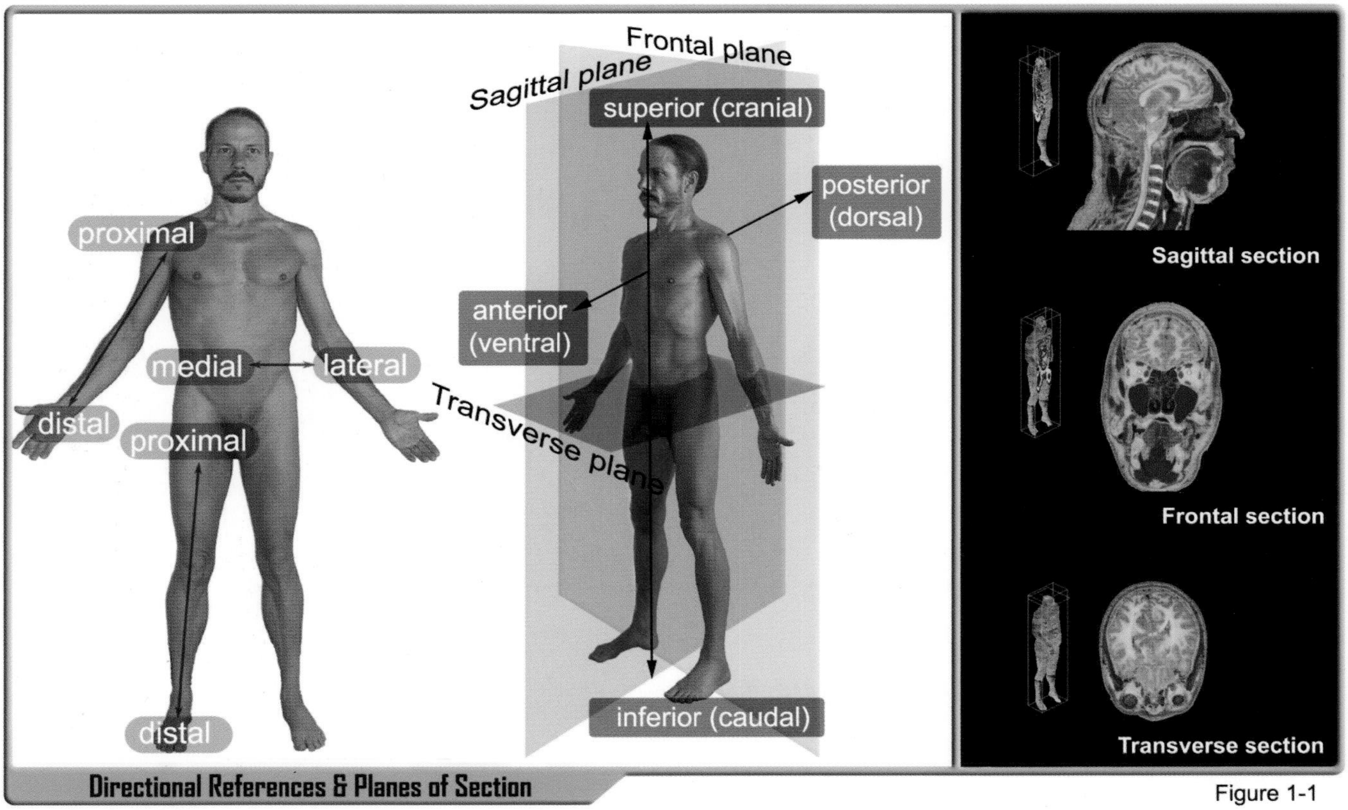

Figure 1-1

produces a **sagittal section** (cutting right between the eyes is called *midsagittal*), and cutting the body in the y plane produces a **frontal section**. To help visualize these planes on yourself, picture this: Standing in the anatomical position, the floor is in the x plane, a midsagittal cut (z plane) would pass between your legs, and a frontal cut (y plane) would separate your front from back. A cut through any plane other than the x, y or z planes produces an *oblique* section. When cutting through the limbs we often refer to the transverse section as a cross-section. Also, we ofter refer to the *longitudinal section* when cutting along the length of the specimen.

In addition to the above directional references, *deep* & *superficial* describe the location of parts relative to the body surface. Deep parts are farther from the surface than superficial parts.

Body Regions & Landmarks

Anatomists divide the human body into major regions and identify a number of body landmarks. It's important to commit these regions and landmarks to memory because they're used abundantly in the study of anatomy (i.e., we will use these terms throughout the course). The major body regions and landmarks include

- **cephalic** – the head region
- **frontal** – the forehead region
- **nasal** – the nose region
- **buccal** – the cheek region
- **oral** – the mouth region
- **mental** – the chin region
- **cervical** – the neck region
- **acromial** – the point of the shoulder
- **thoracic** – the chest region
- **sternal** – the region above the sternum
- **mammary** – the breast region
- **axillary** – the armpit region
- **brachial** – the (upper) arm
- **antecubital** – inside of elbow
- **olecranal** – the posterior elbow
- **antebrachial** – the forearm
- **carpal** – the wrist
- **manual** – the hand
- **abdominal** – the anterior upper extremity

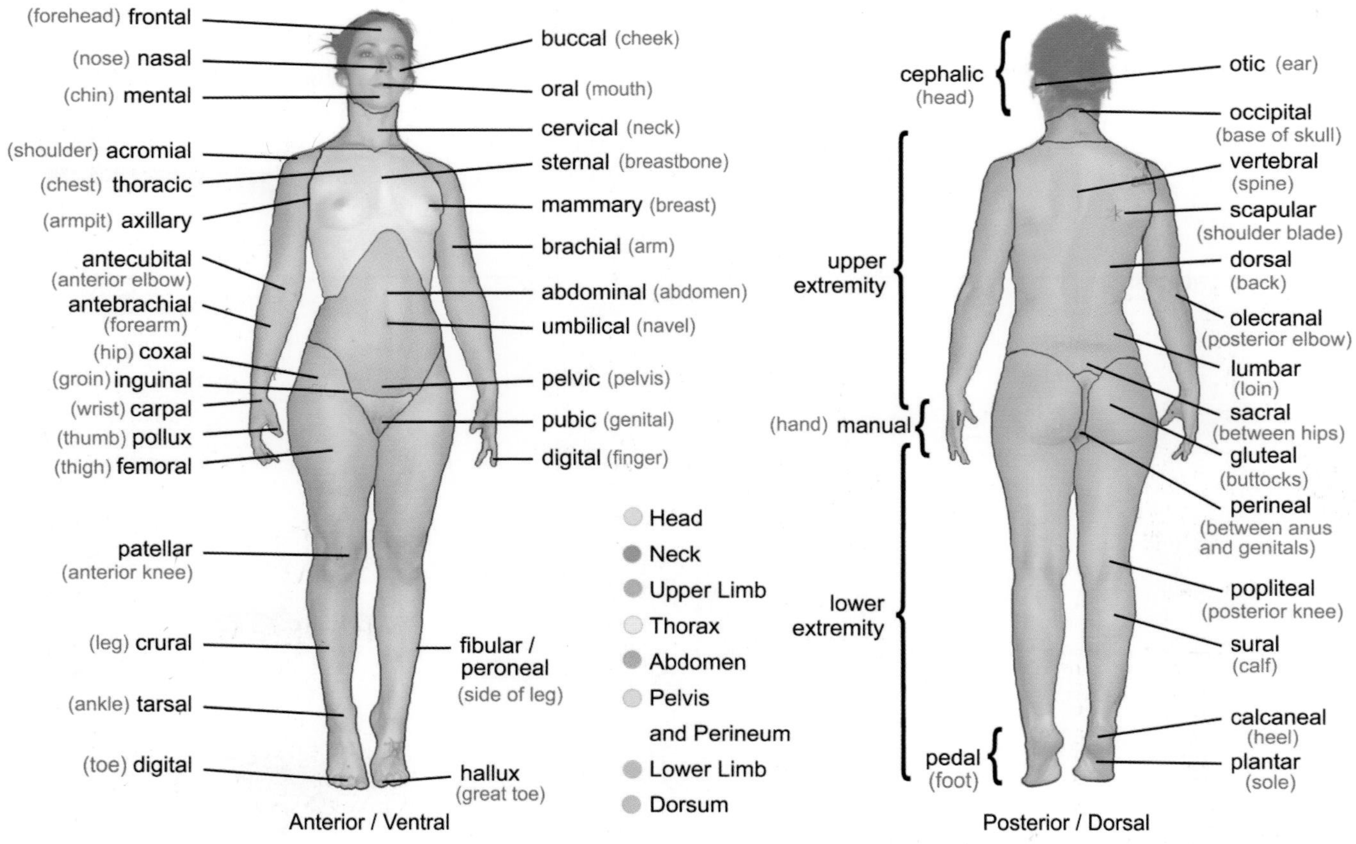

Body Landmarks & Regions Figure 1-2

beneath the ribs

- **umbilical** – the region around the naval
- **coxal** – the hip region
- **inguinal** – the groin region
- **pelvic** – the anterior region enclosed by the pelvic bone
- **pubic** – the genital region
- **femoral** – the thigh region
- **patellar** – the anterior knee
- **crural** – the (lower) leg
- **fibular** / **peroneal** – the side of the leg
- **tarsal** – the ankle
- **pedal** – the foot
- **digital** – the toes & fingers
- **hallux** – the big toe
- **pollux** – the thumb
- **otic** – the ear region
- **occipital** – the back of the head
- **vertebral** – the middle of back over spine
- **scapular** – the shoulder blade
- **dorsal** – the back
- **lumbar** – lower back
- **sacral** – lower back region
- **gluteal** – the buttocks
- **perineal** – the region between the anus and the external genitalia
- **popliteal** – the posterior knee
- **sural** – the posterior leg (calf)
- **calcaneal** – the heal of the foot
- **plantar** – the sole of the foot

Abdominal Regions

Because so many organs are located within the abdomen, this region is subdivided into smaller areas. These areas and the major organs within them are as follows:

- **right hypochondriac region** – portions of the liver, large intestine and gallbladder
- **epigastric region** – portions of the liver, large intestine and stomach
- **left hypochondriac region** – portions of the stomach, large intestine and spleen
- **right lumbar region** – ascending colon of large intestine
- **umbilical region** – small intestine
- **left lumbar region** – descending colon of large intestine
- **right inguinal region** – cecum of large intestine and appendix
- **hypogastric (pubic) region** – small intestine and bladder
- **left inguinal region** – portions of large intestine

Levels of Organization

The human body is a machine built upon a heirarchy of organizational levels. These levels are defined by increases in size and complexity. The smallest level of organization is the **atomic level**. At this level we consider the nature of atoms and

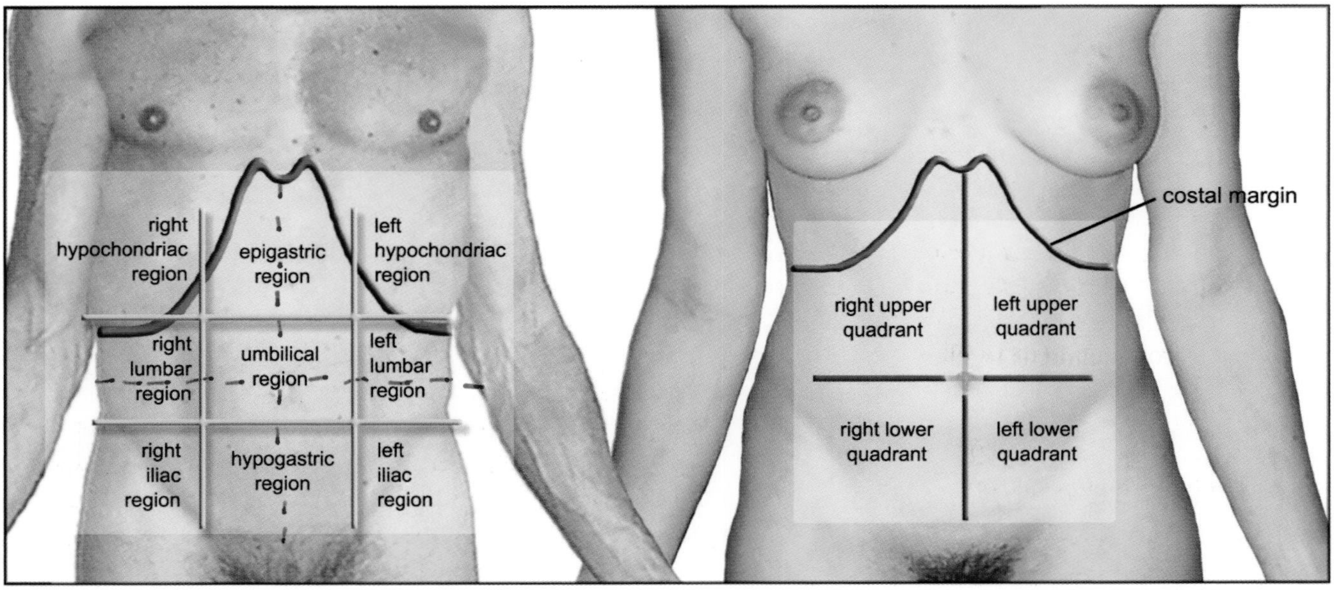

Figure 1-3: Abdominal Regions and Quadrants

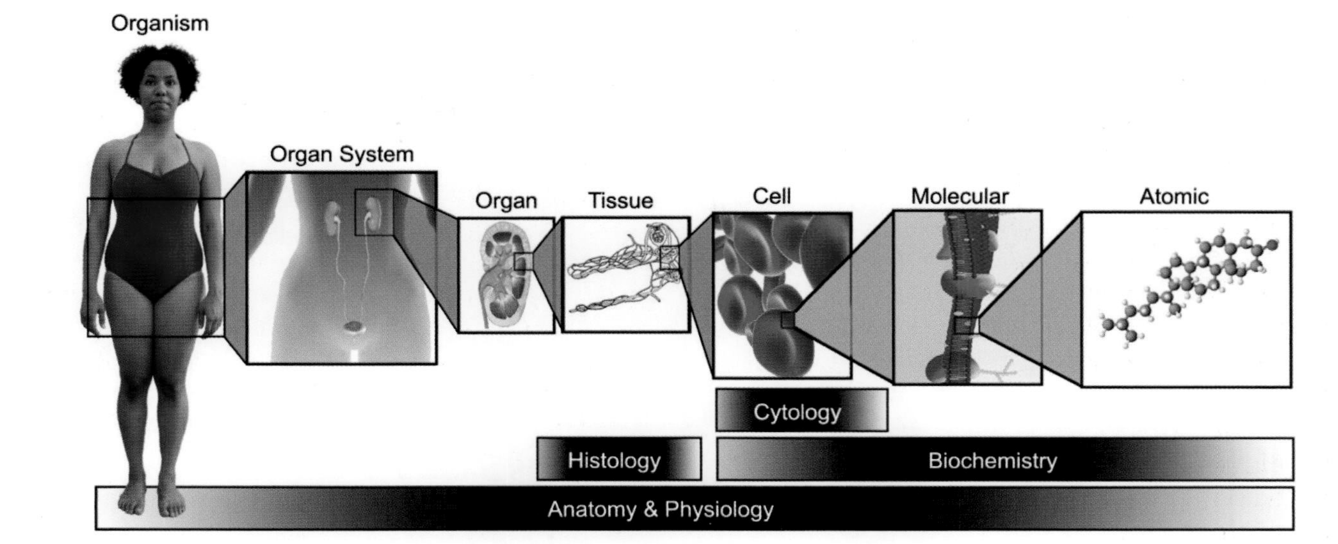

Figure 1-4: The Levels of Organization

how they interact to form small molecules (i.e., chemistry). Atoms are the smallest units of matter and vary in size from about 70 – 500 pm[1] in diameter.

The next level is the **molecular level** of organization. At this level we consider the various biological molecules like proteins, carbohydrates and nucleic acids. The sizes of these molecules vary considerably but are typically in the low nanometer range. For example, the protein hemoglobin is ~4 nm wide and DNA is ~2 nm wide.

Next is the **cellular level** of organization. All living things are made of cells. It's interesting to ponder the nature of life at this level: Cells are living but none of their constituent parts (e.g., proteins and DNA) are alive. A cell may be alive at one moment, then dead the next. The mystical difference between these two states is still a mystery to science. Cells also vary in size, but a typical human cell is 50 – 80 μm across.

Cells rarely live in isolation, rather they group together into communities called tissues to form the **tissue level** of organization. Sheets of cells forming tissues may be visible to the naked eye, ranging from hundreds of micrometers to millimeters in size. In a simple analogy, different tissues can be compared to different types of fabrics, and just as cotton and polyester are stitched together to make blue jeans, different tissues combine to form organs, bringing us to the **organ level** of organization. Most organs are several centimeters in size. Continuing with our fabric analogy, just as blue jeans, T-shirts and jackets can be combined into a wardrobe, different organs work in combination to produce organ systems at the **systemic level** of organization. Finally, eleven organ systems are woven together to produce the **organism** – in our case, the human body – about 2 meters in height.

As indicated in Figure 1-4, there are distinct scientific disciplines that concentrate on a particular organizational level: *Histology* is the study of tissues, *cytology* is the study of cells and *biochemistry* is the study of biological molecules from the cellular to the atomic level. One of the reasons why *Anatomy & Physiology* is such a challenging discipline is that we examine all levels of organization – from the atomic to the organism – and the way each level contributes to the well-being of the individual.

Body Cavities

Most of our internal (or visceral) body organs are enclosed within one of the body cavities (Figure 1-5). These cavities are membrane-lined compartments that allow limited movement of organs within them while simultaneously restricting excessive movements. Until recently, two major body cavities were recognized: The dorsal body cavity and the **ventral body cavity**. Currently, only

[1] pm = picometer = $1x10^{-12}$ meter. See "Units of Metric Measurements" in Exercise 2.

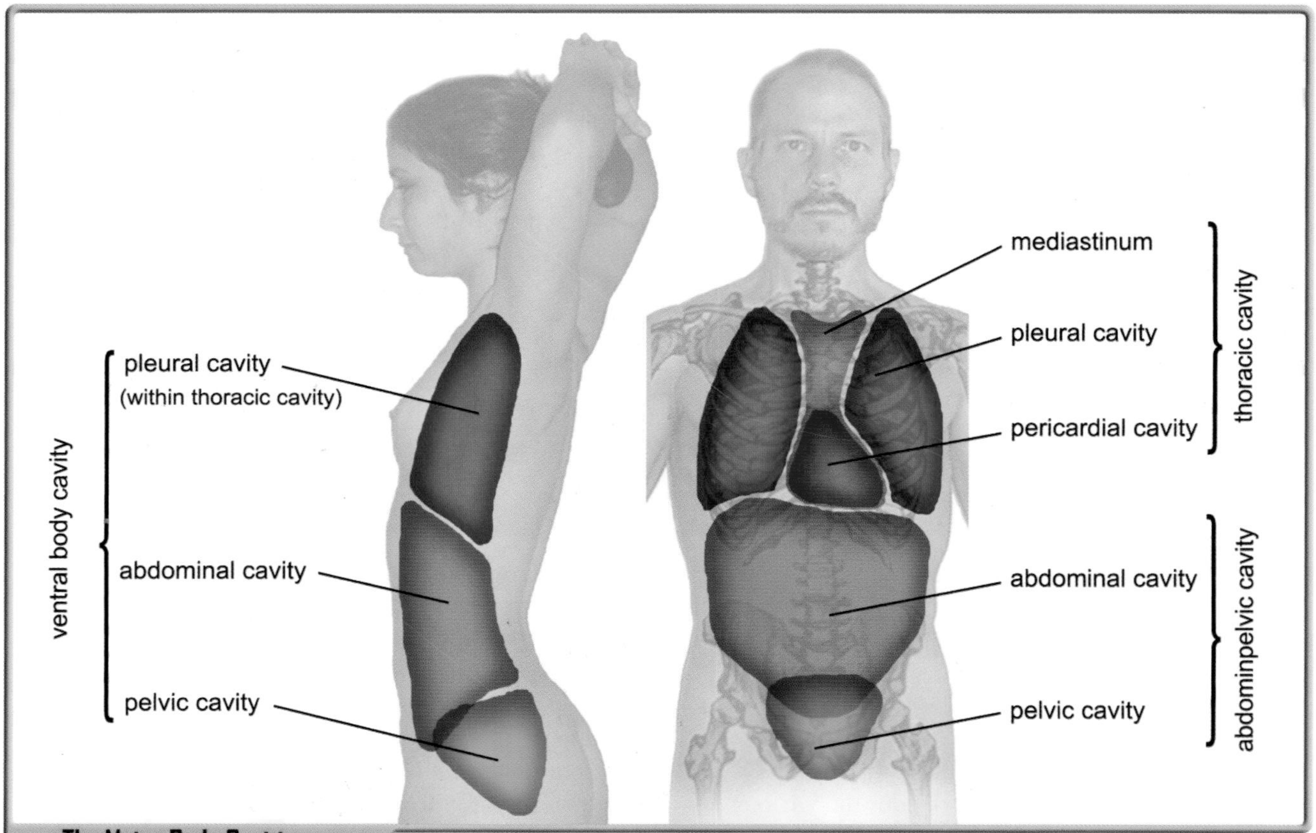

The Major Body Cavities

Figure 1-5

the ventral body cavity – derived from the embryonic coelom – is recognized.

The ventral body cavity is subdivided into the **thoracic cavity** and the **abdominopelvic cavity**. The thoracic cavity contains two **pleural cavities** that house the lungs and the **mediastinum**. Within the mediastinum lies the **pericardial cavity**, which houses the heart.

The thoracic cavity and the abdominopelvic cavity are separated by the diaphragm, a large muscle that facilitates breathing. The abdominopelvic cavity consists of the **abdominal cavity**, which houses organs of the digestive, urinary, lymphatic and other systems, and the **pelvic cavity**, which contains primarily reproductive organs.

As stated previously, each of the above cavities is lined by a membrane, called a *serous membrane*. The serous membrane consists of two layers: the *visceral layer* which lies close to the internal organ and a *parietal layer* which lies against the interior of the body wall. For example, the pleural membrane consists of a visceral pleura against the lung and a parietal pleura against the body wall. In each case there is fluid between the visceral and parietal layers (e.g., pleural fluid between the above mentioned pleural membrane layers).

Activity 1: Memorize Terms

1. Memorize the directional references and planes of section described in the text and figures.
2. Memorize the body landmarks described in the text and figures.
3. Memorize the levels of organization and the body cavities described in the text and figures.

Activity 2: Practicing Terminology
Directional References

1. The wrist is Distal to the elbow.
2. The nose is Distal to the eyes.
3. The head is Superior to the feet.
4. The ears are lateral to the eyes.
5. The bones are deep to the skin.
6. The stomach is inferior to the heart.

Overview of Organ Systems

The human body is a conglomerate of eleven organ systems working in harmony with one another. Each system plays a unique and critical role in the maintenance of homeostasis. We will examine each system in detail as we progress through this manual; however, a brief introduction to each system now will paint a "big picture" that places each organ system in the context of the whole organism.

The eleven organ systems of the body are the **nervous system**, **respiratory system**, **endocrine system**, **cardiovascular system**, **urinary system**, **digestive system**, **reproductive system**, **muscular system**, **lymphatic system**, **skeletal system** and **integumentary system** (shown in figures 1-6 through 1-17). As you first begin to study each system a good question to ask is, "Why does this system exist?" In other words, what does the system do for the body; what is its function? Once you understand the overall function of the system, you can study how the major organs of the system contribute to that function. Often, we will also examine organs at the tissue and cellular levels to see how individual cells allow an organ to perform its job.

As you embark on your study of anatomy, you will become familiar with the eleven organ systems, their overall functions and the major organs of each system.

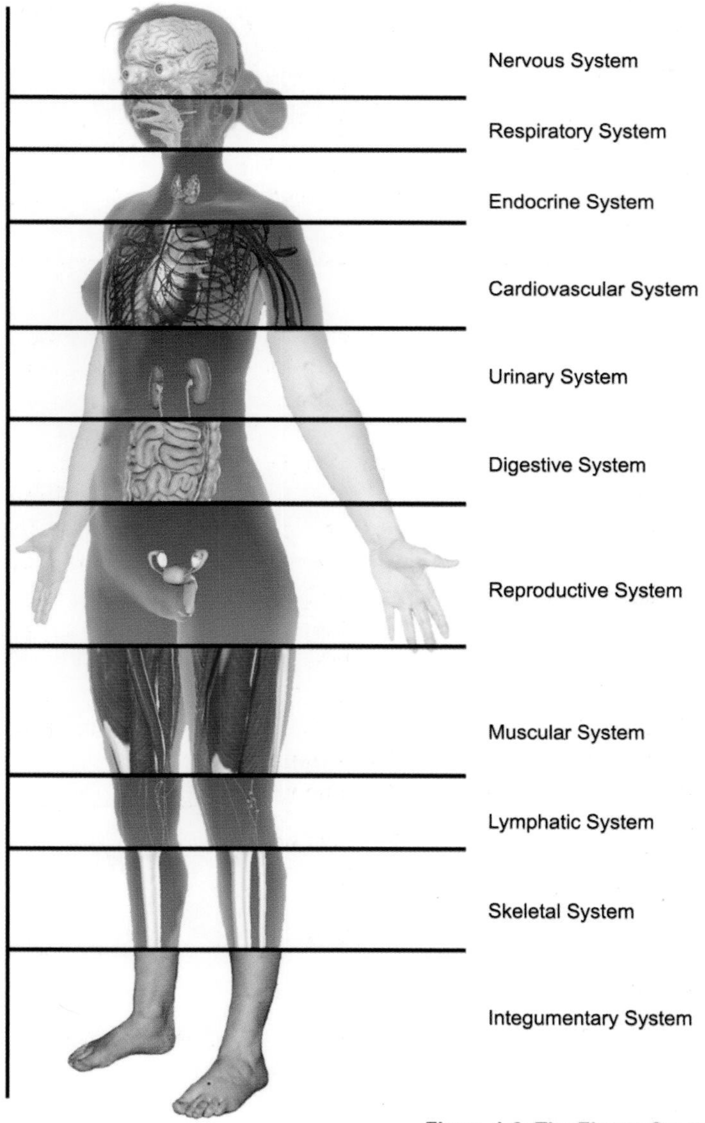

Figure 1-6: The Eleven Organ Systems of the Human Body

The Skeletal System

The skeletal system provides a supporting framework for our bodies, but it also does much more. Our bones work with the cardiovascular system, digestive system and muscular system to help maintain homeostasis and allow body movement.

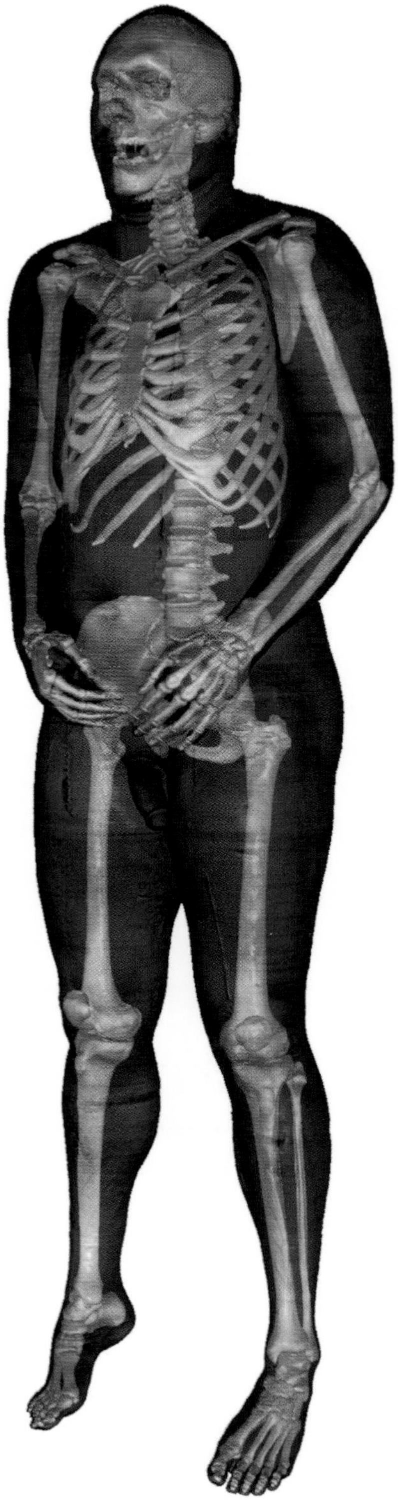

Functions:

- Supporting framework for the body.
- Protects delicate internal organs
- Resevoir for minerals (e.g., calcium)

Major Organs:

- Bones
- Cartilages
- Ligaments
- Joints

Note: The following figures depicting the organ systems – and other figures throughout this manual – were created using the Visible Man database from the Visible Human Project. You can learn more about the Visible Human Project at http://www.nlm.gov/research/visible/

The Nervous System

The nervous and endocrine systems are the two "command-and-control" systems of the body, in that they exert considerable control over the activities of the remaining nine systems. However, the endocrine system, as you will see in exercise 20, is ultimately under the control of the nervous system. Therefore, the nervous system may be thought of as the "master control" system. The nervous system specializes in rapid, real-time communication and information processing.

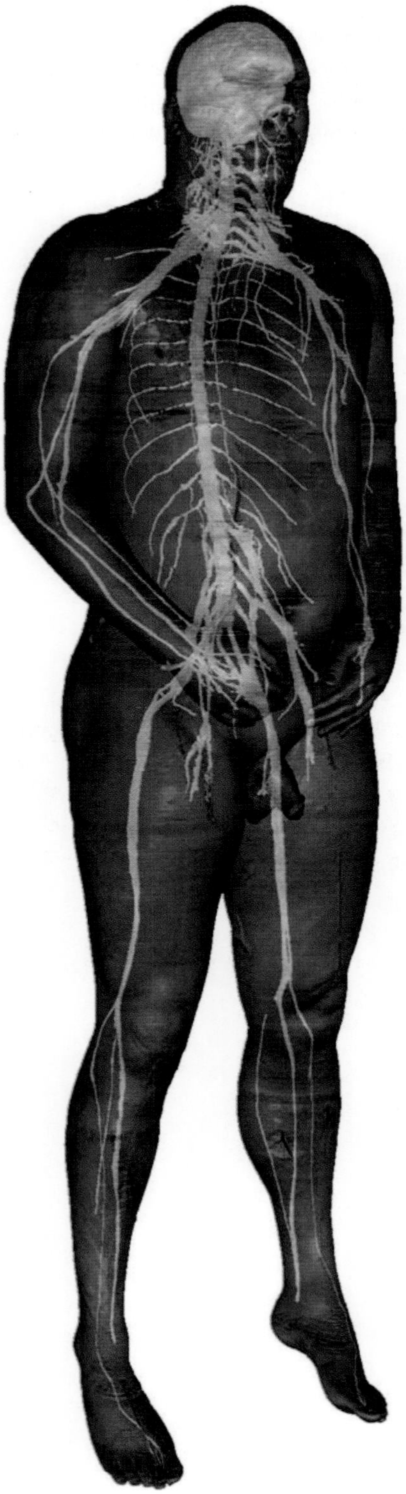

Functions:

- Information processing and transmission.
- Detects internal and external stimuli and allows for rapid responses to potential threats to homeostasis.

Major Organs:

- Brain
- Spinal cord
- Peripheral nerves
- Sensory receptors

The Endocrine System

The endocrine system is one of two "command-and-control" systems of the body. Rather than sending rapid electrical impulses like the nervous system, the endocrine system utilizes chemical messengers (i.e., hormones) that travel through the bloodstream to affect distant parts of the body.

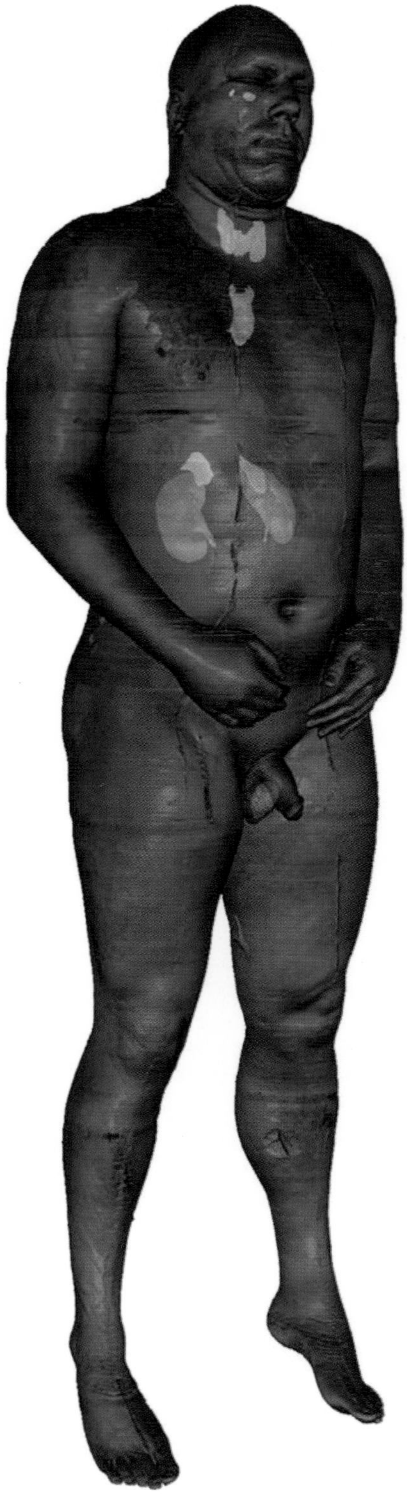

Functions:

- Regulates slow and / or cyclic processes in the body (e.g., puberty and the menstrual cycle).
- Sets the basal metabolic rate of the body
- Maintains homeostasis by responding to changes in the body's internal environment

Major organs:

- Pituitary gland
- Pineal gland
- Thyroid & parathyroid glands
- Adrenal gland
- Pancreas
- Testes & ovaries

Other hormone-producing organs:

not in endocrine system

- Heart
- Stomach
- Kidneys
- Thymus
- Brain

The Muscular System

The muscular system produces body movements, but the muscles of the body also protect softer organs and produce much body heat. Without the contracting abilities of skeletal muscles, we could not eat, walk, talk, smile, grasp objects, or anything else that requires movement.

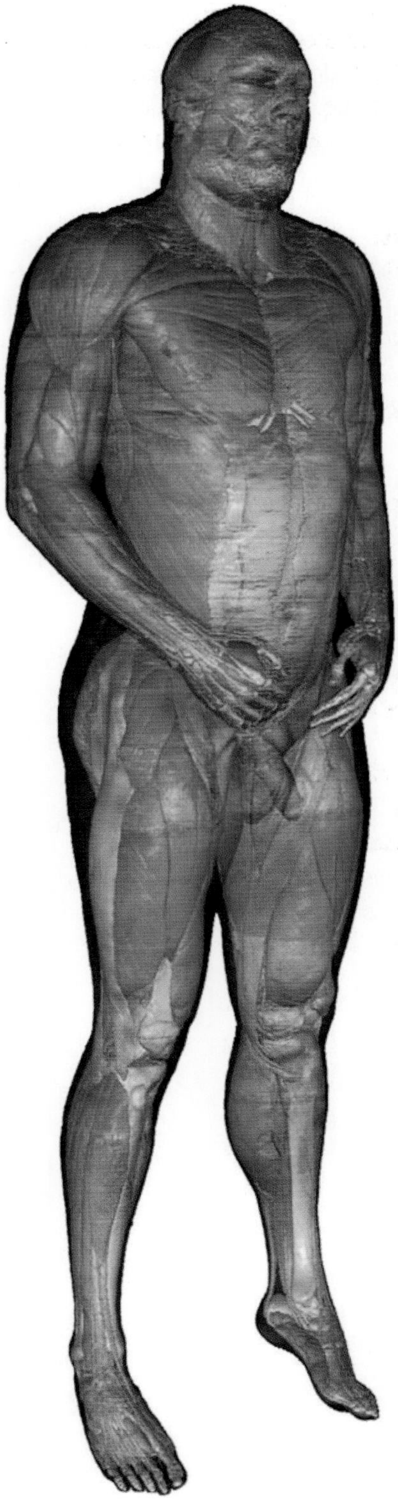

Functions:
- Move bones and skin via contraction of muscle cells
- Maintain homeostasis by generating body heat
- Protects soft, internal organs from blunt impact

Major organs:
- The skeletal muscles
- Tendons
- Aponeuroses

The Cardiovascular System

The cardiovascular system is primarily concerned with transporting substances throughout the body. The transportation system requires a pump (the heart), and transporting medium (blood) and pipes (blood vessels). Hundreds of substances are transported through this system, including oxygen, nutrients, hormones and waste products.

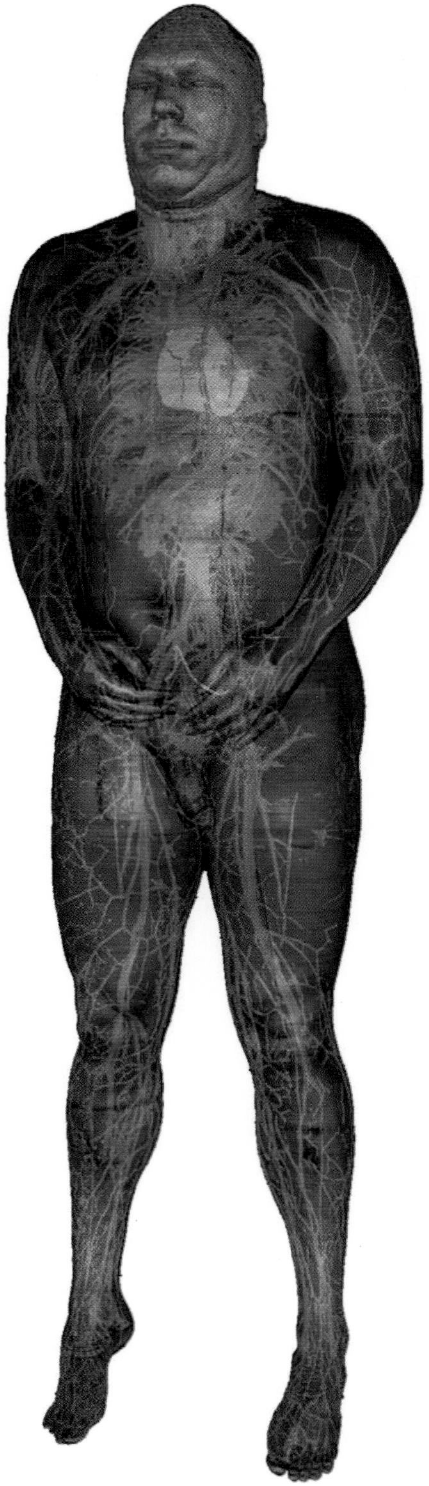

Functions:
- Transport nutrients to body cells & tissues
- Transport waste products away from body tissues
- Transport regulatory substances (e.g., hormones, antibodies) throughout the body
- Distribute heat throughout the body

Major organs:
- Heart
- Blood vessels
- Blood

The Respiratory System

The respiratory system is responsible for exchanging gases between our bodies and the environment. Oxygen is a gas we must obtain continuously from the atmosphere, and carbon dioxide is a waste product gas the system releases into the atmosphere.

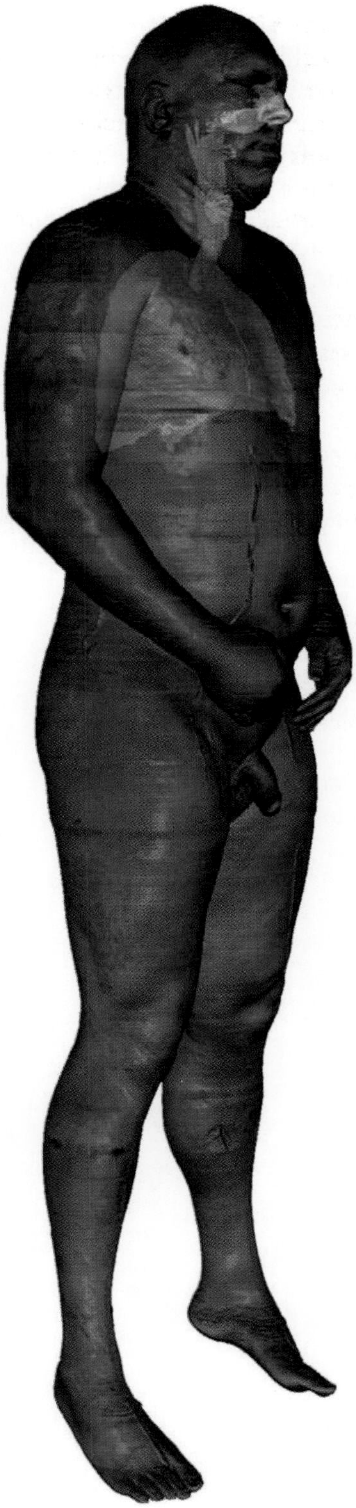

Functions:

- Obtain oxygen gas from the atmosphere
- Release carbon dioxide into the atmosphere
- Maintain pH balance of the blood via the carbon dioxide-carbonic acid-bicarbonate buffer system

Major organs:

- Nasal passages
- Pharynx
- Larynx
- Trachea
- Lungs

The Lymphatic System

The lymphatic system is sometimes called the *immune system*, but this is not entirely correct. There is no immune system, but the body does elicit an *immune response* when invading organisms like bacteria attack our bodies, and the lymphatic system plays many important roles in the immune response. Immunity is a complex undertaking; to work properly, our bodies must be able to recognize "self" from "non-self" and destroy the invading cells before they destroy us!

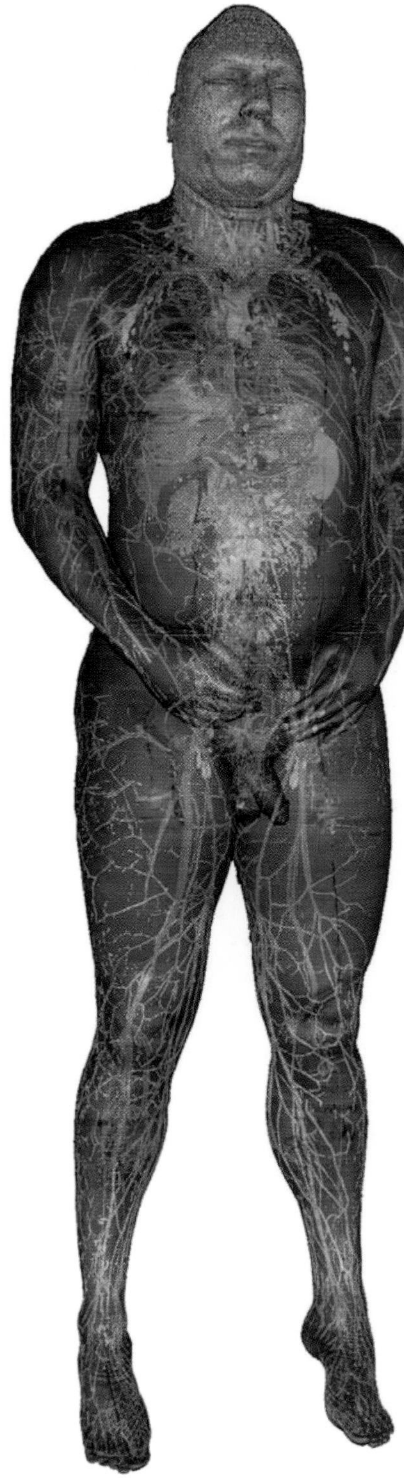

Functions:
- Detect foreign cells and destroy them
- Detect mutant human cells and destroy them
- Cleanse the tissue fluids of pathogens and cell debris from damaged or dead cells
- Produce antibodies

Major organs:
- Lymph nodes
- Lymphatic vessels
- Spleen
- Thymus
- Tonsils

The Digestive System

The digestive system obtains raw materials and energy from the environment that are used to carry out metabolism. The centerpiece of the digestive system is the gastrointestinal tract which – along with the esophagus and oral cavity – extends from the mouth to the anus. Interestingly, foodstuff not absorbed across the wall of this tract never actually enter the body as they enter the tube at the mouth and exit through the anus.

Functions:
- Obtain raw materials and energy from the environment through ingesting, digesting and absorbing nutrients.
- Excreting un-used ingested materials as feces.

Major organs:
- Oral cavity
- Esophagus
- Stomach
- Small intestine
- Large intestine
- Liver
- Pancreas

Other digestive organs:
- Teeth
- Gall bladder
- Salivary glands
- Tongue
- Rectum

The Urinary System

The urinary system removes wastes products – particularly nitrogen wastes – from the body. Cells release those wastes into the bloodstream which is then filtered by the urinary system to produce urine. The urine is stored in the body until a convienent time for disposal.

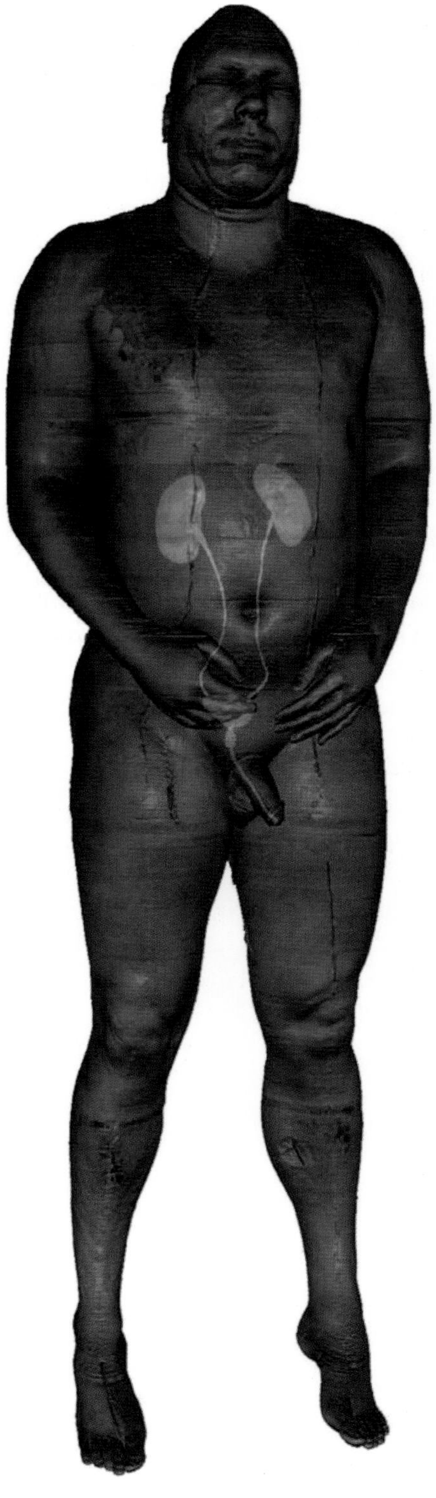

Functions:

- Filter the blood to remove nitrogen waste products (e.g., urea)
- Regulate blood pressure and volume by adjusting the amount of water pulled from the blood and put into urine
- Maintain electrolyte and pH balance of the blood

Major organs:

- Kidneys
- Ureters
- Urinary bladder
- Urethra

The Reproductive System

The reproductive system is unique in two ways: First, it's the only system that comes in two flavors – male and female. Second, it's the only system that is not required for the life of the individual. Many people live just fine without a functional reproductive system. Indeed, it may be argued that the reproductive system causes more harm to the individual than good. Many, many women, for example, have died in childbirth and many others would rather not live with the monthly mentrual cycle. However, the reproductive system is absolutely required for continuance of the species. Without it, we would cease to exist in one generation.

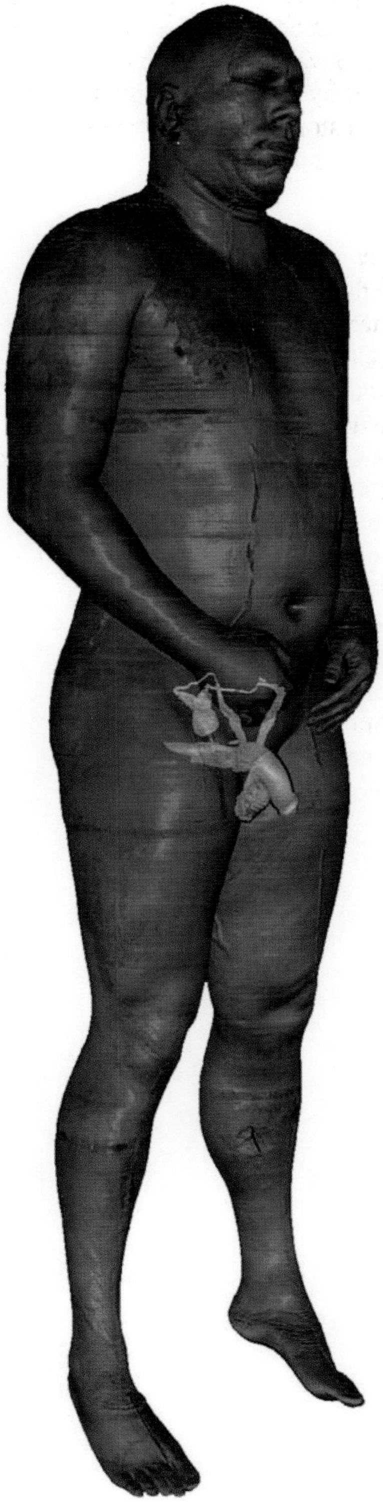

Functions:

Male:

- Produce and maintain sperm (germ cell)
- Deliver sperm to the female reproductive system

Female:

- Produce female ovum (germ cell)
- Receive male reproductive germ cells
- Protect and nourish developing fetus
- Deliver and nourish baby

Major organs:

Male:

- Penis
- Testes
- Scrotum

Female:

- Vagina
- Uterus
- Ovaries
- Breasts (i.e., mammary glands)

The Integumentary System

The integumentary system is the most visible system of the body. We spend countless hours washing it, grooming it, shaving it, tanning it, styling it, perfuming it and more. Entire industries are supported by our obsessions with making it look just right. So the next time you see someone with beautiful skin, tell them what a nice integument they have!

Functions:
- Protect internal organs from dessication, invading pathogens, harsh chemicals, UV radiation and mechanical damage.
- Detect environmental stimuli, such as temperature and touch.
- Excrete excess salts and water.
- Produce vitamin D

Major organs:
- Skin (integument)
- Hair
- Fingernails & toenails
- Cutaneous sensory receptors

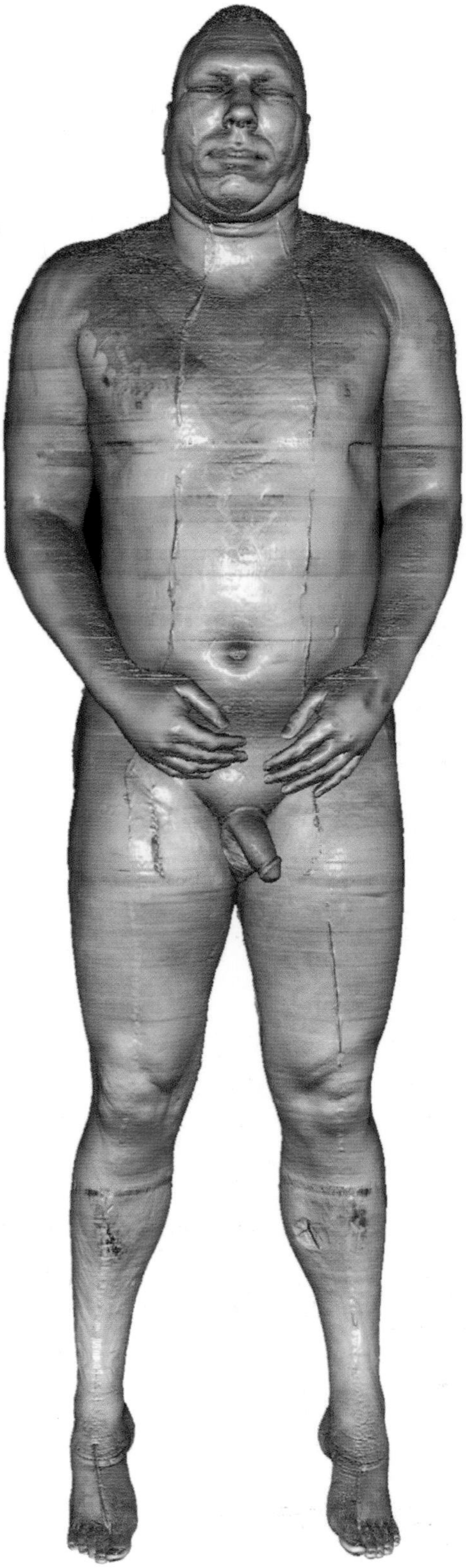

exercise 2

using the MICROSCOPE

- to study anatomy -

He replied, "If you have faith as small as a mustard seed you can say to this mulberry tree, 'Be uprooted and planted in the sea' and it will obey you."

Luke 17:6

An antique brass microscope, likely produced in France between 1840 and 1850.

Gross anatomy can only teach us so much about how the body works: In order to really understand how the body is put together and functions we need to look closer. The building blocks of all organs and tissues are *cells*, but most cells are far too small to be seen with the naked eye. To visualize this most basic component of all living things, we need a *microscope*.

The microscope was invented in the mid-1600's. The microscopes we'll use in anatomy lab work essentially the same way as the original microscopes built nearly 400 years ago. These *compound light microscopes* bend light using a series of glass lenses in order to magnify an image of an object, making it appear larger than it actually is. Our microscopes can magnify objects approximately 400*x*, that is, they can make objects appear 400 times larger than their actual size.

When we think of resolution, we usually think of a digital picture and whether it looks clear and sharp, or pixelated. This is *not* how the word "resolution" is used in microscopy. In microscopy, resolution refers to the amount of magnification required to distinguish two very small, closely-spaced points as two distinct points (as opposed to just one point). If the two very small points appear as a single point, we say that the current magnification cannot *resolve* the points, and a higher magnification is required. The human eye can resolve fingerprints in our skin but cannot resolve the individual cells. A light microscope can resolve the individual cells but cannot resolve the organelles within the cell (except the very large nucleus). An electron microscope can resolve the organelles, but cannot resolve the proteins in the cell. The most powerful microscope, the atomic force microscope, can resolve individual atoms that make up proteins.

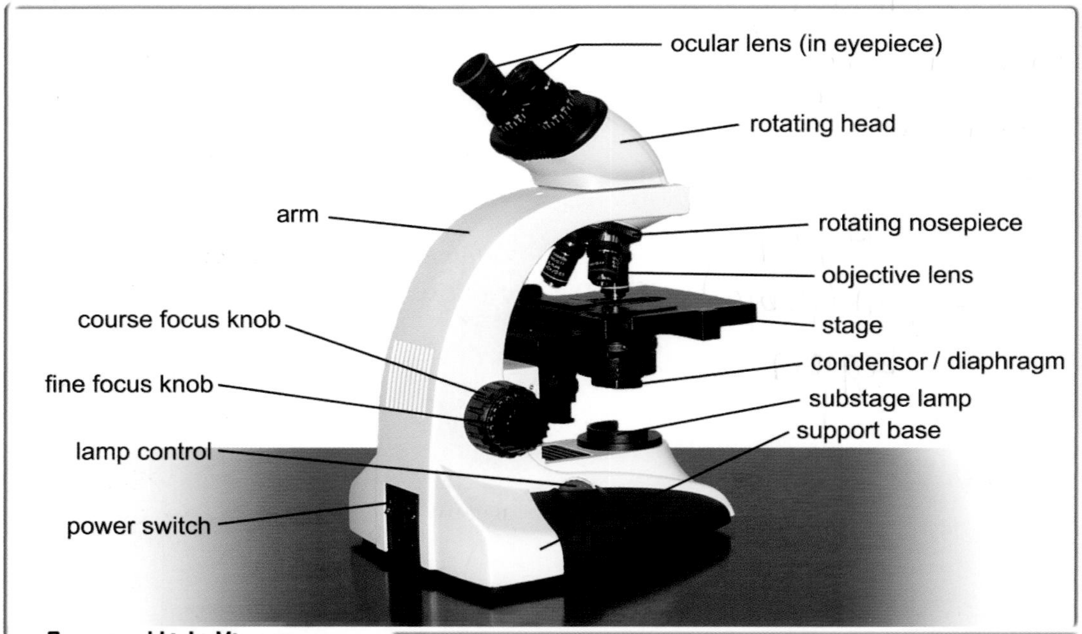

Compound Light Microscope

Figure 2-1

To visualize an enlarged image of an object using a compound light microscope, the specimen is first placed on a stage and illuminated with bright light. The light illuminating the specimen is gathered through a small opening, called an *aperture*, and then passed through a series of lenses to magnify the image. The greater the magnification, the higher the *resolution*. Let us examine the concept of resolution more closely, since its use in microscopy is different than its use in everyday language.

The resolution of the human eye is about 100 micrometers[1] (100 µm). From our discussion above, it follows that this means two small dots separated by less than 100 µm will appear as one dot, but if they are separated by more than 100 µm

[1] See "Units of Metric Measurements" box on the next page

we will see them as two individual dots[2]. Due to the physical properties of light, the theoretical maximum resolution that can be achieved with a compound light microscope is about 0.2 μm (200 nanometers). In practice, such magnification is usually not possible: A good compound light microscope will obtain a resolution of 400-500 nm (0.4-0.5 μm).

Units of Metric Measurements

Scientists use the metric system (technically the SI system) rather than the English system used by the general public in the United States. While the English system is based on arbitrary standards, the metric system is based on physical constants of nature.

The *meter* is the standard unit of length in the metric system. It was originally defined in 1793 as 1 / 10,000,000 the distance from the equator to the pole. Today, it's defined as the distance traveled by light in a vacuum during 1 / 299,792,458 second. Divisions of the metric unit of length useful to the life sciences include

meter (m)	about 39.3 inches
centimeter (cm)	10^{-2} meter
millimeter (mm)	10^{-3} meter
micrometer (μm)	10^{-6} meter
nanometer (nm)	10^{-9} meter
picometer (pm)	10^{-12} meter

Activity 1: Indentify the Parts of a Microscope

1. Obtain a microscope from you lab instructor and carefully place it on your bench. The microscope should always be carried using both hands. Use Figure 2-1 to identify the following parts of the microscope:

Base: Supports the microscope. The base is often weighted to prevent the microscope from toppling over.

Stage: Supports the specimen under examination. On some microscopes the entire stage moves to scan the specimen; on others the slide alone moves and on still others the objective lens moves while the slide and stage remain in a fixed position.

Substage lamp: Provides the light which illuminates the specimen under study. On some microscopes the intensity of the light can be adjusted.

Condensor: Focuses light from the substage lamp onto the specimen.

Iris diaphragm lever: Adjusts the amount of light from the substage lamp illuminating the specimen. Some microscopes employ a lamp dimmer switch instead.

Course adjustment knob: Used to initially bring the specimen into focus. Allows large movements of the objective lens relative to the specimen. On some microscopes this knob moves the stage up and down, while on others it moves the objective lens.

Fine adjustment knob: Allows precise focusing of the specimen.

Objective lens: A lens located immediately above the specimen. Many microscopes utilize 4x, 10x and 40x objective lenses.

Eyepiece: A tube structure through which the viewer examines the specimen.

Ocular lens: A lens located within the eyepiece, usually having a magnification of 10x.

Arm: Connects the stage, objective lenses and eyepiece to the support base.

Rotating nosepiece: Allows selection from multiple objective lenses.

Activity 2: Using the Microscope

1. Obtain a microscope and a letter "e" slide from your instructor. Observe the "e" on the slide and place the slide on the microscope stage with the "e" oriented properly, i.e., as you would write the letter on paper.
2. Turn on the substage lamp and center the letter "e" in the beam of light. Starting with the scan-power objective lens, focus the letter "e" using the course and fine focusing knobs.

[2] A typical human cell is 50–80 μm, just teasingly beyond the resolution of our eyes.

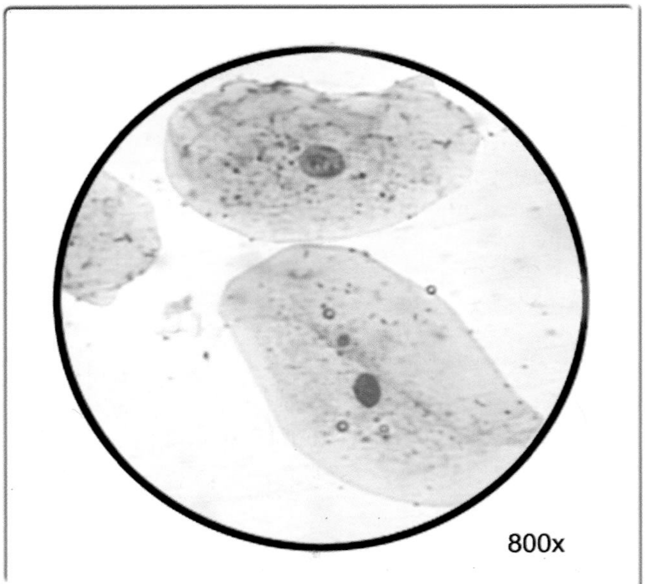

Figure 2-2 **Human Cheek Epithelial Cells**

3. How does the letter "e" appear when observed through the microscope eyepiece?
4. For practice moving a specimen on a microscope, try rotating the pointer and placing the "e" directly beneath the pointer. How do objects appear to move when viewed through the eyepiece?

Activity 3: Measuring Sizes with a Microscope

1. We would like to measure the size of the letter "e" using the microscope. To do this, we must first determine the diameter of the field-of-view (FOV) at each magnification. Remove the letter "e" slide from the stage and obtain a clear metric ruler (the ruler must be transparent). Place the ruler on the microscope stage with the unit markings passing through the middle of the FOV. Using the scanning-power objective lens, how many millimeters wide is the FOV?
2. Rotate the nosepiece until the low-power objective lens is in place. Bring the ruler into sharp focus using fine focus knob. How many millimeters wide is the FOV at this magnification?
3. Rotate the nosepiece until the high-power objective is in place. Most likely you will not be able to directly measure the FOV at high magnification. We must instead calculate the diameter using the empirical measurements obtained at the lower magnifications. Use the formula below to calculate the diameter of the FOV at high magnification.

$$FOV_H = (FOV_L \times Magnification_L) / Magnification_H$$

4. To determine the size of the letter "e", remove the ruler from the stage, return to low magnification and place the "e" slide on the microscope. Move the "e" to the center of the FOV, then estimate how many "e" letters would be needed to cross the FOV. For example, suppose it would take 8 "e" letters to cross your FOV and the diameter of the FOV is 4 millimeters. The width of each "e" would be

$$4\text{mm} / 8\ \text{“e”} = 0.5\ \text{mm} = 500\ \mu\text{m}$$

What is the size of your letter "e"? __________

Activity 4: Observing Cheek Epithelial Cells

In order to view actual human cheek cells we'll need to prepare a *wet mount* as described below.

1. Obtain a clean microscope slide, a cover slip, a toothpick and a bottle of methylene blue stain.
2. Place one small drop of methylene blue in the center of the microscope slide.
3. Use the toothpick to gently scrape cells from the inside of your cheek. You should scrape firmly, but not hard enough to draw blood.
4. Deposit the cheek cells into the drop of methlyene blue on the microscope slide by tapping and / or twirling the toothpick in the stain.
5. Discard the used toothpick into an orange biohazard bag.
6. Place one edge of the coverslip onto the microslide adjacent to the drop of stain. Slowly lower the coverslip over the stain; try to avoid trapping air bubbles under the coverslip. This is a wet mount.
7. Place the wet mount preparation onto the stage of the microscope and observe the cells first under scanning power (4x objective). Once in focus, the cell will appear as tiny blue dots scattered across the field of view.
8. Place some cells to the middle of the field of view and increase the magnification to 100x, then 400x. You should be able to see cells individually or connected together in a sheet. Each cell will have a darkly-stain nucleus near its center. Tiny dark spots on the cheek epithelial cells are harmless bacteria that reside in your mouth.

9. You determined the size of the field of view in Activity 2. Estimate the size of your epithelial cells just as you did for the letter “e.” What is the size of your cheek cells? _______________

Activity 5: Observing Depth in a Microscope

In addition to reversing objects left-to-right and upside-down, the lenses of a compound light microscope also reverse the apparent depth relationships within a specimen. In other words, an object X that is actually above another object Y will appear below object Y in a microscope. This phenomenon is demonstrated in this activity.

1. Obtain a microscope and a slide containing three colored threads from your instructor.
2. Observe the threads in the microscope. The three threads overlap one another. At high magnification only one thread will be in focus at a time. Using the fine focus knob, slowly bring each thread into focus, one at a time. How do the threads appear to be stacked in the microscope? How are they actually stacked?

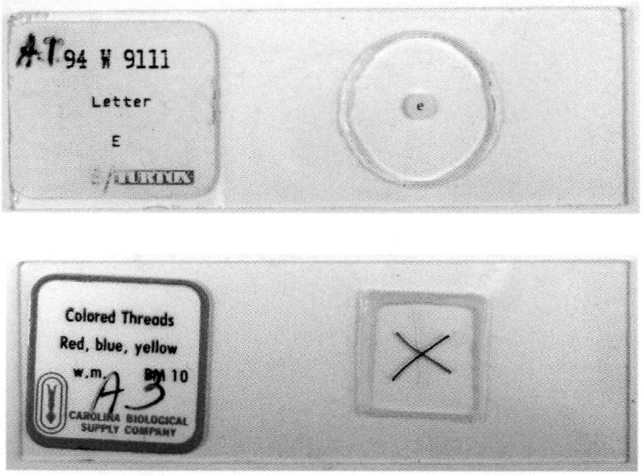

Figure 2-3 **“e” & Thread Microscope Slides**

Activity 6: Practice Using the Microscope

1. Obtain the letter “e” slide and place it on the microscope.
2. Fill out the chart (Table 2.1).

	Scanning Power	Low Power	High Power
Magnification of ocular lens:	10 x	10 x	10 x
Magnification of objective lens:	4 x	10 x	40 x
Total magnification:	40 x	100 x	400 x
Working distance:	______ mm	______ mm	______ mm
Field of view (FOV):	______ mm	______ mm	16 mm
	______ µm	______ µm	______ µm
Observation of letter “e”			

Summary Chart for Your Microscope

Table 2.1

exercise 3

an introduction to CELLS

The body is a unit, though it is made up of many parts;
and though all its parts are many, they form one body.
1 Corinthians 12:12

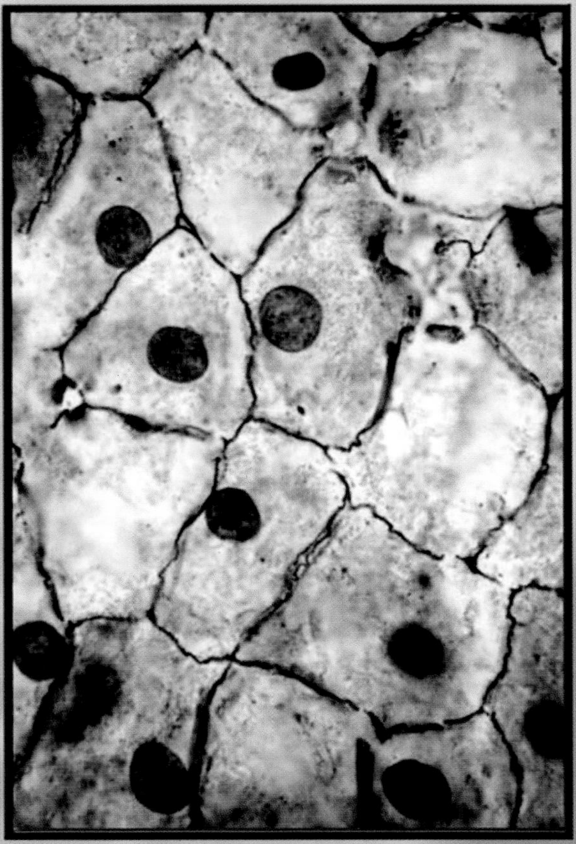

The human body is composed of 60 - 100 trillion cells.

Cells form the building blocks of all living things. If our body is the house, then cells are the bricks. Many cells, such as bacteria, algae and protists, can live independently in nature, but our cells cannot: All of the 100 trillion cells that make up our bodies are dependent upon each other for their own survival. It's been with great difficulty that scientists have learned to "culture" some human cells in a petri dish; most still die when removed from the body. In this exercise, we'll examine the anatomy of a prototypical human cell and survey some of the different types of cells found in our bodies. The study of cells is called *cytology*.

All living things, including people, must be able to maintain a constant internal environment even if the outside environment changes. Maintaining a constant internal environment is called *homeostasis* and is what separates the living from the dead. If, because of injury or disease, we become unable to maintain homeostasis we will die and quickly reach equilibrium with our surroundings. (For example, our body temperature will become the same as the ambient environmental temperature). Cells, too, must maintain a constant internal environment and, like us, if they fail to do so, they will die. In fact, homeostasis at the organismal level is achieved only by maintaining homeostasis at the cellular level.

Organisms possess a number of organs to help them maintain homeostasis. We have, for example, a heart to pump blood, kidneys to filter blood and a urinary bladder to hold the filtration waste product (i.e., urine) until a convenient disposal. These organs help maintain homeostasis by keeping nutrients and waste products moving; if they fail, nutrients will not be delivered to cells and wastes will not be carried away. Likewise, cells possess little "organs" to help them maintain homeostasis. These tiny cellular organs are called *organelles*. Well over a dozen organelles have been discovered in cells; the major ones are depicted in Figure 3-1 and described below. Some of these organelles are surrounded by membranes and are thus called *membranous organelles*; others are not and they're called *non-membranous organelles*.

- **cell membrane** – The boundary of the cell is defined by the cell membrane, also called the *plasma membrane*. The *fluid mosaic model* (Figure 3-2) describes the cell membrane as an oily bilayer of phospholipids with associated proteins. The fluidity of the membrane is controlled by the amount of **cholesterol** present; more cholesterol makes the membrane more viscous. The overall shape of each cell is maintained in part by the **membrane skeleton** just beneath the cell membrane. Some human cells are *polarized*, meaning they have a distinct top and bottom (many human cells are *not* polarized). In polarized cells, the top membrane is called the **apical membrane**; the membranes on the sides and bottom of the cell are collectively called the **basolateral membrane**.
- **nucleus** – Most cells in our bodies contain a large nucleus near the center of the cell. The nucleus is a vault that protects the most precious molecule in the body – DNA. This membranous organelle vault called the nucleus restricts access to DNA and controls gene expression and DNA duplication prior to cell division. The presence of a nucleus defines a class of cells called *eukaryotes* (literally, true nucleus). Bacteria do not possess a nucleus are classified as *prokaryotes* (literally, before nucleus, in reference to the evolutionary presumption that prokaryotes are older and more primitive than eukaryotes). The nucleus is the largest organelle and is the only one visible with a light microscope. One or more dark spots, called the **nucleolus**, are often seen inside the nucleus where there is active gene expression. Everything in the cell between the nucleus and the plasma membrane is called the *cytoplasm*. The cytoplasm is a colloid consisting of watery **cytosol** and suspended organelles, proteins and small molecules.
- **ribosomes** – These are relatively small, non-membranous organelles in the cytoplasm that make proteins from the genetic information provided by the nucleus.
- **endoplasmic reticulum** – The endoplasmic reticulum (ER) is a complex network of membranes sometimes spanning the entire distance from the nucleus to the cell membrane. Two types of endoplasmic reticulum are found in cells: **Smooth ER** and **rough ER**. Rough ER is studded with ribosomes and therefore appears rough when viewed with an electron microscope. Rough ER is a major site of protein production. The proteins produced there are usually modified in some way and travel through the channels of the ER to reach

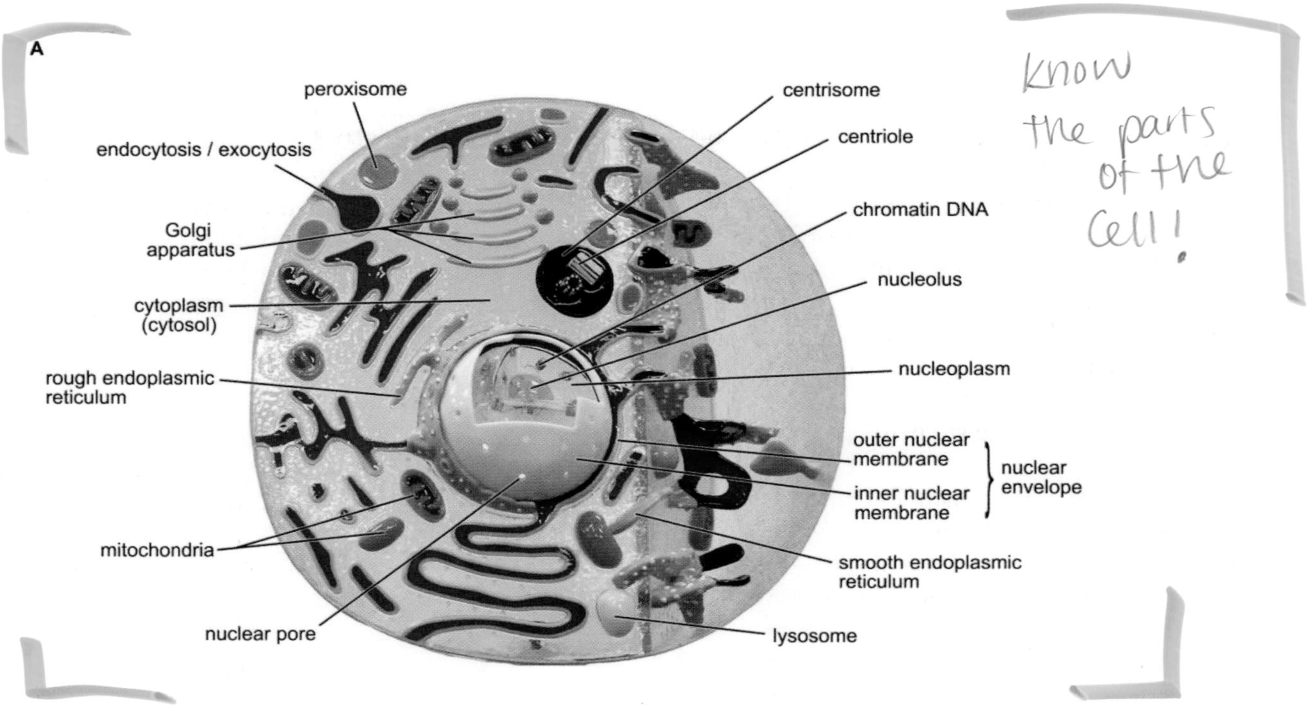

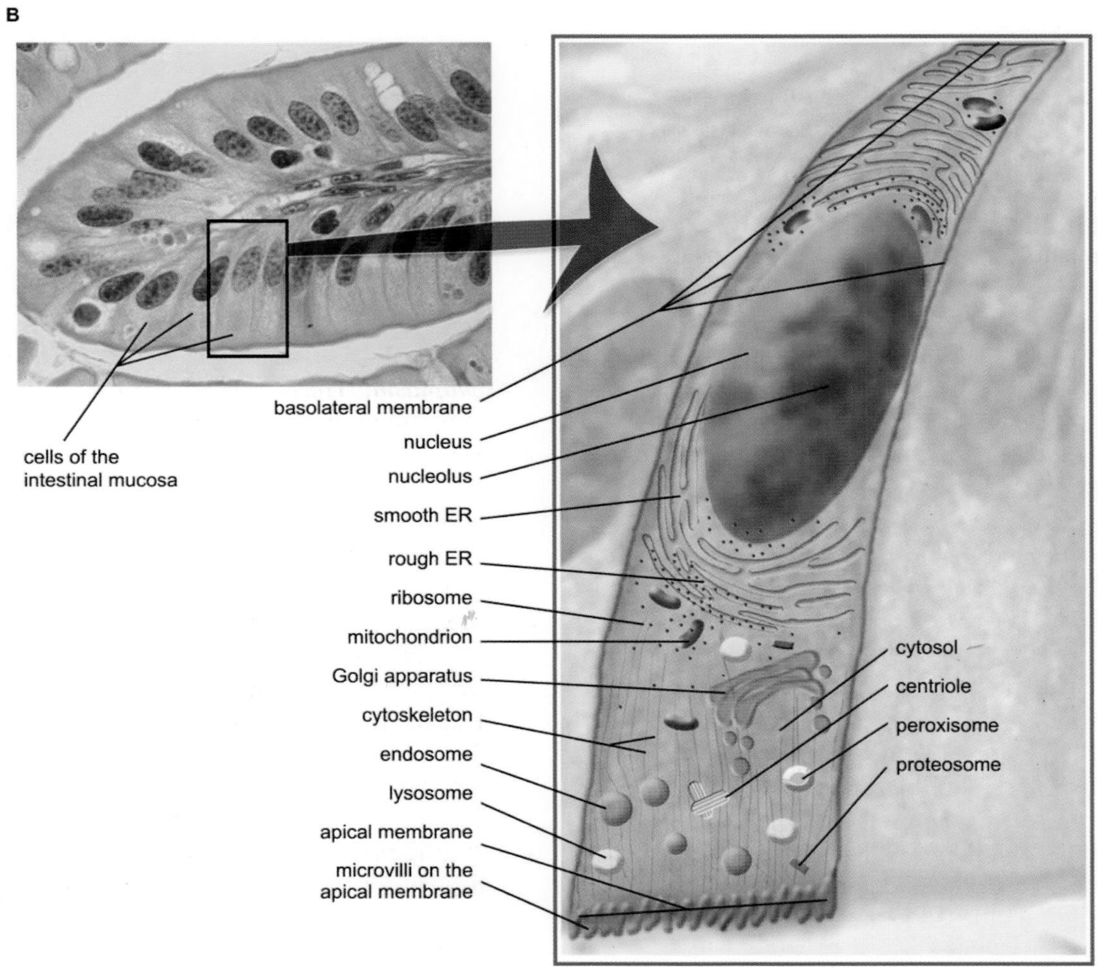

Figure 3-1: Components of a Typical Human Cell

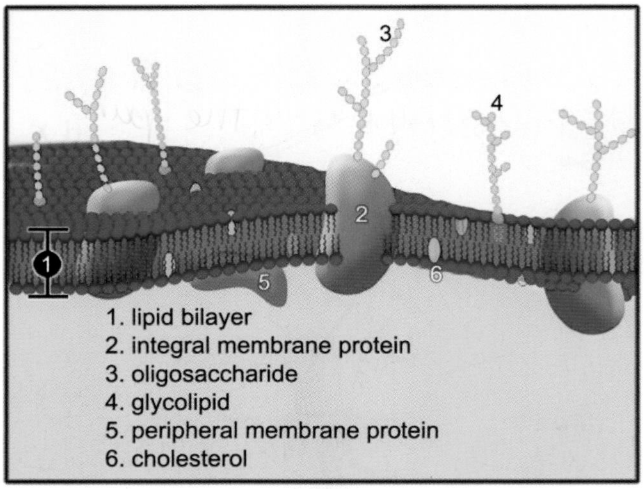

Figure 3-2: Fluid Mosaic Model of Cell Membrane

- specific destinations. Smooth ER contains no ribosomes and is the site of membrane production. Membrane-soluble compounds like steroids and fatty acids are also produced in the smooth ER.
- **mitochondria** – Cells require energy to maintain homeostasis and perform other important cellular functions. This energy is provided in the form of ATP, most of which is produced by the mitochondria, one of the membranous organelles. Because of their important role in ATP production, the mitochondria have been nick-named the "power plants" of the cell.
- **Golgi apparatus** – This membranous organelle acts in some ways like a post office. The Golgi apparatus receives newly-made proteins from the cytoplasm or rough ER on its *cis* face (facing the nucleus) and passes these proteins through a stacked series of membranes until they are released on the *trans* face (facing the plasma membrane). Along the way, proteins are modified and sorted based on their destinations. The sorted proteins are released from the *trans* face in small vesicles that carry the proteins to their proper locations.
- **proteosome** – This non-membranous organelle acts like a cellular recycling bin. Old or damaged proteins enter one side of the proteosome. Inside the proteosome they are disassembled and the building blocks are released from the other side of the organelle. Those building blocks are then ready to be used to make new proteins.

Structure = Function:
Why are Cells So Small?

When learning how to use the microscope in exercise 2 we examined some human cheek cells and determined their size, about 60 μm across. Nearly every cell is microscopic, meaning they're too small to be seen without a microscope. Why are cells so small?

The size of most cells is restricted by the diffusion of nutrients and wastes into and out of the cell. For example, cells use the atmospheric gas oxygen (O_2) to produce energy. If the cell were too big, the amount of O_2 diffusing into the cell would be insufficient to meet the needs of the cell. Likewise, waste products (e.g., CO_2) would not leave a large cell before building up to toxic concentrations. Cells larger than 100 μm are usually too large for adequate diffusion of nutrients; human cells generally range from 50 – 80 μm in diameter.

The size of one human cell is not limited by the diffusion of nutrients and is considerably larger than the others. That cell is the human egg cell, or oocyte. If fertilized, an oocyte must survive for approximately a week with only the nutrients stored within it. As a result, this cell is ~ 1 mm in size, making it the only human cell visible to the naked eye.

- **cytoskeleton** – The cytoskeleton consists of protein fibers that form cables that traverse the cytoplasm. These cables, made primarily of microtubules, intermediate filaments and microfilaments, provide structural support for the cell, aid cell motility (for mobile cells), and help anchor fixed cells to other body structures. Projections of the cytoskeleton may extend beyond the body of the cell as either **microvilli** or *cilia*. Microvilli are found on the apical surface of polarized epithelial cells and increase the surface area of the apical membrane, usually to facilitate absorption of substances into the cell. Cilia actively beat in a rhythmic fashion, usually to move fluids across the surface of the cell.
- **endosome** – This membranous organelle is formed by a portion of the plasma membrane pinching off into the cell. Large extracellular materials can be imported by this method. Phagocytic cells may even "eat" other cells,

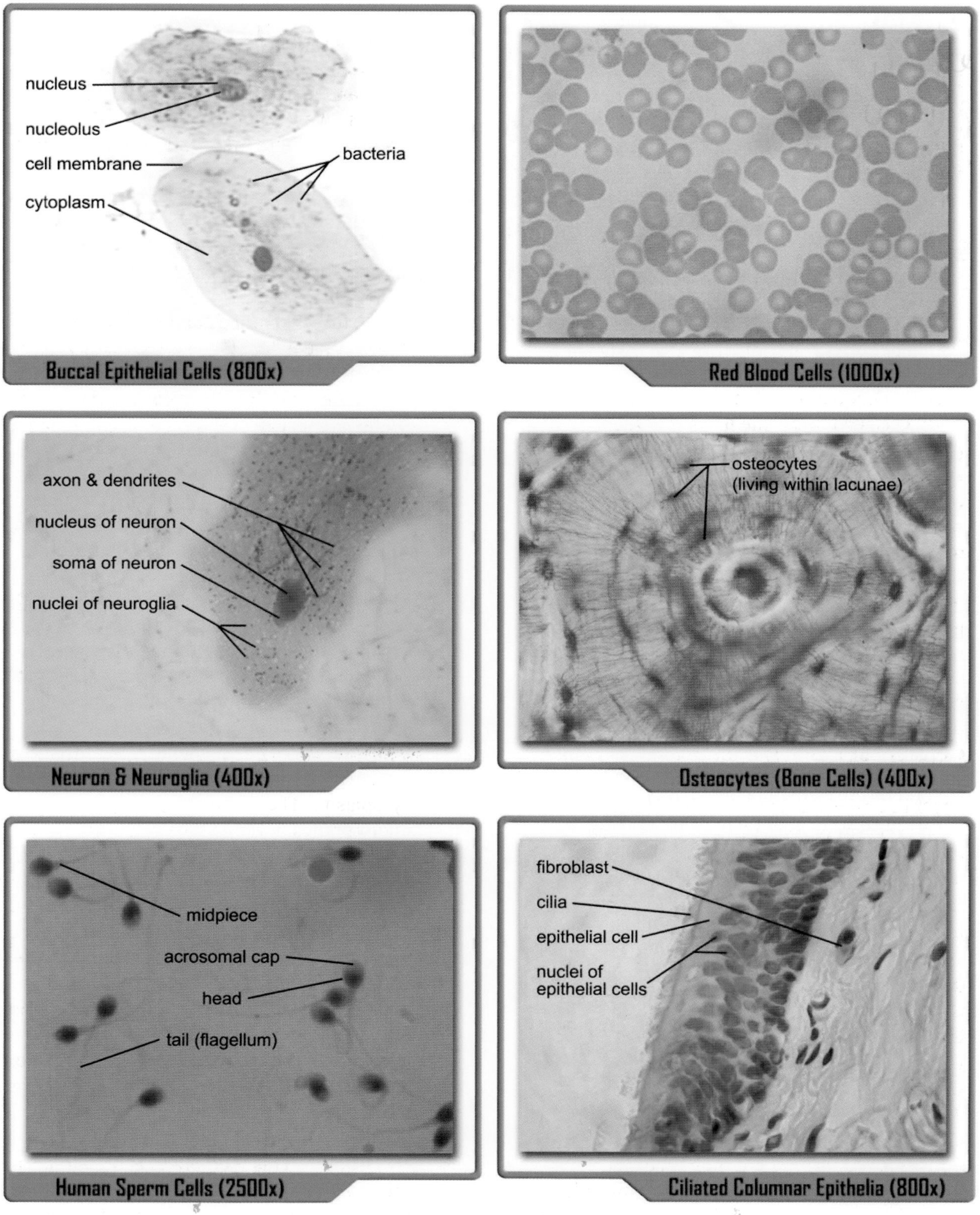

Figure 3-3: Various Types of Cells in the Body

such as bacteria, by engulfing them in endosomes.

- **lysosome** – This membranous organelle is the cell's digestive system. Powerful digestive enzymes are kept safely within the lysosome; if they were to escape, they could digest cellular proteins and thus kill the cell. Lysosomes often fuse with endosomes in order to digest materials taken up by the cell. The digested components are then released into the cytoplasm as nutrients.
- **centriole** – The centriole is a non-membranous organelle that facilitates movement of DNA during cell division. (When a cell divides, a copy of the DNA must be distributed to each daughter cell). Centrioles are also associated with cilia and flagella, cellular projections that cause movement of either the cell or its surrounding fluid.
- **peroxisome** – This membranous organelle also serves a digestive role in the cell. Peroxisomes specifically digest fatty acids. Fatty acid digestion is performed in peroxisomes because it produces some rather toxic waste products, including free radicals and hydrogen peroxide. The peroxisome contains enzymes (catalases and oxidases) that neutralize these hazardous wastes.

Cell Variety

There are about 200 different cell types in the human body, some of which are depicted in Figure 3-3. Human cells vary tremendously in shape and size. These *structural* differences reflect the different *functions* performed by our cells. For example, red blood cells are biconcave in shape and extremely small. These physical atributes maximize the movement of oxygen into and out of these oxygen-transporting cells. Sperm cells are also exceptionally small and possess flagella. These features help sperm swim the long distance needed to reach the egg cell (which happens to be the largest human cell, for reasons discussed in exercise 31).

Cell Division

Cells, like most humans, grow to maturity and reproduce. Most cells in our bodies reproduce through a form of cloning called *mitosis*. (The sex cells – sperm and egg – reproduce via a different process called *meiosis*, discussed in exercise 31). Mitosis occurs rapidly in four phases which takes about 10% of the cell's life cycle. The four phase of mitosis are outlined below and illustrated in figure 3-4.

PMAT

1. **Prophase** – The first stage of cell division. During this phase the DNA will condense into 23 pairs of distinct **chromosomes** as the nuclear membrane disintegrates. Each pair is joined together by protein bridge called the **centromere**. The asters migrate to opposite poles of the cell.
2. **Metaphase** – During this phase the 23 pairs of chromosomes will align themselves along the equator of the cell. Visible centrioles and **mitotic spindles** are attached to each chromosome pair.
3. **Anaphase** – The chromosome pairs will separate during this phase; the daughter chromosomes from each pair will be pulled in opposite directions by the microtubules of the mitotic spindles. This ensures that each daughter cell will have one complete copy of all DNA.
4. **Telophase** – The final stage of mitosis during which the nuclear membrane reforms in each daughter cell and the chromosomes dissolve into chromatin. Simultaneously, the cell membrane will invaginate forming a deep **cleavage furrow**. Eventually, the furrow will become so deep that the cell pinches apart into two separate daughter cells in a process called *cytokinesis*.

As mentioned above, the four phases of mitosis and cytokinesis take up about 10% of the cells life cycle. During the remaining 90%, the cell is in *interphase*, the period of time in which the cell is *not* dividing. During this time the cell is growing and / or performing its prescribed duties. The DNA, existing in a dispersed form called **chromatin**, will be replicated during this phase in preparation for cell division.

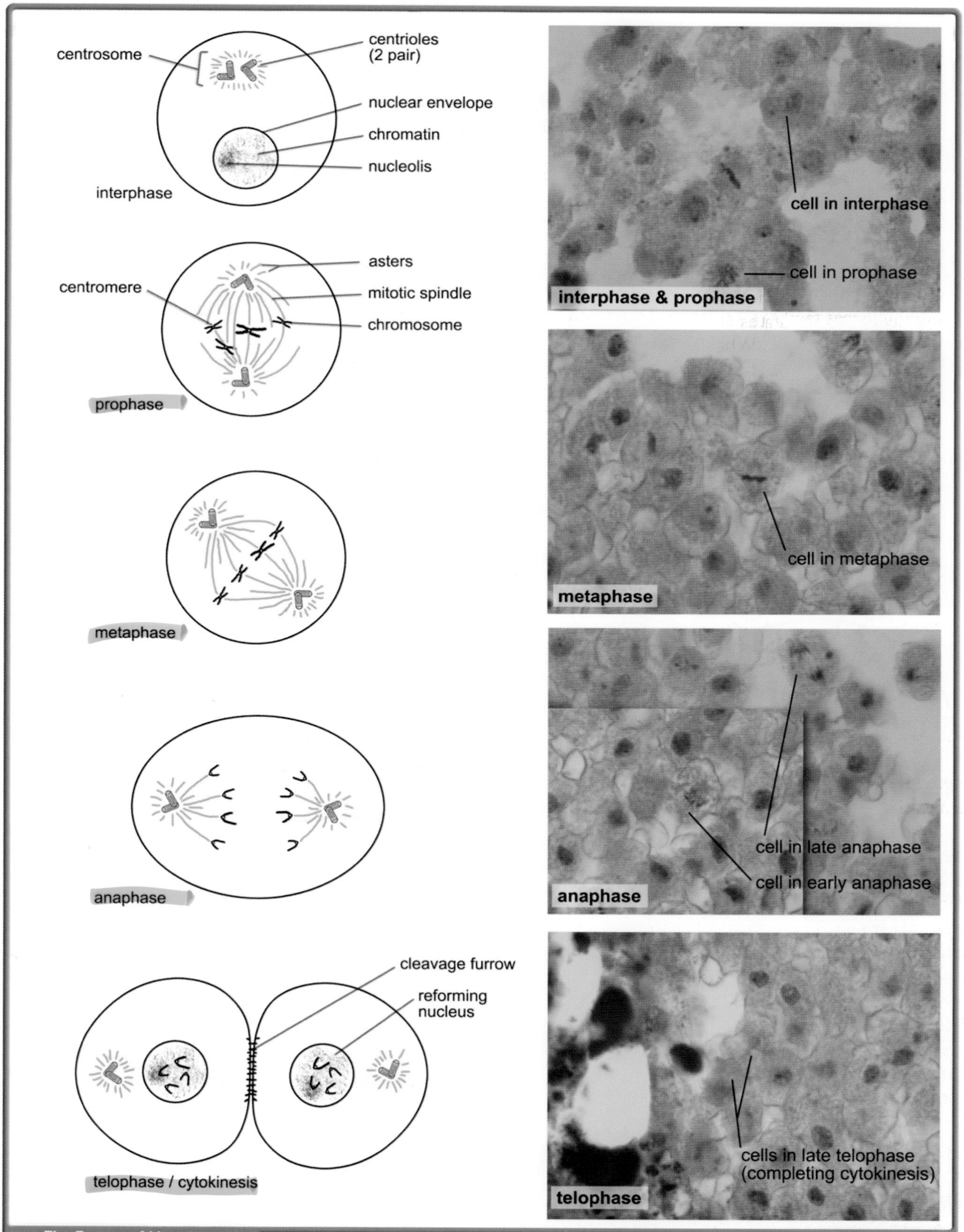

The Stages of Mitosis

Figure 3-4

Activity 1: Indentify the Parts of a Cell

1. Using either Figure 1-1 or a 3D model of a cell, identify the organelles described in this chapter. What role does each of these organelles play in helping the cell maintain homeostasis?

Activity 2: Observe Different Cell Types

1. Observe, either in a microscope or in photomicrographs, the following human cells: Epithelial cells, sperm cells, cardiac (heart) muscle cells and red blood cells. Draw these cells in the circles below (Figure 3-5). How do these cells differ from each other? How do you think these differences help each cell perform its particular function?

Activy 3: Observe the Stages of Mitosis

1. Obtain prepared microscope slides of fish blastula undergoing mitosis. Scan the cells and attempt to find cells in each stage of mitosis.

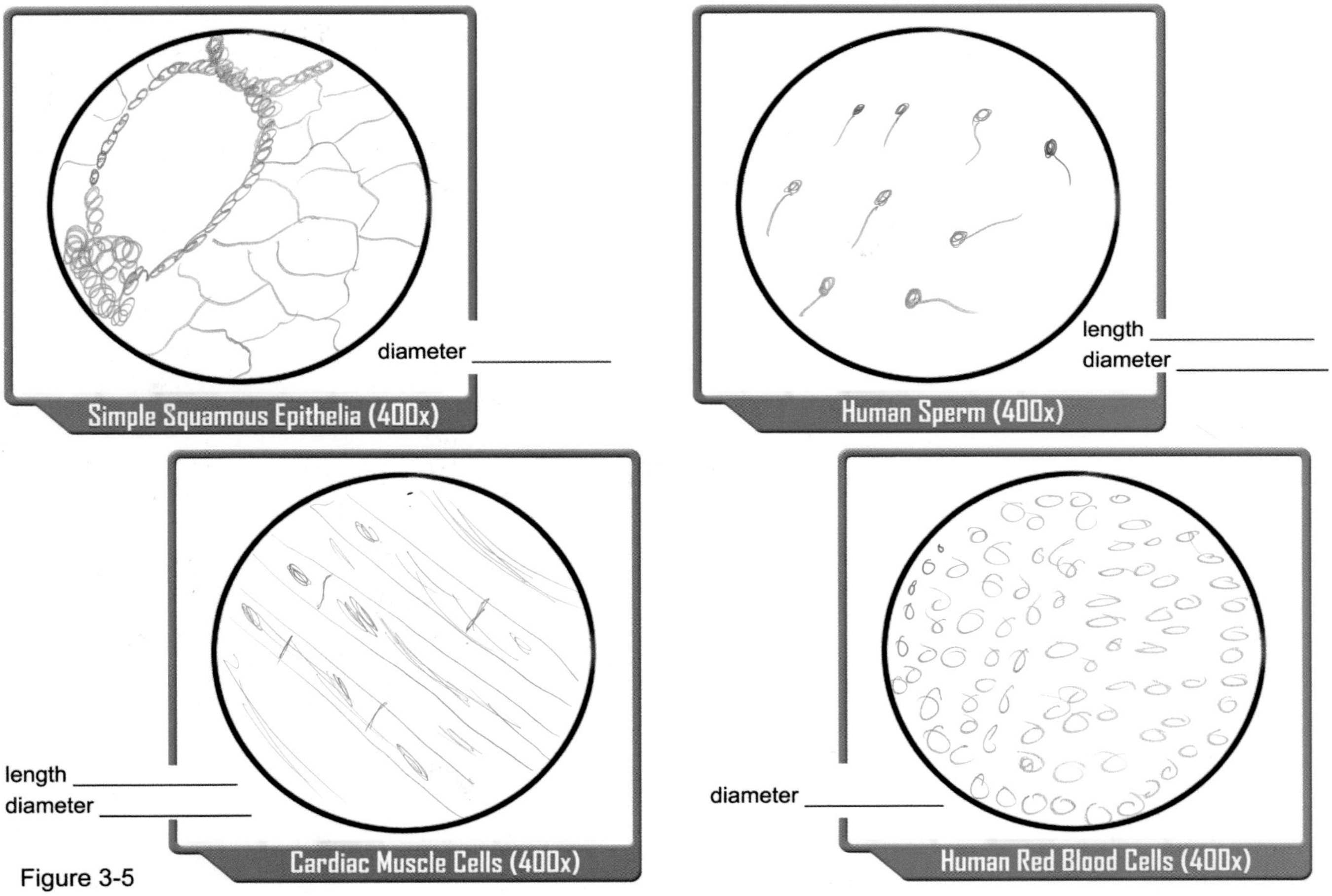

Figure 3-5

exercise 4

an introduction to TISSUES

...the whole body, supported and held together by its ligaments and sinews, grows as God causes it to grow.

Colossians 2:19

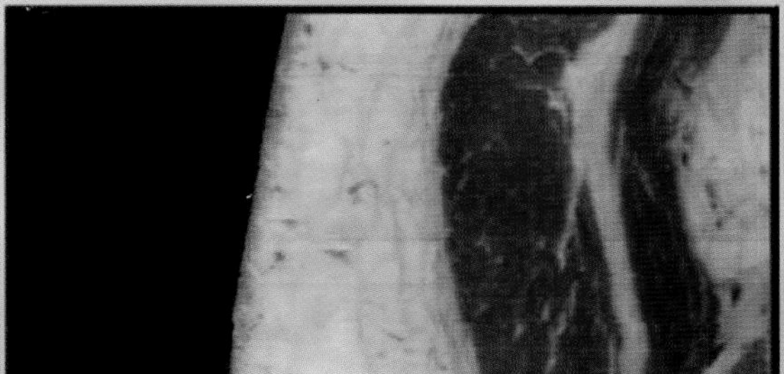

The female breast is composed largely of adipose (i.e., fat) tissue.

We learned in the previous exercise that cells form the building blocks of all living things. In multicellular organsims such as ourselves, many thousands and millions of individual cells exist in communities called *tissues* that perform specific functions. There are just four types of tissues in the human body: Epithelial, Connective, Muscular and Nervous. All of our organs (such as the heart, lungs, blood vessels, skin, etc) are constructed from these four tissue types. In this exercise, we'll examine these tissues closely and discover where and how each type is used in our bodies. The study of tissues is called *histology*.

Epithelial Tissue

Epithelial tissue lines body cavities and any part of the body exposed to the outside world. This includes our skin, intestinal tracts, respiratory tracts, urinary and reproductive tracts and virtually every gland in our bodies.

All epithelial tissues share certain common features. These include

- **cellularity** – Epithelial tissue is very "cellular" compared to other tissue types. In other words, the tissue is composed almost entirely of cells with exceedingly little extracellular material. Thus, the cells are very crowded. To prevent unwanted movement, they are attached firmly to each other and to a *basement membrane*. The basement membrane is a connective tissue structure that connects the epithelial cells to underlying body structures.
- **highly mitotic** – Epithelial cells are generally metabolically active. The *basal metabolic rate* (BMR, set by the hypothalamus and thyroid gland) of the body generally reflects the combined activity of epithelial cells. All together, they contribute significantly to normal, resting body temperature.
- **avascularity** – Epithelial tissue lacks blood vessels entirely. This is a bit ironic given the cellularity and mitotic activity of this tissue; however, all nutrients (including oxygen, glucose, etc) must diffuse into epithelial tissue from near-by tissues, usually connective tissue.
- **polarity** – Epithelial cells have a distinct top and bottom. The bottom and side membranes (collectively called the *basolateral membrane*) of each cell is anchored either to neighboring cells or the basement membrane, but the top membrane is free unattached and exposed. This exposed surface is called the *apical membrane* and is generally very different in composition and function than the basolateral membrane.
- **regenerative** – Epithelial tissues is easily replenished. This is necessary because epithelial tissues often suffer from frictional and abrasive forces (recall that epithelial tissues line body cavities and portions of the body exposed to the outside environment). Consequently, epithelial cells are continually lost and replaced.

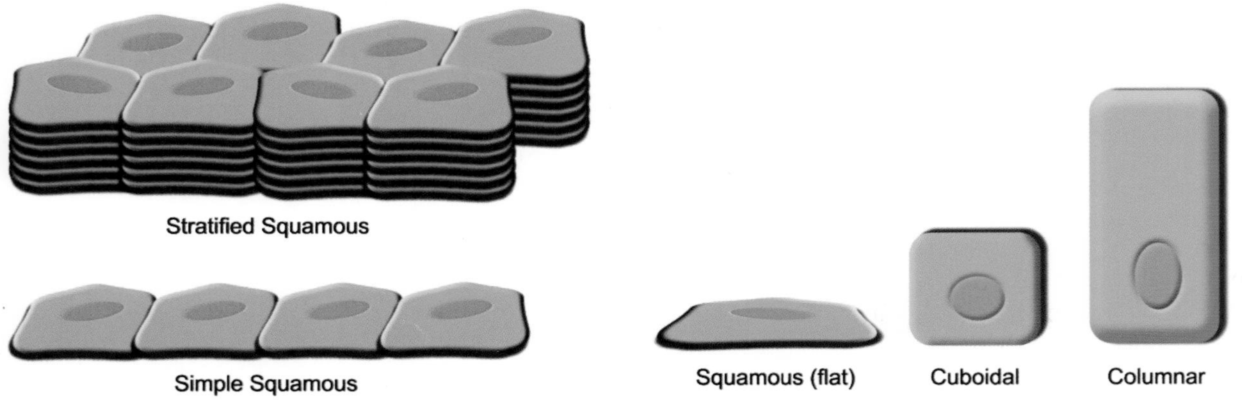

Classification of Epithelial Tissues

Figure 4-1

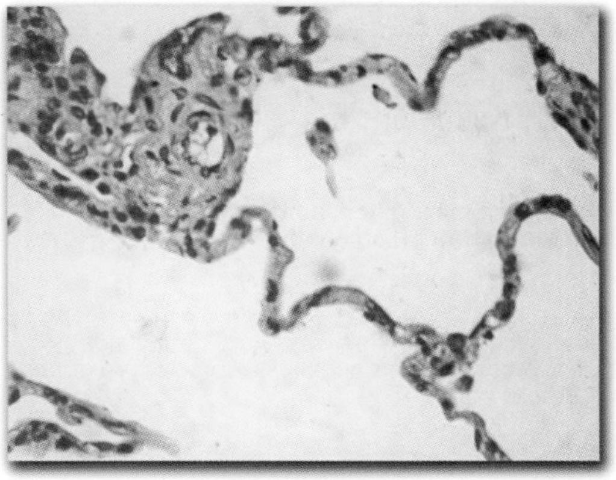

Tissue Type: Epithelial (simple squamous)

Cells: Single layer of flattened cells

Function: Provide for rapid diffusion of gasses and dissolved solutes across membranes

Location: The alveoli of the lungs, the endothelial cells of capillaries, glomeruli of kidneys

Simple Squamous (superior view) (400x)

Figure 4-2

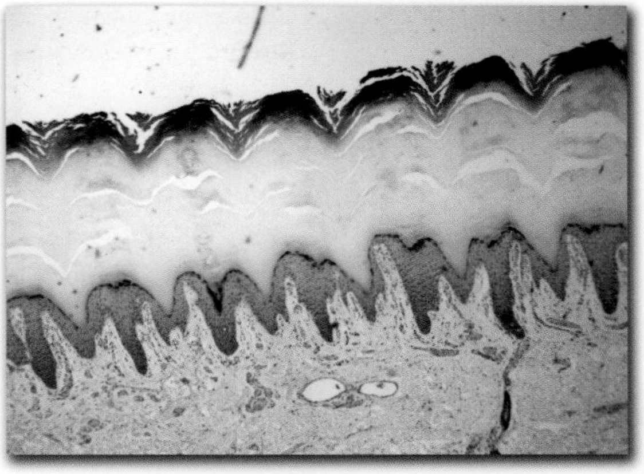

Tissue Type: Epithelial (stratified squamous)

Cells: Multiple layers of flattened cells

Function: Protection from abrasive forces

Location: Keratinized type forms the upper portion of the skin, non-keratinized type formes the wet surfaces of the esophagus, mouth, vagina and rectum.

non-keratinized - lines inside body.

Stratified Squamous Epithelia (40x)

Figure 4-3

There are six basic varieties of epithelial tissues: **Simple squamous**, **simple cuboidal**, **simple columnar**, **stratified squamous**, **stratified cuboidal** and **stratified columnar**. These terms describe the shapes of the cells and the number of layers of cells you find in each type.

Each of the six basic types of epithelial tissue, plus two additional exceptional types **(transitional & pseudostratified)**, are described in more detail in the figures on the next few pages.

Structure defines function

Cell Layers:

- Simple = there is only <u>one</u> layer of epithelial cells
- Stratified = there are two or more layers of epithelial cells

Cell Shape:

- Squamous = flat cells
- Cuboidal = cube-shaped cells
- Columnar = tall cells

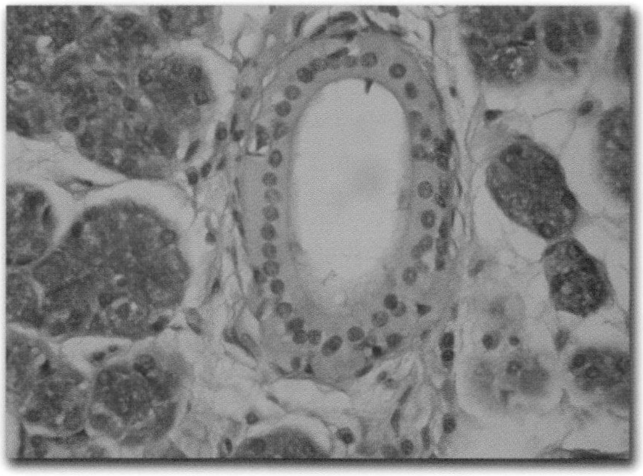

Tissue Type: Epithelial (simple cuboidal)

Cells: Single layer of cube-shaped cells

Function: Secretion and absorption, sometimes ciliated-driven movement of materials

Location: Lines the lumens of small secretory ducts, kidney tubules; portions of bronchioles, reproductive ducts, and ureters

vessles

Simple Cuboidal Epithelia (400x)

Figure 4-4

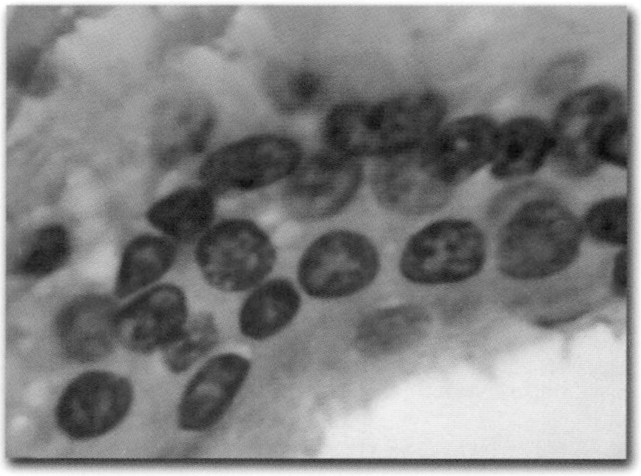

Tissue Type: Epithelial (stratified cuboidal)

Cells: Multiple layers of square cells

Function: Protection; secretion of mucus.

Location: Sweat glands, mammary glands and salivary glands

sufface

Stratified Cuboidal Epithelia (1200x)

Figure 4-5

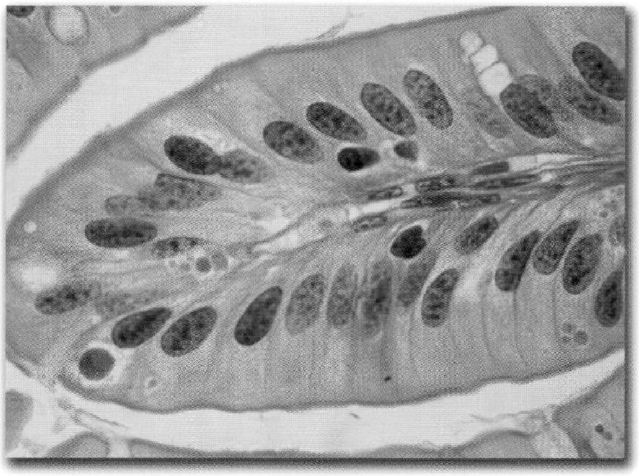

Tissue Type: Epithelial (simple columnar)

Cells: Single layer of tall cells

Function: Secretion and absorption, sometimes ciliated-driven movement of materials, often possess microvilli to increase surface area of apical membrane

Location: Lines the intestinal tract and the lumens of some secretory ducts, lines bronchi and uterine tubes

Simple Columnar Epithelia (400x)

Figure 4-6

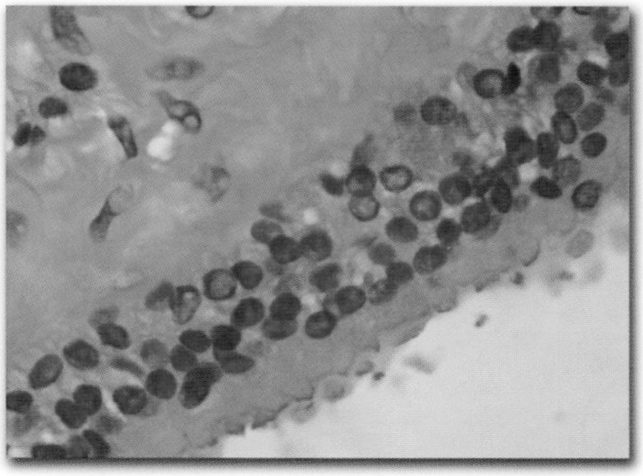

Tissue Type: Epithelial (stratified columnar)

Cells: Multiple layers of tall cells

Function: Protection; secretion of mucus.

Location: Rare in the body; some found in male urethra and ducts of large glands

Stratified Columnar Epithelia (800x)

Figure 4-7

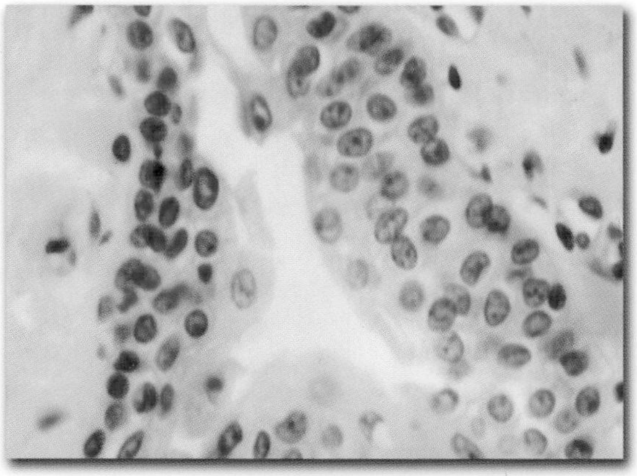

Tissue Type: Epithelial (transitional)

Cells: Single layer of cells that may appear stratified

Function: Allows extensive stretching or expansion of an organ.

Location: Lines the lumens of urethra and ureters; lines inside of urinary bladder.

Transitional Epithelium (400x)

Figure 4-8

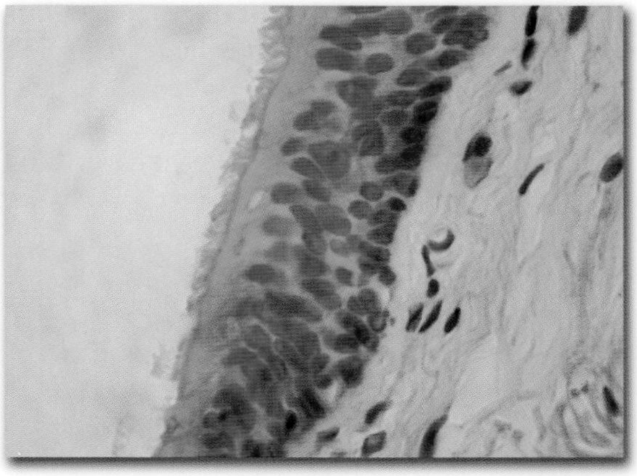

Tissue Type: Epithelial (pseudostratified columnar)

Cells: Single layer of tall cells, appears like multiple layers

Function: Secretion of mucus. Ciliated type moves the mucus layer across the surface of the cells; non-ciliated type provides protection to large tracts and ducts.

Location: Ciliated type in the trachea and most of the upper respiratory tract (moves the mucus escalator); non-ciliated type found in the male reproductive tract

Pseudostratified Columnar Epithelia (800x)

Figure 4-9

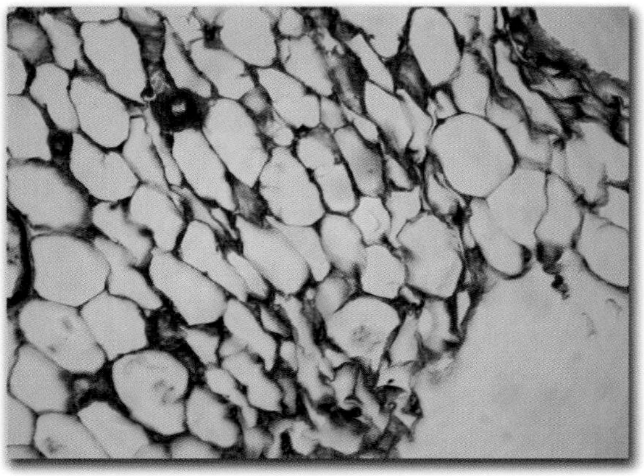

Type: Connective Tissue Proper (Loose)

Cell Types: Adipocytes

Fiber Types: Collagen, elastin and reticular; sparse gel-like matrix

Function: Store energy in the form of triglycerides; soft padding between moving organs and joints; heat conservation

Location: Surrounds most organs and joints; significant amounts beneath the dermis of the skin (i.e., the hypodermis or subcutaneous); major portion of female breasts

Figure 4-10

Adipose (Fat) Tissue (400x)

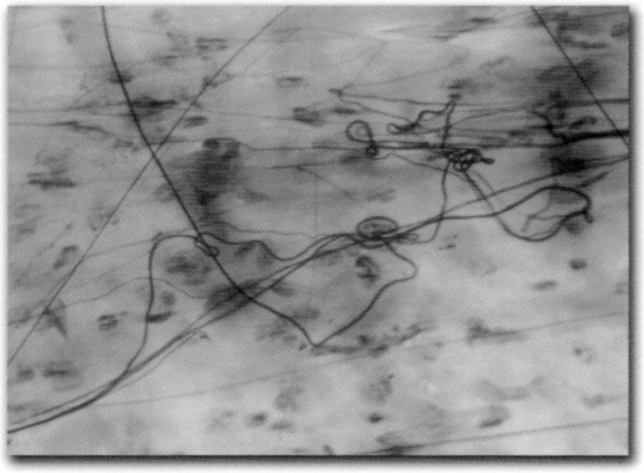

Type: Connective Tissue Proper (Loose)

Cell Types: Fibroblasts, leukocytes, mast cells, macrophages

Fiber Types: Collagen, elastic and reticular

Function: A packing material that cushions and protects soft organs.

Location: Surrounds most organs, forms lamina propia of mucous membranes

Figure 4-11

Areolar Connective (400x)

Connective Tissue

Connective tissues are the most diverse type of tissue in the body, but all connective tissues do basically what the name implies – they connect things. In general, connective tissues anchor epithelial tissues to the body and provide the structural framework for organs. In addition, some connective tissues act like packing material; they fill spaces in and around joints and other moving parts in the body. Connective tissues also store energy, transport substances, distribute heat and fluids, protect soft organs from impact, and many other things.

As diverse as they are, all connective tissues share certain common features, including

- **highly vascular** – With few exceptions (e.g., tendons and ligaments), connective tissues possess a rich blood supply.
- **extracellular material** – Connective tissues consist of relatively few cells dispersed within an extracellular environment called *matrix*. The matrix is composed of a *ground substance* and protein *fibers*. The ground substance varies from liquid to gel-like to downright hard. The fibers may be *collagen fibers, elastic fibers,* and / or *reticular fibers*.
- **cell variety** – Although connective tissues contain relatively few cells compared to epithelial tissue, the types of cells found there vary tremendously. They include *mast cells, fibroblasts, macrophages, monocytes,* and *basophils* among many, many others.

There are four major categories of connective tissue: **Connective tissue proper** (which includes loose and dense types), **cartilage**, **bone** and **blood**. Each type is described more fully in the figures on the next few pages.

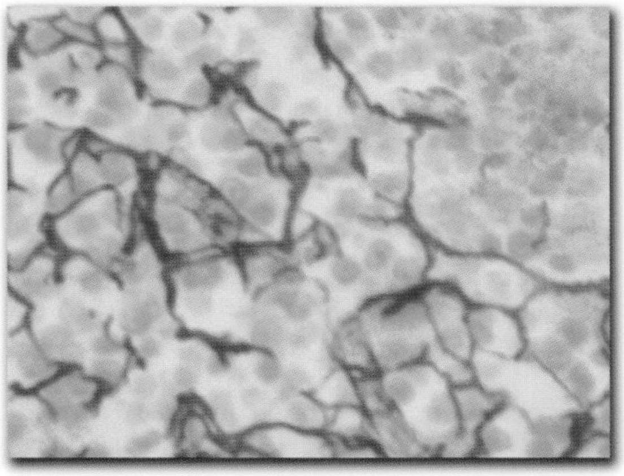

Type: Connective Tissue Proper (Loose)

Cell Types: Lymphocytes, mast cells, macrophages, fibroblasts

Fiber Types: Dark-staining reticular fibers

Function: Reticular fibers create a skeleton-like framework that supports other cell types, including those that support blood cell development.

Location: Spleen, lymph nodes, bone marrow, liver

Figure 4-12

Reticular Tissue (400x)

Type: Connective Tissue Proper (Dense Regular)

Cell Types: Fibroblasts

Fiber Types: Parallel collagen fibers

Function: Forms tendons & ligaments (attaches muscle to bone and bone to bone); withstands great tensile strength from one direction

Location: Tendons, ligaments, aponeuroses

Figure 4-13

Dense Regular Connective (400x)

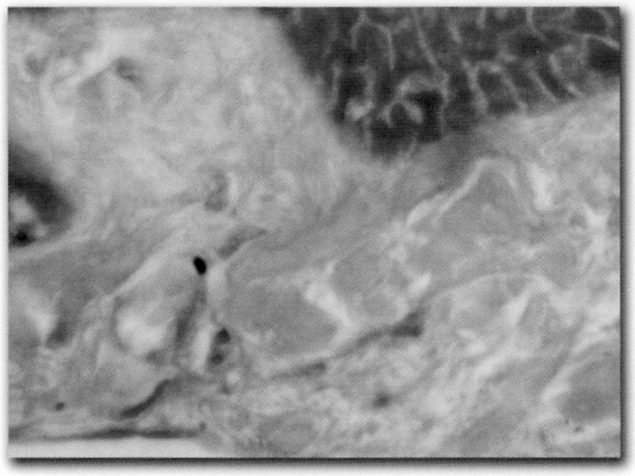

Type: Connective Tissue Proper (Dense Irregular)

Cell Types: Fibroblasts

Fiber Types: Cris-crossing collagen fibers

Function: Allows organs (such as the skin) to be pulled in any direction; withstands considerable tensile strength from many directions

Location: Dermis of the skin, fibrous joint capsules, vessels

Figure 4-14

Dense Irregular Connective (400x)

Type: Cartilage

Cell Types: Chondrocytes in lacunae, chondroblasts

Fiber Types: Collagen

Function: Support & protection

Location: Trachea, larynx, nose, costal cartilages, ends of long bones

Figure 4-15

Hyaline Cartilage (100x)

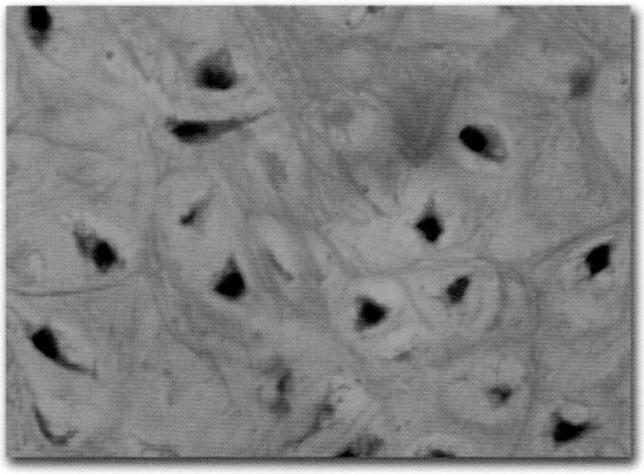

Type: Cartilage

Cell Types: Chondrocytes in lacunae

Fiber Types: Elastic fibers

Function: Provides support with flexibility

Location: The external ear (pinna), epiglottis

Figure 4-16

Elastic Cartilage (400x)

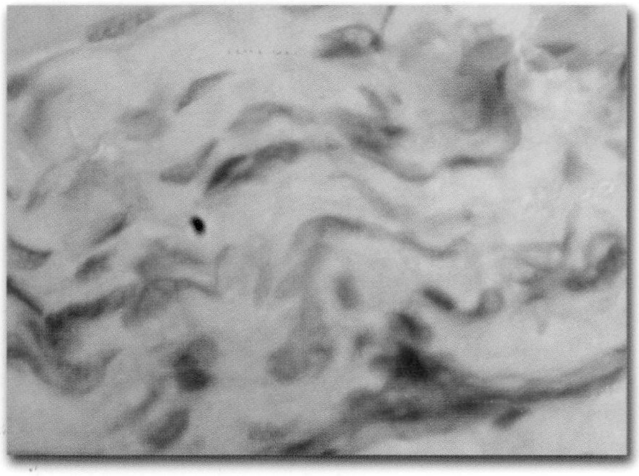

Type: Cartilage

Cell Types: Chondrocytes in lacunae

Fiber Types: Collagen

Function: Absorb compression forces

Location: Intervertebral discs, pubic symphysis, knee joint

Figure 4-17

Fibrocartilage (400x)

Type: Bone (Osseous Tissue)

Cell Types: Osteocytes (osteoblasts, osteoclasts), osteoprogenitor cells

Function: Support for the body and protection for soft tissues and organs; storage of nutrients, especially calcium

Location: The skeleton

Figure 4-18 Osseous Tissue (Bone) (400x)

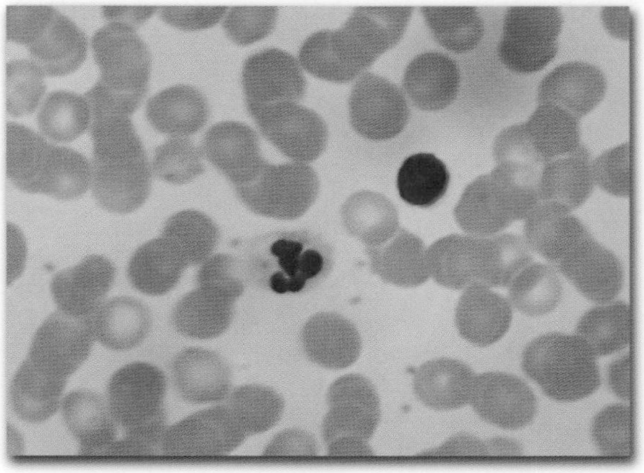

Type: Blood (Connective Tissue, Fluid)

Cell Types: Erythrocytes (red blood cells), leukocytes (white blood cells), thrombocytes (platelets)

Function: Transport of nutrients and waste products throughout the body

Location: Within blood vessels

Figure 4-19 Blood (1000x)

Muscle Tissue

There are three different types of muscle tissue, but all of them are designed for one basic function – to move something. Muscle tissues move things by *pulling action* only; muscles never push. The three types of muscle tissue are **skeletal muscle tissue**, **cardiac muscle tissue**, and **smooth muscle tissue**. Only skeletal muscle can be contracted voluntarily.

Skeletal muscles are all the muscles attached to the skeleton. The primary function of skeletal muscle is to inable voluntary movement of our bones. Important secondary functions of skeletal muscle include heat production to warm our bodies ("shivering" when cold is the act of rapid skeletal muscle movement to produce a burst of heat) and protection of soft organs from blunt impact. As a tissue, skeletal muscle is recognized by the extremely long, straight cells (called *skeletal myocytes*) marked with prominent stripes, called *striations*, from end-to-end. Those striations reflect the nearly crystaline array of proteins in the molecular contractile apparatus called the *sarcomere.* Because the cells are so long (up to 1 foot) they contain numerous nuclei – 50 or more in some cells.

Cardiac muscle cells are found exclusively in the heart. They possess sarcomeres and are striated like skeletal myocytes but are considerably shorter (and usually have only one nucleus). Unlike the long, straight cells in skeletal muscle, *cardiac myocytes* are branched and connected to their neighbors via *intercalated discs*. These connections firmly hold adjacent cells together while allowing ions and other small molecules to freely move among cells. This allows all the cells of the heart to stay in sync with one another and perform essentially as one enormous cell, an effect called *functional syncytium*.

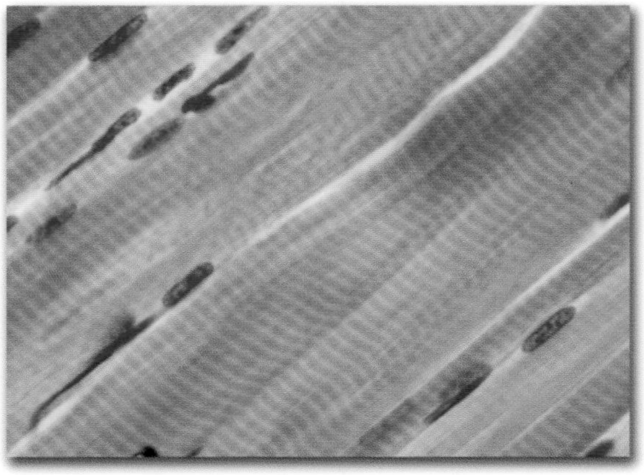

Type: Muscle (skeletal)

Cell Types: Skeletal myocytes (very long, striated due to the presence of sarcomeres); satellite cells

Function: Voluntary movement of the skeleton

Location: Attached to every bone of the skeletal system and to portions of the skin

Figure 4-20

Skeletal Muscle (800x)

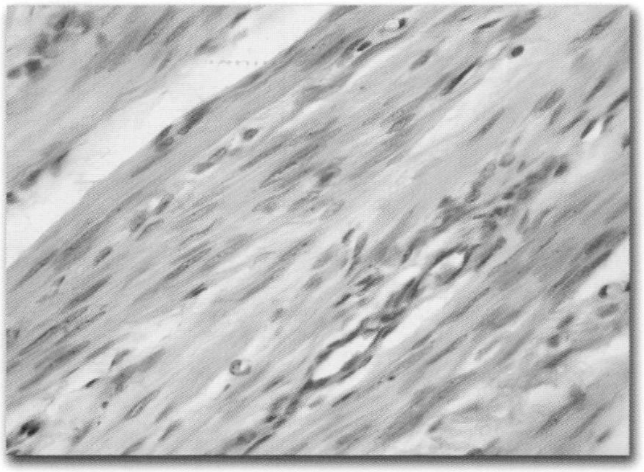

Type: Muscle (smooth)

Cell Types: Smooth muscle myocytes. Do not possess sarcomeres.

Function: Constriction of tubular structures such as blood vessels; movement of substances through tubular structures via peristalsis; not under voluntary control

Location: Around blood vessels the bronchioles; sphincter muscles; the pupil of the eye (i.e., the iris)

Figure 4-21

Smooth Muscle (400x)

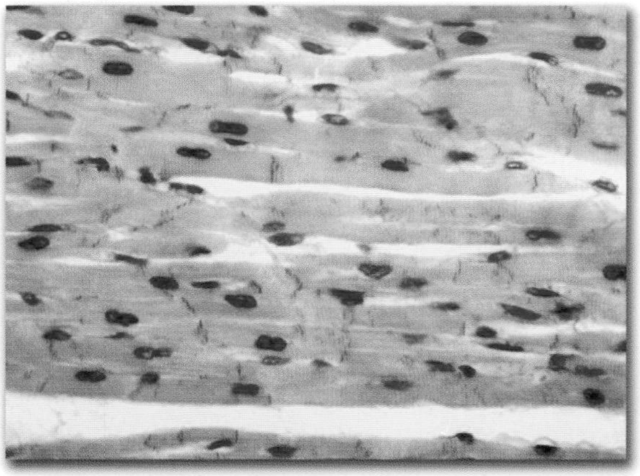

Type: Muscle (cardiac)

Cell Types: Cardiac myocytes (striated due to the presence of sarcomeres, much shorter than skeletal myocytes, branched, connected by intercalated discs, typically one to five nuclei per cell)

Function: Propel blood throughout cardiovascular vessels

Location: Found exclusively in the heart

* Discs set this apart *

Figure 4-22

Cardiac Muscle (400x)

Smooth muscle cells do not possess sarcomeres and thus do not appear striated, but smooth. They are found wrapped around blood vessels, the GI tract, and other tubular structures of the body. Their contractions cause the movement of materials through a tract, or constriction or dilation of a vessel lumen.

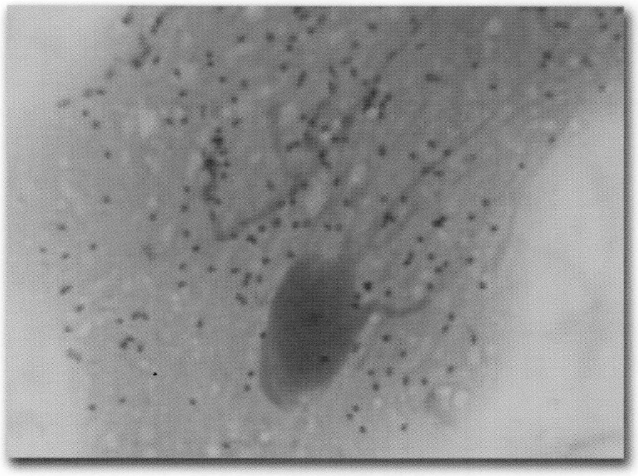

Type: Nervous

Cell Types: Neurons & neuroglia

Function: Transmit and process information rapidly. Transmission is achieved via electrical impulses called "action potentials" propogated through axons and dendrites. Information processing is achieved via neural circuits composed of many neurons.

Location: Brain, spinal cord, ganglia, peripheral nerves

Neuron & Neuroglia (800x)

Figure 4-23

Nervous Tissue

Nervous tissue is composed to two populations of cell: **neuroglia** and **neurons**. There are several types of neuroglia, but they all perform essentially supporting roles for neurons, or "nerve cells."

Neurons are unlike any other cell type in the body. They possess long extensions (up to a meter in length!) that conduct electrical signals to and from other neurons, receptors or effectors (e.g., glands or muscle). Individually, neurons behave like very sophisticated computer transistors. Collectively they give rise to the intelligent consciousness of the brain. How they achieve this remarkable feat is still one of the great mysteries of biology.

Most neurons contain many dendrites but only one axon. The relatively short dendrites received stimuli from receptors or other neurons and provide "input" to the neuron cell body. The single, long axon conducts "output" from that neuron to other neurons or effectors. Although there is only one axon leaving the cell body, the axon often branches so that multiple effectors can receive information from a single neuron.

GFP expressing pyramidal cell in mouse cortex. (reprinted with permission)
Lee W-CA, Huang H, Feng G, Sanes JR, Brown EN, et al. (2006) Dynamic Remodeling of Dendritic Arbors in GABAergic Interneurons of Adult Visual Cortex. PLoS Biol 4(2): e29. doi:10.1371/journal.pbio.0040029

Parts of a Typical Neuron

Figure 4-24

The body contains some 20 billion neurons, most of which are found in the brain and spinal cord. Bundles of axons thread through the body as *nerves*, carrying information rapidly from one part of the body to another (e.g., from sensory receptors in the foot to processing centers in the brain). The structure and function of the nerves, spinal cord and brain will be considered in detail in later exercises.

Body Membranes

Body membranes are composed of epithelial tissue attached to connective tissue. They are found wherever our internal organs interface with the outside environment and they enclose the body cavities introduced in exercise 1. The membranes that enclose the body cavities are moist, as are many of the interfacing membranes (such as the lining of the oral cavity); however, the integumentary membrane, or skin, is dry and water-repellent. *All* body membranes, however, are composed of epithelial tissue firmly attached to an underlying connective tissue. In addition, sheets of tough connective tissue (called *fascia*) compartmentalize muscle groups while anchoring muscle, bone and skin in position. These connections give rise to the **body wall** which surrounds the thorax and abdomen (as shown in Figure 4-25) and the **fascial compartments** which compartmentalize muscle groups of similar action in the limbs (as shown in Figure 4-26).

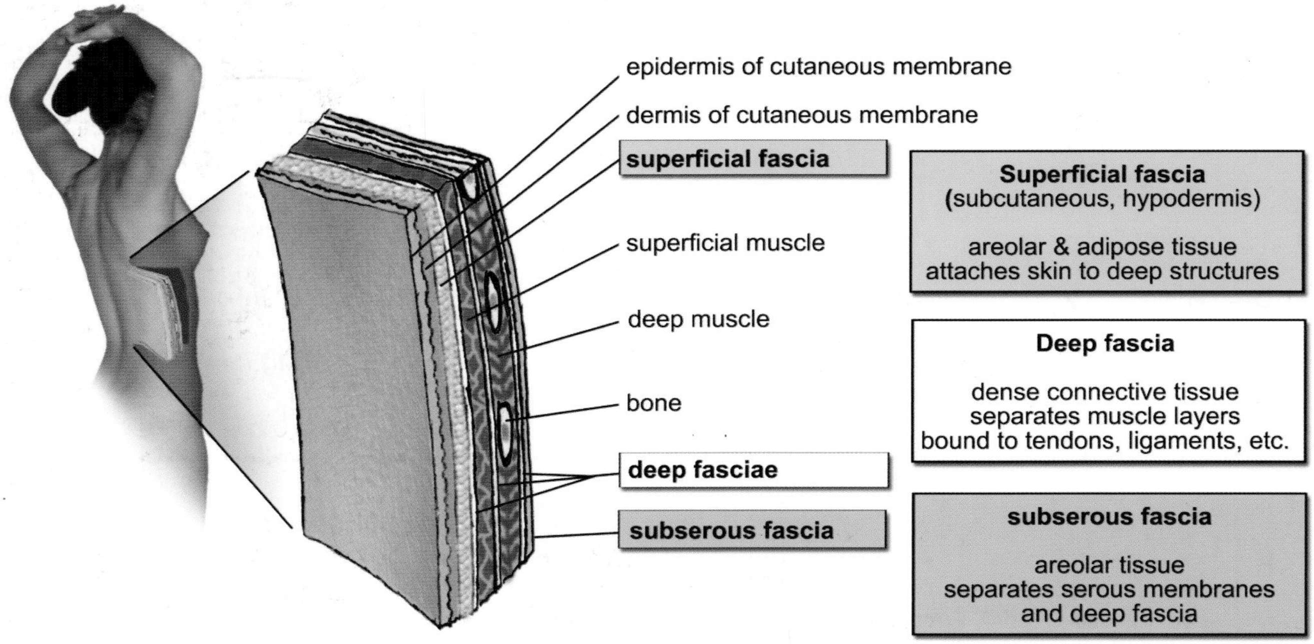

Figure 4-25 **The Body Wall & Fasciae**

Activity 1: Microscopically Examine Various Tissue Types

1. Obtain prepared microscope slides of the various tissue types discussed in this exercise. Be able to distinguish the various types from one another, describe the types of cells and / or fibers found in each tissue, and provide examples of where you might find each tissue in your body.

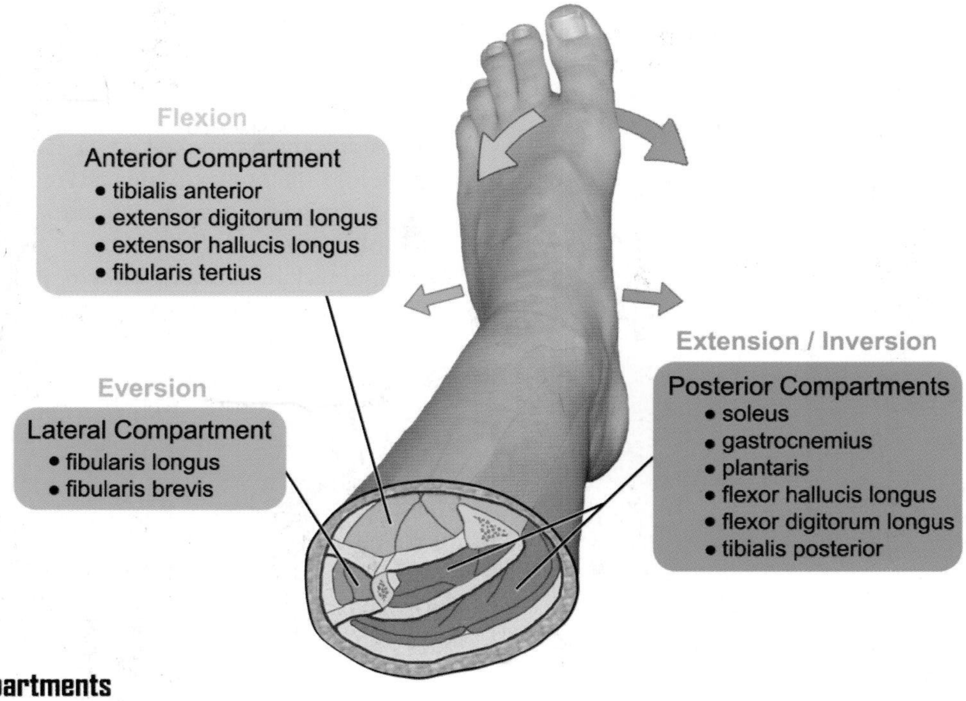

Fascial Compartments Figure 4-26

exercise 5

the INTEGUMENTARY system

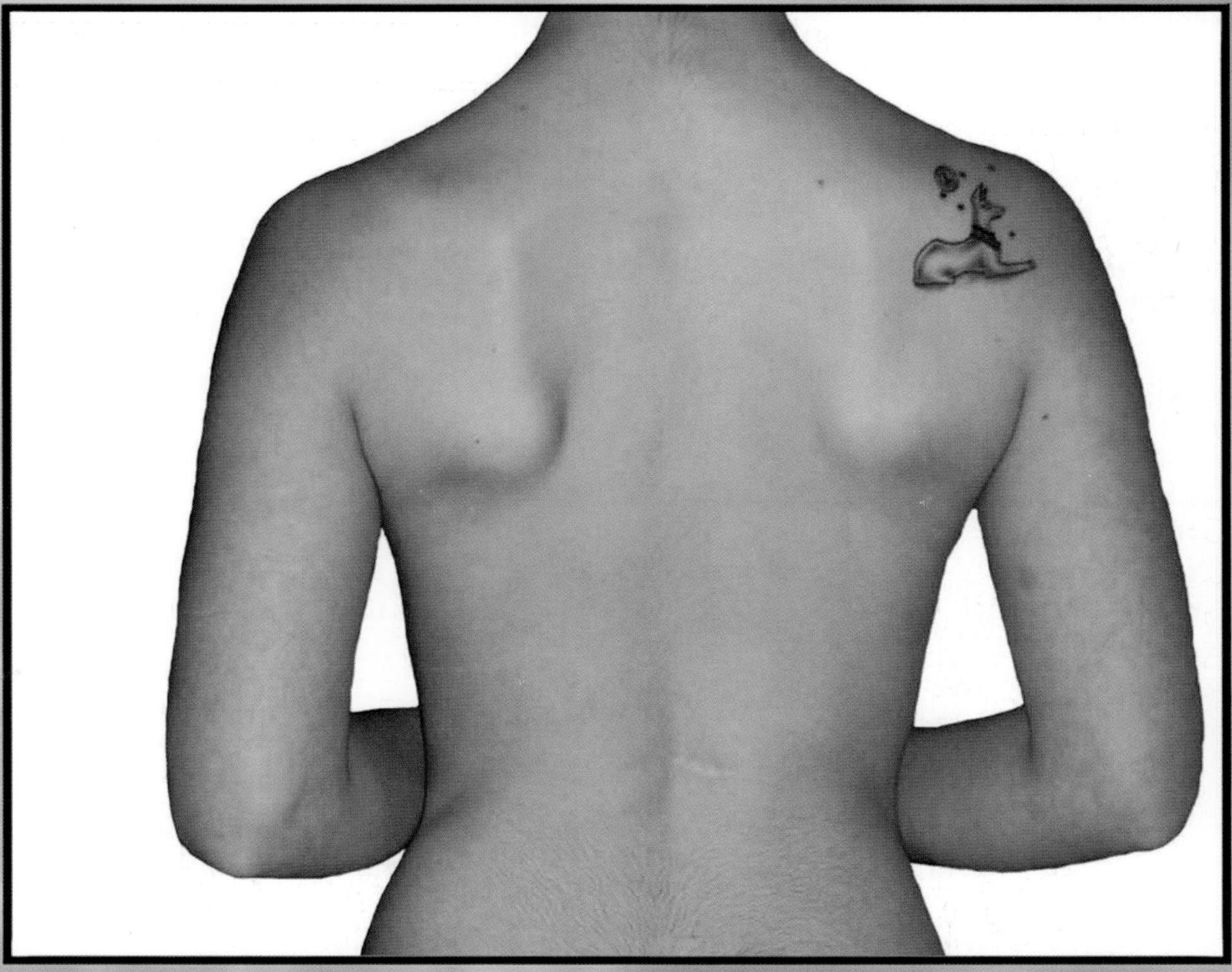

Did you... not clothe me with skin and flesh, and knit me together with bones and sinews?

Job 10:10-11

If beauty is only skin deep, then beauty is truly tenuous. At its thickest skin is less than 2 mm deep; the thinnest skin (covering the eyelids, lips, penis and scrotum) is only 200 µm (0.2 mm) thick. But if this covering we call skin, or *integument*, is thin, it certainly isn't flimsy: One only needs to wear a leather jacket to demonstrate its strength and durability. In addition, our skin is pliable, replenishable, water resistant and extremely sensitive. Together, these remarkable properties make skin the perfect interface between our delicate internal organs and the harsh world outside. The study of this remarkable organ is called *dermatology*.

The Epidermis & Dermis

Human skin is composed of two layers – a relatively thin layer called the **epidermis** and a thicker layer called the **dermis**. A third layer, called the hypodermis, lies just beneath the dermis but is generally not considered part of the integument, rather it's part of the connective tissues (i.e., fascia) that hold the skin to underlying body structures.

The epidermis (epi = above; hypo = below) consists of four or five layers, or strata. From top-to-bottom these are the **stratum corneum**, **stratum granulosum**, **stratum spinosum** and **stratum germinativum**. Thick epidermis is distinguished from thin epidermis by an additional *stratum lucidum* between the corneum and granulosum

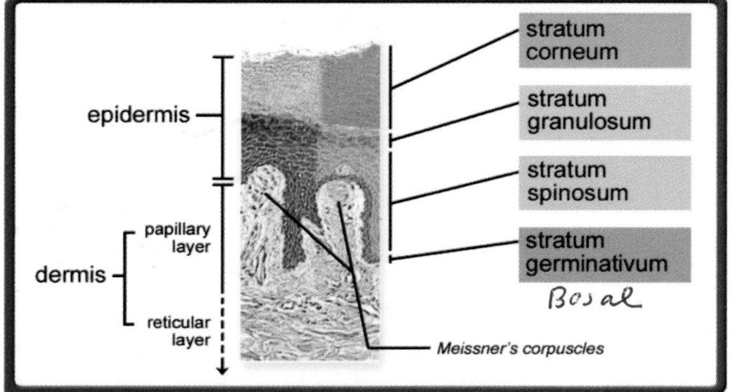

Layers of the Epidermis & Dermis

Figure 5-2

layers. Stem cells (also called germinative or basal cells) live exclusively in the stratum germinativum where they undergo near continuous cell divisions to replenish cells being lost at the skin surface. As the stem cells divide, the daughter cells are pushed up into the *stratum spinosum.* As the cells move through this layer they slowly lose water and begin to dry out. Before drying, however, the cells bolt themselves together tightly and become nearly completely filled with a single protein: keratin. As the cells leave the stratum spinosum and are pushed up into the stratum granulosum and stratum corneum, they become increasingly dry and flattened. Eventually, the now dead cells will get pushed to the skin's surface and be sloughed off. The whole process, from cell birth to sloughing away, takes only about 2 weeks on average.

The epidermis is connected to the underlying dermis through a series of undulating

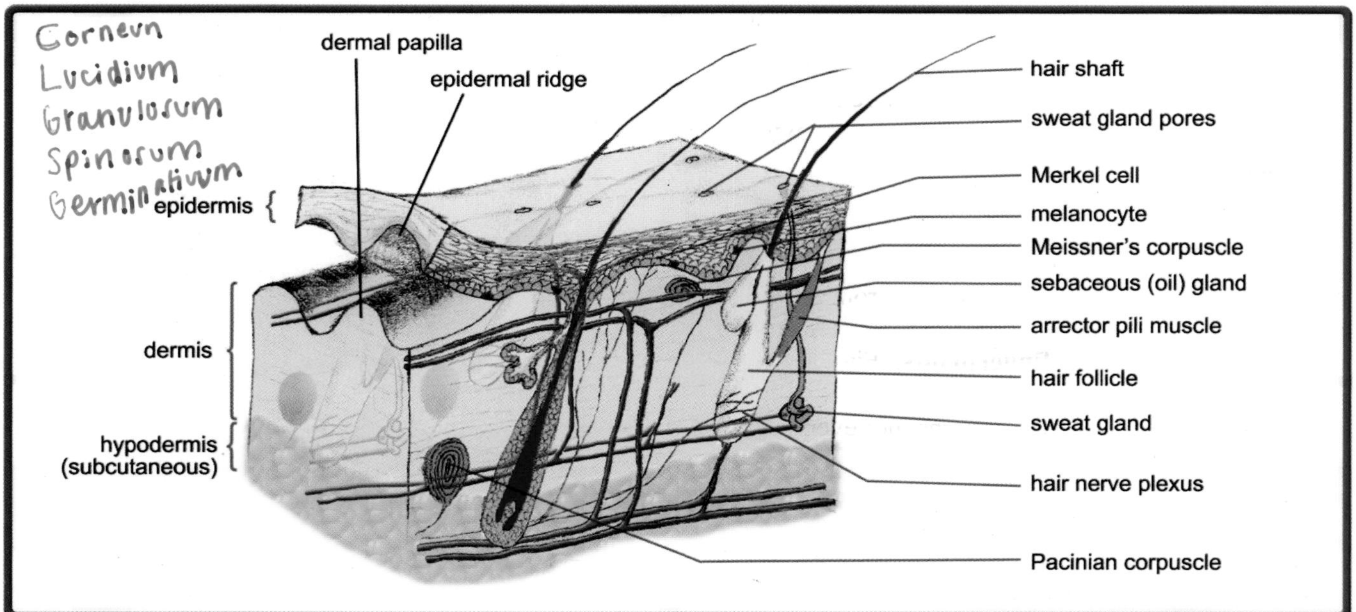

Figure 5-1

Major Components of the Skin

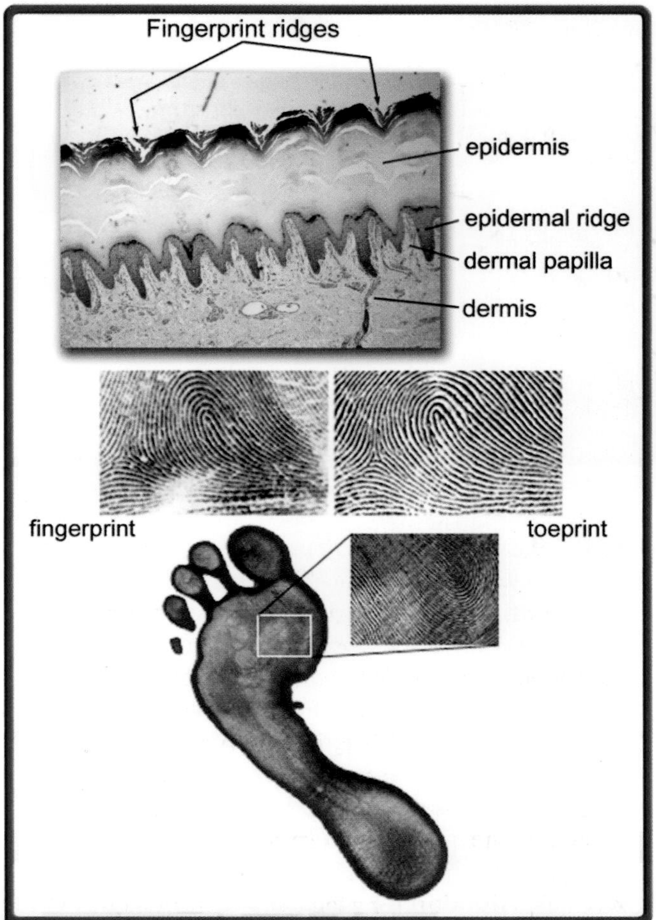

Epidermal Ridges & Skin Prints

Figure 5-3

hills and valleys that fit neatly into one another. The epidermis and dermis can be pictured as two egg-carton matrices lying snugly one on top of the other. These hills and valleys are referred to as **epidermal ridges** in the epidermis and **dermal papillae** in the dermis. They exist to hold the epidermis firmly to the dermis and they're more prominent on areas of the skin subjected to heavy frictional forces. Where the skin is exposed to extreme friction – the palms of the hands, the fingertips, the soles of the feet and toetips – additional ridges are formed in the thickened stratum corneum. These ridges are so prominent they can be seen on the skin surface as what are commonly referred to as **fingerprints**. Fingerprints (and toeprints) are utterly unique – no two people on the planet share identical patterns, not even genetically identical twins. Skin prints are only found on hairless skin.

Excessive frictional forces placed on the skin, such as those experienced while wearing an ill-fitting shoe, may cause the epidermis to pull away from the underlying dermis at the epidermal

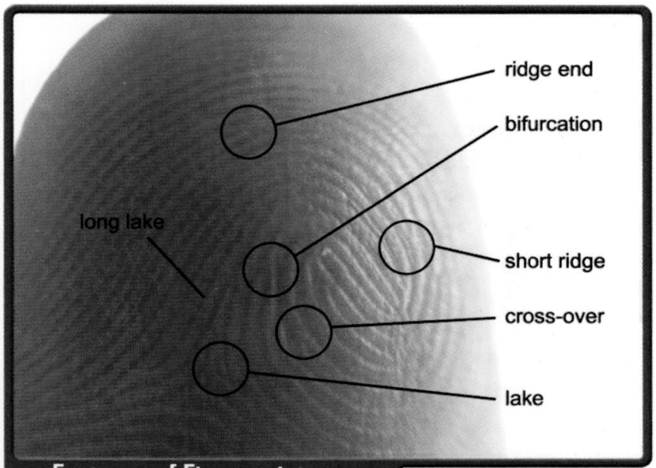

Features of Fingerprints

Figure 5-4

ridges. When this happens, the torn-away area becomes filled with interstitial fluids resulting in a *blister*.

The dermis itself is composed primarily of areolar and dense irregular connective tissues. In a living person or animal this tissue is elastic – stretchy and resilient – but becomes much less so after commercial tanning; it's the dermis that forms the bulk of the material in a leather jacket. The living dermis also holds water extremely well and contributes greatly to *skin turgor* – the healthy plumpness and resiliency of skin. When dehydrated

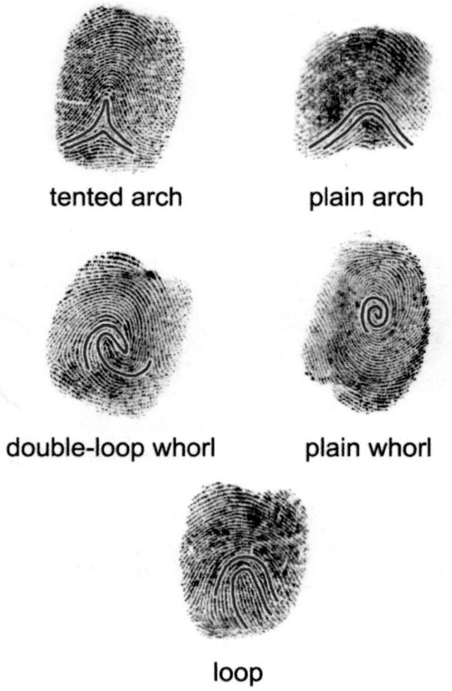

Figure 5-5 Common Fingerprint Patterns

Structure = Function

Epidermal ridges and skin prints are structural features that aid a particular function: grabbing. Just like the tread on a car tire improves its grip to the road, these skin ridges increase the grasping ability of the hands (for picking up objects) and the feet (for walking).

Fingerprints are unique for each person. The ridges that shape fingerprints form randomly during fetal development. After more than 100 years of fingerprinting and more than 100 million prints obtained worldwide, no two individuals have ever been found to have the same pattern. Even genetically identical twins, who may not be distinguishable by their DNA profiles, will have distinct fingerprints. In addition, fingerprints are *immutable*, meaning your prints remain the same throughout your entire life. Because fingerprints are unique & immutable, they are used for identification of people. They can even be used to solve crimes because oils from our fingers remain on the objects we touch in the same pattern as our fingerprints. These left-behind, or latent, prints are usually invisible but can be seen after applying powders or special dyes.

the skin loses water from the dermis and becomes less turgid; dehydrated skin will remain folded when pinched rather than resuming its original shape. Loss of skin turgor and elasticity occurs naturally with age, causing the elderly to take on a wrinkled appearance.

Unlike the epidermis, the dermis is vascular and highly innervated. Superficial blood vessels lie just below the epidermis and provide nutrients to the cells of the stratum germinativum via simple diffusion. Deep blood vessels lie along the bottom of the dermis. Blood may be shunted to either the superficial vessels (when the body is hot) or the deep vessels (when the body is cold) to radiate away or conserve heat to maintain a constant body temperature.

The abundant nerve supply of the dermis makes the skin extremely sensitive to a number of both pleasurable and painful stimuli. Stimulation of free nerve endings is usually interpreted by the brain as pain. Bee stings, for example, stimulate free nerve endings. Non-painful touch, pressure and vibrations are detected by specialized sensory

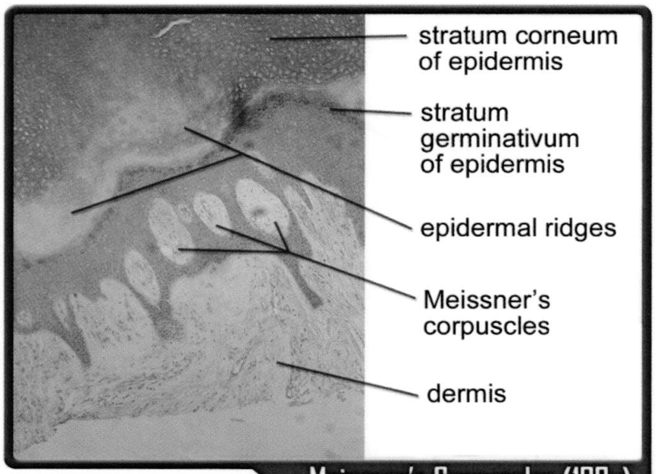

Figure 5-6 Meissner's Corpuscles (100x)

receptors. **Meissner's corpuscles**, located superficially in the dermis, detect light pressure. **Pacianian corpuscles** are deeper and detect heavy pressure on the skin. **Merkel cells** (or, Merkel discs) are spikey cells found in the stratum germinativum associated with sensory nerve endings; they provide sensations of soft touch.

Skin color varies dramatically, from pale ivory to dark ebony (Figure 5-7). The color of skin is dictated primarily by the amount of *melanin* in the lower layers of the epidermis. This dark brown pigment is produced by special cells (*melanocytes*) in the stratum germinativum. Black people do not have more melanocytes than white people, rather the cells are more active and produce substantially more pigment. Melanin is an excellent absorber of UV radiation, which can easily damage DNA in the rapidly dividing stem cells of the epidermis. Consequently, melanin production is increased when the skin is exposed to intense sunlight causing the skin to darken, or "tan."

For those who produce little melanin skin color is determined by the levels of an orange pigment in the skin called *carotene*. As its name implies, this pigment is found plentifully in carrots. For those who lack an abundance of either carotene or melanin, skin color will be affected primarily by the rich blood supply of the dermis, causing the skin to appear rosy or pink. As shown in figure 5-7, Njeri's skin (and hair and eyes) is dark because he has relatively high levels of melanin; Cary's skin is dominated by carotene but her eyes and hair are darkened by melanin; Nicole has little melanin or carotene so her skin is rosy white, her hair blonde and her eyes brightly colored blue.

Figure 5-7

Skin Pigmentation & Color

Local discoloration of the skin can occur upon chemical or physical damage. Indeed, the skin is an excellent resource for doctors when diagnosing numerous pathologies because of this fact. Bruising, for example, is caused by bleeding (and clotting) beneath the epidermis. The blue, brown and yellow colors associated with bruises derive from hemoglobin (blue when deoxygenated) and the breakdown products of heme (e.g., billirubin). In the photo at the beginning of this chapter, notice that the model has a small bruise on her right arm.

The dermis is filled with extracellular protein fibers that confer the properties of pliability and resiliency to our skin. Notice how the skin wraps around the shoulder blades, for example, allowing them to move freely underneath. Many of those fibers are made of the proteins *collagen* and *elastin*. Collagen is a long and extremely tough protein that acts like cables criss-crossing our skin to hold it firmly together. Pound-for-pound collagen is stronger than steel. Elastin is also a long, fibrous protein, but it's stretchy – it can be pulled to nearly twice its original length then bounce back readily when the stress is relieved. Elastin, however, has its limits. With excessive stretching elastin, collagen and other skin proteins can tear leaving scars called *stretch marks*. These injuries are fairly common on the bellies of mothers, whose skin was stretched during pregnancy. (Scars caused by lacerations are created by *fibroblasts* cells laying down new fibers until the damaged epithelial cells can be restored. Most such scars are temporary, but if the laceration was severe, the scar may remain for life).

Although your skin is regularly sloughed off and replaced, tattoos remain. This is because the tattoo ink is deposited beneath the epidermis and into the dermal layer. The dermis contains mostly extracellular fibers and relatively few cells; the fibers – and ink – remain relatively unchanged for decades.

Hair & Nails

Hair and nails are accessory structures to the integument. Both are composed primarily of the protein *keratin*. The nails provide extra protection to the terminal portion of the digits (fingers and toes), while hair increases the padding, water repellency and sensitivity of the skin.

Although nails are found only on the fingers and toes, hair covers the entire body, except for the palms of the hand, the soles of the feet, the sides of the fingers and toes, the lips and portions of the external genitalia in both sexes. *Terminal hairs*, which are relatively long and thick, are restricted to the head, eyebrows, eyelashes and pubic regions of females but are more widely distributed on males due to the effects of testosterone (hair follicles sensitive to testosterone and estrogen are also responsible for the development of *pubic hairs* at puberty). *Vellus hairs* are widely distributed over most of the remaining parts of the body, with the exceptions noted above. Vellus hairs, or "peach fuzz" as they are affectionately called, are much thinner, shorter and typically lighter in color than terminal hairs. These actually make up the bulk of the hairs on your body. An adult has rougly 2.5 million hairs on the body, only 25% (about 600,000) of which are terminal hairs on the head. On average, we lose 50-100 hairs from the head each day, but these are usually replaced at an equal rate.

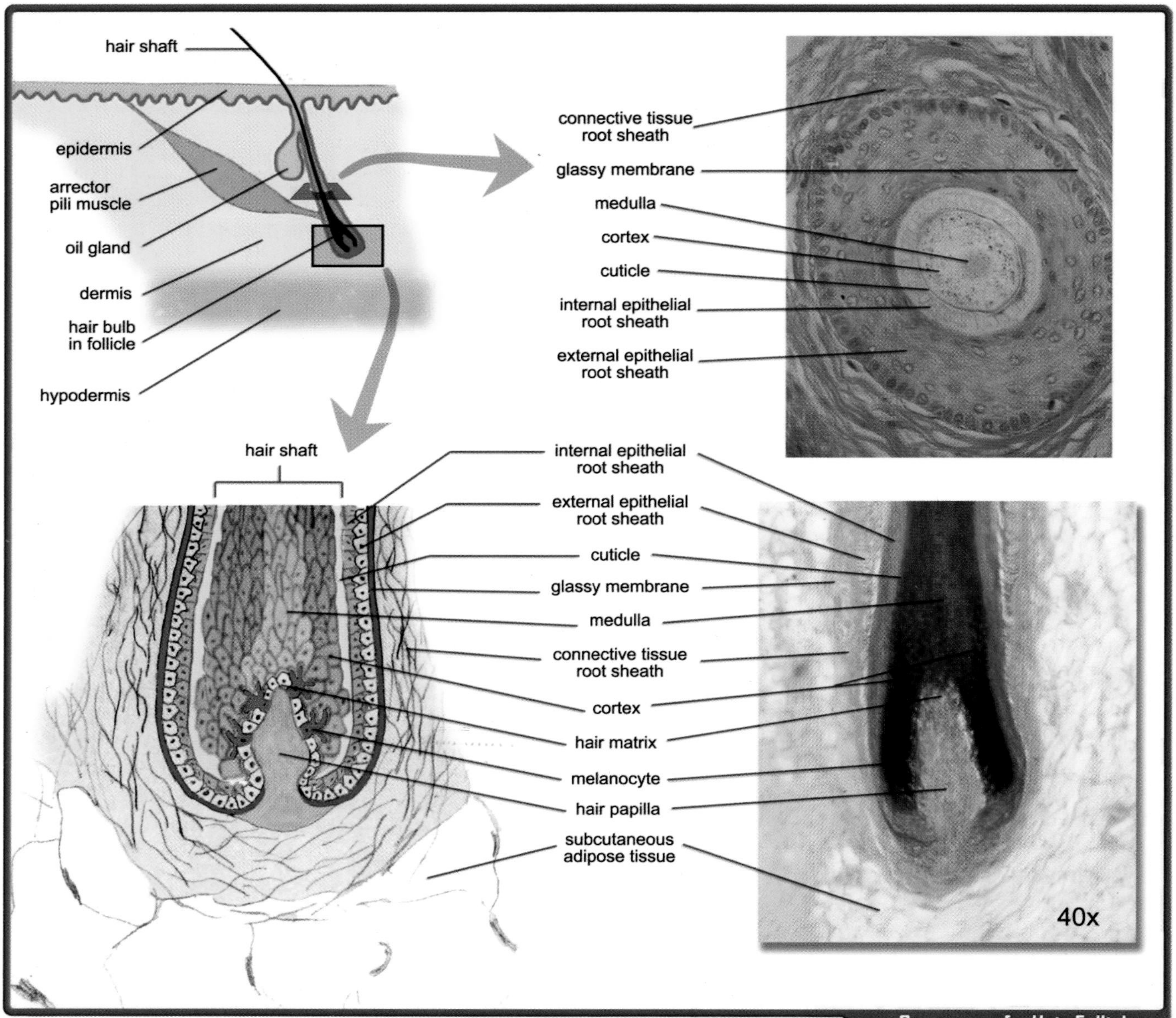

Figure 5-8

Structure of a Hair Follicle

Each hair has an associated oil gland and **arrector pili** muscle (Figure 5-8). This extremely small smooth muscle originates from the basement membrane at the epidermal-dermal interface and inserts on the hair follicle. Upon stimulation by the sympathetic division of the autonomic nervous system, arrector pili muscles contract and lift the hair shaft perpendicular to the skin surface (usually the hair shaft lies down nearly parallel to the skin surface). This action serves to increase the sensitivity of the skin to touch and is an important part of the "fight-or-flight" response.

At the base of each hair follicle is a highly vascular **papilla** which supplies nutrients to the growing **matrix**, where new hair growth occurs. Similar to skin replenishment, stem cells in the hair matrix continually divide pushing their daughter cells upward. As the cells rise they becoming increasingly flattened, dry, bolted together, filled with keratin and melanin (more or less depending on melanocyte activity). Each hair shaft is composed of a central **medulla** surrounded by a **cortex** and **cuticle**. middle

Nails are found on the superior aspect of the terminal portions of each digit (Figure 5-9). The purpose of finger nails and toe nails is to strengthen the termini of the digits – especially when grasping objects and walking. The nails on

Shaft layes: Superficial — Deep
- cuticle
- cortex
- medulla

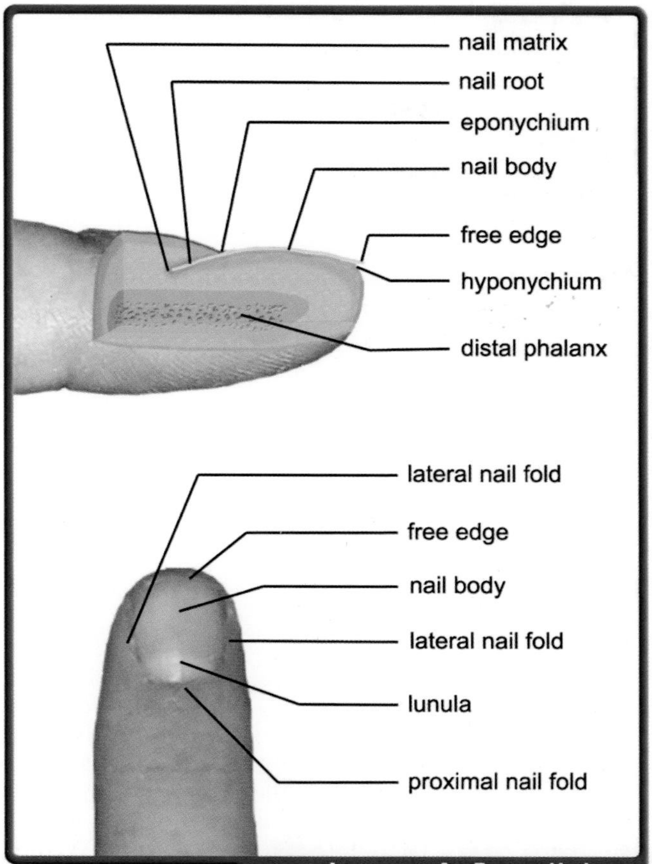

Figure 5-9 Anatomy of a Finger Nail

both fingers and toes are quite similar (Figure 5-10), consisting of a **free edge**, a **nail body**, and a **nail root**. Nail growth occurs at the end of the nail root in a mitotically active zone called the **nail matrix**. The cells of the newly formed nail are not fully differentiated and slightly whiter than the mature cells, producing a white crescent at the proximal edge of the nail called the **lunula**. As the nail grows forward, it drags with it attached epithelial cells from the skin, resulting in a thin covering of skin cells over a portion of the nail called the **eponychium**, or *cuticle*. Similarly, attached skin cells are carried underneath the free edge of the nail forming the **hyponychium**.

Glands

Glands located in the dermis deposit sweat and oils onto the surface our skin. Sweat is a coolant; heat from deep in the body is transferred to the atmosphere when sweat evaporates from the skin. Oils keep the skin from becoming too dry and increase the water-repellency of skin. Four types of glands may be found in the skin: sweat glands, oil glands, ceruminous glands and mammary glands.

Sweat glands, or *sudoriferous glands*, are the most abundant type of glands in the skin. Sudoriferous glands may be categorized as either *eccrine sweat glands* or *apocrine sweat glands*. Eccrine sweat glands are the most numerous and widely distributed throughout the body. Distribution is not uniform, however; some parts of the body possess considerably more eccrine sweat glands than other parts. For example, the palms of the hands contain an abundance of eccrine glands that may become quite active when you get nervous (such as before a lab exam), resulting in "sweaty palms." The sweat produced by eccrine glands is roughly 99% water with a little NaCl, urea and antibiotics.

Apocrine sweat glands are limited to the groin, axillary (armpit) areas and around the nipples. These sweat glands produce a thicker sweat enjoyed by bacteria; excessive bacterial growth produces an unpleasant odor often masked by deodorants and / or perfumes in our culture.

Oil glands, or *sebaceous glands*, are distributed throughout the body, usually associated with hairs. (Those not associated with hairs are called *sebaceous follicles*). These glands produce an oily substance called *sebum* which lubricates hair and the surface of the skin. This natural moisturizer keeps the hair from becoming brittle and the skin from becoming overly dry. Sebum is released by the holocrine mode of secretion, meaning that cells within the gland completely

Sweat Glands on Print Ridges Figure 5-10

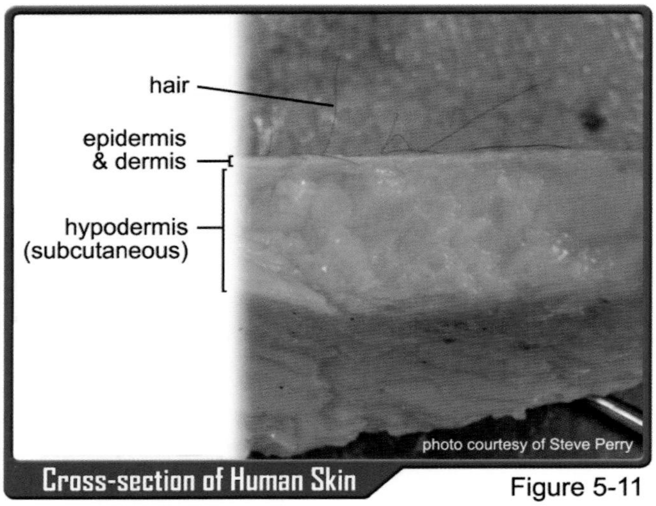

Figure 5-11

rupture. The presence of cellular lipids (such as the ER and plasma membranes) contributes to the oily nature of sebum.

When oil glands become over-active – a common response to the surge of hormones released during puberty – their ducts become clogged causing swelling and bacterial infection. The infection increases the inflammation initiated by the swollen clogged ducts. The result is acne.

Ceruminous glands are found only in the ear and produce the thick secretion called *cerumen*, or *ear wax*. Ear wax protects the ear drum from objects inserted into the external acoustic meatus and discourages the entrance of insects.

Mammary glands are limited to the breasts. The glands are rather undeveloped in children, men and non-pregnant females and only become active in pregnant and nursing women. During lactation, they produce a nutritious milk used to sustain the life of a newborn for many months.

The Hypodermis

Though technically not part of the integument, our discussion of the skin would not be complete without mentioning the hypodermis. This layer of connective tissue, also known as the subcutaneous, dramatically affects the surface appearance of our bodies. It is the adipose, or fat, of the hypodermis that shapes and molds our contours. Muscles, blood vessels and tendons easily seen on men are often masked on women, whose bodies are generally smoother and curvier – less chiseled – than men due to the abundance and distribution of hypodermal adipose. For instance, the breasts of a non-pregnant adult female consist almost entirely of subcutaneous fat whereas the breasts of a male are dominated by the pectoralis major muscles. (The breast of a pregnant female is dominated by active mammary glands). The relative thickness of the hypodermis compared to the integument in a typical skin section can be seen in figure 5-11.

Activity 1: Examine Skin Attachment

1. Use the index finger of one hand to rub the skin back-and-forth on the dorsum of your other hand. Then, rub the skin back-and-forth on the palmer side of your hand.
2. Notice how much more tightly the skin on the palmer side of your hand is attached to underlying fascia than the skin of the dorsum side. This is to insure that the skin on the palmer side is not pulled to far out of place while grasping objects.
3. Is the same true for the dorsum and plantar sides of the foot, as well?

Activity 2: Examine Skin Microscopically

1. Obtain prepared microscope slides of the scalp (thin skin with hair) and the palm (thick hairless skin).
2. Observe the strata in your scalp sample, as well as the numerous hairs. Try to identify as many parts of the hair as possible.
3. Observe the strata in thick skin under high power. Identify the different layers. Also note the prominent epidermal ridges and larger print ridges.

Activity 3: Observe Sweat Gland Activity

1. Sweat glands are activated by the sympathetic nervous system, which in turn can be activated by pain.
2. Observe a fingertip in a dissecting microscope.
3. While observing your fingertip, bite a finger on your other hand, or have a lab partner pinch you painfully.
4. Small droplets of sweat should become visible on your fingertip under the microscope within a few seconds following the painful stimulus.

Activity 4: Sweat Gland Mapping

1. Before beginning this exercise, try to guess which parts of the body might have more sweat glands than others. Why did you select those parts?

2. Obtain 3 pieces of bond paper cut into 1cm x 1cm squares, a bottle of iodine and some adhesive tape.
3. Select 3 patches of skin and have your partner apply a small amount of iodine to each patch using a cotton swab.
4. Wait 3-4 minutes to allow the iodine to dry thoroughly, then have your partner use adhesive tape to secure a square of bond paper over the iodine.
5. After about 15 minutes remove the pieces of bond paper from your skin. Count the number of black dots on each square. Which patches of skin resulted in the most dots (i.e., has the most sweat glands)? Does this agree with your guess above?

The yellow iodine solution soaks into your sweat glands after applying it to your skin. While you were waiting during the 15-minute interval, your sweat glands produced sweat and deposited the sweat, containing iodine solution, onto the bond paper. The iodine chemically reacts with the starch in the bond paper to form a dark blue or black spot, thus providing a “map” of your sweat glands.

Activity 5: Fingerprinting

In this activity you will observe your own fingerprints and demonstrate how fingerprinting is used to solve crimes.

1. Obtain two index cards and an ink pad.
2. Roll the tip of your index finger in the ink pad, then roll it on both index cards.
3. Determine which type of print you have (i.e., whorl, loop or arch). Observe the different features found in fingerprints, such as lakes, bifurcations, etc.
4. Write your name on ONE of the index cards only. Turn in both cards to your lab instructor.
5. The lab instructor will randomly select one card without a name. We’ll pretend that the print on that card was obtained from a crime scene. Compare that print to all the cards with names on them to determine who the print belongs to. Who was the one who left the print at the crime scene?

exercise 6

the SKELETAL system

- tissue & organization -

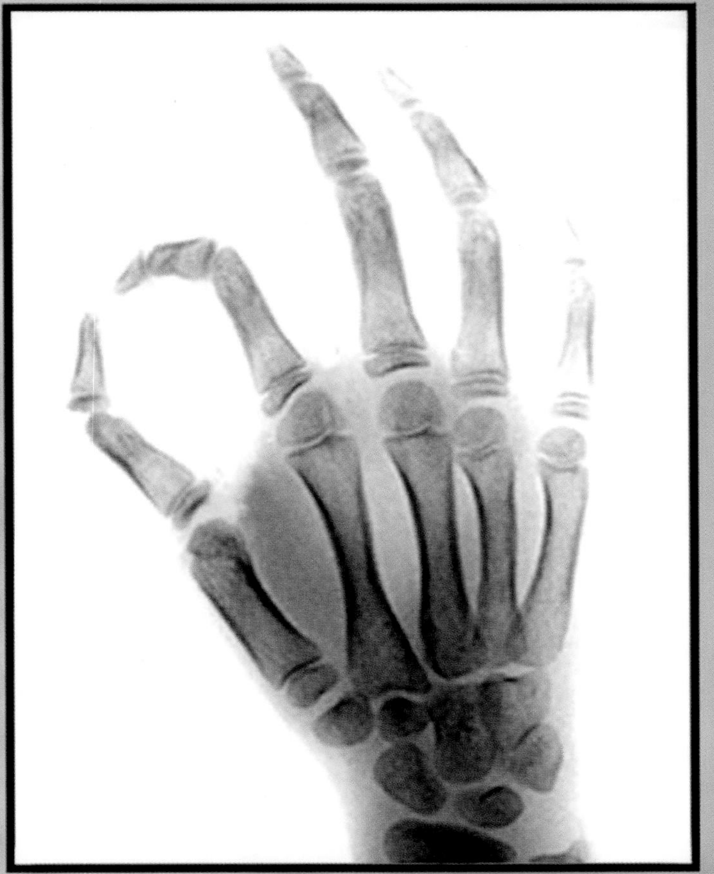

A cheerful look brings joy to the heart,
and good news gives health to the bones.
Proverbs 15:30

The 206 bones of the human skeleton are far from stiff, lifeless props that hold us up. Unlike hair and nails, our bones are fully alive and play crucial roles in maintaining body homeostasis. The bones produce red blood cells, for example, and are largely responsible for preserving calcium and phosphate balance in our blood. Muscles pulling on bones perform body movements and hard bones overlaying soft tissues protect them from blunt impact and punctures. As metabolically active, living organs, our bones are continually being constructed, deconstructed and reconstructed throughout our lives. In fact, the entire skeleton is effectively recycled and replaced every five years.

The bones of the skeleton are separated into two major divisions – those that form the central axis of the body and those that form or support the limbs. The bones forming the central axis are collectively called the **axial skeleton**. The bones of the limbs are called the **appendicular skeleton**. There are 80 bones in the axial skeleton and 126 bones in the appendicular skeleton.

Bone Classification

Bones are classified according to their shapes. All bones fall into one of just five categories: long bones, short bones, flat bones, sesamoid bones, and irregular bones.

Flat bones, as the name implies, tend to be rather thin. Most of the bones that form the brain case are broad, flat and basin-like (e.g., the occipital bones). The ribs are also flat bones, but they are long. thin and curved in shape.

Long bones are distinguished by a central shaft and knob-like endings. The growth of long bones occurs between the shaft (diaphysis) and the knobs (epiphyses) as described later in this chapter. **Short bones** are stubby in appearance and lack a discernable shaft. Long bones and short bones are *not* described (or distinguished) strictly by their lengths. In the foot, for example, the distal phalanges of the toes are shorter in length than the navicular and calcaneus bones; however, the phalanges are long bones while the calcaneus and navicular are short bones.

Sesamoid bones derive their name from the fact that they look like sesame seeds. There are only a few examples of sesamoid bones in the body – the major one is the patella, or knee cap.

Irregular bones do not fit in any of the above categories. Their shapes are variable and highly modified for particular functions. For example, the vertebrae have a large hole in them through which the spinal cord passes and long projections for the attachment of back muscles.

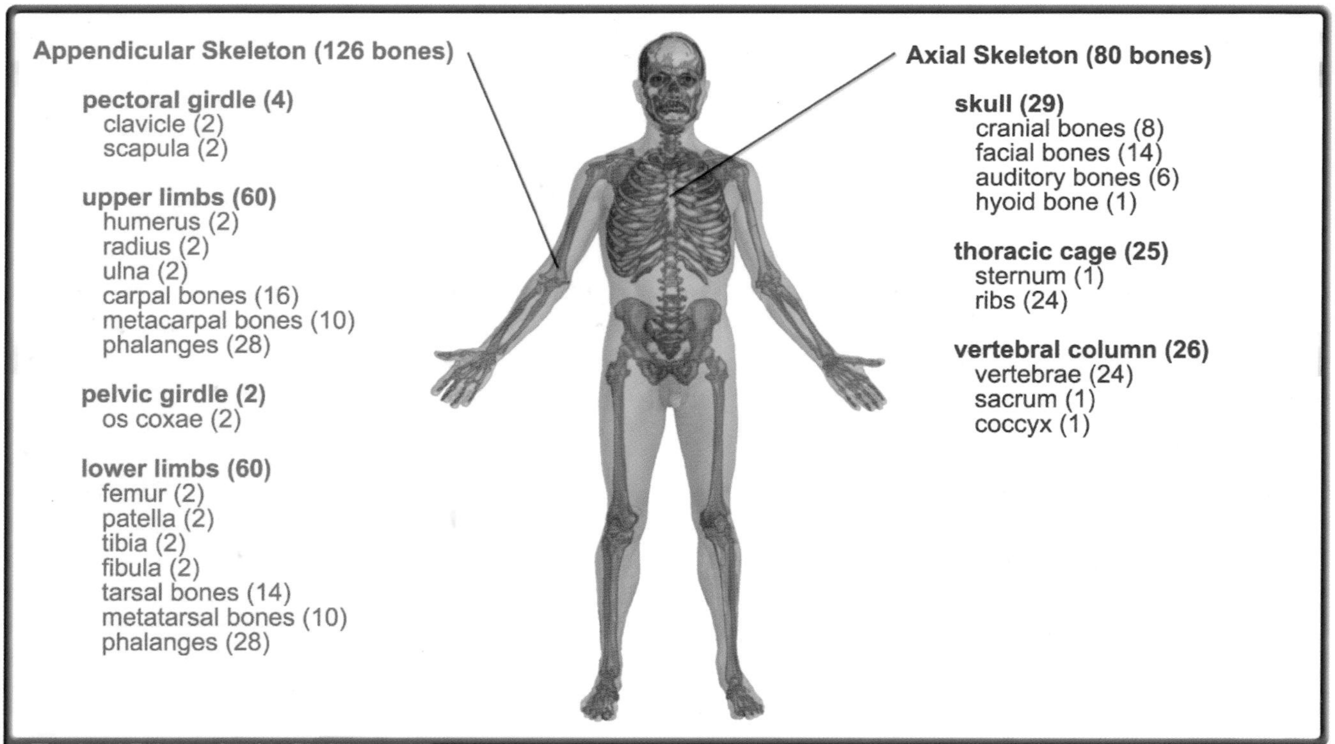

The Axial & Appendicular Skeletons

Figure 6-1

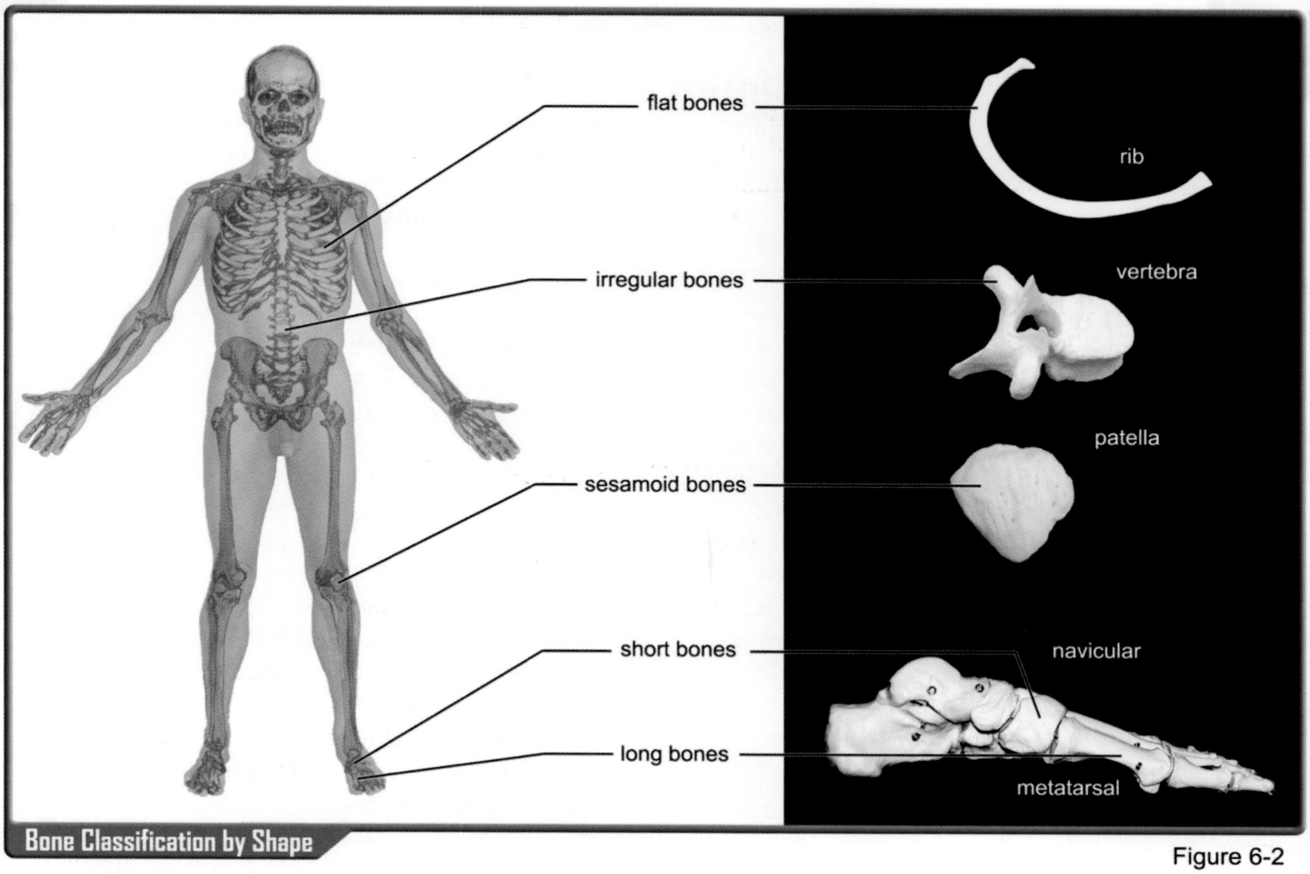

Figure 6-2

Bone Markings

Bones are rarely smooth and featureless, rather they are scarred with numerous markings. As you examine bones in lab, keep in mind that those markings indicate where muscles attached to the living bone, or where nerves and blood vessels passed through the bone or traveled along side it.

Bone markings are divided into two major categories: **Projections** (a.k.a., *elevations*) and **depressions**. Projections are usually part of articulation surfaces, or serve as attachment sites for muscles or ligaments. Examples of projections and depressions commonly found on bones are shown in figure 6-3.

The Internal Structure of Bone

The internal organization of bone may be either **compact** or **spongy**. Compact bone is made of densely-packed *hydroxyapatite* – a crystalline array of calcium phosphate, calcium hydroxide and other mineral salts. The load-bearing portions of long bones are composed of compact bone because it can withstand high compression forces.

Spongy bone is porous, consisting of criss-crossing struts and plates called *trabeculae* which take on the appearance of a sea sponge. Light-weight bones and bones experiencing stress from different directions are made primarily of spongy bone. Most bones contain both spongy and compact regions.

Long bones often possess chambers called **bone cavities**. The cavities are filled with a jelly-like substance called *marrow*. Red marrow found in the larger long bones (e.g., the femur) is the site of blood formation. Yellow marrow found in the smaller long bones are filled with adipose tissue and function primarily to lighten the weight of the bone.

Several skull bones contain hollow cavities called *sinuses*. These chambers are lined with mucus-producing epithelial cells. They lighten the facial bones and perhaps contribute to amplification of vocal sounds. The mucus produced in these chambers drain into the nasal cavity. An infection in these chambers is called a *sinus infection* and is often accompanied by sinus pressure and / or sinus headaches. Sinuses are examined in Exercise 7.

long bones aren't neccessary long; has to do w/ structure!

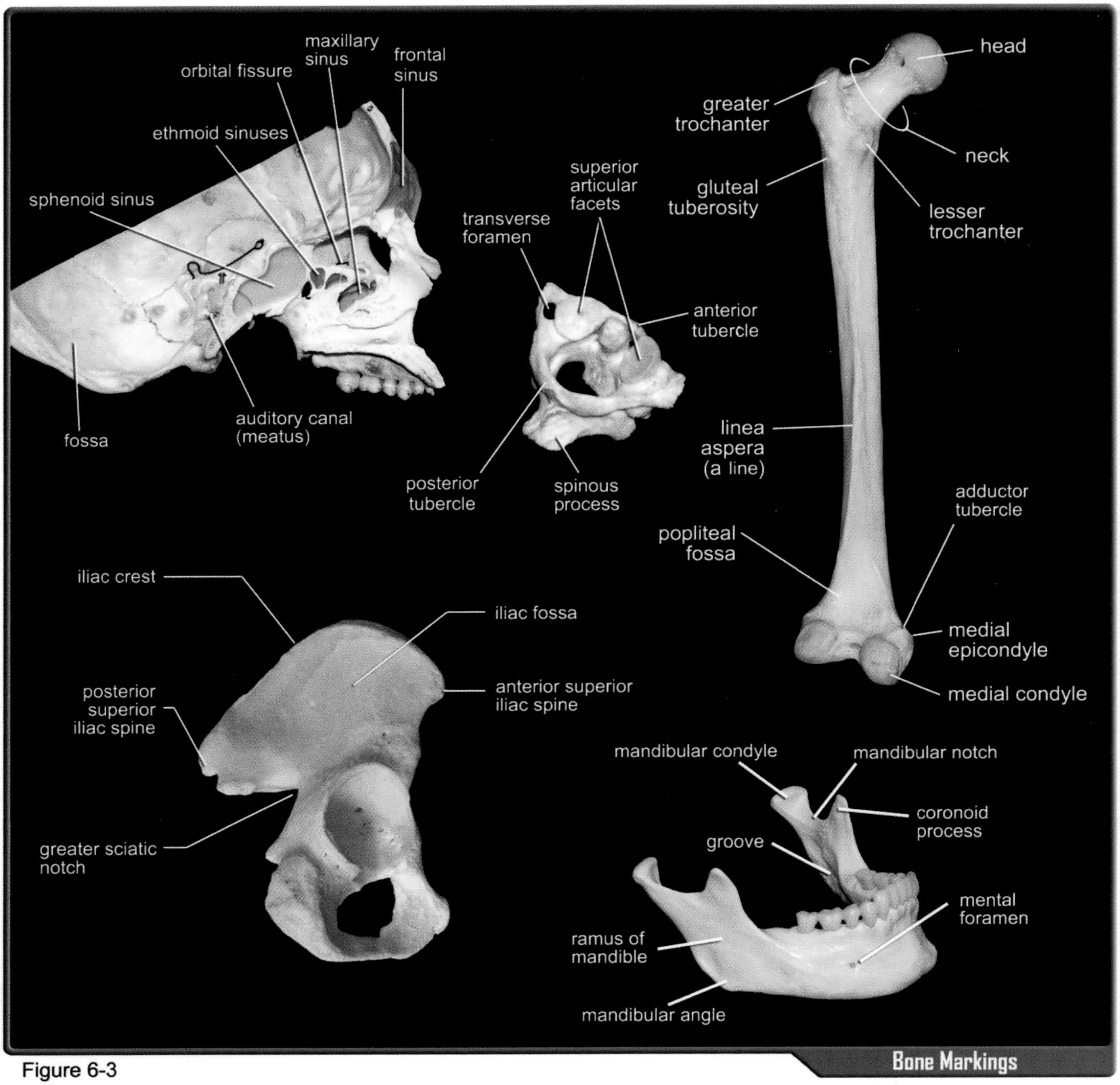

Figure 6-3

Projections for muscle or ligament attachment:

- tuberosity - large rounded often rough projection
- crest - narrow ridge of bone
- trochanter - very large blunt irregularly shaped projects (femur only)
- line - narrow ridge of bone (less prominent than crest)
- tubercle - small rounded projection or process
- epicondyle - raised area on or above a condyle
- spine - sharp slender pointed projection
- process - long prominence or projection

Projections involved in articulations:

- head - bony expansion carried on a narrow neck
- neck - slender support for a head
- facet - small almost flat articular surface
- condyle - rounded articular projection
- ramus - heavy armlike extension of bone
- angle - a sharp turn in a bone

Depressions and cavities:

- sinus - a space enclosed within a bone
- meatus - canal-like passageway
- fossa - shallow depression in a bone
- notch - a deep recess in a bone
- groove - a long furrow along a bone
- fissure - a narrow slit through a bone
- foramen - round or oval passageway through a bone

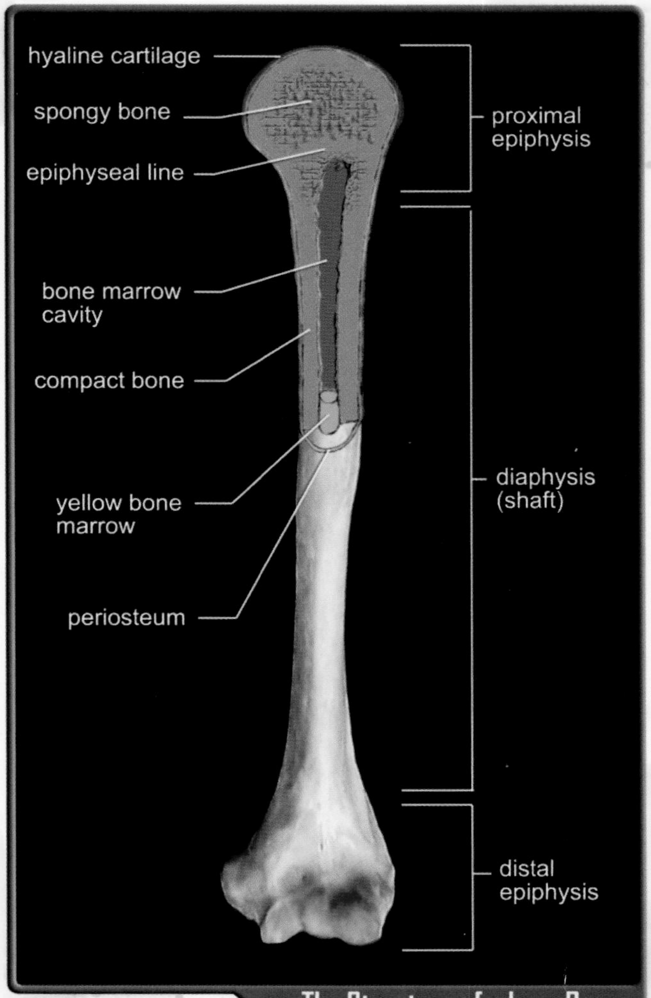

Figure 6-4 The Structure of a Long Bone

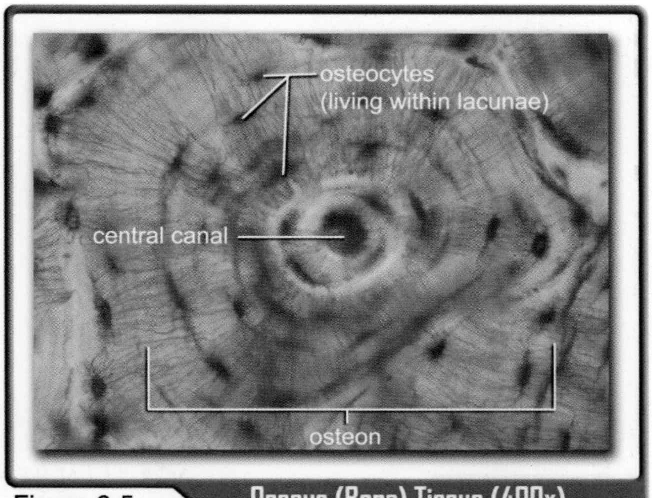

Figure 6-5 Osseus (Bone) Tissue (400x)

Bone (Osseus) Tissue

Compact bone is made of densely-packed inorganic material (hydroxyapatite) around an organic framework (mostly collagen fibers). The material is organized as a bundle of microscopic tubular structures called **osteons** (see Figures 6-5 and 6-6). The osteon forms the basic structural unit of compact bone. In cross section, an osteon looks like an onion with layers of material surrounding a central pore (the **central canal**). In living bone, the central canal is a passageway for nerves and blood vessels. The "onion layers" are called **concentric lamellae**. In an appropriately stained specimen, dark spots are seen scattered throughout each layer; these are bone cells (called *osteocytes*) embedded within small pockets called **lacunae**. The lacunae of different layers are connected to each other and to the central canal via small channels called **canaliculi**. Hard lamellar material between the tubular osteons is called **interstitial lamellae** and they help to secure the osteons togethers. The entire diaphysis is surrounded by **circumferential lamellae** that serve a simliar purpose. The most superficial portion of the bone is wrapped in a connective tissue sheath called the **periosteum**. The periosteum defines the boundary of the bone and provides a route for nerves and blood vessels. The internal cavities and trabeculae are covered by a thin layer of connective tissue called **endosteum**.

Bone Growth

During growth from childhood to adulthood bones must get bigger and stronger. Long bones that contribute to height must gain considerable length. Long bone growth occurs between the **diaphysis** and **epiphysis** in a narrow zone called the

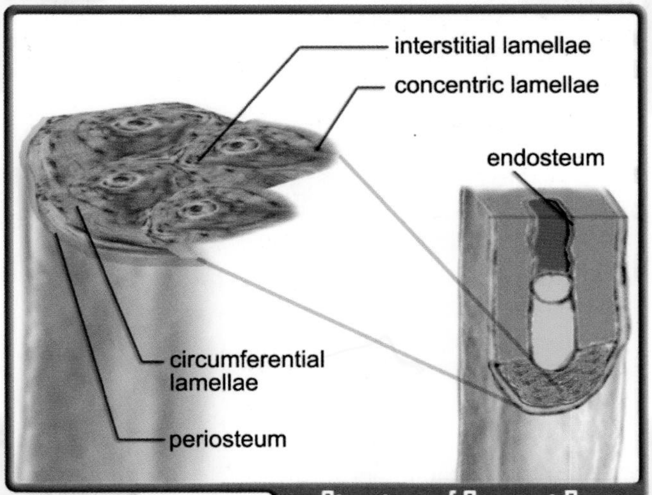

Figure 6-6 Structure of Compact Bone

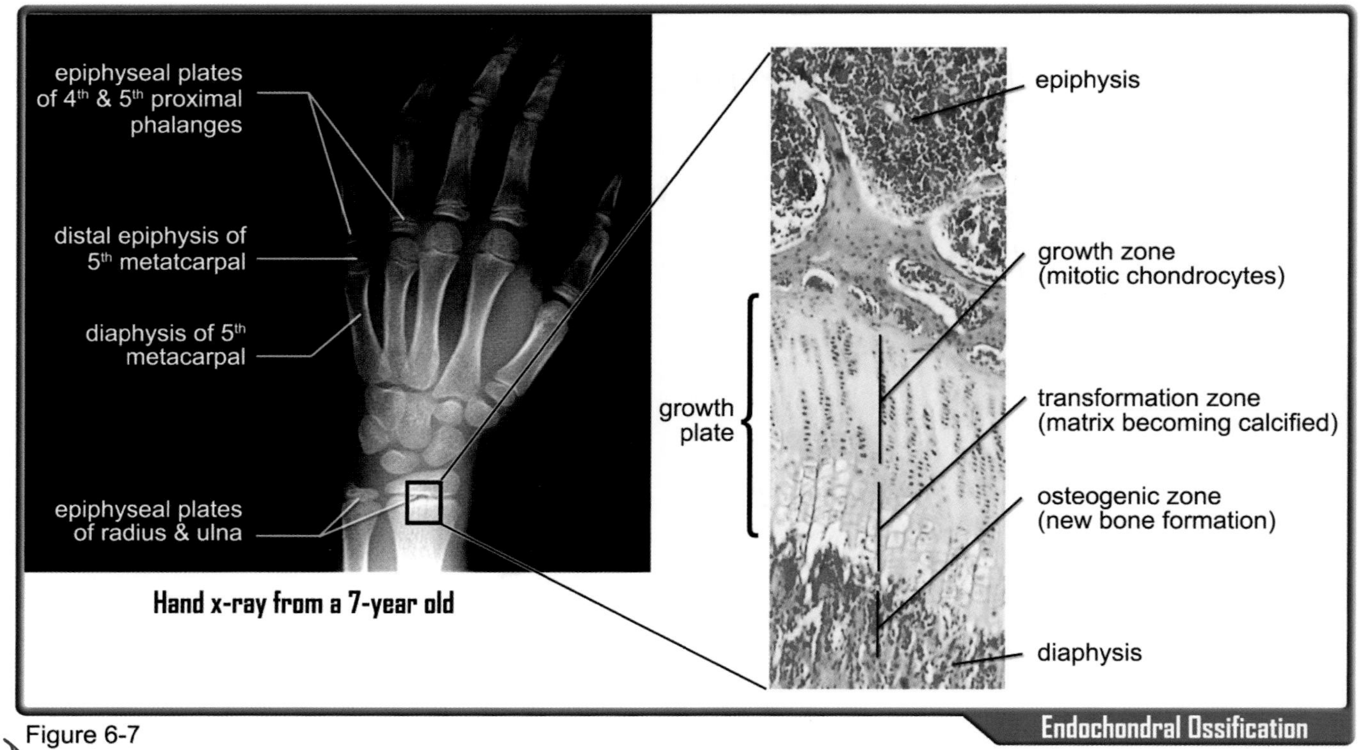

Figure 6-7

epiphyseal plate (Figure 6-7). The epiphyseal plate is composed of cartilage until bone growth is complete. As a bone grows longer, at each end of the bone the cartilage grows on the distal end of the plate and is replaced by bone at the medial end of the plate. If years of bone growth could be filmed and played back in just a few seconds, it would appear as if the epiphyseal plates were pushing the distal bony epiphyses outward in each direction while the bony diaphysis lengthened inside. When bone growth is complete, the cartilaginous epiphyseal plate is replaced with bone. A remnant of the plate is often visible throughout adulthood as the **epiphyseal line**.

Plate allows bone to grow longitudinally

Cartilages of the Skeleton

There are three types of cartilage found in the adult human skeleton: hyaline cartilage, fibrocartilage and elastic cartilage.

Hyaline cartilage is the most abundant of the cartilages. It covers the articulating surfaces of bones within synovial joints and thus is also called *articular cartilage*. This glassy-smooth cartilage reduces friction between articulating bones. Hyaline cartilage is also slightly flexible, and is found in the trachea (which must bend and rotate) and the at the attachment of the ribs to the sternum (which move slightly during breathing). The flexibility of the cartilage can be demonstrated by wiggling your nose, which is also composed of hyaline cartilage.

Fibrocartilage is stiffer, tougher and less flexible than hyaline cartilage. However, it absorbes compression forces very well. Fibrocartilage forms the cartilaginous portions of the intervertebral discs and acts as a shock absorber in the spine. Fibrocartilage also absorbs shock in the knee where it forms part of the meniscus of the knee joint. At the pubic symphysis, fibrocartilage allows a slight twisting motion between the hip bones with each step while absorbing compression forces.

Elastic cartilage is the most flexible type of cartilage, as the name implies. The least abundant of the cartilages, it is only found in the ear and the epiglottis.

All cartilage tissue is primarily composed of extracellular matrix and has very few cells. Cartilage tissue, surrounded by a dense connective tissue sheath called the *perichondrium*, contains neither blood vessels or nerves. Because of the few cells and lack of blood vessels, damaged cartilage tissue is slow to heal.

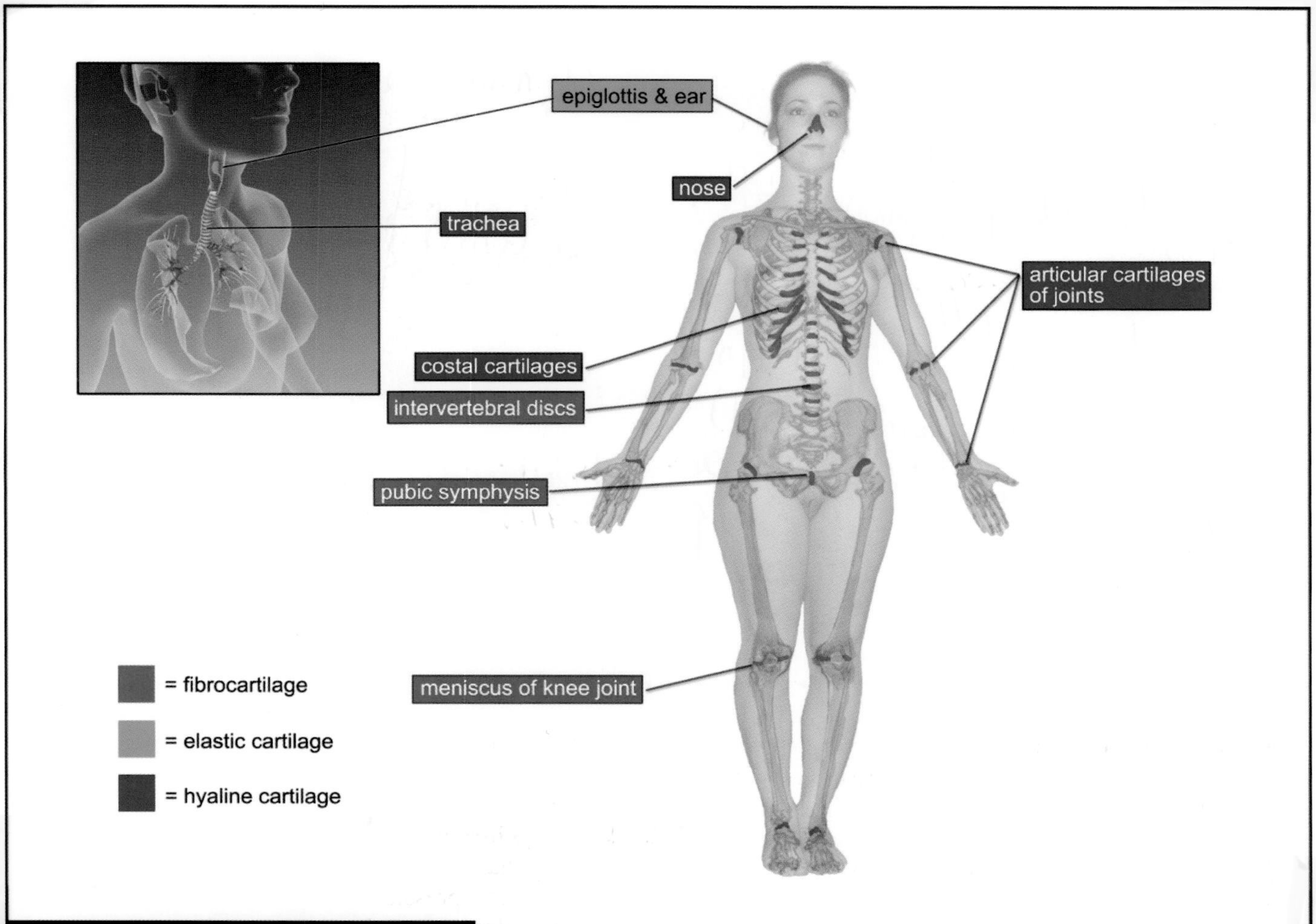

Figure 6-8: Cartilages of the Adult Skeleton

Activity 1: Bone Histology

1. Obtain a prepared slide of compact bone tissue. Observe the osteon, concentric lamellae, interstitial lamellae, circumferential lamellae, lacunae, the central canal and canaliculi.

Activity 2: Bone Markings

1. Using Figure 6-3 in this exercise and / or disarticulated bones, locate two examples of the major types of bone markings, such as tuberosities, crests, spines, etc.

Activity 3: Bone Chemical Analysis

1. Soak a fresh bone sample in hydrochloric acid for one hour or vinegar (weak acetic acid) overnight. The acid dissolves the inorganic mineral matrix of the bone but leaves the organic collagen fibers intact. Describe the physical properties of the acid treated bone.
2. Bake a fresh bone sample for several hours or microwave the sample for 15-20 minutes. Cooking the fresh bone denatures the organic collagen fibers but leaves the mineral matrix intact. Describe the physical properties of the baked bone sample.

Activity 4: Paper-Scissors-Rock

1. Demonstrate to yourself the exceptional load-bearing properties of cylinders (like long bones) using some familiar objects.
2. Roll a sheet of 8 ½ x 11 paper into a cylinder. Use tape to keep the paper from unraveling.
3. Balance a paper plate on top of the cylinder.
4. Place the tape dispensor on the plate.
5. Place a pair of scissors on the plate.
6. Place a rock on the plate.

exercise 7

the SKELETAL system

- the AXIAL skeleton -

So the LORD God caused the man to fall into a deep sleep; and while he was sleeping, he took one of the man's ribs and closed up the place with flesh.

Genesis 2:21

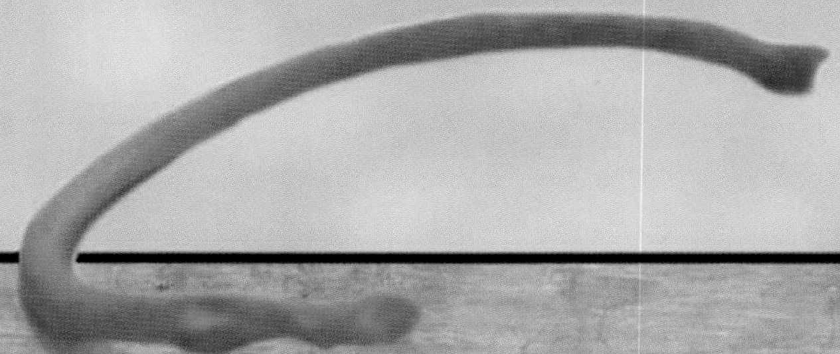

Of the 206 bones of the human body, 80 of them are found in the *axial skeleton* (Figure 7-1). The axial skeleton is composed of the bones that form the central axis of the body, including the skull (cephalic bones), ribcage (thoracic cage) and vertebral column. The primary role of the axial skeleton is *protection*: The skull protects the brain, the ribcage protects the vital organs of the thoracic cavity (lungs and heart) and the vertebral column protects the delicate spinal cord. In addition, the vertebral column also supports the weight of the entire upper body, transferring that weight to the leg bones of the *appendicular skeleton*.

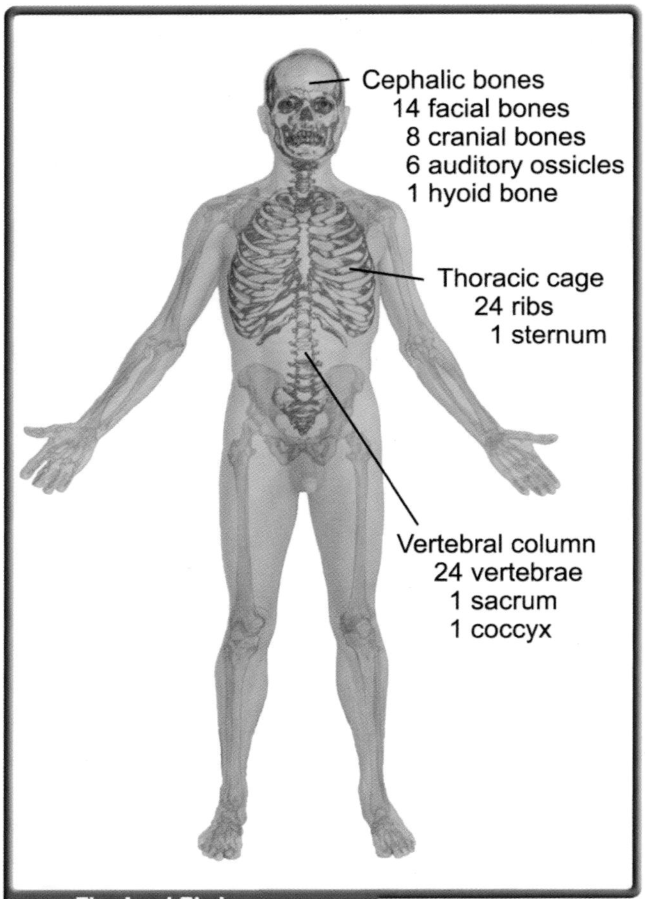

The Axial Skeleton

Figure 7-1

The Cephalic Bones

The bones of the skull can be partitioned into two major divisions: The *cranial bones* and the *facial bones*. Collectively, cranial bones form an enclosed casing for the brain. The facial bones give structure to the face and enclose the openings to the respiratory and digestive tracts.

Cranial Bones

Frontal bone: The frontal bone forms the forehead, superior borders of the orbital sockets and anterior portion of the cranial cavity floor. It possesses two

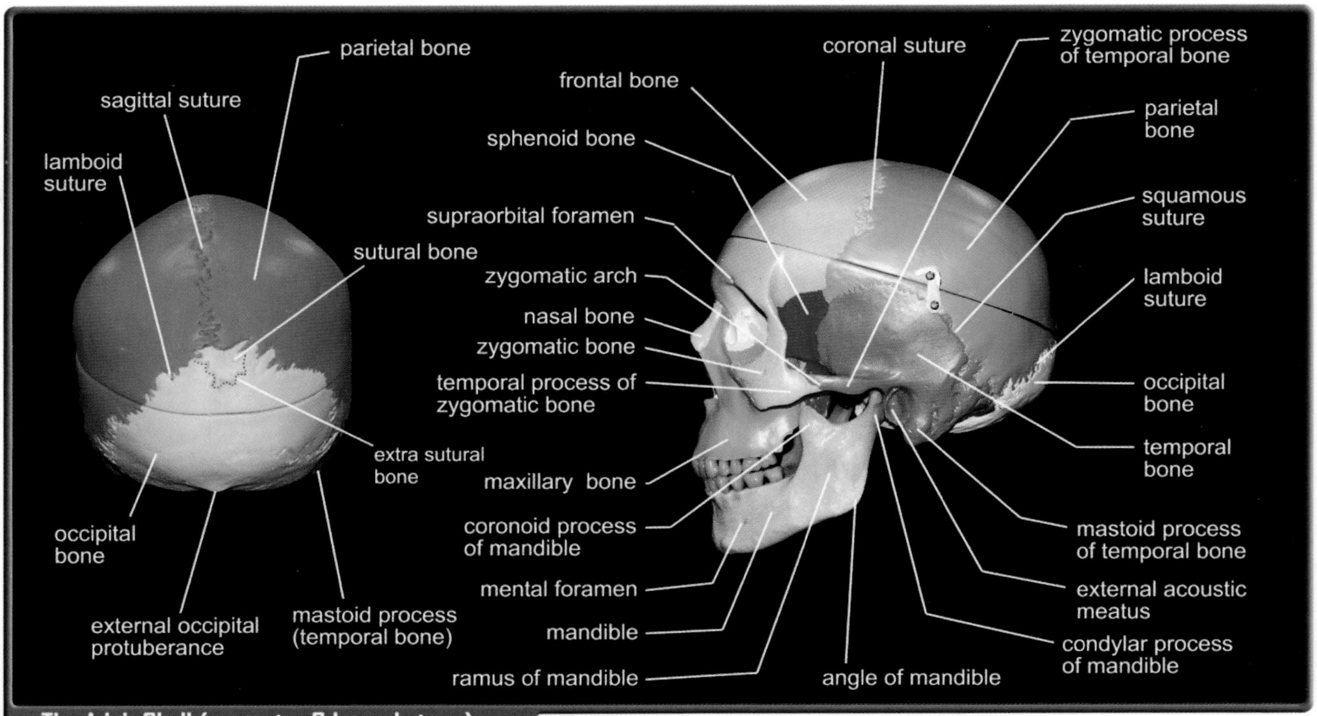

The Adult Skull (posterior & lateral views)

Figure 7-2

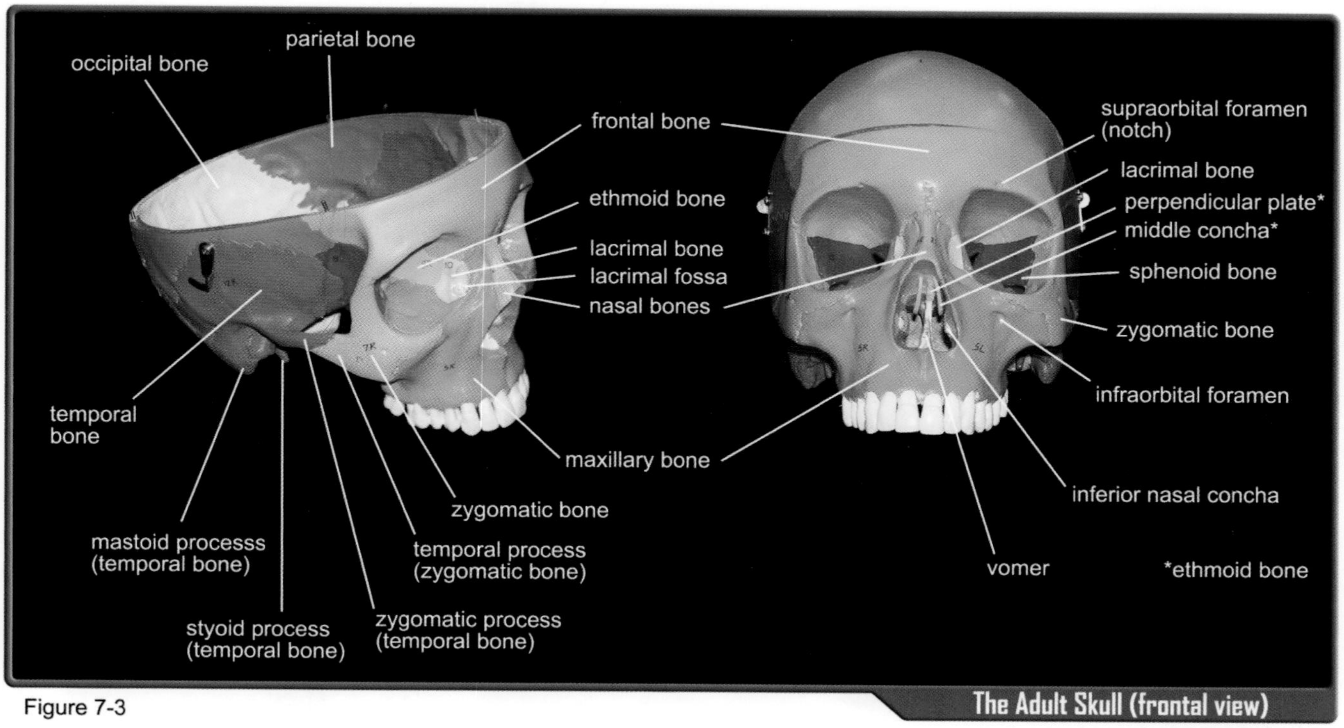

Figure 7-3

supraorbital foramina that allow the passage of nerves and blood vessels to the skin and muscles of the forehead.

Parietal bones: The two large parietal bones form the posterior roof and posterolateral walls of the skull.

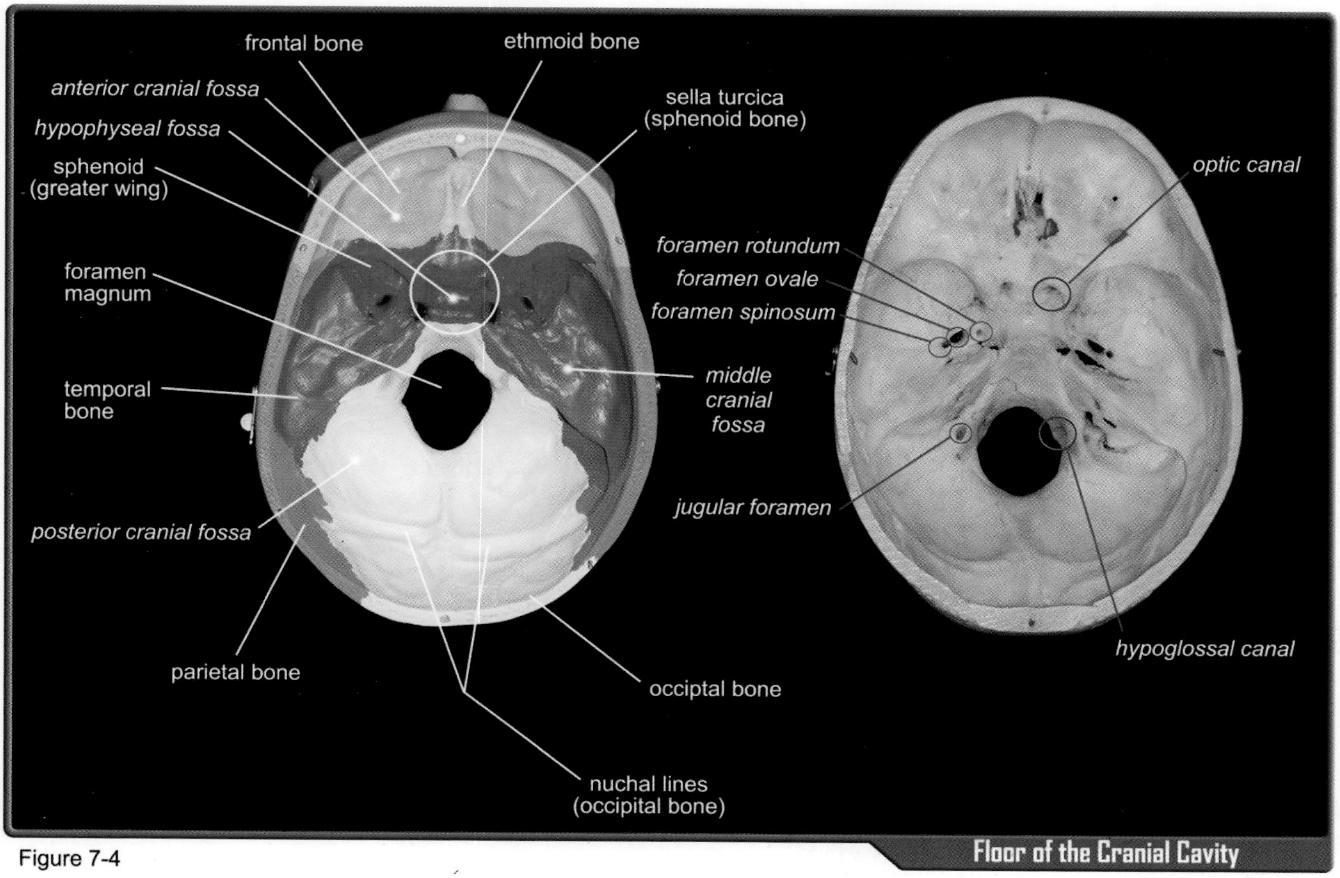

Figure 7-4

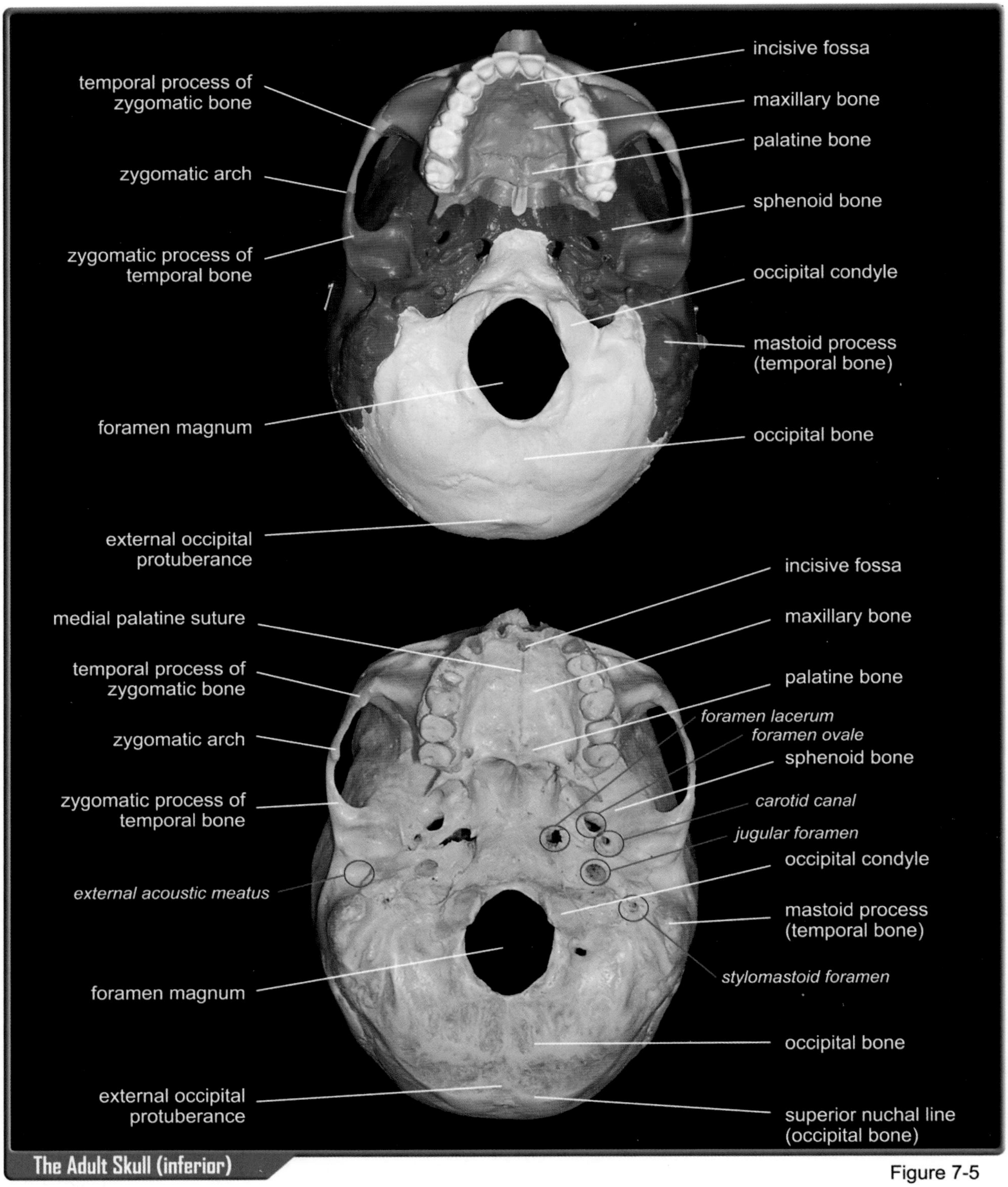

Figure 7-5

Temporal bones: The two temporal bones form the lateral walls of the skull. The temporal bones participate in formation of the cheeks (**zygomatic arch**), movement of the head (via attachment of sternocleidomastoid muscles at the **mastoid processes**), conduction of sound (through the external acoustic meatus) and protection of the hearing and equilibrium sense organs (the cochlea and semicircular canals of the inner ear; the inner ear is actually housed entirely within the temporal bone). The **styloid processes** of the temporal bone support the "floating" hyoid bone in the neck.

Sphenoid: The large and irregularly-shaped sphenoid bone forms portions of the lateral wall of the skull, the nasal septum, the pharanx and the anterior floor of the cranial cavity. A "pocket" within the sphenoid bone, called the **sellica turcica**, supports and protects the pituitary gland.

Ethmoid: The ethmoid is an irregularly-shaped bone that forms part of the orbital socket, the roof of the nasal cavity and superior portion of the nasal septum. Thin curved plates of bone extend medially into the nasal cavity forming the superior and middle conchae. These folds, along with the inferior nasal concha, create turbulence in the air inhaled through the nose. This turbulence helps to warm and humidify the incoming air.

Occipital bone: The large occipital bone forms the posterior floor of the cranial cavity. The most prominent feature of this bone is the large hole (**foramen magnum**) in its base through which passes the spinal cord. The superior and inferior **nuchal lines** on the posterior portion of the bone serve as attachment sites for powerful muscles that extend the head and back.

Facial Bones

Maxillary bone: The maxillary bone forms the front portion of the face. This bone supports the upper teeth and forms most of the brim of the nasal cavity, as well the anterior portion of the roof of the oral cavity. Two prominent foramina (the **infra-orbital foramina**) allow passage of nerves and blood vessels to the skin and muscle of the face.

Palantine bones: These bones form the posterior portion of the roof of the oral cavity.

Nasal bones: These bones form the bony part of the nose.

Vomer: A thin, blade-like bone that forms the posterior portion of the nasal septum.

Inferior nasal conchae: These bones form the inferior walls of the nasal septum and, along with the ethmoid bone, help generate turbulence in air inhaled through the nose.

Zygomatic bones: These bones form the cheeks of the face. Each bone possesses a long slender process that fuses with a similar process from the temporal bone to create the **zygomatic arch**, or cheekbone. Powerful muscles of mastication originate from the arch or pass through it, inserting on the mandible.

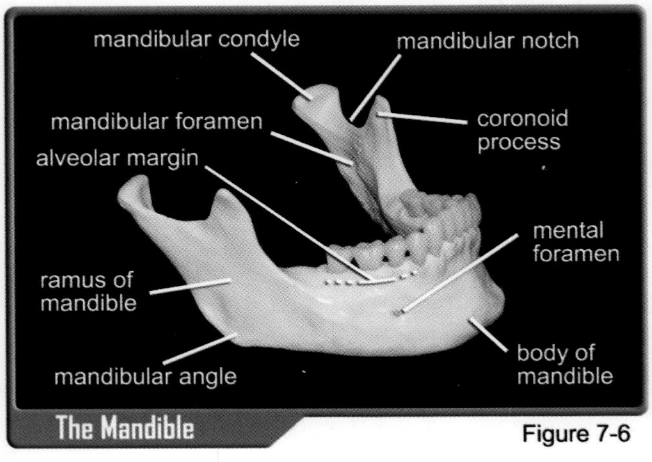

Figure 7-6

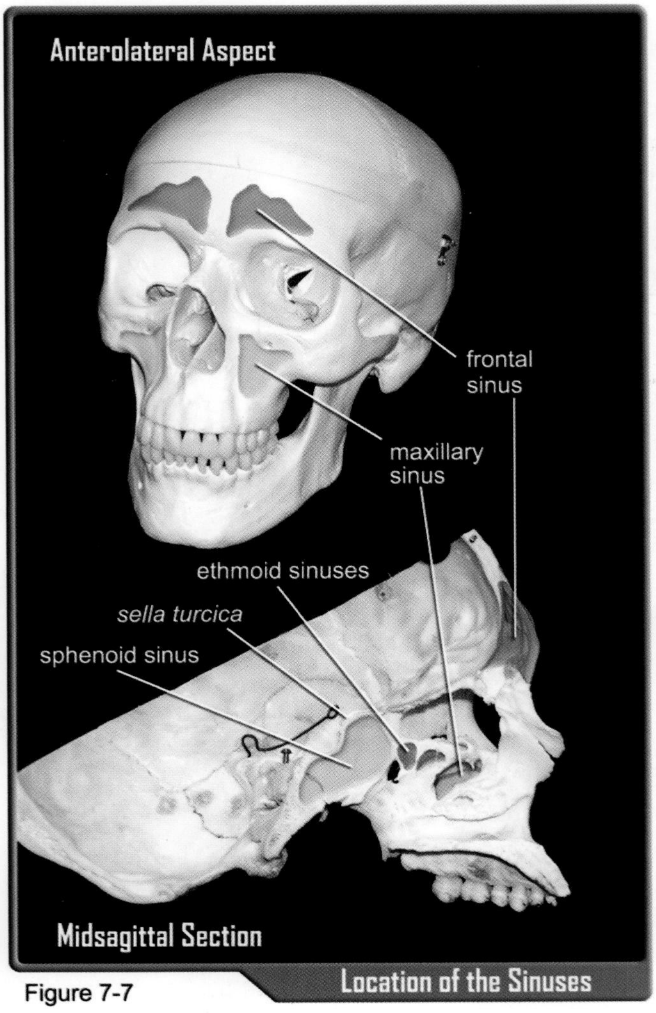

Figure 7-7

Lacrimal bones: The two small lacrimal bones form a small part of the anteromedial walls of the orbits. A small hole, the **lacrimal fossa**, provides a passageway for tears to drain from the eye into the nasal cavity.

Mandible: This U-shaped bone is the only skull bone that moves (Figure 7-6). The mandible, or jawbone, holds the inferior teeth and hinges against the temporal bone just anterior to the mastoid process. Depression and elevation of the mandible opens and closes the mouth, respectively. Two prominent foramina anteriorly, the **mental foramina**, allow nerves and blood vessels to reach the skin and muscle of the chin and lower face. The two **mandibular foramina** provide innervation and blood supply to the teeth.

The Sinuses

Four bones in the skull contain hollow pockets called **sinuses** (Figure 7-7). The sinuses are lined with mucous epithelium and may serve to lighten the weight of the facial bones. Additionally, the hollow cavities likely amplify the voice and contribute to the unique sound of each individual's voice. Unfortunately, these sinuses are also prone to infections and, when filled with fluid, are the source of "sinus pressure" and "sinus headaches" that often accompany such infections. The mastoid process of the temporal bone also contains a sinus.

The Hyoid Bone

The hyoid bone (Figure 7-8) does not articulate with any other bone. Rather, it "floats" in the neck just above the Adam's apple in the throat. The bone is attached by ligaments to the styloid processes of the sphenoid bone and thus hangs like a swing. It serves as an attachment site for muscles that control the tongue and carry out swallowing. The **horns** of the U-shaped hyoid can be palpated by squeezing on the trachea above the Adam's apple.

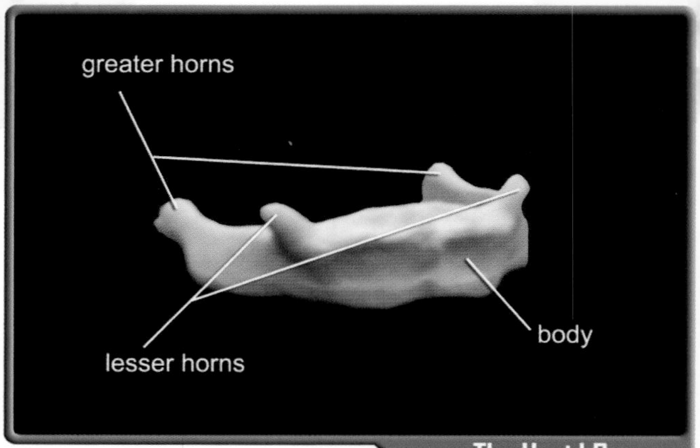

Figure 7-8 The Hyoid Bone

The Spinal Vertebrae

There are 24 vertebrae that stack to form the surprisingly flexible vertebral column (Figure 7-9). Between each vertebra is a joint called the *intervertebral disc*. Flexible as it is, this bony column completely surrounds and protects the delicate spinal cord while allowing spinal nerves to enter and leave the cord to innervate all parts of the body. A healthy adult spinal column contains four curves: The **cervical curve**, the **thoracic curve**, the **lumbar curve** and the **sacral curve**. Each of these curves are antero-posterior in nature. An abnormal lateral curve is called **scoliosis**; an exaggerated thoracic curve is called **kyphosis**; an exaggerated lumbar curve is called **lordosis** (see Figure 7-10).

The vertebral column is divided into three regions: *cervical*, *thoracic* and *lumbar*. It's capped by the skull superiorly and the sacrum inferiorly. The 7 **cervical vertebrae** are found in the neck, the 12 **thoracic vertebrae** articulate with the ribs and the 5 **lumbar vertebrae** are found in the lower back. A convenient way to remember how many of each type there are is to recall when you normally eat breakfast (7am), lunch (12 noon) and dinner (5pm).

Individual vertebra are identified by a letter and a number: The letter indicating the spinal region (C = cervical, T = thoracic, L = lumbar) and the number its position in the sequence. The first vertebra of the spinal column, for example is C1 – the first vertebra in the cervical region – the second is C2, the third is C3, and so on. Likewise, the first vertebra of the thoracic region is called T1, the second T2, etc.

A typical vertebra consists of a **vertebral body** which forms the bulk of the bone and a **vertebral arch** that forms a large opening (**vertebral foramen**) through which the spinal cord passes. The arch is formed by the **laminae** posteriorly, the **pedicals** laterally and the vertebral body ventrally. A prominent **spinous process** projects posteriorly from each vertebra. These processes serve as attachment sites for powerful muscles that extend and flex the vertebral column.

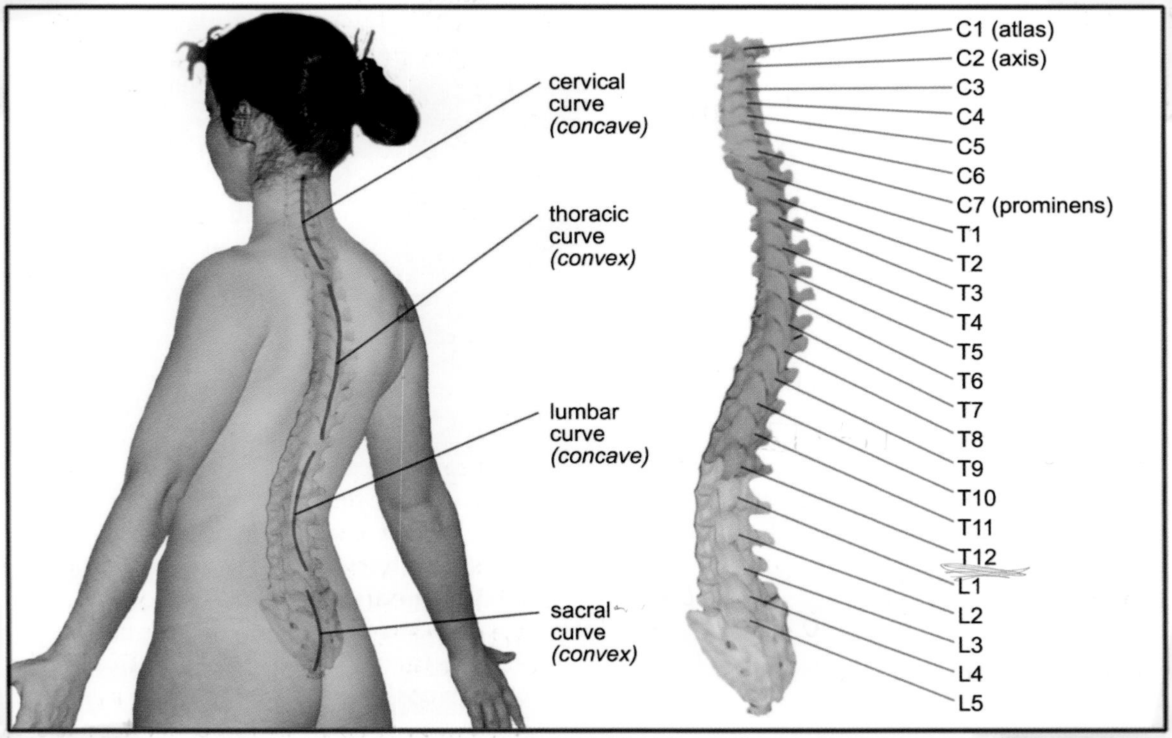

Figure 7-9: Curves of the Spinal Column

Additionally, each vertebra possesses a pair of **superior articular facets** and **inferior articular facets** at which they articulate with the vertebrae above and below, respectively.

The size of the vertebral foramina in each spinal region reflects the size of the spinal cord in that region. In the cervix, the spinal cord is large, but it tapers off as it descends through the thoracic and lumbar vertebrae as spinal nerves emerge to innervate the body. As a result, the vertebral foramina are largest in the cervical region and get progressively smaller in the thoracic and lumbar regions. By contrast, the vertebral bodies grow larger from cervical to lumbar regions. This is because the vertebral bodies support progressively more body weight as you move down the spinal column. The cervical vertebrae must only support the head, while the lumbar vertebrae support the weight of your entire upper body, including the head, arms, thorax and abdomen.

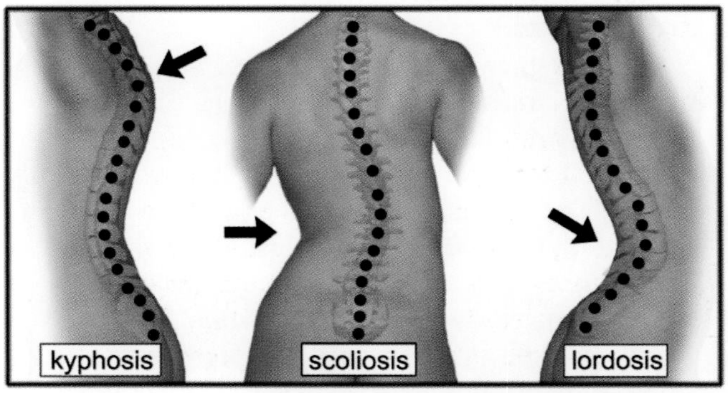

Figure 7-10: Abnormal Spinal Curves

The Cervical Vertebrae

The cervical vertebrae are the smallest of all the vertebrae; however, they possess the largest vertebral foramina (see Figures 7-11 and 7-16). Often the spinous process of the cervical vertebrae are split on the ends (referred to as *bifid*). The cervical vertebrae are also unique in possessing **transverse foramina** through which pass the carotid arteries which supply blood to the brain.

The cervical vertebrae C1 and C2 do not look like the other vertebrae and they possess unique functional features, as well (Figure 7-12). C1 (a.k.a., ***atlas***) articulates with the two elongated occipital condyles on the occipital bone of the skull. The up-and-down "yes" motion of the head is achieved by piveting the skull between those condyles and the **superior articular surfaces** of C1. Cervical vertebra C2 (a.k.a., ***axis***) possesses a large, vertical-pointing process called the **dens**. The atlas rests upon C2 snugly around the dens (held in place by a tough band of ligament). The atlas can rotate around the dens producing the side-to-side "no" motion of the head. Simultaneously rocking the skull on the superior articular surfaces of C1 and rotating C1 around the dens of C2 produces complex angular motions of the head. These movements can be further compounded by flexion / extension of the other cervical vertebrae. The last cervical vertebra, C7, possesses an unusually large spinous process that often leaves a visible bump at the base of the neck; hence it is also known as the *vertebra prominens* (or simply, **prominens**).

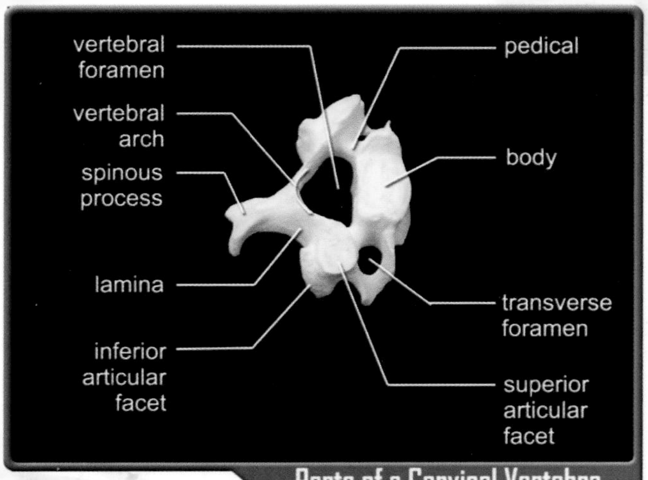

Figure 7-11 Parts of a Cervical Vertebra

The Thoracic Vertebrae T1-T12

The thoracic vertebrae possess a medium-sized body that resembles a heart shape. Unique to each of the 12 thoracic vertebrae is a pair of transverse processes that articulate with a pair of ribs. The long, slender, downward-pointing spinous processes and the laterally-pointing transverse processes give the thoracic vertebrae the appearance of a giraffe head when viewed from the side (Figure 7-14).

The Lumbar Vertebrae L1 - L5

The lumbar vertebrae are recognized by their massive bodies and small vertebral foramina. These vertebrae are large because they support the weight of the entire upper body, including the internal organs of the abdomen and thorax, the arms and the head. From the lateral perspective, the lumbar vertebrae resemble a moose (Figure 7-14).

> triangular vertebral foramina

The Sacrum & Coccyx

The sacrum is formed by the fusion of 5 large vertebrae. It articulates with L5 superiorly, the coccyx inferiorly and the ox coxae (hip bones)

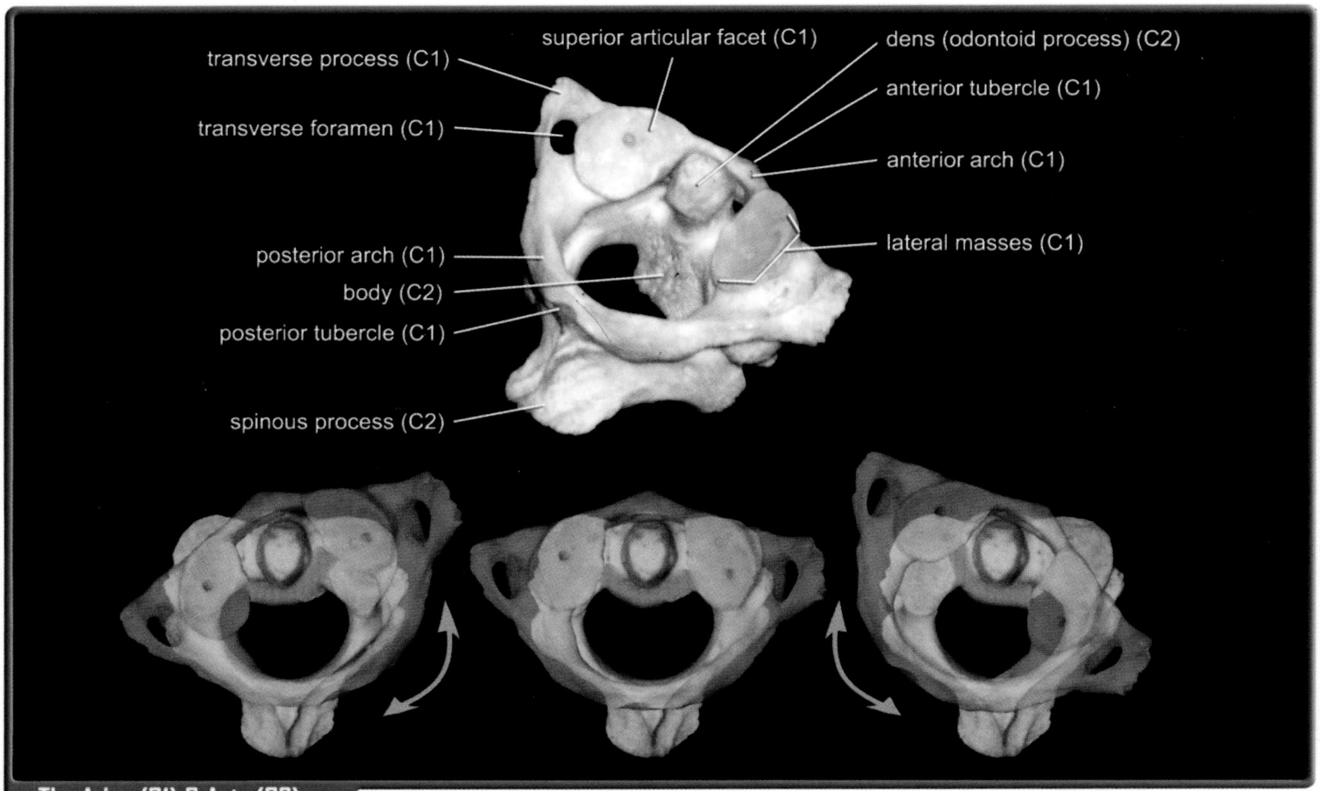

The Atlas (C1) & Axis (C2)

Figure 7-12

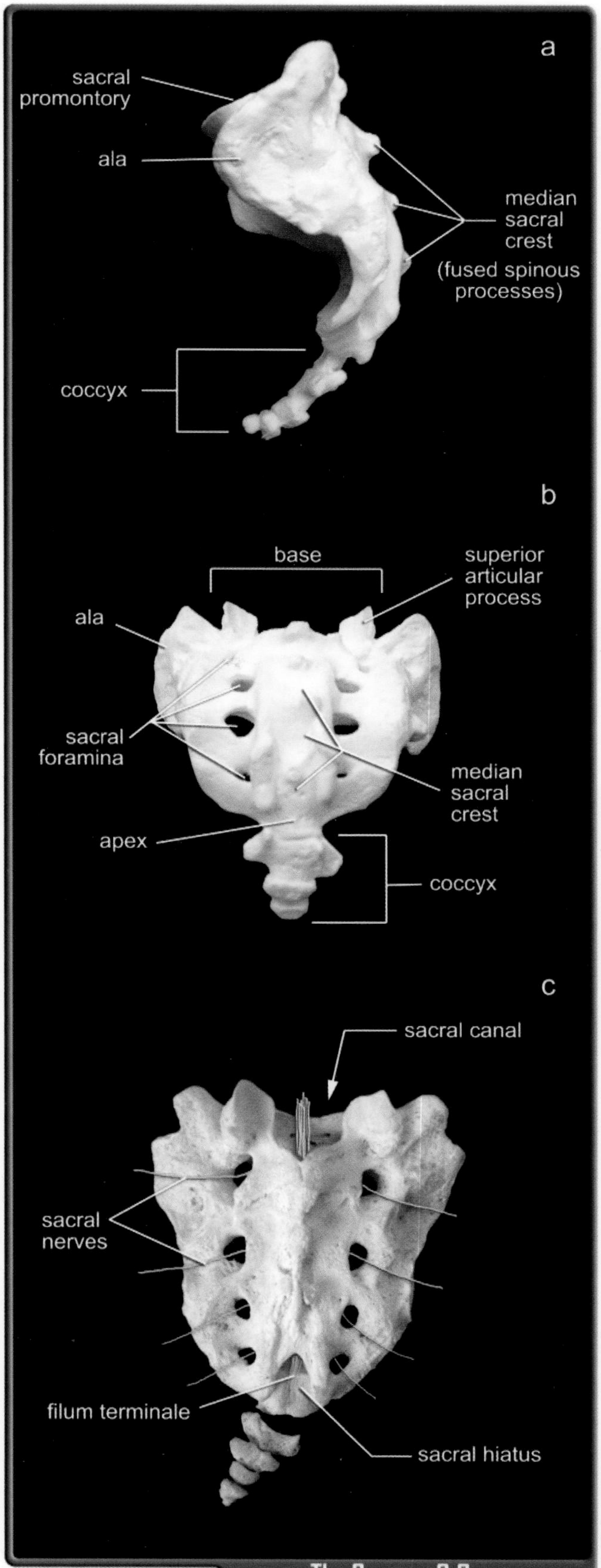

Figure 7-13 The Sacrum & Coccyx

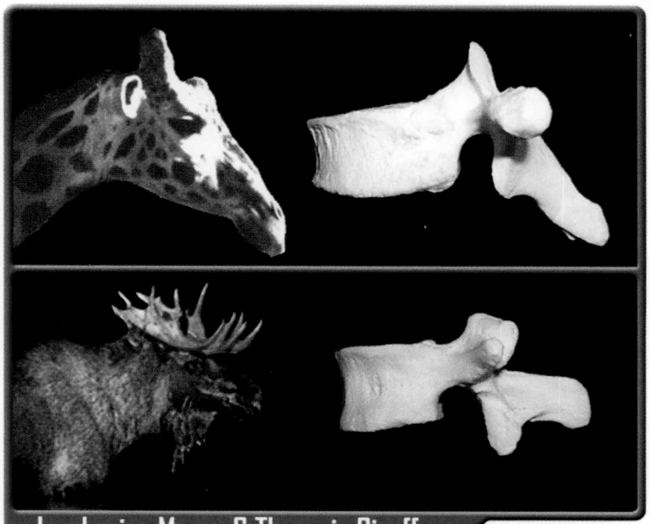

Lumbaring Moose & Thoracic Giraffe Figure 7-14

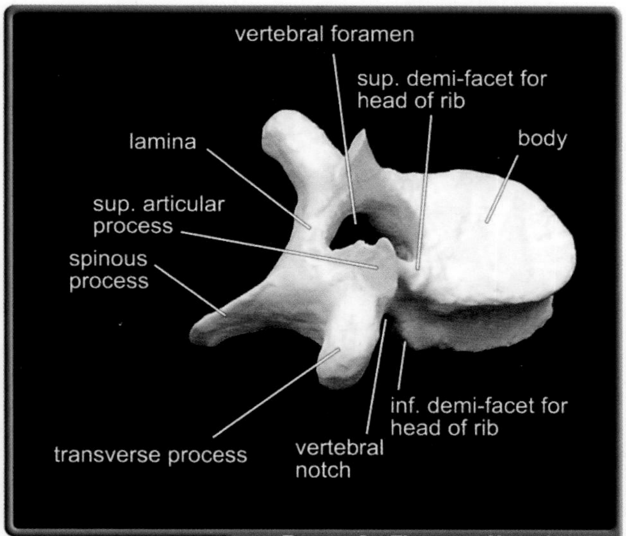

Figure 7-15 Parts of a Thoracic Vertebra

anterolaterally. The body of the sacrum curves anteriorly (more so in men than women). Four pair of **sacral foramina** allow spinal nerves and blood vessels to traverse the bone. Connective tissues from the spinal cord pass through the **sacral canal** and attach firmly to the sacrum at the **sacral hiatus**.

The **coccyx**, also called the tailbone, is a small but extremely important bone. If you break your coccyx there are only three uncomfortable positions: sitting, standing and lying down! Like the sacrum, the coccyx is formed by the fusion of ~5 vertebrae. You will notice that the human coccyx differs dramatically from the those of four-legged animals. Unlike the tails of cats and dogs, for example, the human coccyx is attached to numerous pelvic floor muscles and contributes greatly to the strength and stability of the pelvic floor. The bone in humans is curved anteriorly and the attached muscles support the organs of the abdominopelvic cavity. In four-legged mammals, no curvature of the coccyx is found; rather it articulates with the remaining bones in the tail.

Viewed posteroinferiorly, the disarticulated sacrum & coccyx resembles an elephant (Figure 7-13). Note the relatively straight shape of the real female sacrum shown in Figure 7-13c and that the sacral canal & hiatus are not depicted in the plastic models of the male sacrum (Figure 7-13a,b).

The Thoracic Cage

The thoracic cage is composed of 25 bones: 24 **ribs** and 1 **sternum**. This "cage" encloses the vital organs of the thorax, especially the heart (which lies immediately deep to the sternum). The floor of the thoracic cage is formed by the *diaphragm*, a large sheet of muscle that expands the thoracic cage when contracted. The expansion of the thoracic cage by the diaphragm pulls air into the lungs during inhalation.

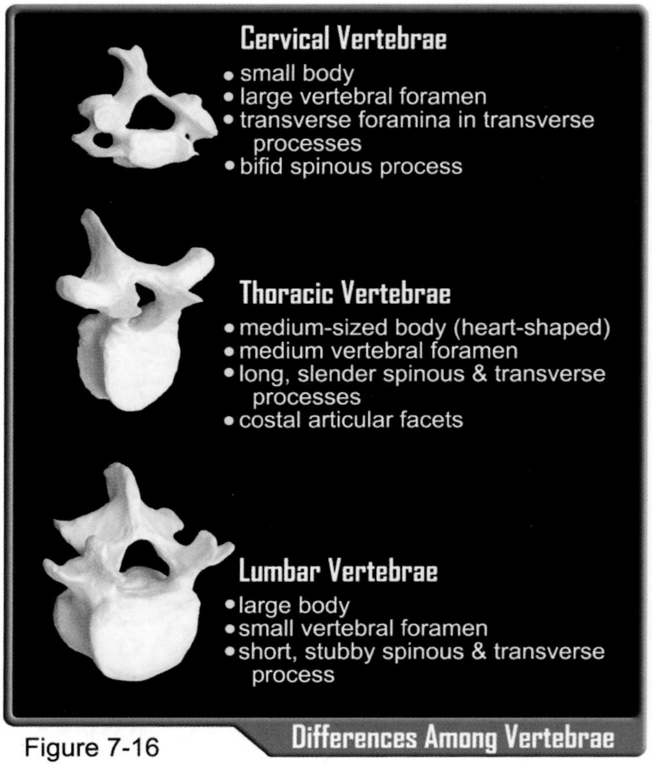

Figure 7-16

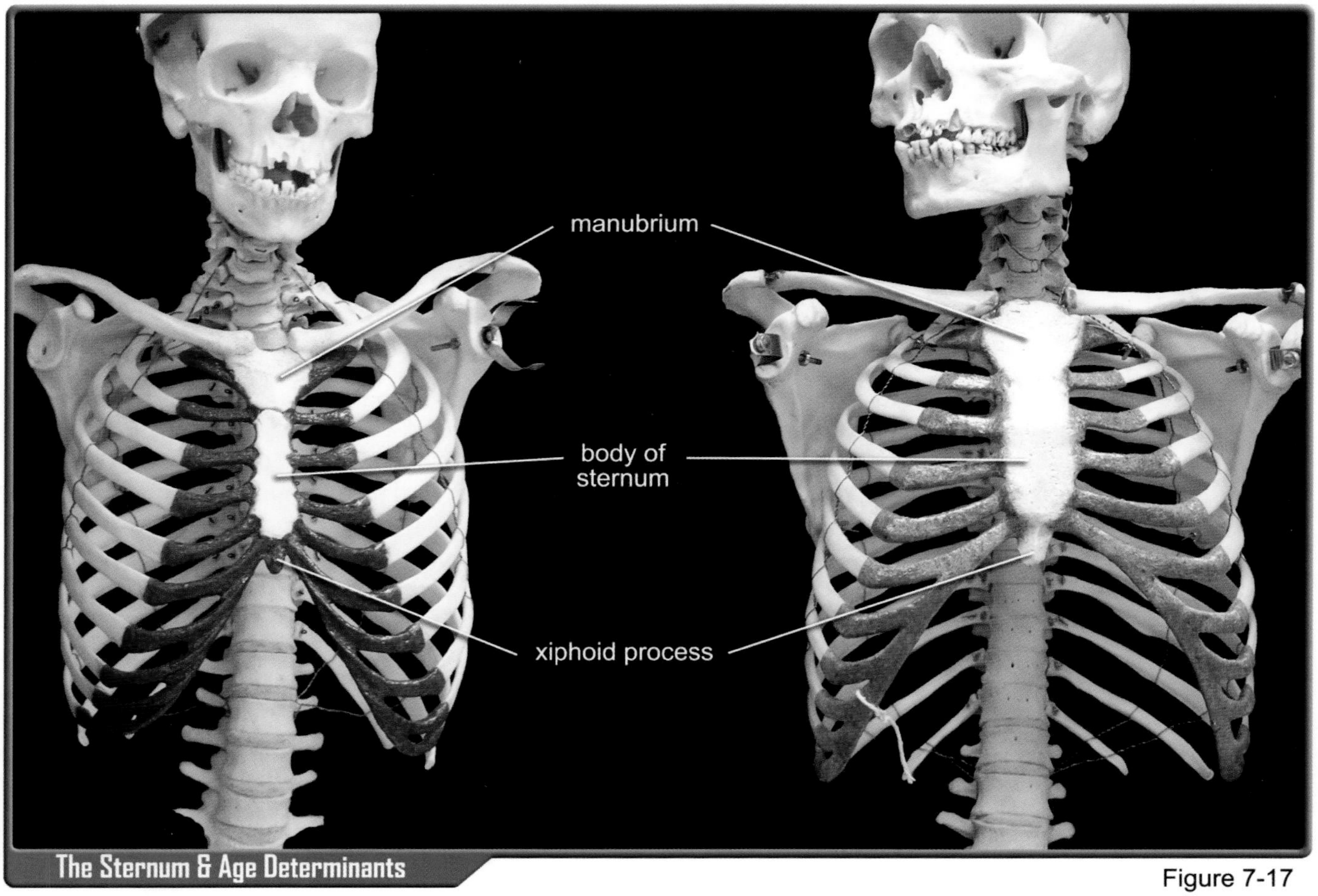

Figure 7-17

>Ribs are flat bones

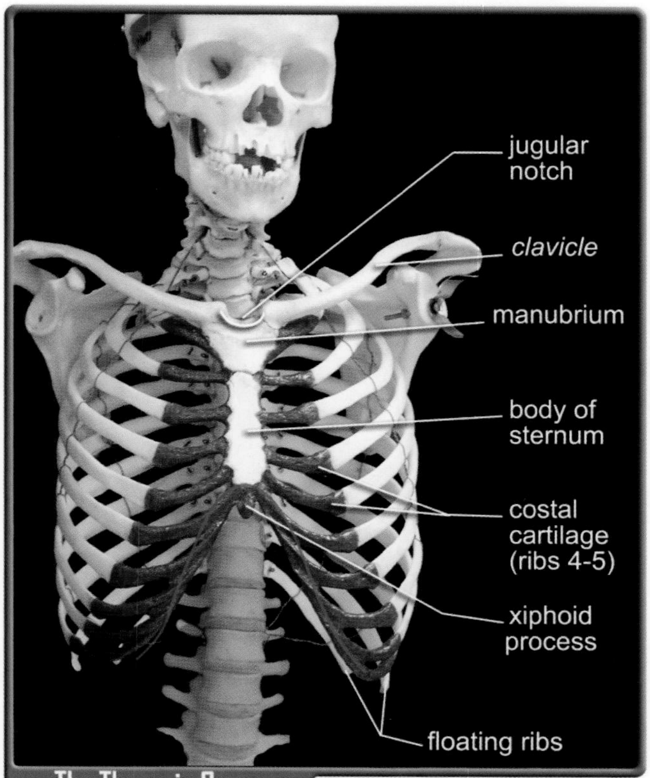

The Thoracic Cage

Figure 7-18

The sternum is made of three separate components in young people, but those components fuse to form one continuous bone in adults. The top portion of the sternum is a triangular bone called the **manubrium**. The manubrium articulates with the clavicles and the first pair of ribs. A cleft is present at the top of the manubrium, the depth of which is exacerbated by the attached clavicles. This cleft is called the **jugular notch**. The second component, the **body** of the sternum, articulates with the ribs. The third component, the **xiphoid process**, is an important attachment site for the diaphragm. The xiphoid process is the last part of the sternum to ossify and fuse; the process is usually complete by the age of 25. In Figure 7-17, the skeleton on the left is from a young adult whereas the skeleton on the right is from an elderly adult.

The ribs are attached to the sternum via hyaline cartilage, called the **costal cartilages**. The body of the sternum articulates directly with ribs 2-7 and indirectly with ribs 8-10 (via the costal cartilage of rib 7). Rib 1 articulates with the manubrium. Ribs 11 and 12 have no connection with the sternum. Because of the arrangements described above, ribs 1-7 are called *true ribs*, ribs 8-

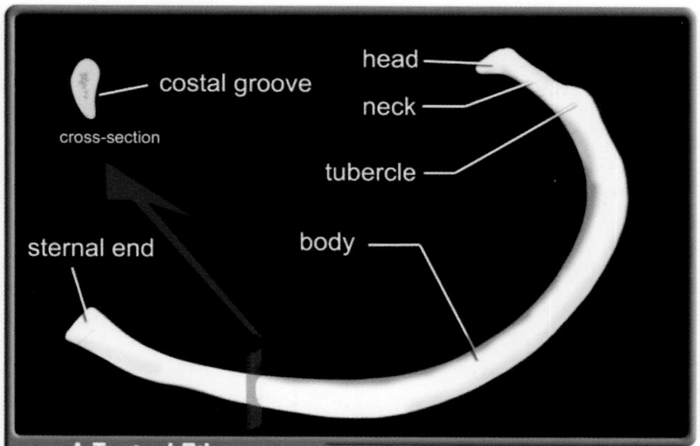

A Typical Rib

Figure 7-19

12 are called *false ribs* and ribs 11-12 are called the *floating false ribs*.

Anteriorly, the margin of the 7th – 10th ribs form an arch called the **costal dome** (or, **costal margin**). This dome defines the boundary between the thorax and the abdomen.

Activity 1: Examine Bones of the Axial Skeleton

1. Using the photos in this lab manual, disarticulated and articulated bones, and / or a complete skeleton, critically examine the bones of the axial skeleton.

Activity 2: Construct a Complete Skeleton

1. Using disarticulated bones, arrange the bones on your lab bench to form a complete skeleton. By careful observation of bone markings you should be able to distinguish bones from the right or left side of the body.

Activity 3: Palpate Bones of the Axial Skeleton

1. Palpate as many bones of the axial skeleton as you can on yourself or your lab partner.

exercise 8

the SKELETAL system

- the APPENDICULAR skeleton -

You made him ruler over the works of your hands; you put everything under his feet.
Psalm 8:6

Of the 206 bones of the human body, 126 of them are found in the **appendicular skeleton** (Figure 8-1). The majority of those bones are found in the hands and feet.

The Pectoral Girdle

The pectoral girdle is responsible for holding the upper limbs in place and anchoring many of the muscles that move the arms. Interestingly, the only articulation of the upper limbs with the axial skeleton occurs between the clavicles (collar bones) and the manubrium of the sternum (breast bone).

The Clavicles & Scapula

The two **clavicles** are S-shaped bones that, as stated above, are the only part of the upper limbs to articulate with the axial skeleton (Figure 8-2). The medial **sternal end** of the bone is thick and triangular from the lateral perspective. By contrast, the lateral **acromial end** appears flattened. Based on these features and the S-shape of the bone, you should be able to determine whether a disarticulated clavicle comes from the left or right side of the body.

The **scapulae**, or shoulder blades, are basically flat and triangular in shape (Figure 8-3). These "floating" bones have no direct attachment to the axial skeleton but lie over the posterior portion of the rib cage held in place by muscles. The scapulae slide up-down and side-to-side to allow a wide range of arm movements.

Being shaped like a triangle, each scapula has three angles and three borders: The **superior**, **lateral** and **inferior angles** and the **lateral**, **medial** and **superior borders**. The posterior surface of the bone is divided by the **spine**. The flattened area above the spine is the **supraspinous fossa** and the larger, flattened area beneath the spine is the **infraspinous fossa**.

The scapula articulates with the humerus of the arm at the **glenoid cavity** – a large, concave surface that forms the floor of the shoulder joint. The **acromion** and **coracoid process** wrap around the head of the humerus superiorly.

Much of the scapula can be both seen and felt depending on the position of the arms. When the scapulae are pulled together (i.e., stretching the chest) the medial & lateral borders, inferior angle and spine can be seen on the back. In the same

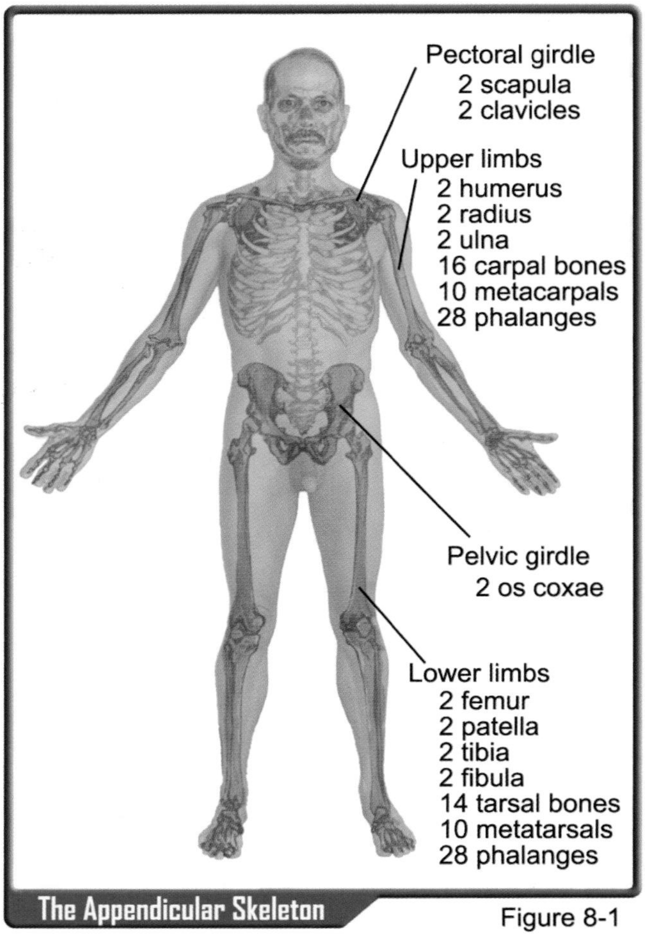

Figure 8-1

position, the coracoid process can sometimes be seen on the anterior aspect of the shoulder (i.e., on the upper chest) just below the clavicle. With the arms down, the acromion can be easily seen and felt

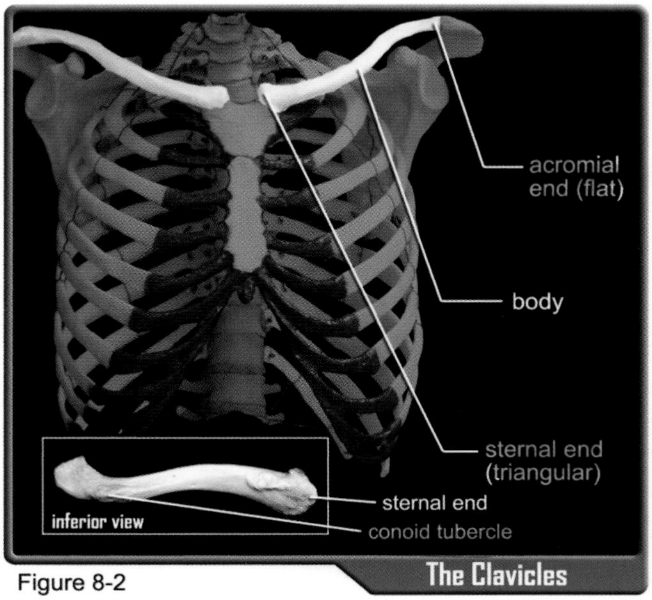

Figure 8-2

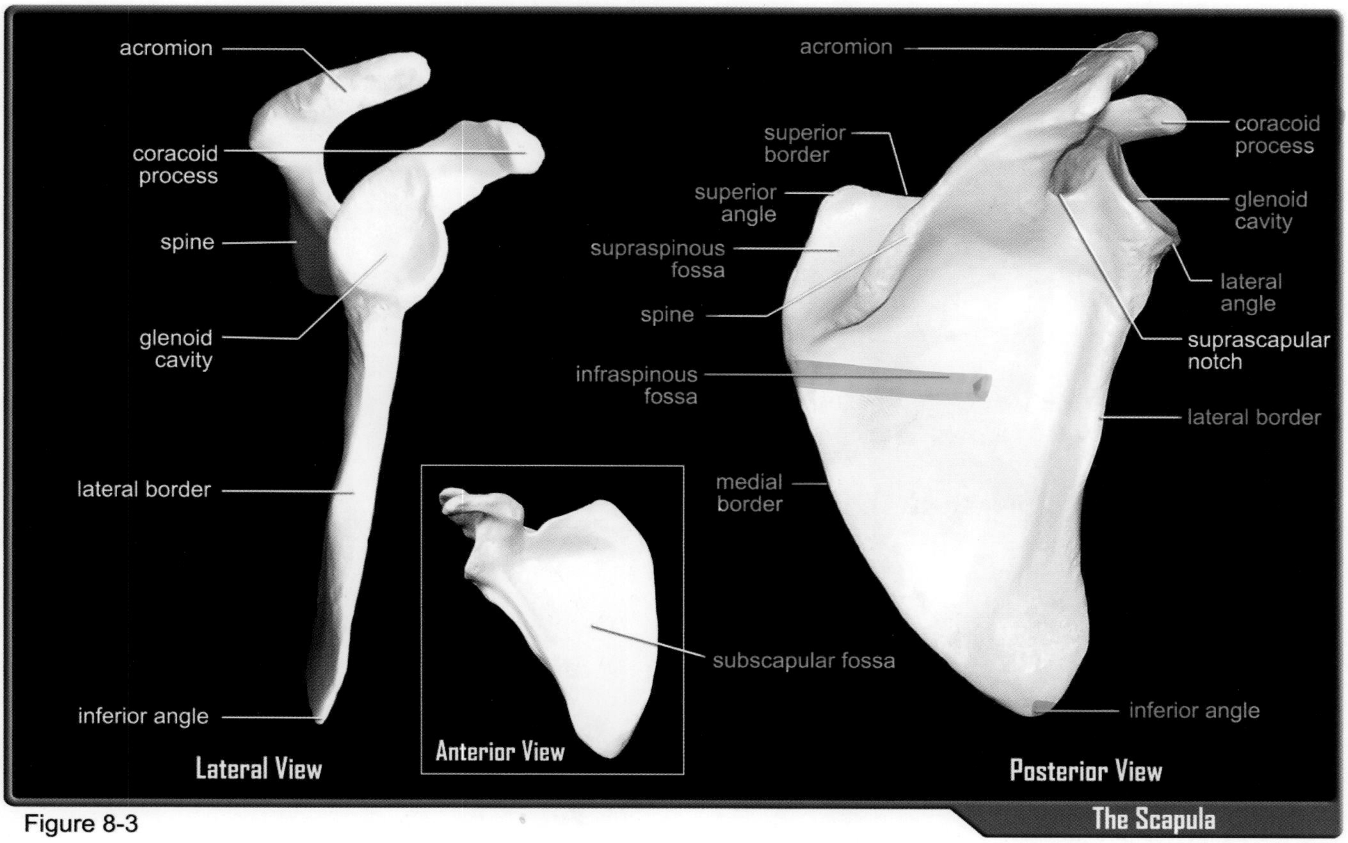

Figure 8-3

as a bump on the superior aspect of the shoulder.

The Upper Limbs

Sixty bones are found in the upper limbs, which consist of the arms, forearms, wrists and hands.

The Arm

The arm contains only one bone – the **humerus** – which articulates proximally with the clavicle and scapula of the pectoral girdle and distally with the **radius** and **ulna** of the forearm (see Figures 8-4 and 8-6). The proximal end of the humerus is a large rounded articular surface called the **head**. The **anatomical neck** marks the boundary of the glenohumoral joint as defined by the synovial cavity and the **surgical neck** is a narrowing region of the bone distal to the joint.

Approximately midway down the length of the diaphysis is the **deltoid tuberosity**, an enlargement that marks the attachment site of the deltoid bone. The distal end of the bone contains several noteworthy structures. The **lateral epicondyle** and **medial epicondyle** are projections that stabilize the elbow joint. Both epicondyles can be easily palpated. Between the epicondyles posteriorly is a deep cleft called the **olecranon fossa**. This cleft receives the olecranon of the ulna when the arm is fully extended. The fossa can sometimes be felt when the arm is partially flexed. Between the epicondyles anteriorly are two clefts: The **coronoid fossa** and the **radial fossa**, which accept coronoid process of the ulna and the head of the radius, respectively, when the arm is fully flexed.

The most distal portion of the humerus is marked by the **capitulum** and the **trochlea**. The capitulum articulates with the radius and the trochlea articulates with the ulna.

The Forearm

The forearm is composed to two bones, the ulna and the radius (Figure 8-5). The ulna is primarily responsible for movement of the forearm while the radius supports and allows movement of the hand and fingers.

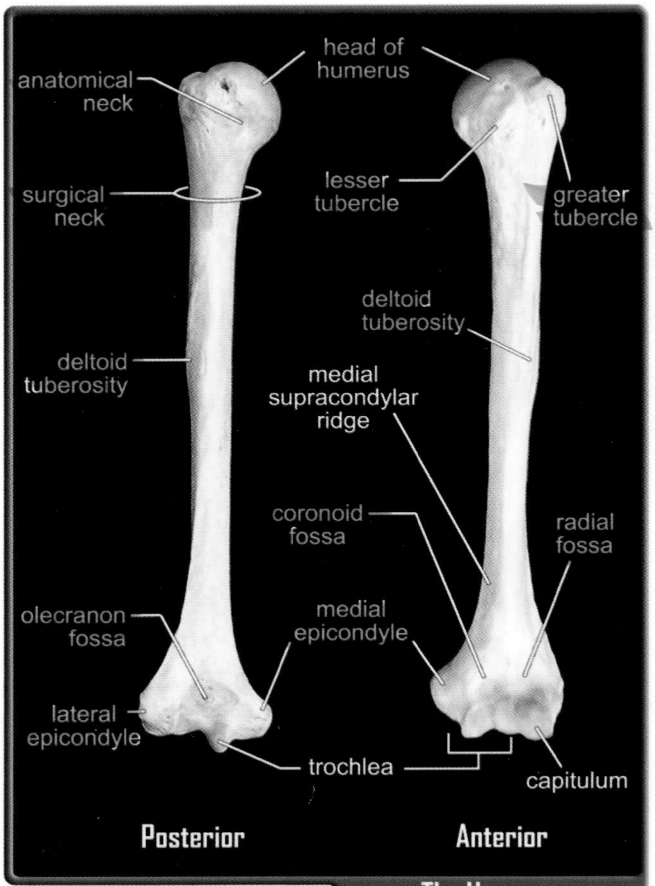

Figure 8-4 The Humerus

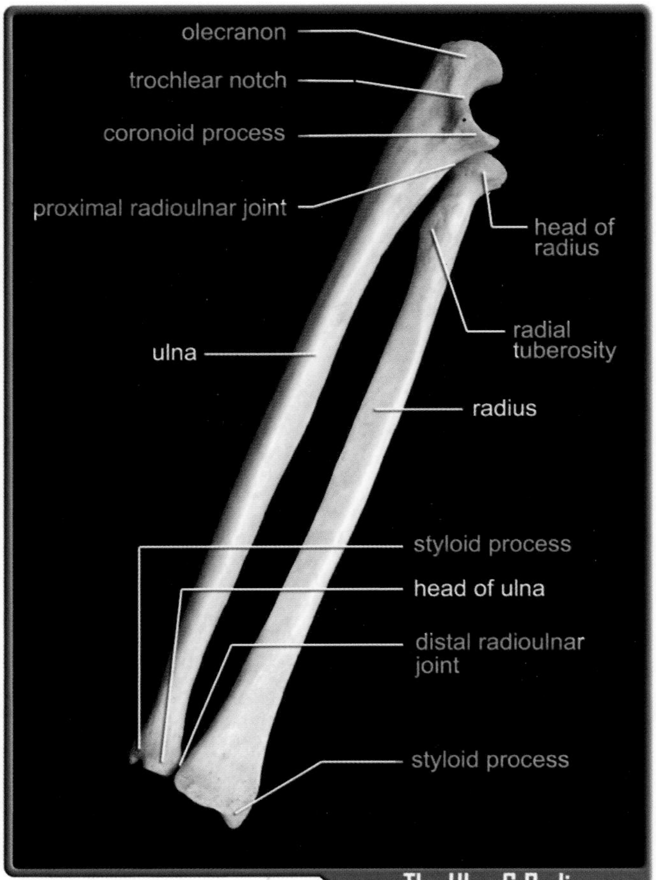

Figure 8-5 The Ulna & Radius

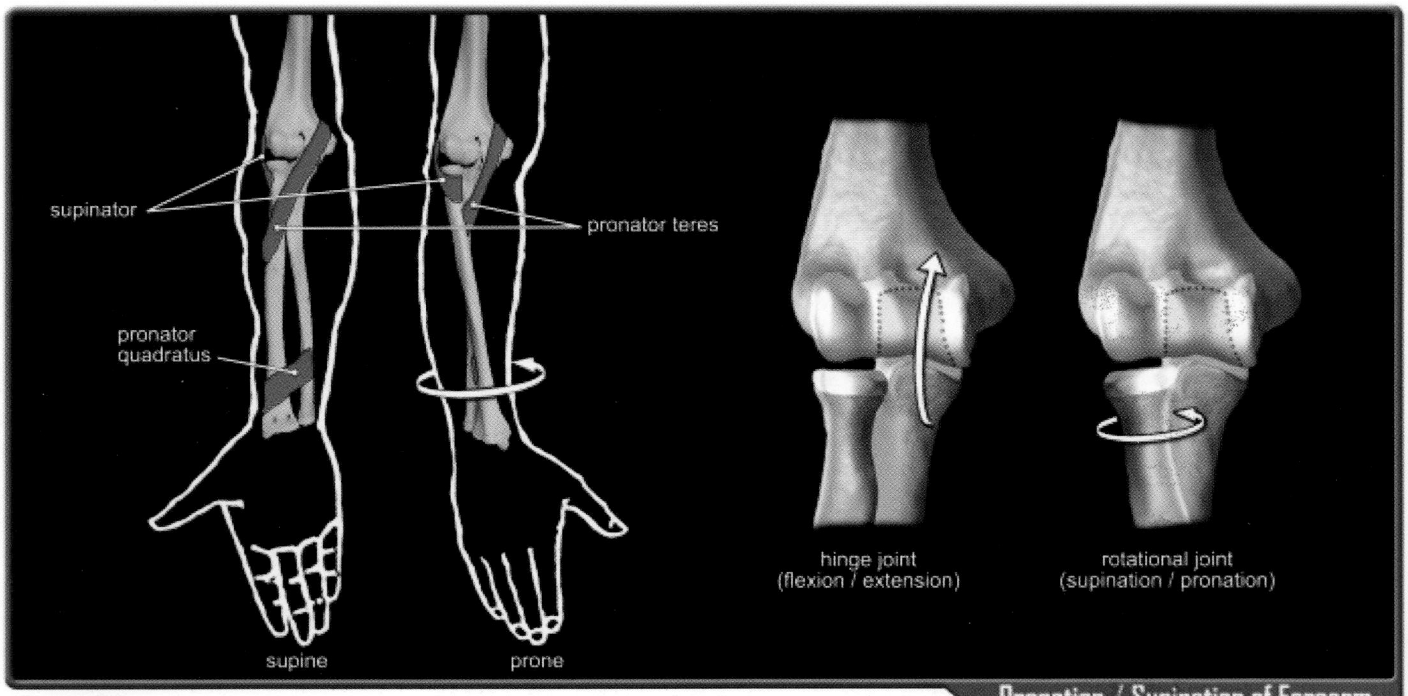

Figure 8-6 Pronation / Supination of Forearm

carpal bones go clockwise

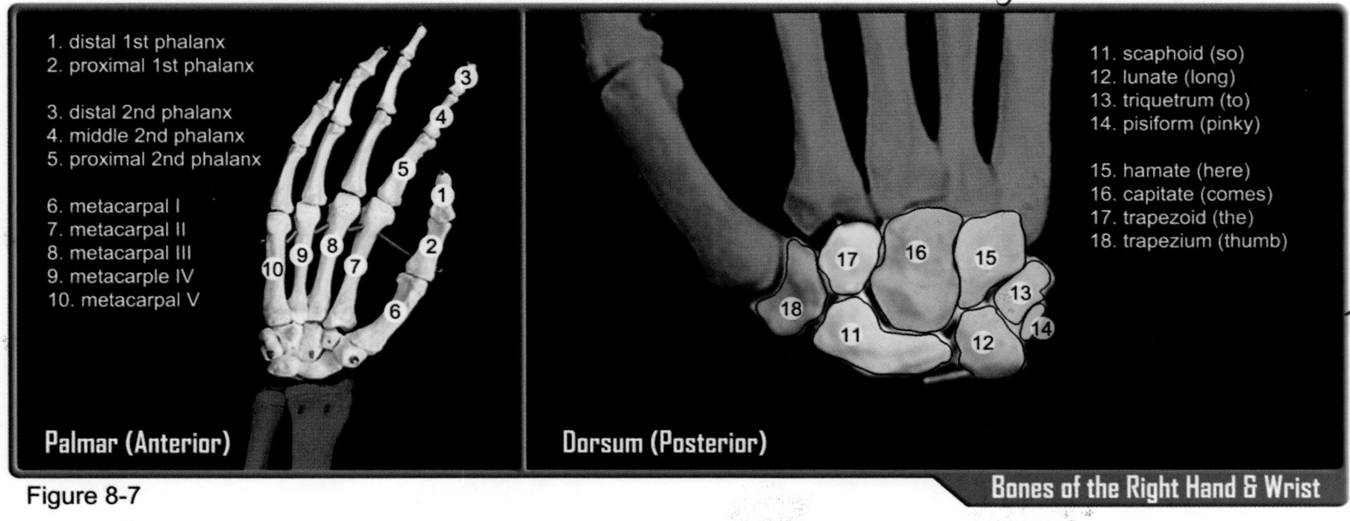

Figure 8-7

So Long To Pinky Here Comes The Thumb

The ulna is large proximally and tapers off distally. The bone articulates with the radius at both ends and with the humerus proximally via a large curved projection called the **olecranon process**. The olecranon is forms the bony point of the elbow and locks the forearm in position during full extension of the elbow. The olecranon also prevents overextension of the elbow joint. The **trochlear notch** of the olecranon rotates about the trochlea of the humerus during flexion / extension of the elbow. The **coronoid process** opposite the - olecranon fits snugly into the coronoid fossa of the humerus during full flexion of the elbow.

Distally, the **head of the ulna** articulates with the ulnar notch of the radius. The radius rotates around the head of the ulna when the hand undergoes pronation & supination.

The Wrist & Hand

There are 27 bones in each hand and wrist (Figure 8-7). The wrist is composed of 8 bones in two rows of four. The proximal row contains the **pisiform**, **triquetrum**, **lunate** and **scaphoid** bones. The distal row contains the **hamate** (which articulates with the pinky and ring fingers), the **capitate** (which articulates with the middle finger), the **trapezoid** (which articulates with the index finger) and the **trapezium** (which articulates with the thumb). All of the wrist bones can be felt, but it's

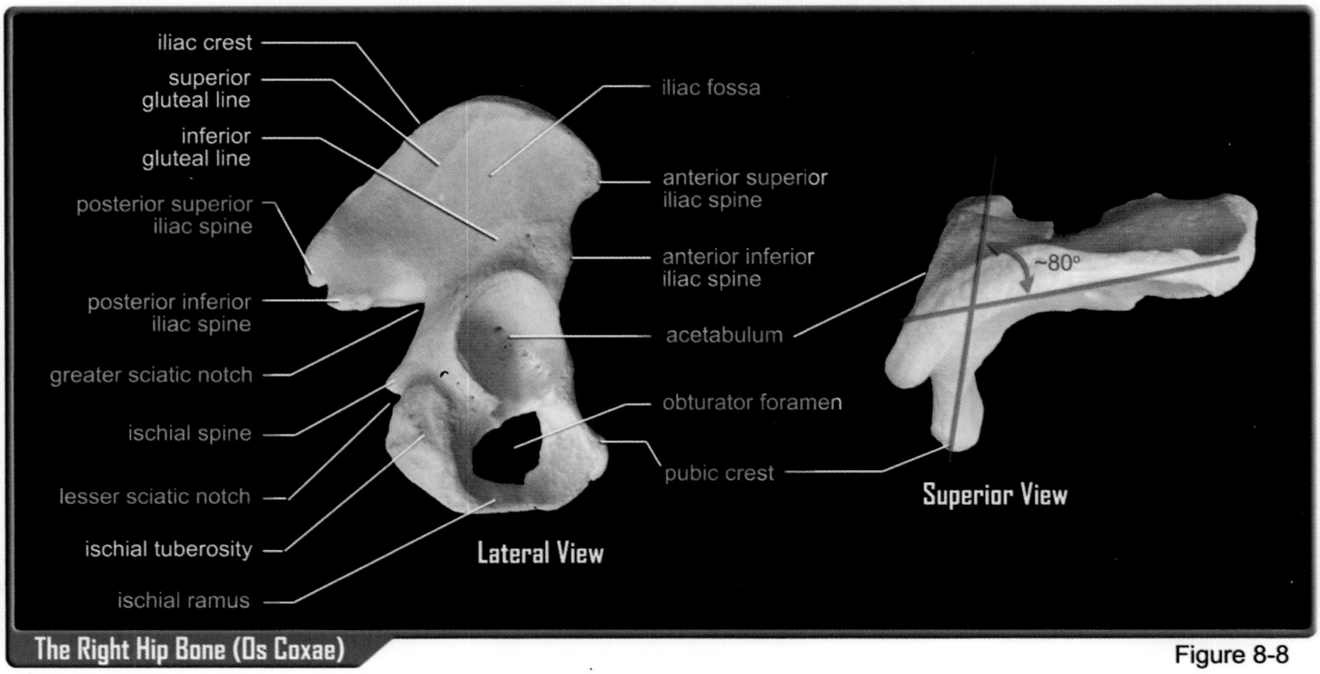

Figure 8-8

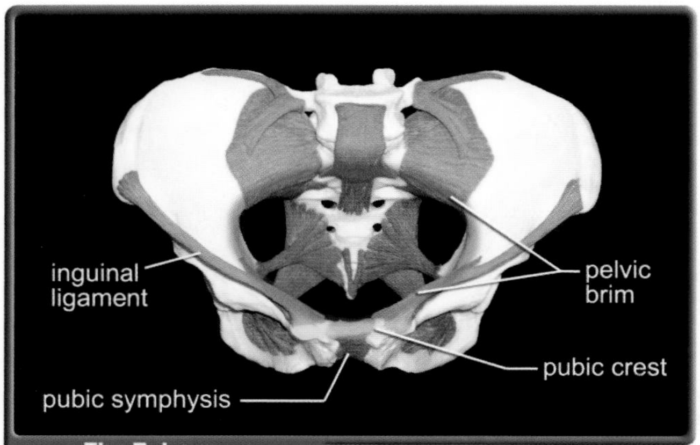

The Pelvis
Figure 8-9

often difficult to distinguish one from another. However, the triquetrum can be felt as a bump on the wrist at the base of the hypothenar eminence, and the pisiform can be felt as a bump just distal to the styloid process of the ulna.

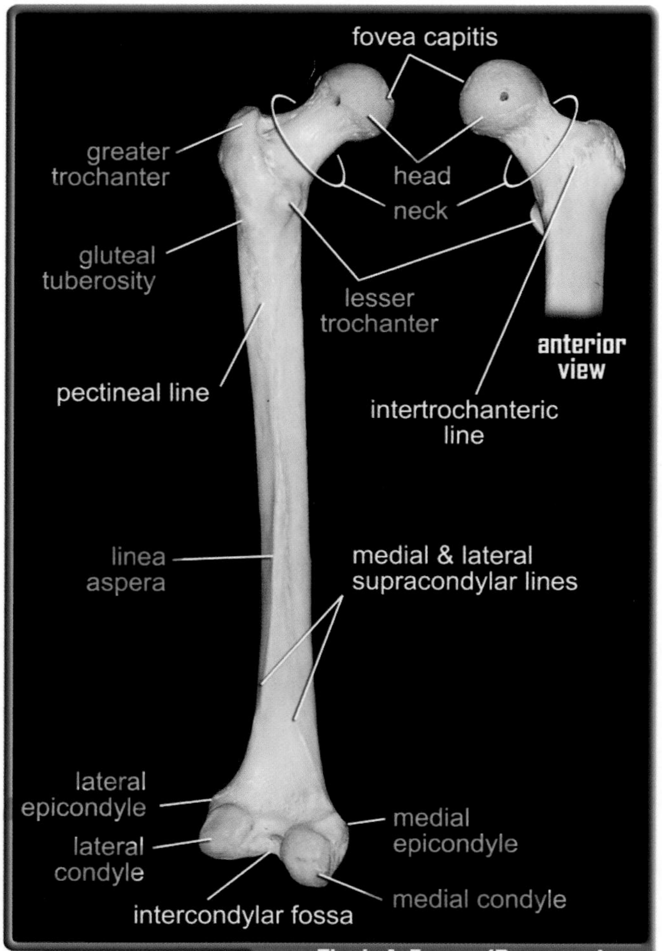

Figure 8-10
The Left Femur (Posterior)

The Pelvic Girdle

The pelvic girdle is actually composed of bones from both the appendicular and axial skeletons. The posterior wall of the pelvic girdle is formed by the sacrum and coccyx of the axial skeleton; the lateral and anterior portions are formed by the coxal bones of the appendicular skeleton.

The Hip Bones

The two coxal (hip) bones, the **os coxae**, are each formed by the fusion of three bones: the **ilium**, **ischium** and **pubis** bones (Figure 8-8). The two coxal bones articulate directly with each other only in the front of the body at a joint called the **pubic symphysis**. The **pubic crest** above this joint is easily felt on men but is usually more difficult to feel on women because of a fat pad (the mons pubis) above it.

All three bones of the os coxae contribute to the formation of the **acetabulum**, a deep socket which accommodates the head of the femur and forms the hip joint.

The **ischial bones** form the posteroinferior portion of the pelvis. The rami of the ischial bones support your body weight while you sit and have thus been nick-named the "sitz bones." The ischial and pubis bones form a large opening called the **obturator foramen**.

The **iliac bones** are the largest of the 3 bones that form the os coxae. The most prominent feature of the ilium is the long ridge – the **iliac crest** – that extends along the superior border of the bone. Pointed projections called **spines** mark each end of the crest. Each ilium possesses a large **articular surface** where it articulates with the sacrum.

The pelvis surrounds and protects the organs of the pelvic cavity and supports the organs of the abdominal cavity (Figure 8-9). The **pelvic brim** is formed by the sacral promontory posteriorly and the arcuate lines of the ilia anterolaterally. The pelvic brim is considerably wider is women as compared to men, in order to facilitate passage of the baby during childbirth. (Additionally, the entire pelvis is wider and shorter in women than in men, making the hips the widest part of the female body). The **greater sciatic notch** provides a route for the sciatic nerve and blood vessels to pass into the leg; the **lesser sciatic notch**

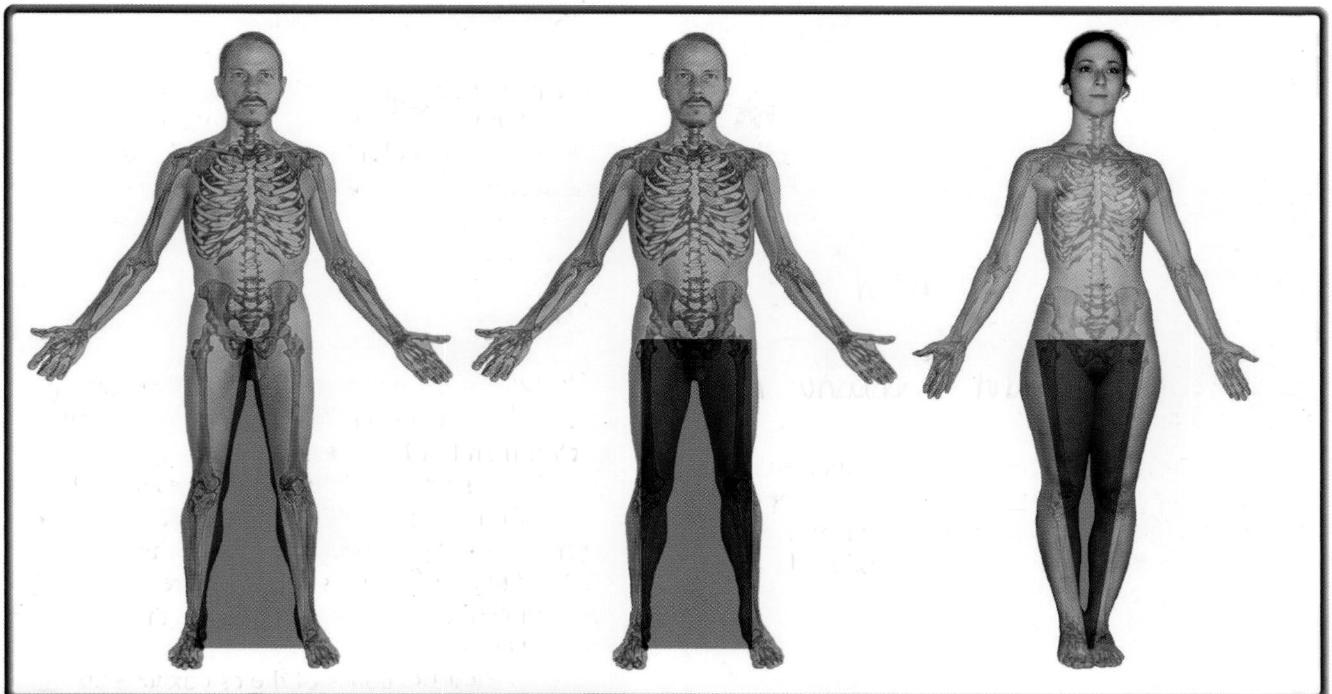

Weight Distribution by the Pelvic Girdle & Lower Limbs

Figure 8-11

similarly allows passage of nerves and blood vessels.

From the surface, only a few parts of the pelvis can be palpated or seen. The iliac crests are easily seen and felt on men and can be felt on women with more difficulty. The anterior superior iliac spines are easily seen on both men and women anteriorly as small bumps on the skin; by contrast, the posterior superior iliac spines are seen as dimples on either side of the sacrum. As stated above, the pubic crest can be felt just above the pubic symphysis, just above the penis on the male and deep to the mons pubis on the female. The **inguinal ligament**, which connects the anterior superior iliac spine to the pubic crest, is also more easily seen on men. The ischial rami can be felt best by pressing hard against the buttocks at the level of the gluteal fold while standing or walking. The coccyx can be felt immediately superior to the anus.

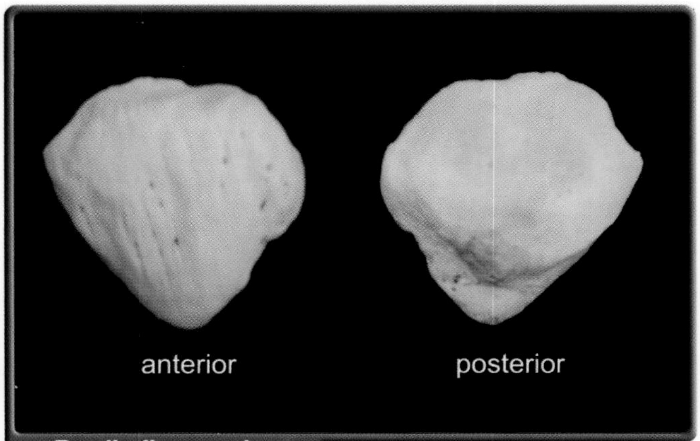

Patella (kneecap)

Figure 8-12

The Lower Limbs

The lower limbs consists of the thigh, leg, ankle and foot. The arrangement of the bones in the lower limbs is similar to that of the upper limbs.

The Thigh

The thigh contains just one bone, the **femur** (Figure 8-10). However, the femur is the largest and heaviest bone of the body. The large **head** of the femur fits snugly into the acetabulum of the coxal bone to form the ball-and-socket hip joint. The rather long **neck** of the femur causes the bone to project laterally from the axis of the body. As a result, when standing with feet slightly apart, the skeleton actually forms a rectangular shape even though the legs appear to make a triangle (with the apex up). Conversely, when standing with the feet close together, the skeleton makes a triangle with the apex down. This unstable position makes it

The
Circus
Needs
More
Interesting
Little
Clowns

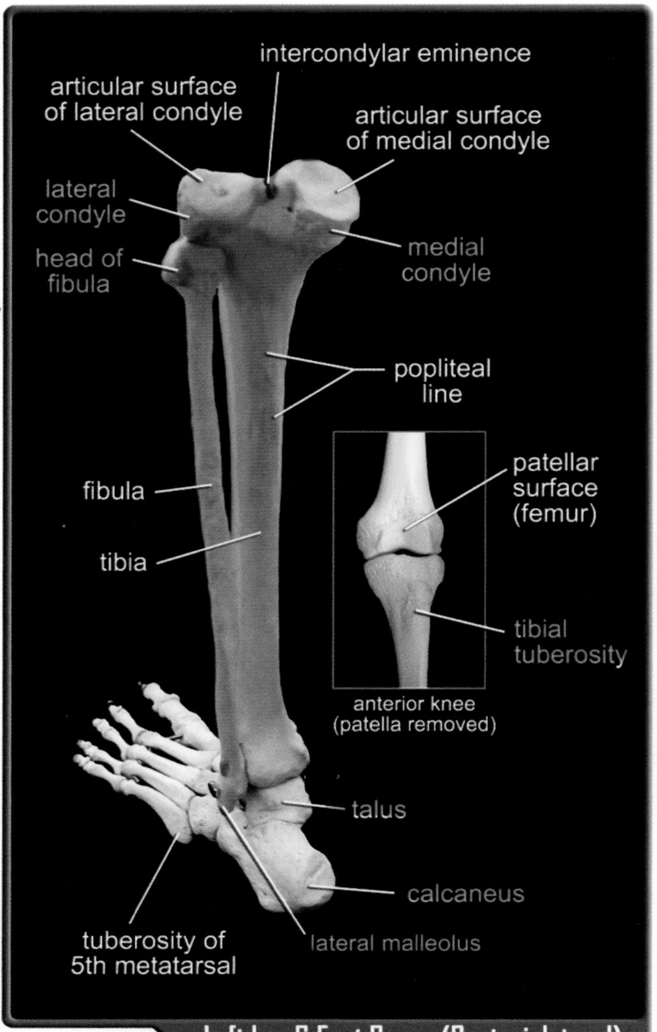

Figure 8-13 Left Leg & Foot Bones (Posteriolateral)

more difficult to stand with the feet together than with the feet apart (see Figure 8-11).

The **greater trochanter** of the femur serves as an attachment site for powerful muscles that abduct the thigh. Muscles that adduct and flex the thigh attach to the **lesser trochanter**. At the distal end of the bone, the large **medial** and **lateral condyles** articulate with the tibia bone in the leg.

Only the distal end of the femur can be easily palpated or seen. The **lateral** and **medial epicondyles** can be felt high on either side of the knee. Additionally, the **patella**, or *kneecap*, can be seen and felt at the knee joint (Figure 8-12).

The Leg

The leg, defined anatomically as the region between the knee and the ankle, contains two bones: The **tibia** and the **fibula** (Figure 8-13). The tibia is the

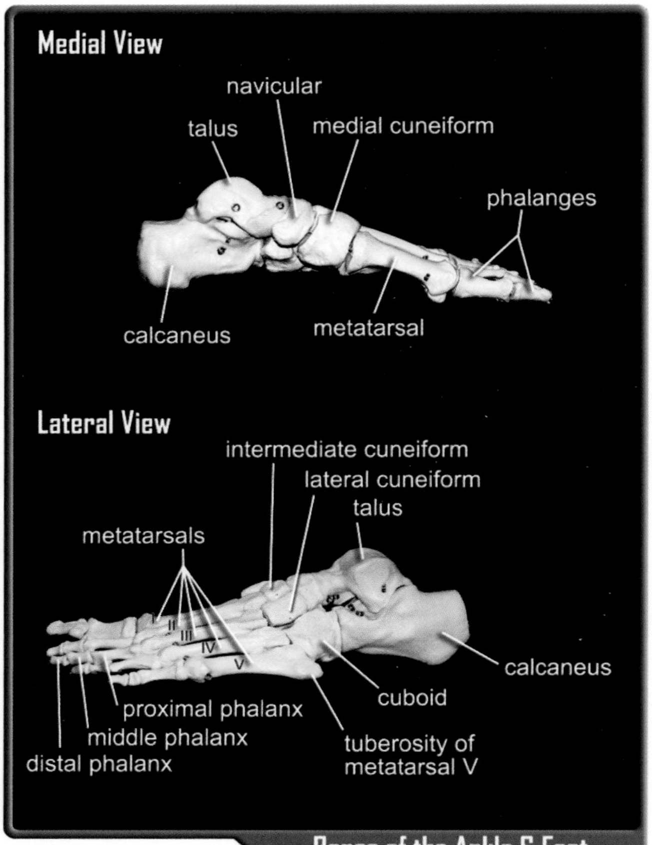

Figure 8-14 Bones of the Ankle & Foot

larger of the two bones and transfers body weight from the femur to the ankle and foot. The smaller fibula serves as an anchor for muscles that move the foot and toes.

The medial and lateral condyles of the femur rest upon the expansive **articular surfaces** of the **medial** and **lateral condyles** of the tibia. Anteriorly, the large **tibial tuberosity** serves as an attachment site for powerful thigh muscles that extend the leg (e.g., when kicking a football). The patella is a bone embedded in tendons that slides above the femur-tibia joint and stabilizes the joint. The **head of the fibula** articulates with the tibia laterally just beneath the lateral condyle of the tibia at the **proximal tibiofibular joint**.

Distally, the tibia and the fibula terminate in what are commonly (but mistakenly from an anatomical point of view) called the "ankle bones." The **medial malleolus** of the tibia forms the medial "ankle bone" and the **lateral malleolus** of the fibula forms the lateral "ankle bone." The lateral malleolus is lower than the medial malleolus. Between the malleoli, the two bones articulate again at the **distal tibiofibular joint**.

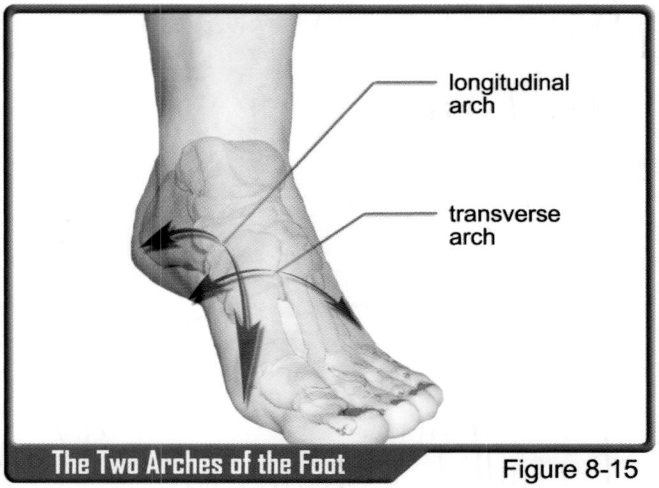

Figure 8-15

When standing with your legs slightly apart, your legs appear to make a triangle (apex up), but the bones actually form a rectangle. This combination makes standing in that position easy. With the legs closed, however, both the flesh of the legs and the bones make a triangle with the apex down. This combination makes it relatively difficult to stand with your feet close together.

In the leg, several parts of the the tibia and fibula can be seen and/or palpated. The lateral and medial condyles of the tibia form two large bumps on the sides of the leg just beneath the knee joint. The tibial tuberosity can be felt on the front of the leg just beneath the knee joint. The head of the fibula can be felt (and seen) as a small bump on the lateral side of the leg in the same plane as the tibial tuberosity. The anterior margin of the tibia (i.e., the "shin bone") can be felt all the way down the front of the leg. Finally, the lateral malleolus of the fibula and the medial malleolus of the tibia can be felt and seen as the "ankle bones" as described above.

The Ankle & Foot

There are seven ankle, or tarsal, bones (Figure 8-14). The tibia in the leg rests upon the **talus**, which in turn rests upon the **calcaneus**. Thus, when standing, body weight is transferred from the femur to the tibia to the talus to the calcaneus. Four tarsal bones are arranged in a row and articulate with the metatarsal, or foot bones. Laterally, the **cuboid** bone is found between the calcaneus and 5th metatarsal. The other three bones in the row are the **lateral cuneiform**, **intermediate cuneiform** and **medial cuneiform** bones. The **navicular** bone bridges the talus and the three cuneiform bones.

The five metatarsal bones are the bones of the foot. Together with the tarsal bones, the metatarsals form two arches: The **longitudinal arch** which runs from heel to toe, and the **transverse arch** which runs across the foot medially and laterally (Figure 8-15). The arches form the "instep" and act as shock absorbers when walking. The arches are held in place largely by supporting ligaments. A significant portion of the population has elongated ligaments resulting in a "fallen arch", or "flat feet."

The toes contain 14 bones. The first toe, or great toe, contains two bones (proximal and distal phalanges) while the other toes possess three bones (proximal, middle and distal phalanges). The base of the metatarsals articulates with the ankle bones; the head of the metatarsal articulates with the phalanges of the toes. When walking, your body weight is transferred from the femur to the tibia to the talus to the calcaneus, along the lateral edge of the foot through the 5th metatarsal, across the heads of the metatarsals and finally to the phalanges of the great toe which lifts you through the next step.

Many of the bones of the ankle and foot can be felt and seen. The calcaneus forms the bulk of your heel. The navicular bone can often be felt and seen as a large bump on the medial side of your foot, high on the arch. The highest point of the foot is the base of the 2nd metatarsal. The large tuberosity of the 5th metatarsal can be felt as a bump on the lateral side of your foot, exactly halfway between your heel and "pinky" toe.

Activity 1: Examine Bones of the Appendicular Skeleton

1. Using the photos in this lab manual, disarticulated and articulated bones, and / or a complete skeleton, critically examine the bones of the axial skeleton.

Activity 2: Construct a Complete Skeleton

1. Using disarticulated bones, arrange the bones on your lab bench to form a complete skeleton. By careful observation of bone markings you should be able to distinguish bones from the right or left side of the body.

Activity 3: Determine Your Arch Type

1. Obtain a plain white sheet of paper and a sheet of paper coated with charcoal from your instructor.
2. Step on the paper coated with charcoal, then onto the clean sheet of paper. A footprint

should be left behind. You may want to trace the outline of your footprint.

3. As shown in figure 8-16, mark the middle of the second toe and the middle of the heel. Draw a line between these two points (the *longitudinal foot axis* line).
4. Mark the center of longitudinal foot axis line as point C.
5. Draw a line perpendicular to the longitudinal foot axis line, passing through point C.
6. Draw a line from the most medial part of the forefoot to the most medial part of the heel.
7. Measure the length of lines MC and lines MA. The transverse arch index (TAI) is the ratio of MC/MA.
8. Use the table below to determine your arch type from your TAI.

Your TAI = ____________

Your arch type is ____________

Arch Type	TAI
High arch	<0.74
Normal arch	0.75-1.25
Low arch	1.26-2
Flat arch	>2

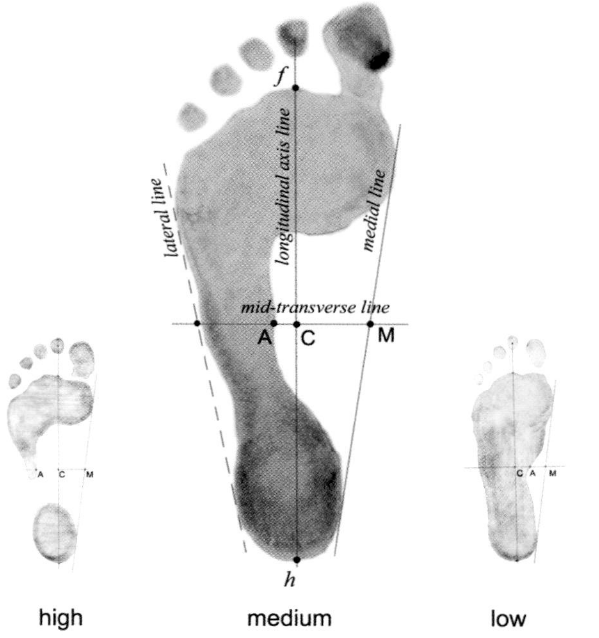

Measuring Arch Types Figure 8-16

Activity 4: Surface Anatomy Examination

Pectoral Girdle & Upper Limbs

1. Palpate or visually examine as many bones as possible on yourself and / or your lab partner.

- **Clavicles** – The clavicles, or collar bones, can be felt along their entire lengths. Each clavicle articulates with the axial skeleton at the manubrium of the sternum. The articulation creates a highly visible V- or U-shaped indentation at the base of the neck called the jugular notch. Trace the clavicle from its sternal end to the acromial end. The articulation of the clavicle with the acromion process of the scapula creates a bump at the top of the shoulder. The bump can also be located by lifting the arm and feeling within the deep depression created in the shoulder by the deltoid muscle.
- **Humerus** – The humerus of the arm can only be felt at the distal end because the proximal end is within the shoulder joint and surrounded by large muscles. Distally, the two epicondyles of the humerus are obvious bumps on the lateral and medial sides of the elbow joint.
- **Ulna** – The ulna can be felt from one end of the bone to the other. Distally, the head of the ulna makes a large and obvious bump on the medial side (i.e., pinky finger side) of the wrist. Press firmly on the bone and trace it all the way up the forearm to its proximal end. The bone terminates with a large projection called the olecranon, which forms the point of the elbow.
- **Radius** – Unlike the ulna, the radius cannot be felt from end-to-end. However, the distal and proximal ends of the bone can be palpated. Distally, the styloid process can be seen and felt as a bump on the lateral (i.e., thumb side) of the wrist. Proximally, the head of the radius can be felt best with the elbow in full extension. It's a small bump immediately distal to the lateral epicondyle of the humerus. Try to feel the head of the radius rotate as you supinate-pronate the forearm.
- **Carpal bones** – Distal to the head of the ulna is a smaller bump which can be felt rather easily. This bump is from the triquetral bone of the wrist. On the opposite side of the wrist at the base of the hypothenar emminence the pisiform bone can be palpated. Several other carpal bones may be felt in the wrist, but accurately identifying them is difficult.

- **Metacarpals** – Each of the five metacarpal bones of the hand can be palpated by squeezing one hand firmly with the other. In particular, the head of the each bone is readily seen and felt at the distal ends (also known as the "knuckles"). Note that the metacarpals are not usually seen, only felt. The lines you might see on the dorsum side of the hand are not the metacarpal bones but are tendons of the extensor muscles that extend your fingers.
- **Phalanges** – Each of the 14 phalanges can be felt by massaging the fingers.

Pelvic Girdle & Lower Limbs

- **Os coxae** – Various parts of the hip bones can be seen and felt. The iliac crest forms a prominent ridge across either side of the hips from front-to-back. These are where you commonly place your hands when standing with "hands on your hips." The crest terminates anteriorly with the anterior superior iliac spine – a point that is quite visible through the skin. The crests terminate with the posterior superior iliac spines which usually appear as dimples in the lower back. The pubic crest (and sometimes the pubic tubercles) can be felt anteriorly by pressing firmly on the pelvis just above the pubic region. This is sometimes harder to feel on women than on men because of a fat pad (mons pubis) present on women. The ramus of the ischium can be felt by pressing firmly on the buttocks while standing with the gluteal muscles relaxed. These may also be felt while sitting if you sit on your hands.
- **Femur** – Only the ends of the femur can be palpated. Proximally, the greater trochanter can be felt by pressing firmly against the side of the thigh. Locating this bony projection may be aided by slowly moving the hip joint by swinging your leg front-to-back. Distally, the two condyles of the femur can be felt low on the thigh on the lateral and medial sides of the knee joint. These and other knee structures can be felt best with the knee fully flexed.
- **Tibia** – Like the ulna, the tibia can be felt from one end to the other. With the knee fully flexed, the epicondyles of the tibia can be felt and seen as medial and lateral bumps low on the knee joint. Between them, the prominent tibial tuberosity is evident just below the patella. From the tibial tuberosity, trace the anterior margin of the tibia all the way to the ankle. The tibia ends distally with a large projection called the medial malleolus.
- **Fibula** – Like the radius, only the ends of the fibula can only be felt and/or seen. Proximally, the head of the fibula can be located by first finding the tibial tuberosity, then sliding your fingers laterally to the outside of the leg. At the same height as the tibial tuberosity, the head of the fibula is a small bump on the lateral side of the leg. The bone cannot be traced liked the tibia because of surrounding leg muscles, but the distal end of the fibula can be seen and felt as the large lateral malleolus. Note that the lateral and medial malleoli, often called the "ankle bones", belong in fact to the leg bones, not bones of the ankle.
- **Tarsal bones** – The calcaneus can be seen and felt as the large bony projection of the heel ("heel bone"). On some people, the cuboid bone forms a large, broad bump on the lateral side of the foot; on others, this bump is not at all prominent. And again, the navicular bone forms a prominent bump on the medial side of the foot just above the arch on some individuals, but not others.
- **Metatarsals** – Each of the five metatarsal bones can be felt by massaging the foot. The tuberosity of the fifth metatarsal presents as a large bump on the lateral side of the foot exactly halfway between the heel and the small toe. This bump can often be seen as well as felt.
- **Phalanges** – Most of the phalanges can be felt in the toes, but some of the smaller ones may be masked by surrounding tissues.

exercise 9

the SKELETAL system

- articulations -

It is written: "As surely as I live," says the Lord, "Every knee will bow before me; every tongue confess to God."

Romans 14:11

Virtually every bone in the body is connected to at least one other bone. These bone-to-bone connections are called **articulations**, or joints. Without joints between bones, body movements would be severely limited. Articulations allow adjoining bones to move relative to one another as they are pulled on by attached muscles.

Joint Movements

A wide variety of movements can be accomplished by your body's joints. Most of the movements discussed below are made by synovial joints (discussed later) since they are the most mobile. As you will see, synovial joints primarily allow movements of the appendicular skeleton.

Joint motions are described relative to the anatomical position, which is standing upright with feet slightly apart, arms by the sides, hands facing forward with fingers extended. In this position, all of the joints of the body are in the "extended" position, except for the ankles. The types of motions made by joints are as follows.

- **Abduction / Adduction** – Abduction / adduction describe movements in the frontal plane, i.e., side-to-side motions. Abduction is movement of the limbs *away* from the body, or spreading of the fingers or toes, or movement of the wrist away from the body. Adduction is closure of the fingers or toes and the movement of the limbs back to the body (i.e., back to the anatomical position). Examples of abduction and adduction are shown in Figure 9-1 and Figure 9-3.
- **Flexion / Extension** – Flexion / extension describe movements in the sagittal plane, i.e., front-to-back motions. Flexion is achieved when the angle between two articulating bones is *decreased* by their movements. Extension is achieved when the angle between articulating bones is *increased* and the limbs are returned to the anatomical position. Flexion and extension of the knee joint are shown in Figure 9-2.
- **Hyperextension** – Hyperextension is achieved when joint extension is continued past the anatomical direction. Not all joints that undergo flexion/extension can achieve hyperextension. For example, the elbow can be flexed and extended, but the olecranon of the ulna prevents hyperextension of that joint. Likewise, the knee can be flexed and extended, but hyperextension is prevented by strong ligaments (e.g., the PCL and ACL). The wrist, neck, back, shoulder and hip can by hyperextended. Flexion, extension and hyperextension of the wrist is shown in Figure 9-3.

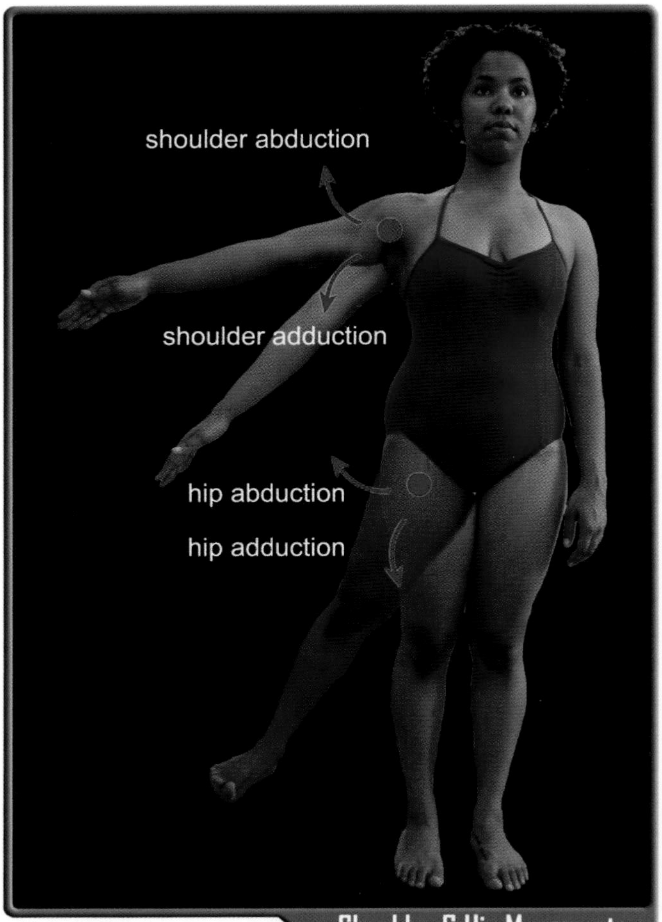

Figure 9-1 Shoulder & Hip Movements

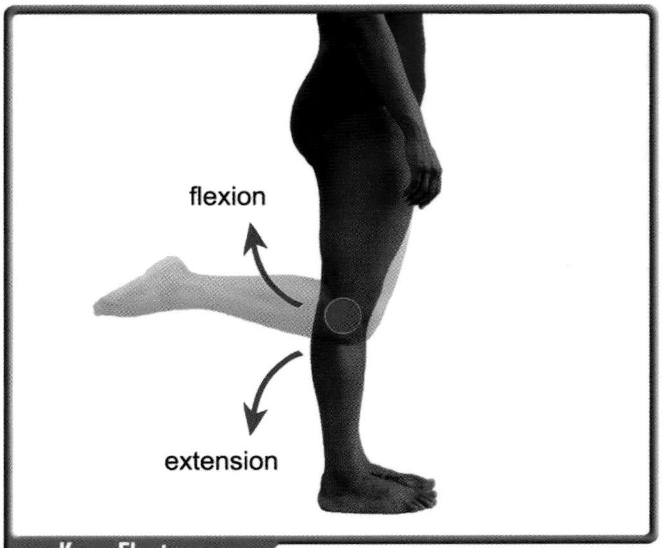

Knee Flexion Figure 9-2

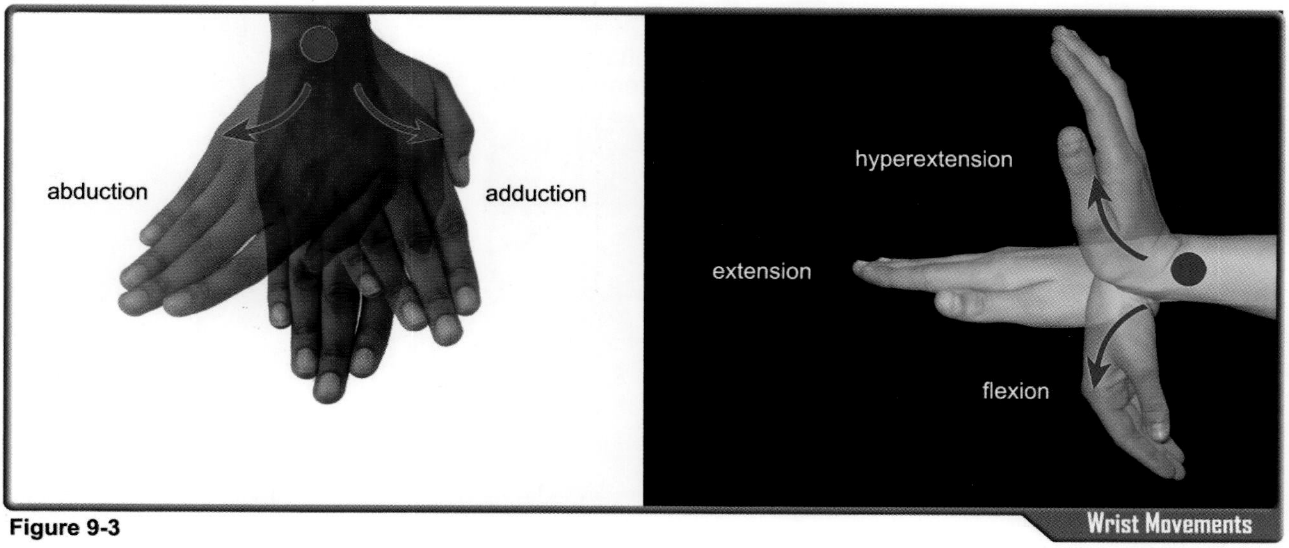

Figure 9-3

- **Rotation** – The hip and shoulder joints can undergo lateral and medial rotation, as shown in Figure 9-4. The vertebral column and neck can also achieve left and right lateral rotation (Figure 9-5).
- **Circumduction** – Circumduction is the circular movement of a limb such that it traces an arch (Figure 9-6). The hip and shoulder joints, as well as the ankles, wrists and certain fingers can achieve circumduction.

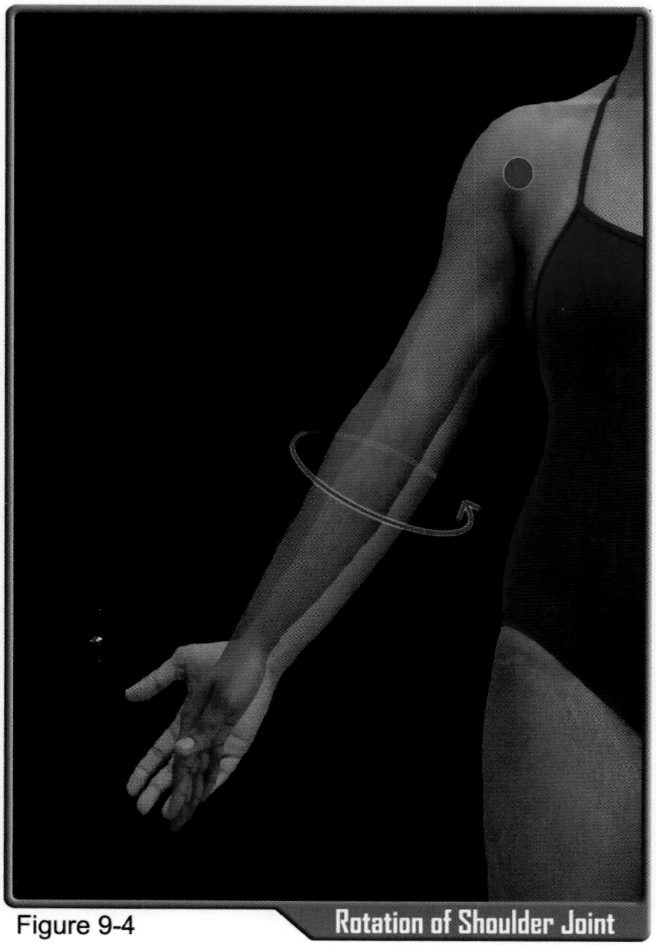

Figure 9-4

Special Movements

Recall that the ankles are the only joints not extended in the anatomical position. Movements of the ankle have traditionally been given special terms, but newer terms more in line with the above descriptions are also becoming popular. Pointing the toes may be referred to either as **plantar flexion**, or as **ankle extension**. The opposite motion (i.e., raising the foot toward the knee) has been traditionally called **dorsiflexion**, but also is known as **ankle flexion**. The ankles can also be tilted side-to-side. Turning the foot inward is called **inversion**; turning the foot outward is called **eversion**. These movements are depicted in Figure 9-7.

The human hand is a remarkable instrument. It can at times curl up into a fist and punch through a wall, and at other times grip a pencil and delicately trace minuscule markings on paper. Much of the versatility of the hand is made possible by the thumb, which is alone capable of touching the tips of the other fingers. The special motion of touching the tip of the thumb with the tip of another finger is called **opposition** (Figure 9-8). Other special movements of the body include

- protraction / retraction of the jaw
- elevation / depression of the jaw and shoulders
- supination / pronation of the forearm (see Figure 8-6)

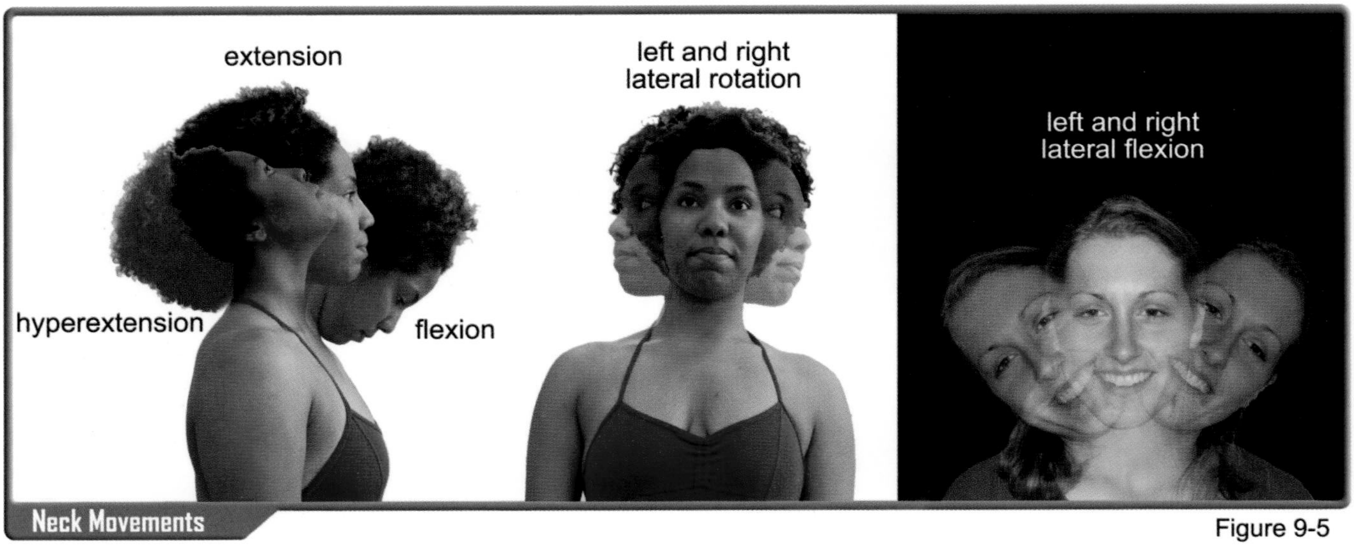

Figure 9-5

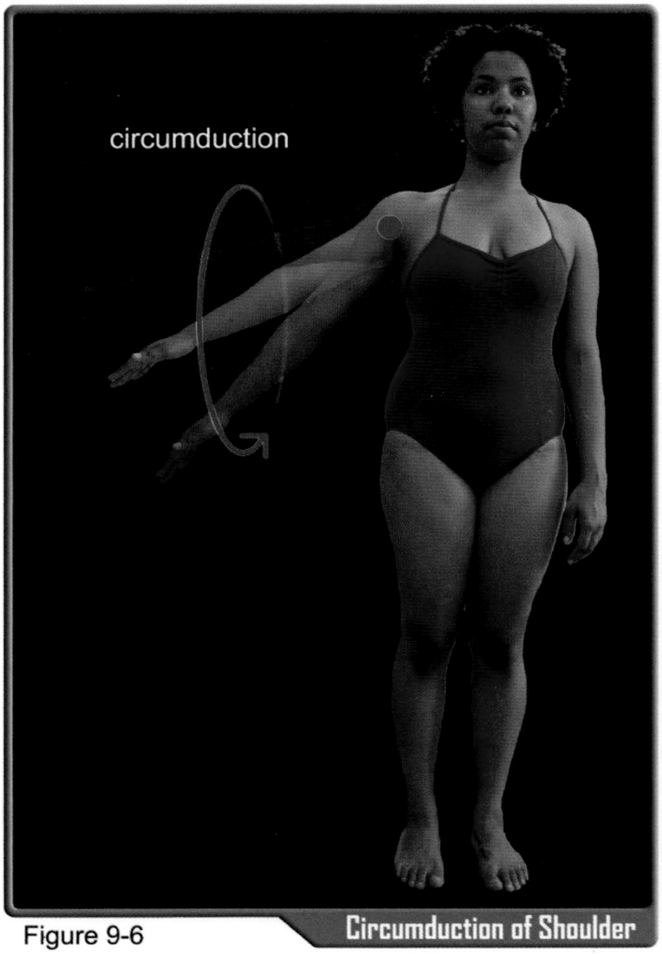

Figure 9-6

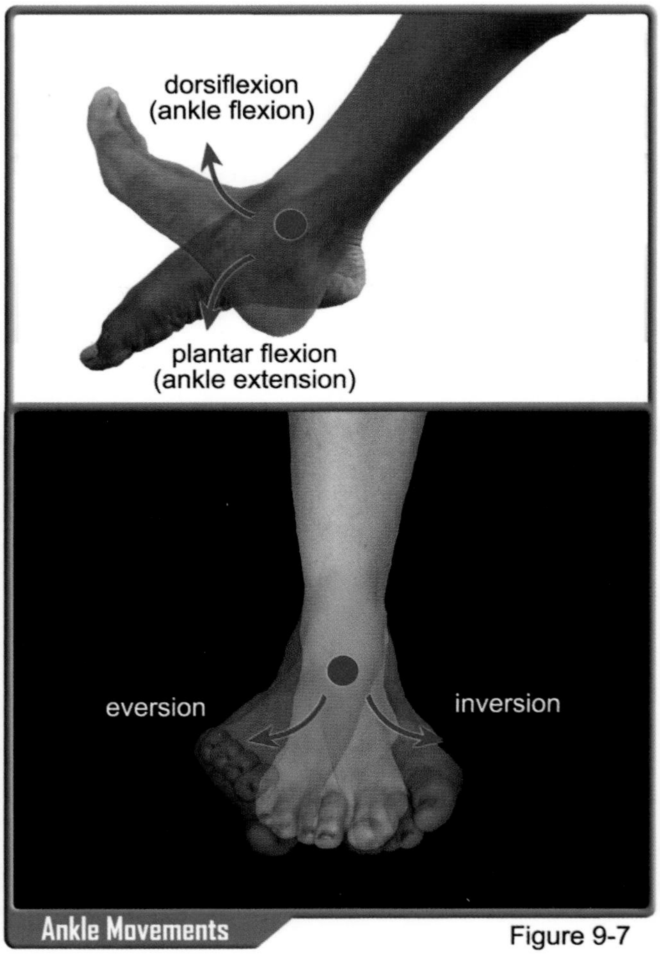

Figure 9-7

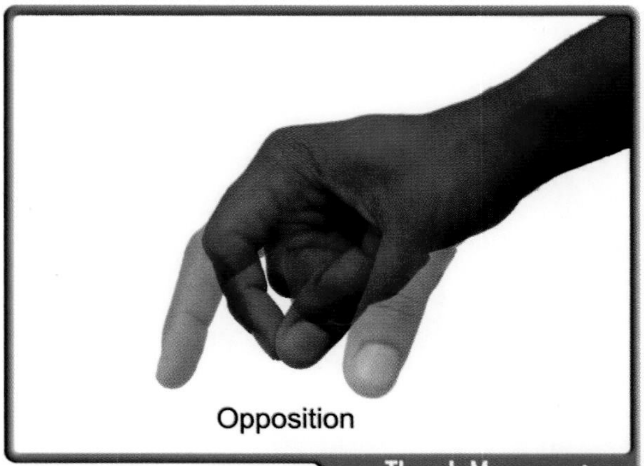

Figure 9-8 Thumb Movements

Types of Joints

Joints may be classified either functionally or structurally (i.e., physiologically or anatomically). Physiologically, joints are classified as (1) freely movable joints, called **diarthroses**, (2) slightly movable joints, called **amphiarthroses** or (3) immovable joints, called **synarthroses**. Not surprisingly, diarthroses predominant in the appendicular skeleton whereas many bones of the axial skeleton are connected by less mobile synarthrotic and amphiarthrotic articulations. As you study the different types of joints, notice the inverse relationship between joint mobility and joint stability.

Anatomically, joints are classified as either

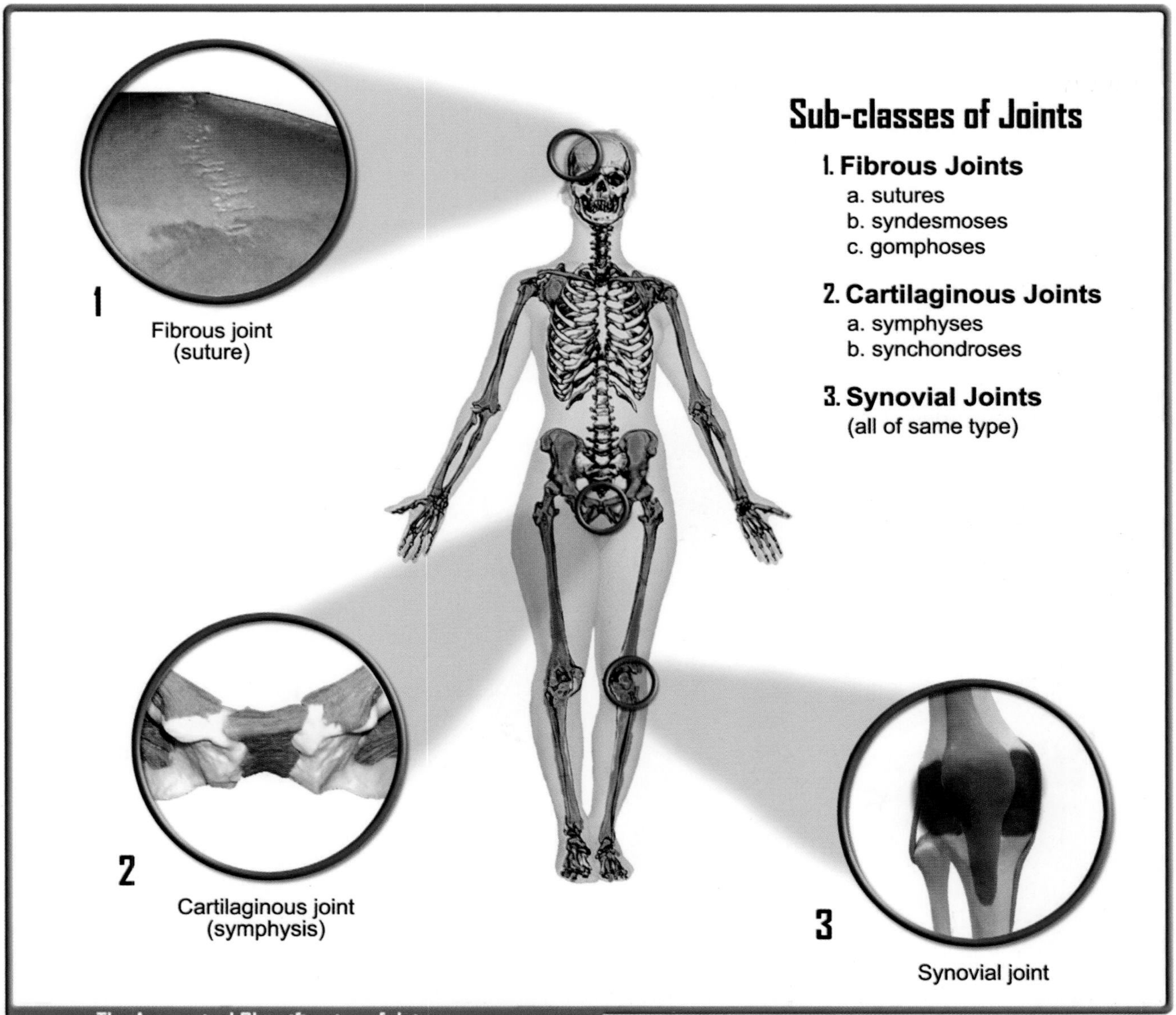

The Anatomical Classification of Joints

Figure 9-9

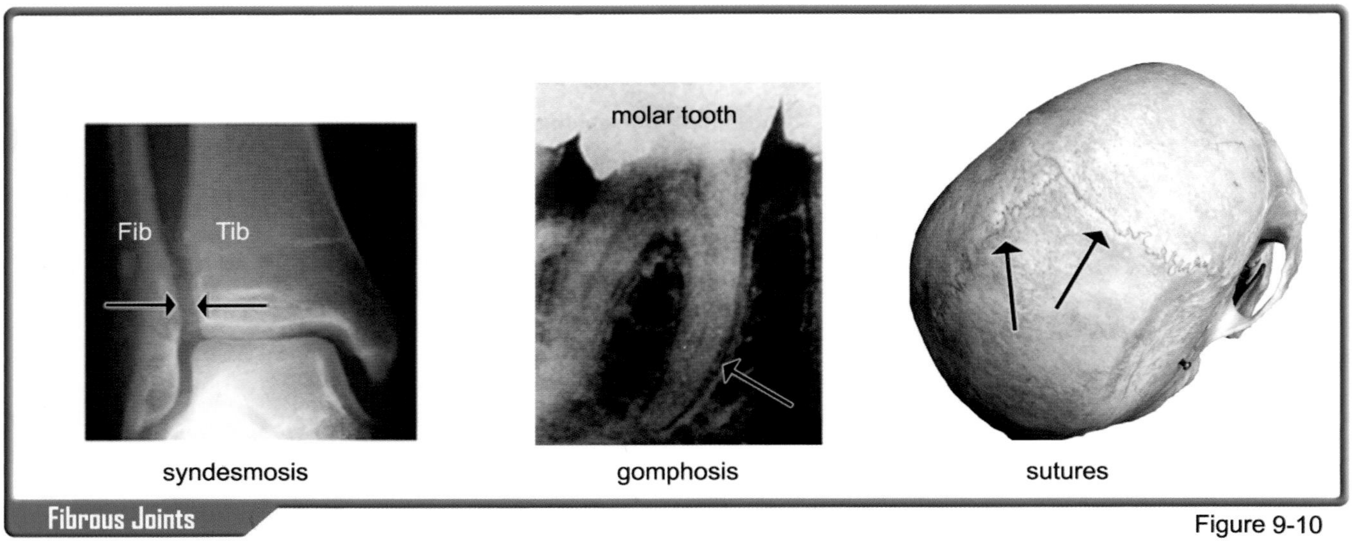

Figure 9-10

fibrous, **cartilaginous** or **synovial** (Figure 9-9). Based on what you already know about the Structure-Function law, you might predict a strong correlation between the anatomical and physiological classifications. This, indeed, is the case. For example, fibrous joints tend to be immovable (synarthrotic) whereas synovial joints are freely movable (diarthrotic). Cartilaginous joints provide a compromise of rigidity and flexibility and are thus usually amphiarthrotic. Here, we will use the anatomical classification of joints and briefly examine the properties of each.

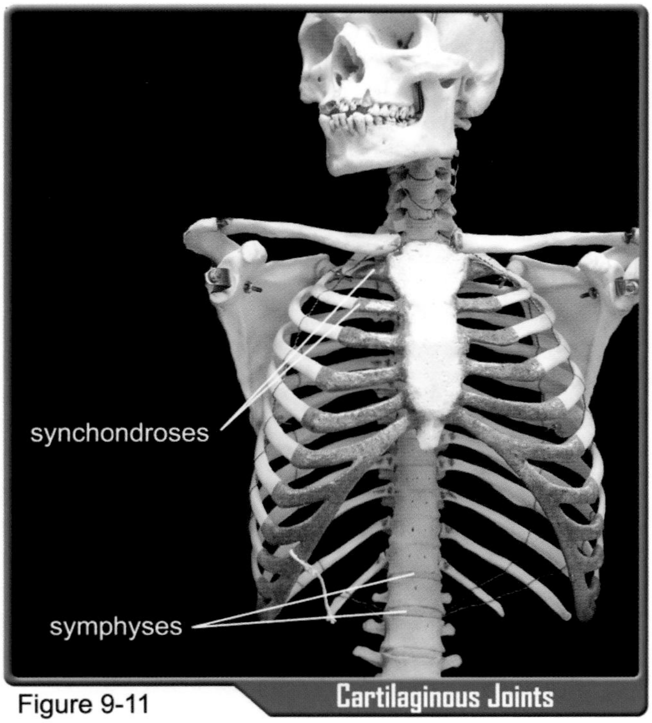

Figure 9-11 Cartilaginous Joints

Fibrous Joints

As the name implies, fibrous joints are held together by fibrous connective tissue. In general, fibrous joints are the least mobile of all joints.

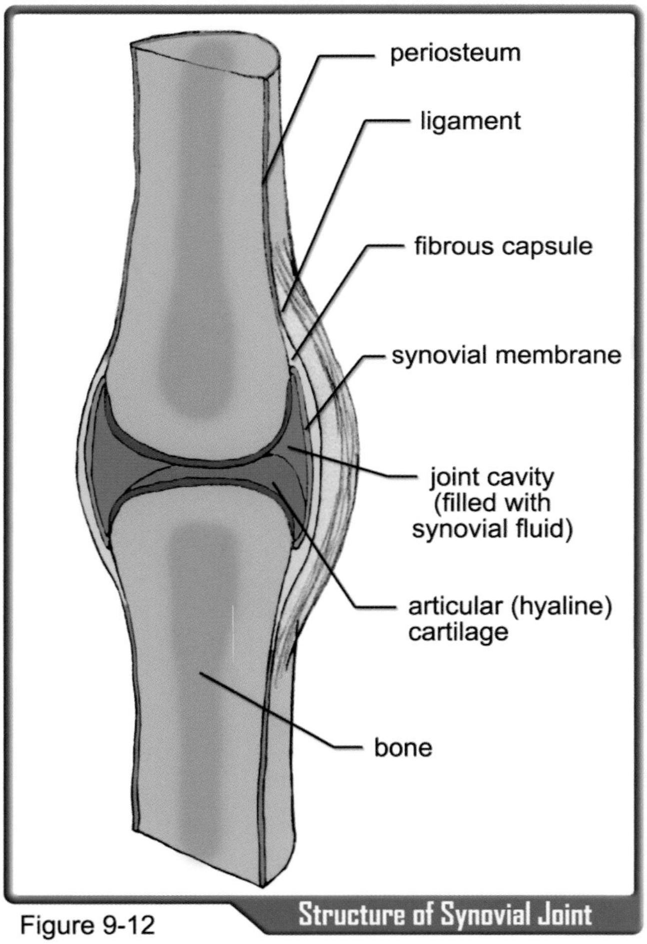

Figure 9-12 Structure of Synovial Joint

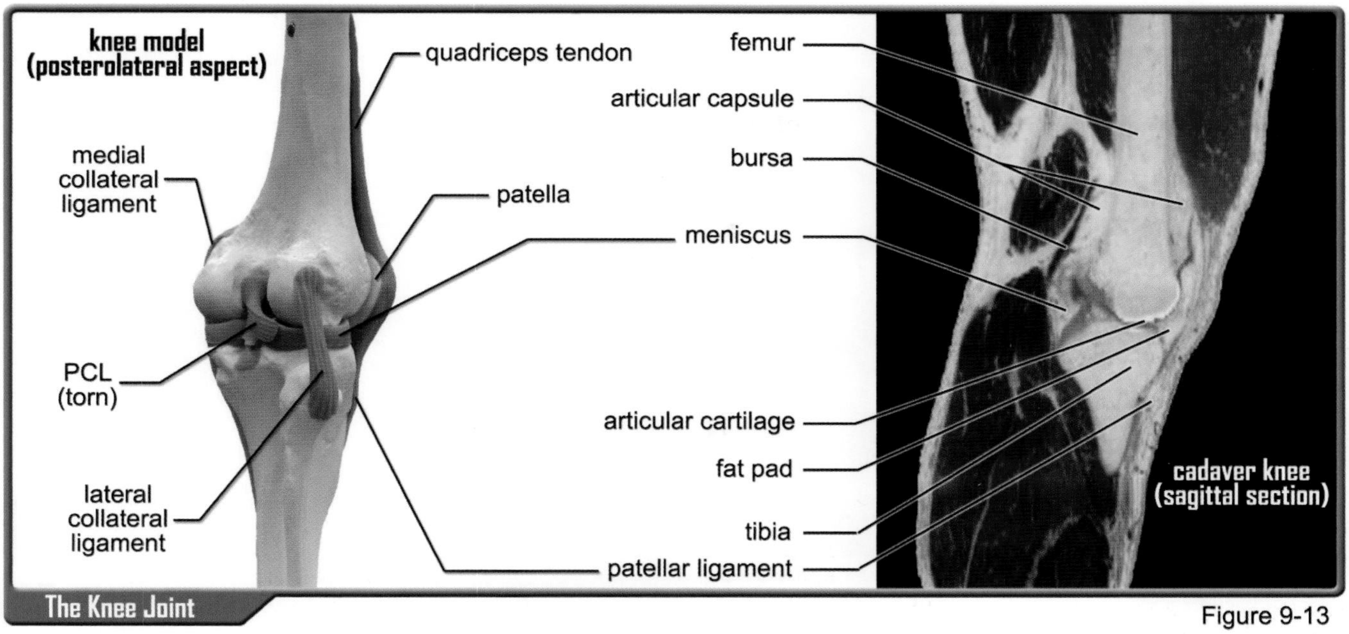

Figure 9-13

Some fibrous joints do allow slight movement, but most allow no movement at all. There are three basic types of fibrous joints: sutures, syndesmoses and gomphoses (Figure 9-10). **Syndesmoses** attach bones together by a short, tough fibrous ligament. The bones do not interlock and limited movement is allowed. The distal portions of the tibia and fibula are held together just above the talus by a syndesmotic joint.

The teeth are firmly held in place by a special fibrous joint called a **gomphosis**. A short span of ligament (the periodontal ligament) attaches each embedded tooth to the facial bone. This ligament allows for slight movement, so it's normal for healthy teeth to wiggle slightly or feel "loose."

Suture joints are found predominantly in the skull. The cranial bones are firmly attached by interlocking with each other at the joint. Absolutely no movement is allowed by a suture joint. Sutures are extremely stable and rarely become disarticulated in life.

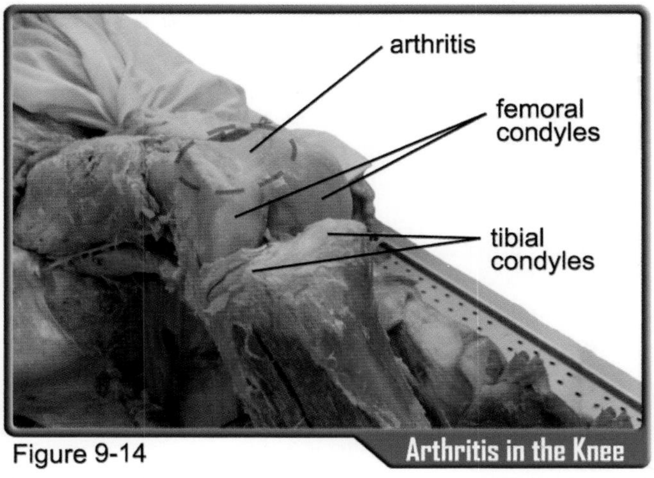

Figure 9-14

Cartilaginous Joints

Bones connected by **cartilaginous joints** are held together by a thin pad of cartilage. Most cartilaginous joints are slightly movable, or amphiarthrotic. There are two types of cartilaginous joints: **symphyses** and **synchondroses** (Figure 9-11).

Symphyses are formed when two bones are connected by a thin pad or sheet of fibrocartilage. Slight movement is allowed by this type of joint. The pubic symphysis connecting the two pubic bones, and the intervertebral joints between the vertebrae are symphyses.

In a synchondrosis the articulating portion of bone is padded with hyaline cartilage. The connections between the first rib and the sternum is an example of a synchodroses. No movement is allowed at these joints. The slightly movable joints between ribs 2-6 and the sternum typically become synchondrotic in older individuals.

Synovial Joints

Synovial joints are characterized by articulation sites enclosed within a joint capsule, or joint cavity. These joints are highly mobile (diarthrotic). The joint cavity is filled with a lubricating fluid called **synovial fluid** and the terminal portions of the

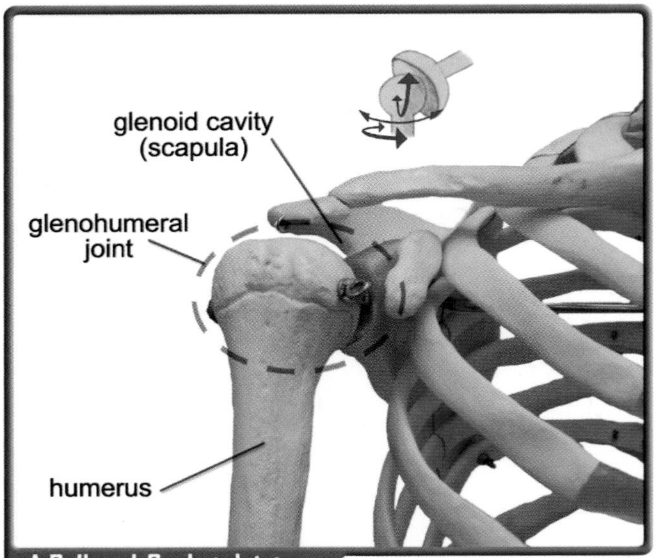

A Ball-and-Socket Joint
Figure 9-15

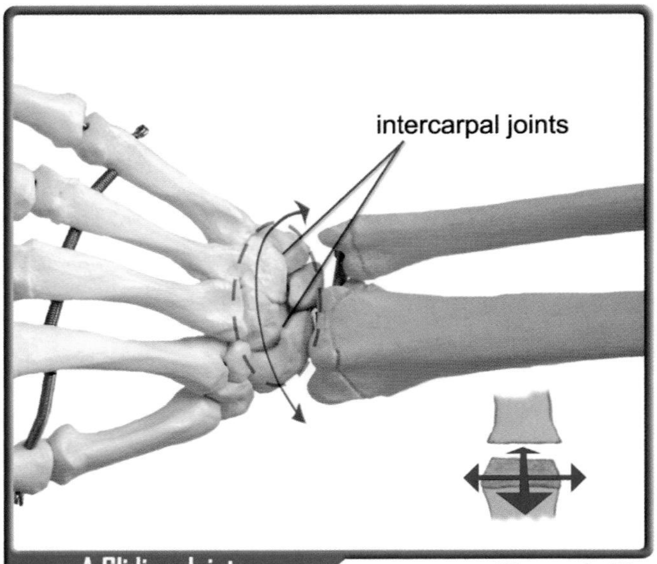

A Gliding Joint
Figure 9-17

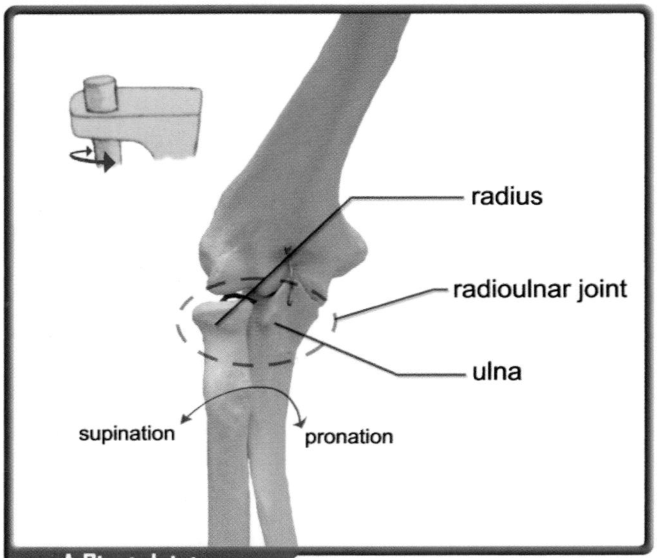

A Pivot Joint
Figure 9-16

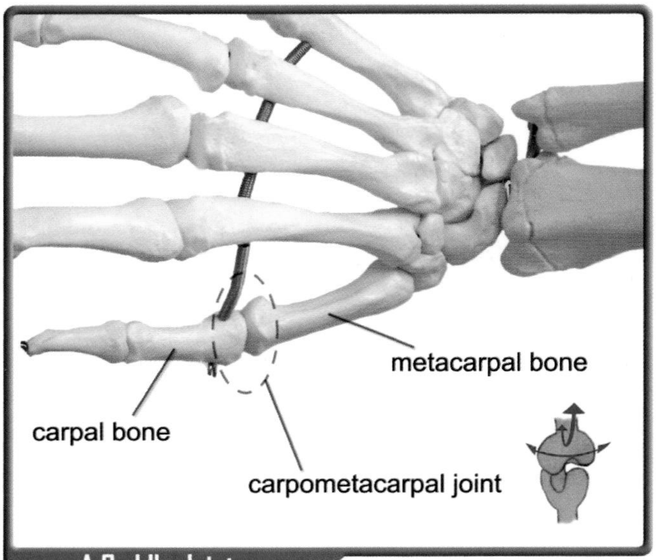

A Saddle Joint
Figure 9-18

articulating bones are covered with glassy smooth hyaline cartilage, also called **articular cartilage**. These features protect the bones during joint movements. Because of the high mobility of synovial joints they are the least stable. It is not uncommon for bones at the shoulder, knee or hip to become disarticulated, or "pulled out of joint."

The common features of a synovial joint are shown in figure 9-12. As stated above, synovial joints are characterized by a surrounding joint capsule composed of an outer **fibrous capsule** and an inner **synovial membrane**. The fibrous capsule is made primarily of dense irregular connective tissue. The synovial membrane is composed of epithelial cells and areolar connective tissue which secrete synovial fluid into the joint cavity. The entire articular capsule is usually reinforced by ligaments. In some cases, a bursa may form within or near a synovial joint cavity (described below).

The knee joint is perhaps the most complex joint in the body (Figure 9-13). The joint possesses the usual components of a synovial articulation, but also has other accessory structures, as well. **Fat pads** are soft, adjustable connective tissue structures that can change shape as the joint moves. **Menisci** (singular, meniscus) is a tough ligamentous disc of fibrocartilage that provides extra padding between the opposing bones.

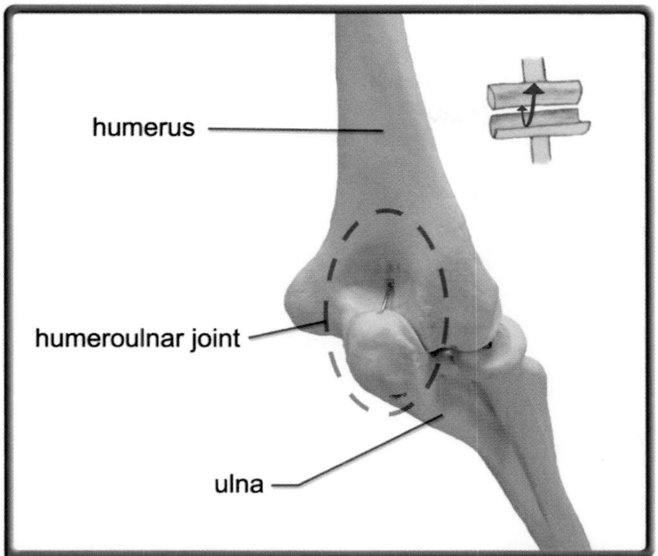

A Hinge Joint Figure 9-19

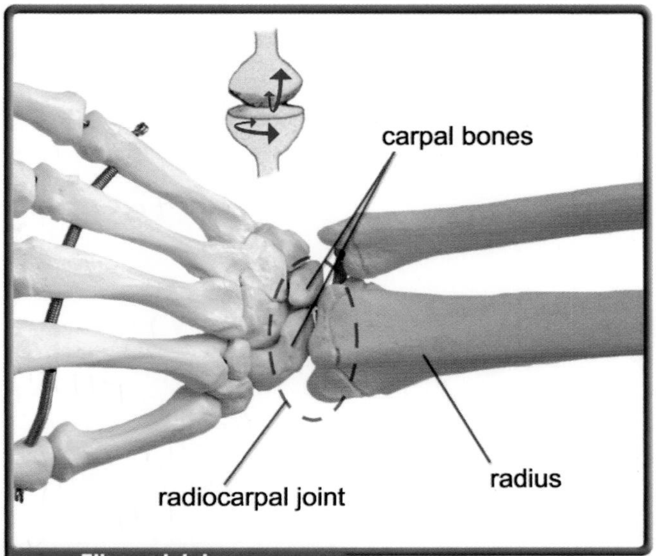

Ellipsoidal Joint Figure 9-20

Ligaments, such as the ACL (anterior cruciate ligament) and PCL (posterior cruciate ligament) prevent over-extension of the joint. **Bursae** (singular, bursa) are small pockets within connective tissue. The bursae are lined with a synovial membrane and filled synovial fluid.

Arthritis is a common synovial joint ailment for older people (Figure 9-14). The condition is characterized by pain and stiffness in a joint. It's caused by the wearing away of the articular (hyaline) cartilage that protects adjoining bones, sometimes by the immune system. Sprains and dislocations are other ailments of synovial joints. A *sprain* occurs when supporting ligaments are stretched beyond normal capacity. A *dislocation* occurs when one of the articulating bones is pulled out of the joint cavity.

Types of Synovial Joints

There are six types of synovial joints. Each one provides a unique type and / or range of motion.

- **Ball-and-socket joint** – The most versatile joint (and the least stable) is the ball-and-socket joint (Figure 9-15). This type of synovial joint is *multiaxial* and can undergo flexion, extension, hyperextension, abduction, adduction and circumduction.
- **Pivot joint** – The pivot is joint is a *uniaxial* synovial joint that allows rotation in one plane only. The articulation between the atlas (C1) and axis (C2) is an example of a pivot joint, as well the the radioulnar joint at the elbow (Figure 9-16). The radius pivots across the ulna during pronation and supination.
- **Gliding joint** –The gliding joint, or plane joint, is a *nonaxial* synovial joint that allows gliding movements in two directions within one plane. Articulations between (most of) the carpal bones are gliding joints (Figure 9-17).
- **Saddle joint** – The saddle joint is a *biaxial* joint allowing two-way movement. The joint is so named because of its saddle shape: The articulating surface of one bone is convex while the reciprocal surface on the other bone is concave. The carpometacarpal joint of the thumb is a saddle joint (Figure 9-18), as well the thumb's metacarpotrapezium joint.
- **Hinge joint** – The hinge joint is a *uniaxial* joint that allows movement in only one plane. The humeroulnar joint at the elbow is an example of a hinge joint (Figure 9-19).
- **Ellipsoidal (condyloid) joint** – This is another *biaxial* synovial joint that allows two-way movement. It is named by the ellipsoid shape of the articulating bone surfaces. The radiocarpal joint in the wrist is an example of this type of joint (Figure 9-20).

Activity 1: Examine Motions of the Appendicular Skeleton

1. Using the figures in this exercise and a lab partner, demonstrate the following types of motions:
   - Adduction / abduction
   - Flexion / extenstion / hyperextension
   - Circumduction
   - Lateral flexion
   - Rotation
   - Pronation / supination
   - Dorsiflexion / plantar flexion
   - Inversion / eversion
   - Protraction / retraction
   - Elevation / depression

Special Focus

Fetal Skeleton

The adult skeleton consists of 206 bones, but a newborn baby has closer to 275 bones. This is because many adult bones (such as the sternum and the phalanges) originally start out as several pieces that fuse later in life.

The fetal skeleton differs from the adult skeleton in other ways, as well. The skull of the fetus is disproportionately large, as is the ribcage. The limbs, on the other hand, are disproportionately short. The wrist and ankle bones are small and mostly cartilage. The mandible is almost straight, and this undoubtedly makes nursing easier for the mother since the amount of leverage produced by the baby's jaw is dramatically reduced.

The skull bones of the fetus are not fused, but they are held loosely together by connective tissues called **fontanels**. This design feature allows the skull (the widest part of the fetus) to be compressed and distorted during the birthing process. This is often necessary to allow successful passage through the narrow birth canal. They

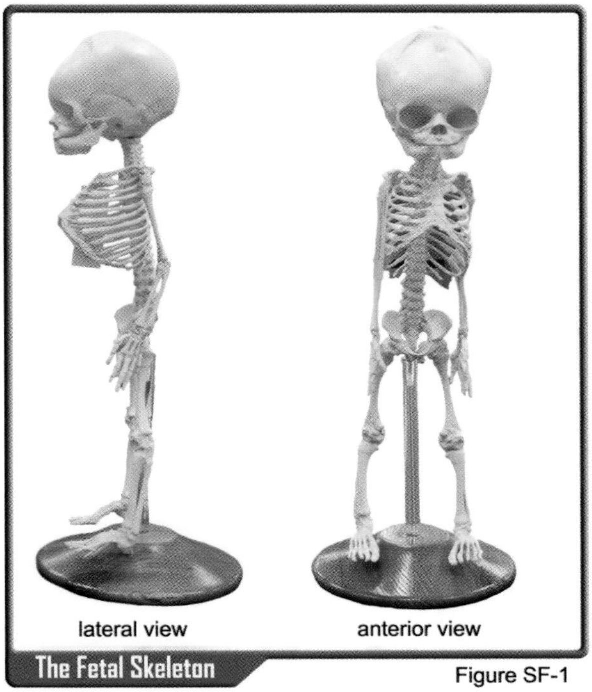

Figure SF-1

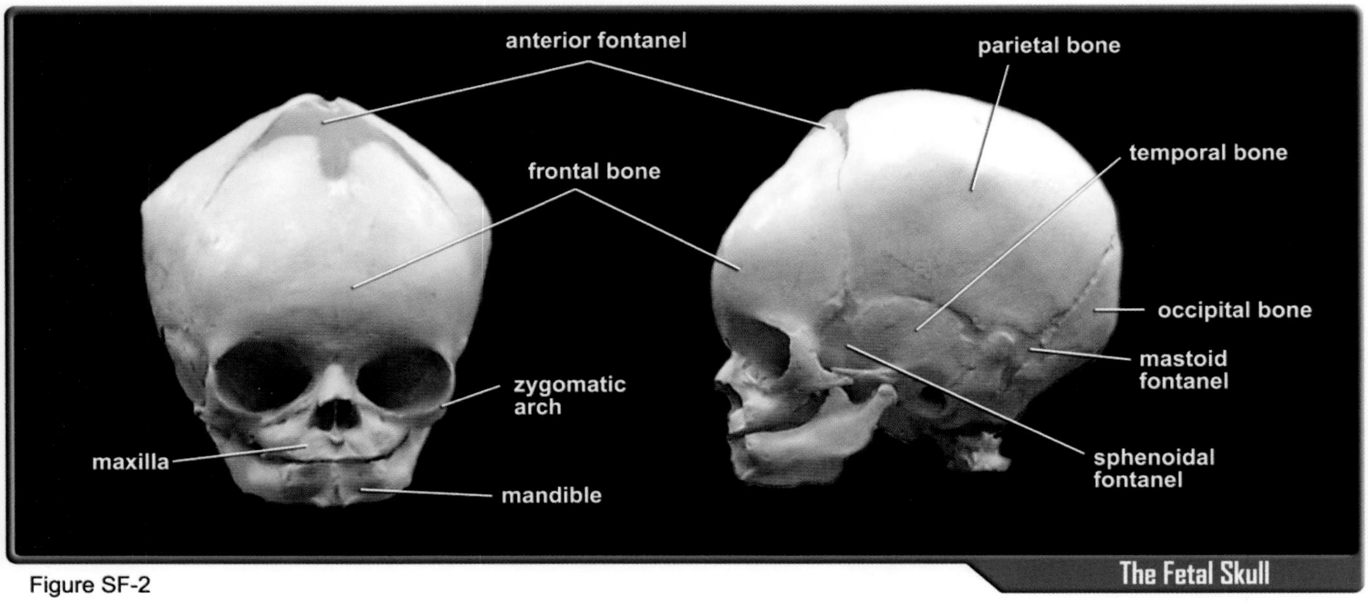

Figure SF-2

persist for several months after birth and are often referred to as "soft spots."

Activity 1: Examine the Fetal Skeleton

1. Obtain a fetal skeleton from your lab instructor or use the figures in this exercise. Pay close attention to the relative sizes of the limbs, skull and ribcage.
2. Observe the lack of curvature in the spine, the straight jaw and the un-ossified regions of the sternum, wrists and ankles.
3. Note the fontanels on the fetal skull.

Review of the Fetal Skeleton

1. How does the size of the fetal face compare to the cranium?

2. What is a fontanel? What is its function?

3. Compare the following bony features of the adult and the fetus and describe their differences.
   a. Vertebrae

   b. Os coxae

   c. Carpals & tarsals

   d. Sternum

   e. Rib cage

   f. Patella

exercise 10

the MUSCULAR system

- tissue & organization -

The joy of the Lord is your strength.
Nehemiah 8:10

Muscle cells and muscle tissue are designed for *movement*. Muscles are responsible for moving food through the digestive tract, air through the respiratory tract and blood through arteries and veins, among many other things. However, when we speak of the Muscular System we are referring primarily to movements of the skeleton. Indeed, the muscle cells responsible for moving the bones of the skeleton are called **skeletal muscle cells**. (By contrast, heart muscle is made of cardiac muscle cells and muscles that moves air, food and other substances through vessels are called smooth muscle cells.) The relationship between the muscular system and the skeletal system is so strong that some anatomists simply refer to them as the *musculoskeletal system*. Because skeletal muscles can be contracted at will, they are also known as *voluntary muscles*.

Before studying the muscles of the body and the movements they produce, we will first describe muscle cells and how they're organized to achieve the objectives of the muscular system. Muscle cells, also called *muscle fibers* or *myocytes*, are highly differentiated cells. Though only 60 – 100 μm wide they can be up to 30 centimeters long (i.e, 12 inches)! Many thousands or millions of muscle cells bundled together constitute a muscle (such as the biceps brachii muscle). During contraction, these long, slender cells can shorten to about 2/3 their normal resting length. Typically, each end of the muscle is attached to bone via a strong connective tissue attachment, called a **tendon** (Figure 10-1). During normal body movements, the bone attached to one end of the muscle is fixed in position while the bone attached at the other end is allowed to move. The fixed end of the muscle is called the **origin**; the movable end is called the **insertion**. The movement produced by contraction of the muscle is called its *action* (Figure 10-2).

As mentioned above, a muscle is composed of many individual muscle cells bundled tightly together. A number of important connective tissues are important in holding the muscle together, especially when it's under tension. Each muscle cell is wrapped in a sheath called the **endomysium**. Hundreds or thousands of individually-wrapped myocytes are bundled together into **fascicles**, each fascicle covered with a sheath called the **perimysium**. Finally, many hundreds or thousands of fascicles are bundled together to form the complete muscle. The fascicle bundles are wrapped in a sheath called the **epimysium**. The epimysium is continuous with the fibers of the **tendon**, which

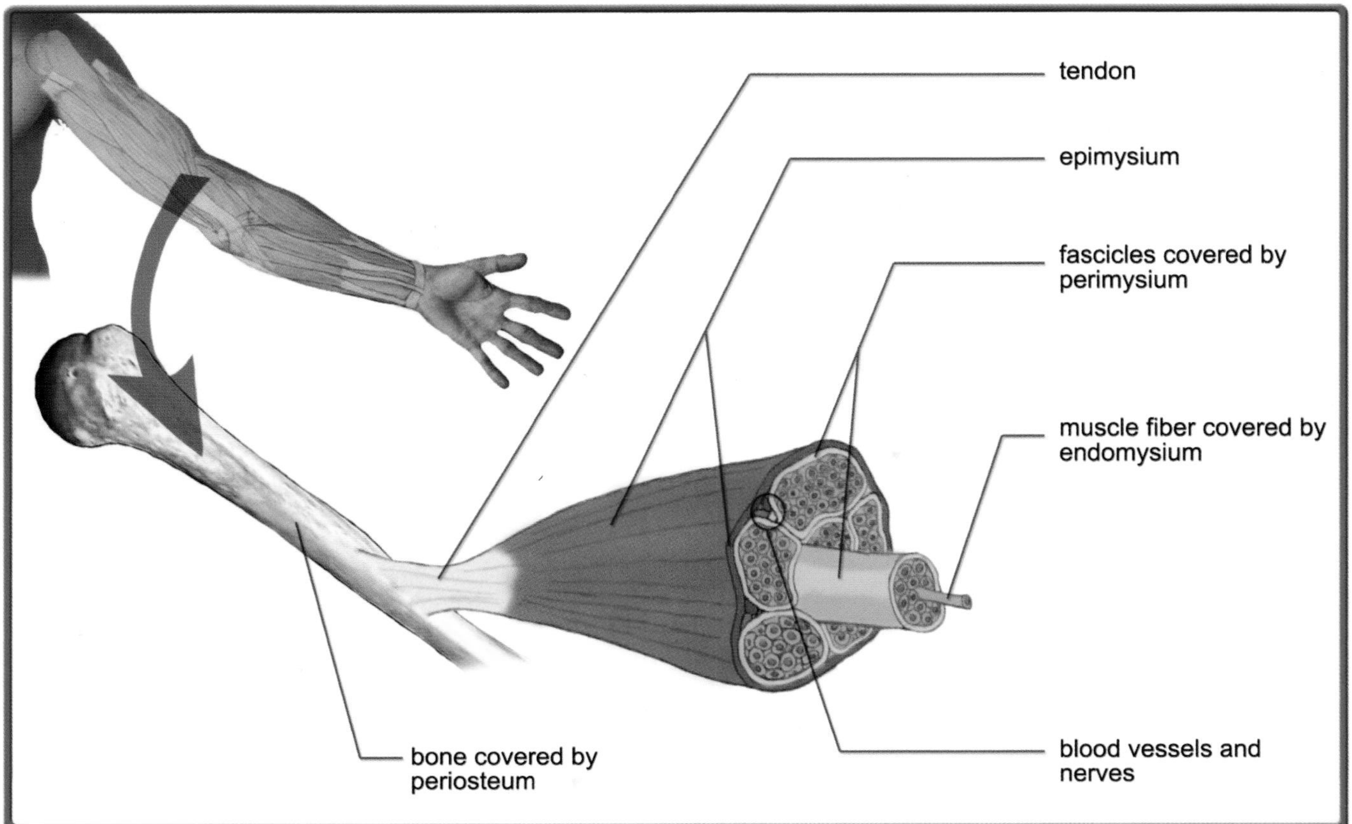

Figure 10-1 Connective Tissue Coverings in Muscle

insertion: Mastoid process of temporal bone

origin: Manubrium of sternum and medial portion of each clavicle

action: Head flexion, rotation and lateral flexion

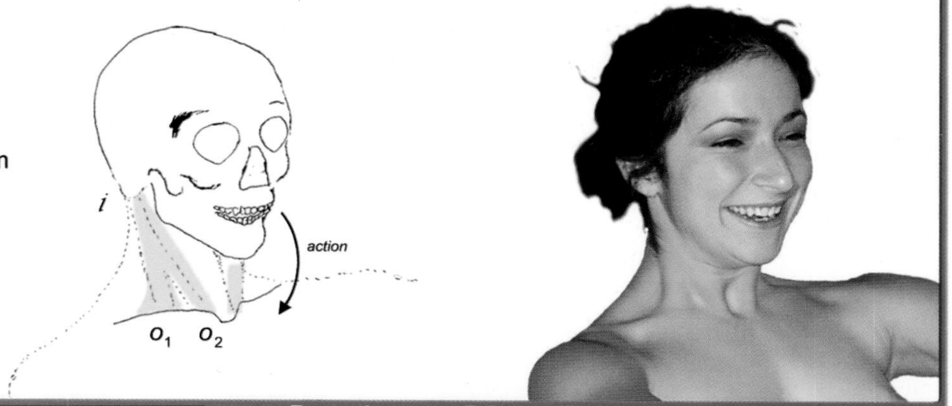

Figure 10-2 Origin, Insertion & Action (The Sternocleidomastoid Muscle)

are continuous with the **periosteum** covering of the attached bone. The connective tissue coverings are shown in Figure 10-1.

Skeletal Muscle Histology

Microscopically, skeletal muscle cells appear long, striated and multi-nucleate (Figure 10-3). Because mature myocytes develop by the fusion of many immature cells, they may possess up to 50 nuclei. The nuclei can be seen immediately beneath the cell membrane, called the **sarcolema** in muscle cells. The striated, or striped, appearance of the cell is due to the intracellular arrangement of **sarcomeres**, the contractile units responsible for shortening skeletal and cardiac muscle (smooth muscle uses a different mechanism of contraction; discussed later in this exercise). Sarcomeres nearly fill the entire cytoplasmic space (called *sarcoplasm* in muscle cells). They are composed of interlocking thin and thick *myofilaments* that slide past each other during contraction (Figure 10-4). The **thin filaments** are composed of a long, filamentous protein called *actin*, attached at one end to a protein "wall" called the **z-line**. **Thick filaments** are composed of bundles of *myosin* proteins attached at one end to another protein "wall" called the **M line**. At rest, there is a small zone of overlap between thick and thin filaments (called the **A band**), but during muscle contraction, thick filaments attach to thin filaments and pull them using a ratcheting motion. The effect is to increasing the zone of overlap between the myofilaments and shorten the muscle cell. This mechanism of muscle contraction is called the *sliding filament theory*.

The movement of certain ions initiate and maintain muscle cell contraction. Upon stimulation by a motor neuron, a muscle cell will allow Na^+ ions to pass through the sarcolema and enter the sarcoplasm. This action triggers the release of Ca^{2+} ions from the endoplasmic reticulum (called the **sarcoplasmic reticulum**, or **SR**, in muscle cells). The Ca^{2+} ions then interact with the myofilaments to allow them to slide past each other.

To ensure that all the myofilaments within a cell contract simultaneously, there must a way of delivering Na^+ and Ca^{2+} ions to all of them at once. The delivery of sodium ions presents a particular problem since some myocytes are nearly 100 μm thick. Simple diffusion of Na^+ from the outside would cause myofilaments near the cell surface to contract much sooner than myofilaments deep inside the cell. To compensate for this problem, the sarcolema periodically penetrates the cell in the form of **T tubules** (Figure 10-5). These

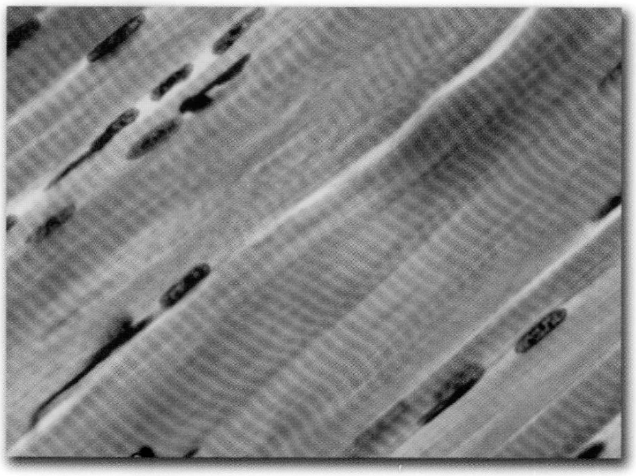

Figure 10-3 Skeletal Muscle (800x)

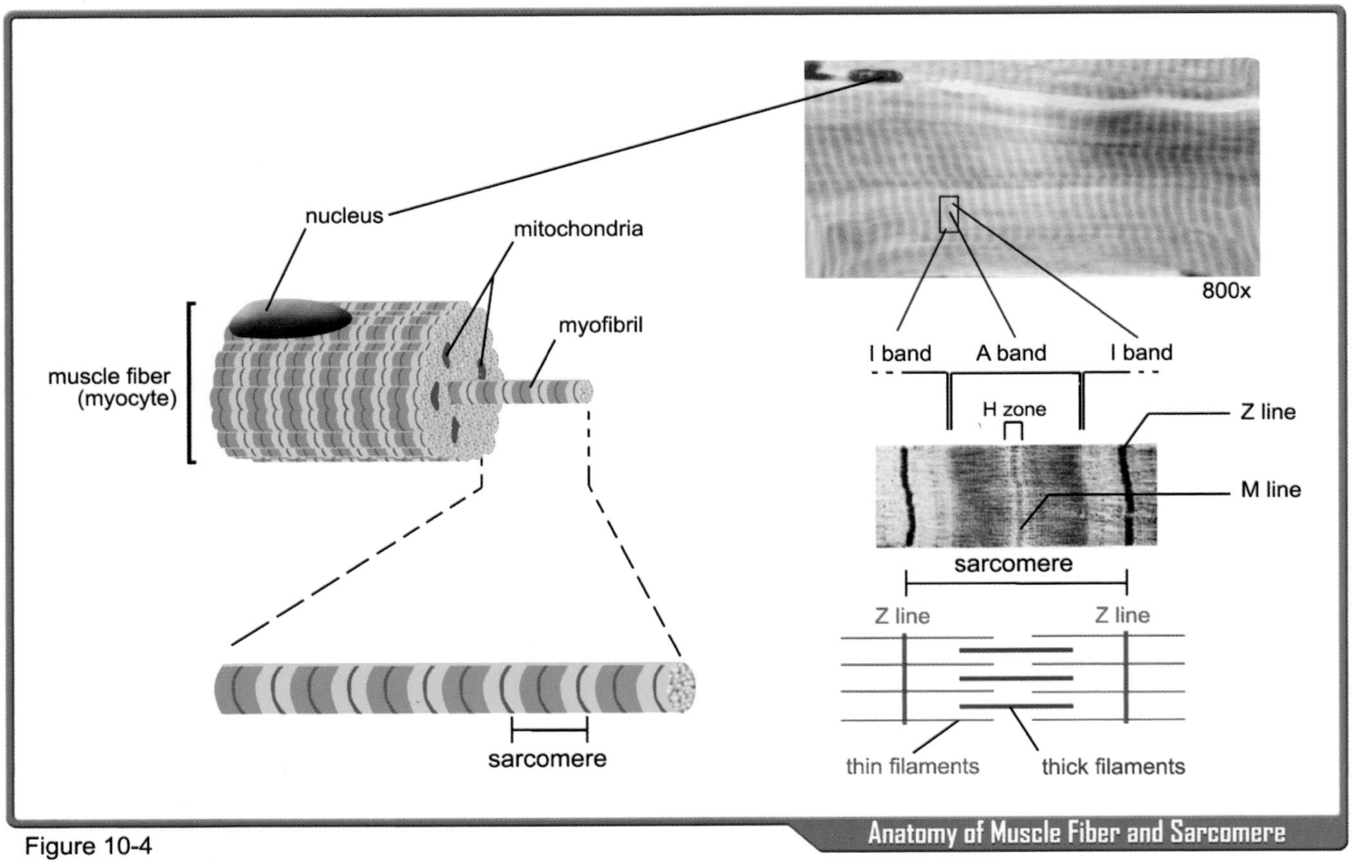

Figure 10-4

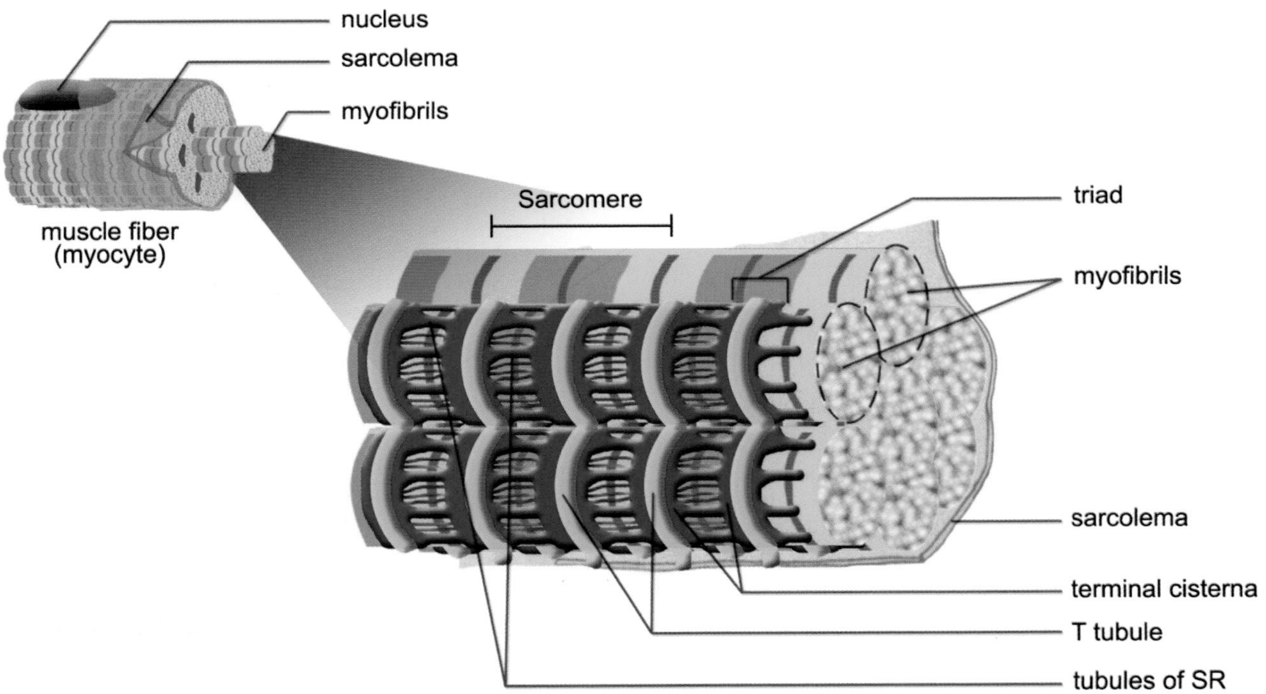

Figure 10-5

Relationship Between Sarcomere, Sarcoplasmic Reticulum & T Tubules

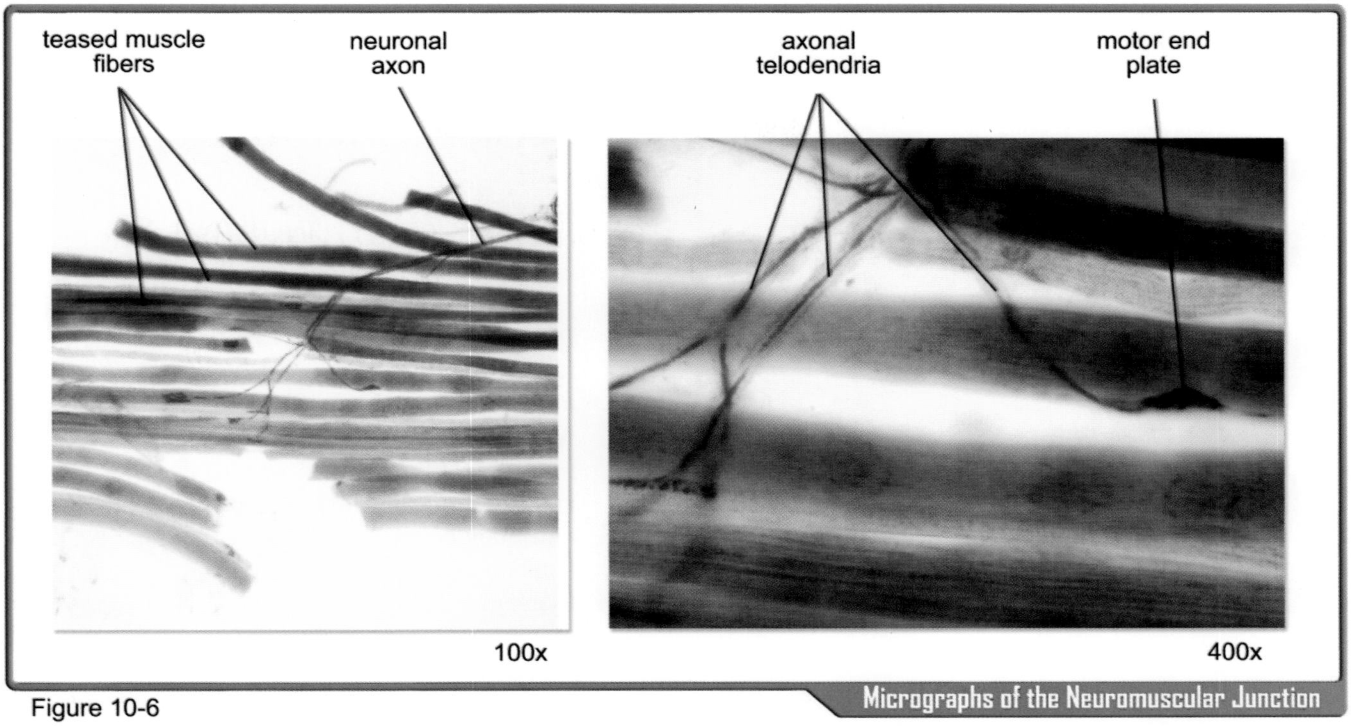

Figure 10-6

invaginations surround the zones of overlap in each sarcomere. In addition, they surround an enlarged area of the sarcoplasmic reticulum called the **terminal cisternae**. These enlarged areas store calcium ions and release them when stimulated. The portions of the terminal cisterna and T tubules that surround the sarcomere are called the **triad**.

The Neuromuscular Junction

Voluntary skeletal muscles only contract when instructed to do so by the nervous system. Those instructions generally originate from the cerebral

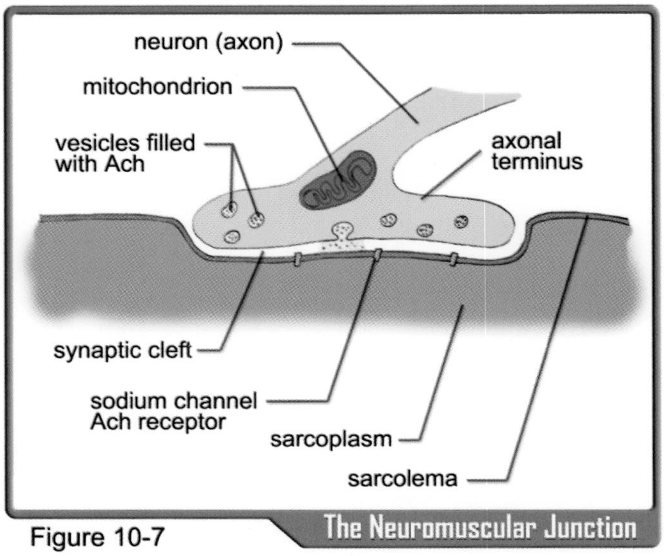

Figure 10-7

cortex where decisions to move voluntarily are made. The instructions are delivered to the muscle cells by *motor neurons* whose long axons penetrate the connective tissue sheaths surrounding the cells and terminate on the sarcolema in a swollen area called the **motor end plate** (Figure 10-6). A narrow gap of 2-4 nm, called the **synaptic cleft**, separates the axon membrane from the myocyte membrane. When an action potential arrives at the axon terminus, vesicles containing the neurotransmitter *acetylcholine* (*Ach*) release this chemical into the synaptic cleft. The Ach diffuses quickly across the cleft and binds to receptors on the myocyte membrane (i.e., the sarcolema). Upon binding of Ach, sodium channels in the sarcolema open and allow the influx of extracellular Na^+ into the muscle cell. The influx of Na^+ opens calcium ion channels in the SR directing the release of Ca^{2+} into the sarcoplasm. The Ca^{2+} interacts with the myofibrils to trigger contraction.

Cardiac & Smooth Muscle

Besides skeletal muscle, there are two other muscle types in the body (Figure 10-8). **Cardiac muscle** is found exclusively in the heart. Cardiac muscle contracts in a similar way to skeletal muscle using sarcomeres and therefore the cells appear striated. However, cardiac cells are considerably shorter than skeletal muscle and they are branched.

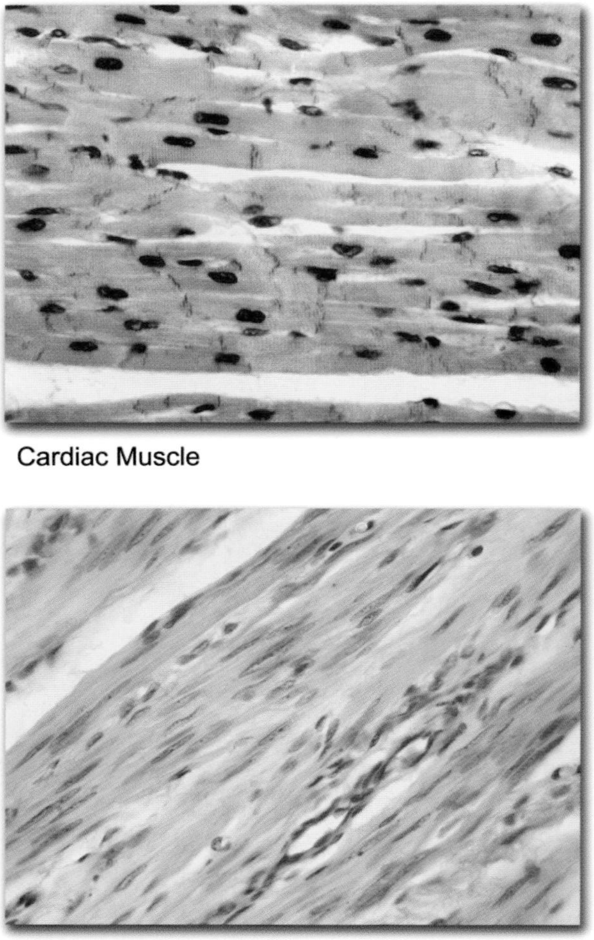

Smooth & Cardiac Muscle (400x)

Figure 10-8

Neighboring cardiac muscle cells are tightly connected to each other by *intercalated discs*. Gap junctions between cardiac myocytes allow neighboring cells to share cytoplasm and thus the sodium and calcium ions required for contraction. Because of the gap junctions and intercalated discs, cardiac muscle tissue functions as one huge cell, a phenomenon called *function syncytium*.

In addition to skeletal muscle attached to bones and cardiac muscle in the heart, we find **smooth muscle** scattered throughout the body. Smooth muscle contracts by a different mechanism than skeletal and cardiac muscle; it lacks sarcomeres and thus doesn't appear striated. It's controlled entirely by the involuntary (autonomic) nervous system and cannot therefore be contracted at will. Smooth muscle lines tubular structures, such as blood vessels, bronchioles and the GI and urinary tracts. Contraction of smooth muscle may adjust the lumen size of vessels or push materials through tracts.

Types of Skeletal Muscles

There are several ways to describe and classify skeletal muscles. For example, muscles may be described by their functions as follows:

- **Prime mover (agonist)** – a muscle primarily responsible for producing a particular movement
- **Antagonist** – a muscle that resists the movement produced by a prime mover. An antagonist for one action (such as extending the arm) may be a prime mover for another action (such as flexing the arm).
- **Synergist** – a muscle that assists a prime mover. Synergists will often initiate large movements, such as swinging the arms or legs, until the prime mover takes over the motion.
- **Fixator** – a muscle that holds a bone or bones into a fixed position to alter the action of another contracting muscle. They often fix the origin of a prime mover so that only its insertion will move.

Muscles may also be classified by their anatomical features, particularly by the arrangement of fascicles within the muscle (Figure 10-9):

- **Unipennate** – a muscle in which the fascicles emerge from one side of the muscle and run largely parallel to each other.
- **Bipennate** – a muscle in which the fascicles emerge from a central tendon running longitudinally down the length of the muscle.
- **Multipennate** – a muscle in which the fascicles emerge from two or more central tendons running longitudinally down the length of the muscle.
- **Convergent** – a muscle in which the fascicles start from a broad tendon on one end of the muscle and converge into a narrow, strap-like tendon on the other end of the muscle.
- **Circular** – also known as a *sphincter*; a muscle in which the fascicles run circularly around an orifice, constricting it when the muscle is contracted.
- **Parallel** – also known as *fusiform*; a muscle in which the fascicles run parallel to each other

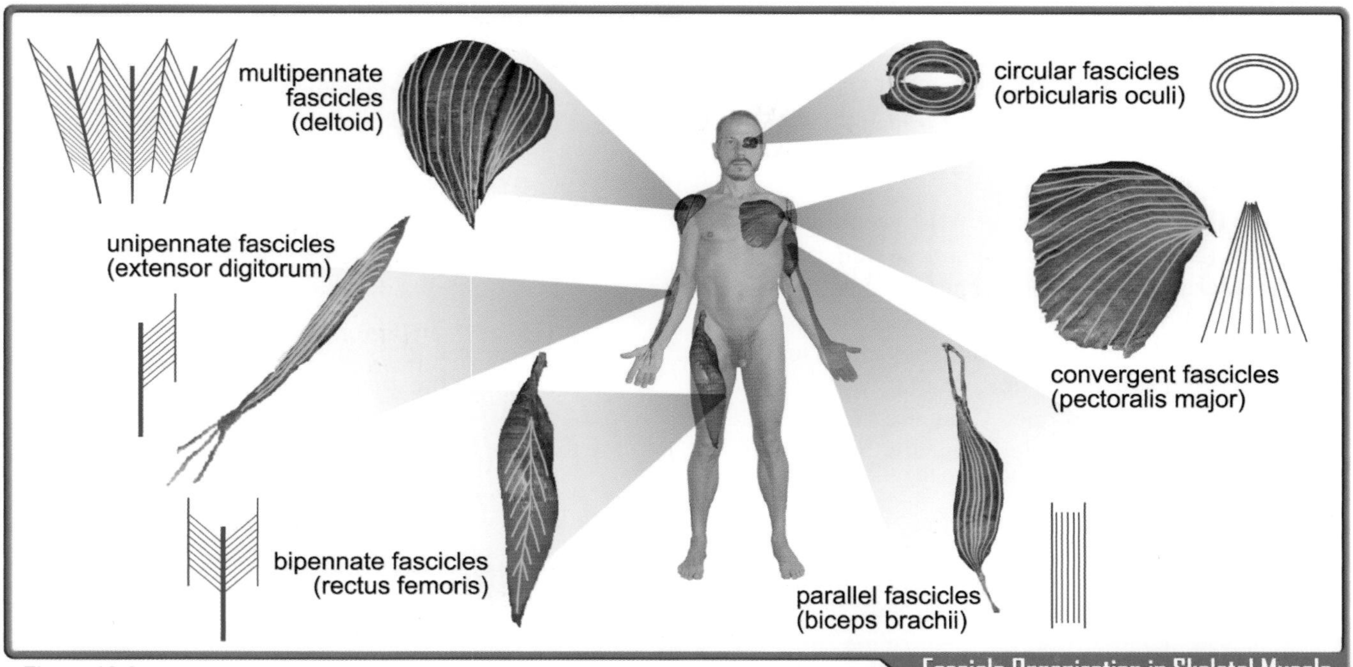

Figure 10-9 Fascicle Organization in Skeletal Muscle

and converge into a narrow tendon at each end of the muscle.

Naming Muscles

At first glance, the names of muscles often appear long and unnecessarily complicated. However, the names of muscles usually convey significant amounts of information about the muscle, such as its action, location, or primary function. Most muscles are named according to the following criteria:

- **Action of the muscle** – example, *flexor digitorum superficialis* describes the action of this muscle as flexing the digits.
- **Shape of the muscle** – example, *deltoid* describes the triangular shape of this muscle (delta = triangle).
- **Size of the muscle** – example, *gluteus maximus* describes the largest of the gluteal muscles.
- **Number of origins** – example, *biceps brachii* has two origins.
- **Direction of the muscle fascicles** – example, *rectus abdominis* contains straight, parallel fascicles, *transversus abdominis* contains fibers traversing the body, *external oblique* contains fibers running obliquely (not transversely or longitudinally) to the body.
- **Location of the muscle** – example, *flexor digitorum superficialis* describes the superficial location of this muscle.
- **Location of muscle origin & insertion** – example, *sternocleidomastoid* has its origin on the sternum and clavicles and its insertion on the mastoid process of the temporal bone.

Types of Muscle Contraction

There are three modes of muscles contraction: **concentric**, **eccentric**, and **isometric** (Figure 10-10). During concentric contraction, the force generated by the muscle is sufficient to overcome resistance and the muscle shortens. In eccentric contraction, tension on the muscle is slowly and

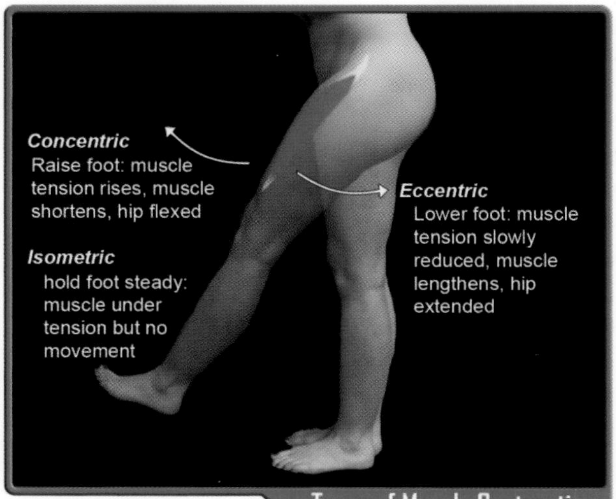

Figure 10-10 Types of Muscle Contraction

methodically reduced as the muscle lengthens. This type of contraction is used during deceleration. During isometric contraction the muscle is under tension but neither lengthens or shortens.

Activity 1: Examine Muscles Microscopically

1. Obtain a microscope and examine skeletal muscle at low and high magnifications. Notice the striated appearance of the muscle cells, the length of the cells and the number of nuclei.
2. Also examine cardiac muscle and smooth muscle in a microscope. Compare these muscle types to skeletal muscle. How are they similar? How are they different?

Activity 2: Examine a Neuromuscular Junction

1. Examine the structure of a neuromuscular junction in a microscope. Identify the structures described in this exercise.

Activity 3: Examine Fresh Muscle

1. Obtain a microscope, dissecting needles, forceps, a glass microscope slide and a cover slip.
2. Obtain a small piece of chicken muscle (thigh or breast) and carefully tease the muscle fibers apart using the forceps and dissection needles.
3. Place the teased muscle on a microscope slide and add 1 drop of saline solution. Cover with the cover slip and examine the specimen under high power magnification. Notice the banding pattern on the fresh muscle preparation. Regulate the light carefully to obtain the highest possible contrast..

Activity 4: Examine Muscle Contraction

These instructions are based on the 'Contraction of Glycerinated Muscle with ATP' kit from Carolina Biological.

1. Obtain a petri dish containing glycerinated muscle fibers cut to 2-cm lengths; obtain a millimeter ruler.
2. Place the petri dish on the stage of a dissecting microscope, or use a magnifying glass to carefully observe the muscle.
3. Use a teasing needle to separate muscle fiber strands. Ideally, isolate a single stand. Strands more than 0.2 mm thick are too thick to be used.
4. Mount a thin strand on a microscope slide with a coverslip. Examine the strand under magnification; note the striations.
5. Transfer several thin strands to a small drop of glycerol on a microscope slide. Do not use a cover slip. The less glycerol employed, the easier to observe contraction.
6. Measure and record the lengths of the muscle fibers using the dissecting scope or magnifying glass.
7. Add several drops of ATP solution; observe the reaction of the muscle fibers.
8. After 30-45 seconds, re-measure the lengths of the fibers.

Length of fibers (step #6): ____________________

Length of fibers (step #8): ____________________

exercise 11

the MUSCULAR system

- muscles of the body -

He gives strength to the weary and increases the power of the weak.

Isaiah 40:29

The muscular system includes all of the skeletal muscles that move the upper and lower limbs of the appendicular skeleton and the head, neck and trunk of the axial skeleton. With few exceptions, all skeletal muscles are attached to at least one bone. Because of the intimate relationship between the skeletal and muscular systems, they are sometimes refered to as the *musculoskeletal system.*

There are several ways to classify the 600+ muscles[1] of the human body, such as by location (i.e., body region), origin, action, etc. In this exercise, the muscles are grouped and discussed by location. As discussed in Exercise 1, the body is divided into eight major regions: Head, neck, thorax, abdomen, dorsum, pelvis/perineum, upper limbs and lower limbs (Figure 11-1). In the tables that follow, representative muscles from each region are described by their origins, insertions and actions. Approximately one hundred muscles are discussed, but remember that this represents less than 17% of all the skeletal muscles of the body! Also, recall from Exercise 10 that a skeletal muscle is attached to bone at its two ends: a fixed end called the *origin* and a movable end called the *insertion.* (And the movement produced by a contracting muscle is called its *action*). However, in many cases the roles for origin and insertion are reversed depending on the action desired. For example, contraction of the sternocleidomastoid (STM) can flex the head if the sternum is fixed and the head is allowed to move. In that case, the origin for the STM is the sternum and its insertion is on the temporal bone. However, if the head is fixed in position by the trapezius and other neck muscles but the thorax is allowed to move, then contraction of

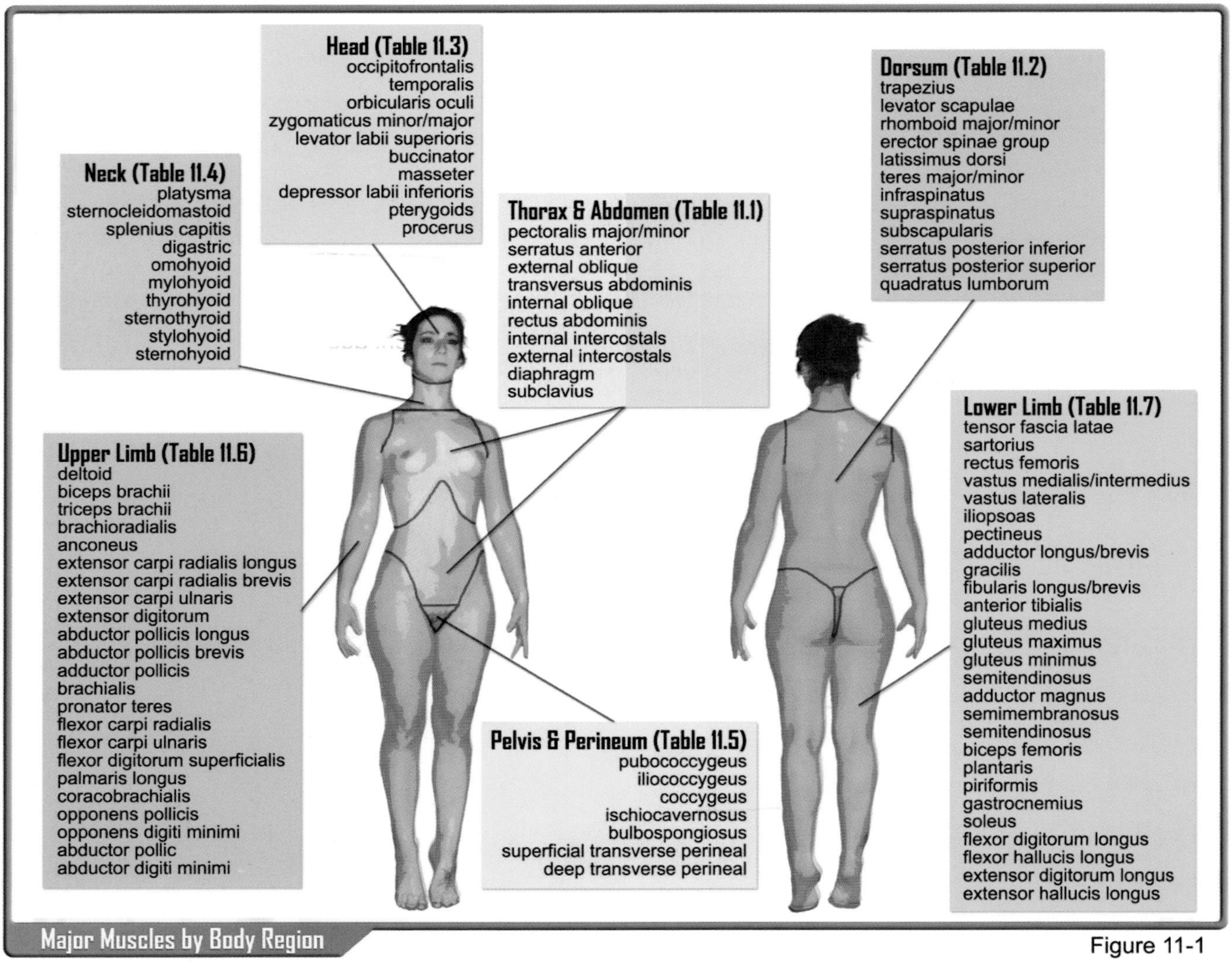

Figure 11-1

[1] Interestingly, the exact number of muscles in the body is a matter of debate. The number varies from 600 to 850 depending on who you ask and how muscles are defined. The general consensus is 630.

the STM lifts the sternum and expands the ribcage. Thus, its origin would be defined as the temporal bone and its insertion the sternum & clavicle.

As you study the muscles described in this exercise, try to identify as many as you can on yourself or a friend.

Muscles of the Thorax & Abdomen

Most of the muscles in the thorax are either directly or indirectly involved with arm movement, or with movement of the ribcage (primarily to assist respiration). Most of the abdominal muscles move the vertebral column.

TABLE 11.1 Muscles Of The Thorax & Abdomen (Anterior Trunk)

muscle	*origin*	*insertion*	*action*	*figure(s)*
diaphragm	xiphoid process, costal cartilage of ribs 7-12, lumbar vertebrae	central tendon	expand thorax, compress abdomen (respiration)	11-4
external intercostals	inferior border of rib	superior border of rib below rib of origin	expand ribcage	11-4
external oblique	anterior surface of ribs 5-12	linea alba, pubic crest & tubercles, iliac crest	compress abdomen, depress ribs, flex or rotate spine	11-3
internal intercostals	superior border of rib	inferior border of rib above	compress ribcage	11-4
internal oblique	lumbodorsal fascia, iliac crest	inferior aspect of ribs, xiphoid process, linea alba	compress abdomen, depress ribs, flex or rotate spine	11-3
pectoralis major	sternum, costal cartilages 1-6, medial aspect of clavicles	intertubercular groove & greater tubercle of humerus	flexion, adduction, & medial rotation of shoulder	11-3 11-4
pectoralis minor	anterior medial aspect of ribs 3-5	coracoid process of scapula	depress & protract shoulder, rotate glenoid cavity inferiorly or elevate ribs (scapula fixed)	11-4
rectus abdominis	superior aspect of pubic symphysis	inferior aspect of costal cartilages 5-7, xiphoid process	flex spinal column	11-3 11-4
serratus anterior	anterolateral aspect of ribs 1-9	anterior medial border of scapula	protract shoulder, rotate glenoid cavity superiorly or elevate ribs (scapula fixed)	11-3 11-6
subclavius	medial aspect of first rib	inferior lateral border of clavicle	depress & protract shoulder	11-4
transversus abdominis	costal cartilages 6-12, iliac crest, lumbodorsal fascia	linea alba, pubis	compress abdomen	11-3

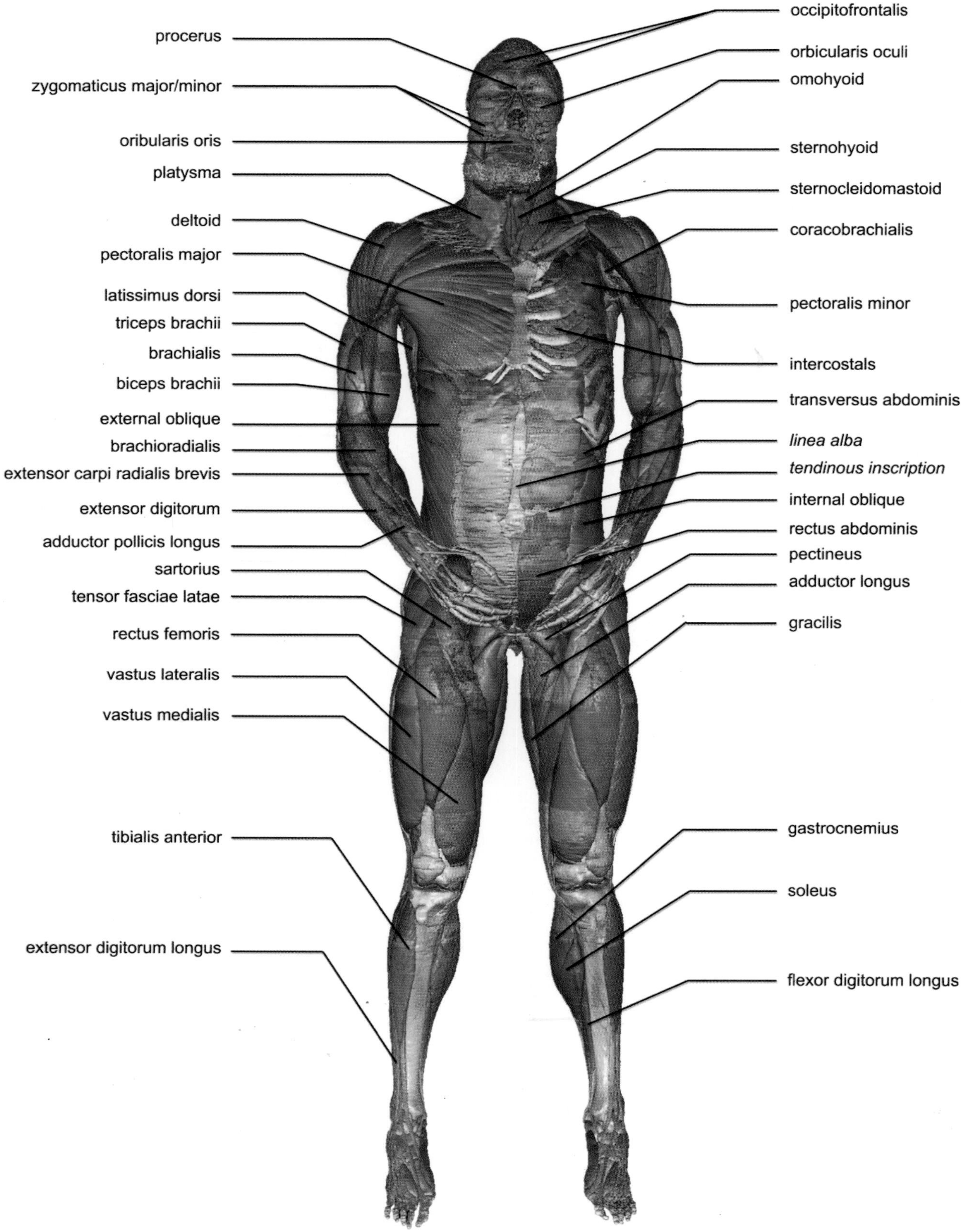

Figure 11-2 **Muscles Overview (Anterior)**

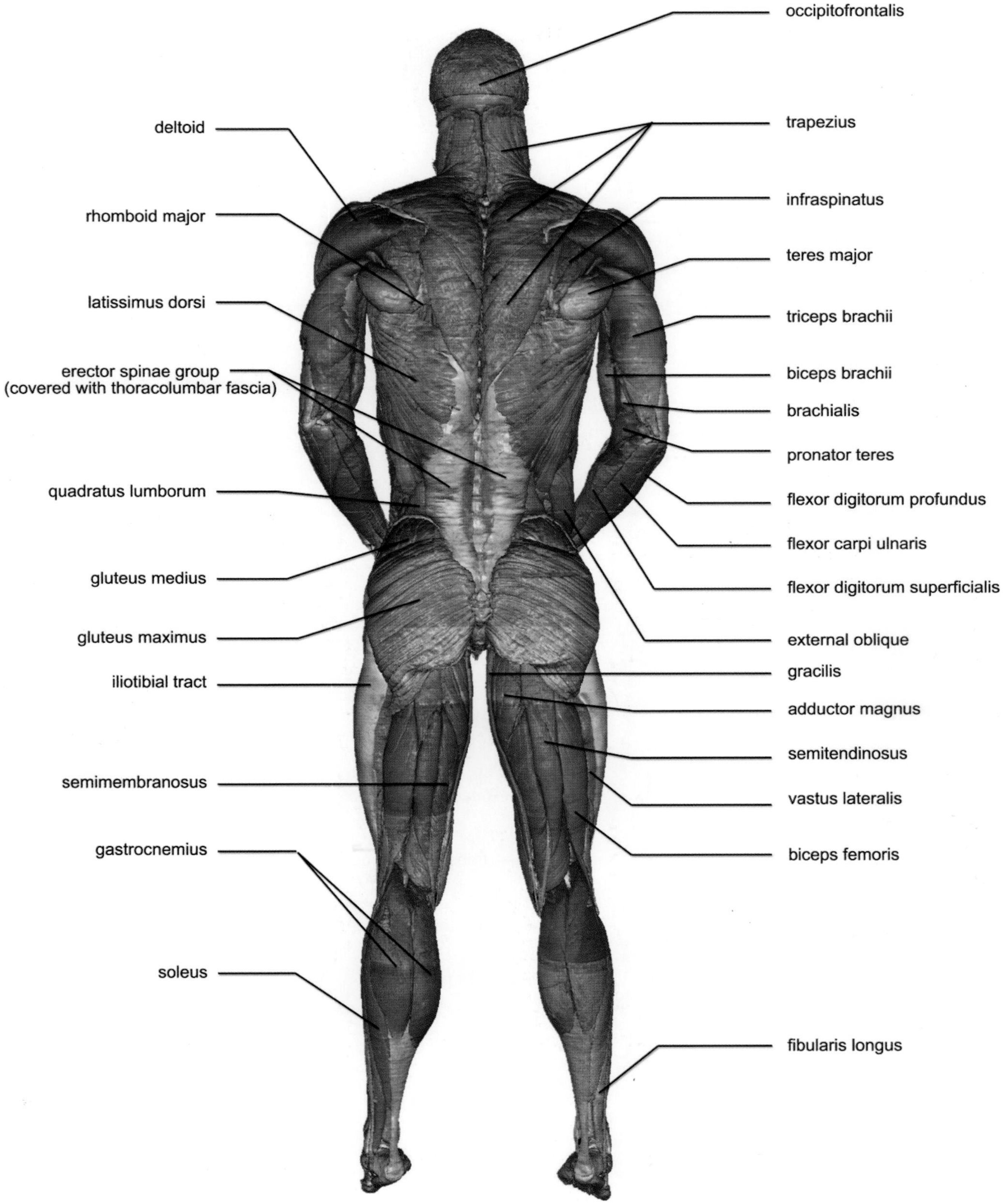

Figure 11-2 (cont)

Muscles Overview (Posterior)

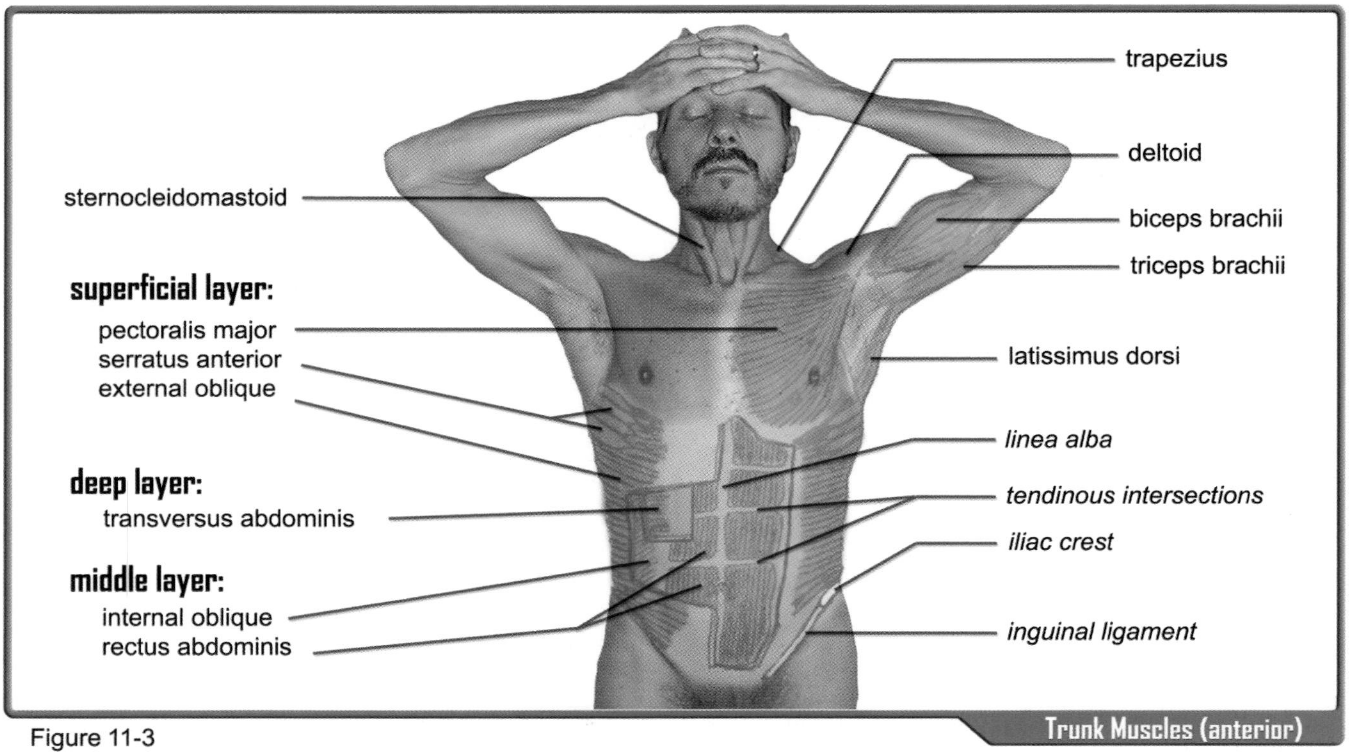

Figure 11-3

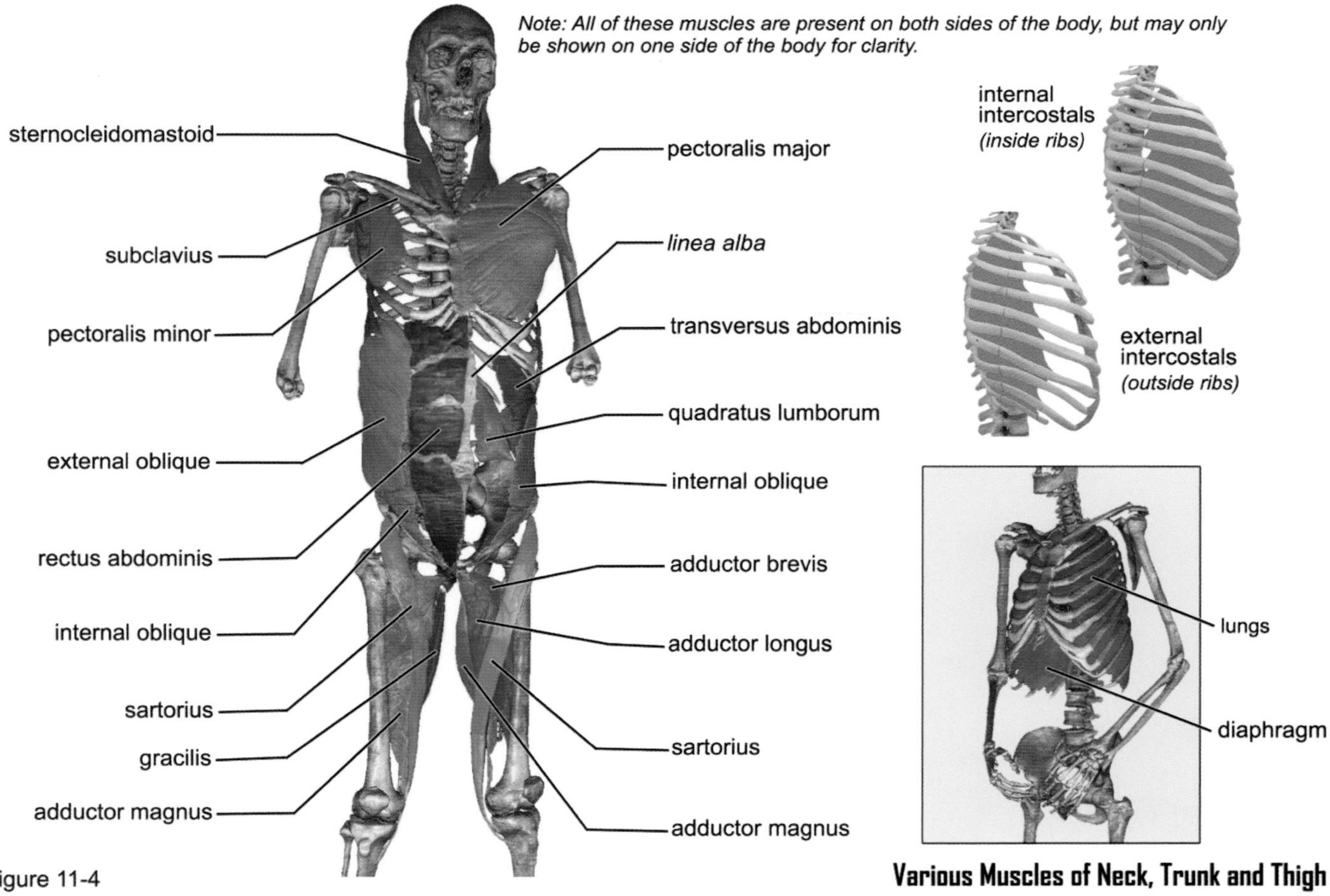

Figure 11-4

Various Muscles of Neck, Trunk and Thigh

TABLE 11.2 Muscles of the Back (Posterior Trunk)

muscle	*origin*	*insertion*	*action*	*figure(s)*
erector spinae group (eight muscles)	iliac crest, sacrum, spinous processes of lumbar vertebrae	posteromedial aspect of ribs 2-12	extend spine, flex spine, extend neck	11-5 11-7
infraspinatus*	infraspinous fossa of scapula	greater tubercle of humerus	lateral rotation of shoulder	11-5 11-6 11-8
latissimus dorsi	spinous processes of lumbar vertebrae and inferior thoracic vertebrae, ribs 8-12, lubodorsal fascia	intertubercular groove of humerus	extension, medial rotation, adduction of shoulder	11-3 11-5 11-6 11-7
levator scapulae	transverse processes of C1-C4	superior aspect of the medial border of scapula	elevate scapula	11-5
rhomboid major	spinous processes of superior thoracic vertebrae	inferior aspect of the medial border of scapula	adduct scapula, downward rotation of scapula	11-5
rhomboid minor	spinous processes of vertebrae C7-T1	medial border of scapula	adduct scapula, downward rotation of scapula	11-5
serratus posterior, inferior	aponeuroses of T10-L3 spinous processes	inferior aspect of ribs 8-12	pull ribs inferiorly and outwardly	11-5
serratus posterior, superior	spinous processes of C7-T3	superior aspects of ribs 2-5	elevates ribs, expands thorax	11-5
subscapularis*	subscapula fossa of scapula	lesser tubercle of humerus	medial rotation of shoulder	11-8
supraspinatus*	supraspinous fossa of scapula	greater tubercle of humerus	abduction of shoulder	11-5 11-7
teres major	inferior angle of scapula	intertubercular groove of humerus	extension, medial rotation, adduction of shoulder	11-5 11-6
teres minor*	lateral border of scapula	greater tubercle of humerus	lateral rotation of shoulder	11-5 11-6
trapezius	occipital bone, spinous processes of thoracic vertebrae	clavicle, acromion & spine of scapula	1-extend neck, 2-elevate, retract, depress or rotate scapula upward, 3-elevate clavicle	11-2 11-5 11-6 11-7 11-9
quadratus lumborum	iliac crest, iliolumbar ligament	transverse processes of lumbar vertebrae, rib 12	together, depress ribs; individually, cause lateral flexion of spine	11-4

* Collectively called the "SITS" muscles of the rotator cuff. These muscles produce the complex actions required to throw a baseball.

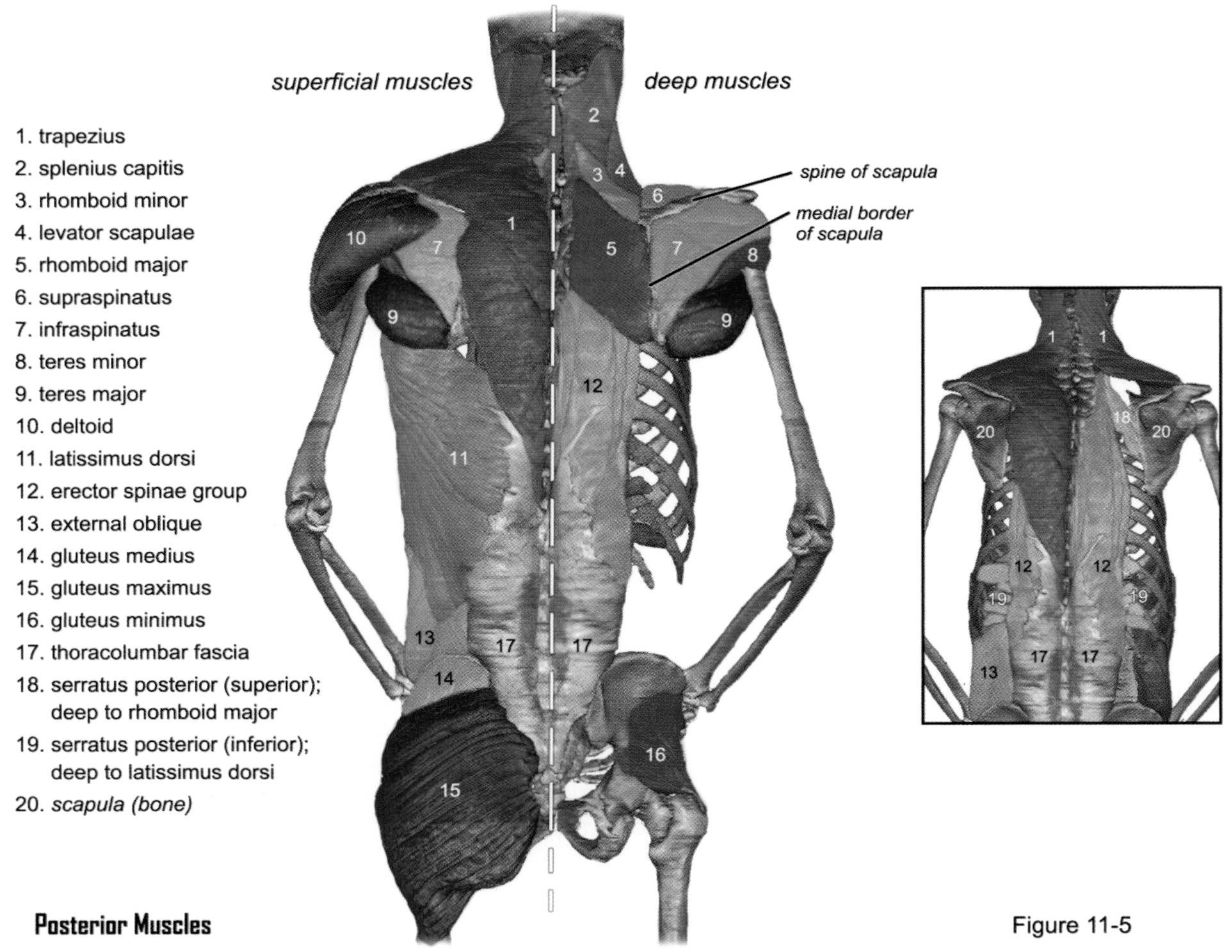

Figure 11-5

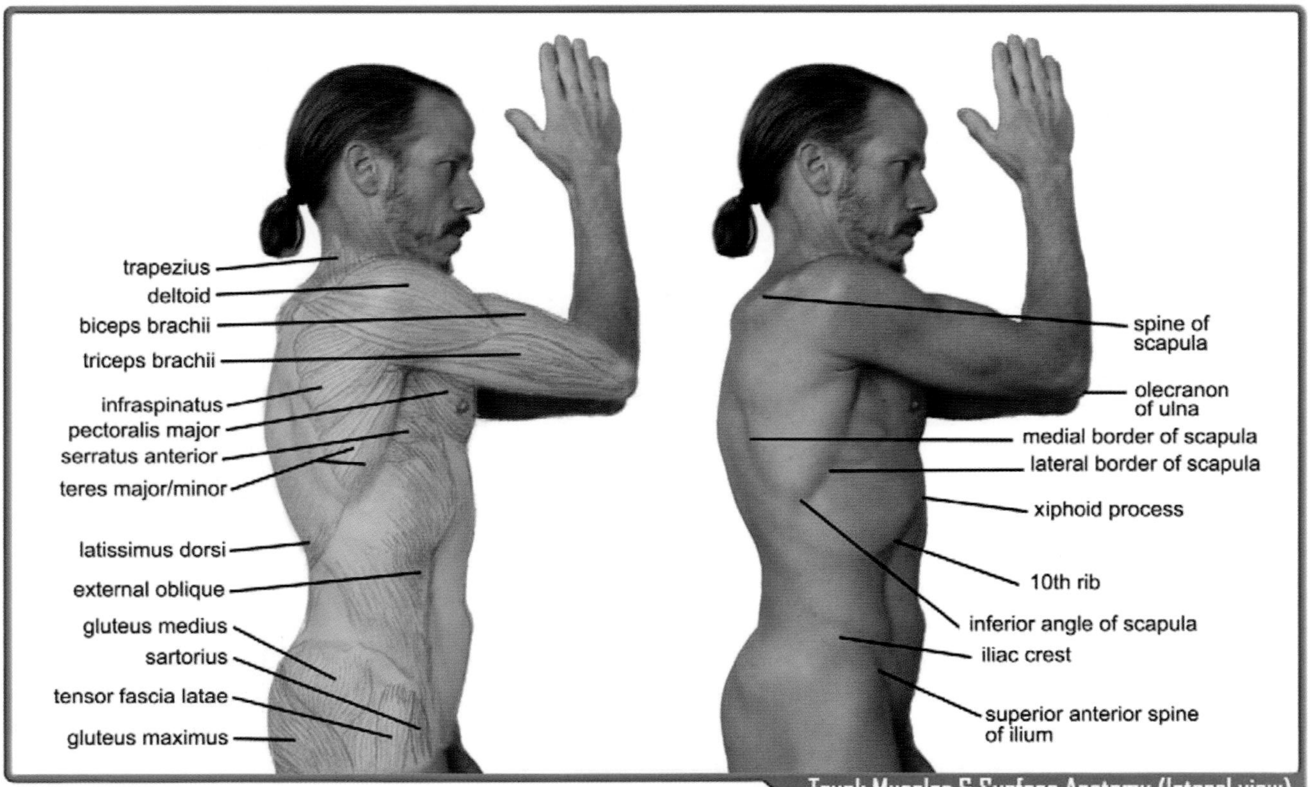

Figure 11-6

TABLE 11.3 Muscles Of The Head & Face (Facial Expression)

muscle	origin	insertion	action	figure(s)
buccinator	mandible, alveolar process of maxilla	orbicularis oris	pull back corners of lips	11-9
depressor labii inferioris	mandible	orbicularis oris	depress lower lip	11-9
levator labii superioris	inferior aspect of orbit, nasal bone	orbicularis oris	elevate upper lip	11-9
masseter	zygomatic arch	lateral aspect of angle of mandible	elevate mandible	11-9 11-10
occipitofrontalis	orbicularis oculi, procerus	superior nuchal line of occipital bone	raise eyebrows, wrinkle forehead	11-9
orbicularis oculi	anterior aspect of orbit	skin of eyelids	close eyelids (blink)	11-9
orbicularis oris	maxilla, mandible, zygomaticus, levator labii & depressor labii	skin of the lips	compress lips, pucker lips (kissing muscle)	11-9
procerus	nasal bone, lateral nasal cartilages	frontal belly of occipitofrontalis	flare nostrils, wrinkle forehead	11-2
pterygoid, lateral	lateral pterygoid plate	medial aspect of mandibular ramus	depress mandible, protrude mandible, lateral excursion	11-10
pterygoid, medial	lateral pterygoid plate	medial aspect of mandibular ramus	elevate mandible, lateral excursion	11-10
temporalis	temporal fossa	coronoid process of mandible	elevate mandible	11-10
zygomaticus major	zygomatic bone	corner of mouth	retract & elevate corner of mouth	11-9
zygomaticus minor	zygomatic bone	upper lip	retract & elevate upper lip	11-9

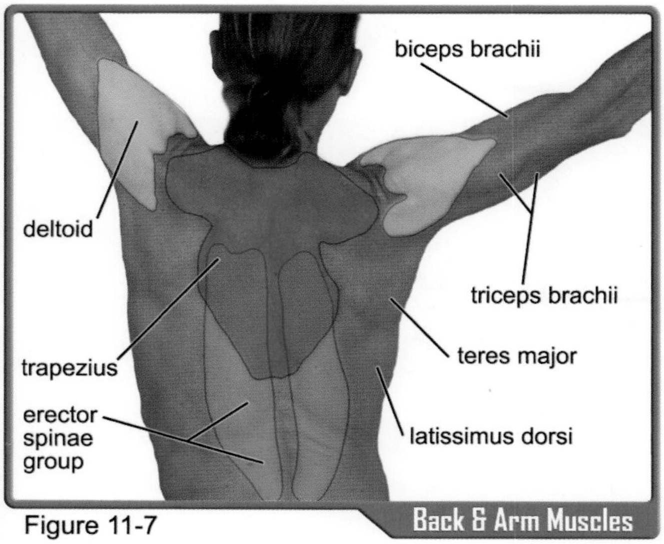

Figure 11-7

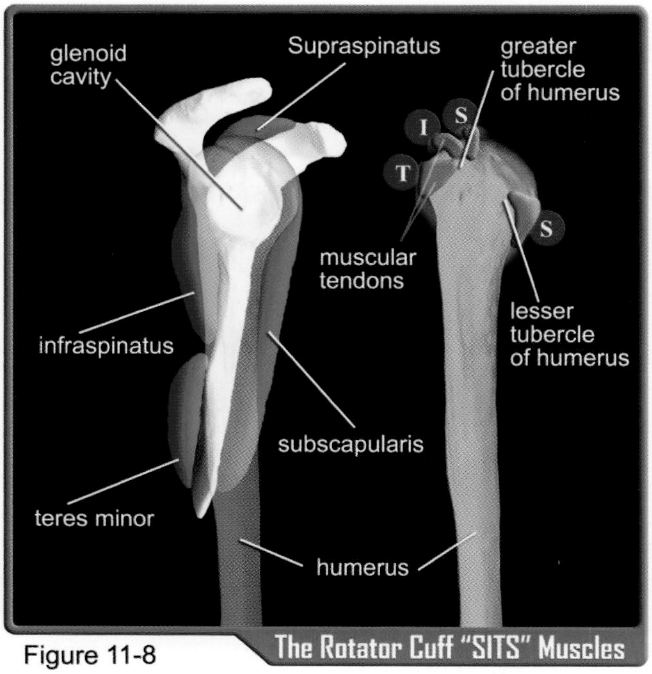

Figure 11-8

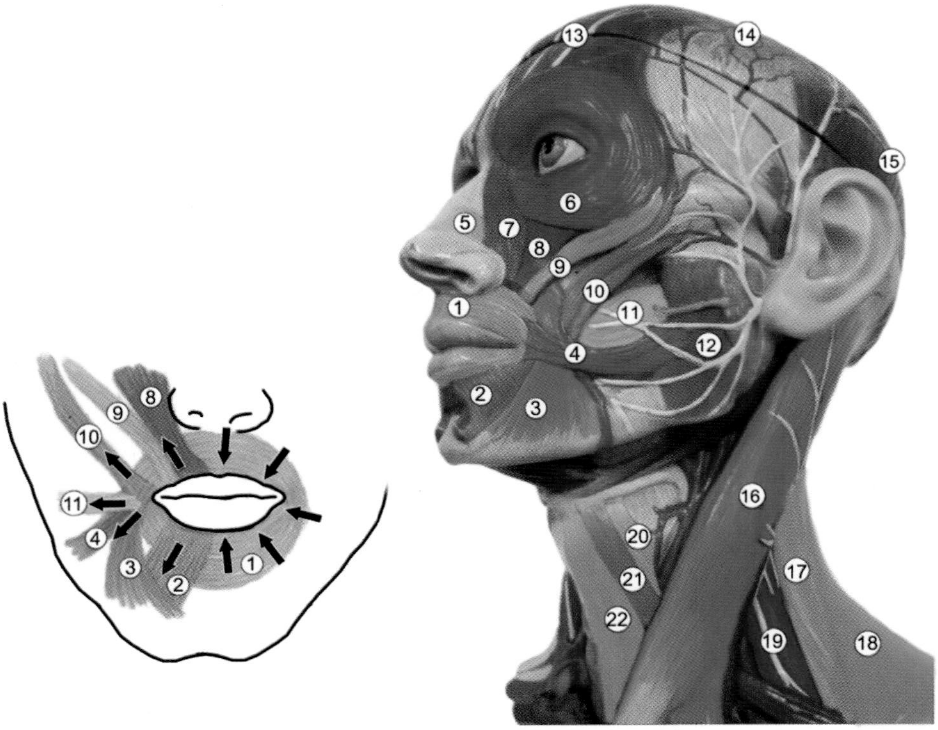

1. orbicularis oris
2. depressor labii inferioris
3. depressor anguli oris
4. risorius
5. nasalis
6. orbicularis oculi
7. levator labii superioris alaeque nasi
8. levator labii superioris
9. zygomaticus minor
10. zygomaticus major
11. buccinator
12. masseter
13. frontalis*
14. epicranial aponeurosis*
15. occipitalis*
16. sternocleidomastoid
17. scalene
18. trapezius
19. longus capitis
20. thyrohyoid
21. omohyoid
22. sternohyoid

*collectively called occipitofrontalis or epicranius

Figure 11-9

Face, Head & Neck Muscles

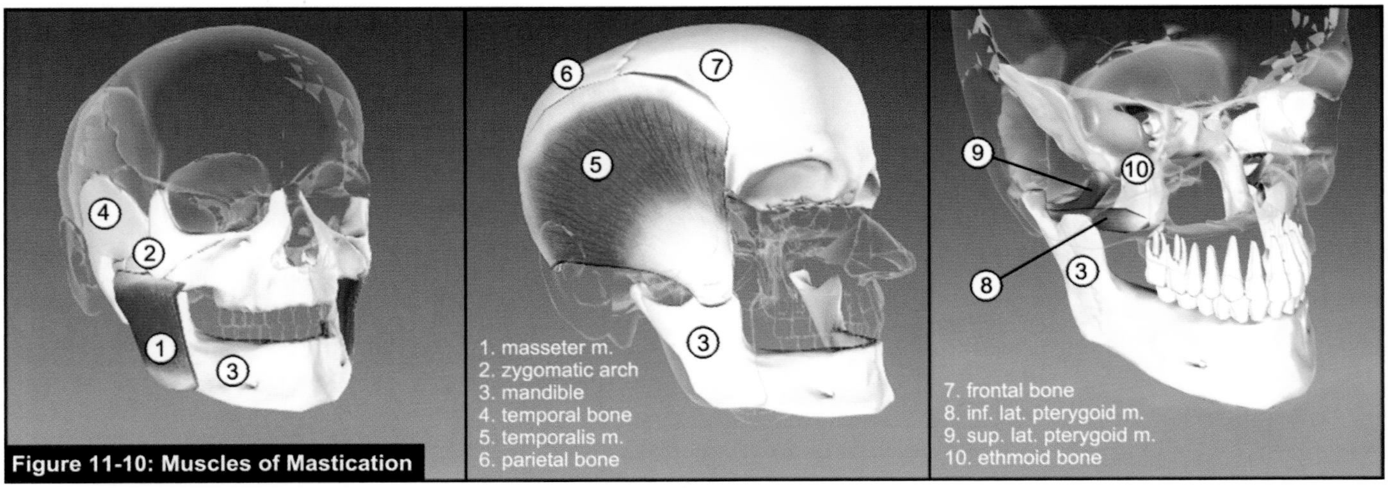

Figure 11-10: Muscles of Mastication

TABLE 11.4 Muscles of The Neck

muscle	*origin*	*insertion*	*action*	*figure(s)*
digastric	*anterior belly*: deep aspect of mental proturberance of mandible. *posterior belly*: mastoid process of temporal bone	hyoid bone	depress mandible or elevate hyoid bone (larynx)	11-11
mylohyoid	medial aspect of mandible	hyoid bone	depress mandible, elevate hyoid bone, elevate floor of mouth	11-11
omohyoid	*inferior belly*: superior border of scapula. *superior belly*: central tendon connecting inferior & superior bellies	*inferior belly*: central tendon connecting inferior & superior bellies. *superior belly*: hyoid bone	depress hyoid bone & larynx	11-11
platysma	superficial fascia covering pectoralis	mandible and skin of cheeks	tense skin of neck, depress mandible	11-10
splenius capitis	spinous processes and ligamentum nuchae of cervical and upper thoracic vertebrae	mastoid process of occipital bone	together they extend the neck; alone they rotate or laterally flex the neck	11-5
sternocleidomastoid	clavicular head attaches to sternal aspect of clavicle; sternal head attaches to manubrium	mastoid process of occipital bone	together they flex the neck; alone they rotate head	11-2 11-4 11-9 11-11
sternohyoid	manubrium of sternum	hyoid bone	depress hyoid bone & larynx	11-11
sternothyroid	dorsal aspect of manubrium & first costal cartilage	thyroid cartilage of larynx	depress hyoid bone & larynx	11-11
stylohyoid	styloid process of temporal bone	hyoid bone	elevate larynx	11-11
thryohyoid	thyroid cartilage of larynx	hyoid bone	elevate larynx, depress hyoid	11-11

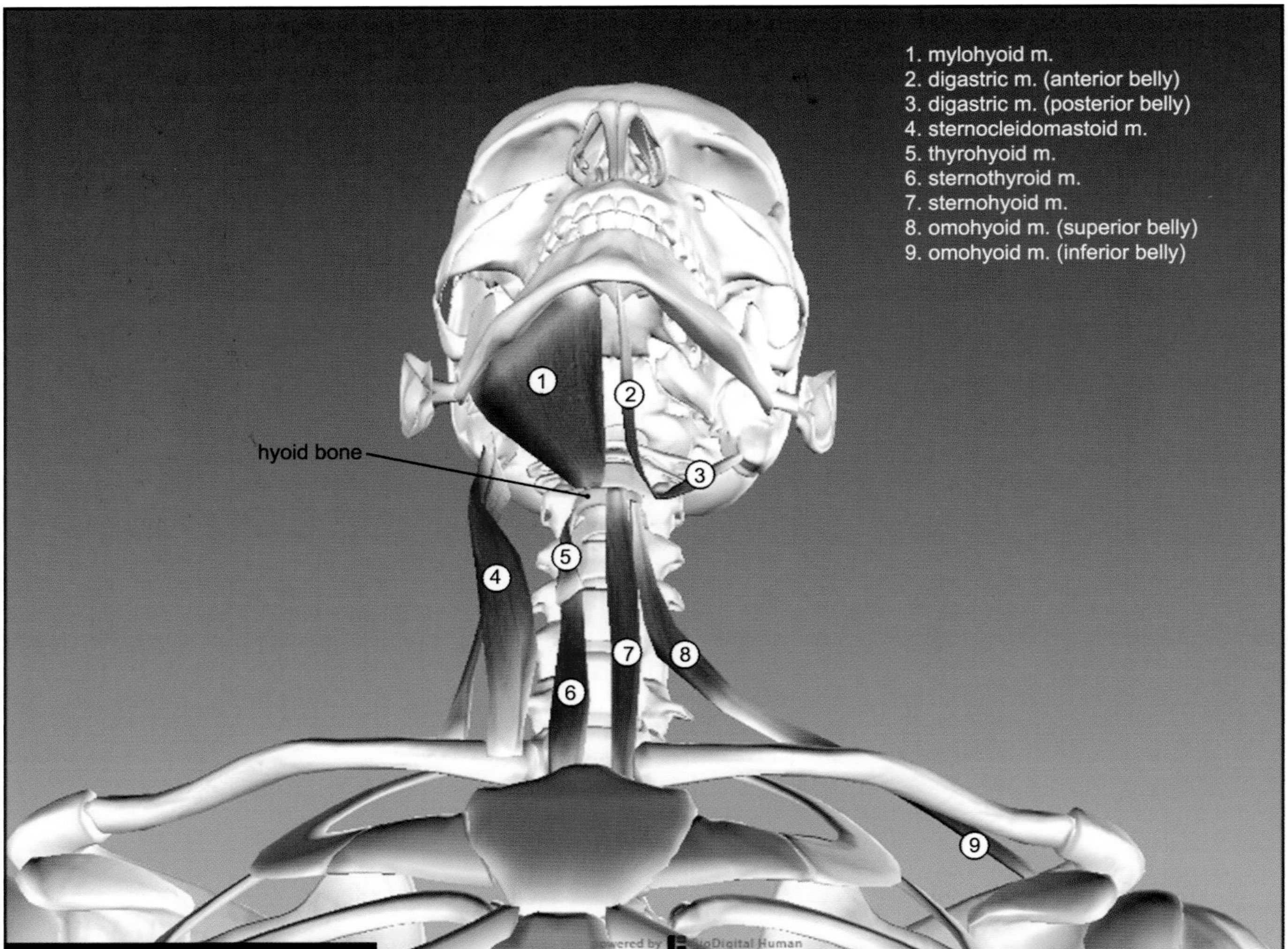

Figure 11-11: Muscles of the Neck

Muscles of the Pelvis & Perineum

The muscles of the pelvis and perineum form the pelvic floor (which supports visceral organs of the pelvis and abdomen) and contribute to urinary, digestive and sexual functions.

TABLE 11.5 Muscles Of The Pelvis & Perineum

muscle	*origin*	*insertion*	*action*	*figure(s)*
bulbospongiosus	*males*: connective tissue sheath surrounding bulb of penis. *females*: connective tissue sheath surrounding the clitoris (fibers pass on either side of urethra and vagina)	central tendon of perineum	*males*: contributes to erection, ejaculation & feeling of orgasm. *females*: contributes to feelings of orgasm and constricts vagina	11-12 11-13
coccygeus*	ischial spine	lateral, inferior borders of sacrum and coccyx	tense & support the pelvic floor	11-12 11-13
deep transverse perineal	ischial ramus	central tendon of perineum	stabilize central tendon, support pelvic floor	11-12 11-13
iliococcygeus*	ischial spine, pubis	coccyx	tense pelvic floor, elevate anus	11-12 11-13
ischiocavernosus	ischial ramus and tuberosity	inferior aspect of pubic symphysis	contributes to erection of penis and clitoris	11-12 11-13
pubococcygeus*	inner margins of pubis	coccyx	tense pelvic floor, elevate anus	11-12 11-13
superficial transverse perineal	ischial ramsu	central tendon or perineum	stabilize central tendon, support pelvic floor	11-12 11-13

*collectively called the levator ani

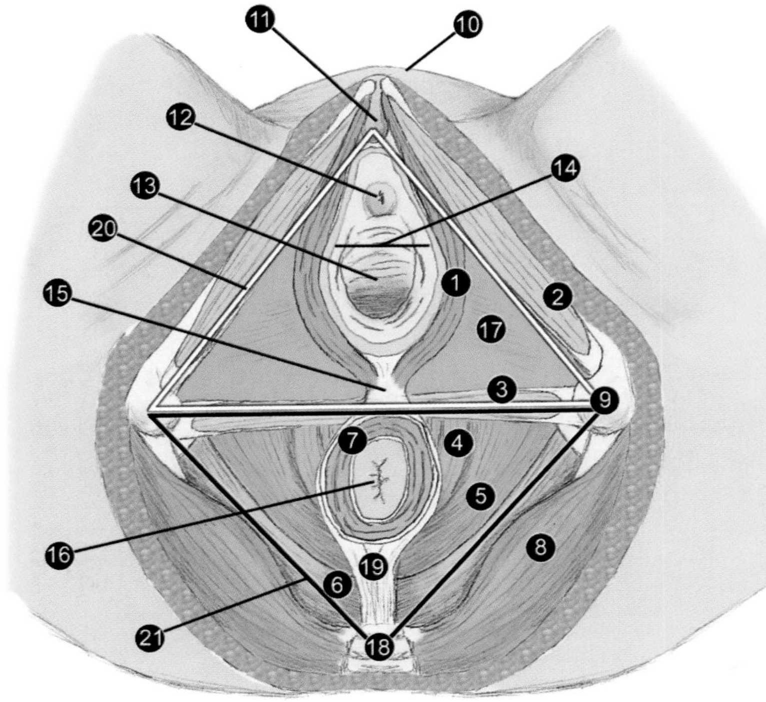

1. bulbospongiosus muscle
2. ischiocavernosus muscle
3. superficial tranverse perineus (STP) muscle
4. puborectalis*
5. pubococcygeus*
6. illiococygeus*
7. anal sphincter
8. gluteus maximus
9. ischial tuberosity
10. mons pubis
11. clitoris
12. external urethral meatus
13. vaginal orifice
14. vestibule
15. perineal body (central tendon)
16. anus
17. deep transverse perineal muscle
18. coccyx
19. anococcygeal ligament
20. urogenital triangle
21. anal triangle

*collectively = levator ani

Muscles of the Female Perineum

Figure 11-12

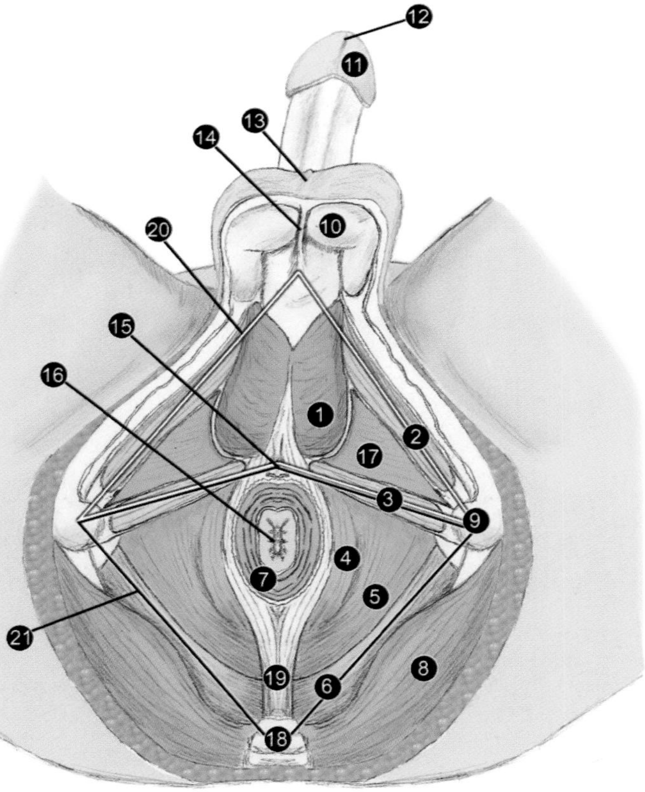

1. bulbospongiosus muscle
2. ischiocavernosus muscle
3. superficial tranverse perineus (STP) muscle
4. puborectalis*
5. pubococcygeus*
6. illiococygeus*
7. anal sphincter
8. gluteus maximus
9. ischial tuberosity
10. testicle
11. glans penis
12. external urethral meatus
13. raphe
14. scrotal septum
15. perineal body (central tendon)
16. anus
17. deep transverse perineal muscle
18. coccyx
19. anococcygeal ligament
20. urogenital triangle
21. anal triangle

*collectively = levator ani

Muscles of the Male Perineum

Figure 11-13

TABLE 11.6 Muscles of Upper Limb

muscle	*origin*	*insertion*	*action*	*figure(s)*
abductor digiti minimi	pisiform bone	ulnar side of proximal 5th phalanx	abduction of little finger	11-15
abductor pollicis brevis	scaphoid & trapezium	radial side of proximal aspect of first proximal phalanx	abduction of thumb	
abductor pollicis longus	proximal dorsal aspect of ulna and radius	lateral margin of first metacarpal	abduction of thumb and wrist	11-14
adductor pollicis	metacarpal and carpal bones	proximal first phalanx	adduction of thumb	11-15
anconeus	posterior, inferior aspect of lateral epicondyle of humerus	lateral margin of olecranon of ulna	extension of elbow	11-14
biceps brachii	*short head*: coracoid process of scapula. *long head*: supraglenoid tubercle of scapula	radial tuberosity	flexion of elbow, flexion of shoulder, assist supination	11-6 11-7 11-15
brachialis	anteriodistal aspect of humerus	ulnar tuberosity	flexion of elbow	11-15
brachioradialis	ridge superior to the lateral epicondyle of humerus	styloid process of radius	flexion of elbow	11-15
coracobrachialis	coracoid process of scapula	medial aspect of humerus	shoulder flexion and adduction	11-15
deltoid	lateral 2/3 of clavicle, acromion of scapula	deltoid tuberosity of humerus	*together*: abduction of shoulder. *anterior part*: flexion & medial rotation of shoulder. *poster part*: extension & lateral rotation of shoulder	11-5 11-6 11-7
extensor carpi radialis brevis	lateral epicondyle of humerus	base of 3rd metacarpal	extension and abduction of wrist	11-14
extensor carpi radialis longus	lateral supracondylar ridge of humerus	base of 2nd metacarpal	extension and abduction of wrist	11-14
extensor carpi ulnaris	lateral epicondyle of humerus, dorsal aspect of ulna	base of 5th metacarpal	extension and adduction of wrist	11-14
extensor digitorum	lateral epicondyle of humerus	posterior aspect of phalanges 2-5	extension of fingers and wrist	11-15
extensor pollicis longus & brevis	anterior shaft of ulna & radius	base of distal (longus) & proximal (brevis) 1st phalanx	extension of thumb	11-14
flexor digitorum profundus	medial, posterior surface of ulna; interosseus membrane	base of distal phalanges 2-5	flexion of fingers	11-15
flexor digitorum superficialis	medial epicondyle of humerus	anterior aspect of middle phalanges 2-5	flexion of fingers and wrist	11-15
flexor carpi radialis	medial epicondyle of humerus	base of 2nd and 3rd metacarpals	flexion and abduction of wrist	11-15
flexor carpi ulnaris	medial epicondyle of humerus	base of 5th metacarpal	flexion and adduction of wrist	11-15
Flexor pollicis longus	anterior shaft of radius; interosseus membrane	base of distal 1st phalanx	flexion of thumb	11-15

TABLE 11.6 Muscles of Upper Limb (cont)

muscle	*origin*	*insertion*	*action*	*figure(s)*
opponens digiti minimi	hamate bone	5th metacarpal	opposition at 5th metacarpal	11-15
opponens pollicis	flexor retinaculum	first metacarpal	opposition of thumb	11-15
palmaris longus	medial epicondyle of humerus	palmar aponeurosis and flexor retinaculum	flexion of wrist	11-15
pronator quadratus	distal aspect of anterior ulna	distal aspect of anterior radius	pronation of forearm	11-15
pronator teres	medial epicondyle of humerus, coronoid process of ulna	midlateral surface of radius	pronation of forearm	11-15
Supinator	lateral epicondyle of humerus, proximal ulna	proximal aspect of radius	supinate forearm	11-14 11-15
triceps brachii	*lateral head*: superior lateral margin of humerus. *long head*: infraglenoid tubercle of scapula *medial head*: posterior aspect of humerus inferior to radial groove	*all heads*: olecranon of ulna	extension of elbow (long head also contributes to extension and adduction of shoulder)	11-6 11-7 11-15

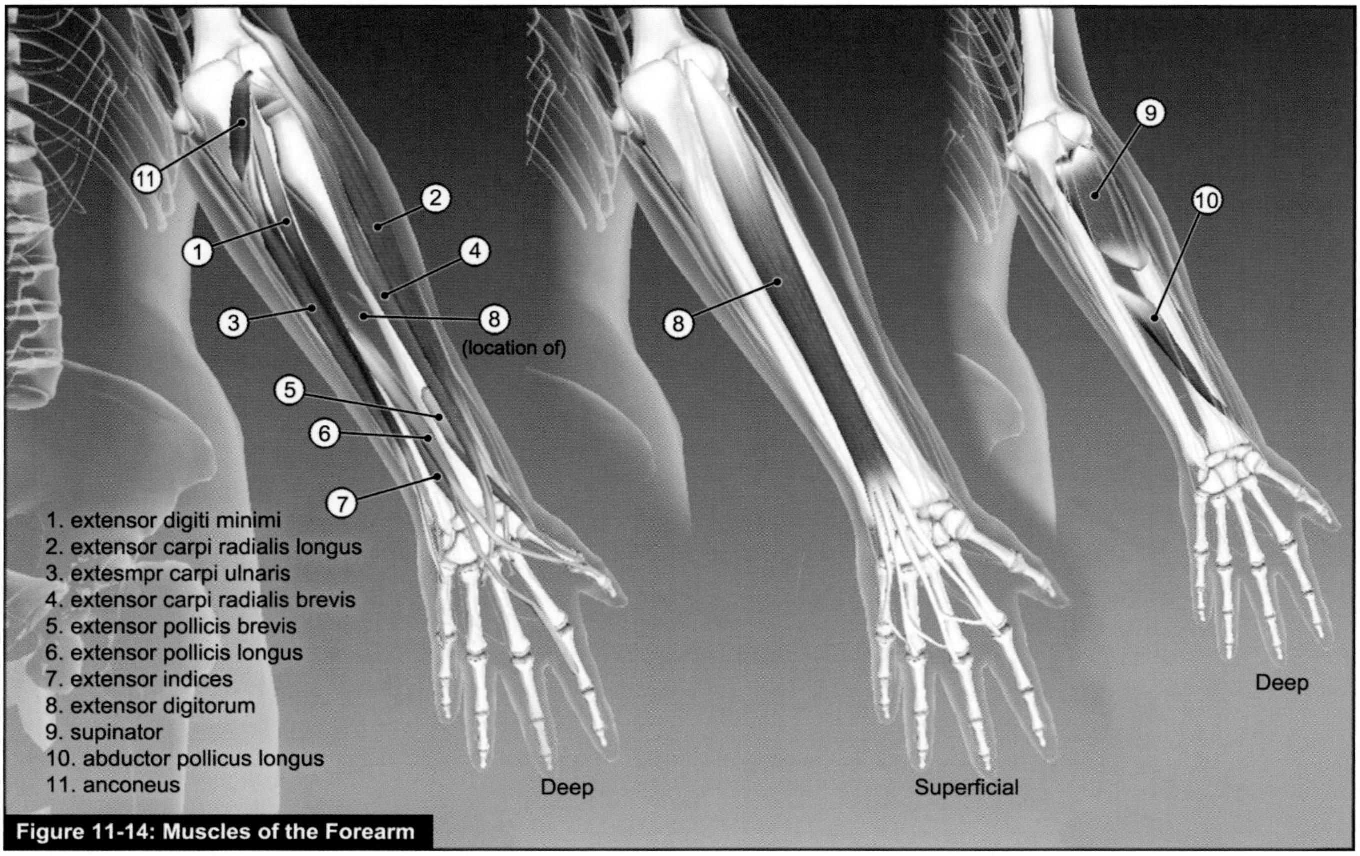

Figure 11-14: Muscles of the Forearm

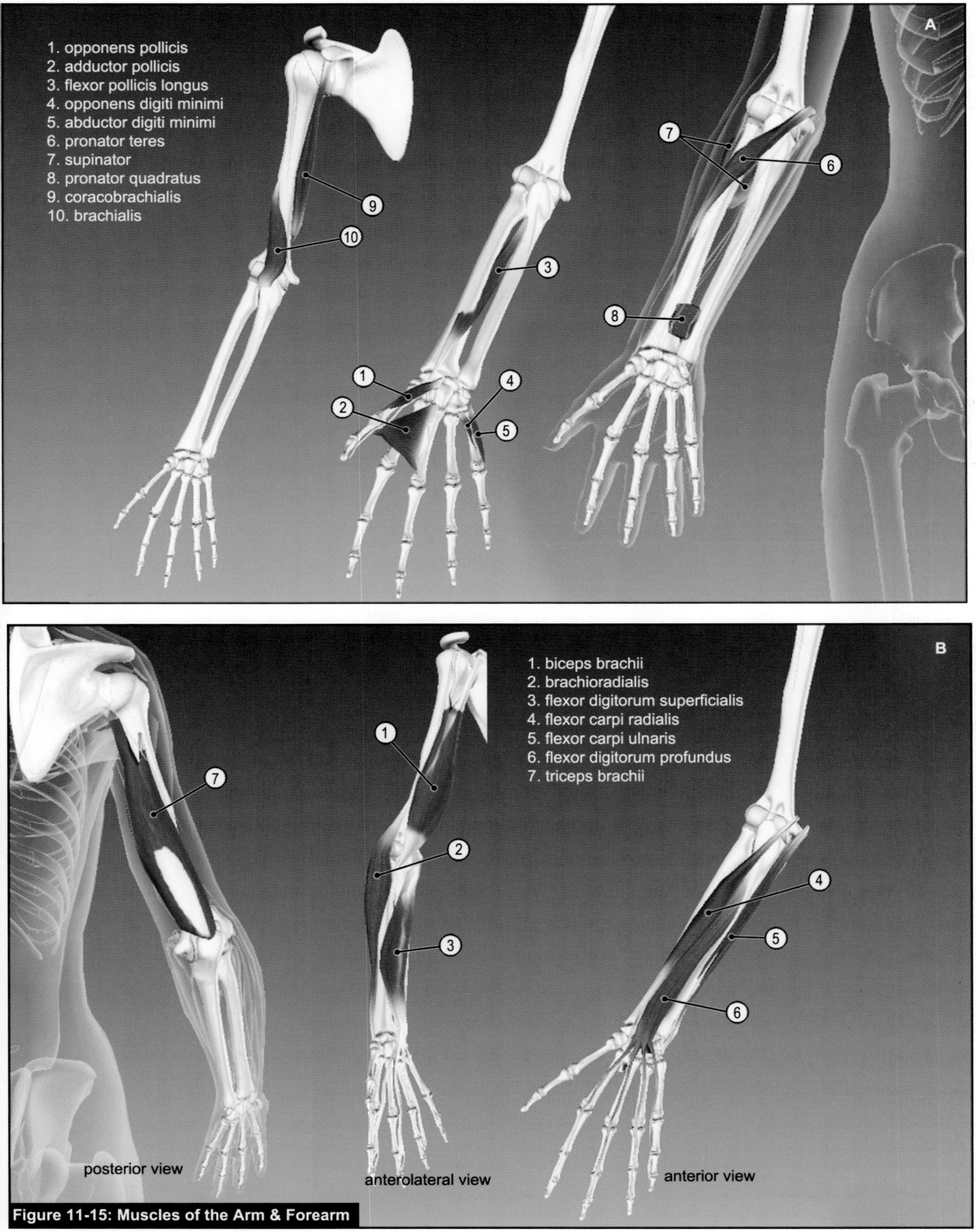

Figure 11-15: Muscles of the Arm & Forearm

TABLE 11.7 Muscles of Lower Limb

muscle	*origin*	*insertion*	*action*	*figure(s)*
adductor brevis	inferior aspect of pubic ramus	linea aspera of femur	adduction, flexion and medial rotation of hip	11-4 11-20
adductor longus	inferior aspect of pubic ramus	linea aspera of femur	adduction, flexion and medial rotation of hip	11-16
adductor magnus	ischial tuberosity, ischial & pubic rami	linea aspera, adductor tubercle of femur	adduction & medial rotation of hip	11-17 11-18 11-20
biceps femoris*	ischial tuberosity, linea aspera of femur	head of fibula, lateral condyle of tibia	flexion of knee, extension and lateral rotation of hip	11-16 11-18 11-19
extensor digitorum longus	lateral condyle of tibia, anterior aspect of fibula	superior aspects of phalanges 2-5	extension of toes 2-5	11-17
extensor hallucis longus	anterior surface of fibula	superior aspect of distal 1st phalanx	extension of great toe	11-17
fibularis brevis	lateral margin of fibula	base of 5th metatarsal	foot eversion, ankle extension	11-17
fibularis longus	lateral condyle of tibia, head & proximal shaft of fibula	base of 1st metatarsal	foot eversion, ankle extension	11-16 11-17
flexor digitorum longus	posteromedial aspect of tibia	inferior aspect of distal phalanges 2-5	flexion of toes 2-5	11-20
flexor hallucis longus	posterior aspect of fibula	inferior aspect of distal 1st phalanx	flexion of great toe	11-20
gastrocnemius	femoral condyles	calcaneus	ankle extension, foot inversion, knee flexion	11-16 11-17 11-18
gluteus maximus	posterior iliac crest, gluteal line of ilium, sacrum, coccyx	iliotibial tract, gluteal tuberosity of femur	extension and lateral rotation of hip	11-16 11-18
gluteus medius	middle portion of iliac crest	greater trochanter of femur	abduction and medial rotation of hip	11-16 11-18 11-20
gluteus minimus	lateral surface of ilium	greater trochanter of femur	abduction and medial rotation of hip	11-5 11-17 11-20
gracillis	inferior aspect of pubic ramus	medial surface of tibia inferior to medial condyle	flexion of knee, adduction and medial rotation of hip	11-16
iliopsoas	iliac fossa, anterior aspect of transverse processes of T12-L5	lesser trochanter of femur	flexion of hip	11-17
pectineus	superior aspect of pubic ramus	pectineal line of femur	flexion, medial rotation and adduction of hip	11-16
piriformis	anterolateral aspect of sacrum	greater trochanter of femur	abduction of hip	11-17

TABLE 11.7 Muscles of Lower Limb (cont)

muscle	origin	insertion	action	figure(s)
plantaris	lateral supracondylar ridge	calcaneus	ankle extension, knee flexion	11-17 11-18
rectus femoris**	anteroinferior aspect of iliac spine, superior rim of acetabulum	tibial tuberosity via patellar ligament	extension of knee, flexion of hip	11-16 11-18 11-19
sartorius	anterosuperior aspect of iliac spine	medial surface of tibia near tibial tuberosity	flexion of knee, flexion and lateral rotation of hip	11-16 11-18
semimembranosus*	ischial tuberosity	posterior aspect of medial tibial condyle	flexion of knee, extension and medial rotation of hip	11-16 11-18 11-19
semitendinosus*	ischial tuberosity	proximal medial aspect of tibia	flexion of knee, extension and medial rotation of hip	11-16 11-18 11-19
soleus	head & proximal shaft of fibula, posteromedial shaft of tibia	calcaneus	ankle extension	11-16 11-17 11-8
tensor fascia latae	iliac crest, lateral aspect of anterior superior iliac spine	iliotibial tract	flexion and medial rotation of hip, support knee joint	11-16 11-18
tibialis anterior	lateral condyle and proximal shaft of tibia	base of 1st metatarsal	ankle flexion, inversion of foot	11-16 11-17
tibialis posterior	interosseous membrane between tibia and fibula	tarsal and metatarsal bones	adduction and inversion of foot, ankle extension	11-17
vastus intermedius**	anterolateral aspect of femur and distal portion of linea aspera	tibial tuberosity via patellar ligament	extension of knee	11-18 11-19
vastus lateralis**	anterior aspect of femur inferior to greater trochanter, proximal portion of linea aspera	tibial tuberosity via patellar ligament	extension of knee	11-16 11-18 11-19
vastus medialis**	linea aspera of femur	tibial tuberosity via patellar ligament	extension of knee	11-18 11-19

* Collectively called the "hamstrings"
** Collectively called the quadriceps femoris, or "quads"

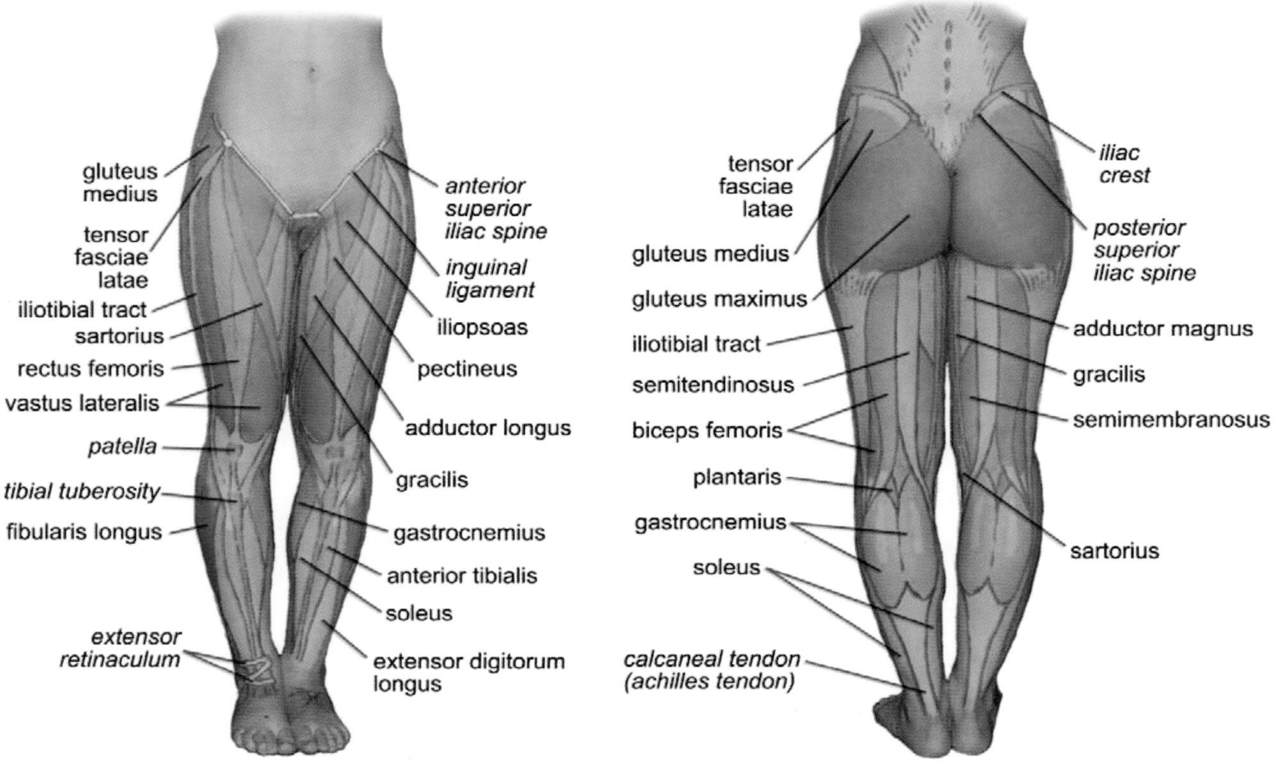

Figure 11-16

Thigh & Leg Muscles

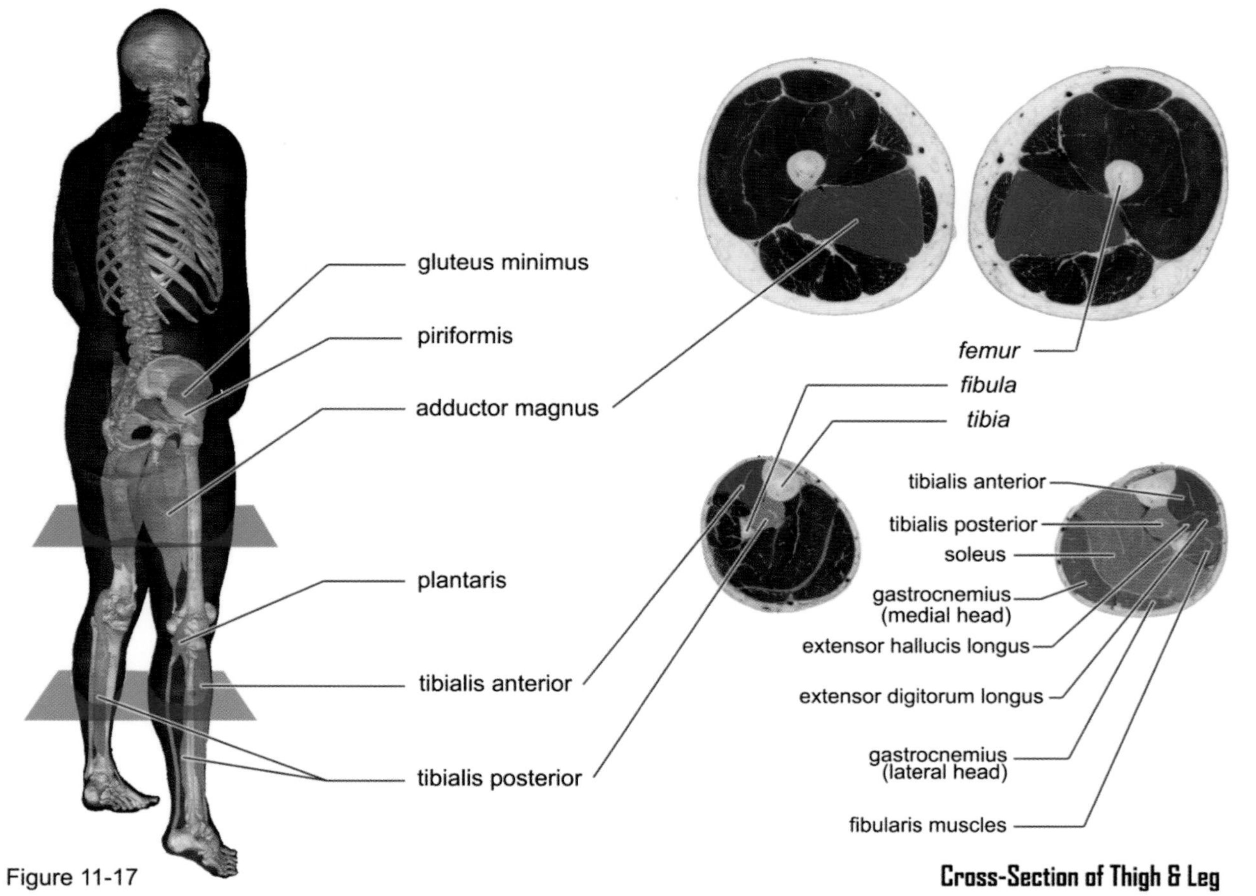

Figure 11-17

Cross-Section of Thigh & Leg

1. psoas major*
2. iliacus*
3. gluteus medius
4. gluteus maximus
5. tensor fasciae latae
6. sartorius
7. rectus femoris
8. iliotibial tract
9. biceps femoris
   short head, deep
   long head, superficial
10. vastus lateralis
11. vastus medialis
12. gastrocnemius
    (lateral head)
13. soleus
14. fibularis longus
15. extensor digitorum
    longus

* collectively called "iliopsoas"

16. tibialis anterior
17. pectineus
18. adductor longus
19. gastrocnemius
    (medial head)
20. flexor digitorum longus
21. flexor hallucis longus
22. gracilis
23. adductor brevis
24. adductor magnus
25. semimembranosus
26. semitendinosus
27. vastus intermedius
28. quadratus femoris
29. sup. and inf. gemelli
30. piriformis
31. gluteus minimus
32. obturator internus
33. plantaris

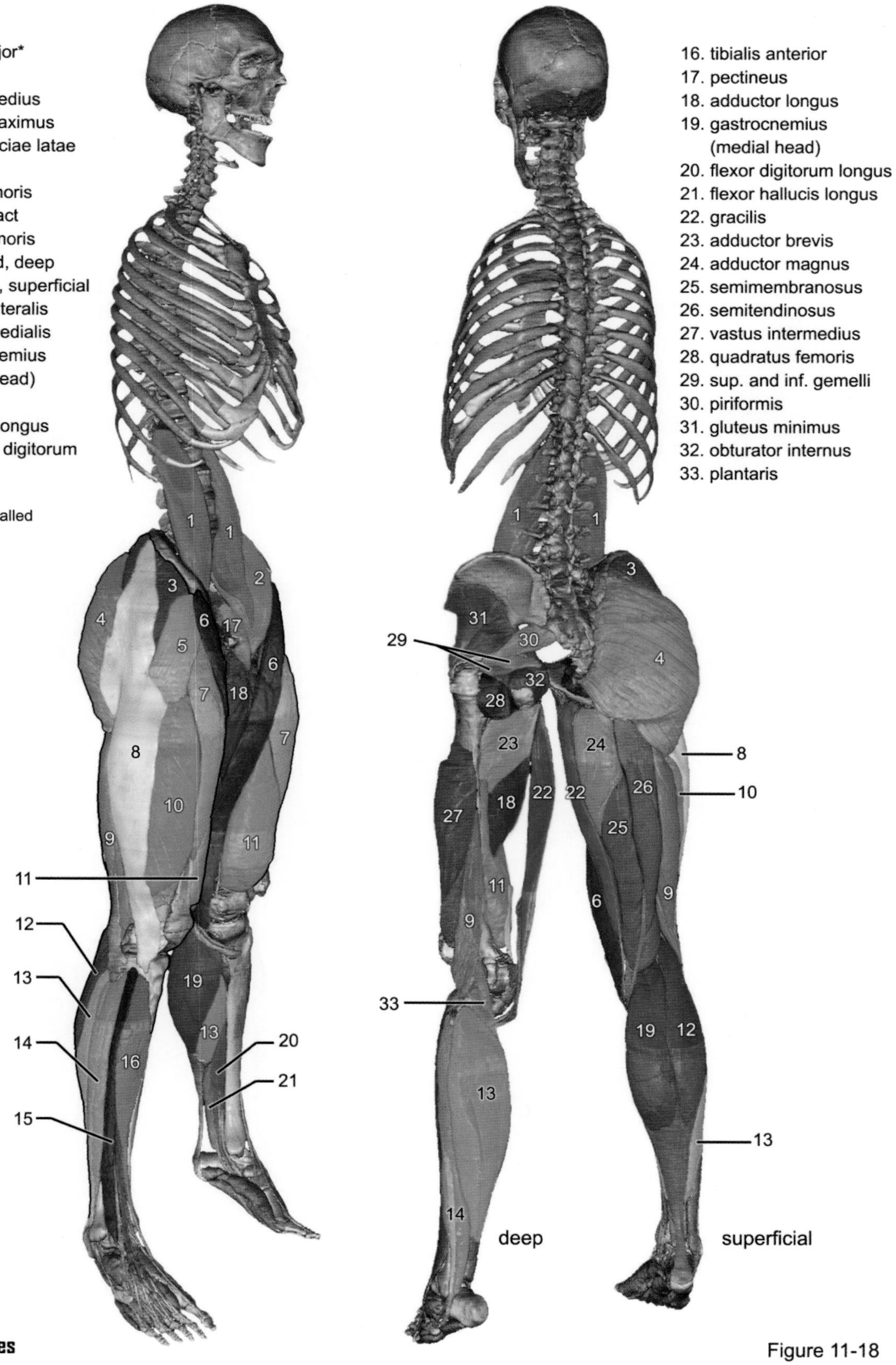

Lower Limb Muscles

Figure 11-18

anterior compartment

1. vastus lateralis
2. vastus intermedius
3. rectus femoris
4. vastus medialis
5. sartorius

(1–4: "quads")

posterior compartment

6. biceps femoris
7. semitendinosus
8. semimembranosus

(6–8: "hamstrings")

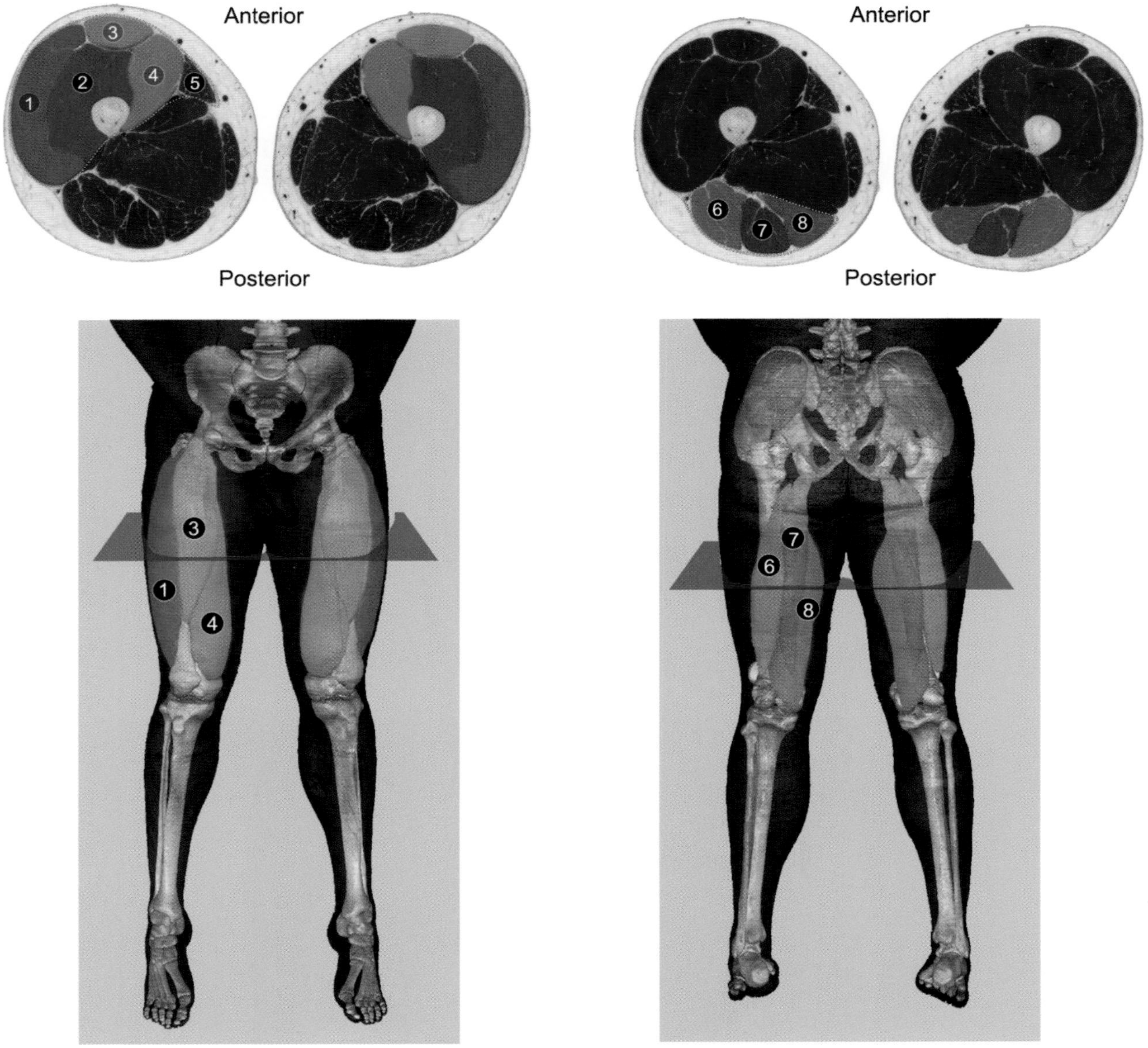

Figure 11-19

The "Hamstrings" & "Quads"

Activity 1: Examine Body Musculature
Using the figures and tables in this exercise, examine the origins, insertions and actions of the major skeletal muscles.

Activity 2: Palpating Trunk Muscles
1. *Pectoralis major* – Press your hands together at chest level with your elbows wide apart. The large pectoralis major can be seen and felt in the thoracic region.
2. *Deltoid* – Attempt to adduct your shoulder against resistance. The deltoid can be seen and felt on the superior aspect of the shoulder. Now lift your hand above your head (elbow extended). In this position the three portions of the deltoid can be seen surrounding the acromion process.
3. *Trapezius* – Attempt to elevate your shoulder against resistance. The upper portion of the trapezius can be seen and felt along the superior aspect of the shoulder.
4. *Latissimus dorsi* – Fully abduct the arm and extend your elbow. Now attempt to adduct the arm against resistance. The latissimus dorsi may be seen and felt contracting along the lateral aspect of the body trunk.

Activity 3: Palpating Muscles of the Upper Limb
1. *Biceps brachii* – Attempt to flex your forearm against resistance. The biceps is easily felt and seen on the frontal aspect of the arm. Its tendon can be traced crossing the antecubital fossal.
2. *Triceps brachii* – Extend your elbow against resistance. The large triceps brachii can be seen and felt on the posterolateral aspect of the arm.

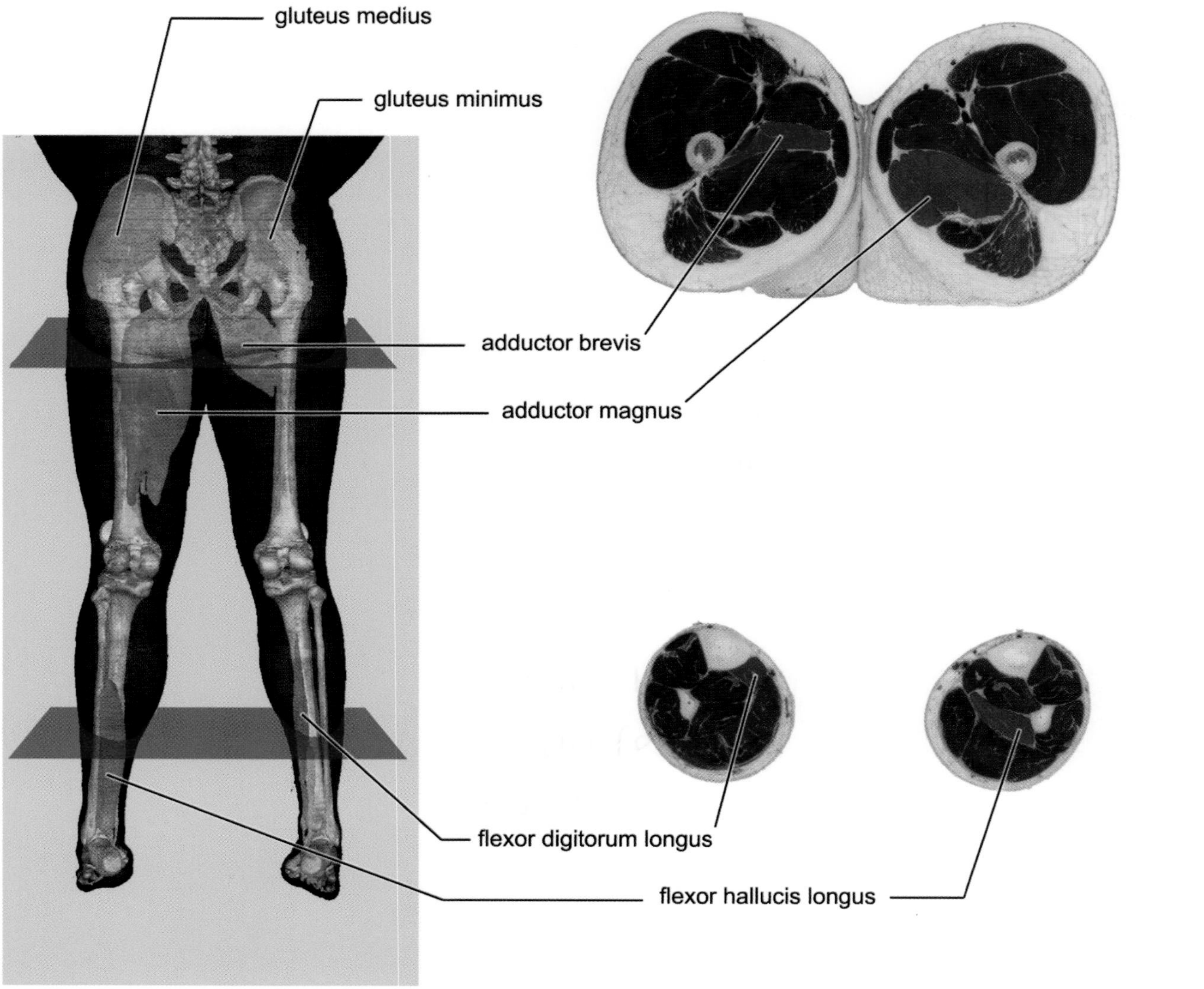

Figure 11-20

Cross-Section of Thigh & Leg

Sometimes, the lateral head of the triceps creates a sharp bulge on the lateral aspect of the arm.

3. *Forearm flexors & extensors* – Grasp your forearm tightly several inches above your wrist. Alternately flex and extend your fingers and palpate the various muscles contracting in your forearm. Alternately flex and extend each finger individually and notice the difference muscles utilized for each motion.
4. *Extensor digitorum* – Extend and flare your fingers. Observe and palpate the tendons of the extensor digitorum crossing the dorsum of your hand.

Activity 4: Palpating Muscles of the Lower Limb

1. *Gluteus maximus* – From a squating position, palpate the gluteus maximus as you extend your hip to resume an upright position. Alternatively, palpate the action of the muscle while walking.
2. *Gastrocnemius* – Have your partner stand on his or her toes. Palpate both heads of the gastrocnemius muscle to the calcaneus.
3. *Tibialis anterior* – Place your hand firmly on the lateral side of the shin bone. Feel the tibialis anterior contract as your partner dorsiflexes the foot.
4. *Quadriceps femoris* – Palpate contraction of the quads by placing your hands firmly on the front of the thigh while your partner attempts to extend the knee against resistance.
5. *Biceps femoris* – Palpate contraction of the biceps femoris by placing your hand firmly against the back of the thigh while your partner attempts to flex the knee against resistance.

Activity 5: Muscle Painting

1. Choose one or more male students to be painted. The student(s) should wear shorts and be shirtless for this exercise.
2. Obtain paint brushes and water-based paint of various colors from your instructor. Paint the following muscles on your subject:

- Pectoralis major
- Serratus anterior
- Latissimus dorsi
- Rectus abdominis
- External oblique
- Trapezius
- Deltoid
- Infraspinatus
- Teres major
- Sternocleidomastoid
- Biceps brachii
- Triceps brachii
- Brachioradialis
- Rectus femoris
- Vastus lateralis
- Vastus medialis
- Biceps femoris
- Semimembranosus
- Semitendinosus
- Gastrocnemius
- Soleus
- Tibialis anterior
- Fibularis longus

Activity 5: Color Muscle Groups by Action

1. The body is moved primarily by muscle groups, not individual muscles. Color the superficial muscles on the following page using a different color for each number. This will allow you to visualize opposing muscle group actions (such as flexors vs extensors).

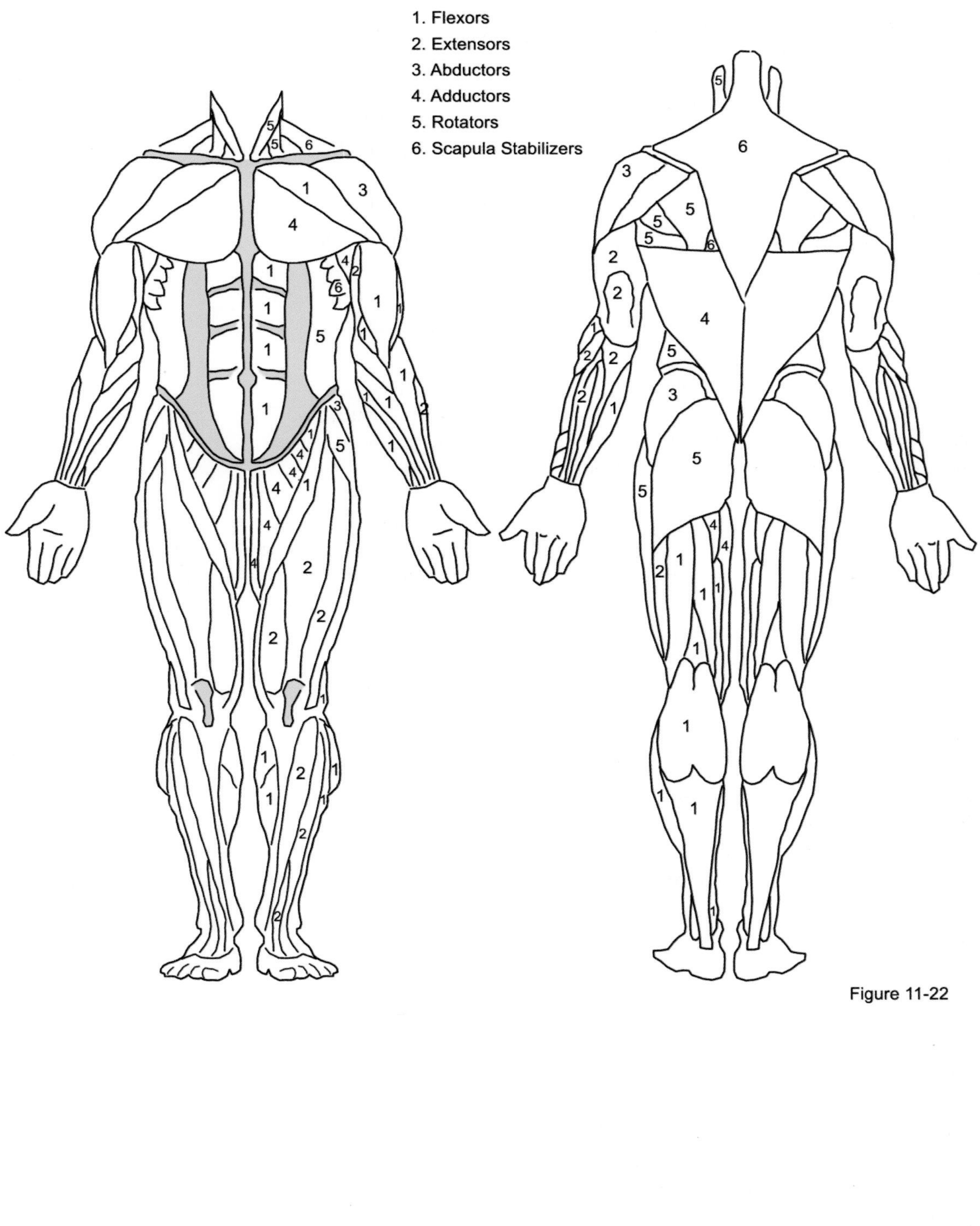
1. Flexors
2. Extensors
3. Abductors
4. Adductors
5. Rotators
6. Scapula Stabilizers

Figure 11-22

exercise 12

the NERVOUS system

- tissue & organization -

Like a scarecrow in a melon patch, their idols cannot speak; they must be carried because they cannot walk. Do not fear them; they can do no harm nor can they do good.
Jeremiah 10:5

Without a nervous system, willful movements such as walking and talking are not possible.

The nervous system is one of two "command-and-control" systems of the human body (the other being the endocrine system). The role of the nervous system is to gather information from within and without the body, process that information and generate appropriate responses – all in real time. In these respects the nervous system is similar to a computer system, but even the most sophisticated computer pales in comparison to the human nervous system. Beyond processing information basic to survival, the nervous system achieves conscious awareness, feels emotions, and performs intellectual and abstract thought.

Despite the complex functions performed by the nervous system, there are relatively few cell types found in nervous tissue. The **neuron**, or *nerve cell*, is the basic functional unit of the nervous system (Figure 12-1). It is the only cell capable of processing information and generating a response. Neurons, however, are incredibly fragile cells that require supporting cells to maintain their three-dimensional configurations. In addition, neurons are extremely energy demanding – when thinking hard, your brain may consume 20% of your body's energy! However, neurons produce little energy of their own. The supporting cells that prop up and energize neurons are collectively called **neuroglia** (literally, "nerve glue"), or *glial cells*. Glial cells of the central nervous system (CNS = brain & spinal cord) include astrocytes, microglia, oligodendrocytes, and ependymal cells (Figure 12-2). Glia of the peripheral nervous system (PNS = ganglia & peripheral nerves) include Schwann cells and satellite cells (Figure 12-3).

Neuroglia of the CNS

Astrocytes are so named because of the star-like appearance of these cells. Processes from the cells surround blood capillaries in the brain and spinal cord and carefully regulate what gets into and out of the nervous tissues (the so-called *blood-brain barrier*).

Microglia, the smallest of the glial cells, are phagocytic. The engulf and destroy pathogens and CNS debris from aging cells. In effect, they serve as the immune system for the nervous system.

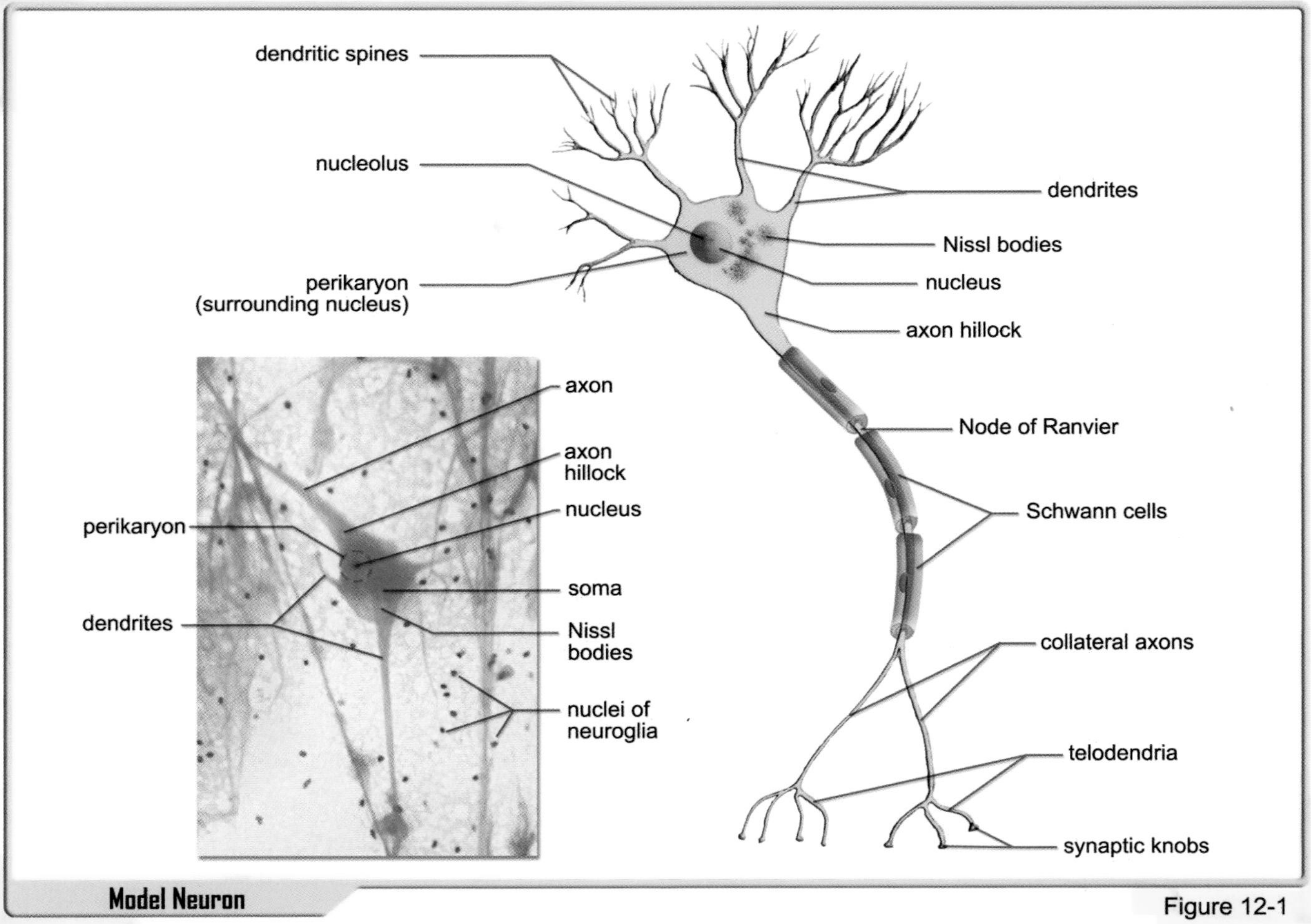

Figure 12-1

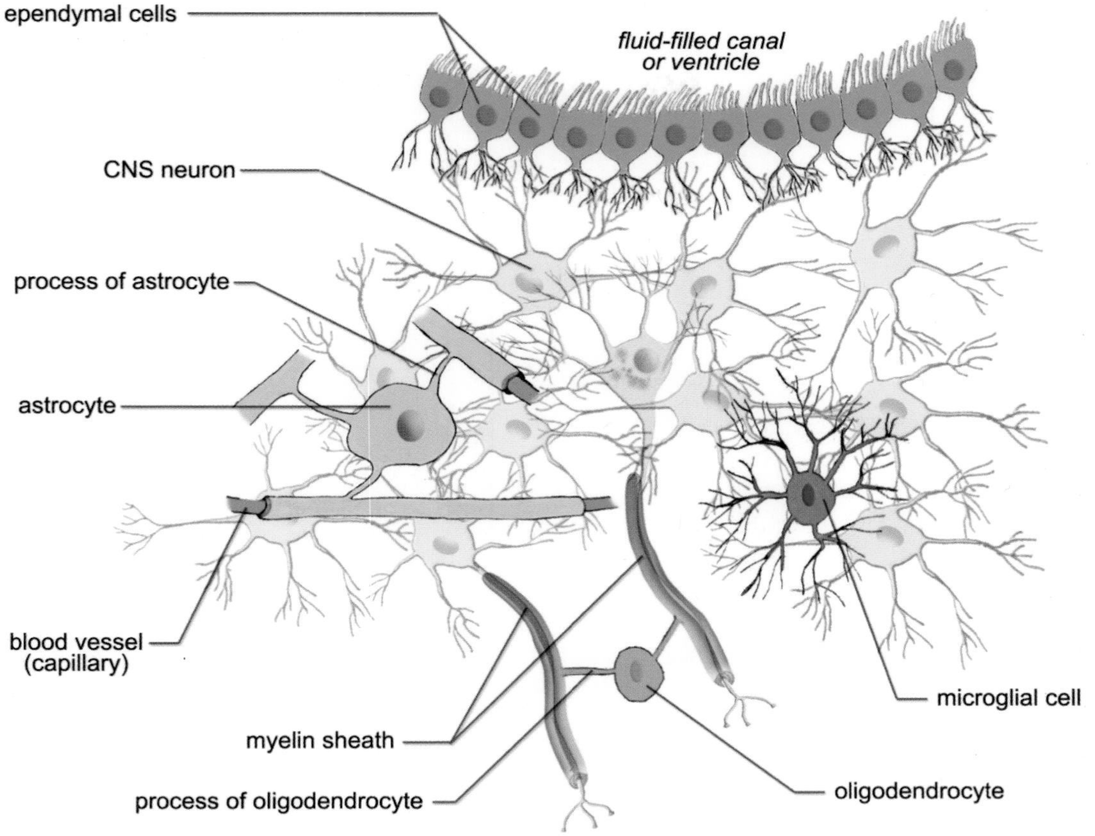

Figure 12-2

Supporting Cells of the Central Nervous System

Oligodendrocytes provide the *myelin sheath* for CNS axons. This sheath surrounds the axons of nerve cells and dramatically increases the speed at which axons transmit information. Processes from oligodendrocytes wrap repeatedly around the axon producing a lipid-rich coating around it. In some ways, this is like the rubber coating that surrounds an electrical wire.

Ependymal cells have properties characteristic of both neurons and epithelia. These "neuroepithelial cells" possess excitable membranes and dendrite-like processes similar to neurons, but they also possess cilia and produce secretions like epithelia. Ependymal cells form the walls of the

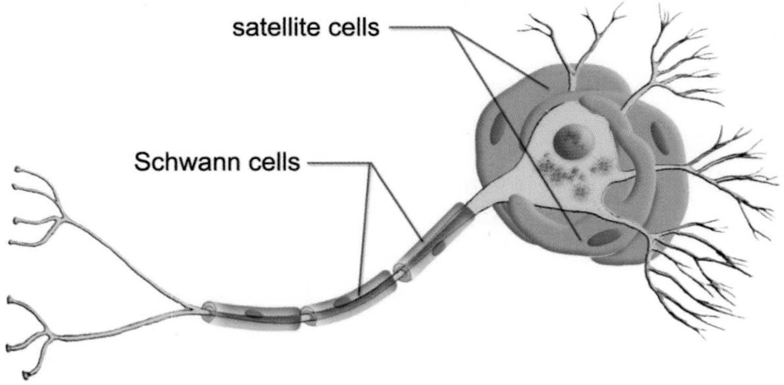

Figure 12-3

Neuroglia of the Peripheral Nervous System

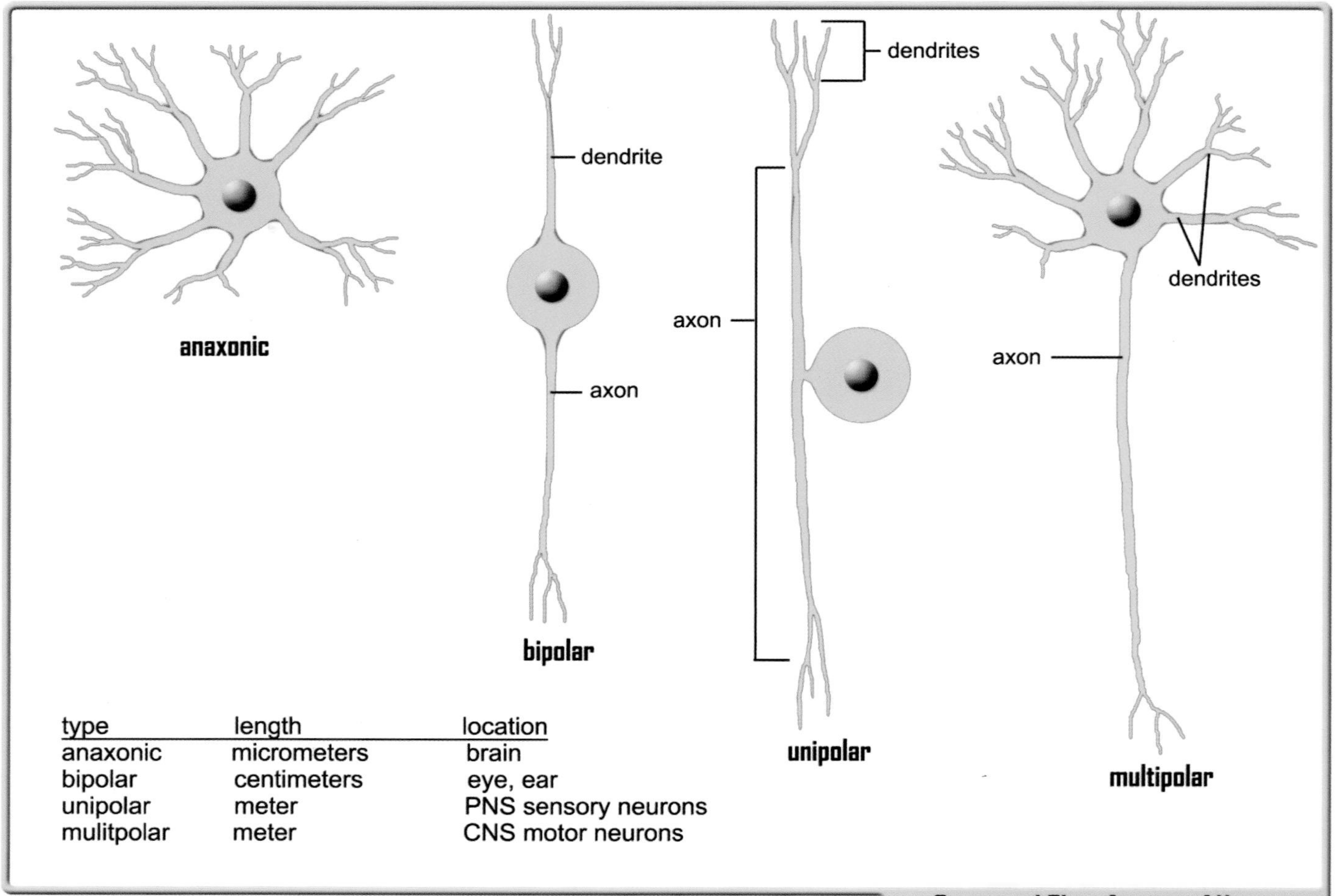

type	length	location
anaxonic	micrometers	brain
bipolar	centimeters	eye, ear
unipolar	meter	PNS sensory neurons
mulitpolar	meter	CNS motor neurons

Figure 12-4 **Structural Classification of Neurons**

central canal in the spinal cord and line the ventricles in the brain. They produce and circulate a fluid called *cerebrospinal fluid* (CSF) which supports CNS nervous tissues.

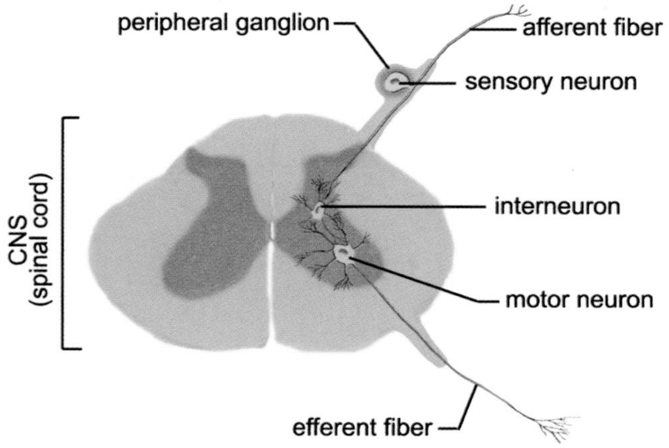

Figure 12-5 **Functional Classification of Neurons**

Neuroglia of the PNS

The major neuroglia of the PNS are Schwann cells and satellite cells. **Schwann cells** form the myelin sheath that surrounds axons of peripheral neurons. A small gap between the cells, called **nodes of Ranvier**, allow ions to be exchanged between the axoplasm (i.e., axonal cytoplasm) of the neuron and the surround interstitial fluid. Schwann cells are the PNS analogs of oligodendrocytes of the CNS.

Satellite cells surround the cell body, or **soma**, of a peripheral neuron. Like CNS astroctyes, they regulate the exchange of materials from the interstitial environment and the inside of the neuron (another blood-neuron barrier).

The Neuron

As stated above, the neuron is the basic functional unit of nervous tissue. Collections of neurons enable complex information processing, consciousness, intellectual pursuits, interpersonal communication, and much more. Individually, neurons behave like electronic transistors in that multiple inputs are received and a single output is generated. The inputs are received either via processes called **dendrites** or directly through soma. The output signal is propogated through the **axon**.

Neurons vary widely in shape and size, but all have multiple dendrites and a single axon. The dendrites branch into numerous smaller processes and finally terminate as **dendritic spines**. In general, the single axon is longer than most of the dendrites. It emerges from the cell body from an enlarged area called the **axon hillock**. Long axons in PNS nerves are sometimes surrounded by glial cells called Schwann cells. These cells create a lipid, non-conducting coat (called the myelin sheath) around the axon. The output signal (called an *action potential*) propogates down the axon as an electrical event that requires the movement of ions across the axon membrane. The movement of those ions is prevented by the myelin sheath and only occurs in small gaps between Schwann cells called the nodes of Ranvier. The signal thus skips from node to node as it travels down the axon. This skipping action speeds up signal transmission up to 100-fold.

Axons may divide one or more times to produce **collateral axons**. In this way, the single output signal from a neuron can be simultaneously delivered to more than one receiving neuron or effector. Near the terminus of the axon several more branches may be observed, called **telodendria**. Each *telodendrion* terminates with an enlarged **synaptic knob** filled with chemicals (i.e., neurotransmitters) that chemically communicate an action potential to the receiving neuron or effector (e.g, muscle or gland).

The nucleus of a neuron is generally large and filled with multiple *nucleoli* (singular = **nucleolus**), regions of active DNA expression. Surrounding the nucleus in an area called the **perikaryon** are dense granuoles called **Nissl bodies**, which are collections of rough endoplasmic reticulum (RER).

Classes of Neurons

Neurons may be classified anatomically or physiologically. Anatomically, there are four basic types of neurons: anaxonic, unipolar, bipolar and multipolar (Figure 12-4).

Anaxonic neurons are relatively short (micrometers in length) and located primarily in the brain. The name is a bit of a misnomer (anaxonic = no axon) in that the cell *does* possess an axon; however, the short axon can't be distinguished from the dendrites.

Unipolar neurons possess a long axon from which the cell body is attached by a thin stalk. The axon and the dendrites are continuous (i.e, fused together). The name is derived from the fact that the cell body has a single, stalk-like attachment to the axon. They are usually found as PNS sensory neurons and may be up to a meter in length.

Bipolar neurons have two processess eminating from the cell body: an axon and a single dendrite. The axon may be longer than the dendrite, but otherwise may only be distinguishable by its knob-like synaptic terminals (as opposed to the thin dendritic spines). They are found predominantly in the eye and ear and may be up to a centimeter in length.

Multipolar neurons have many processes emerging from the cell body. All are dendrites except for a single axon, which is considerably longer than the dendrites. Multipolar neurons are generally found as CNS motor neurons and the axon may be up to a meter in length.

structure

Physiologically neurons are classified as either sensory neurons, motor neurons, or interneurons (Figure 12-5).

Sensory neurons, or afferent neurons, deliver information *from* sensory receptors *to* the CNS. They are unipolar neurons with the cell bodies located in peripheral **ganglia** (gray matter outside the CNS). There are approximately 10 million sensory neurons in the body.

Motor neurons, or efferent neurons, are multipolar and deliver information *from* the CNS *to* peripheral effectors, such as a skeletal muscle. The cell bodies of motor neurons are found in the CNS (i.e., the brain or spinal cord) while the axons form peripheral nerves that innervate muscles, glands and other tissues. There are approximately 500,000 motor neurons in the body.

Interneurons are by far the most abundant type with more than 20 billion in all. One interneuron may connect a sensory neuron to a motor neuron. More often, thousands or millions of interneurons will process received sensory information before issuing commands to motor neurons. Quick reflexes possess few interneurons, but the response is predictable. More complex responses utilizing many interneurons may be for

Functionale

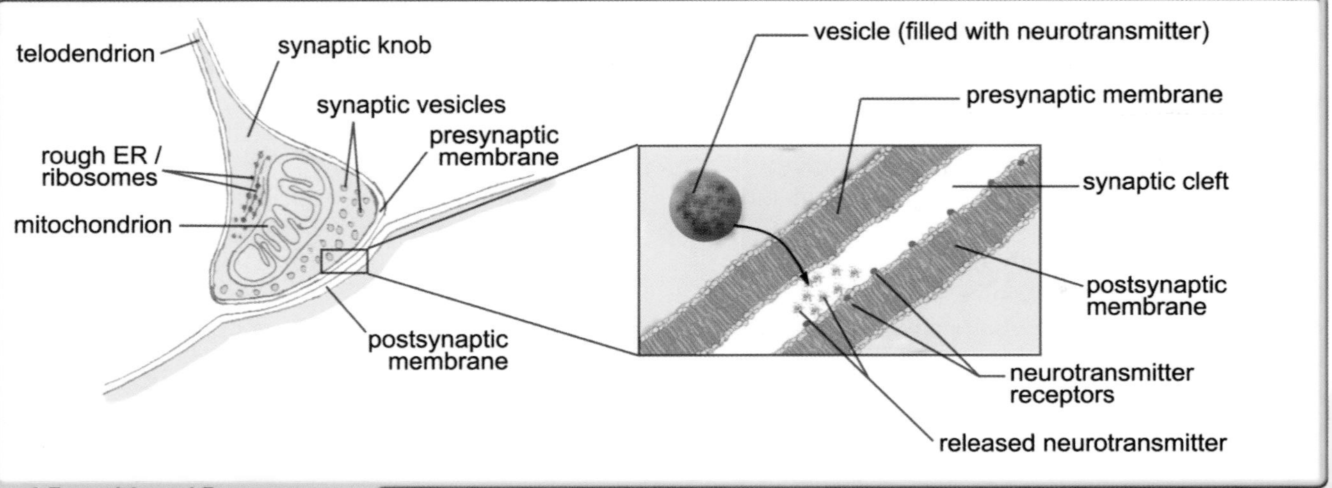

A Typical Axonal Synapse

Figure 12-6

flexable, but they are slower due to the prolonged processing by so many interneurons.

The Axonal Synapse

The terminal portion of a neuronal axon ends with a **synapse**. The role of the synapse is to convey to the receiving neuron (or effector) that an action potential was transmitted down the axon. This is achieved by the use of chemical messengers called **neurotransmitters**.

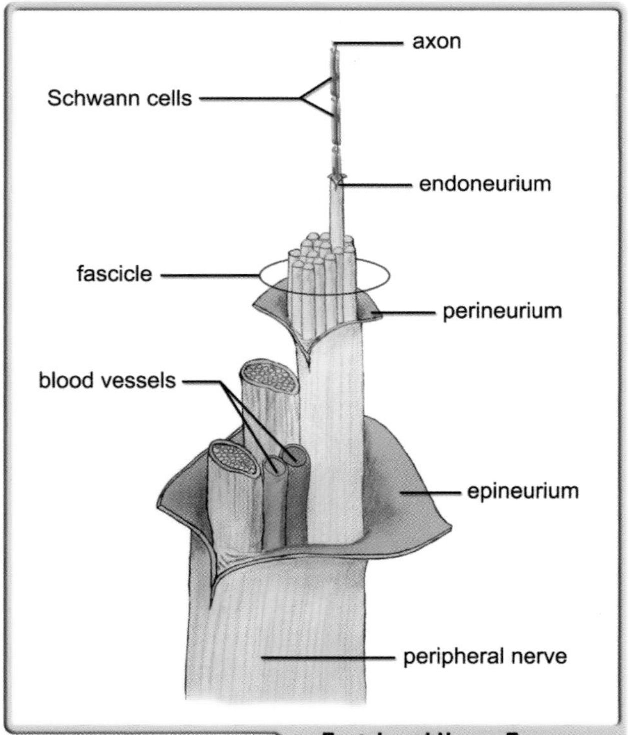

Figure 12-7 Peripheral Nerve Structure

The axon terminates with an enlarged area called the **synaptic knob**. This knob contains a mitochondrion to make ATP and rough ER to make proteins and **synaptic vesicles**. The synaptic knob is filled with hundreds of vesicles containing neurotransmitter molecules. When an action potential reaches the synaptic knob, vesicles merge with the **presynaptic membrane** and release neurotransmitter into the **synaptic cleft**. The neurotransmitter molecules quickly diffuse across the narrow cleft and bind to neurotransmitter receptors on the receiving cell **postsynaptic membrane**. Binding of neurotransmitter to these receptors informs the receiving cell that an action potential has just arrived. A typical axonal synapse is illustrated in figure 12-6, and a specific type of synapse – the neuromuscular junction – is also discussed in exercise 10.

The Structure of a Nerve

Neuron fibers (i.e., axons) travelling back and forth from the CNS to the body tissues rarely travel alone. In stead, fibers traveling to/from the same general location usually bundle together into **nerves**. Fibers from motor neurons emerging from the brain or spinal cord and going to the same body region travel as *motor nerves* (or *efferent nerves*). Similarly, sensory fibers coming from the same body region travel to the CNS in bundles called *sensory nerves* (or *afferent nerves*). Sometimes a nerve may contain both motor and sensory fibers and is therefore called a *mixed nerve*.

All nerves – motor, sensory or mixed – possess several layers of connective tissue sheaths that support and protect the bundle of axons. These sheaths not only provide structural support and protection for the nerve, but also electrically insulate the nerve.

The innermost protective wrapping is the **endoneurium**, which surrounds each individual axon. Hundreds or thousands of individually wrapped axons bundle together to form a **fascicle**. Fascicles are wrapped by a connective tissue sheath called the **perineurium**. Numerous fascicles bundle together within a thick, course sheath called the **epineurium**. Usually, blood vessels and lymphatic vessels travel with nerve fascicles in the epineurium.

Activity 1: Examine Microscopic structure of Nervous Tissue

1. Obtain slides of nervous tissue, a neuromuscular junction, and a cross-section of a peripheral nerve. Identify as many of the structures discussed in this exercise as possible.
2. Draw a neuron and label it.

Special Focus

Neurophysiology

A neuron has the unique ability to transmit electrical signals across long distances along its axon. This is achieved by the propogation of an *action potential* – a localized, momentary reversal of the cell's *transmembrane potential*. What are these "potentials" and how do they allow neurons to transmit information?

A neuron at rest has a slightly negative charge inside compared to the extracellular environment. This is due primarily to the abundance of negative proteins and phosphates inside the cell and an abundance of positively-charged sodium ions (Na^+) outside the cell. This uneven distribution of charges produces a measurable voltage difference across the cell

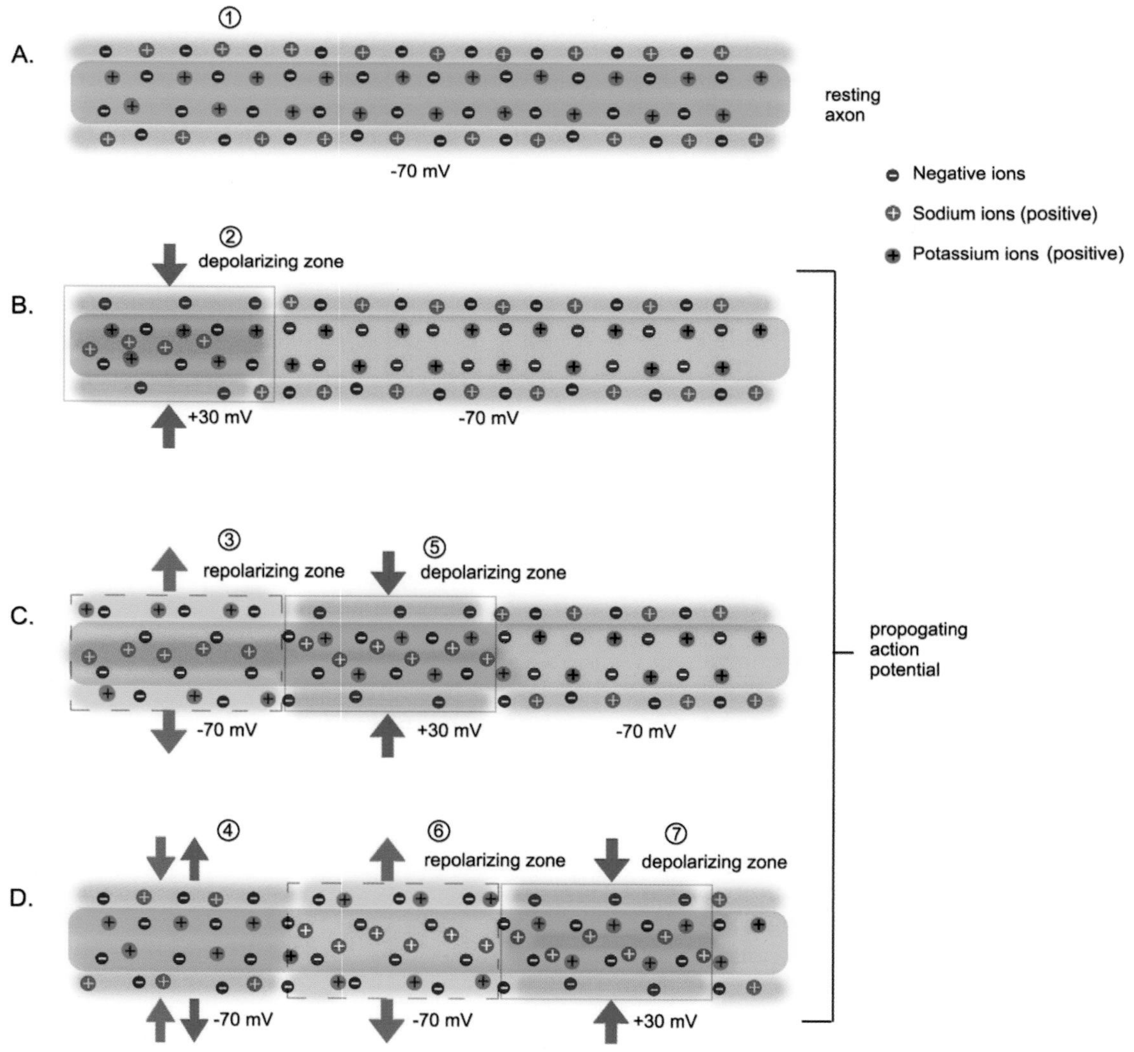

Figure SF-1

The Nerve Impulse

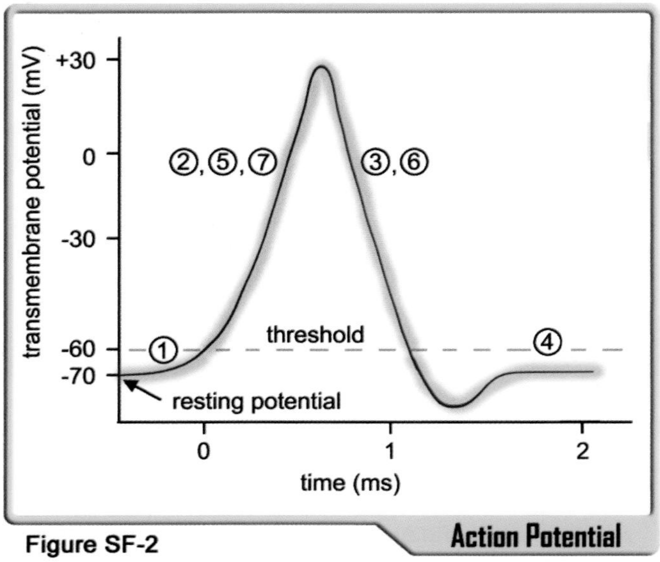

Figure SF-2

membrane called the **transmembrane potential**. At rest, a typical neuron has a transmembrane potential of -70 mV (millivolts).

An **action potential** is a localized "flip-flop" of charges (negative-to-positive) across the cell membrane moving down the axon of the neuron. The progression of the action potential down an axon can be visualized as falling dominoes; at the point where the dominoes are falling the action potential is switching from -70 mV to +30 mV, an event called **depolarization**. In an axon, however, the membrane potential quickly goes back to -70 mV following the action potential (as if the dominoes automatically set themselves back up after falling!). The return to -70 mV is a process called **repolarization**.

Figure SF-1 depicts a portion of an axon at rest and three snapshots of the axon as an action potential passes through. As stated above, the resting potential is established by negative ions inside the cell and positive sodium ions outside (1). There are also positive potassium ions (K^+) inside the cell but not enough to overtake the negative charges. An action potential begins as a neuron is stimulated and sodium channels are opened at the site of stimulation. If enough sodium enters to lower the transmembrane potential to -60 mV (i.e., **threshold potential**), then an action potential will begin. Sodium ions rush into the cell by the millions (driven by a large concentration gradient). As the sodium ions rush in, they bring with them positive charge and the membrane depolarizes (2). Eventually, the inside of the cell becomes positive. At +30 mV, the sodium channels close and potassium channels open, allowing potassium ions to move *out* of the cell (also driven by a concentration gradient). Enough potassium leaves the cell to swing the positive charge outside the cell again, eventually restoring the -70 mV resting potential (3). Although the resting transmembrane potential is restored to -70 mV, the sodium is inside the cell and potassium is outside. An ATP-driven pump called the Na^+,K^+-exchange pump (or, Na^+,K^+ ATPase) pumps sodium out and potassium in to restore the ions to their proper locations (4).

An action potential is depicted graphically in figure SF-2. Note that the circled numbers and line colors in SF-2 correspond to those in SF-1.

Review of Action Potentials

1. Define the following terms.
   a) Transmembrane potential

   b) Action potential

   c) Depolarization

   d) Repolarization

   e) Threshold potential

   f) Resting potential

2. Would a substance that decreases membrane permeability to sodium stimulate or inhibit the generation of an action potential? Why?

exercise 13

the NERVOUS system

- brain & cranial nerves -

Whatever is pure, whatever is noble, whatever is right, whatever is lovely, whatever is admirable - if anything is excellent or praiseworthy - think about these things.
Philippians 4:8

The brain is perhaps the most fascinating organ in the human body. Despite having learned much about this organ in the past few decades, the brain may still be considered the last "black box" of human physiology. This remarkable 3-pound mass of nervous tissue can form and maintain memories, achieve self-awareness and pursue intellectual and abstract thoughts (even pursues a better understanding of itself, as yours is doing now). How the brain accomplishes these feats remains a mystery.

The brain is just one part – albeit a central part – of the larger **nervous system**. The brain relies entirely on the other peripheral parts of the system to obtain information and execute its commands. The nervous system is thus divided into two main partitions: The **central nervous system (CNS)** and **peripheral nervous system (PNS)** (Figure 13-1). The brain and the spinal cord constitute the CNS. The PNS is composed of cranial and spinal nerves, ganglia, and sensory receptors scattered throughout the body (Figure 13-2).

The major function of the PNS is to deliver information to the CNS (i.e, the brain & spinal cord) from sensory receptors and then to deliver commands from the CNS to peripheral effectors (e.g., muscle or glands). Thus, the PNS is partitioned into two divisions: The *sensory division* (a.k.a., **afferent division**) and the *motor division*. (a.k.a., **efferent division**). The motor division is in divided into the **somatic nervous system (SNS**; a.k.a., *voluntary system*) and the **autonomic nervous system (ANS**; a.k.a., *involuntary system*). Finally, the ANS is divided into the *sympathetic* and *parasympathetic* branches. An overview of this arrangement of the nervous system is depicted in figure 13-1.

Regions of the Human Brain

The brain is divided into six major regions. The largest and most complex region is the **cerebrum**, followed by the **cerebellum**. The other four regions – the **diencephalon**, the **mesencephalon**,

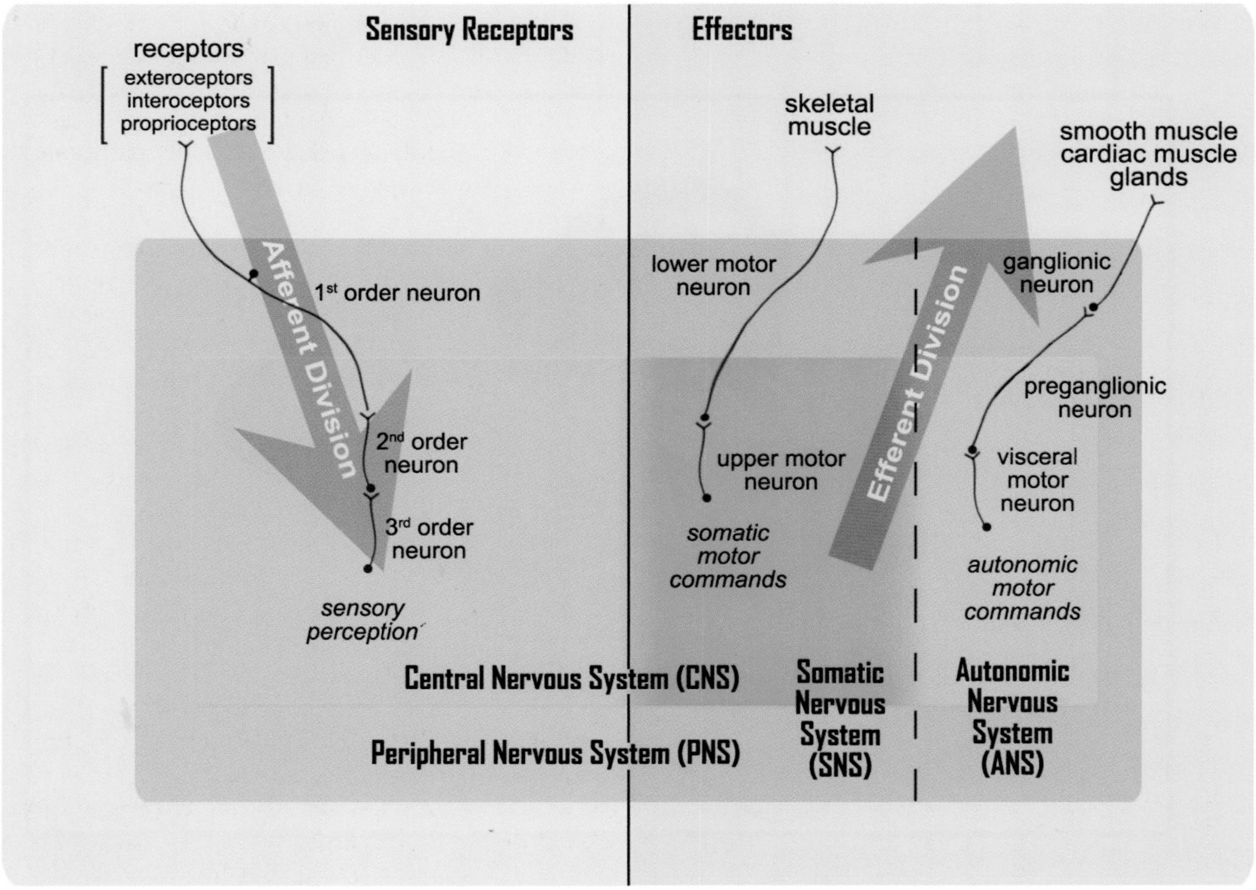

Overview of Neural Integration

Figure 13-1

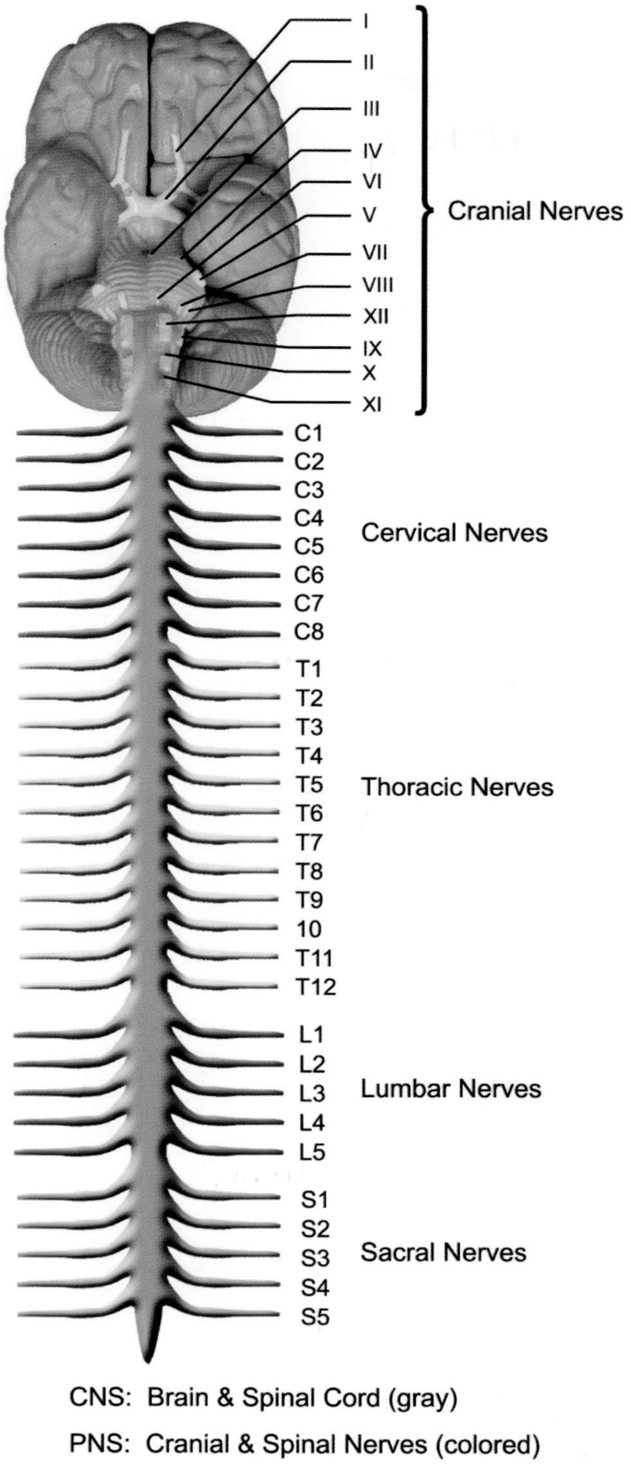

The CNS & Peripheral Nerves Figure 13-2

the **pons** and the **medulla oblongata** – are found deep with the brain and are collectively called the the *brain stem* (Figure 13-3).

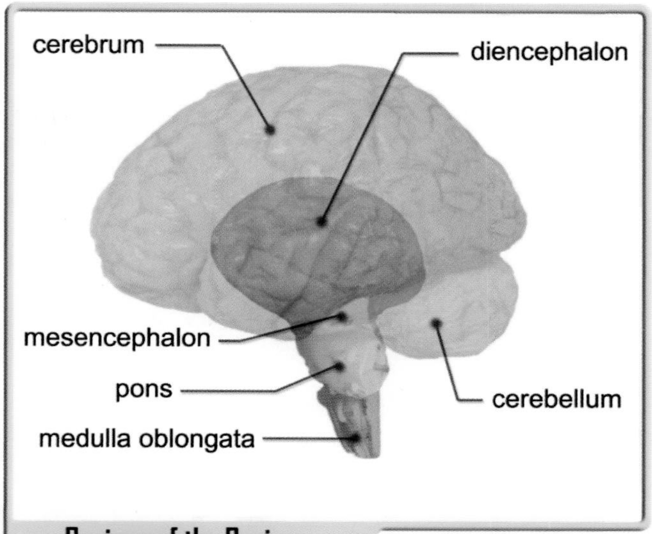

Regions of the Brain Figure 13-3

Cerebrum

The cerebrum is by far the largest of the brain regions (Figures 13-3 & 13-4). It is responsible for all conscious thought and higher learning. Most notably, the cerebrum has a convoluted surface made of numerous folds and valleys. These folds (called **gyri**; singular = *gyrus*) and valleys (**sulci**; singular = *sulcus*) increase the surface area of the cerebrum, effectively allowing more brain in less space. The cerebrum is also noticeably partitioned into right and left hemispheres by a deep **longitudinal fissure**. In general, the right hemisphere controls the left side of the body and the left hemisphere controls the right side of the body. Posteriorly, a **transverse fissure** separates the cerebrum from the cerebellum.

The cerebrum is divided into a number anatomically- and functionally-based lobes. The lobes are named according to the skull bones which cover them. The most anterior portion of the cerebrum is the **frontal lobe**, where problem-solving and analytical thought takes place. The **parietal lobes** possess the **precentral** and **postcentral gyri**, separated by the **central sulcus**. The precentral gyrus is the originator of somatic motor (i.e., skeletal muscle) commands, while the postcentral gyrus is the seat of somatosensory perceptions. Most of the **occipital lobe**, covering the posterior aspect of the cerebrum, is devoted to visual interpretation. Laterally, the **temporal lobes** contain portions of the limbic system. Whereas the other lobes enable you to understand and perform complex operations, the *limbic system* seems

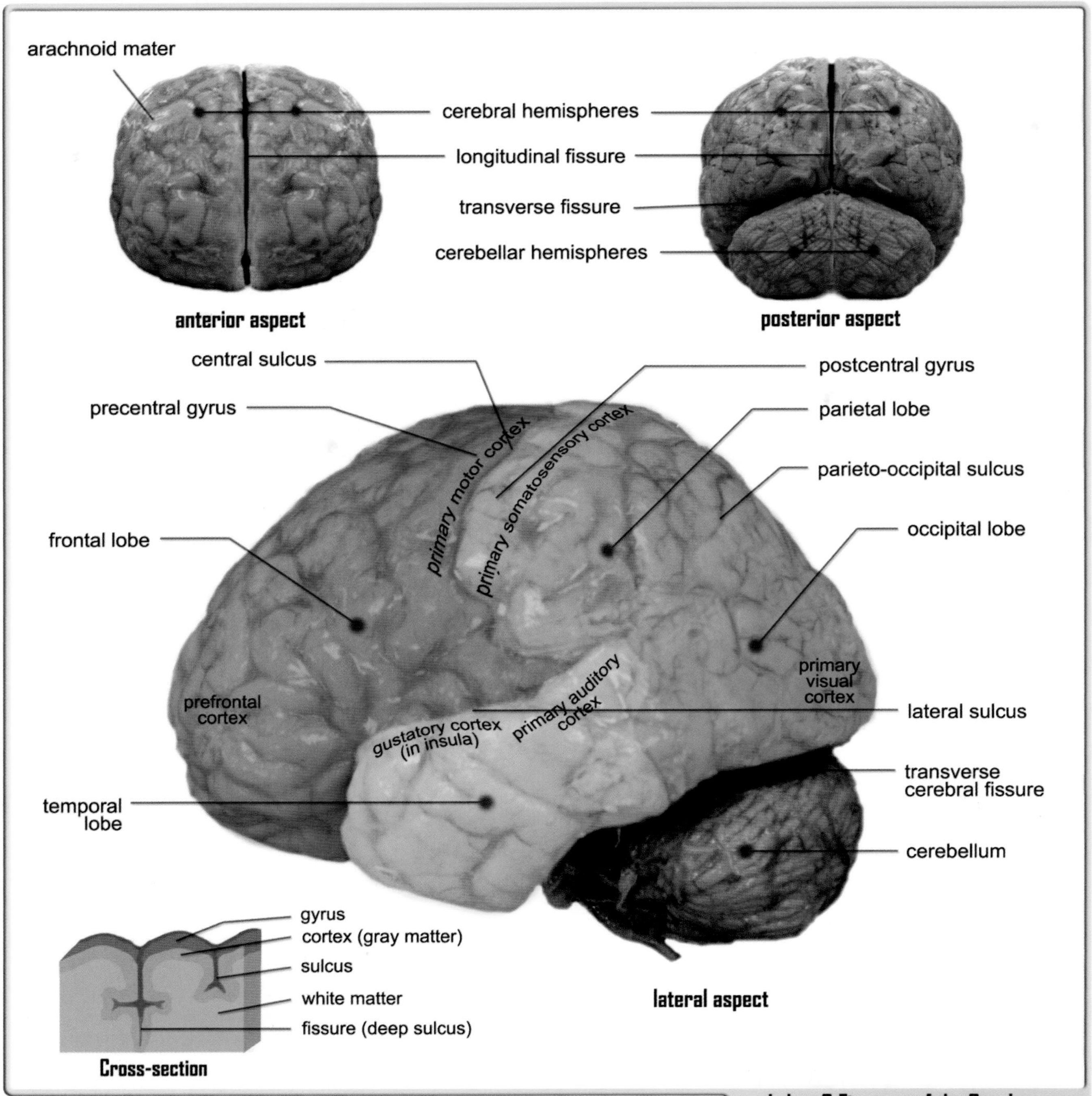

Figure 13-4 Lobes & Fissures of the Cerebrum

important in making you *want* to understand and do them. For this reason it's sometimes called the *motivational system*.

Internally, the cerebrum is organized with **gray matter** superficially in a region called the **cortex** and **white matter** deep to the cortex. Gray matter is composed primarily of neuron cell bodies; white matter is predominantly myelinated neuronal processes. Large, compact tracts of white matter connect different regions of the brain. The **corpus callosum**, for example, provides communication between the two hemipheres of the cerebrum (Figures 13-5 & 13-6). Likewise, the **fornix** carries information between the hippocampus in the lateral lobe and the **mammillary bodies** (Figure 13-9) on the inferior surface of the cerebrum. Patches of gray matter, called *cerebral nuclei*, are also found deep in the cerebrum. Cerebral cortex, white matter and several nuclei can be seen in figure 13-6.

Cerebellum

The cerebellum is the second largest region of the brain (Figures 13-4 and 13-5). The main functions of the cerebellum is to monitor body position and make movements smooth and fluid. For example, when you pick up a book, the cerebellum receives information from receptors within your muscles and tendons about the weight of the book. It uses that information to adjust muscle activity so the book is elevated at the right speed and placed in the desired location. Without the dedicated involvment of the cerebellum, body movements would be jerky and awkward.

Like the cerebrum, the cerebellum is divided into two hemispheres and contains gray matter in a superficial cortex with white matter deep to the cortex. Gyri and sulci are also present, but tend to be much smaller than those of the cerebrum. A midsagittal section of the cerebellum (Figure 13-5) reveals a tree-like arrangement of white matter tracts referred to as the **arbor vitae** (latin for "tree of life").

Brain Stem

The brain stem is composed of the diencephalon, mesencephalon, pons and medulla oblongata. These parts of the brain manage the basic housekeeping and survival tasks of the body (many of which are mediated by cranial reflexes). The parts of the brain stem discussed below are shown in figures 13-3, 13-5 and 13-6.

The **medulla oblongata** is the lowest portion of the brain stem. It's continuous with the spinal cord and helps coordinate breathing and heart patterns, as well as simple reflexes like the swallowing reflex.

The **pons** (latin for "bridge") contains white fibers connecting the medulla oblongata to the midbrain, cerebrum and cerebellum. It appears to function primarily as a relay station.

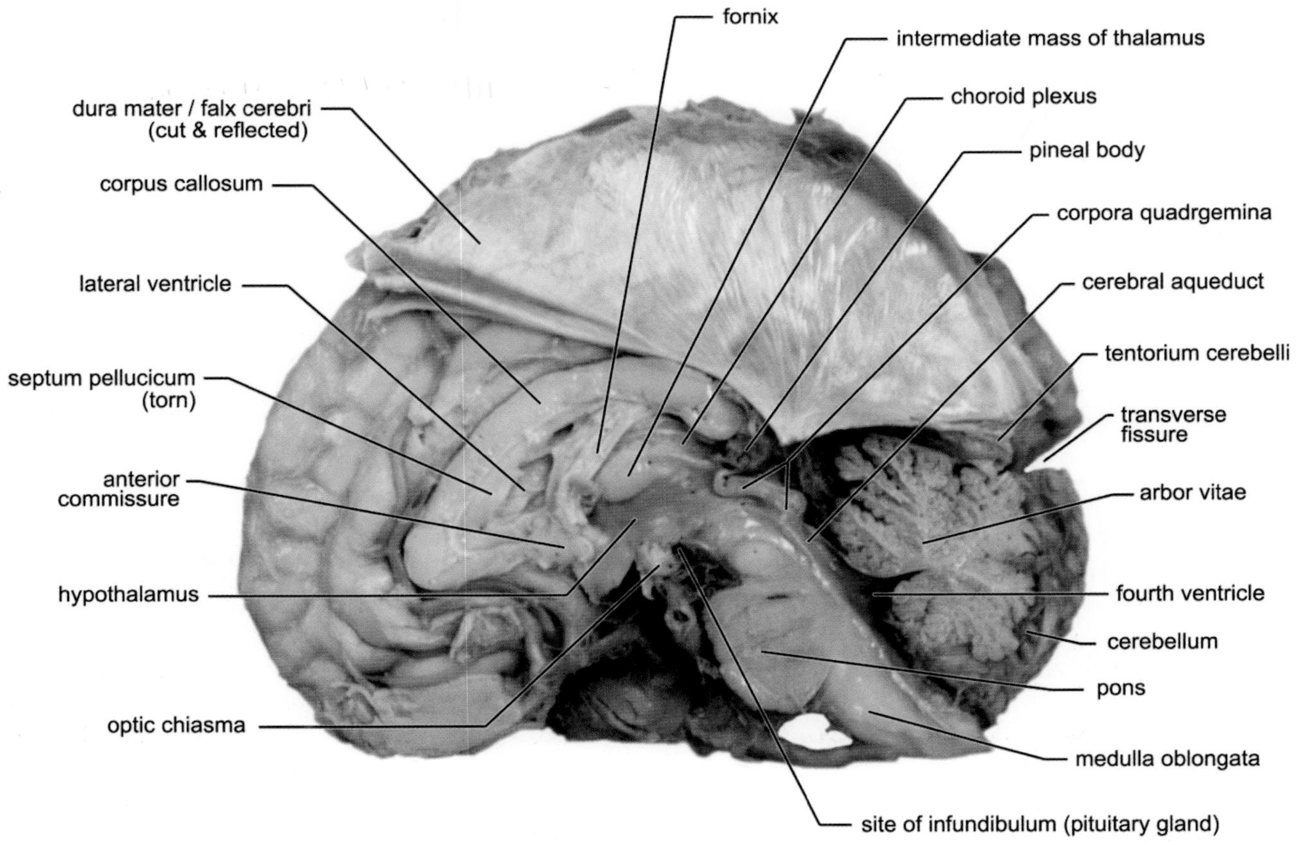

Human Brain (Midsagittal Section)

Figure 13-5

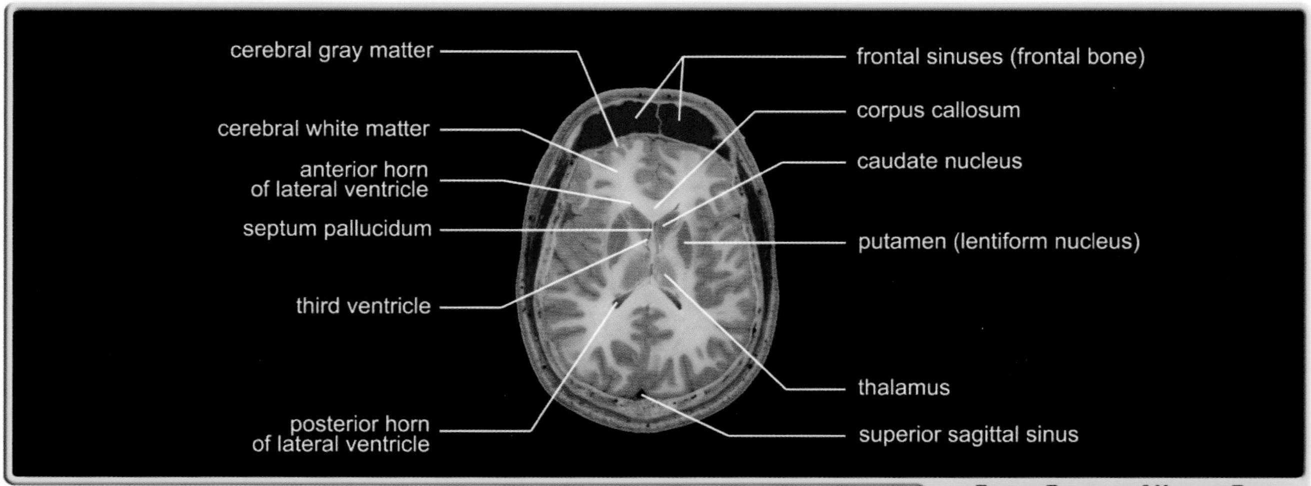

Figure 13-6 **Cross-Section of Human Brain**

The **mesencephalon**, or *midbrain*, contains centers responsible for processing (subconsciously) visual and auditory information. Visual and auditory reflexes (such as flinching at an unexpected loud noise) are mediated by the midbrain.

The **diencephalon** is the highest and most complex part of the brain stem. Indeed, some anatomists do not consider the diencephalon to be part of the brain stem at all. Central within the diencephalon is a fluid-filled chamber called a ventricle. The left and right walls of this chamber are the left thalamus and right thalamus. Each **thalamus** contains processing centers for interpreting sensory information. The floor of the thalamus is called the **hypothalamus**. This small part of the brain is the seat of emotions, basic animal instincts (like sex drive and hunger) and the nervous system's link to the endocrine system. In addition to producing its own hormones, the hypothalamus is connected to the pituitary gland – the master gland of the endocrine system – via a small stalk called the **infundibulum**. Here is where the two "command-and-control" systems coordinate their activities.

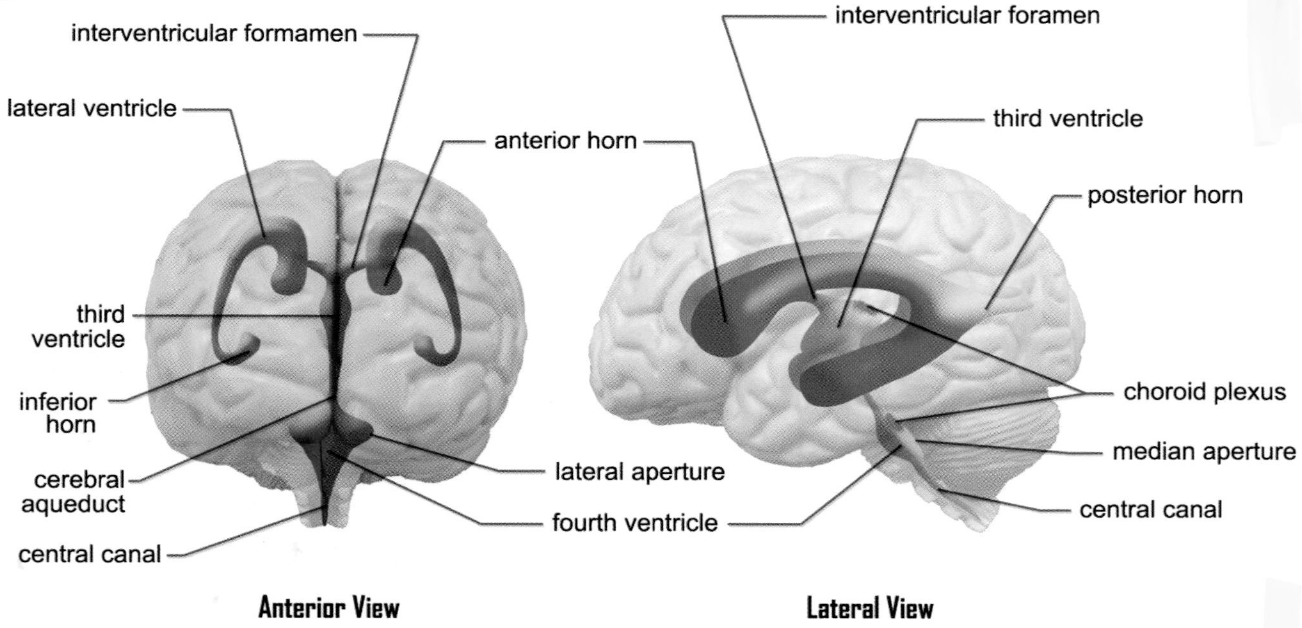

Figure 13-7 **Ventricles in the Brain**

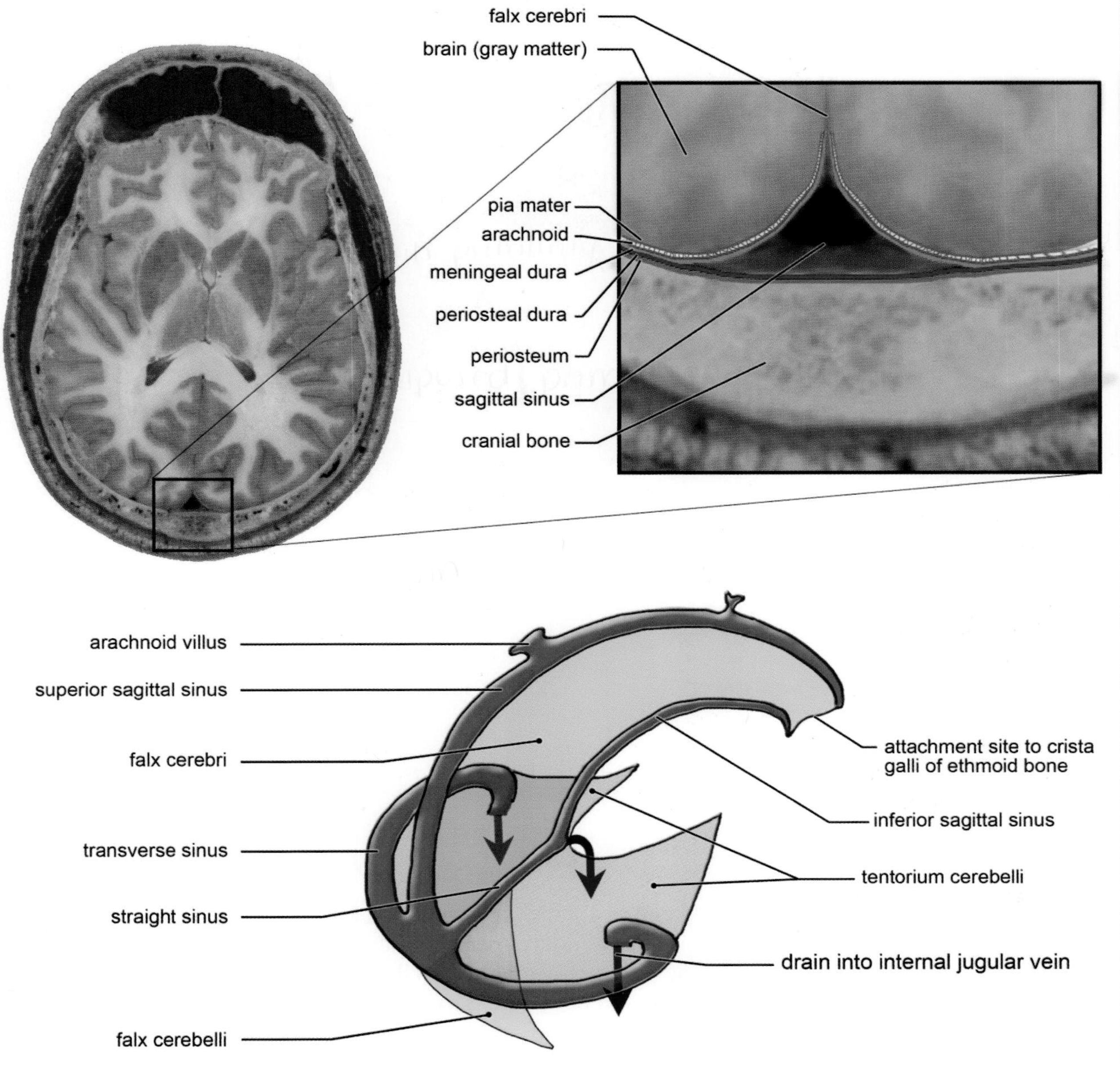

Meninges of the Brain

Figure 13-8

The Ventricles & CSF

Deep within the brain are four fluid-filled cavities called **ventricles** (Figure 13-7). These chambers produce and circulate the fluid within them called *cerebral spinal fluid (CSF)*. Most of the CSF is produced by the **choroid plexus**, a tangled mass of capillaries hanging from the roof of the third and fourth ventricles.

CSF is similar to blood plasma but with fewer proteins. It's produced by ependymal cells which filter the blood plasma and create a blood-brain barrier. The fluid fills the interior of the brain and surrounds the brain exteriorly, acting like a fluid cushion that supports and protects the delicate neural tissue.

The CSF produced by the ependymal cells first fills the **lateral ventricles** and then passes from the **third ventricle** through the **cerebral aqueduct** into the **fourth ventricle**. The fluid may then leave the fourth ventricle through the **median** and **lateral apertures** to enter the subarachnoid space surrounding the outside of the brain. From

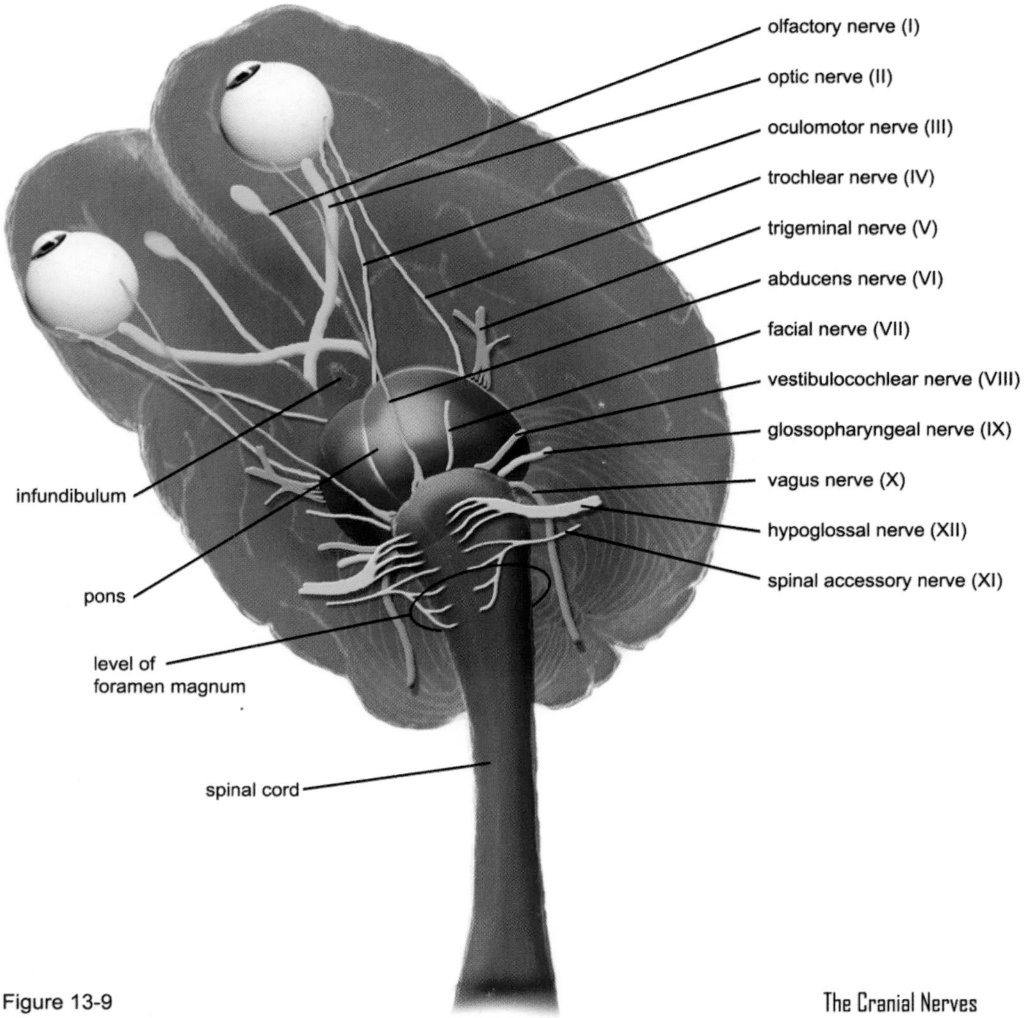

Figure 13-9 The Cranial Nerves

there the fluid exits through the **arachnoid villi** to reinter the blood. Alternatively, the fluid may leave the fourth ventricle passing through the **central canal** of the spinal cord. The CSF passing through the central canal circulates back up to the cranium on the outside of the spinal cord, entering the arachnoid space and finally the blood.

Meninges of the Brain

The brain is protected by several layers of connective tissue coverings called **meninges** (singular = *meninx*). The outermost layer is the **dura mater** (Figure 13-8; see also Figure 13-5). This layer is the thickest and most durable – almost like leather in texture. The dura mater surrounding the brain is divided into two parts – the **periosteal dura** fused with the periosteum of the cranial bones, and the **meningeal dura** deep to the periosteal layer. These two layers are fused in all but three places where the meningeal layer penetrates deep into the brain case. At the **falx cerebri**, the meningeal dura dips into the sagittal fissure and attaches to the crista galli of the ethmoid bone. The cavity created by the separation of the dural layers at this point is called the **superior sagittal sinus**, which collects and drains blood from surrounding brain tissue. At the **falx cerebelli** the meningeal dura delves inward between the two hemispheres of the cerebellum. At the **tentorium cerebelli** the meningeal dura separates the cerebellum and the cerebrum. In each case, blood collects in the surrounding sinuses (**sagittal sinuses**, **straight sinus**, **transverse sinuses**) and drains into the internal jugular veins.

The middle meninx is called the **arachnoid mater**. This weblike tissue has threadlike projections that span the tissue. The *arachnoid space* between the threads are filled with cerebral spinal fluid (CSF). Projections of the arachnoid called arachnoid villi penetrate the dura mater and

*menigitis = infection Of meninges
Dura
arachnoid
Pia
> superficial to deep

Cranial Nerve:	Type:	Major Functions:
I - Olfactory	Sensory	smell
II - Optic	Sensory	vision
III - Oculomotor	Motor	eyelid and eyeball movement
IV - Trochlear	Motor	innervates superior oblique turns eye downward and laterally
V - Trigeminal	Mixed	chewing face & mouth touch & pain
VI - Abducens	Motor	turns eye laterally
VII - Facial	Mixed	controls most facial expressions secretion of tears & saliva taste
VIII Vestibulocochlear (auditory)	Sensory	hearing equillibrium sensation
IX - Glossopharyngeal	Mixed	taste senses carotid blood pressure
X - Vagus	Mixed	senses aortic blood pressure slows heart rate stimulates digestive organs taste
XI - Spinal Accessory	motor ~~Mixed~~	controls trapezius & sternocleidomastoid controls swallowing movements
XII - Hypoglossal	Motor	controls tongue movements

Oh once one takes the anatomy final very good vacations seem heavenly

Sensory/motor: Some say many money but my brother says big brains matter more

The Cranial Nerves

Table 13.1

provide a route for CSF to drain into the venous blood supply.

The innermost meninx is the **pia mater**. This exceptionally thin covering is fixed tightly to the surface of the neural tissue of the brain.

An infection of the meninges is called *meningitiis*. This condition can be life-threatening because the infection may spread to the neural tissue in the brain.

Cranial Nerves

Like the spinal nerves, the cranial nerves are part of the peripheral nervous system (PNS).

There are 12 pair of cranial nerves, numbered I-XII with Roman numerals and named according to their functions (Figure 13-9). They are numbered anteriorly-to-posteriorly (when several nerves appear in the same frontal plane they are numbered medially-to-laterally). All 12 pair of cranial nerves service the head and neck region with the exception of cranial nerve X (the vagus nerve) which penetrates into the thorax and abdomen to serve visceral organs in those body cavities. Five of the cranial nerves are *mixed nerves*, containing both afferent and efferent fibers. Cranial nerves I, II and VIII are purely sensory, while cranial nerves III, IV, VI and XI are primarily motor.

The cranial nerves and their functions are summarized in Table 13-1. The information in that table should be committed to memory. A mnemonic that's often used to memorize the order of the nerves is "*O*h, *O*nce *O*ne *T*akes *T*he *A*natomy *F*inal, *V*ery *G*ood *V*acations *A*re *H*eavenly." The first letter of each word in the mnemonic is the same as the first letter for each cranial nerve, in order.

* memorize nerve
>names / Roman numerals
>types (sensory/motor/mixed)
>major functions *

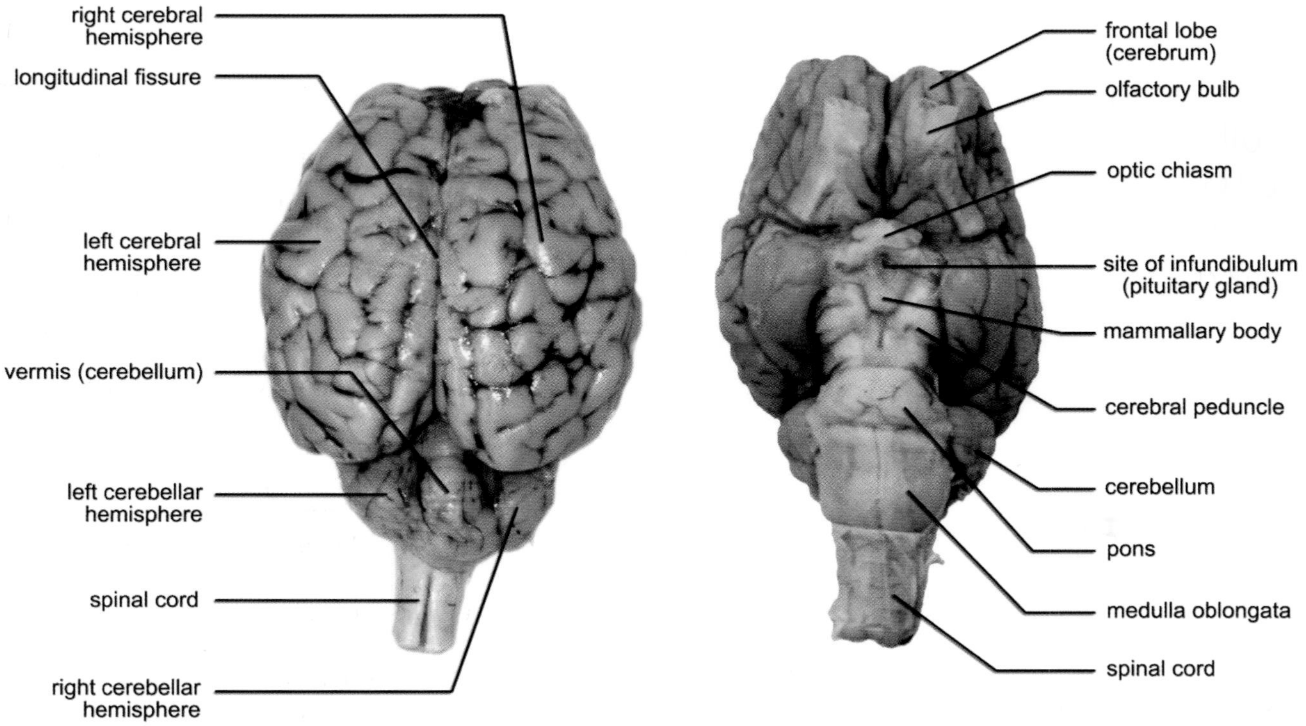

Figure 13-10 **The Sheep Brain**

Activity 1: Examine a Model of the Human Brain

1. Obtain a model of the human brain. Using the figures in this exercise, identify the major structures of the brain.

Activity 2: Identify the Cranial Nerves

1. Using Figure 13-9 and / or a model of the human brain, identify the locations of the cranial nerves.
2. Using Table 13-1, study the functions of the cranial nerves.

Activity 3: Sheep Brain Dissection

External Brain Structures

1. Obtain a preserved sheep brain from your instructor.
2. Observe the undissected sheep brain from the lateral perspective. Compare the appearance of the sheep brain to the human brain (Figure 13-4). How is the sheep brain similar to the human brain? How is it different?
3. A portion of the dura mater is often left on the ventral aspect of the sheep brain. Observe the color, texture and durability of the dura mater. Is it easy or difficult to tear this connective tissue?
4. Examine the bulb-like olfactory bulbs on the ventral aspect of the sheep brain. How does the olfactory bulb of the sheep brain compare to those on the human brain?
5. Identify the optic nerve (cranial nerve II), optic chiasma and optic tracts.
6. In life, the pituitary gland is located immediately posterior to the optic chiasma. This endocrine gland is attached to the hypothalamus of the brain by a thin stalk called the infundibulum. The gland is not present on the preserved sheep brains, but the infundibulum (or part of it) is usually visible just posterior to the optic chiasma.
7. The mammillary body is immediately posterior to the infundibulum. Notice that the mammillary body in the sheep is a single large eminence, but is two rounded projections on the human brain.
8. Identify the cerebral penducles on the sheep midbrain, just posterior to the mammillary body. These are fiber tracts connecting the midbrain to the cerebrum.

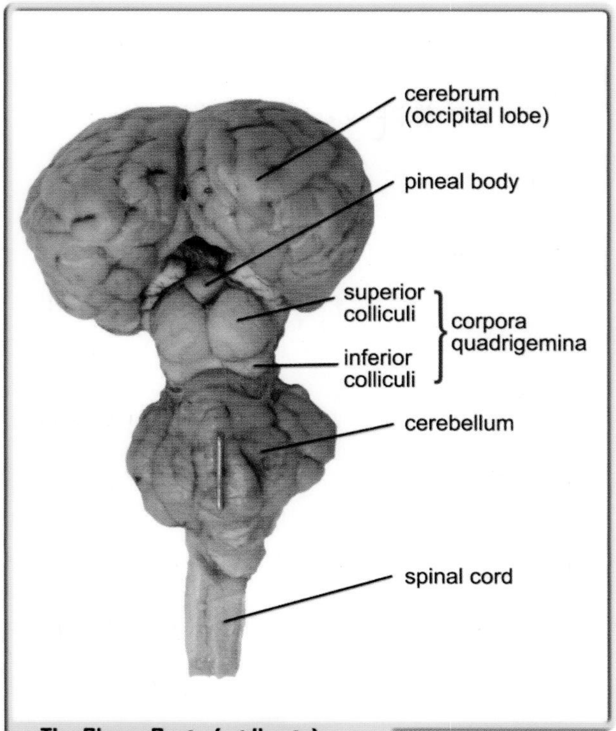

The Sheep Brain (midbrain) Figure 13-11

9. Identify the pons and medulla oblongata posteriorly on the ventral aspect of the brain. These are called the hindbrain on sheep.
10. Observe the dorsal (i.e., superior) aspect of the sheep brain. Notice the deep longitudinal fissure separating the left and right hemispheres of the cerebrum. Carefully pry apart the two hemispheres of the cerebrum to expose the corpus callosum.
11. Carefully examine the cerebellum of the sheep brain and compare it to the human brain. Notice that the sheep cerebellum is not divided longitudinally like the human cerebellum. Consequently, which dural fold is missing in the sheep brain that is present in the human brain? Notice also the large vermis of the sheep cerebellum.
12. Expose the dorsal surface of the midbrain by gently separating the cerebellum from the cerebrum. Identify the large superior colliculi and the smaller inferior colliculi of the corpora quadrigemina. Identify the pineal body just anterior to the superior colliculi.

Internal Brain Structures

1. Place the sheep brain on the dissecting tray ventral side down.
2. Make a sagittal cut through the brain in a superior to inferior direction (through the longitudinal fissure, corpus callosum and vermis of the cerebellum).
3. Two tracts of white matter are evident: the corpus callosum superiorly and the fornix inferiorly. Between them is a thin membrane called the septum pellucidum that separates the left and right lateral ventricles.
4. The rather large pineal body is seen inferior to the posterior aspect of the corpus callosum. Beneath the pineal body anteriorly is the intermediate mass of the thalamus. Beneath the

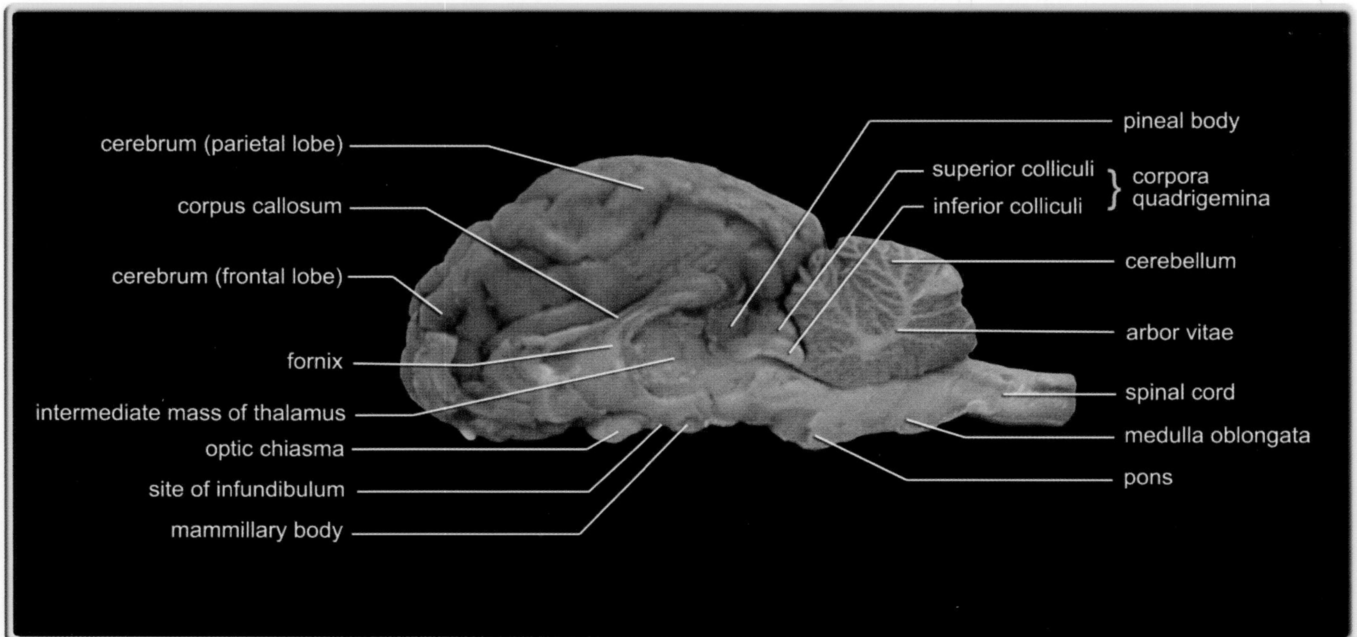

Figure 13-12 The Sheep Brain (midsagittal)

pineal body posteriorly is the corpora guadrigemina.

5. The midsagittal cut through the cerebellum reveals a treelike structure of white matter called the arbor vitae. The cerebellum monitors and smoothes skeletal muscle movements.
6. If possible, obtain a second sheep brain and make a frontal cut which passes through the optic chiasma.
7. Notice the lateral ventricles separated by the thin septum pellucidum. The roof of the ventricles is formed by the corpus callosum; the floor of the ventricles by the fornix. Identify the third ventricle beneath the fornix.

Sensory/motor	Nerve names
Some	~~Optre~~ Olefactory
say	Optic
marry	Oculomotor
Money	Throclar
But	Trigamal
my	Abdcus
Brother	Facial
says	Vaso
Big	Glossopharygnal
Brains	Vagus
matter	Spinal awarness?
more	Hypoglossal

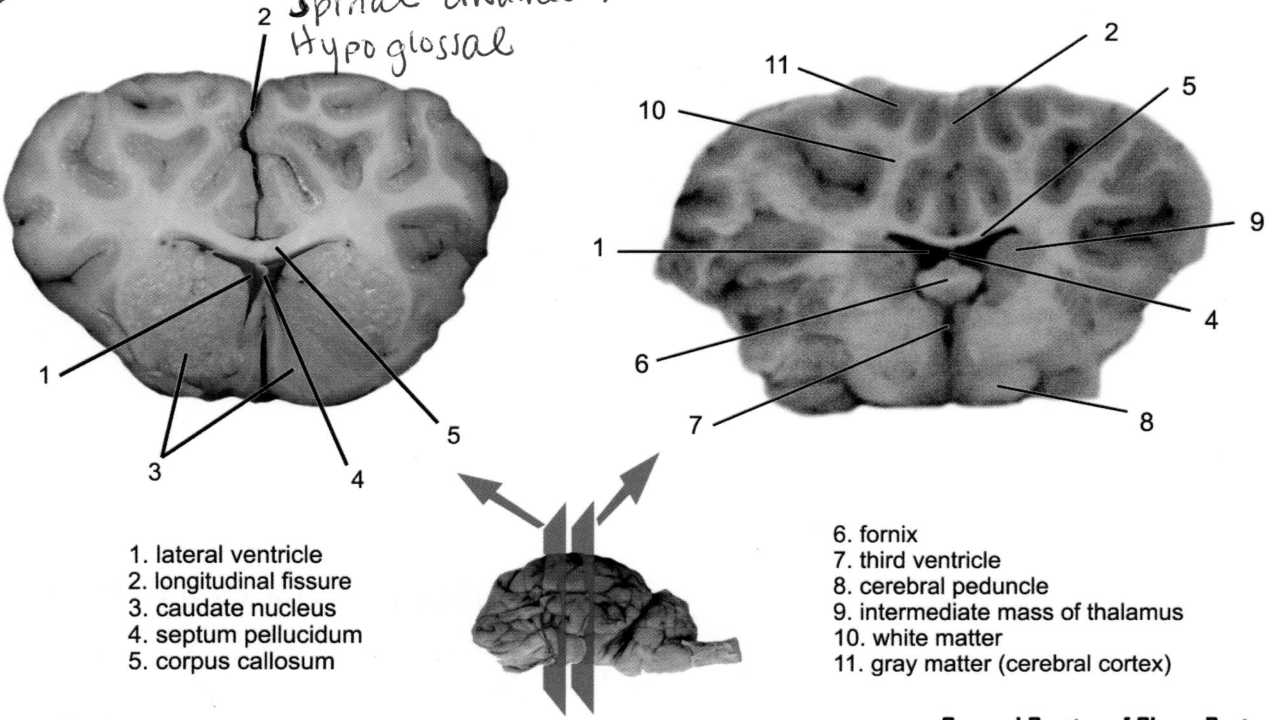

Figure 13-13

Coronal Section of Sheep Brain

exercise 14

the NERVOUS system

- spinal cord & spinal nerves -

He said to the paralyzed man, "I tell you, get up, take your mat and go home."

Luke 5:24

Like telephone lines, the peripheral nerves of the body transmit information quickly over long distances. If a line is broken, communication will cease.

As discussed in Exercise 13, the Nervous System is divided into two major divisions: the *central nervous system* (*CNS*) and the *peripheral nervous system* (*PNS*). The CNS is composed of the brain and spinal cord; the PNS is composed of the peripheral nerves and ganglia. In the previous exercise we discussed the brain and cranial nerves. Here, we'll examine the spinal cord (part of the CNS) and the spinal nerves (part of the PNS). Spinal nerves issue from the spinal cord to innervate the neck, trunk and limbs (Figure 14-1). These nerves send motor commands from the CNS to distal parts of the body and delivery sensory information from receptors to the central nervous system. The spinal cord, essentially an extension of the brain, controls simple movements of the limbs and coordinates spinal reflexes.

Regions of the Spinal Cord

There are 31 pair of spinal nerves arising from the spinal cord (Figure 14-2). The spinal cord and spinal nerves are divided into regions in the same way as the bony vertebral column (see exercise 7). You will recall from studying the skeletal system that the 24 vertebrae are divided as follows: 7 cervical vertebrae, 12 thoracic vertebrae and 5 lumbar vertebrae. In addition, 4-5 sacral vertebrae fuse to form the sacrum. The spinal nerves are named like the vertebrae from top-to-bottom within each region. For example, C1, C2 and C3 are the first three spinal nerves in the cervical region; T1, T2 and T3 are the first three nerves in the thoracic region. The first seven spinal nerves are named according the vertebrae below the nerve (for example, spinal nerve C4 is above vertebra C4). The remaining spinal nerves are named according to the vertebra above the nerve (for example, spinal nerve T7 is below vertebra T7; see the inset in Figure 14-2). The transition occurs at vertebra C7: Spinal nerve C7 is above vertebra C7 and spinal nerve C8 is below it. Thus, there are 7 cervical vertebrae but 8 cervical spinal nerves.

Throughout its length the spinal cord is approximately the size of a dime. However, there are obvious enlargements in the cervical and lumbar regions and a tapering off of the cord at its terminus inferiorly (Figure 14-2). Spinal nerves from the **cervical enlargement** innervate the upper limbs and spinal nerves from the **lumbar enlargement** innervate the lower limbs. These areas of the spinal cord receive sensations and coordinate spinal motor reflexes for the limbs.

The spinal cord itself ends in the upper lumbar region. It tapers off at the **conus medullaris** until only a thin filament remains – the **filum terminale** – attached to the sacrum. The lumbar and sacral spinal nerves travel inferiorly through the vertebral foramina before emerging from their respective intervertebral or sacral formamina. The roughly parallel strings of nerve fibers resemble a horse tail and is aptly named the **cauda equina**.

Like the brain, the spinal cord is protected by three layers of connective tissue sheaths – the *spinal meninges*. The delicate *pia mater* is the deepest sheath, the *arachnoid* forms the middle sheath, and the tough *dura mater* forms the outer sheath.

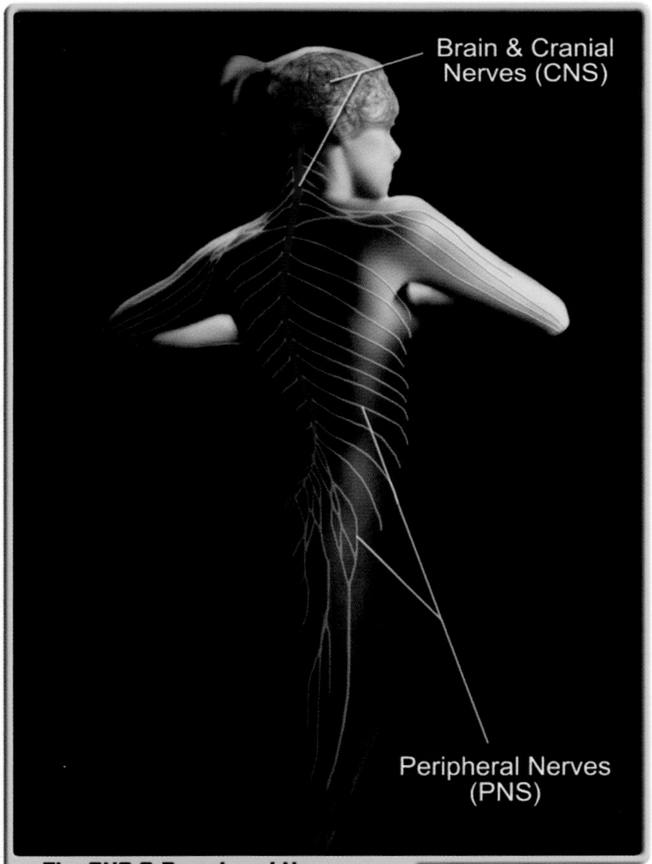

The CNS & Peripheral Nerves

Figure 14-1

Spinal Cord in Cross-Section

In cross section, the spinal cord reveals distinct white and gray matter (Figure 14-3). As in the brain, **gray matter** in the spinal cord is composed primarily of neuron cell bodies and unmyelinated processes; **white matter** consists primarily of

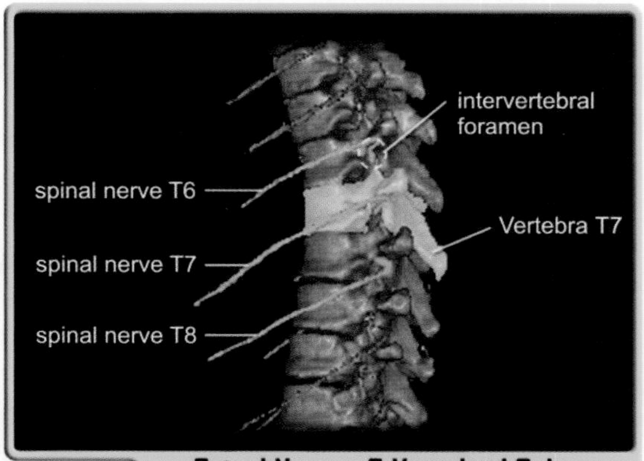

Spinal Nerves & Vertebral Column

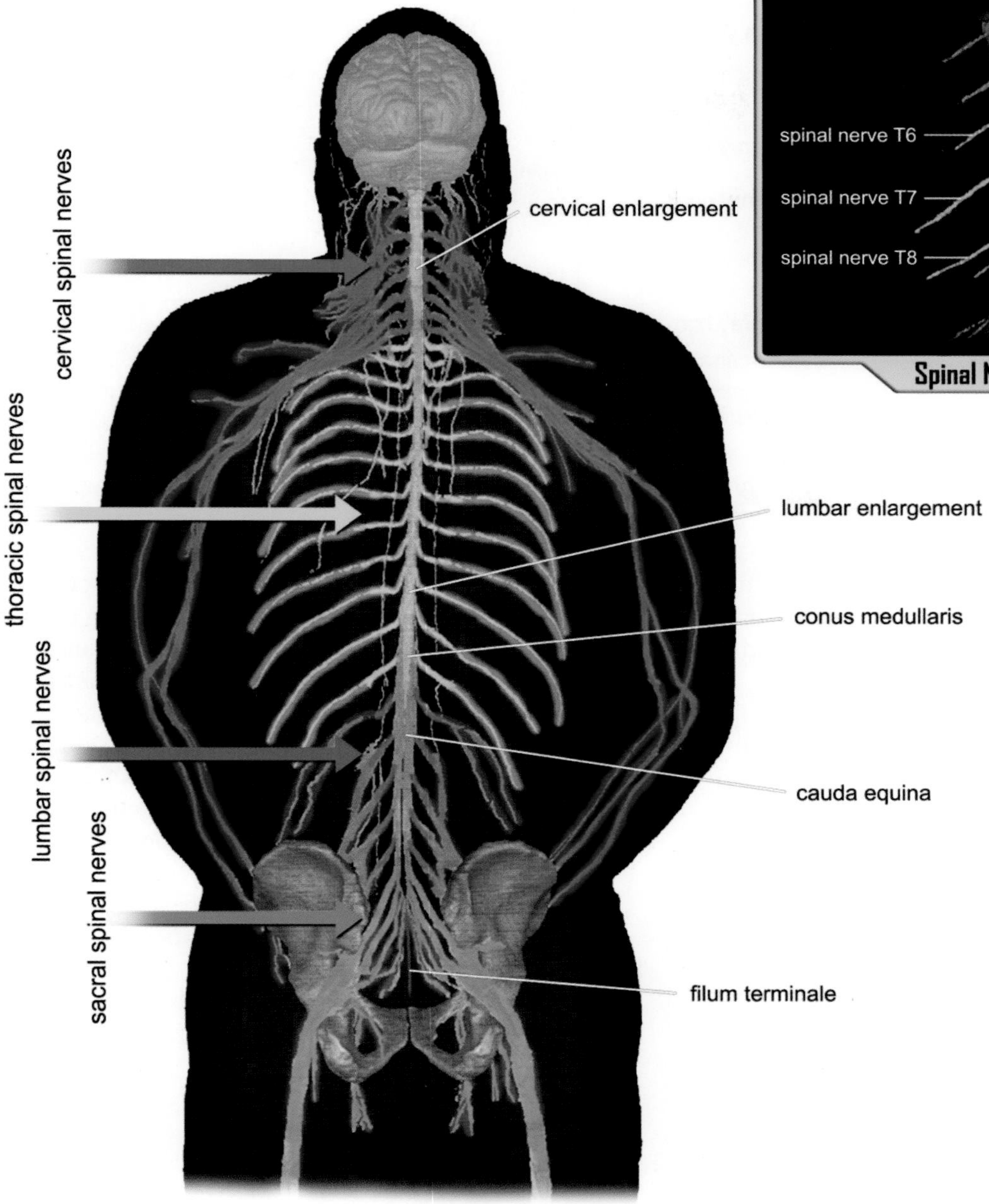

Figure 14-2 **The Spinal Cord & Spinal Nerves (posterior view)**

myelinated axons. The white matter is found superficially surrounding the butterfly-shaped gray matter. The gray matter is pierced by the **central canal** passing through the center of the cord throughout its length. The cord is nearly bisected by two fissures – the **anterior median fissure** ventrally and the **posterior median sulcus** posteriorly. The left and right halves of the spinal cord are symmetrical. The gray matter in each half displays three enlargements called horns; thus, there are six horns total. The **anterior gray horn** is the largest and is nearly completely surrounded by white matter. The **posterior gray horn** is smaller than the anterior horn and often has a thin wing extending to the outer edge of the spinal cord. The **lateral horn** is the smallest of the horns and is often absent in the thoracic and cervical regions. The two halves of gray matter are joined by the **anterior gray commissure** and **posterior gray commissure** near the central canal.

The white matter of the spinal cord is divided into **columns**, also called **funiculi** (Figure 14-3). These columns consist of myelinated axons traversing up and down the spinal cord. Like the

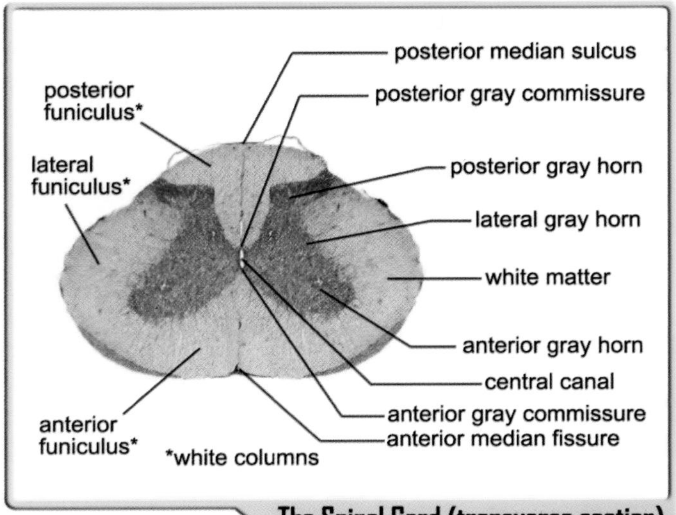

Figure 14-3 **The Spinal Cord (transverse section)**

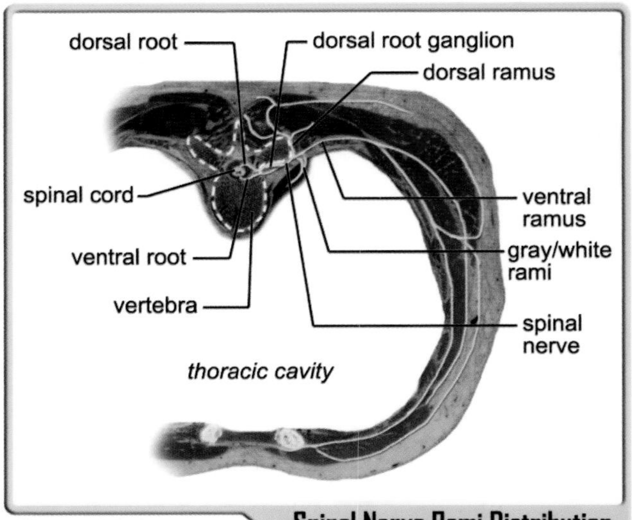

Figure 14-5 **Spinal Nerve Rami Distribution**

horns, there are three columns in each half of the spinal cord and they are named according to their locations (**anterior white column**, **lateral white column** and **posterior white column**).

Spinal Nerve Roots & Rami

The 31 spinal nerves are *mixed nerves*, containing both sensory and motor fibers. As shown in Figure 14-4, sensory fibers in each nerve enter the spinal cord on its dorsal side as the **dorsal root**. Motor nerve fibers exit the spinal cord on its ventral side as the **ventral root**. These two roots converge to form the actual spinal nerve. Upon exiting the bony vertebral column, the spinal nerve soon branches into four **rami** (Figure 14-5). Thus, the spinal nerve is only a centimeter or two long in most cases. The **dorsal ramus** innervates the skin and muscles of the back; the **ventral ramus** follows the body wall to innervate the skin & muscles of the thorax and abdomen, as well as the upper and lower limbs. The **white and gray rami** (together called the *rami communicantes*), serve the visceral organs of the thoracic and abdominal cavities.

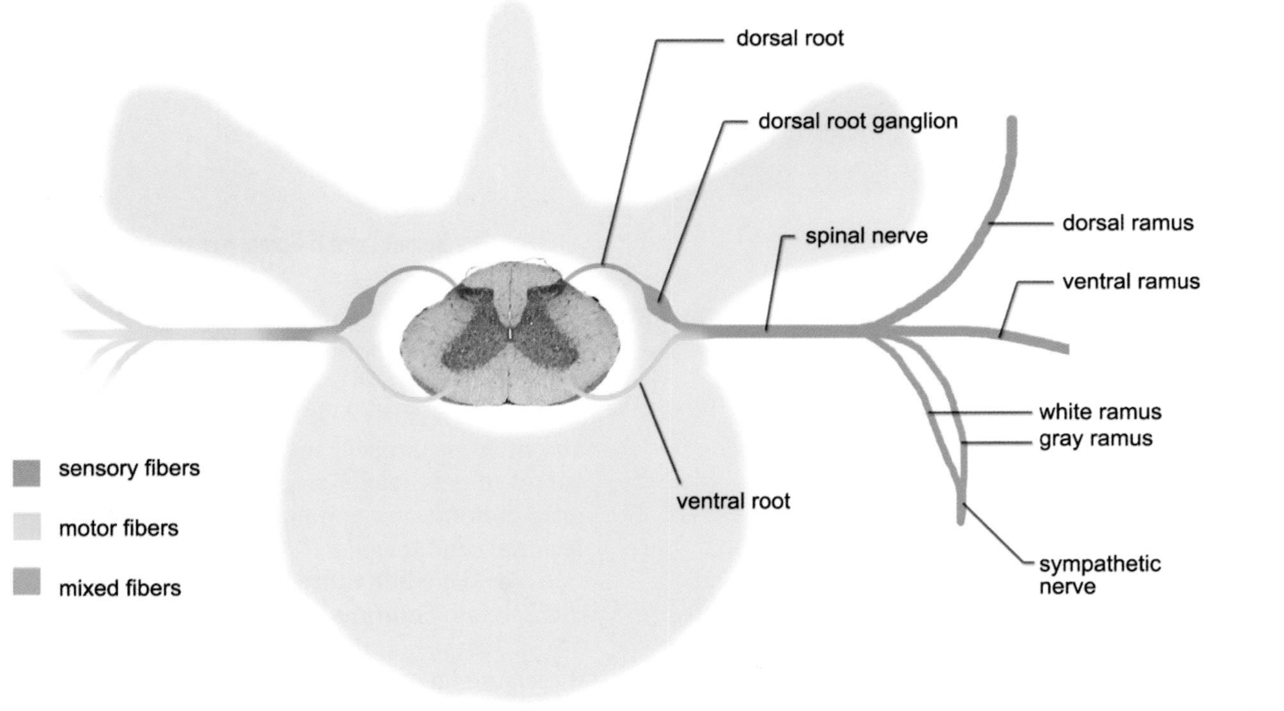

The Spinal Cord Roots & Rami Figure 14-4

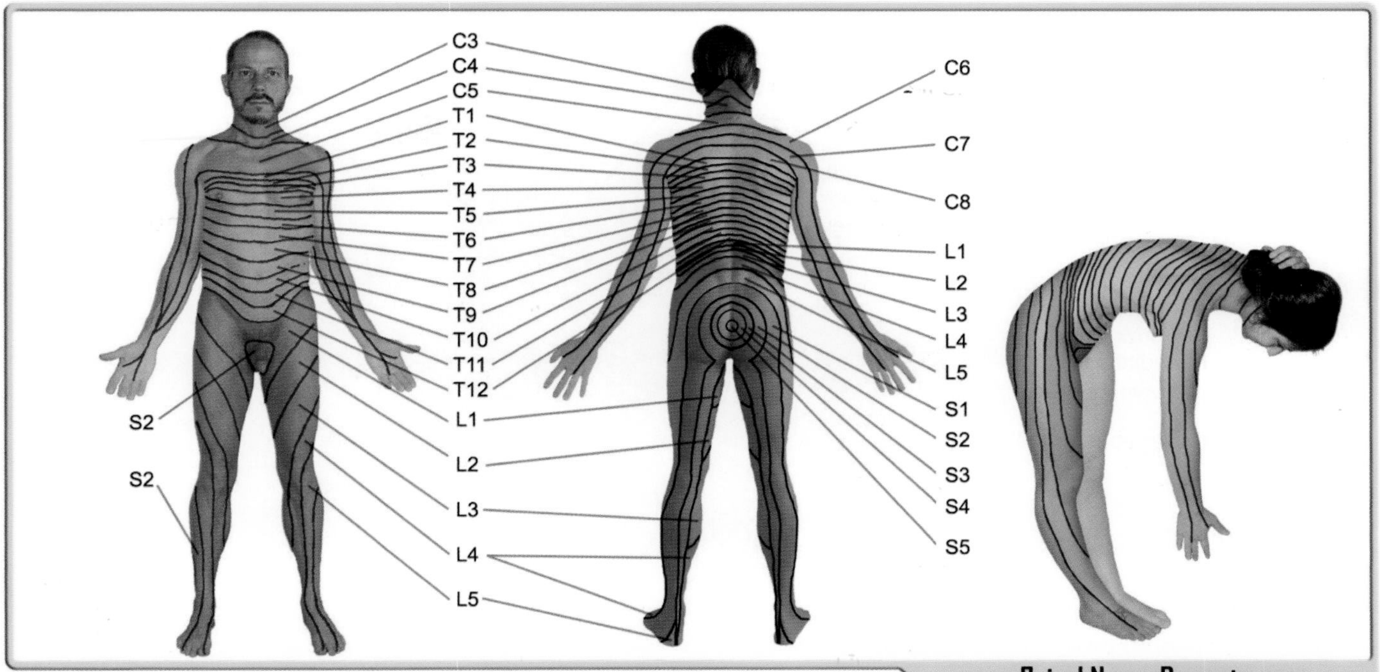

Figure 14-6 Spinal Nerve Dermatomes

The Dermatome

Each spinal nerve serves a particular "zone" of the body called a **dermatome** (Figure 14-6). The cervical spinal nerves serve the superior portion of the back and the posterior portion of the upper limbs. The thoracic spinal nerves serve the body trunk and anterior aspect of the upper limbs. The lumbar spinal nerves serve the inferior portion of the back and the anterior aspect of the lower limbs. The sacral spinal nerves serve the buttocks, perineum & pubic regions and the posterior aspect of the lower limbs. The dermatome lines appear curvy and somewhat haphazzard when viewed from the anatomical position, but the logic of spinal nerve distribution is clearly seen when one is bent over (as a four-legged animal).

Nerve Plexus

The ventral rami of spinal nerves T2-T12 pass anteriorly as the *intercostal nerves* to innervate the anterior and lateral portions of the body trunk. These nerves run parallel courses without intermingling. The ventral rami of the most superior and inferior spinal nerves, however, intertwine with one another forming complex networks called *plexuses*, from which emerge peripheral nerves that serve the limbs.

The **cervical plexus** (Figure 14-7) is formed by the interweaving of ventral roots C1 through C4. The major nerve emerging from this

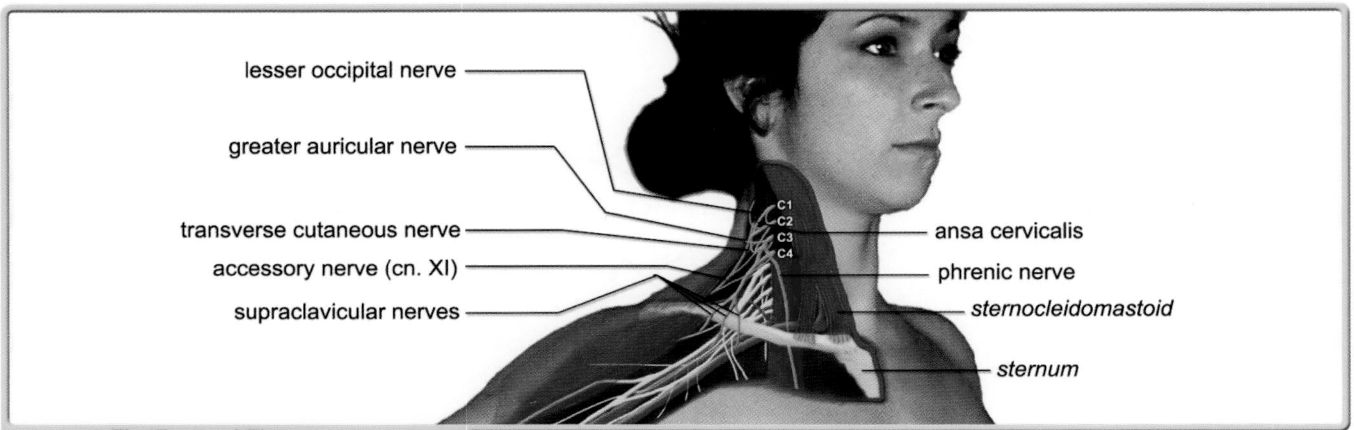

The Cervical Plexus Figure 14-7

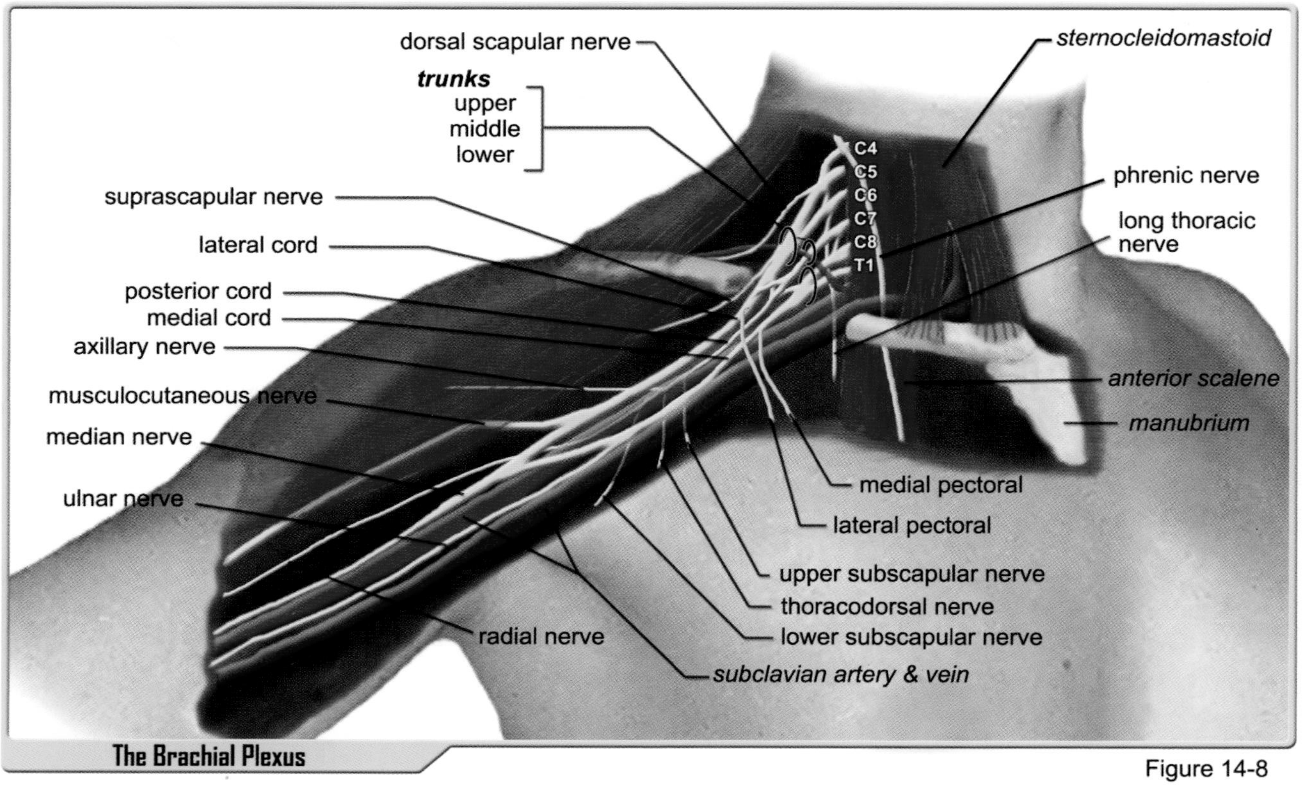

The Brachial Plexus

Figure 14-8

Innervation by the Brachial Plexus

ulnar nerve
intrinsic hand muscles
flexor muscles of anterior forearm

median nerve
palmaris longus
flexor muscles of anterior forearm

radial nerve
brachioradialis
supinator

musculocutaneous nerve
biceps brachii
brachialis
coracobrachialis

axillary nerve
teres minor
deltoid

long thoracic nerve
serratus anterior

pectoral nerves
pectoralis major & minor

suprascapular nerve
supraspinous
infraspinatus

dorsal scapular nerve
rhomboids
levator scapulae

subscapular nerves
subscapularis
teres major

thoracodorsal nerve
latissimus dorsi

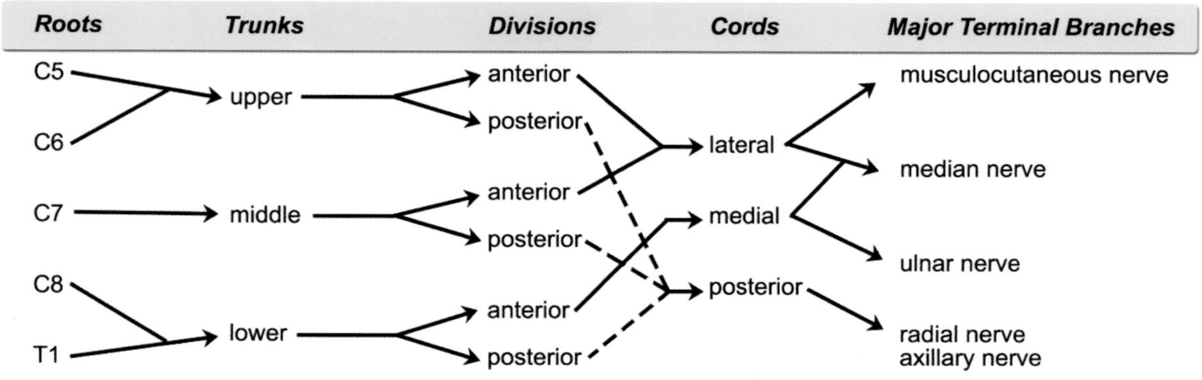

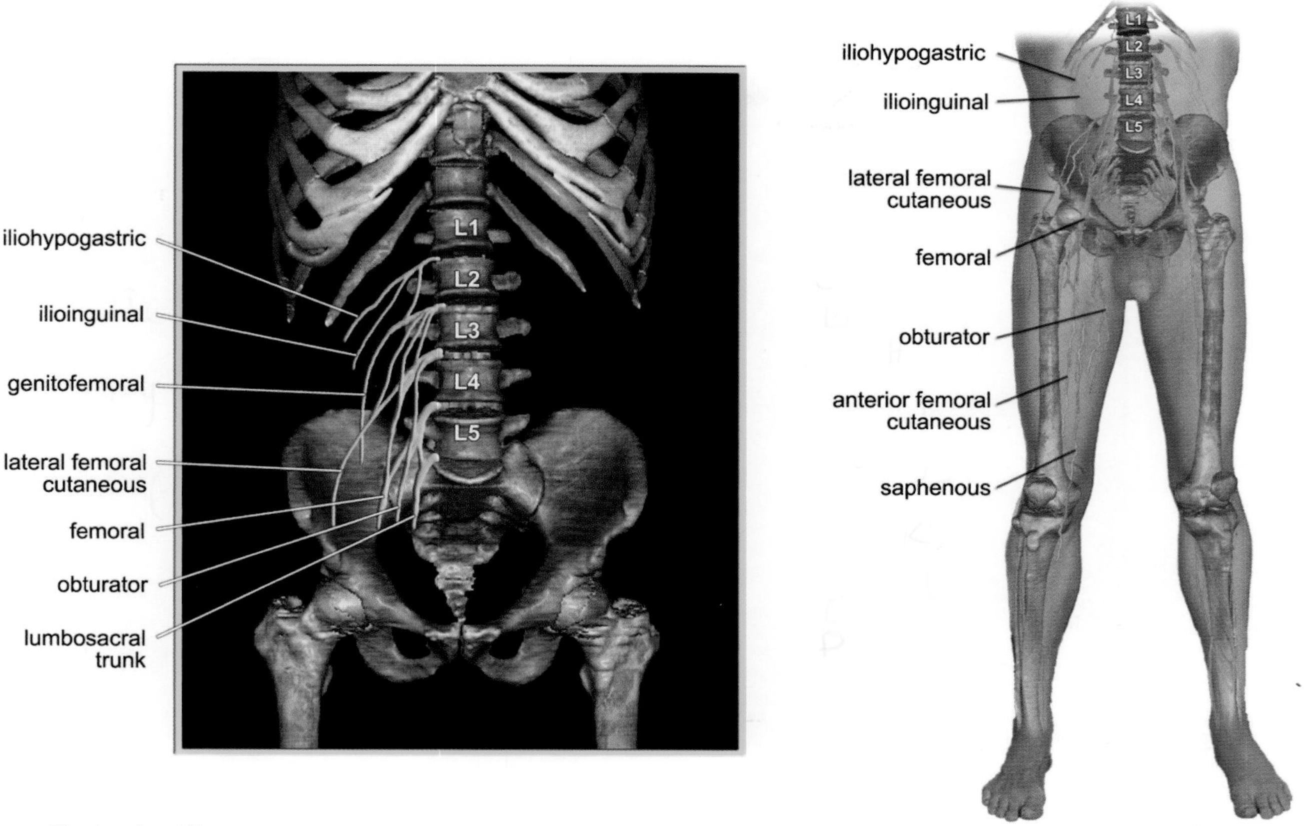

The Lumbar Plexus

Figure 14-9

plexus is the ***phrenic nerve*** which innervates the diaphragm. The primary danger of a broken neck is severence of the phrenic nerve (or the roots supplying it) and subsequent paralysis of the diaphragm muscle. Without immediate intervention, the victim of such an accident will die of asphyxiation.

The **brachial plexus** (Figure 14-8) is formed from the ventral roots of spinal nerves C5 through T1. These rami first converge into three **trunks** (upper, middle and lower) which subsequently branch into anterior and posterior divisions. These divisions interweave to form three **cords** (lateral, posterior and medial). The three cords then branch into five major peripheral nerves: ***musculocutaneous nerve***, ***median nerve***, ***ulnar nerve***, ***radial nerve*** and ***axillary nerve***.

The radial nerve supplies the extensor muscles of the forearm and can be injured by excessive use of crutches. The ulnar nerve courses down the posteriomedial aspect of the arm around the medial epicondyle of the humerus. Striking the ulnar nerve at the elbow can lead to strange sensations commonly referred to as "hitting the funny bone."

The **lumbar plexus** (Figure 14-9) arises from the ventral rami of nerves L1 through L4. The largest nerve emerging from this plexus is the ***femoral nerve*** which innervates the anterior thigh muscles.

The **sacral plexus** (Figure 14-10) is formed from the ventral rami of nerves L4 through S4. Peripheral nerves arising from this plexus innervate the buttocks and virtually all of the leg and foot. The largest nerve from this plexus (indeed, the largest nerve of the body) is the ***sciatic nerve***. Entering the leg through the greater sciatic notch of the os coxae, this nerve divides into the ***common fibular nerve*** and the ***tibial nerve***. *Sciatica* is a term referring to stabbing pains generated by damage to the sciatic nerve. If the sciatic nerve is severed, there is a total loss of motor function in the leg.

Referred Pain

Nociceptors are free nerve endings in the body that detect painful stimuli. Visceral pain results from nociceptors activated in visceral organs due to damage or a disturbance of homeostasis. Often,

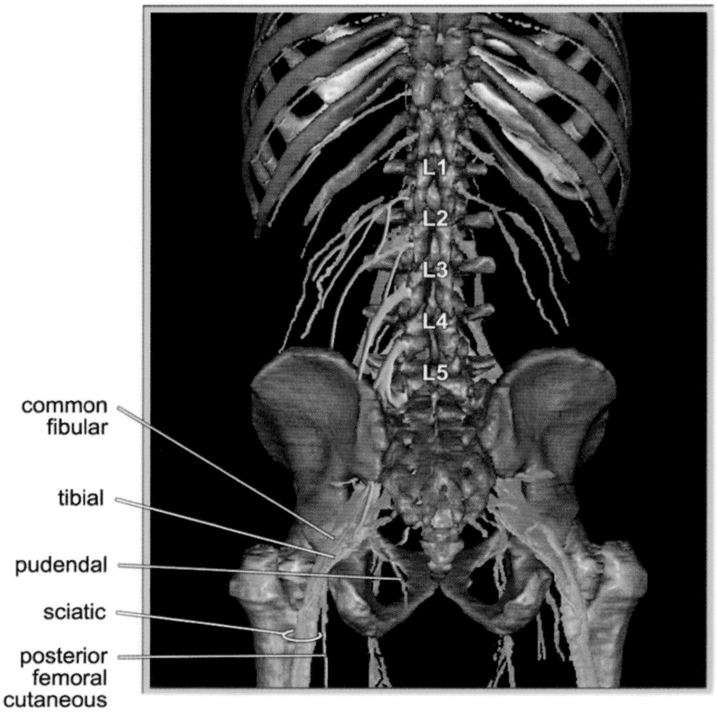

The Sacral Plexus

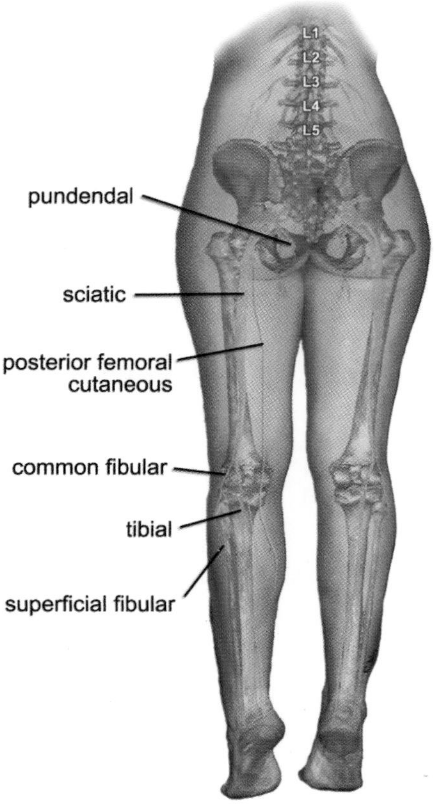

Figure 14-10

pain originating from deep visceral organs is perceived as coming from superficial skin areas, a phenomenon known as **referred pain** (Figure 14-11). This phenomenon is generally caused by nerves innervating the visceral organ being in close proximity to nerves serving more superficial areas. Recall that conscious awareness is achieved only by the cerebrum. Sensory fibers from visceral organs do not generally reach the cerebrum, but electrical activity of sensory neurons from visceral nociceptors may activate near-by neurons that do reach the cerebrum. The conscious perception of pain is then felt coming from a different part of the body. For example, sensory fibers from the heart as well as those from the skin over the heart and the medial aspect of the left arm all enter the spinal cord as the same segments (T1 through T5). Activation of the sensory nerves from the heart stimulate activity in the nerves serving the shoulder and arm. As a result, pain from a heart attack is often felt as pain in the left shoulder and arm.

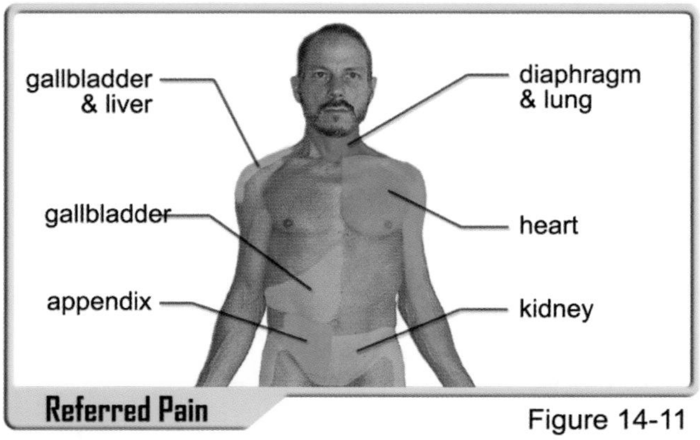

Referred Pain

Figure 14-11

Activity 1: Examine a Model of the Human Spinal Cord

1. Obtain a model of the human spinal cord and spinal nerves. Using the figures in this exercise, identify the major structures of the cord and nerves.

Activity 2: Identify the Nerves Plexuses

1. Identify each of the four major nerve plexuses and the main peripheral nerves emerging from each plexus.

exercise 15

the NERVOUS system

- reflex physiology -

My steps have held to your paths, my feet have not slipped.

Psalm 17:5

Reflexes help us maintain our posture and balance.

There are two "command-and-control" systems in the human body: The endocrine system and the nervous system. Both systems exert control over the other body systems by gathering information about the outside world or internal environment and then appropriately altering the activities of other systems in response to that information. Some responses are extremely complex and deliberate, others are simple and automatic. ***Reflexes*** are comparatively simple.

A neural reflex is a *rapid, predictable, automatic response to a stimulus*. They can be considered as "preprogrammed" responses to frequent stimuli. Most neural reflexes are designed to *i*) maintain our balance and posture to keep us from falling, *ii*) protect us from imminent danger or injury, or *iii*) carry out routine but complex motor patterns such as walking and chewing.

The Reflex Arc

Reflexes consists of five steps called the ***reflex arc*** (Figure 15-1). The components of a reflex arc are as follows:

know these

1. **Receptor** – Detection of a stimulus by a sensory *receptor*.
2. **Sensory relay** – Detection of stimulus is relayed to the CNS via a *sensory neuron*.
3. **Integration** – The CNS processes the sensory information and determines a response.
4. **Motor command relay** – The CNS issues a motor command via a *motor neuron*.
5. **Effector** – The body responds to the stimulus through the action of an *effector*.

Types of Reflexes

There are several ways to classify reflexes, and any particular reflex may be classified as more than one type. We will consider two classification schemes: ***monosynaptic*** vs ***polysynaptic*** (based on the number of neurons involved) and ***somatic*** vs ***autonomic*** (based on the nervous system involved).

Monosynaptic vs Polysynaptic

The simplest neural reflexes are monosynaptic reflexes. These reflexes require only two neurons – a sensory neuron and a motor neuron – joined by a single synapse. The synapse between the neurons

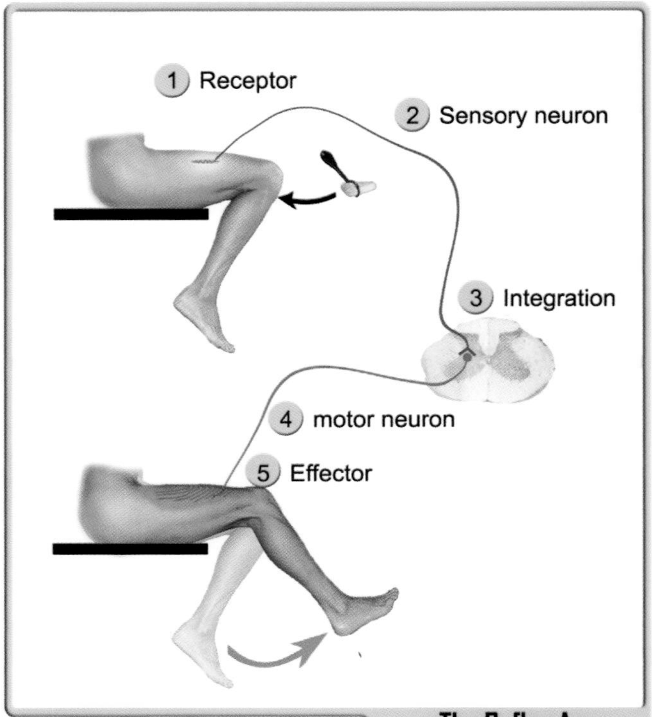

Figure 15-1 **The Reflex Arc**

represents the integration center. Obviously, not much integration can occur in such a simple system. Consequently, monosynaptic reflexes produce extremely stereotypical responses. The patellar (or, knee-jerk) reflex is an example of a monosynaptic reflex (Figure 15-1).

Polysynaptic reflexes contain at least one interneuron between the sensory neuron and the motor neuron and thus possess two or more synapses. Most polysynaptic reflexes actually possess hundreds or thousands of interneurons and many synaptic connections. As a result, complex integration of sensory data is possible and more diverse responses may be elicited. In general, the more synapses there are, the more varied the response may be. Unfortunately, the more synapses that are involved, the slower the response will be.

Somatic vs Autonomic

Reflexes may be either somatic or autonomic. Somatic reflexes involve the skeletal muscles as primary effectors. Most somatic reflexes are postural reflexes aimed at helping you maintain your balance and posture.

Autonomic reflexes involve glands, smooth muscles or visceral organs as primary effectors. These reflexes are used to coordinate certain metabolic functions or protect you from harm. For

mono - based on # of neurons
→ reflexes are faster & integrated in the spinal cord

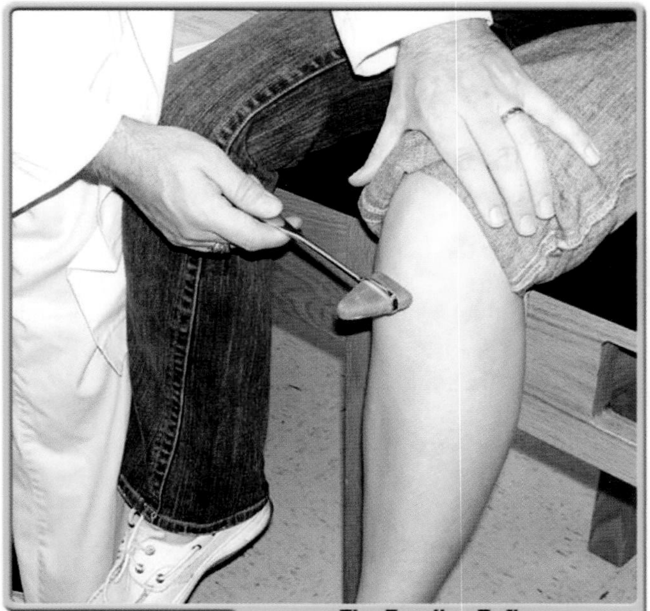

Figure 15-2 The Patellar Reflex

example, smooth muscles in the eye (i.e., the iris) reflexively constrict the size of the pupil when the eye is exposed to bright light. This defensive reflex protects the retina of the eye from damage by too much light energy.

Acquired Reflexes

Acquired reflexes are *learned through experience*. All complex motor skills (such as driving, skiing, typing, or even walking) depend on aquired reflexes. Walking, for example, is achieved primarily by reflexes of the spinal cord. The main involvement of the brain is only to issue the command to walk; the actual details of moving the proper muscles at the proper time is achieved by the spinal cord. In simplistic terms, walking is achieved when the brain initiates a fall forward and spinal reflexes then manipulate the arms and legs to prevent the fall. The result is a step forward.

Reflex Activities

Students should work in pairs and perform the following reflexes on one another. In each case, the subject should try not to think too much about the reflex being tested since most reflexes (even spinal reflexes) can be easily inhibited by the brain.

Activity 1: Patellar reflex (Figure 15-2)

1. The subject should sit comfortably on the lab bench, as far back as possible so the entire thigh is supported by the bench.
2. The examiner should lightly tap the patellar tendon with the broad side of a rubber reflex hammer. Best results are obtained by striking the tendon between the patella and tibial tuberosity. If the reflex is small or absent, try stiking the tendon a little harder.
3. After observing one or two "knee jerk" reactions, have the subject clasp their hands and squeeze them together as tightly as possible and simultaneously count backwards from ten to zero. While the subject is couting, strike the patellar tendon again. Was there any difference in the reflex observed?

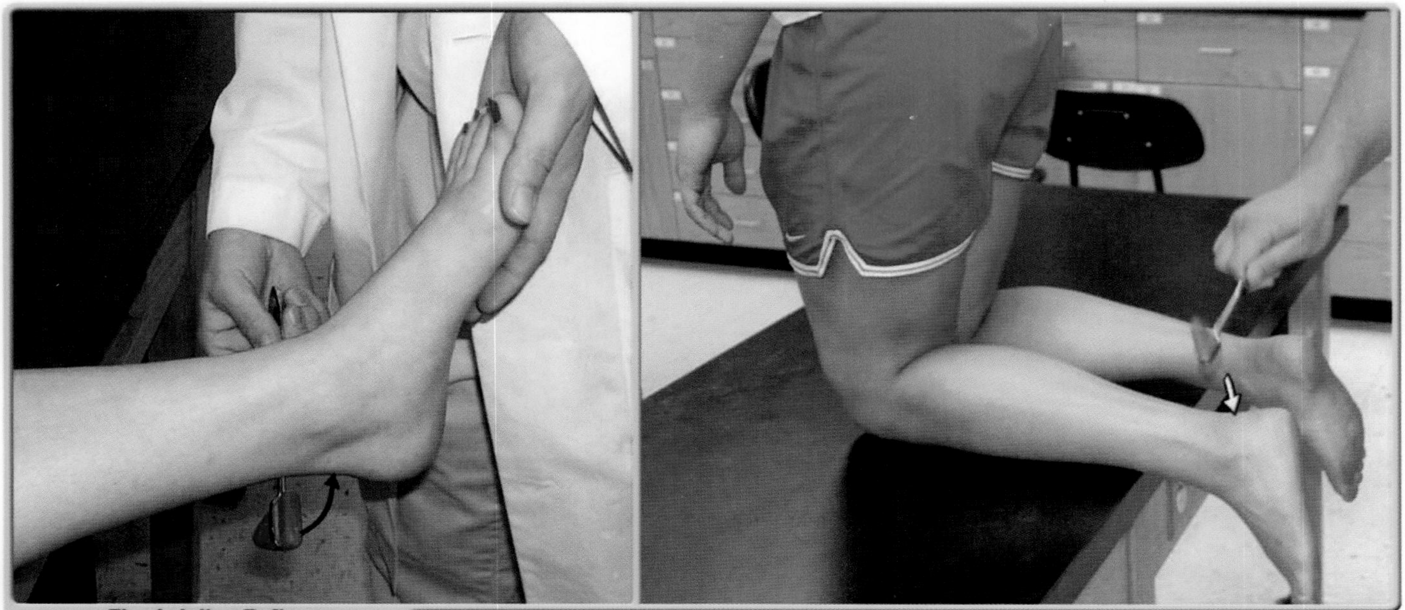

The Achilles Reflex

Figure 15-3

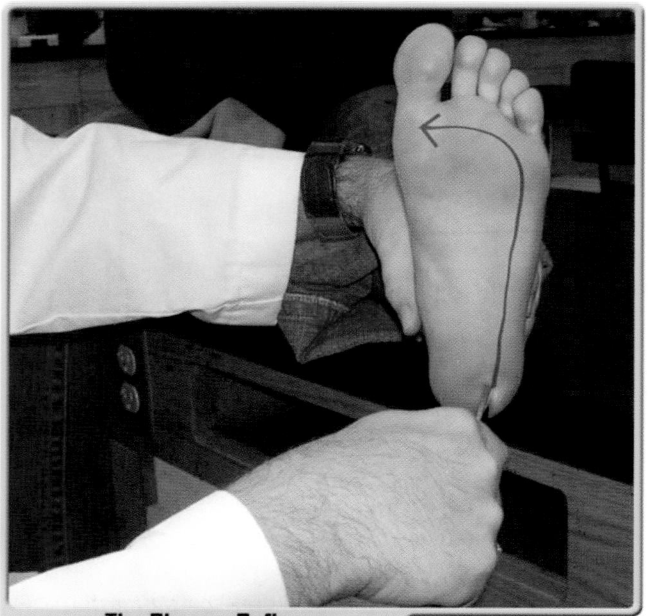

The Plantar Reflex Figure 15-4

Activity 2: Achilles Reflex (Figure 15-3)

1. Have the subject remove a shoe and sock and sit on the lab bench with only their foot and ankle extending over the edge of the bench (i.e., the weight of the leg should be supported by the bench).
2. The subject must completely relax their leg and foot.
3. The examiner should press on the bottom of the foot at the base of the toes to slightly dorsiflex the subject's foot.
4. Holding the relaxed foot in a dorsiflexed position, the examiner should strike the achilles tendon superior to the calcaneus. What reflex action is observed?
5. Alternatively, have the subject "stand" on their knees as shown in Figure 15-3 and gently tap the Achilles tendon.

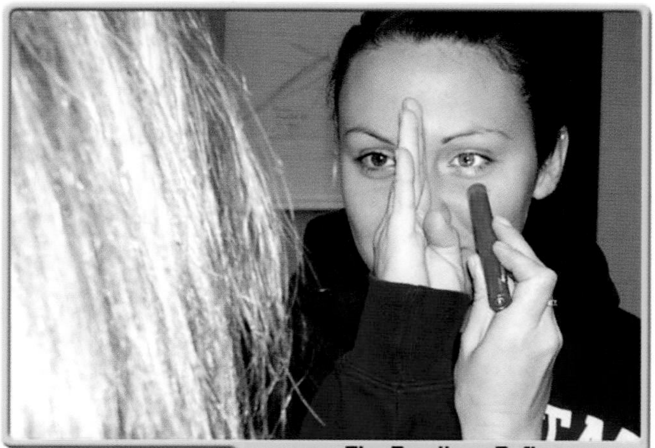

Figure 15-5 The Pupillary Reflex

Activity 3: Plantar Reflex (Figure 15-4)

The plantar, cremaster and abdominal reflexes are *superficial cord reflexes* that involve both the spinal cord and the brain. Perform the plantar reflex as follows:

1. Have the subject remove a shoe and sock and sit on the lab bench with only their foot and ankle extending over the edge of the bench (i.e., the entire leg should be on the bench).
2. The subject must completely relax their leg and foot.
3. Using the handle of a reflex hammer, the examiner should firmly trace a path from the heel along the lateral edge of the foot and along the base of the toes. During this movement, the toes of the subject should reflexively curl. If the toes flare out instead (the *Babinski sign*), this is taken as an indication of spinal cord injury.

Activity 4: Crossed Extensor Reflex

(Note: Only the examiner should read these instructions)

1. The subject should sit comfortably in a chair with both hands resting on the lab bench, palms facing upward and eyes closed.
2. Attempt to catch the subject by surprise by quickly jabbing the index finger of one hand with a sharp pencil or toothpick (*not hard enough to bleed!*).
3. What was the response of the subject? Did both hands move or just one hand? How did the hand(s) move?

Activity 5: Pupillary Light Reflex (Figure 15-5)

The pupillary light reflex is an autonomic, cranial nerve reflex. This exercise is best done under dim light conditions.

1. Use a light pen to shine a light into one of the subject's eyes. How does the pupil respond to the light?
2. Now use your hand to shield one eye from the light. Shine the light onto one eye. Does the eye in the dark respond to the light?
3. Repeat this experiment using blue and Red LED lights and a remote control (IR light). Were the results the same?

Activity 6: Ciliospinal Reflex

The ciliospinal reflex is a cranial nerve reflex.

1. The examiner should gently stroke the skin (or even just the hairs) on the back of the right side of the subject's neck.

2. While stroking the neck, observe the subject's pupils. Why do you think the pupils respond to this stimulus?

Activity 7: Gag Reflex (Figure 15-6)
(Note: The gag reflex should not be performed on those with a strong regurgitation reflex)
1. Using a long cotton swab or tongue depressor, the examiner should lightly stroke one side of the subject's uvula. The uvula should move upwards in response.

Activity 8: Salivary Reflex
(Note: Subjects for this exercise must not be eating, drinking, or chewing gum)
We continuously produce saliva and swallow it throughout the day. The amount of saliva we produce can be reflexively altered by stimulation of taste receptors on the tongue.
1. The subject should refrain from swallowing for 2 minutes.
2. After 2 minutes, collect the saliva by spitting into a test tube.
3. Place 3-4 drops of lemon juice onto the subject's tongue. The subject should mix the juice in their mouth for several seconds, then swallow it.
4. The subject should again refrain from swallowing for another 2 minutes.
5. After 2 minutes, collect the saliva by spitting into a second, clean test tube.
6. Compare the amounts of saliva collected before and after application of lemon juice on the tongue. Did the lemon juice stimulate or inhibit salivary gland activity?

Activity 9: Corneal Reflex
1. Have the subject look away from you without blinking.
2. *Gently* touch the subject's cornea with a soft tisue or wisp of cotton.
3. What reflexive action occurred in response to the cornea being touched?

Activity 10: Acquired Reflex
1. The subject will repeatedly catch a meter stick dropped by the examiner between their index finger and thumb. Record the centimeters or inches that pass through the subject's fingers each time before catching the meter stick.
2. After several iterations of step #1, repeat the procedure except play word-association at the same time. The examiner will say a word just before dropping the meter stick; the subject must say the first word that comes to mind *before* catching the stick.
3. Did the subject's performance catching the stick improve with each iteration? How did introducing word-association affect the subject's performance?

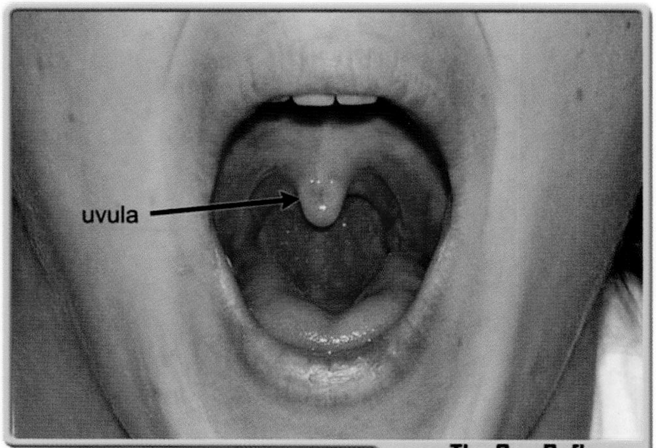

Figure 15-6 **The Gag Reflex**

exercise 16

the NERVOUS system

- general senses -

But Jesus said, "Someone touched me; I know that power has gone out from me." Then the woman, seeing that she could not go unnoticed, came trembling and fell at his feet. In the presence of all the people, she told why she had touched him and how she had been instantly healed.

Luke 8:46-47

Many millions of receptors make our skin extremely sensitive to touch.

Many different types of sensations are delivered to the central nervous system (CNS) every second of every day. Those sensations originate at sensory receptors that are sensitive to particular types of stimuli. Sensations that arise from highly complex sensory receptors restricted to special sense organs are called the *special senses*. There are five special senses: vision, hearing, equilibrium, taste and smell. Sensations that arise from simple receptors widely scattered throughout the body are called the *general senses*. There are literally hundreds (perhaps thousands) of general senses in the body, responding to such diverse stimuli as temperature, pressure or pH. In this exercise, we will examine a few general senses and the receptors that provide those sensations.

General sensory receptors are classified according to the source of their stimulus. **Exteroceptors** respond to stimuli in the external environment and thus monitor the external conditions in which our bodies are immersed. They respond to such stimuli as heat, cold, touch, pain and pressure. They may be as simple as free nerve endings in the skin (which detect pain) or as complex as the photoreceptors of the eye (which detect light).

Interoceptors monitor the internal condition of the body. *Chemoreceptors* are interoceptors that respond to changes in blood pH, tissue oxygen levels and many, many other types of chemical stimuli. *Visceral stretch receptors* monitor distension of visceral organs like the GI tract.

Proprioceptors are a distinct class of interoceptors that provide postural information to the CNS. Proprioceptors are embedded in skeletal muscles, tendons, ligaments and joints.

Structure of General Sensory Receptors

A number of distinct types of general sensory receptors have been identified in the skin (Figure 16-1). The simplest of these are ***free nerve endings*** (also called *naked nerve endings*). These are dendrites of neurons that terminate in the papillary layer of the dermis or the lower strata of the epidermis. They are primarily responsible for detecting pain; however, free nerve endings associated with hair roots detect movement of hair. In addition, free nerve endings associated with **Merkel cells** detect light touch.

More complex skin receptors include Paccinian corpuscle and Meissner's corpuscle. These receptors are called *encapsulated receptors* because the nerve endings are enclosed within layers of connective tissue. The **Meissner's corpuscle** is located in the papillary layer of the dermis and detects light touch. The **Pacinian corpuscle** is located deeper in the dermis and detects forceful pressure and vibrations.

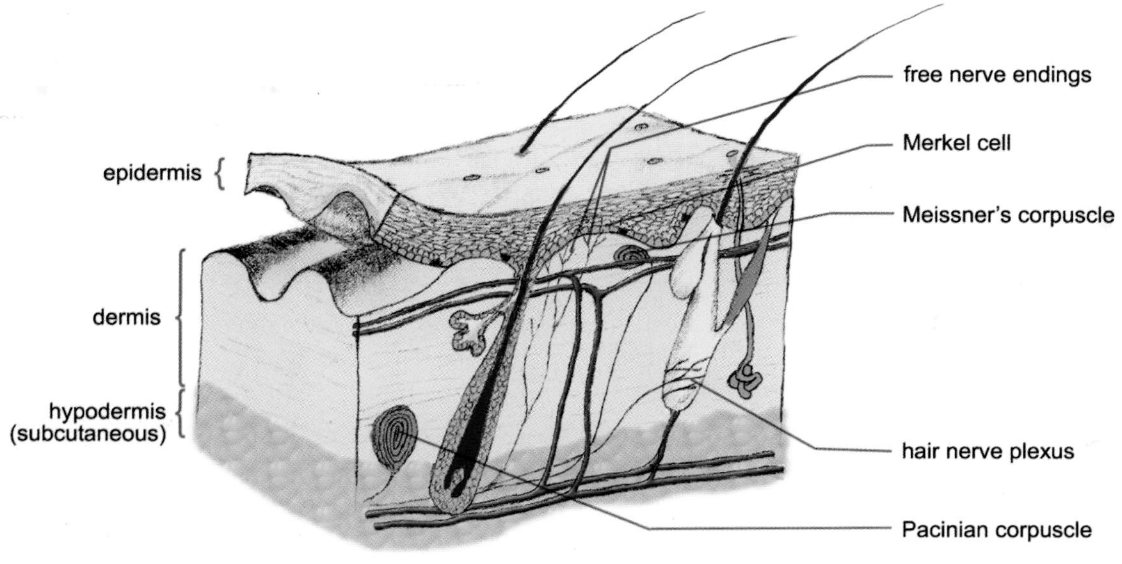

Figure 16-1

Exteroceptors of the Skin

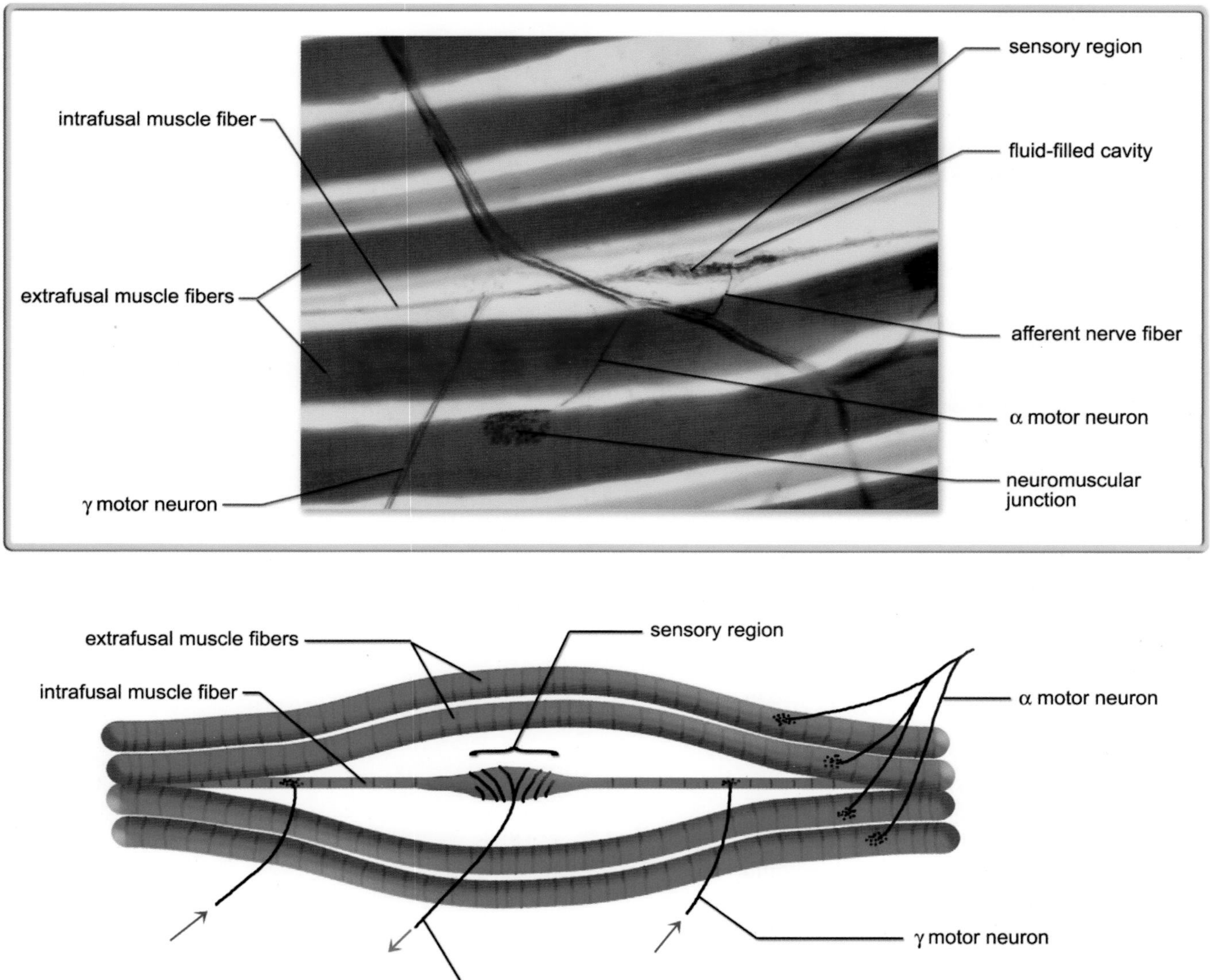

Figure 16-2 **The Muscle Spindle**

Proprioceptors

Proprioceptors monitor the position of the body's parts in space. They are found scattered throughout moving parts of the body, such as muscles and tendons. They ensure that skeletal muscles don't become over-stretched, and they're important components of stretch reflexes. The **muscle spindle** is the sensory receptor for stretch reflexes (Figure 16-2).

The muscle spindle is composed of **intrafusal fibers** embedded within regular fibers of the skeletal muscle (called **extrafusal fibers**). The intrafusal fibers are innervated by a **sensory neuron** whose dendrites spiral around the **sensory region** of the muscle spindle. This neuron continuously sends pulses of action potentials to the CNS and motor neurons (**α motor neurons**) → extra fusal fiber innervating the extrafusal fibers When the muscle spindle is compressed (due to skeletal muscle contraction) the pulse frequency is slowed. In response, α motor neurons decrease muscle tone in the extrafusal fibers and the muscle relaxes. When the muscle spindle is stretched the pulse frequency increases. Higher frequencies cause the α motor neurons to increase contraction in the extrafusal fibers.

These stretch reflexes help maintain body position and posture. For example, when standing the muscles of the leg maintain your balance. If you lean forward, the calf muscle is stretched. The stretched muscle spindles cause the calf muscle to contract pulling you back to the upright position. If

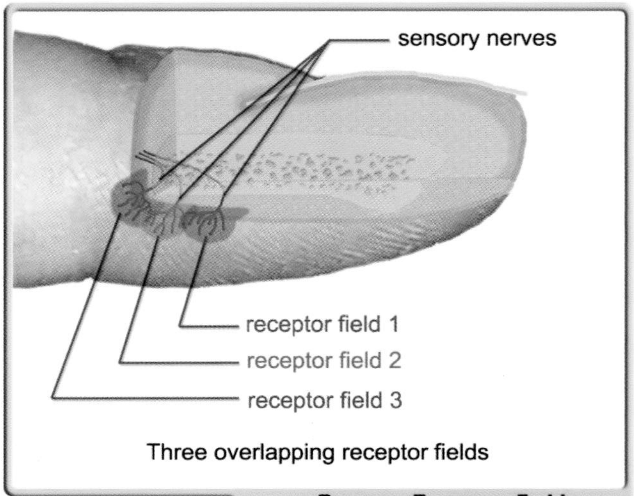

Figure 16-3 **Sensory Receptor Fields**

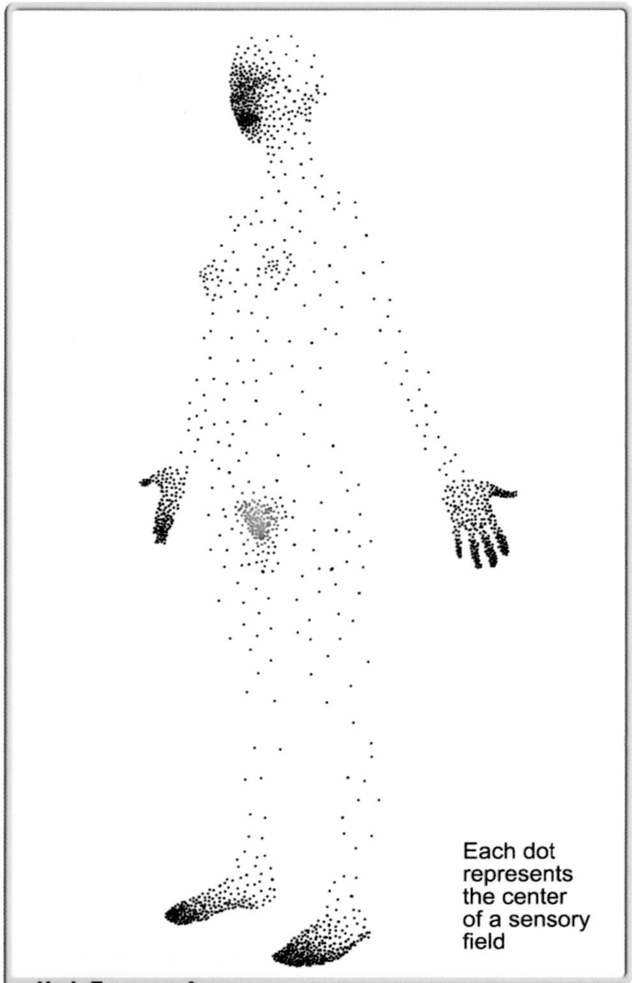

High Sensory Areas Figure 16-4

you lean back, the muscle spindle in the calf is compressed causing the calf muscle to relax. At the same time, muscle spindles in the shin and thigh are stretched and cause anterior leg muscles to contract, pulling you forward.

If you think carefully about the above description of muscle spindle action, you may discover an interesting dilemma. If compression of a muscle spindle causes the extrafusal fibers of a skeletal muscle to relax, how is willful muscle contraction attained? The brain might tell the biceps muscle to contract, for example, but as the muscle shortens the muscle spindle is compressed causing the biceps to relax. Without some solution to this problem, muscle spindles would make it impossible to contract any skeletal muscles in your body. This problem is overcome by the brain sending contraction signals to both the extrafusal fibers and the intrafusal fibers. The γ **neuron**—intrafusal fiber delivers contraction information to the intrafusal fiber of the muscle spindle. As the surrounding muscle contracts, each end of the intrafusal fiber is told to contract, as well. As a result, the length of the sensory region is unchanged, as is the pulse frequency. In this way, the whole muscle can shorten without triggering relaxation of the extrafusal fibers.

Receptor Physiology

Sensory receptors are *transducers* because they convert stimuli to action potentials. This is true of all sensory receptors, regardless of the type of stimuli being detected. Since *all* stimuli are converted to action potentials, how are unique stimuli – such as touch, sound and light – distinguished by the brain? The answer to this question must lie in the destination of the action potential. Action potentials received by one area of the cerebral cortex are interpreted as pain, for example, while those received by a different area of the cortex are interpreted as touch (or taste or sound).

Most pain and touch receptors are located in the skin. Each sensory receptor in the skin monitors a particular area called the *receptor field* (Figure 16-3). The smaller the receptor fields and the more dense the sensory receptors, the more sensitive that area of the body will be to stimuli. On the other hand, the larger the receptor fields and the less dense the receptors, the less sensitive that area of the body will be to stimuli. Only a few parts of the body have dense receptors with small receptor fields, as shown in figure 16-4.

Most skin receptors become desensitized when exposed to constant stimulation. For

Testing Tactile Localization

Body area tested	Error of localization (millimeters)
back of hand	
palm of hand	
fingertip	
back of neck	
top of foot	
bottom of foot	

example, you feel your clothes (or a wristwatch) when you first put them on but quickly forget about them. Likewise, when you step into an air-conditioned room it may feel cool at first, but you stop noticing the temperature after just a few minutes. This phenomenon is called *adaptation*.
desensitization to constant stimuli

Activity 1: Histological Examination of Sensory Receptors

1. Obtain microscope slides of a muscle spindle. Observe the extrafusal fibers, intrafusal fibers and the dendrites the sensory neurons coiled around the intrafusal fibers.
2. Obtain a microscope slide of a Golgi tendon organ. These receptors are made of dendrites that branch through the tendon near the muscle attachment site. Stretching of these dendrites trigger action potentials received by the cerebellum of the brain.
3. Obtain a microscope slide of human skin. Observe the Meissner's and Pacinian corpuscles in the dermis layer.

Activity 2: Testing Tactile Localization

1. Obtain two fine-tip pens or markers of different colors and a millimeter ruler.
2. With the subject's eyes closed, the examiner should lightly touch the subject with a marker on the dorsum (i.e., back) of the hand.
3. Without looking, the subject should use the other marker to try to touch the exact same spot. Use the millimeter ruler to measure how close the subject came to the original mark.

location ____________ [ ] 2 cm

location ____________ [ ] 2 cm

location ____________ [ ] 2 cm

4. Repeat the test at several locations on the body, such as the palmar side of the hand, the leg, foot, arm, etc.
5. Which parts of the body have the smallest receptor fields (i.e., the "highest touch resolution")?

Activity 3: Density Mapping of Touch Receptors

1. Obtain a sharp pencil, a black marker and a red marker for this exercise.
2. With the black marker, draw a 2-cm x 2-cm square on the subject's forearm.
3. With the subject's eyes closed, use the pencil and *lightly* touch the subject somewhere in the square. Touch the subject in 10 different locations within the square. *Important: Use only a very light touch; you only want to stimulate superficial Meissner's corpuscles.*
4. Using the squares in this manual, generate a "map" of sensory receptors by recording the location of felt touches with the black marker and the location of unfelt touches with the red marker.
5. Repeat this test on several different parts of the body.

Activity 4: Two-Point Discrimination Test

1. Using a caliper, forceps, or two toothpicks, test the ability of the subject to differentiate two distinct touch sensations. The caliper contains two fine tips whose separation can be carefully controlled. If the two touches occur within a single receptor field, it will be perceived as a single touch. If the two touches occur in

separate receptor fields, they will be felt as two simultaneous touches.

2. With the caliper or forceps tips close together, lightly touch the subject on the arm. Separate the tips slightly and touch the subject again in the same place. Continue separating the tips until the subject feels not one but two touches. Record the distance between the tips.
3. Repeat the above test at different locations on the body, such as the lips, hands (front & back), fingertips, feet (front & back), legs, thighs and stomach. What parts of the body have the highest density of touch receptors?

Activity 5: Demonstrating Sensory Adaptation

1. With the subject's eyes closed, the examiner should place a coin on the subject's forearm.
2. Determine how long (in seconds) it takes for the subject to no longer feel the coin.

Activity 6: Temperature Detection, Part 1

1. Draw a square on your partner's palm with 1-inch (2.5 cm) sides. Prepare a grid by dividing the square into smaller squares with 0.5 cm sides.
2. Have your partner rest the marked palm on the bench top with their eyes closed.
3. Remove a blunt probe from a beaker of hot water (110°F). *Be sure the probe is not hot enough to burn the skin.*
4. Wipe the probe dry and touch your partner's skin on some part of the grid. Ask your partner if the probe feels warm or cold and record the result.
5. While the prove remains warm, randomly test ten locations on the grid. Record your results.
6. Repeat the procedure above using a probe cooled in ice water.

Activity 7: Temperature Detection, Part 2

1. Prepare three beakers of water: ice-cold, lukewarm, and hot (110°F).
2. At the same time, place the index finger of one hand in the hot water and the index finger of the other hand in the cold water.
3. After two minutes, remove both fingers from the water and place them into the beaker of lukewarm water. What temperature is sensed by each finger?

Two-Point Threshold Test

Body area tested	Two-point threshold (millimeters)
face	
back of hand	
palm of hand	
fingertips	
lips	
back of neck	
ventral forearm	

warm

cold

Temperature Dection Grids

exercise 17

the NERVOUS system

- special senses: VISION -

"What do you want me to do for you?" "Lord, I want to see," he replied. Jesus said to him, "Receive your sight; your faith has healed you." Immediately he received his sight and followed Jesus, praising God.

Luke 18:41-43

Vision is something most of us take for granted, yet most of the information we receive concerning the world around us comes through our eyes. Our eyes are beautifully equipped to provide us with information about an object's size, distance, color, luminosity, texture and 3-dimensional shape, as well as its relative position to other objects and its motion – all in real time and in exquisite detail. However, it's the brain that "makes sense" of the flood of sensory information provided by the eyes, and as any Master of Illusion will tell you, appearances are not always reality.

In this lab we'll explore the perception of objects and colors by our eyes, and consider the role the brain plays in interpreting the vast amount of information delivered to it from the eyes. Specifically, we'll examine our ability to see colors when viewed under different environmental conditions, demonstrate color adaptation by our cone cells and lateral inhibition by (primarily) our rods cells; we'll examine how binocular vision helps us establish a 3-D view of the world, and take a look at some familiar objects in unfamiliar ways to demonstrate the role the brain plays in visual interpretation.

In addition to receiving visual information, our eyes play a significant role in the formation of most facial expressions. Because of this, they have sometimes been called the "windows to the soul." Let us now throw open the shutters and explore the fascinating world of vision!

Anatomy of the Eye

The external structures of the eye are shown in figure 17-1. A closable gap, called the **palpebral fissure**, in the skin of the face produces an opening that exposes the anterior surface of the eye to the outside environment (specifically, to light). The medial and lateral junctions of the upper and lower eyelids, or **palpebrae**, are called the **medial canthus** and **lateral canthus**, respectively. The palpebral fissure can be opened or closed at will by lifting or dropping the upper eyelid. Along with the eye lashes, the primary function of the palpebrae is to protect the soft tissues of the eye from injury caused mainly from airborne debris and dust particles.

Tears are produced by the **lacrimal system** (Figure 17-2). The **lacrimal gland**, situated just deep to the upper eyelid laterally and superior to the eyeball, produces a dilute salt solution (tears) that

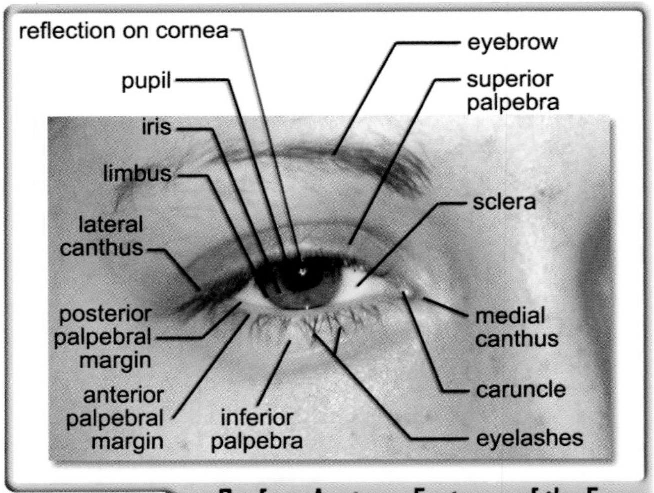

Figure 17-1 **Surface Anatomy Features of the Eye**

washes and keeps moist the soft tissues of the eye exposed to air. After washing the eye, tears are directed by the **lacrimal caruncle**, a fleshy protrusion located within the medial canthus, to the **lacrimal sac** and are then emptied into the nasal cavity via the **nasolacrimal duct**. (When crying, tears sometimes flood the draining capacity of the nasal cavity causing your nose "to run"). The **ciliary glands** (located between eyelash hair follicles), the **tarsal glands** (located along the **palpebral margin**) and the lacrimal caruncle all secrete various lipid and protein rich secretions that moisten the eye and protect it from invasion. However, the glands sometimes fall prey to bacteria, causing a *cyst*. A bacterial infection of a ciliary gland is called a *sty*.

A mucous membrane called the **conjuctiva**

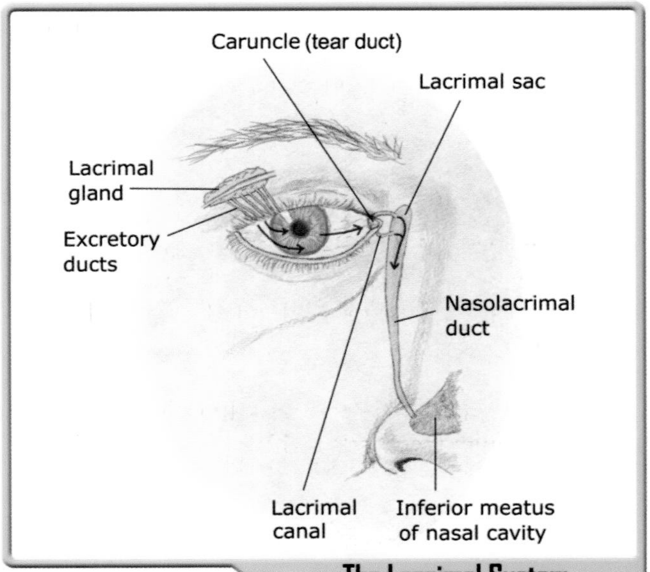

Figure 17-2 **The Lacrimal System**

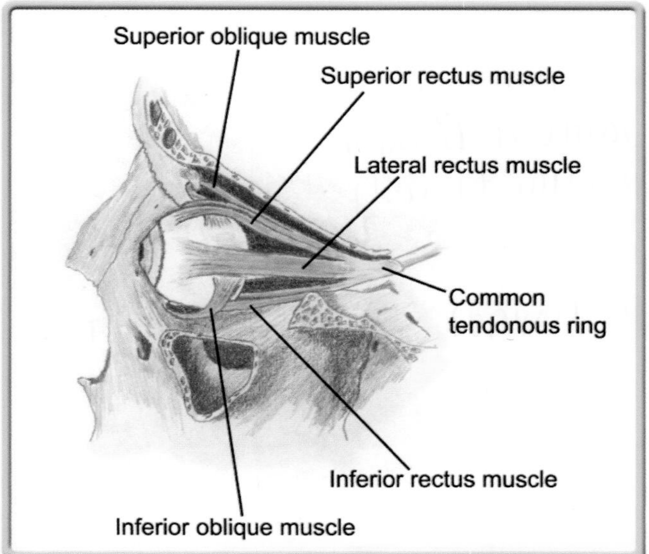

Figure 17-3 **Extrinsic Eye Muscles**

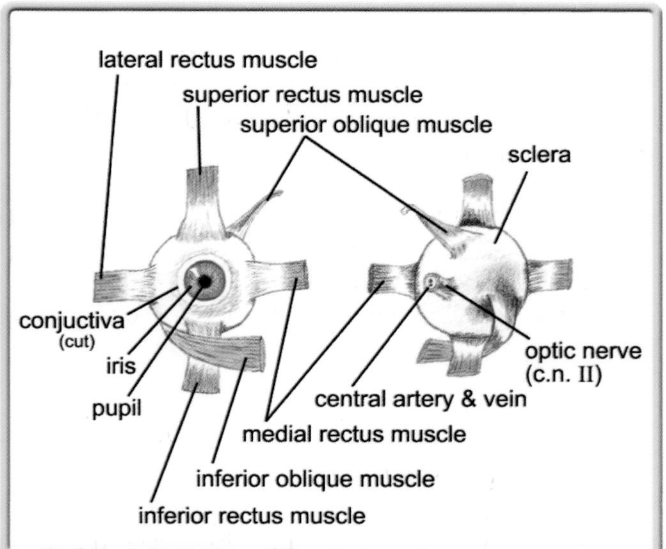

Features of the Eyeball Figure 17-4

lines the inner surface of the eyelids as well as the anterior surface of the eyeball. Along the eyelids the membrane is called the **palpebral conjuctiva**; on the eyeball it's called the **ocular**, or **bulbar, conjuctiva**. The conjuctiva consists of a thin layer of stratified epithelial cells that are kept moist by tears and obtain their oxygen directly from the air. Inflammation of this membrane is called *conjuctivitis* (or, "*pink eye*").

Movement of the eyeball is mediated by the extrinsic muscles of the eye (Figures 17-3 & 17-4). The **laterial**- and **medial rectus** muscles move the eyeball laterally and medially, respectively, and the **superior**- and **inferior rectus** muscles move the eyeball up and down, respectively. The **superior oblique** muscle turns the eyeball down and laterally, while the **inferior oblique** muscle turns the eyeball up and laterally. All of these muscles originate from the tendonous **common tendinous ring** (or, *annular ring*) surrounding the optic nerve.

Light enters the eye through an opening called the **pupil**. The pupil appears dark black because light enters there but usually does not come back out. The **iris** is the colored portion of the eye surrounding the pupil; it consists of smooth muscles which constrict the pupil under high light and dilate the pupil under low light. The pupil and iris are covered by the transparent **cornea**, which protects the interior of the eye (by preventing the entry of debris through the pupil) and bends light to help focus it inside the eye. Once light passes through the cornea and pupil it is further focused by the **lens**. Unlike the cornea, the lens is flexible and can be adjusted so that objects both near and far can be properly focused inside the eye.

Internally, the eye is divided into two cavities - the **anterior cavity** and the **posterior cavity** - separated by the lens (Figure 17-5). The anterior cavity is filled with a watery fluid called **aqueous humor** and the posterior cavity is filled with a gelatinous material called the **vitreous body**. The **sclera**, also called the "white" of the eye, and the cornea make up the outer layer of the eye called the *fibrous tunic*. The area where the sclera and the cornea join is called the **limbus**. Underneath the outer fibrous tunic, which contains relatively few blood vessels, is a blood-rich layer called the *vascular tunic*. The iris is part of the vascular tunic, as is the **choroid** (which provides nutrients to the retina) and the **ciliary bodies** (which support the

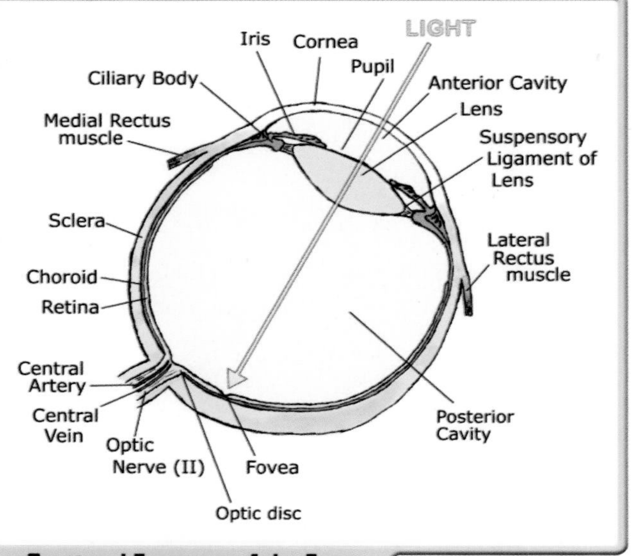

Sectional Features of the Eye Figure 17-5

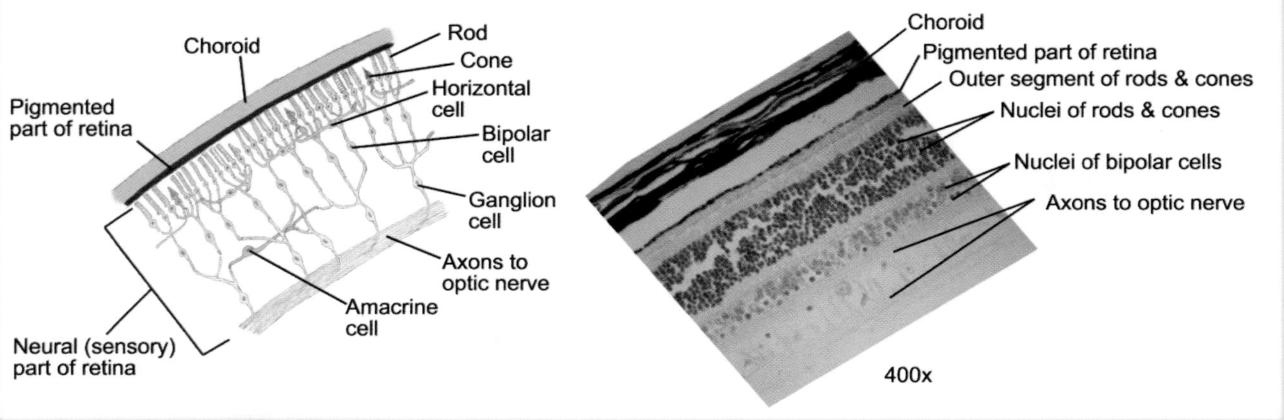

Organization of the Retina

Figure 17-6

lens). The inner-most layer is called the ***neural tunic***, or ***retina*** (Figure 17-6). The retina contains the photoreceptor cells which detect light and the neural tissues that deliver signals to the brain. The axons from retinal neurons gather at the **optic disc** and exit the eyeball as the **optic nerve**. The portion of the retina lying directly behind the lens, called the **fovea**, is especially rich in photoreceptor cells and produces the sharpest and brightest images. However, there are no photoreceptor cells where the neural axons exit the eyeball, and this produces a *blind spot* on the retina.

Physiology of Vision

Vision begins with the perception of light. The biochemical steps of vision are described below and depicted in figure 17-7.

After passing first through the cornea, then the aqueous humor of the anterior chamber, then the lens and finally the gelatinous vitreous body of the posterior chamber, a photon (λ) will either be absorbed by a photoreceptor cell in the sensory part of the retina or by the pigmented part of the retina just deep to the choroid. If the photon is absorbed by the pigmented part of the retina it will go undetected by the eye. If the photon is absorbed by a photoreceptor, then a chain of biochemical events is initiated which ultimately leads to the brain's recognition that light of a certain color and intensity has been detected from a particular point in space.

The biochemical chain of events begins with the absorption of a photon by a protein called **rhodopsin**, which is founded abundantly on the stacked **membranous disks** of the **outer segment** of photoreceptors cells. The rhodopsin protein changes shape when excited by light; the altered rhodopsin protein quickly interacts with a protein called **transducin** which then activates a protein called **phosphodiesterase (PDE)**. Activated PDE removes a small molecule called **cGMP** from **cGMP-activated sodium channels** in the photoreceptor's plasma membrane. Without cGMP, sodium channels close, stopping the usual influx of sodium ions into the outer segment of the photoreceptor cell. This causes a change in the membrane potential of the cell which stops the release of a neurotransmitter (glutamate) at the photoreceptor's synapse with a bipolar neuron. The loss of glutamate informs the neuron that the photoreceptor has just detected a photon and the neuron relays this information to the brain.

The brain continuously receives a deluge of information from the eyes and interprets this information on both subconscious and conscience levels. Conscious visual perceptions are made in the occipital lobe of the left and right cerebral hemispheres. Each photoreceptor ganglion in the

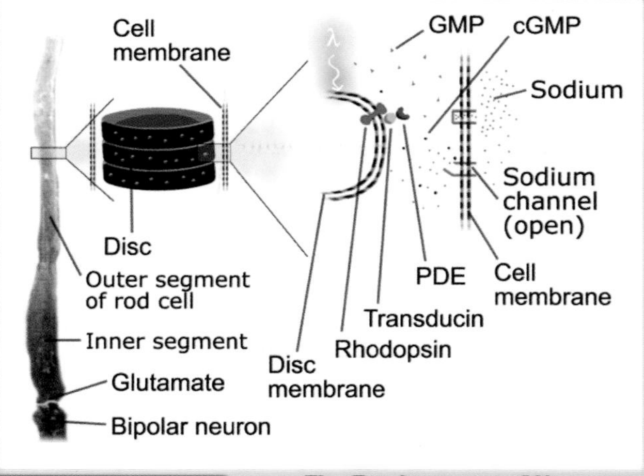

Figure 17-7

The Biochemistry of Vision

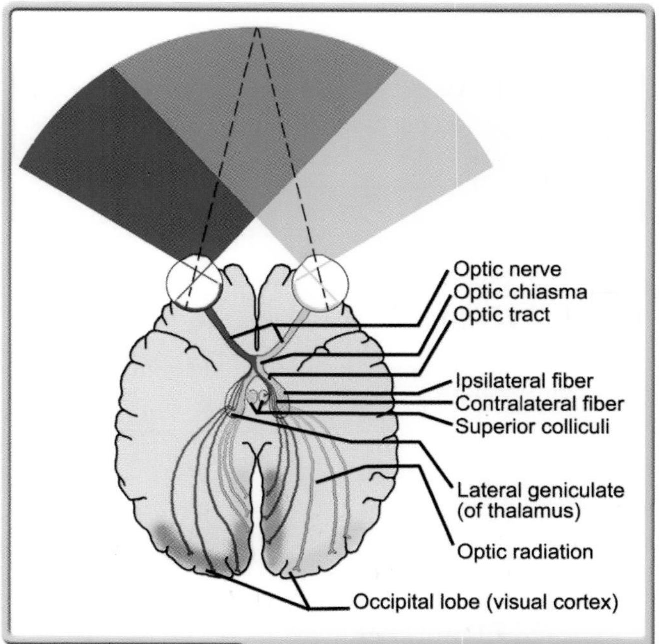

Figure 17-8 **Visual Pathways in the Brain**

eye sends its signal to a specific area of the occipital lobe, and in this way a map of the retina is produced in the brain.

Visual Neural Pathways

Axons from the ganglion cells in the retina converge at the optic disc at the posterior of the eyeball. There, they exit the eye together as the **optic nerve** (cranial nerve II). The two optic nerves converge at the **optic chiasma** inferior to the brain where axons from the medial side of each retina cross to the opposite side of the head while axons from the lateral side of each retina do not. The ganglion cell axons synapse with neurons in the **lateral geniculate body of the thalamus**, whose axons fan out to form the **optic radiation**. These axons synapse with neurons in the **visual cortex** of the occipital lobe of the brain, where visual interpretation takes place (Figure 17-8).

Activity 1: Dissection of a Cow Eye

1. Don disposable gloves and obtain a preserved cow eye and dissecting instruments from your instructor.
2. Examine the external features of the eye. The eye is surrounded on all but the anterior surface by thick adipose. This fatty tissue protects and cushions the eyes within their boney sockets. The extrinsic eye muscles and the optic nerve may or may not be visible protruding from the posterior of the eyeball. Anteriorly, a thin membrane called the cornea covers the iris and pupil. Transparent in life, the preserved cornea is nearly opaque.

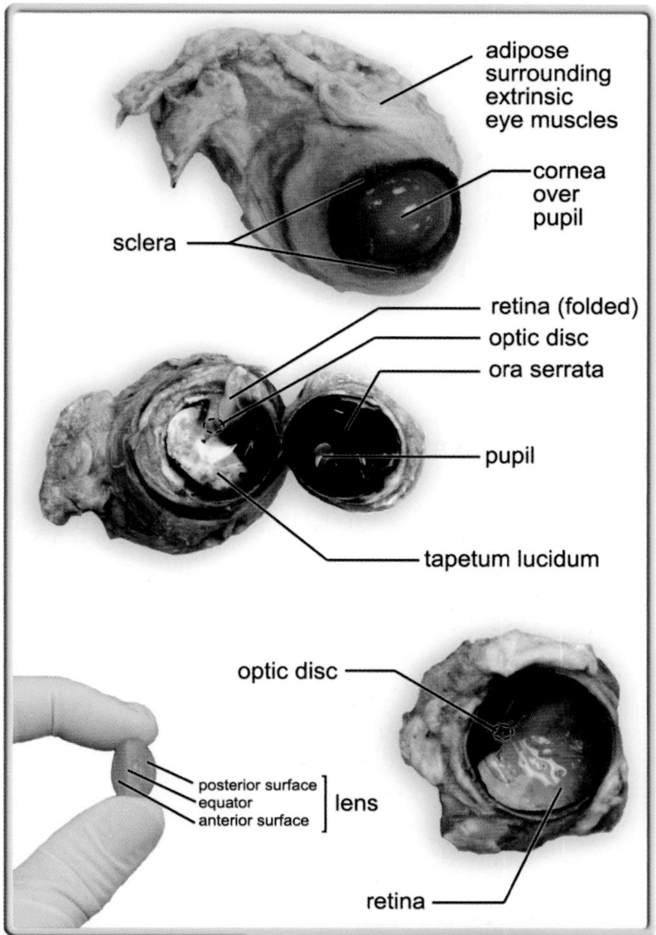

Figure 17-9 **Dissected Cow Eye**

3. Carefully remove the adipose tissue surrounding the eyeball to reveal the sclera, optic nerve and extrinsic muscles that move the eye. Six in all, these muscles turn the eye left - right and up – down.
4. Using a sharp scalpel, carefully make an incision through the sclera about 6 mm (¼ inch) away from the cornea. (The sclera may be extremely tough, so you may need to apply considerable pressure to penetrate it). Using a pair of scissors, cut the sclera around the circumference of the eyeball paralleling the edge of the cornea
5. Lift away the anterior portion of the eyeball; the vitreous body should remain in the posterior portion of the eyeball.
6. Identify the following structures on the anterior part of the eye:

- Cornea
- Ciliary body
- Orra serrata
- Lens
- Iris

7. Examine the posterior portion of the eyeball. Remove the vitreous body and observe the retina as a glistening yellow-white membrane and the pigmented choroid layer beneath.

Activity 2: Color Perception – Light vs Dark

1. Turn out the room lights and perform this experiment under *very dim* light conditions. (One small LED lamp can be used to illuminate the entire room).
2. Allow 10 minutes to let your eyes adjust to the darkness.
3. Examine the letters and numbers in the Color Perception Chart. Try to correctly determine the colors of the characters as well as the background colors. Below each character, write what you think is its color.
4. Turn on the lights and examine the chart in bright light conditions.

1. Did any student see all the colors correctly under all of the conditions? ____________
2. Which colors were the easiest and which were the most difficult to see on each background?

____

3. What difference do the lighting conditions make? ______________________________

____

____

4. How do roads sign designers use this type of information when designing road signs?

____

____

____

Activity 3: Color Perception – Benham's Disk & Color Adaptation

The Benham's disk was invented by a nineteenth century toymaker who noticed colors in a black-and-white pattern he mounted on a spinning top. Like Benham, most people see colors of various intensities while staring at a spinning Benham's disk. The reason can be found in the excitation of cone receptors in the retina of the eye.

There are three types of cone receptors on the retina: red-sensitive cones, blue-sensitive cones and green-sensitive cones. We perceive white light when each of these receptors is stimulated equally.

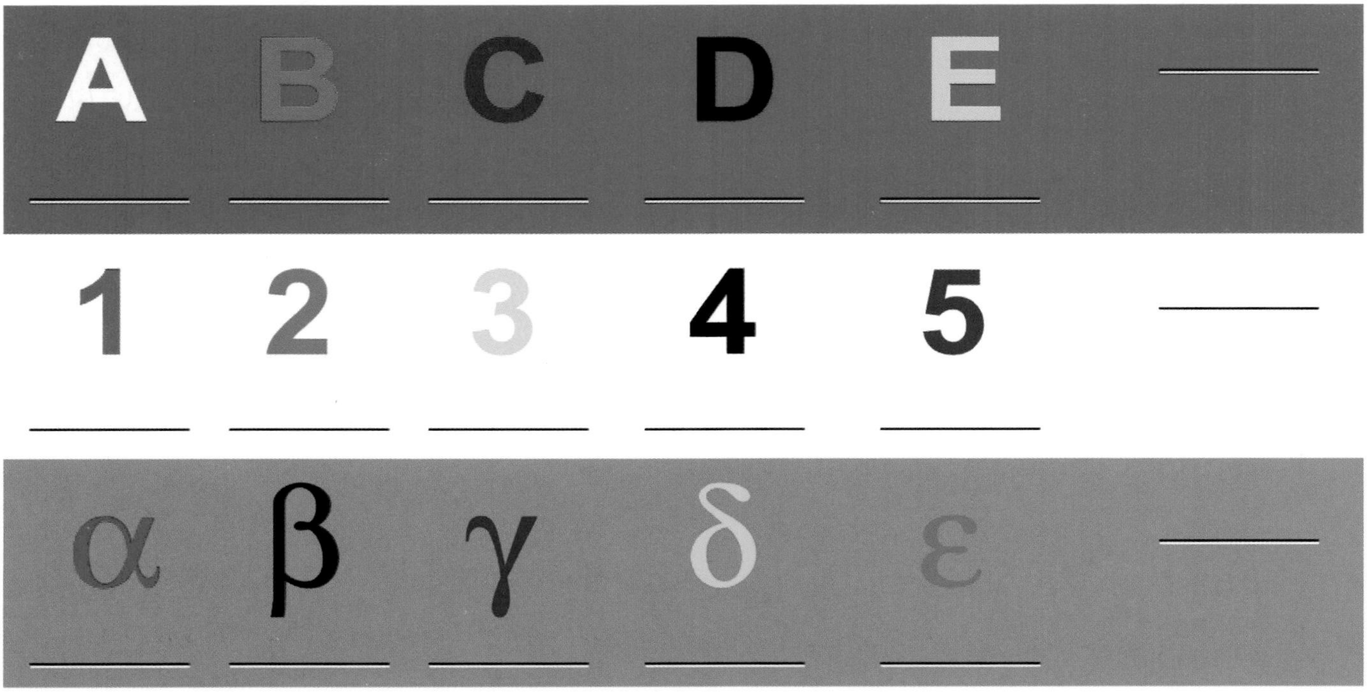

Color Perception Chart

It is known that the three cones cells differ in more ways than just the color of light to which they respond. For example, each receptor type has a distinct *latency time* (the time it takes to respond to a photon) and a distinct *persistence time* (the time it keeps responding once stimulated). Blue cones, for instance, have the longest latency time and the longest persistence time.

When you stare at one place on a spinning Benham's disk you're seeing alternating flashes of black and white. However, as stated above, you only see white when all three cone types are responding equally. Since some cones respond more quickly and / or keep responding longer than others (i.e., different latency and persistence times), an imbalance ensues as the disc spins, and excitation of the different cones is not in sync. The result is that we perceive streaks of colors on the disk. The colors you perceive vary across the disk because at different radial positions on the disk the black arcs have different lengths, so that the flashing rate they produce on the retina is also different.

I. Benham's Disk

1. If a Benham's disk is not provided by the instructor, one can easily be made by cutting out the pattern at the back of this exercise, mounting it on a cardboard backing with adhesive and then attaching it to a pencil eraser with a thumbtack (mount it loosely enough to allow it to spin without resistance).
2. Spin the disk under a bright incandescent light while staring at one point on the disk. Notice the colored bands that appear on the disk. Reverse the direction of the spin and try different speeds.

1. What color is seen toward the center of the disk? ______________________________
2. Toward the outside of the disk? ________ ___________________________________
3. In what order were the colors when you reverse the spin direction? __________________ ___________________________________
4. How do the colors change with different rates of spinning? ________________________ ___________________________________

II. Color Adaptation

1. Stare at the flag while counting *slowly* to twenty, then shift your gaze to the white space below it. A faint image of the flag will appear in the white space (blinking hard once or twice may help you see it better).

The faint image that appears in the white space is called an *afterimage*. Afterimages appear because the cones in your retina become adapted when exposed to the same color for a prolonged period of time. Interestingly, the image that appears is not the same color as the original image, rather the complementary color. To explain this, let's consider what happens to the cones observing the cyan (greenish-blue) stripes. When you stare at the flag, the cyan stripes remain fixed on the same spot of your retina. Over time, those cones become adapted and less sensitive to cyan. When you shift your gaze to a white area of the page, faint red stripes appear because the green-sensitive cones and blue-sensitive cones are not responding to the white paper with the same intensity as the red cones. It's as if the green and blue portions of the white paper have been "turned down", and white light minus green and blue light = red. But this only happens on the cyan-adapted portion of your retina! The portion of the retina observing the yellow field

Color Adaptation

Figure 17-10

Figure 17-11 Binocular Vision Test

becomes desensitized to yellow and the afterimage there appears blue. The afterimage of the flag appears red, white and blue because they are the complementary colors of cyan, black and yellow.

Activity 4: Demonstrating Binocular Vision & Lateral Inhibition

I. Binocular Vision

1. Take a sheet of white paper and roll it into a tube 11in. long and about ½ inch in diameter. Use clear tape to keep the paper from unrolling.
2. Hold the tube with your right hand, looking through the tube with your right eye. Place the medial side of your left hand against the tube about 4 to 6in. from your face in front of your left eye – as shown in figure 17-11. Focusing on a distant object, you should notice what appears to be a hole in your left hand! Wiggling your fingers may help you see this effect better.
3. Move your left hand back and forth along the tube and notice how the hole in your hand changes.

Your right eye sees objects in the distance while your left eye sees your hand. Your brain fuses the images from each eye to produce a hand with a hole in it!

II. Lateral Inhibition

1. Stand directly beneath a light (fluorescent lights work well) and look through the tube at the floor beside your feet. The portion of the floor seen through the tube will appear considerably brighter than the floor seen outside the tube.
2. Now turn your gaze upward and look at a portion of the ceiling about 1ft. away from a light source (*do not look directly at the light!*). The portion of the ceiling seen through the tube will appear darker than the ceiling seen outside the tube.

Figure 17-12 The Blind Spot Test

We already know that when your photoreceptors detect light they send a signal to your brain, but they also send inhibitory signals to neighboring photoreceptors telling them to be less sensitive to incoming light. When you look through the tube at the floor, the walls of the tube are dark and photoreceptors detecting the floor are not inhibited by surrounding photoreceptors detecting the wall of the tube. Thus, the floor appears brighter looking through the tube. By contrast, when you look at the ceiling near the light source, the white tube reflects a lot of light and appears bright. The photoreceptors detecting the bright wall of the tube inhibit nearby receptors detecting the ceiling, therefore the ceiling seen through the tube appears darker.

Activity 5: Demonstrating the Blind Spot

1. Hold your head about 12 in. above the blind spot test figure (Figure 17-12). Cover or close your left eye and stare at the footprint with your right eye. Slowly move your face toward the figure keeping your eye focused on the footprint. The handprint will disappear when it becomes focused on your blind spot. If you continue moving toward the figure the spot will exit the blind spot and once again be visible.
2. The above procedure can be repeated using your left eye and staring at the handprint. The footprint will disappear as it becomes focused on the blind spot.

Activity 6: Testing visual acuity

1. Have your lab partner stand 20 feet from the posted Snellen eye chart and cover one eye with their hand. As your partner reads each line on the chart, check them for accuracy. If your partner wears glasses perform the test twice,

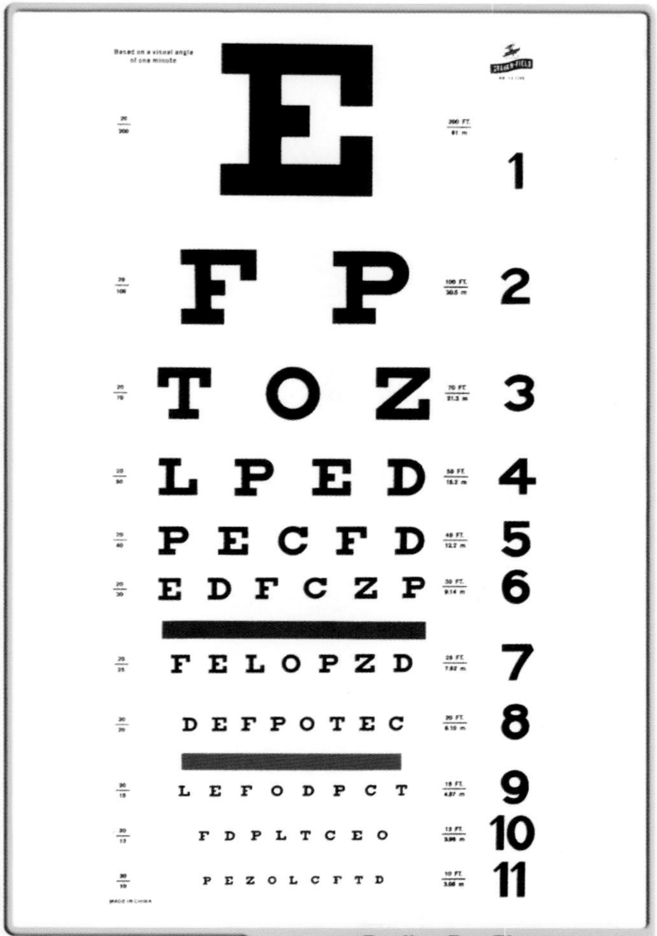

Figure 17-13 Snellen Eye Chart

first without the glasses and then with the glasses. *Do not remove contact lenses.*

2. Record the lowest row for which all letters were read accurately. If that row is labeled 20/20, then your partner has normal vision. If the row is labeled 20/30 or higher (any ratio with the value less than one), then he or she has less than normal visual acuity. If the row is labeled 20/15 or less (any ratio with a value greater than one), then your partner has better than average visual acuity.
3. Repeat the above test for the other eye.

Visual acuity, right eye (without glasses):________

Visual acuity, right eye (with glasses): __________

Visual acuity, left eye (without glasses): _________

Visual acuity, left eye (with glasses): ___________

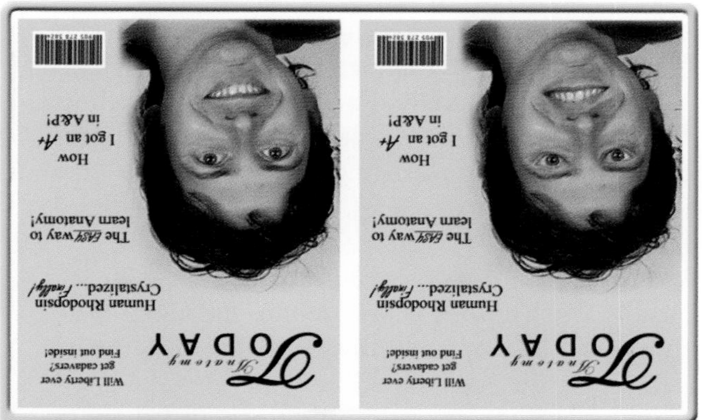

Not-So-Familiar Faces Figure 17-14

Activity 7: Not-So-Familiar Faces

Together the eyes send a tremendous amount of information to the brain, and it's the brain's job to sort out this information to make sense of it all. To help do this, the brain gets used to seeing many things a certain way so that when presented with the same or similar information in the future it can recall past representations rather than fully analyze the latest image. This phenomenon is illustrated clearly in this activity.

1. Without turning the images right-side up, look briefly at the pair of upside-down magazine covers shown in figure 17-14. Do you recognize the person in the picture? At first glance, many people are unable to correctly identify the personality, although you may figure it out with a long examination.
2. Look more closely at the pair of upside-down magazine covers. Do you notice any differences between them? If yes, do you consider the differences to be subtle or glaring?
3. Now turn the pictures right-side up. Do you still think the same way about the differences?

The eyes and mouth of the personality have been turned upside down in one magazine cover. This is hardly noticeable when viewing the covers upside-down because our brains are used to seeing the eyes and mouth right-side up. Consequently, the alteration appears subtle. When the faces are turned right-side up, however, the eyes and mouth are revealed as upside-down and the face takes on a bizarre, even grotesque appearance because this is so unusual to our brains.

Activity 8: Test for Astigmatism

1. Observe the astigmatism chart in figure 17-15. If any of the parallel lines appear bold, then you have astigmatism. Usually, if any lines appear bold they so in pairs (e.g., lines 11 & 5 or lines 2 & 8).

Astigmatism is caused by deformed corneas. Usually, each cornea is perfectly round along the limbus and forms a smooth sphere that cups the iris. If the cornea is egg-shaped, contains elevations or depressions, or is not uniformly thick, then light is not bent consistently by the cornea. The un-even bending of light causes blurry spots on the retina.

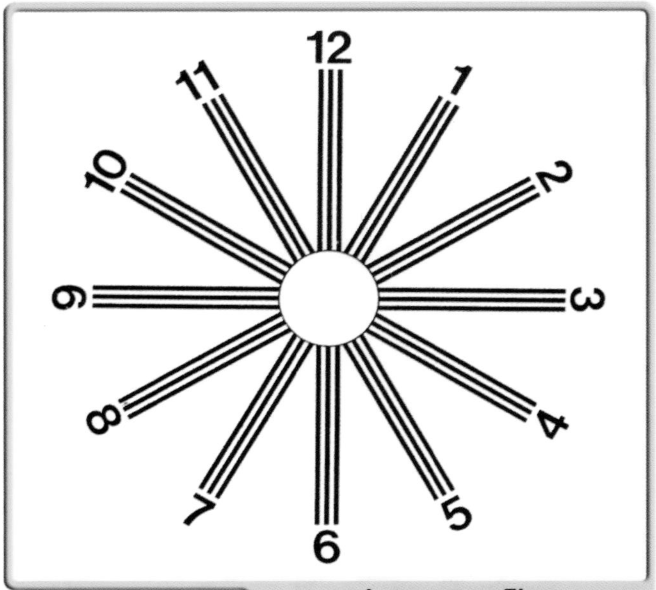

Figure 17-15 Astigmatism Chart

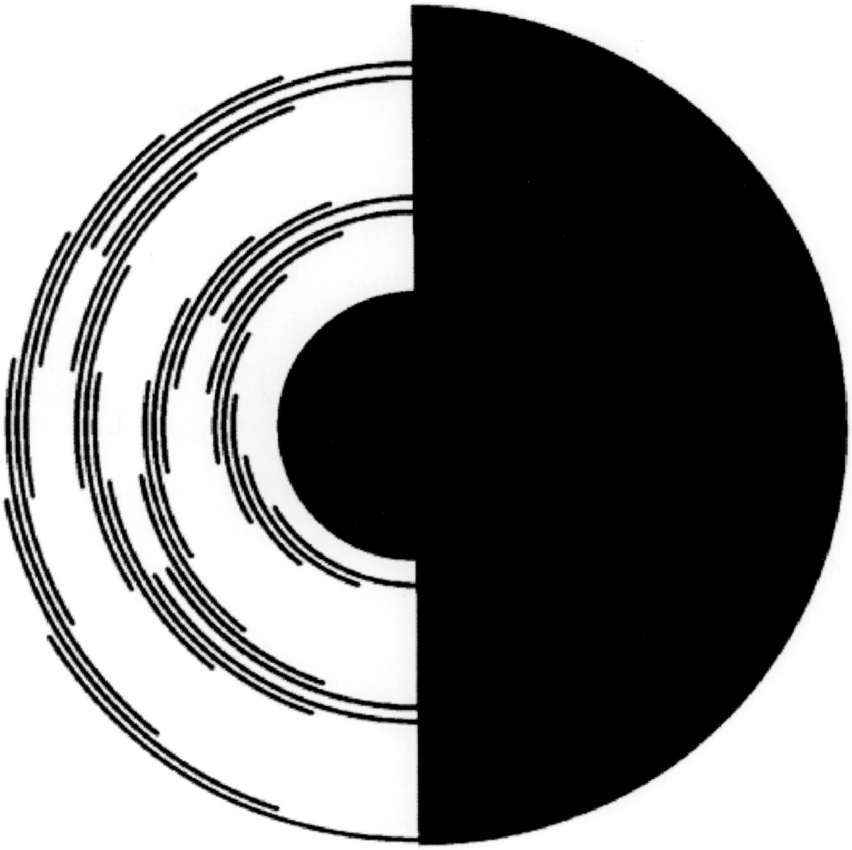

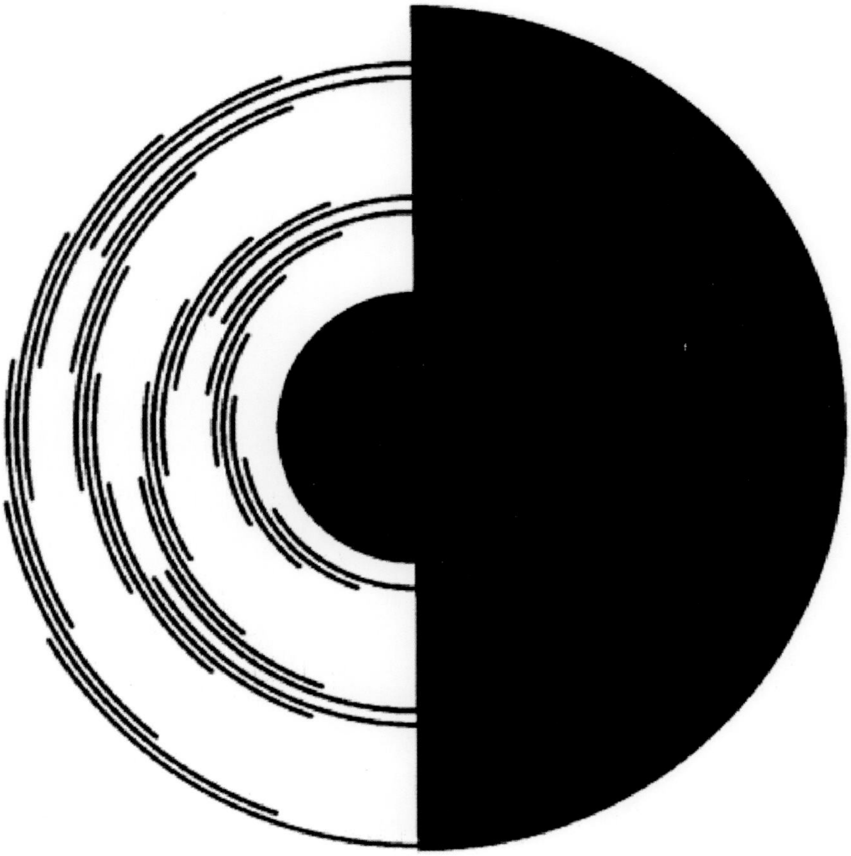

exercise 18

the NERVOUS system

- special senses: HEARING & BALANCE -

People were overwhelmed with amazement. "He has done everything well," they said. "He even makes the deaf hear and the mute speak."
Mark 7:37

Hearing and balance are achieved by specialized compartments of the same sensory organ – the ear. At first it may appear that hearing and balance have little to do with each other and so it may seem odd that the same organ would detect both sensations. However, hearing and balance are both achieved by detecting *motion*: Motion of your head in the case of balance and motion of air molecules in the case of hearing. In both cases, the ear exploits mechanoreceptors to obtain information about movement.

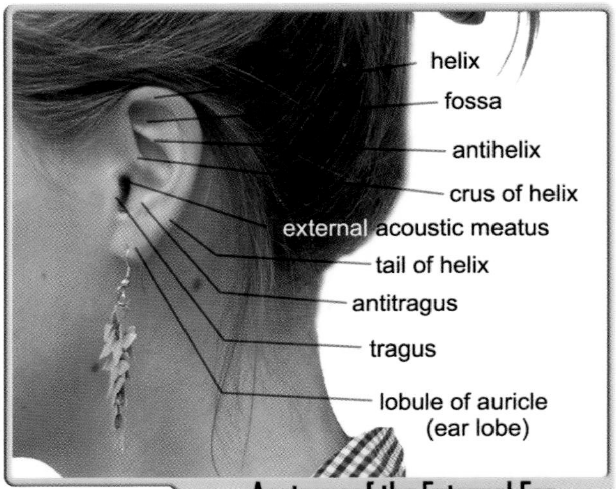

Figure 18-1 Anatomy of the External Ear

Anatomy of the External Ear

Externally, the ear is composed of folds of skin supported by cartilage (Figure 18-1). These folds are designed to direct sound into the **external acoustic meatus**, or *ear canal*. A major fold called the **helix** forms a ring enclosing a flattened cavity called the **fossa**. The cartilage of the helix begins at the **crus of the helix** superior to the ear canal and terminates above the **ear lobe** at the **tail of the helix**. The ear lobe (a.k.a., *lobule* of *auricle*) is composed almost entirely of adipose tissue and is consequently soft and highly flexible. (In figure 18-1, the lobe has been pierced to allow wearing of pierced earrings). A smaller, internal fold called the **antihelix** forms the internal border of the fossa. This fold terminates at the **antitragus**. The external acoustic meatus is guarded anteriorly by the **tragus**, which also serves to direct sound into the ear canal.

Internal Anatomy of the Ear

Internally, the ear canal extends about 1 ½ inches into the skull (Figure 18-2). Much of the internal components of the ear are housed within and protected by the temporal bone. The ear canal terminates at the **tympanic membrane**, or *ear*

1. vestibular nerve (cn VIII)
2. cochlear nerve (cn VIII)
3. stapes
4. incus
5. malleus
6. tympanic cavity
7. round window
8. pharyngotempanic (auditory) tube
9. cochlea
10. vestibule
11. tympanic membrane (eardrum)
12. semicircular canals
13. temporal bone
14. external acoustic meatus (ear canal)
15. helix
16. fossa
17. lobe

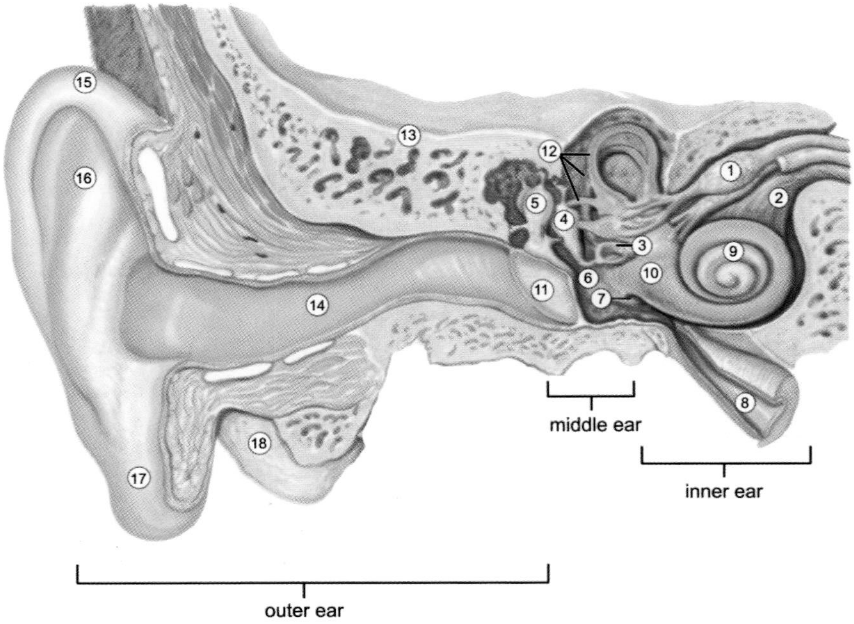

Figure 18-2 Internal Anatomy of the Ear

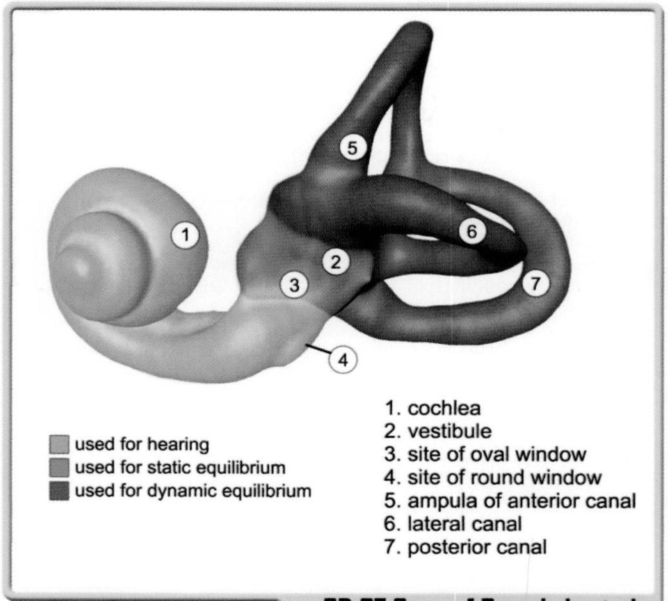

Figure 18-3 **3D CT Scan of Bony Labyrinth**

drum. This membrane vibrates when struck by sound waves (much like a speaker vibrates to *produce* sound waves). The vibrational motion of the ear drum is tranferred to the **cochlea** via three tiny bones – the **malleus, incus** and **stapes**. The cochlea, housed within the bony labyrinth (Figure 18-3), contains the organ of Corti. The organ of Corti is the organ actually responsible for detecting sound by converting the vibrational energy transferred from the ear drum into action potentials delivered to the brain via the nerve fibers of the **vestibulocochlear nerve**. The **semicircular canals** detect motions of the head to provide the sensation of balance, i.e., equilibrium.

The above components of the ear are divided into three sections: The external ear and the ear canal make up the **outer ear**; the tympanic membrane, malleus, incus and stapes make up the **middle ear**; the cochlea and semicircular canals make up the **inner ear** (or, *labrynth*).

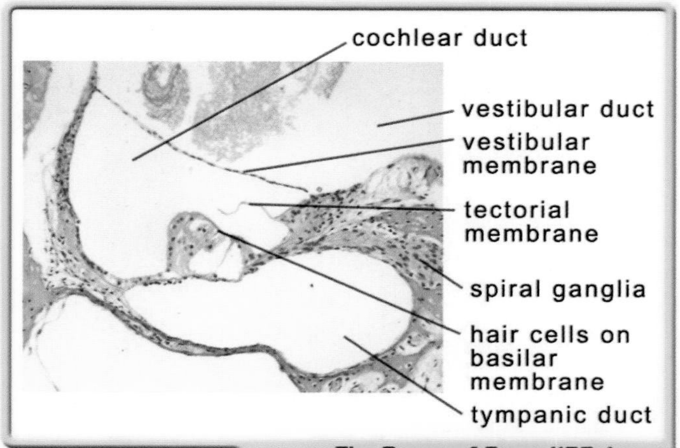

Figure 18-4 **The Organ of Corti (100x)**

Physiology of Hearing

Vestibular nerve = Balance

"Hearing" is the successful conversion of mechanical motion of air molecules into electrochemical action potentials detected by the brain. This conversion is achieved by a sophisticated organ – the **organ of Corti** – housed within the cochlea (Figure 18-4). The detection of sound begins at the tympanic membrane. Vibrational motion of the membrane (induced by sound) is translated to the oval window of the cochlea by the three small auditory ossicles. Vibrational motion of the oval window induces vibrational waves in the fluid (perilymph) within the vestibular duct. These fluid waves cause the flexible **basilar membrane** to rise and fall as the waves pass by. As the basilar membrane rises, the **stereocilia** of **hair cells** bend against the inflexible

Cochlear = sound

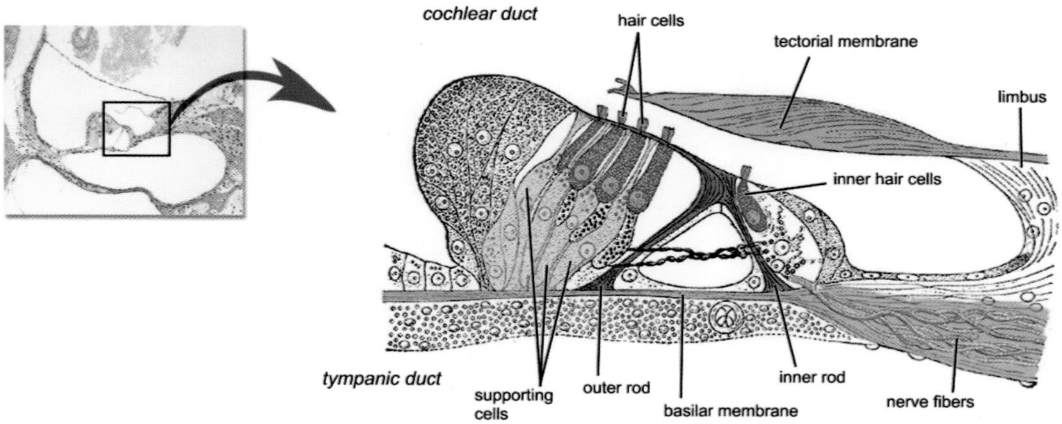

Organ of Corti Structure

Figure 18-5

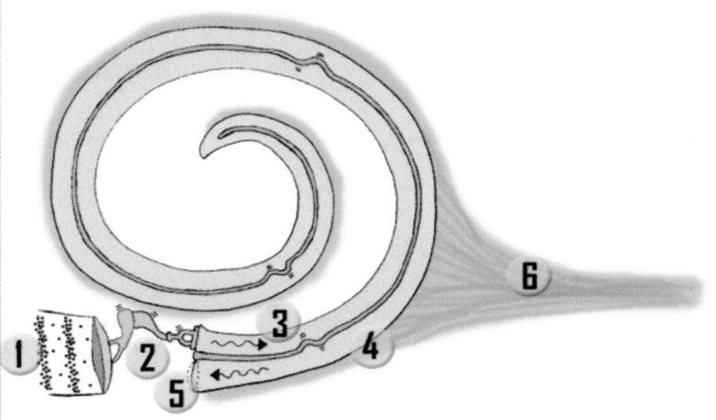

1. Sound enters the ear and vibrates the tympanic membrane.
2. Vibrations of the tympanic membrane are carried to the oval window of the cochlea by the auditory ossicles.
3. Vibrations (i.e, pressure waves) in the perilymph spiral to the tip of the cochlea, inducing vibrations of the basilar membrane.
4. Vibrations of the basilar membrane bend stereocilia on hair cells, triggering neuronal action potentials.
5. The pressure wave in the perilymph spirals back through the cochlea via the tympanic duct and is relieved at the flexible round window.
6. Action potentials from the stimulated hair cells are sent to the brain via the vestibulocochlear nerve (cranial nerve VIII).

Sound Frequency Determination

Figure 18-6

tectorial membrane above them. Bending of the stereocilia triggers an action potential in the underlying neuron associated with the hair cell. The action potential is received by the brain and is interpreted as sound. The hair cells possess stereocilia of various lengths; the number of stereocilia bent by the vibrating basilar membrane provides an indication of the strength of the passing wave, which is directly related to the volume of the sound. The steps of sound detection are summarized in figure 18-6.

The pressure wave in the perilymph spirals its way to the tip of the cochlea through the vestibular duct and then spirals back through the tympanic duct. The pressure is finally relieved at the round window at the end of the tympanic duct where a thin membrane bulges and retracts with each pressure wave.

When the basilar membrane is exposed to sound of just one frequency, only a small part of the

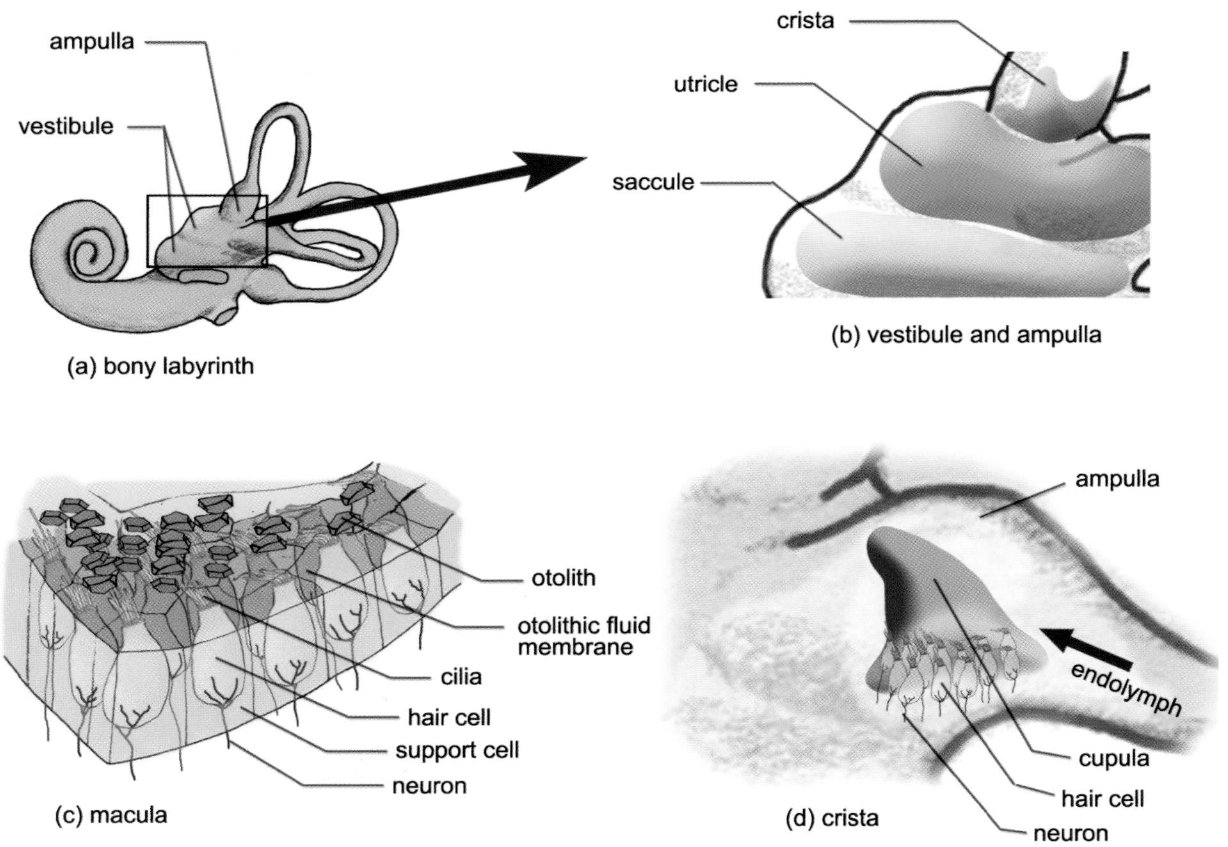

Figure 18-7: Structure of Vestibular Apparatus

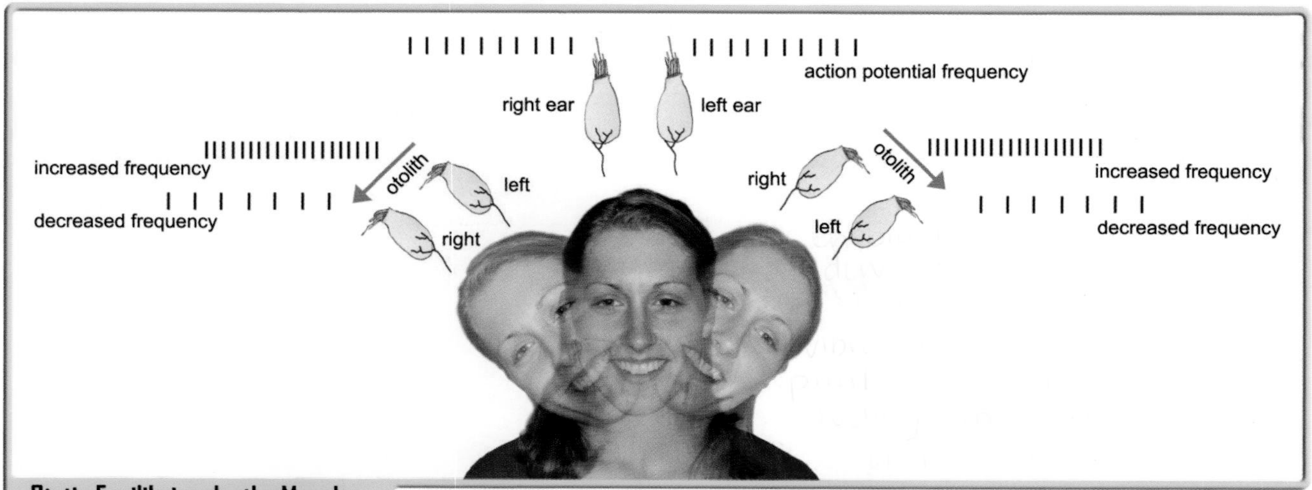

Static Equilibrium by the Macula

Figure 18-8

membrane will vibrate. High frequency sounds cause vibrations at the beginning of the basilar membrane near the oval window; low frequencies cause vibrations near the tip of the basilar membrane. Thus, which part of the basilar membrane vibrates is determined by the the sound wave frequency (or *note*). That is, *sound frequency information is converted to positional information on the basilar membrane.* Most sounds we hear are a mixture of many frequencies, so multiple parts of the basilar membrane vibrate simultaneously. While listening to complex sounds (e.g., music), the barrage of information is sorted out by the auditory cortex of the brain.

Physiology of Balance

Balance and equilibrium are achieved by the **vestibule** and **semicircular canals** of the inner ear (Figure 18-7). There are two types of balance – *static equilibrium* and *dynamic equilibrium*. Static equilibrium allows you to maintain your body position when sitting or standing still; it's achieved primarily by the **saccule** and **utricle** housed within the **vestibule**. Dynamic equilibrium allows you to maintain your posture while your body is in motion. Dynamic equilibrium is achieved by the **cristae** housed within the **ampulla** of the **semicircular canals**.

Static Equilibrium

Two sac-like structures are found within the vestibule of the inner ear: the **saccule** and the **utricle**. Contained within the walls of both of these sacs are sensory structures called **maculae**. Each macula, situated 90° degrees to the other, consists of **hair cells** possessing ~70 stereocilia submerged in a gelatinous matrix (also called the **otolithic membrane**). Embedded in the matrix are small crystals of calcium carbonate, called **otoliths**.

When the head is tilted the gelatinous matrix with embedded otoliths are pulled downward by gravity (Figure 18-8). The shifting of the matrix bends the stereocilia of the hair cells. A bend in one direction dramatically increases the frequency of action potentials from neurons associated with the hair cells; a bend in the opposite direction decreases the frequency of action potentials. These signals are transmitted through the vestibular branch of cranial nerve VIII to the brain. The brain, particularly the cerebellum, responds by adjusting muscle tone to balance the body. The static equilibrium system is so sensitive that a mere ½° tilt of the head is detectable.

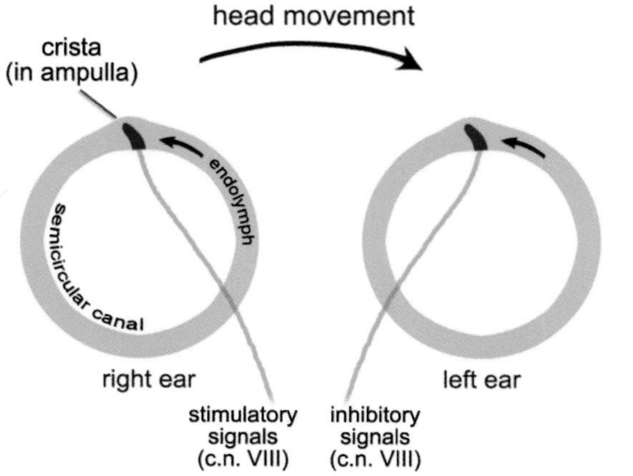

Figure 18-9 Dynamic Equilibrium by the Cristae

Dynamic Equilibrium

Acceleration and deceleration (or, more precisely, *angular momentum*) is detected by the semicircular canals. The three semicircular canals are arranged in perpendicular planes to each other (i.e., one each in the *x*, *y* and *z* planes) so that movement in any direction can be easily detected. Each canal is filled with a fluid – endolymph – which is free to circulate through the canal. A swollen area at the base of each canal (called the **ampulla**) houses a flap-door called a **crista**. The crista is a thick gelatinous protrusion into the flow of the endolymph. When the head moves, the endolymph *resists* movement due to inertia. The crista is bent due to the drag of the endolymph and, as with the macula, bending of the crista affects action potentials from the associated neurons. Bending in one direction stimulates action potentials; bending in the opposite direction inhibits action potentials. The potentials are sent via the vestibular branch of cranial nerve VIII to the brain for interpretation. The two inner ears are arranged as mirror images of one another, like your left and right hands are mirror images. Consequently, when your head moves in a given direction, stimulatory signals are received from one ear while inhibitory signals are received from the other (Figure 18-9).

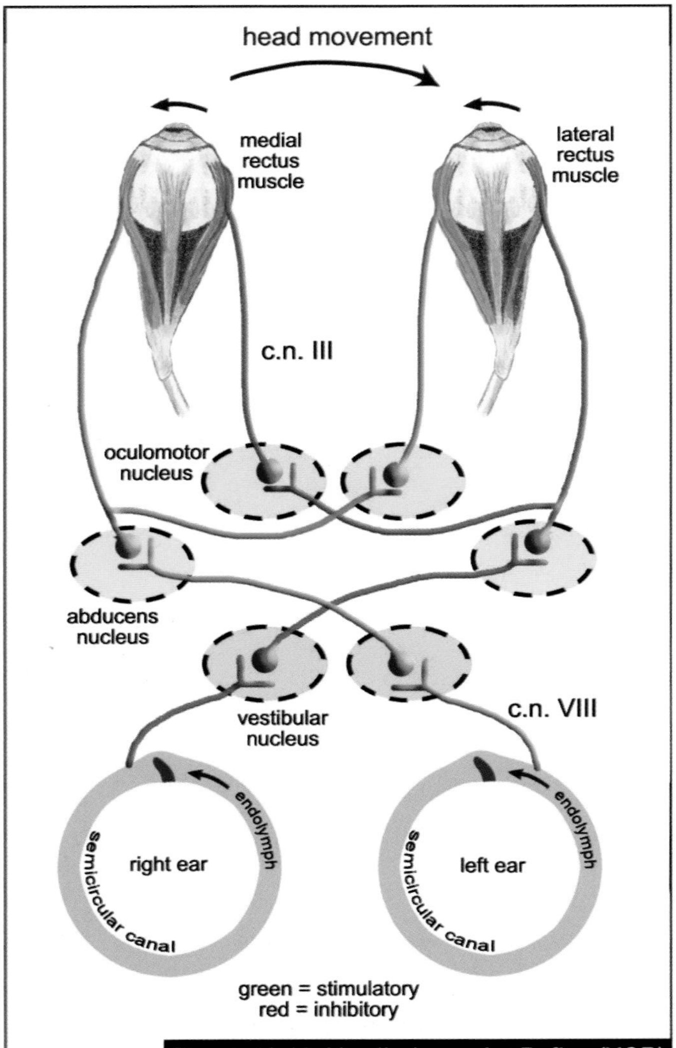

Figure 18-10: Vestibulo-ocular Reflex (VOR)

1. stapedius m.
2. tensor tympani m.
3. malleus
4. incus
5. stapes
6. post. semicircular canal
7. lat. semicircular canal
8. ant. semicircular canal
9. vestibule
10. cochlea
11. vestibular branch*
12. cochlear branch*
13. tympanic membrane
14. tympanic cavity
15. pharyngotympanic tube

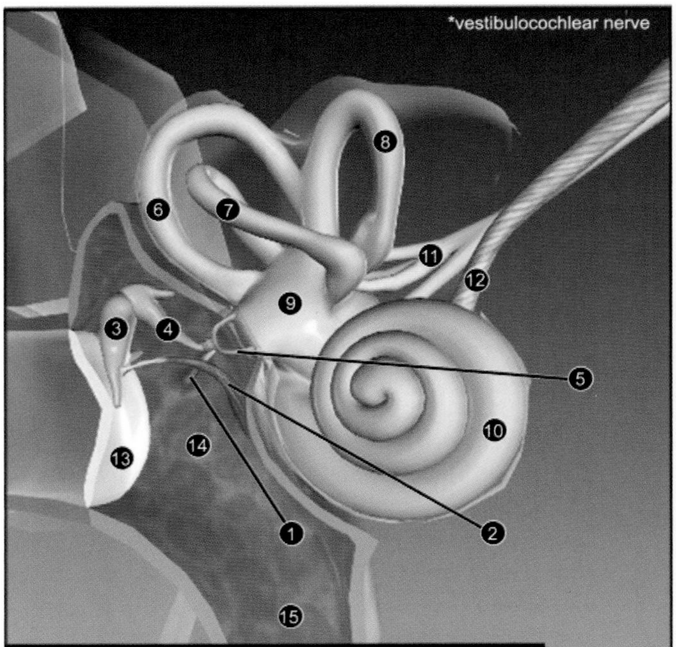

Figure 18-11: Inner Ear & Muscles Protecting the Ear

Auditory Neural Pathways

One of the fastest reflexes in the human body is the **vestibulo-ocular reflex** (**VOR**; figure 18-10). Head movements and eye movements must be quickly coordinated to prevent blurry vision when your head moves (like the blurry image produced by the rapid movement of a movie camera). The VOR reflex arc, which consists of only three neurons, takes only 10 milliseconds to complete. Also, recall that the external eye muscles are among the fastest twitch muscles in the body.

Dynamic Range of the Ear

The human ear has a dynamic range of more than 1 trillion! This means there's an astounding trillion-fold difference between the lowest audible sound

Decibel (Db)	Sound
0	soft whisper
30	quiet office
60	conversational speech
80	typical music
110	power tools
130	*(pain threshold)*
150	rock concert
160	jet engine *(close)*

Table 18-1: Decibel Levels of Common Sounds

and the loudest bearable sound. Sound volumes are measured using the Decibel scale. Decibel levels for some common sounds are listed in Table 18-1.

Damage to the ear (and loss of hearing) can result from excessively loud sounds. Two muscles in the middle ear dampen loud noises to protect the delicate tympanic membrane and organ of Corti. The **tensor tympani muscle** inserts on the malleus; the **stapedius muscle** inserts on the stapes (Figure 18-11). These muscles reflexively contract when the ear is exposed to loud noises. Contraction of the tensor tympani muscle restricts movement of the eardrum; contraction of the stapedius limits movement of the stapedius and the oval window.

Activity 1: Identifying Ear Structures

1. Using the figures in this exercise as a guide, identify ear structures on a dissectible ear model and, for external structures, on a lab partner.

Activity 2: Microscopic Examination of the Cochlea

1. Obtain a prepared slide of the cochlea. Using the figures in this exercise, identify the structures on the cochlea, including parts of the Organ of Corti.

Activity 3: Hearing Tests

Note: Perform the following tests in a quiet location.

3-A. Acuity Test

1. Have your partner pack *one* ear with cotton. Place a ticking watch near the subject's *unpacked* ear, then slowly move the watch away from the subject's ear. Record the distance (in centimeters) where the watch ticking is no longer detectable by the subject. Repeat this process for the other ear.

   right ear ___________ left ear ___________

   Did the ticking sound fade abruptly or gradually?

3-B. Sound Localization Test

1. Have your partner close both eyes. Hold the ticking watch an audible distance from the subject and move it around to various locations. Is the subject able to successfully track the sound? Can the sound be localized equally well in all directions?
2. Repeat the above procedure using a louder sound (such as headphones connected to an iPod or MP3 player). Try the location test using various volume settings.

   The brain determines the location of a sound by i) comparing the relative volumes of the sound at each ear, and ii) determining which ear receives the sound first.*

3-C. Frequency Range Test

1. A tuning fork generates a sound of one frequency (i.e., a pure note). Obtain tuning forks of various frequencies ranging from 100 to 5000 Hz (cps).
2. Strike the lowest frequency tuning fork against the heel of your hand – Do NOT pluck the tuning fork or strike it against a table.
3. Place the tuning fork 5-10 cm from your partner's ear. Does the subject hear the note?
4. Repeat the procedure for several tuning forks of various frequencies.
5. Mosquito Tones™ are ring tones for cell phones that employ very high frequencies. The high-frequency tones can be heard by high-school and college students, but not by their teachers. Test the frequency range of an older student (or your instructor) and compare it with the range of the younger students.

   Which tuning fork was heard loudest by the subject?
   frequency _______________

---

* The speed of sound is 768 miles per hour. If a sound is approaching you from your left side, how much sooner will the sound reach your left ear than your right ear? Assume the width of your head is 6 inches.

Which tuning fork was heard least by the subject?
frequency _______________

3-D. Weber Test for Conductive and Sensorineural Deafness

1. Strike a tuning fork and place the handle of the fork medially on the subject's head. If the tone is heard equally well in both ears, the subject's hearing is normal. If the subject has sensorineural deafness in one ear, the tone will be softer (or absent) in the affected ear. If the subject has conduction deafness in one ear, the tone will be heard louder on the affected side. Conduction deafness can be simulated by stuffing cotton into one ear to interfere with the conduction of sound into the inner ear.

   Is the tone heard equally in both ears, or does the subject exhibit sensorineural or conduction deafness?

3-E. Rinne Test for Conduction Deafness

1. Strike a tuning fork and place the handle of the fork on the subject's mastoid process.
2. When the subject can no longer hear the tone, move the still vibrating fork next to the subject's ear (not touching his body).
3. If the subject can once again hear the tone, then conduction is normal and the test result is positive.
4. Now strike the tuning fork and place it immediately next to the subject's ear (not touching the body).
5. When the subject can no longer hear the tone, place the handle of the fork against the subject's mastoid process. If the subject once again hears the tone via bone conduction, then air conduction is impaired and the subject has some conduction deafness. The test result is negative.
6. Repeat the test for the subject's other ear.

   Does the subject exhibit air conduction impairment in either ear?

Activity 4: Equilibrium Tests

4-A. Balance

1. Have your partner walk a straight line, with arms down by their side and placing one foot directly in front of the other.

   Was the subject able to walk without wobbling?

2. If a person's nervous system is depressed (perhaps by illness or stress), mental activity may impact balance and equilibrium. Have your partner stand quickly from a seated position while rapidly counting backward from ten.
   Did the subject shows signs of dizziness or loss of balance?

4-B. Barany Test

CAUTION: This test should not be performed on students prone to motion sickness.

CAUTION: Several students should surround the subject during testing to catch them if they fall.

1. Have the subject sit on a rotating stool with hands firmly clasping the stool. The subjects head should be tilted downward (chin-to-chest).
2. Four students should surround the subject. One should rotate the stool about 10 rotations in a 10 second time period, then stop rotation abruptly.
3. Immediately note the subject's nystagmus*, then ask the subject to stand and walk. Does the subject experience vertigo (the feeling of spinning or dizziness).

   Healthy subjects should exhibit nystagmus after rotation. While rotating, the fluid in the semicircular canals will bend the cupula (flexible tip of crista), causing brief nystagmus. (Under constant movement the cupula adjusts to compensate and nystagmus discontinues). When the rotation suddenly stops the cupula over-compensates causing nystagmus in the opposite direction of the rotation. When standing or walking, the subject should tend to fall in the opposite direction of rotation.

---

* Nystagmus is the involuntary slow tracking of the eyes in one direction followed by rapid movement in the opposite direction (like an old typewriter cylinder).

4-C. Romberg Test

The cerebellum maintains normal balance by continually monitoring information from the vestibule of the ear and proprioceptors scattered throughout the body. This information is compared with the intent of the cerebrum regarding body posture and movement, and appropriate muscle actions are taken to maintain balance. The Romberg test determines the fitness of the proprioceptors, cerebellum and connecting neural circuits in maintaining balance.

1. Have the subject stand with his back to the blackboard (but not touching the board) and with feet close together.
2. Aim a light source toward the subject so that a shadow is cast onto the blackboard.
3. The subject should now stand erect as still as possible for two minutes, with eyes open and staring straight ahead. During this time, use chalk to mark on the blackboard any movements of the subject's shadow. Does the subject display any side-to-side swaying movements?
4. Repeat the above test with the subject's eyes closed. Does the subject exhibit more or less swaying?
5. Repeat the above test with the subject turned sideways to the blackboard so you can observe front-to-back swaying motions.

The above tests can also be performed with the subject standing on just one foot.

exercise 19

the NERVOUS system

- special senses: TASTE & SMELL -

*Flowers appear on the earth...
the blossoming vines spread
their fragrance.
Song of Solomon 2:12-13*

The nose knows ~ Our noses can identify an estimated 50,000 unique odors.

Taste and smell are the two special senses that make use of *chemoreceptors*; that is, they are designed to detect chemical stimuli. Other chemoreceptors are scattered throughout the body as part of our general senses, but those for taste and smell are restricted to the tongue and nose and specialize in detecting chemicals from the external environment. Both detect chemicals dissolved in solution – saliva on the tongue, mucus in the nose – even if the chemicals originate from dried foods or the air. These chemicals are detected by **gustatory receptors** on the tongue and **olfactory receptors** in the nasal cavity.

There are only five basic tastes (sweet, salty, sour, bitter and umami), but the nose can distinguish some 20,000-50,000 unique smells. As we will see in this exercise, however, olfaction significantly affects our appreciation of foods.

Anatomy of the Tongue

The tongue is a muscular organ that forms the floor of the mouth. The organ is actually composed of many skeletal muscles that function as a *muscular hydrostat* (like the arm of an octopus) since the muscles do not originate from bony attachments.

The tongue is divided into two major parts: the **oral part** and the **pharyngeal part** (Figure 19-1). The pharyngeal part is firmly anchored to the oropharynx and consists primarily of the **root** of the tongue. The highly dexterous oral part consists of the **corpus** (i.e., body) of the tongue and the **apex** (tip) of the tongue. On many people a **median sulcus** divides the tongue longitudinally. Additionally, a **terminal sulcus** divides the oral and pharyngeal parts of the tongue.

The primary functions of the tongue are *i*) to assist the formulation of words during speech and *ii*) to manipulate food while chewing and swallowing. As part of its digestive function, the tongue *tastes* objects brought into the oral cavity. That is, the tongue performs a quick chemical analysis of foods we eat before it's swallowed. ***Gustatory receptors*** are associated with **taste buds** scattered primarily on the dorsum of the tongue (Figure 19-2). The taste buds themselves are usually affiliated with **papillae**, four types of which are found on the tongue. The small and abundant **filliform papillae** (also called *lingual papillae*) are distributed uniformly across the dorsum of the tongue. They give the tongue its velvet, or carpeted, appearance. The slightly larger **fungiform papillae** are also distributed widely on the dorsum of the tongue. These papillae are easily seen on a tongue that has been discolored (by a blue lollipop, for example). The **circumvalate papillae** usually appear as large rounded structures forming a V-shape at the posterior portion of the oral part of the tongue. Finally, the **foliate papillae** are restricted to the lateral edges of the tongue near the circumvalate papillae. The foliate papillae have the appearance of shark gills.

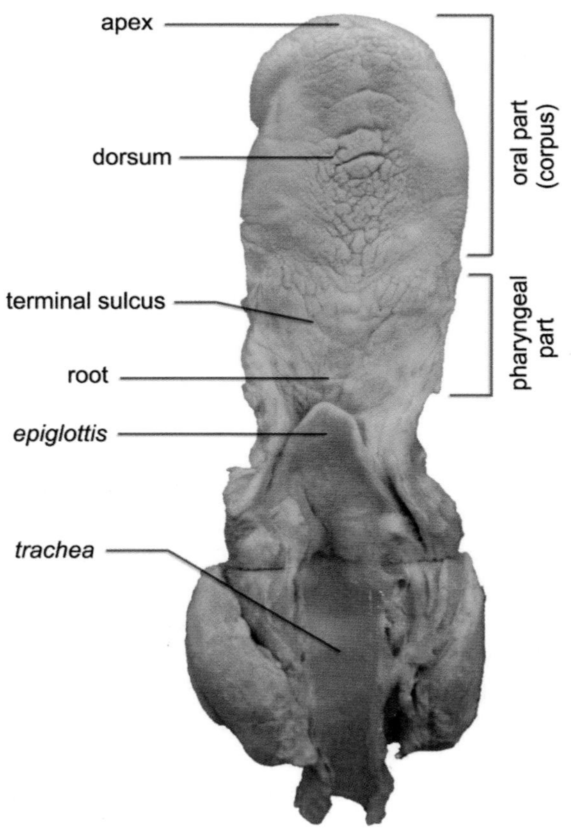

Figure 19-1 **Surface Anatomy of the Human Tongue**

Gustatory Receptors

As stated above, gustatory receptors (i.e., taste buds) are scattered throughout the tongue in association with papillae. The inset in figure 19-2 shows taste budes associated with filliform papillae. Deep grooves called **taste pores** allow dissolved chemicals to reach the taste buds while simultaneously protecting the receptors from the harsh and abrasive environment of the mouth. Long microvilli (called *gustatory hairs*) extend

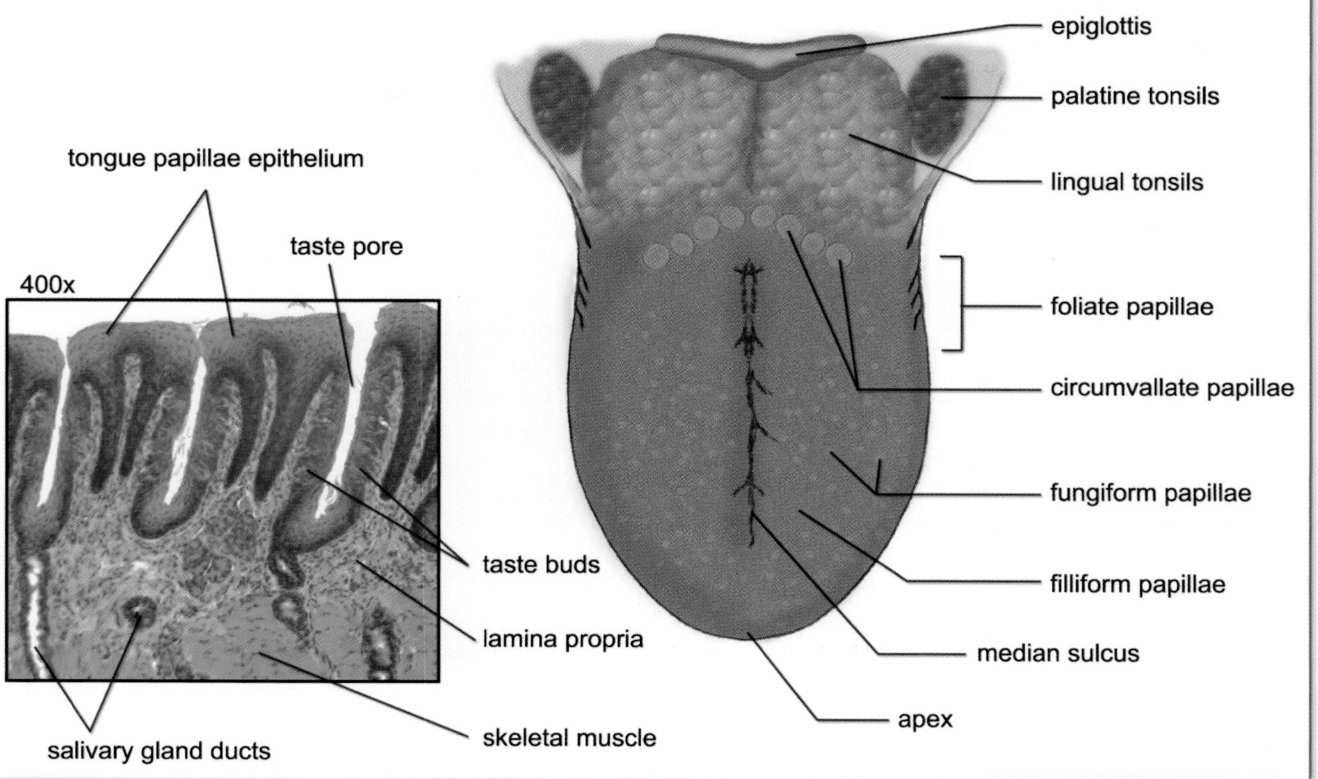

Figure 19-2

Structures of the Tongue

from the receptor cells into the taste pore. Binding of appropriate dissolved chemicals to the microvilli triggers depolarization of the gustatory receptor cell. Afferent nerve fibers convey stimuli information to the sensory cortex (i.e., the postcentral gyrus of the brain) via cranial nerves VII, IX and X.

The Nasal Cavity and Olfaction

The sense of smell is achieved by specialized neuroepithelial tissue called the **olfactory epithelium** (Figure 19-3) which occupies an area of about 5 cm^2 in the nasal cavity. The olfactory epithelium is not in the direct pathway of inhaled air, so our sense of smell is not particularly great under most circumstances. The act of sniffing, however, draws more air toward the olfactory epithelium and therefore improves our ability to smell.

The olfactory receptor cells are bipolar neurons that project numerous **olfactory cilia** toward the lumen of the nasal cavity. They are supported by non-sensory epithelial cells. The olfactory cilia contain receptor proteins that bind to different classes of organic and inorganic molecules. Axons emerge from the basal ends of the receptor cells and pass through the pores of the cribiform plate of the ethmoid bone. They synapse with nerves in the olfactory bulbs on either side of the eithmoid bone and convey their signals to the olfactory cortex as the olfactory nerve (*cranial nerve I*).

Olfactory Receptors

Olfactory receptors are quite different from other types of receptors in the body. Most receptors exhibit high specificity for a particular molecule, that is, they bind one and only one molecule (called a *ligand*). Usually, an inactive receptor is activated upon binding its ligand. Olfactory receptors don't bind to a single, unique ligand molecule, however. Instead, each receptor binds to a *class* of molecules that often share similar atomic features. As a result, many different odorants can bind to a given receptor. Likewise, a given odorant will often bind to more than one type of olfactory receptor. Because of these properties, molecules that have never been encountered before can be analyzed by

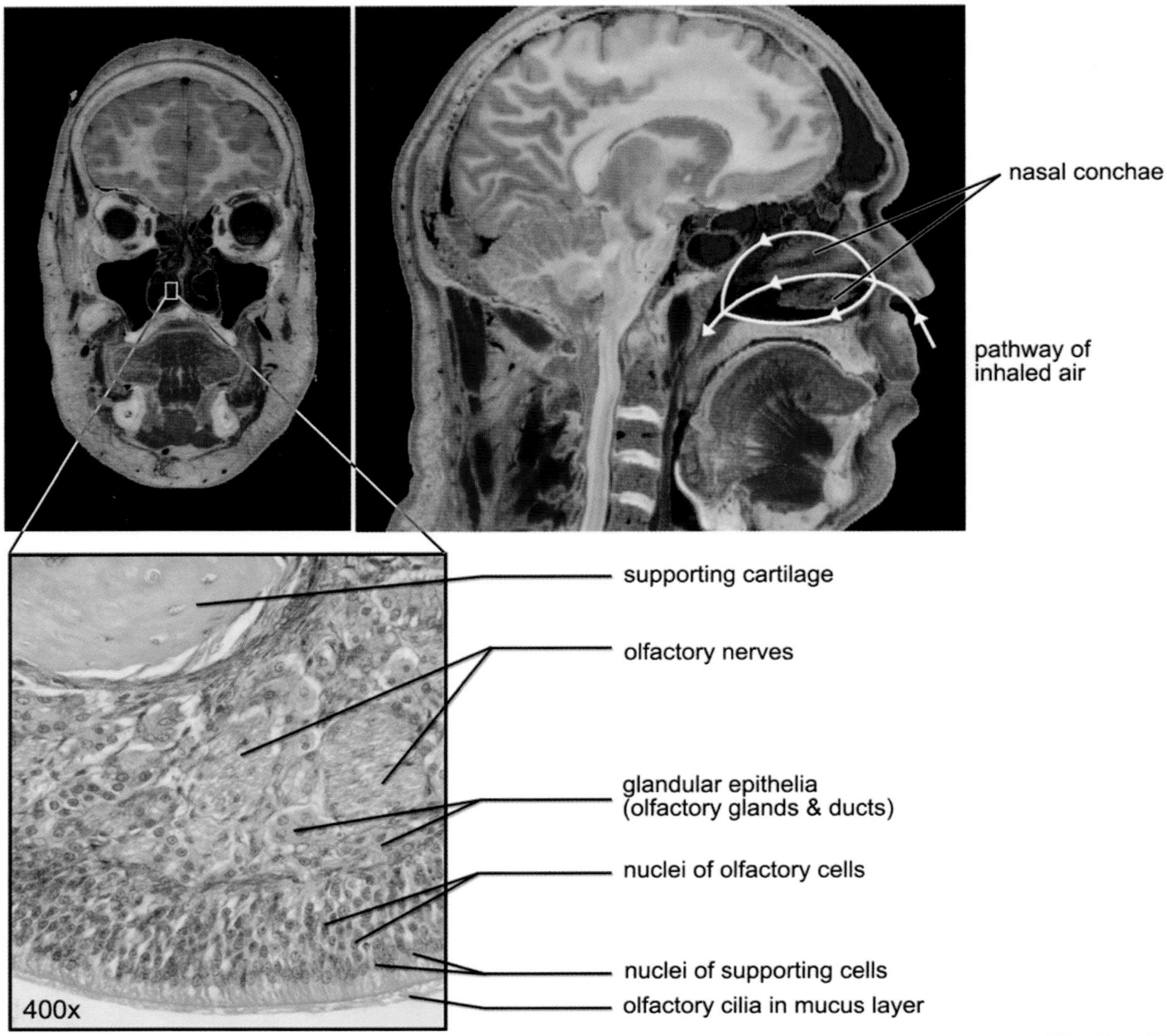

Figure 19-3 **The Nasal Cavity**

our sense of smell. Also, a virtually endless number of smells can be characterized even though we probably have less than 500 different types of olfactory receptors. There is still much to be learned about the sense of smell. In 2004 Linda Buck and Richard Axel won the *Nobel Prize in Physiology or Medicine* for their work related to olfaction.

Activity 1: Microscopic Examination of the Tongue

1. Obtain a microscope slide of the tongue and a microscope. Locate the papillae and taste buds embedded within the deep taste pores.

Activity 2: Mapping Taste Buds on the Tongue

1. Obtain 4 cotton swabs and flavored solutions (salty, sour, bitter and sweet) from your instructor.
2. Have you lab partner rinse his mouth with water and then lightly dry his tongue with a paper towel.
3. Dip a cotton swab into one of the four flavors and gently apply the solution to varies locations on the tongue. Label the figure provided to indicate where the flavor could be detected.
4. Repeat steps 2 & 3 for each flavor, being sure to use a clean cotton swab for each flavor.
5. Was your partner able to taste all of the flavors on all parts of the tongue?

Activity 3: Microscopic Examination of the Olfactory Epithelia

1. Obtain a microscope slide of olfactory epithelium and a microscope. Examine the tissue, noting the olfactory cilia of the olfactory receptors and the nerves that pass through the supporting tissues.

Activity 4: Effect of Smell on Taste

1. Obtain cotton swabs and several bottles of flavored extracts (e.g., banana extract, cherry extract, etc.).
2. Have your partner close her eyes.
3. Dip a clean cotton swab into one of the flavored extracts.
4. While waving an open bottle of a *second* flavored extract under your partner's nose, lighly dab her tongue with the *first* flavor.
5. What flavor does your partner taste?
6. Have your partner rinse her mouth with water and smell coffee beans. Then repeat the experiment using different combinations of flavored extracts.

Activity 5: Effect of Smell & Texture on Taste

1. Ask the subject to sit with eyes closed and pinched nose.
2. Obtain samples of the food items provided by your instructor. ***Do not*** allow the subject to see the food being tested. Handle the food with toothpicks.
3. For each test, place a cube of food into the subject's mouth and ask him/her to identify the food by
    a. manipulating the food with the tongue, then
    b. chewing the food, then
    c. releasing the nostrils while continuing to chew the food
4. Record your results in the chart provided (Table 19.1).

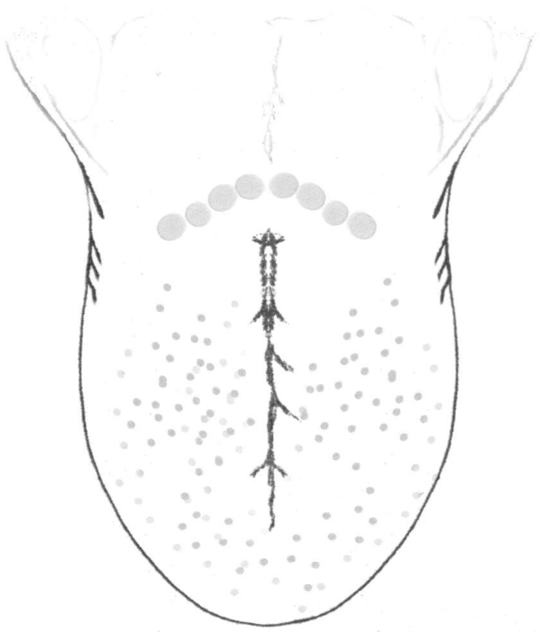

Food tested	Texture only	Chewing with nostrils closed	Chewing with nostrils open	Identification unsuccessful

Table 19.1 **Identification by Texture & Smell**

1-4. List the four types of papillae found on the tongue and briefly describe each.

Type: ___________________________

Description:

Type: ___________________________

Description:

Type: ___________________________

Description:

Type: ___________________________

Description:

5. What are the primary functions of the tongue?

6. Which cranial nerve(s) conveys sensory information to the brain from the tongue?

7. Which cranial nerve(s) conveys sensory information to the brain from the olfactory epithelium?

8. How do olfactory receptors differ from other chemical receptors in the body?

9. In what ways are the senses of smell and taste similar?

 Name ______________________________

exercise 20

the ENDOCRINE system

Praise the LORD, O my soul, and forget not all his benefits - who forgives all your sins and heals all your diseases.

Psalm 103:2-3

A ritual dancer of the Dogon people of Mali in west Africa wearing a mask depicting goiter (thyroid gland swelling) due to iodine deficiency.

The endocrine system is one of the two "command-and-control" systems of the body (the other being the nervous system). Whereas the nervous system is best at gathering information about the external environment and responding rapidly (such as jumping out of the way of an oncoming bus), the endocrine system is especially designed to monitor internal conditions and control slow or cyclic body functions. The most familiar examples include the female menstrual cycle, which occurs monthly, and the gradual progression through puberty, which occurs only once in a lifetime over a decade-long time span.

Organs of the Endocrine System

Organs of the endocrine system are scattered throughout the cephalic, cervical, thoracic, abdominal and pubic regions (Figure 20-1). Many endocrine tissues are rather soft, making them difficult to palpate or mend surgically. A number of endrocrine organs are exclusively endocrine while others perform both *endocrine* and *exocrine* functions. In addition, several organs from other organ systems release hormones into the bloodstream and are thus technically endocrine organs, as well (for example, the brain and the heart). The major hormone-releasing organs are described individually below. If possible, microscopically examine each of the endocrine tissues as they are described.

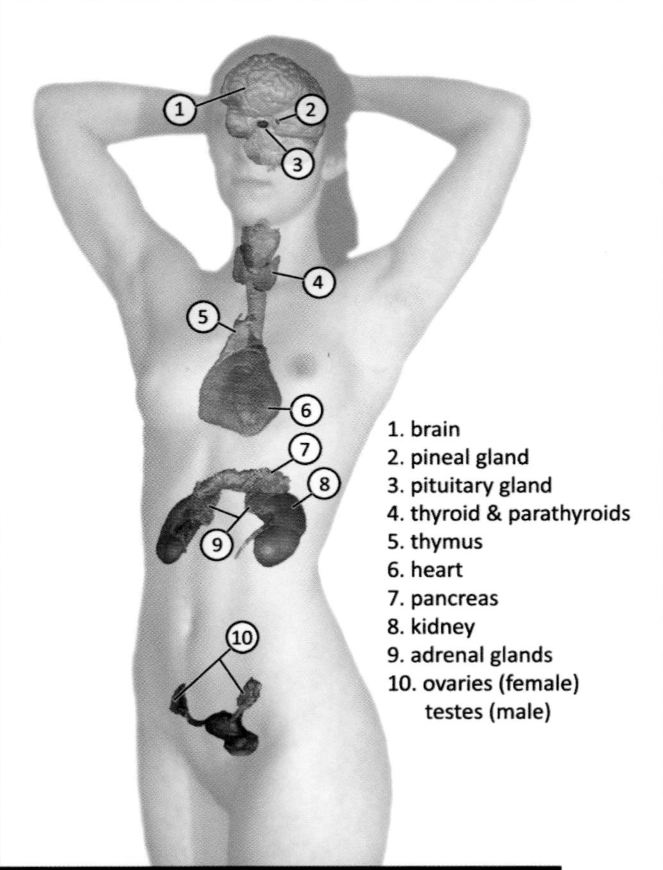

Figure 20-1: Some Endocrine Glands & Tissues

The Pituitary Gland

The **pituitary gland**, located within the cranial cavity, is often called the "master gland" of the endocrine system for two important reasons: First, it produces hormones that directly control the activities of other endocrine glands (causing them to produce their own hormones); Second, it has a close physical and functional relationship with the hypothalamus of the brain (Figure 20-2). For instance, the hypothalamus produces hormones that directly affect the pituitary gland and axons from hypothalamic neurons penetrate deep into the pituitary. Thus, it's between these two structures (the pituitary gland and the hypothalamus) that the two "command-and-control" systems of the body communicate and coordinate their activities.

The hypothalamus and pituitary gland share an unusual physical connection. Usually, hormones released by endocrine glands use the bloodstream to travel throughout the body to distant target cells. Blood, of course, circulates through the body, flowing from the heart through arteries, then capillary beds and back to the heart through veins. Usually, blood passes through just one capillary bed as it flows from artery to vein. In a cardiovascular *portal system*, however, the blood passes through two sequential capillary beds (connected by *portal veins*) before entering the veins and returning to the heart. Portal systems are rare in the body, but a very important one called the *hypophyseal portal system* carries blood from a capillary bed in the hypothalamus to a capillary bed in the pituitary gland. This allows hormones produced by the hypothalamus to travel quickly to the pituitary gland without having to first go the heart and then throughout the whole body. The pituitary gland responds to hypothalamic hormones to regulate the rest of the endocrine system.

The pituitary gland is divided into two lobes: The anterior lobe and the posterior lobe (Figure 20-2). The anterior pituitary contains hormone-producing epithelial cells and the second

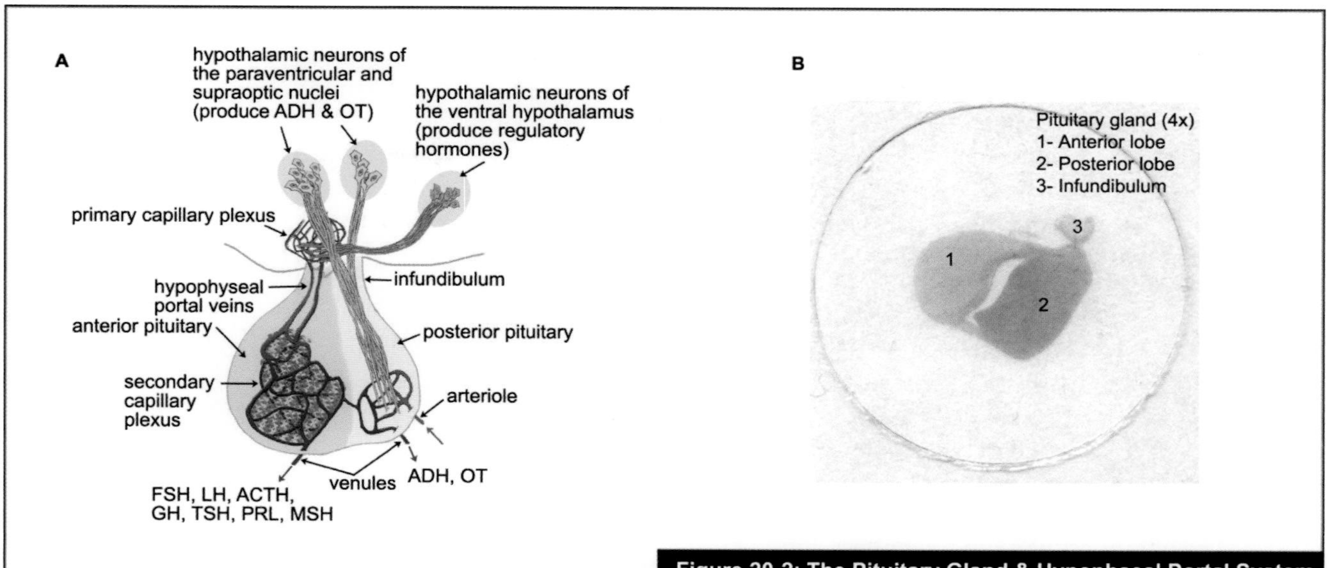

Figure 20-2: The Pituitary Gland & Hypophseal Portal System

capillary bed of the hypophyseal portal system. Several hormones of the anterior pituitary regulate the hormone production of other endocrine organs. The posterior pituitary is technically not an endocrine organ at all because it doesn't produce any hormones; however, it stores and releases two hormones (OT and ADH) produced by the hypothalamus and transported to the posterior lobe through neuronal axons.

The hormones produced by the anterior pituitary are under the control of the hypothalamus of the brain. The hypothalamus releases *regulatory hormones* (*releasing and inhibitory hormones*) to increase or decrease the levels of circulating anterior pituitary hormones. For example, when the body temperature gets too cold, the hypothalamus releases TRH (thyroid releasing hormone) which then causes the anterior pituitary to release TSH (thyroid stimulating hormone). TSH stimulates the thyroid gland to release T3 (triiodothyronine) and T4 (thyroxin). T3 and T4 increase the metabolic rate of cells throughout the body, elevating body temperature. A summary of the hormones released by the hypothalamus and pituitary gland can be found in figure 20-3.

The Adrenal Gland

The two **adrenal glands** rest superiorly on the kidneys (Figure 20-4). Each gland is divided internally into two layers: The inner **medulla** and the outer **cortex**. Each division releases hormones, but the hormones released and their triggers are vastly different.

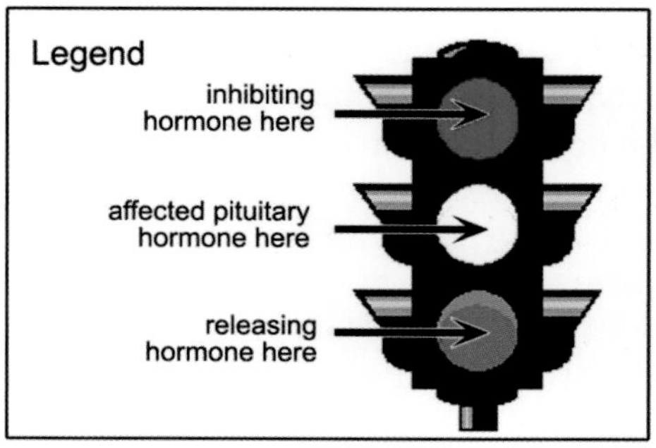

GH = Growth Hormone
GH-RH = GH Releasing Hormone
GH-IH = GH Inhibiting Hormone
TSH = Thyroid Stimulating Hormone
TRH = TSH Releasing Hormone
ACTH = Adrenocorticotropic Hormone
CRH = Corticotropic Releasing Hormone
PRL = Prolactin
PRF = Prolactin Releasing Factor
PIH = Prolactin Inhibiting Hormone
LH = Leutinizing Hormone
GnRH = Gonadotropic Releasing Hormone
FSH = Follicle Stimulating Hormone
MSH = Melanocyte Stimulating Hormone
MRF =MSH Releasing Factor

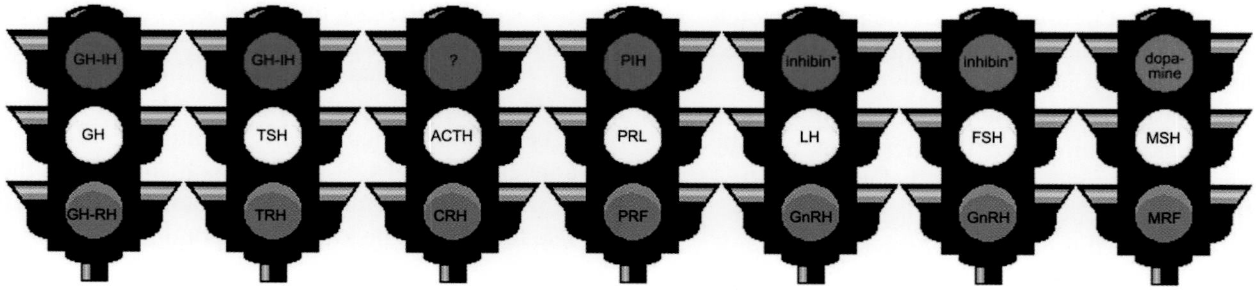

Figure 20-3: Hypothalamic Regulatory Hormones

*produced by gonads

Compared to other endocrine organs, the adrenal medulla is unique in the way it's triggered to release its hormones: The hormone-releasing epithelial cells of the medulla are stimulated directly by the nervous system. Because they form direct connections (i.e., synapses) with neuronal axons they're referred to as *neuroepithelial cells*. The adrenal medulla is under the control of the sympathetic division of the autonomic nervous system (ANS). When the sympathetic division is stimulated, the medulla releases epinephrine (E) and norepinephrine (NE) into the bloodstream. These hormones assist the nervous system in producing the "fight-or-flight" response.

The adrenal cortex is subdivided into three regions: The outermost **zona glomerulosa**, the middle **zona fasciculata** and the inner **zona reticularis**. All three regions release steroid hormones. The zona reticularis produces sex hormones (primarily *androgens*) of unknown function called gonocorticoids. Although their functions are not completely understood, hyperactivity of this region of the adrenal gland produces enhanced male secondary sexual characteristics, such as facial hair, even on women. The zona glomerulosa produces *mineralocorticoids* (mostly aldosterone), which are steroid hormones important in the regulation of water and electrolyte balance. The zona fasciculata releases *glucocorticoids* into the bloodstream in response to circulating adrenocorticotropic hormone (ACTH) released by the pituitary gland. Glucocorticoids control the body's use of glucose and overall metabolic rate. Interestingly, these hormones also exhibit anti-inflammatory properties and are thus administered to reduce pain and inflammation. Hydrocortisone, for example, is a glucocorticoid.

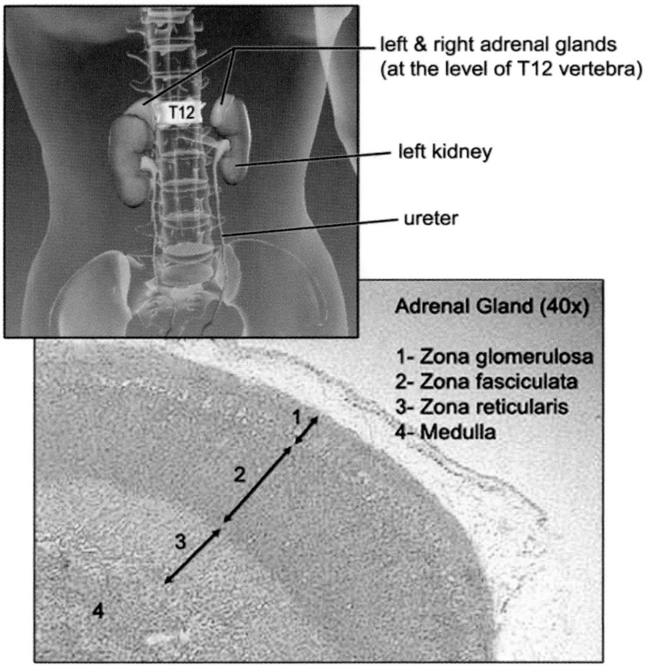

Figure 20-4: The Adrenal (Suprarenal) Glands

The Thyroid & Parathyroid Glands

The bilobed **thyroid gland** is located at the base of the neck (Figure 20-5). The gland can be palpated by finding your "Adam's apple" and then gently tapping on your trachea while moving your hand inferiorly. Just before reaching the jugular notch you should feel the hard trachea give way to the soft tissue of the thyroid.

The thyroid gland produces two hormones: T3 (triiodothyronine) and T4 (thyroxine). These hormones are produced in small chambers called **follicles** by follicular cells. Both T3 and T4 are released by the thyroid in response to circulating thyroid-stimulating hormone (TSH) produced by the pituitary gland. Although both T3 and T4 can be found circulating in the blood (bound to thryoid-binding globulin proteins), T3 is the one responsible for affecting target cells (which, by the way, is virtually every cell in the body). Most circulating T4 is converted to T3 inside target tissues. Once inside the cell, binding of T3 to thyroid hormone receptors on the mitochondria stimulates mitochondrial ATP production. More generally, cells respond to thyroid hormones by increasing overall metabolic activity, resulting in the consumption of energy and the generation of heat. Because of the dramatic effects of thyroid hormones on body metabolism, people with *hyperthyroidism* tend to be alert, thin, heat-intolerant and active. By contrast, those with *hypothyroidism* tend to be more lethargic and over-weight. Both T3 and T4 contain iodine and a form of hypothyroidism called *goiter* is caused by a lack of iodine in the diet. In the United States, goiter is rare because of the addition of iodine to table salt (i.e., iodized salt).

Entrenched between the follicles of the thryoid gland are parafollicular cells, also known as C cells. Parafollicular cells monitor the concentration of Ca^{2+} in the blood and release the hormone calcitonin (CT) when blood calcium levels rise too high. The kidneys respond to CT by

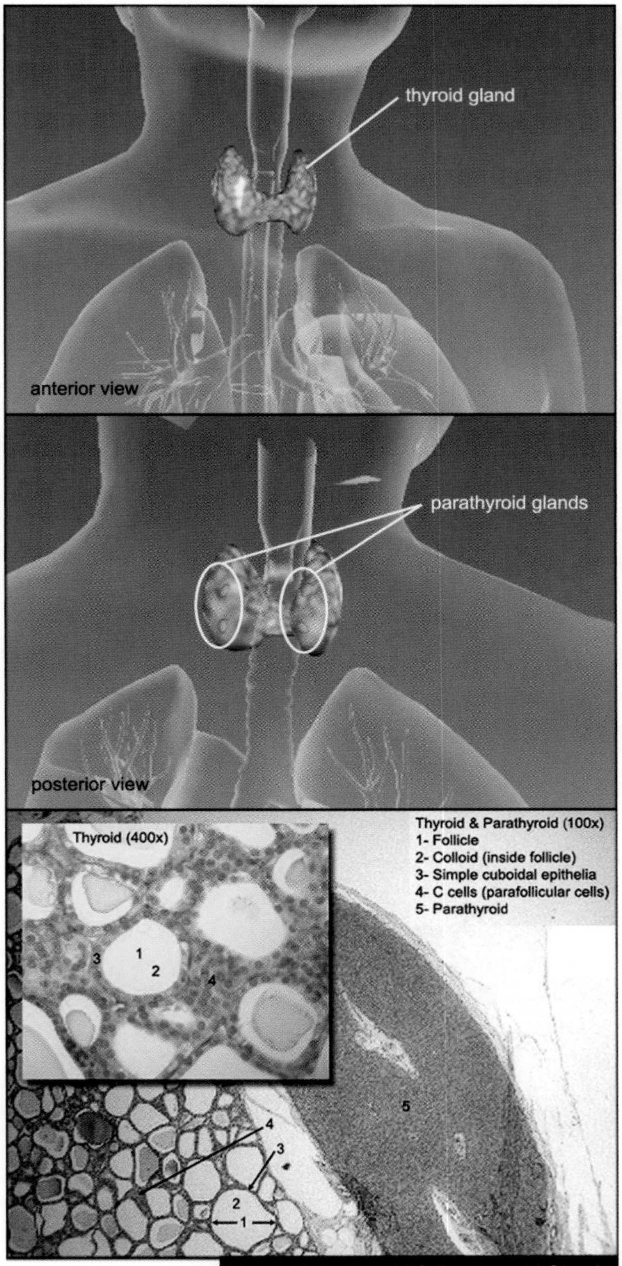

Figure 20-5: Thyroid & Parathyroid Glands

excreting calcium into urine, thus lowering its concentration in the blood.

The **parathyroid glands** are four small nodules embedded within the posterior portion of the thyroid gland; two on the left lobe and two on the right lobe. These small glands produce parathyroid hormone (PTH) which also helps regulate blood calcium concentration. PTH is released when blood Ca^{2+} levels fall too low. The kidneys respond to PTH by keeping Ca^{2+} in the blood and releasing the hormone calcitriol, which aids absorption of calcium from the digestive tract. In bones, PTH stimulates osteoclasts that in turn dissolve calcium from the bony matrix and release it into the bloodstream.

The Pancreas

The **pancreas** is a rather large organ located in the superior portion of the abdomen, outside and behind the peritoneal cavity (i.e., it is *retroperitoneal*). It possesses both endocrine and exocrine functions. As an exocrine organ the pancreas produces numerous digestive enzymes that are secreted into the gastrointestinal tract. Pockets of hormone-producing cells are scattered throughout the pancreas (Figure 20-6). These pockets of endocrine cells, called the **islets of Langerhans**, are 100 – 200 μm in size and contain two populations of cells: Alpha cells that produce glucagon and the more numerous beta cells that produce insulin. Insulin and glucagon function antagonistically in the regulation of blood glucose levels. Following a meal, when glucose levels in the blood begin to rise, pancreatic beta cells release insulin into the bloodstream. Target cells throughout the body respond to insulin by absorbing glucose from the blood and storing it away as glycogen. When blood glucose levels fall too low, pancreatic alpha cells release glucagon. Target cells respond to glucagon by turning to their stored glycogen supplies as their primary source of glucose, or by manufacturing glucose from scratch.

The Pineal Gland

Like the pituitary gland, the pineal gland is located within the cranial cavity and is surrounded by the brain. The gland produces melatonin, a hormone believed to regulate daily cycles (i.e., circadian rhythm). Collateral axons from visual pathways enter the pineal gland to presumably inform the gland of available sunlight. Melatonin production is lowest during the daylight hours and highest at night during the early morning hours. Interestingly, blood melatonin levels are higher in children than adults and the decline of melatonin may trigger puberty. In adults, blood melatonin levels are higher during the winter months – when days are short and nights are long – and may play a role in *seasonal affective disorder* (*SAD*), a condition marked by depression and melancholy.

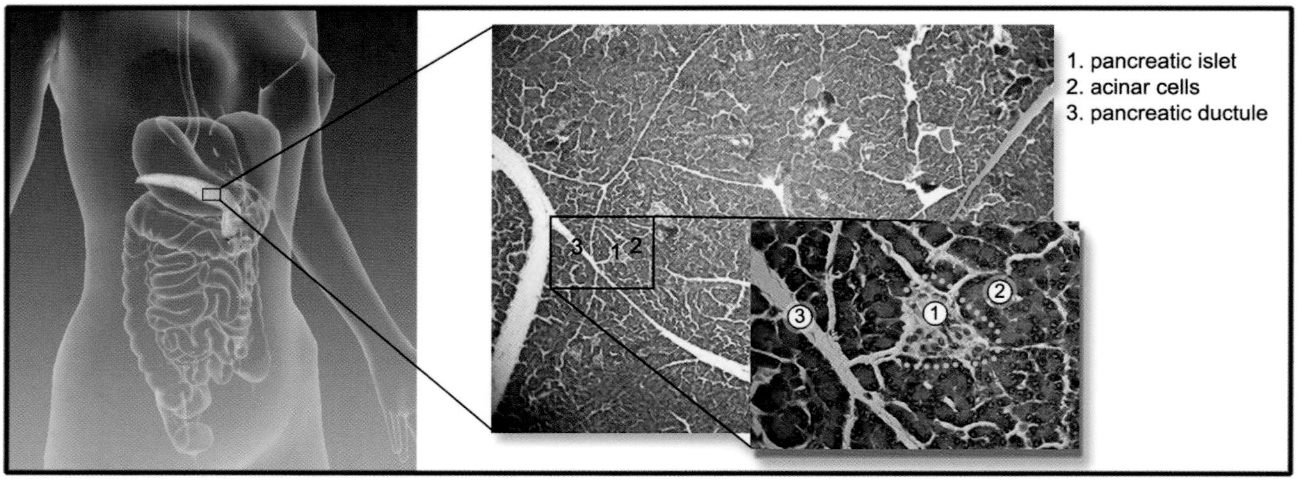

Figure 20-6: The Pancreas

Endocrine Functions of Other Organs

Several organs belonging to various different organ systems produce hormones and thus are also considered endocrine tissues. Endocrine activity of a few major organs are discussed below.

The Heart

The major organ of the cardiovascular system – the heart – contains endocrine tissues that produce hormones. Atrial natriuretic peptide (ANP) is released by the myocytes of the right atrium and brain natriuretic peptide (BNP) is produced by myocytes of the right ventricle (BNP was originally thought to be produced in the brain). These hormones are released when the chambers of the heart become over-stretched, an indication that blood volume – and blood pressure – is too high. The kidneys respond to natriuretic peptides by increasing urine production, i.e., removing more water from the blood, thus lowering blood volume and pressure.

The Brain

We've already discussed the important endocrine activity of the hypothalamus of the brain. More than a dozen hormones are produced by the hypothalamus which exert influence over every organ system in the body. Thus, the brain ultimately controls the entire endocrine system and the functions of visceral organs.

The Kidneys

The kidneys – major organs of the urinary system – produce several hormones that help regulate blood volume and composition. Erythropoietin (EPO) is released by the kidneys when blood volume is too low. EPO targets cells in red bone marrow and stimulates the production of erythrocytes, or red blood cells. Likewise, renin is released by the kidneys when renal blood flow is reduced by low blood pressure. Renin stimulates the release of ADH and aldosterone, leading to water retention by the kidneys and increased thirst. The kidneys also produce calcitriol in response to circulating PTH. Calcitriol stimulates osteoclast activity in bone causing the release of Ca^{2+} into the bloodstream and elevating blood calcium levels. Calcitriol works in conjunction with calcitonin to increase calcium absorption from the gut.

The Intestines

The stomach and small intestine both produce hormones that regulate digestion. Gastrin (produced by the stomach) and cholecystokinin (produced by the duodenum of the small intestine) are examples. These and other digestive hormones will be considered further when we examine the digestive system.

Adipose

Adipose tissue releases a hormone called leptin. This hormone has received a lot of attention lately because of its impact on body weight. Obese mice

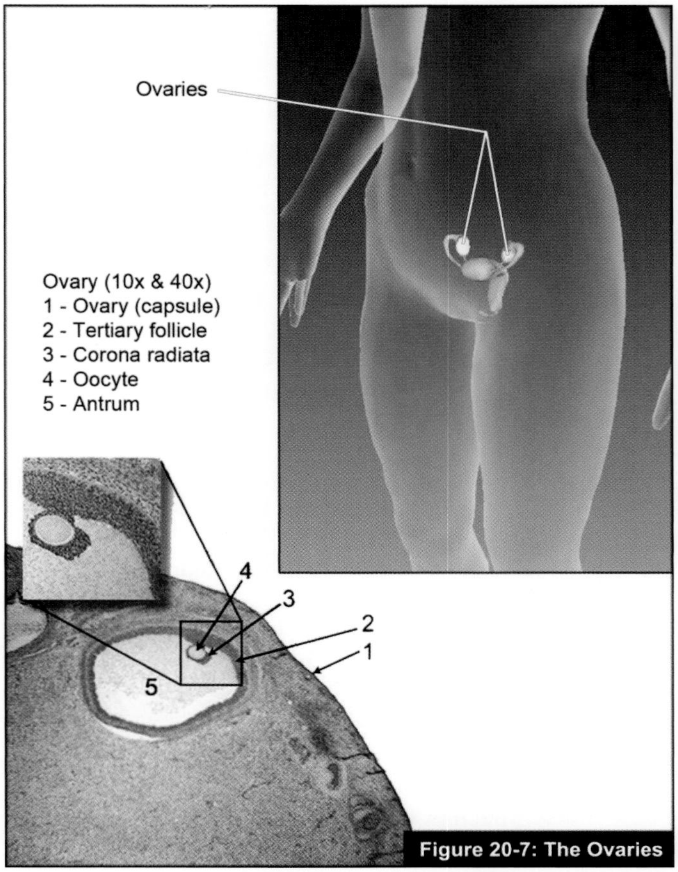

Figure 20-7: The Ovaries

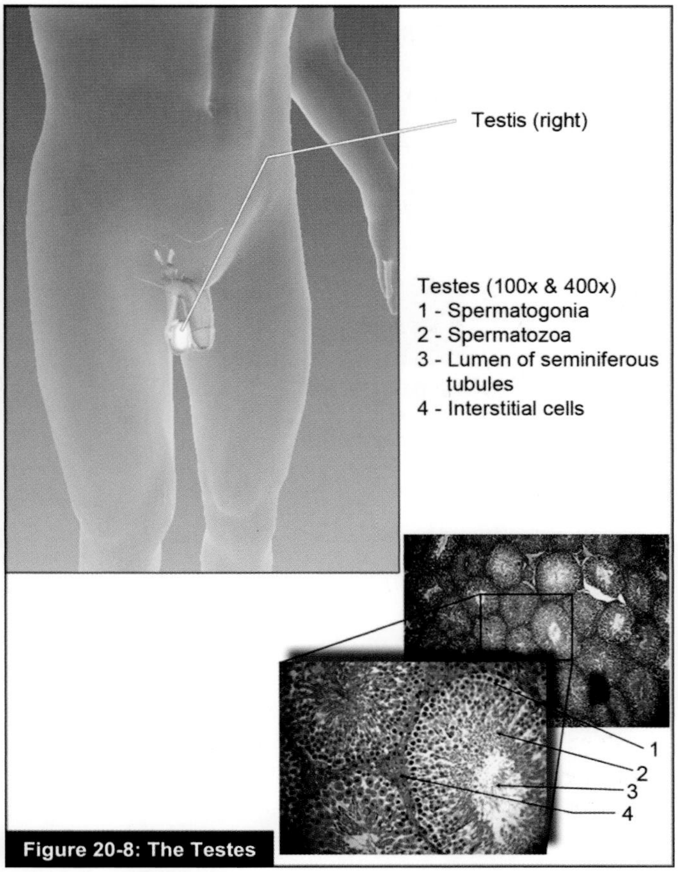

Figure 20-8: The Testes

with mutant genes for making leptin returned to normal body weight when leptin was administered by injection; however, the medicinal use of leptin in humans is still under investigation.

The Thymus

The thymus is an organ of the lymphatic system located in the mediastinum deep to the sternum. It's an unusual organ in that it atrophies with age. The gland is relatively large in children, but shrinks and undergoes fibrosis in the decades following puberty. In most people, the thymus has lost nearly all function by the end of their 50's. Hormones of the thymus regulate maturation of immune defense cells.

The thymus produces a number of hormones collectively called thymosins. These hormones direct the differentiation of T cells, a special population of lymphocytes responsible for cell-mediated immunity and coordinating the immune response to foreign cells. T cells live for decades, but their slow decline over time following atrophy of the thymus may make the elderly more susceptible to microbial attack. This is especially a concern for those who travel the world following retirement, since they'll be exposed to new microbes they've never experience before and that without a functional thymus to develop T cells against the new antigens.

The Gonads

The **ovaries** in the female (Figure 20-7) and the **testes** in the male (Figure 20-8) are reproductive organs that produce the sex hormones, primarily estrogen and testosterone. Testosterone – the male sex hormone – is produced by interstitial cells inside each testis and is responsible for developing secondary sexual characteristics in men (such as facial hair and lower voices). Estrogen – the female sex hormone – is produced by follicles within the ovary and brings about feminine characteristics in women, and helps regulate the monthly menstrual cycle. Effects of testosterone and estrogen are summarized in figure 20-9.

Activity 1: Locating the Endocrine Organs
1. Memorize the locations of the endocrine organs and the tissues discussed in this chapter.

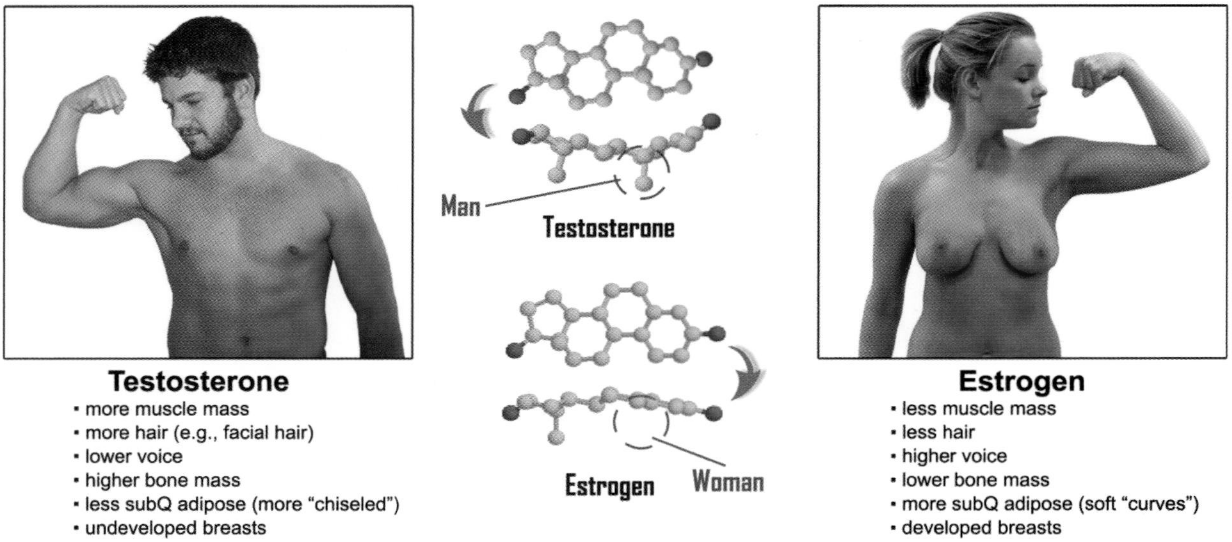

Figure 20-9: Secondary Sexual Characteristics

2. Attempt to locate as many endocrine organs as possible in the cat. Your instructor can find the pituitary gland by cutting the head of a cat mid-sagittally using a sharp hand saw.

Activity 2: Histological Examination of Endocrine Tissues

Obtain prepared slides of the pituitary gland, thyroid & parathyroid glands, adrenal gland, pancreas, ovary and testis. In the circles on the page at the end of this chapter, draw the endocrine tissues found in these organs at the recommended magnification levels. You should be able to identify these tissues in a microscope and list the hormones they produce.

Activity 3: Hormone Actions

Using this lab manual, the internet, and your A&P textbook, complete the table at the end of this chapter.

Activity 4: Endocrine Disorders

**Special thanks to Mary Gribbin*

Using this lab manual, the internet, and your A&P textbook, seek out the information on each endocrine disorder described below and link it to the patient symptoms and lab tests in the following table (beginning on the next page). Your task: match each patient with one of the following disorders or conditions:

- Acromegaly
- Addison's disease
- Cretinism
- Cushing's disease
- Decrease in gonadotropins
- Decrease in PRL
- Diabeties insipidus
- Gigantism
- Graves' disease
- Myxedema
- Sheehan syndrome
- Type I diabetes mellitus
- Type II diabetes mellitus

Endocrine Disorders Table

Patient	Symptoms / Lab tests	Condition / Gland / Hormone
#1: Avery	• High glucose in the urine • High ketones in the urine • Blurred vision • Weakness • Frequent urination • Intracellular dehydration • Thirst center activated	Condition: Gland: Hormone:
#2: Bill	• High glucose in the urine • Patient is obese • Low energy level • Frequent urination	Condition: Gland: Hormone:
#3: Carla	• Dilute urine (low density) • Excessive thirst • Frequent urination • When water intake was restricted, urinary output remained high	Condition: Gland: Hormone:
#4: Daniel	• High urinary glucose • High urinary ketone • Patient complains of jaw pain and joint pain • Asymmetrical growth • Increased size of hands, feet, and lower jaw • Increased blood somatotropin levels, especially after puberty	Condition: Gland: Hormone:
#5: Ethan	• Exhibits goiter • Exhibits protruding eyes • Has tachycardia at rest • Excessive sweating	Condition: Gland: Hormone:
#6: Frank	• Increased blood levels of ACTH which has led to an increase in cortisol levels, which has led to an increase in blood glucose levels • Upon stress, ACTH levels do not rise • Patient does not show any circadian pattern of ACTH secretion • Purple striation in the chest and abdomen areas • Weight gain • Rounded cheeks • Lump of fatty tissue on cervical region • Hypertension	Condition: Gland: Hormone:
#7: Gillian	• Exhibits a decline in ACTH levels • Hypoaldosteronism • Shows weakness and fatigue • Pigmentation in the skin and nipple areas • Hypotension	Condition: Gland: Hormone:

#8: Heather	• Patient experiences postpartum failure to lactate • Patient is 25 years old	Condition: Gland: Hormone:
#9: Irene	• Patient gave birth recently • Experiencing headaches • Has vision problems • Stiff neck • Tests show intracranial pressure • As time (years) goes by, the patient experiences numerous hormonal deficiencies	Condition: Gland: Hormone:
#10: James	• Has cardiac hypertrophy • Shows symmetrical growth • Experienced an increase in somatotropin before puberty • Patient showed excessive growth before puberty and after puberty	Condition: Gland: Hormone:
#11: Kimberly	• Lab tests showed low body temperature (35C) • Often tired • Very sensitive to cold temperatures • Hair and nails are brittle • Eventual development of thick skin • Patient is 35 years old	Condition: Gland: Hormone:
#12: Linda	• Patient is 7 years old • Appears dwarf-like • Arms and legs are short compared to trunk • Broad, puffy face • Protuberant abdomen • Sparse hair	Condition: Gland: Hormone:
#13: Mary	• Patient is 13 years old • Lack of pubic hair • Lack of axillary hair	Condition: Gland: Hormone:

Hormone / Class	produced by…	in response to…	causes…	antagonized by…
ADH = antidiuretic hormone class: peptide	hypothalamus, secreted via posterior pituitary	rise in blood [electrolyte] fall in blood volume fall in blood pressure	decrease water loss via the kidneys reduces [electrolyte] increases blood volume and pressure	natriuretic peptide
OT = class:				XXXXX
ACTH = class:				
TSH = class:				
GH = class:				
LH = class:				
MSH = class:		XXXXX		
T3 = class:				XXXXX
T4 = class:				XXXXX
E = class:				XXXXX

Hormone / Class	produced by…	in response to…	causes…	antagonized by…
NE = class:				XXXXX
PTH = class:				
EPO = class:				
FSH = class:				
PRL = class:				
calcitonin class:				
calcitriol class:				
melatonin class:				XXXXX
inhibin class:				XXXXX
androgens class:				

Hormone / Class	produced by…	in response to…	causes…	antagonized by…
estrogens class:				
renin class:				
natriuretic peptide class:				
insulin class:				
glucagon class:				
aldosterone class:				
regulatory hormones class:				XXXXX

1. What are interstitial cells? Which organ produces interstitial cells?

2. What are the zona glomerulosa, the zona fasciculata and the zona reticularis? In what part of which endocrine organ would you find these "'zones" or "layers"? What hormones are produced by the zones?

3. What two hormones are produced by the adrenal medulla? What stimulates the release of these hormones?

4. What are the "islets of Langerhans"? In which organ would you find these islets? What hormones are produced by these islets?

5. Does the posterior pituitary produce any hormones? Is yes, which ones?

6. What are the tropic hormones produced by the pituitary gland? Give examples of non-tropic hormones produced by the anterior pituitary gland.

7. Which endocrine gland contains follicles filled with colloid? What hormones are produced by this gland?

8. What is the major hormone produced by the pineal gland? What is thought to be the function of the pineal gland? Where would find the pineal gland?

9. Which endocrine organ atrophies with age?

10. Provide two examples of purely endocrine organs. Provide two examples of mixed endocrine/exocrine organs. Provide two examples of organs that produce hormones, yet are not traditionally considered "endocrine organs."

11. Draw the following structures as they appear in a microscope.

Adrenal gland (40x)

Pituitary gland (4x)

Thyroid & Parathyroid (400x)

Pancreas (400x)

Ovary (10x)

Testis (400x)

exercise 21

the CARDIOVASCULAR system

- BLOOD -

In the same way, after the supper he took the cup, saying, "This cup is the new covenant in my blood, which is poured out for you."

Luke 22:20

The cardiovascular system is composed of three main components: 1/ The *blood*, which forms the transportation medium for gases, proteins, cells, hormones, etc, 2/ *blood vessels*, which conduct the blood to every cell in the body, and 3/ the *heart*, which pumps the blood through the blood vessels. We'll first examine the blood, then the blood vessels and finally the heart in subsequent exercises.

Blood is a rather unusual human tissue in that it's a fluid. The only other fluid tissue in the body is lymph, a component of the lymphatic system. Blood is a transportation medium that must continuously move substances (including solids, liquids and gases) to and from every cell in your body. If this transportation process stops for even a few minutes, death will ensue. In this chapter we'll examine some of the unique properties of blood that allow this extraordinary fluid to move so many things to so many places so effectively.

Properties & Composition of Blood

Blood is classified as a connective tissue and, like all connective tissues, it's composed of specialized cells suspended in an extracellular matrix. For blood, the matrix is a liquid called **plasma** (Figure 21-1). Blood plasma is a viscous watery solution containing numerous different solutes. The specialized cells in blood are collectively called the **formed elements**. None of the formed elements possess cilia or flagella; thus, they do not "swim." Rather, they float freely in the plasma and are carried along within the current of flowing bloodstream. Together, the plasma and formed elements are called **whole blood**. Whole blood is an extremely useful tissue clinically as alterations in its properties can provide clues to many pathological conditions.

Blood Plasma

Blood plasma is about 92% water; the remaining 8% is composed of more than 100 different solutes, including proteins (e.g., albumins and antibodies), small organic molecules (e.g., glucose and urea), ions (e.g., Na^+ and K^+) and dissolved gases (e.g., N_2 and CO_2).

One protein found abundantly in blood plasma is fibrinogen. In fact, this one protein represents about 4% of all plasma proteins. Fibrinogen is soluble in water but when a blood vessel is torn fibrinogen is converted to a non-soluble form called fibrin. Insoluble fibrin fibers catch cells floating in the bloodstream. The result is a blood clot, which eventually plugs the tear in the vessel. When storing blood plasma it's often useful to remove fibrinogen to prevent unwanted clotting. Blood plasma with fibrinogen removed is called *serum*.

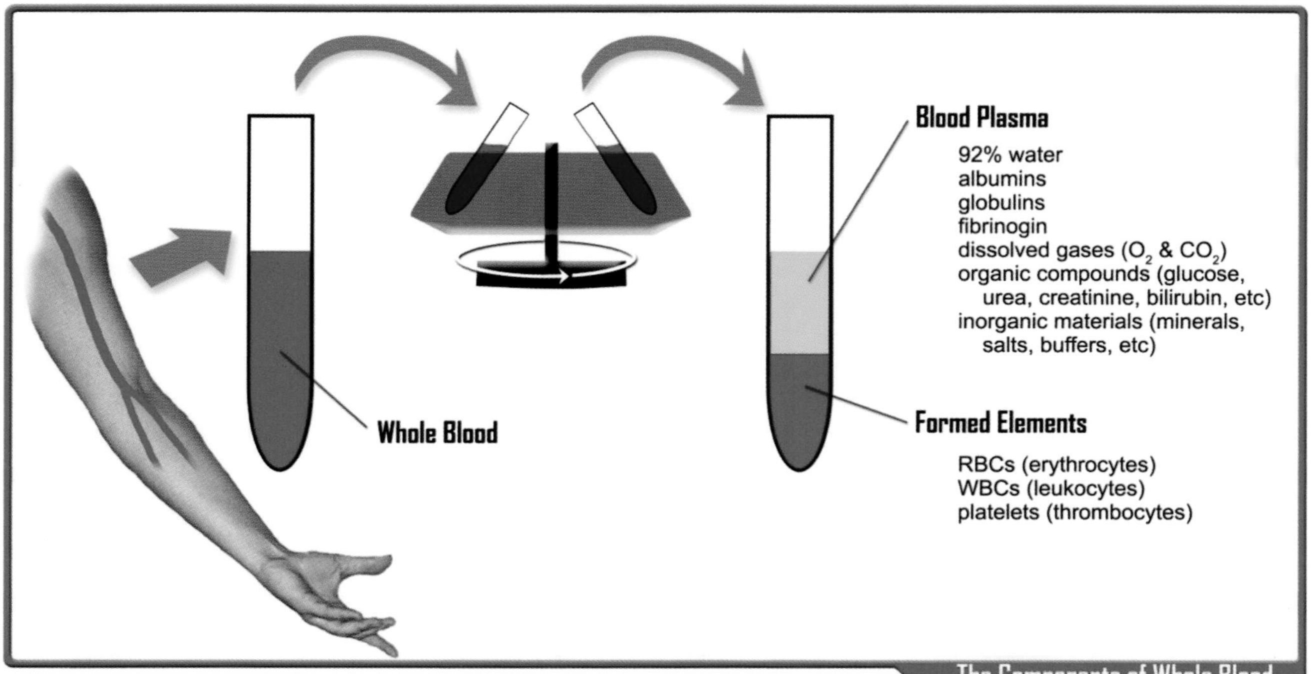

Figure 21-1 The Components of Whole Blood

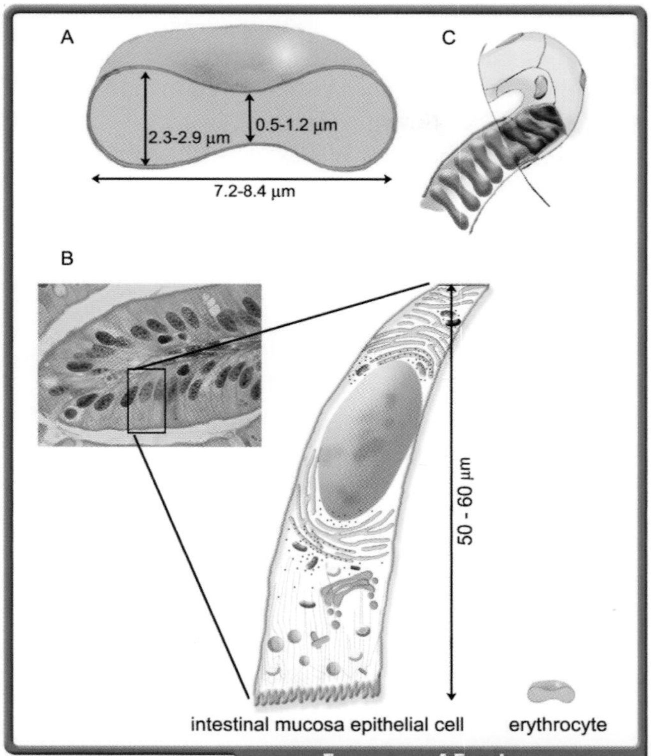

Figure 21-2 Features of Erythrocytes

The Formed Elements

As stated above, the cells suspended in blood plasma are collectively called the formed elements. Three populations of cells are found in the formed elements: **Red blood cells** (**RBCs**), whi**te blood cells** (**WBCs**) and **platelets** (shown in figure 21-4). Red blood cells, or erythrocytes, are by far the most abundant with roughly 5 million RBCs per microliter of whole blood (approximately 99.9% of the formed elements). Since the average adult has ~5 liters of blood, the total erythrocytes in the body is approximately 25 trillion; thus, 25-40% of all cells in the body are RBCs.

Red blood cells are among the most differentiated cells in the body (Figure 21-2). They are extremely small – less than 10 µm in diameter. Technically, they're not actually living cells since they lack a nucleus and other organelles and are not metabolically active. Rather, RBCs are essentially sacs filled almost entirely with a single protein: Hemoglobin (Hb). Hemoglobin reversibly binds dissolved oxygen and carries this gas from the lungs to cells throughout the body. To facilitate oxygen uptake and transport red blood cells are flat, biconcave discs. The biconcave shape gives RBCs the maximal surface area-to-volume ratio, which allows rapid diffusion of oxygen into and out of the cells. Their flatness allows them to stack like dinner plates. Most capillaries are so small that RBCs must pass through in single file; stacking the RBCs moves more of them through capillaries faster. Finally, red blood cells are relatively short-lived, circulating through the bloodstream only about 120 days before being replaced.

White blood cells, or leukocytes, account for less than 0.1% of the formed elements. There are five types of leukocytes (Figure 21-3) and each plays an essential role in "clean-up and defense" within the body. Unlike RBCs, all WBCs contain nuclei and other organelles and are metabolically active, and most leukocytes live for decades. The five types of WBCs are lymphocytes, monocytes, neutrophils, basophils and eosinophils (shown in figure 21-3). In each photo, white blood cells – stained blue – are surrounded by red blood cells).

Lymphocytes are cells of the lymphatic system. Most lymphocytes are found in lymphatic vessels and tissues (e.g., lymph nodes), but when circulating in the bloodstream they are catagorized as one of the white blood cells, or leukocytes. Lymphocytes participate in the immune response by attacking foreign cells and producing antibodies.

The other leukocytes are also involved in "clean up and defense" of the body. **Basophils**

Structure = Function

Red blood cells are highly differentiated cells. They possess several structural features that aid their function, which is to deliver oxygen to all body cells.

1/ RBCs are extremely small. This increases the rate at which oxygen can get into and out of the cells and it allows RBCs to travel through tiny capillaries surrounding larger body cells.

2/ RBCs are flattened. This allows them to stack like dinner plates as they pass single-file through tiny capillaries. This moves more RBCs through the capillaries faster.

3/ RBCs are biconcave discs. This shape has the maximum surface area-to-volume ratio, again speeding the rate at which oxygen can get into and out of the cell. A red blood cell only spends about two seconds in the lungs gathering oxygen before it's off to the body.

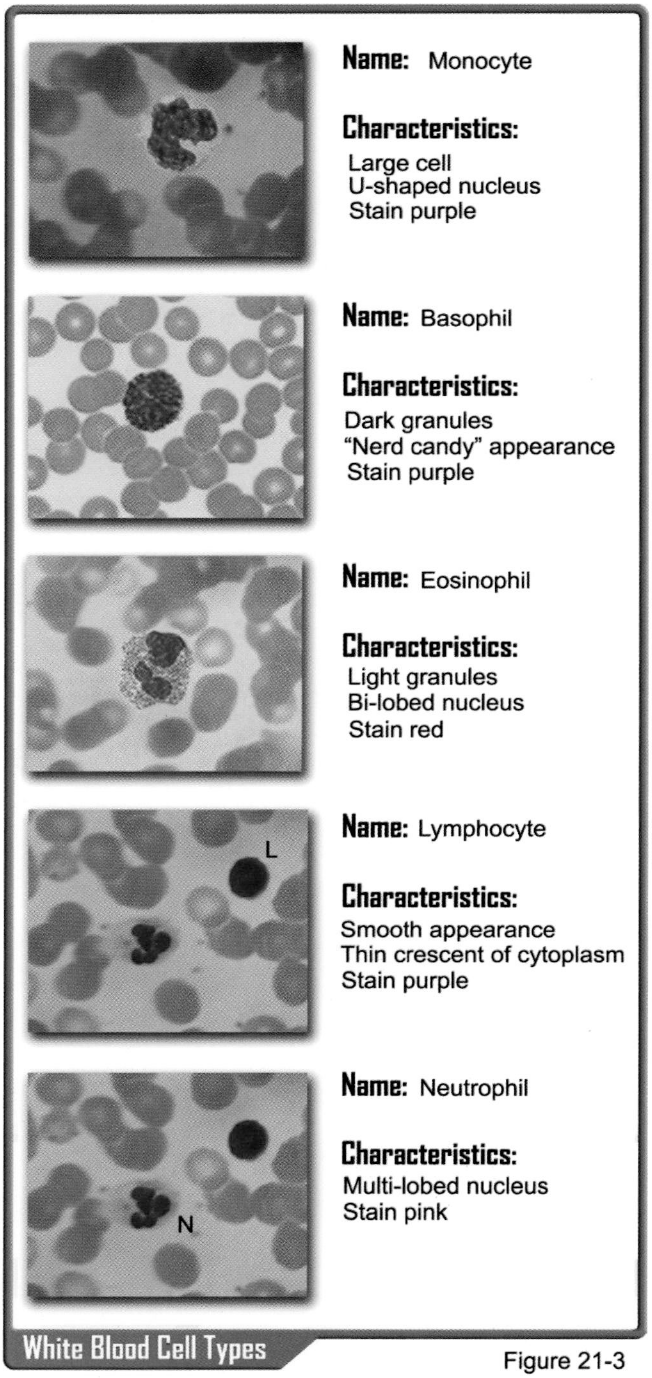

Figure 21-3

accumulate at injury sites and release histamine and heparin; histamine causes local inflammation (dilation of blood vessels) and heparin slows blood clotting. Together these help wash out an injured site with blood and recruit other leukocytes to the area. **Neutrophils** are phagocytic, that is, they engulf and destroy foreign cells (e.g., bacteria) or dead cells. They are the most abundant of the WBC's and account for the white/yellow appearance of pus in a wound. **Monocytes** are also phagocytic, but they can destroy not only the invading pathogen but also infected body cells. **Eosinophils** attack and destroy large invading organisms like parasitic worms.

Platelets, like WBCs, constitute only a small fraction to the total number of formed elements in blood. Like RBCs, platelets lack organelles and are not metabolically active; rather, they are small sacs filled with several proteins essential for blood clotting. Those proteins are required during the cascade of reactions that convert fibrinogen to insoluble fibrin.

Blood Typing

There are many different "blood types" found in the human population. The different types of blood are determined by the set of proteins (called antigens) found in the cell membranes of erythrocytes. The ABO-Rh blood types are the most important clinically.

The type of blood a person has is determined (biochemically) as follows: Individuals possessing the Rh antigen on their red blood cells would be Rh-positive; those lacking that particular antigen would be Rh-negative. About 85% of the American population is Rh-positive. Individuals possessing the A antigen have A-type blood; those with the B antigen have B-type blood. If a person possesses both the A and B antigen they have AB-type blood. Finally, if a person has neither the A or B antigen they have O-type blood. Thus, a person with the A and Rh antigens would be A+. A person with the A and B antigens but not the Rh antigen would be AB-.

It is crucial that blood of different types not be mixed in the body. If a person of blood type A, for example, is given blood type B by a transfusion, the blood mixture will *agglutinate*, or clump up. This could be fatal for the person receiving the transfusion.

Blood Pathologies

Two blood abnormalities common in the United States will be considered here: Sickle cell anemia and leukemia (Figure 21-4).

Sickle cell anemia is a genetic disease caused by a mutation in the gene encoding hemoglobin. The mutant hemoglobin protein still binds oxygen reversibly but fails to pack properly within the RBC, distorting the shape of the erythrocyte into a cresent, or sickle, form. These distorted cells don't transport oxygen as effectively as their wildtype counterparts and they tend to clump together inside small blood vessels.

Leukemia is a cancer affecting the leukocytes, or white blood cells. One common form of this cancer is lymphatic leukemia, a condition marked by abundant, mutant lymphocytes and severely reduced number of erythrocytes.

One of the most commonly ordered clinical tests in the United States is the *complete blood count, or CBC*. A CBC is actually a series of lab tests designed to provide an overall picture of a patient's blood. Abnormalities can be indicative of certain infections or problems with blood-forming organs. In the following activities we will perform the basic tests associated with the CBC.

Always Use caution when working with human blood. Always wear gloves and clean up all blood spills with 10% bleach solution.

Activity 1: Microscopic Examination of Blood

1. If you are preparing your own blood smear, start with the next step. If you are using a prepared blood slide skip to step 12.
2. Obtain two glass slides, a dropper bottle of Wright stain, a lancet, distilled water and alcohol swabs. Thoroughly clean the glass slides and dry them.
3. Wipe a finger with the alcohol swab. Shake your hand vigorously for 10-15 seconds to engorge your fingers with blood.
4. Using a lancet, prick your finger to begin bleeding. Do *not* squeeze or "milk" blood from your finger; this will only mix blood with interstitial fluids. Immediately dispose of the lancet in a proper container.
5. Once a large drop of blood has formed on your finger, lightly touch it on a glass slide about ½ inch from the end.
6. Quickly (to prevent clotting) use the second slide to smear the blood droplet uniformly across the first slide. Allow the blood to dry on the slide.
7. Place the slide on a paper towel and flood the slide with Wright stain (about 10 drops).
8. Allow the stain to remain on the slide for 3-4 minutes, then flood the slide with 10 drops of distilled water.
9. Allow the slide to rest undisturbed for another 4-5 minutes.

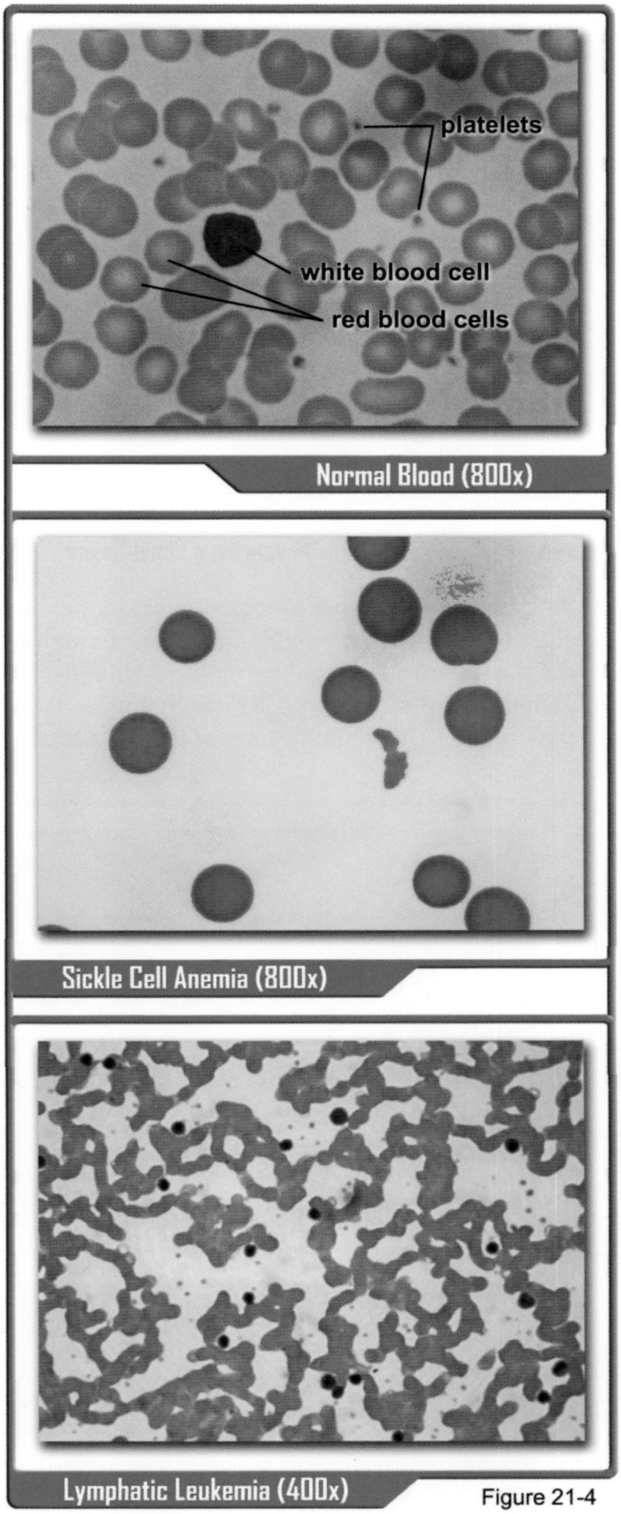

Figure 21-4

10. Rinse the slide under a stream of distilled water to wash away the excess stain.
11. Place the slide on a paper towel and allow it to dry completely. Once the slide is dry, you may observe the preparation under the microscope.

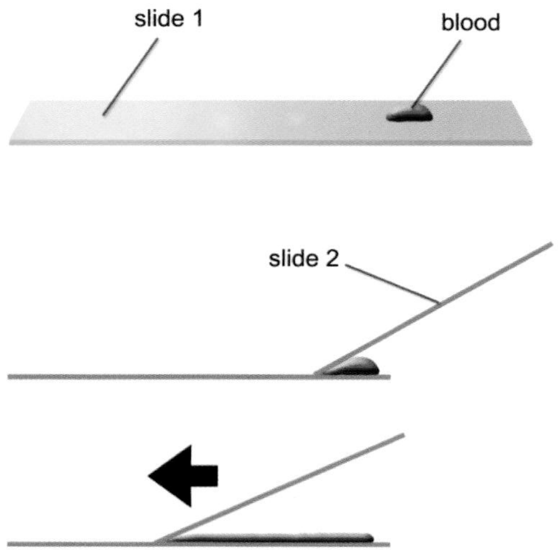

Figure 21-5 **Preparing a Blood Smear**

12. Alternatively, obtain a prepared microscope slide of a normal human blood smear. Examine the blood under high power (400x). Note the abundance of red blood cells which appear as pink halos. The white centers of the cells result from light penetrating the thin center of the cell more readily than the thicker outer edges. Based on the area of the field of view, estimate the abundance of RBCs per microliter of blood. Also, estimate the relative abundance of WBCs and platelets as compared to RBCs. Finally, estimate the size of these cells using the method described in exercise 2.
13. Examine prepared microscope slides of blood from a leukemia patient and a patient with sickle-cell anemia. Note the differences between these samples and the normal blood sample.

Activity 2: The Hematocrit

A hematocrit is usually performed when anemia is suspected. A hematocrit is obtained by subjecting a blood sample in a small tube to centrifugation, causing the formed elements to settle to the bottom of the tube. Because the plasma is squeezed out from between the cells, a hematocrit is also known as the *packed cell volume (PCV).* Follow these steps (and refer to figures 21-6 and 21-7) to

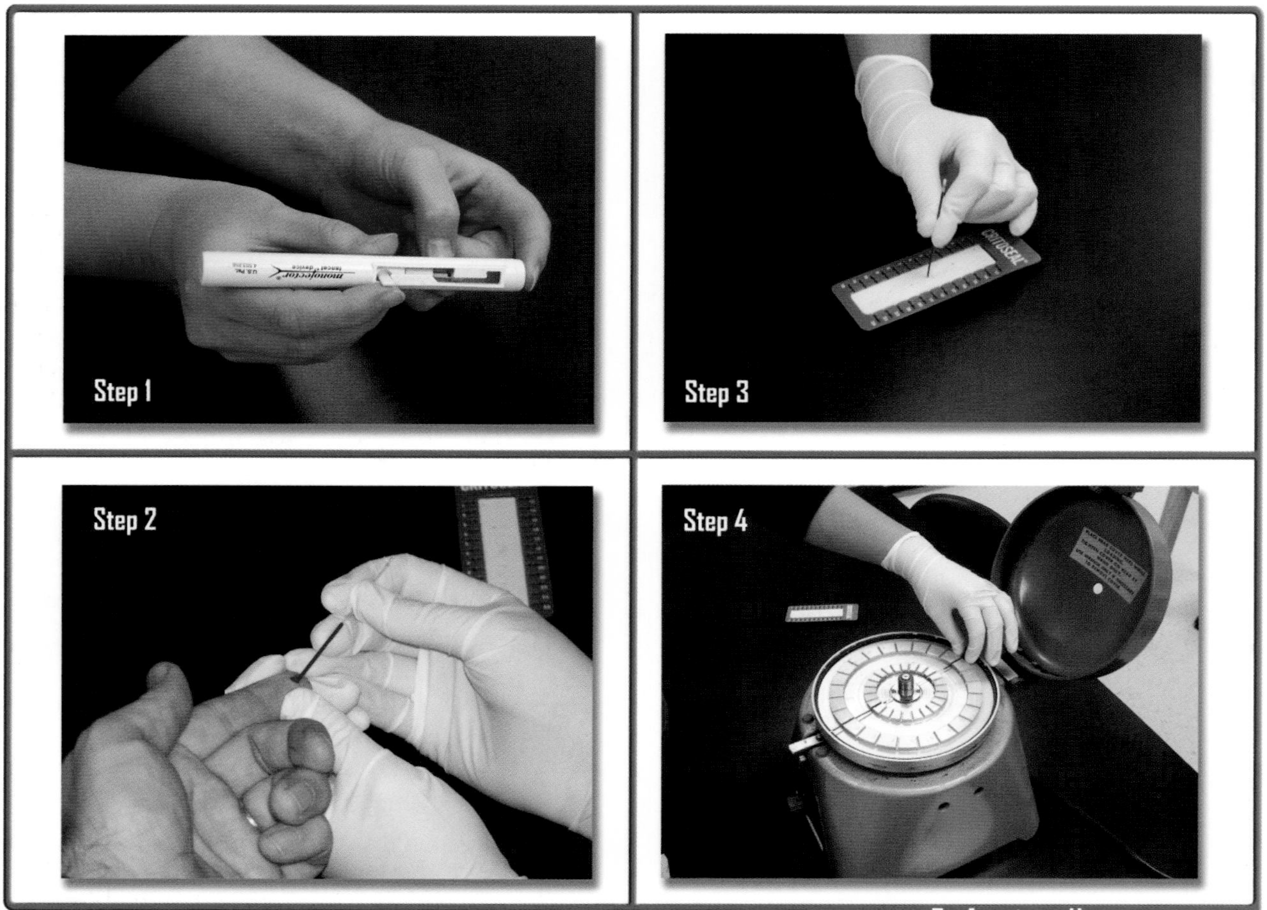

Figure 21-6 **Performing a Hematocrit**

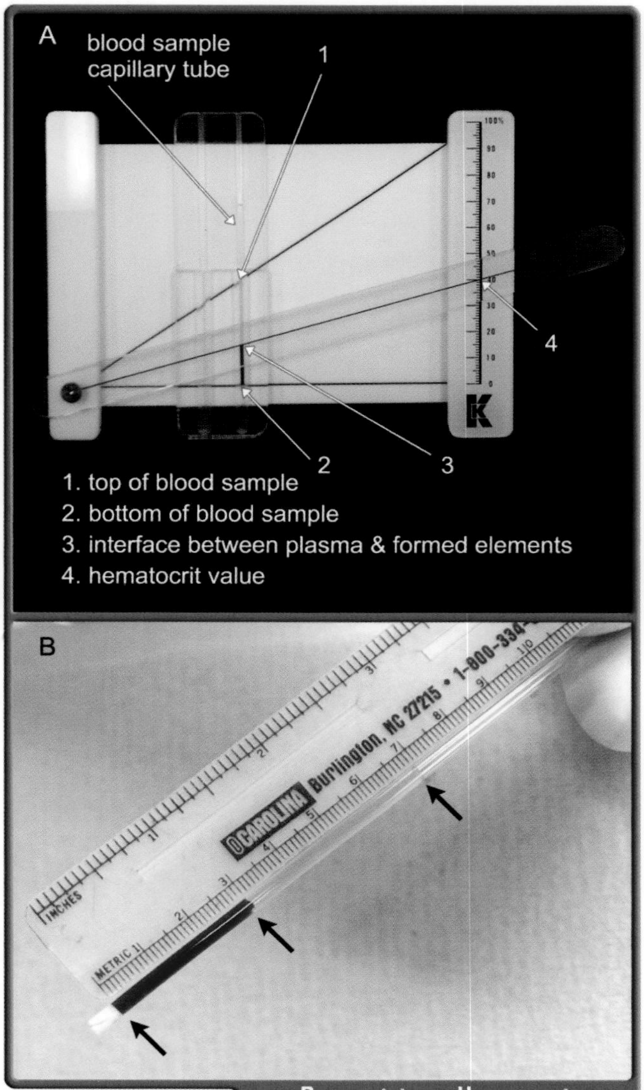

Figure 21-7 Determining a Hematocrit

determine the hematocrit, or PCV, of your blood:

1. Use a lancet to prick one of your fingers.
2. Once the blood begins flowing freely, draw up blood into a hematocrit capillary tube using capillary action (not gravity). The hematocrit capillary tubes contain heparin to prevent blood clotting and are marked with a line on one end. Place the end opposite the blue line into the drop of blood on your finger. DO NOT ALLOW AIR TO ENTER THE TUBE OR YOU MUST START OVER!
3. Once the capillary tube is filled at least three quarters, plug the end of the tube used to draw blood with clay.
4. Place the tube in a microhematocrit centrifuge, with the clay-plugged end facing outward. Balance the centrifuge with an even number of samples.

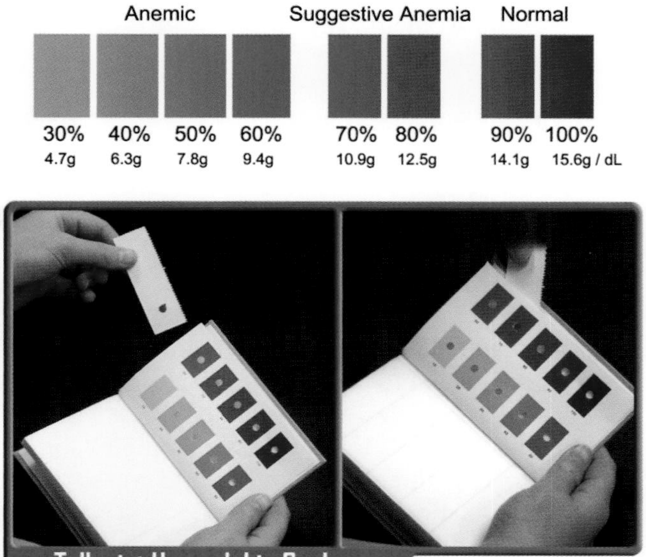

Tallquist Hemoglobin Scale

Figure 21-8

5. Centrifuge the samples for 3 minutes. Once the centrifuge rotor has come to a complete stop, remove your sample from the centrifuge.
6. Observe the blood in the tube. The red blood cells should be packed tightly at the bottom of the tube while the blood plasma appears as a pale yellow fluid above the packed cells. Sometimes, a thin white line is apparent between the RBC's and plasma; these are packed white blood cells.
7. Using a metric ruler, measure the height of the packed blood cells from the top of the clay plug, then measure the total height of packed blood cells + plasma from the top of the clay plug. Make your measurements in millimeters.
8. The hematocrit value, or PCV, is the height of the formed elements divided by the height of the whole blood (formed elements + plasma). This value should be in the range of 42-54% for men, 38-48% for women. If your PCV is less than 40%, you may be anemic.

Activity 3: Measuring Hb Content of the Blood

1. Use a lancet to prick one of your fingers.
2. Place a drop of blood onto the special paper provided by your instructor.
3. After 1 minute, compare the color of your blood drop with the Hb scale provided by your instructor (see Figure 21-8). Do not allow the blood to dry too long (more than 2-3 minutes) before comparing to the Hb scale because the blood continues to darken as it dries.
4. A hemoglobin (Hb) content of 14-18 grams per deciliter of blood is normal for men (12-16

g/dL for women). If your Hb value is low, you may be anemic.

Activity 4: Determining Blood Type

1. Use a lancet to prick one of your fingers.
2. Once the blood has started flowing, place one drop of blood in each circle on the Blood Test Card.
3. Place a drop of anti-A antibody next to one drop of blood, a drop of anti-B antibody next to the second drop of blood and a drop of anti-D antibody next to the third drop of blood.
4. Using a toothpick, mix the blood drops with the antibody drops. Use a separate toothpick for each of the three reactions to avoid cross-contamination.
5. Within 1-2 minutes agglutination should become apparent if any of the reactions are positive. No agglutination will occur with negative reactions. A positive reaction indicates the presence of A, B or D antigens on the blood sample RBCs.
6. Observe the agglutination patterns shown in figure 21-9 to help you determine your blood type.

Activity 5: Determining Coagulation Time

1. Use a lancet to prick one of your fingers.
2. Once the blood has begun to flow freely, draw some blood up into a capillary tube (using capillary action, not gravity). After the tube is nearly filled with blood, begin measuring the time. At 45 second intervals break the tube in half. After several intervals the blood should begin to coagulate, as evidenced by the blood becoming string-y rather than fluid. How many seconds did it take before the blood began clotting?

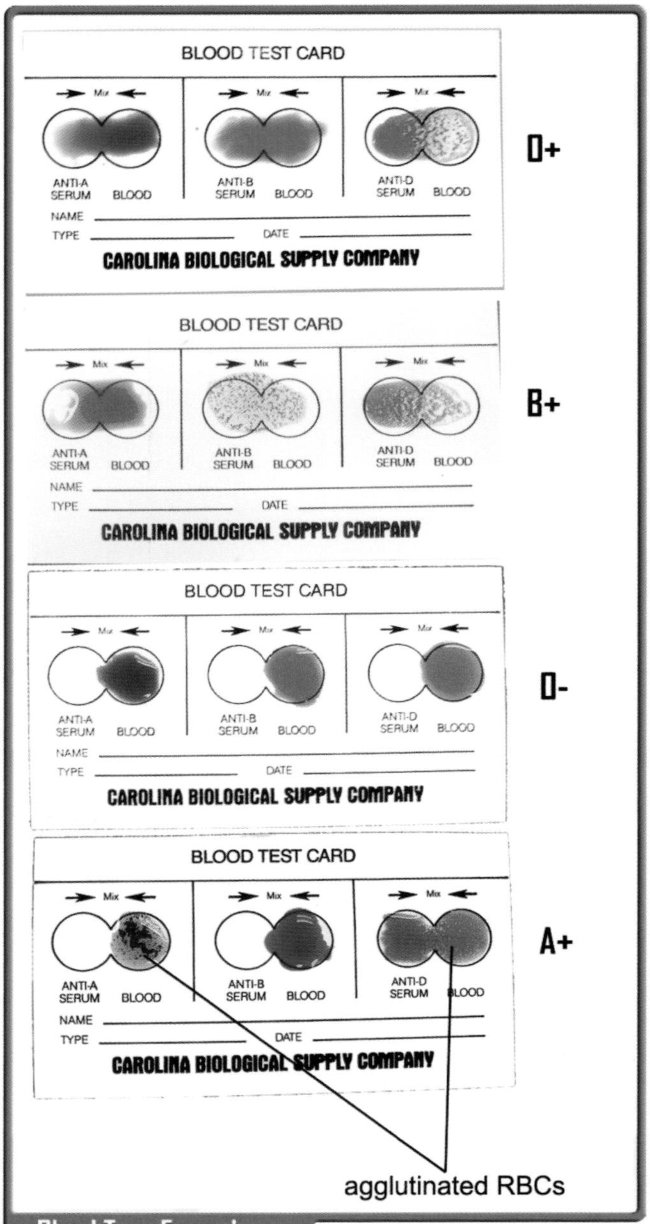

Blood Type Examples

Figure 21-9

1. What is the difference between *whole blood*, *blood plasma* and *blood serum*?

2. What are the three classes of cells making up the formed elements of blood? In general terms, what role does each class play in the function of blood?

3-10. Match the following terms with the correct description.

Leukocyte	Biconcave discs that transport oxygen
Monocyte	Small protein-filled cells involved in blood clotting
Erythrocyte	A white blood cell
Lymphocyte	The most abundant white blood cell; found in pus
Basophil	Found abundantly in lymph nodes and lymphatic vessels
Thrombocyte	Attack large, multicellular parasites
Eosinophil	Phagocytic cells that can destroy infected body cells
Neutrophil	Release histamine & heparin in injured tissues

11. How does the structure of red blood cells aid their function?

 Name ______________________________

12. List five nutrients found in blood.

13. Fibrinogen is one of the most abundant proteins in blood. What is the role of fibrinogen?

14. Define *hematocrit.*

15. How do the diseases sickle-cell anemia and leukemia affect the blood?

16. Heparin is often used during invasive surgeries. Why?

17. What is the biochemical basis for different blood types? Why can't different blood types be mixed?

exercise 22

the CARDIOVASCULAR system

- HEART -

Create in me a pure heart, O God, and renew a steadfast spirit within me.

Psalm 51:10

The heart is a sophisticated pumping instrument that propels blood through the miles of blood vessels traversing your body. It beats tirelessly day and night throughout your life – up to 1 billion beats! In this lab exercise we'll examine the gross anatomy of the heart and discuss the *conducting system* that coordinates each heartbeat.

The Heart: A Double Pump

The heart is actually two pumps in one. Each pump sends blood through a distinct *circuit*. Inside, the heart is divided into left and right halves. The left side of the heart collects blood from the **pulmonary circuit** and pumps blood through the **systemic circuit**. The right side of the heart collects blood from the system circuit and pumps it through the pulmonary circuit (Figure 22-1).

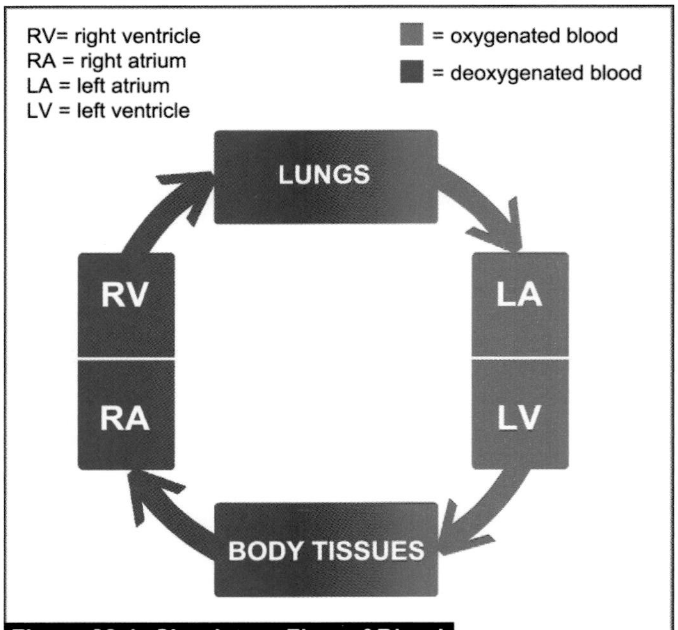

Figure 22-1: Circulatory Flow of Blood

Surface Anatomy of the Heart

One of the most notable features of an intact heart is the small size of the **atria** compared to the **ventricles** (Figure 22-2). The two atria act as collecting tanks for blood returning from the vascular circuits: Blood returning from the systemic circuit drains into the **right atrium**; blood returning from the pulmonary circuit drains into the **left atrium**. Inside the heart blood freely flows from the atria into the ventricles. Once the atria have filled they will contract together, emptying their contents into the ventricles below. (The nearly full ventricles are essentially "topped-off" by atrial contractions). Subsequent, simultaneous contraction of the much larger ventricles sends blood coursing through the pulmonary and systemic circuits. Because the systemic circuit is much larger than the pulmonary circuit, the **left ventricle** is considerably larger and more powerful than the **right ventricle**.

The heart is roughly shaped like an upside-down pyramid. Thus, the **base** is superior to the **apex**. The apex of the heart is part of the large left

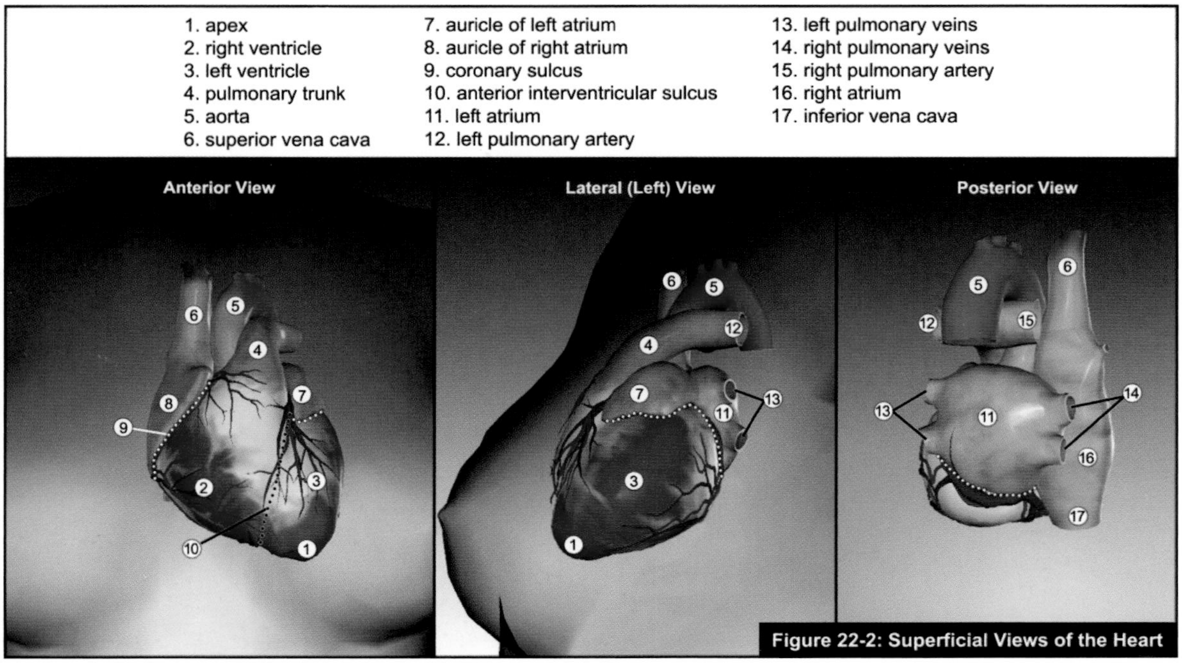

Figure 22-2: Superficial Views of the Heart

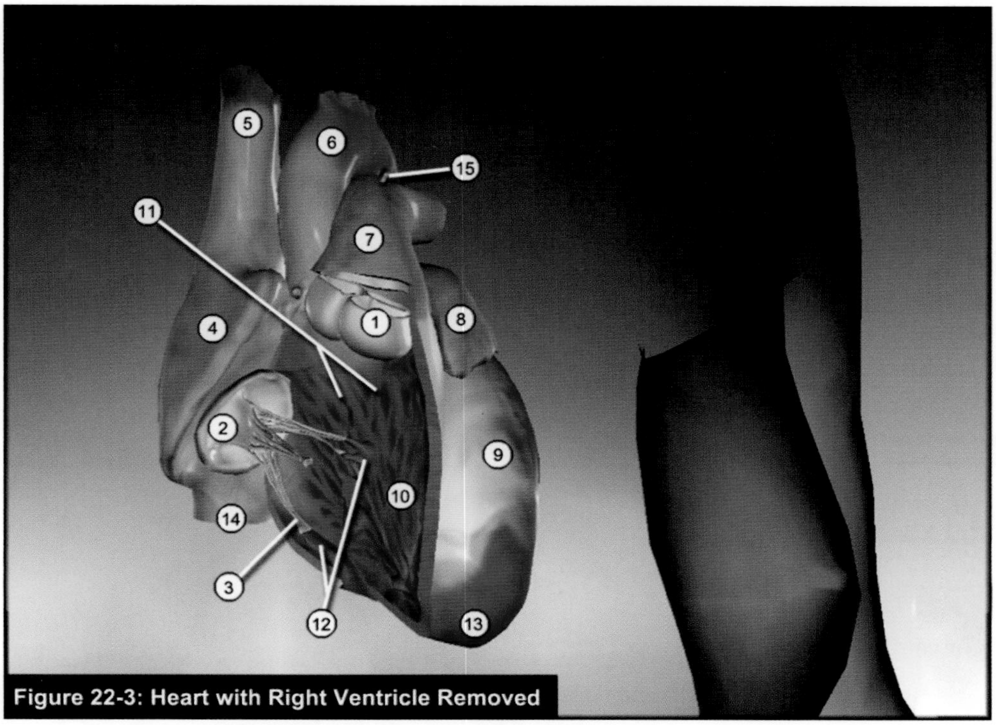

Figure 22-3: Heart with Right Ventricle Removed

1. pulmonary semilunar
2. tricuspid AV valve
3. chordae tendinae
4. right aurical (atrium)
5. superior vena cava
6. aortic arch
7. pulmonary trunk
8. left aurical (atrium)
9. left ventrical
10. interventricular septum
11. trabeculae
12. papillary muscles
13. apex of heart
14. inferior vena cava
15. ligamentum arteriosum

ventricle, which pumps blood through the systemic circuit. The right ventricle sits like a pocket attached to the side of the left ventricle (this is clearly seen on figures 22-11 & 22-12). A depression on the heart surface called the **interventricular sulcus** (often filled with adipose) defines the border between the two ventricles. The **coronary sulcus** is a depression that circumnavigates the heart and delineates the atria above and the ventricles below. The superior portions of the atria are called **auricles** because they appear deflated in isolated hearts and resemble ears.

Internal Features of the Heart

Besides the size differences between the atria and ventricles noted above, the internal walls of these chambers are notably distinct. The walls of the atria appear white and smooth, while the walls of the ventricles appear dark and rough. The rough projections of the ventricular walls are called **trabeculae**. The wall of the left ventricle is considerably thicker than the wall of the right ventricle, and this feature may be the best way to determine which is which (recall also that the apex is part of the left ventricle). These walls consist of a thick layer of muscle called the **myocardium**.

The passageways between the atria and ventricles are guarded by large valves called the **antrioventricular** (**AV**) valves (Figures 22-3 and 22-8). These valves allow blood to enter the ventricles from the atria but prevent backflow of blood from the ventricles into the atria during ventricular contractions. The left AV valve consists of two flaps, or *cusps*, and is called the **bicuspid valve**. The right AV valve consists of three cusps and is called the **triscuspid**. The cusps of both AV valves are attached to the inner walls of the ventricles by tough bands called the **chordae tendinae**, or *heart-strings*. The strings hold the cusps of the AV valves in the closed position during ventricular contractions. Specialized muscles attached to the ventricular wall – the **papillary muscles** – pull on the heart-strings to keep the valves closed when intraventricular pressures are highest.

Two other valves prevent the backflow of blood into the ventricles. The **aortic semilunar**

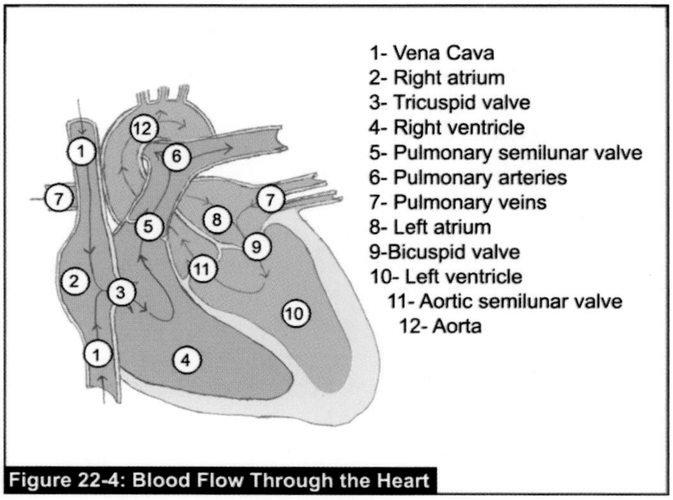

Figure 22-4: Blood Flow Through the Heart

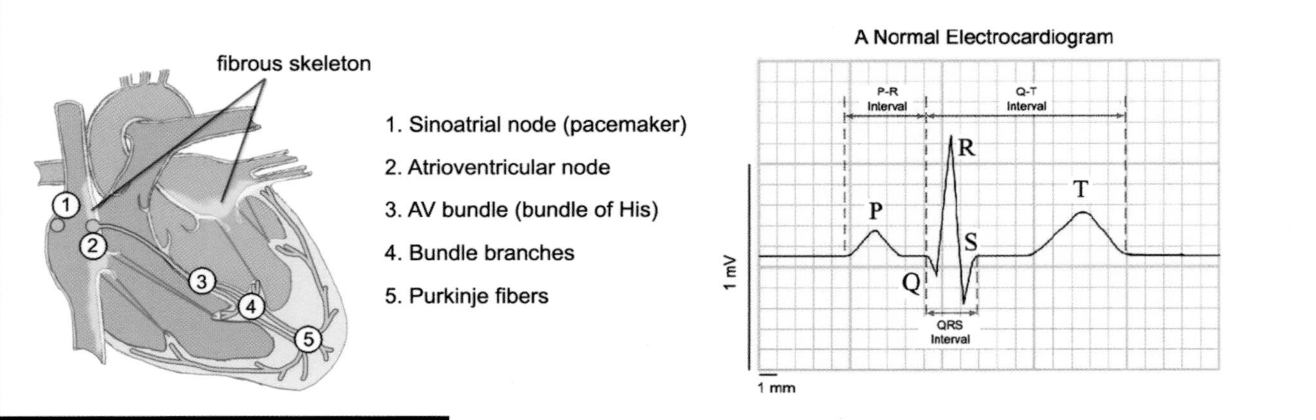

Figure 22-5: Electrical Events in the Heart

valve keeps blood from falling from the aorta into the left ventricle when the ventricle is relaxed. Likewise, the **pulmonary semilunar** valve prevents blood from falling into the right ventricle from the pulmonary artery when the right ventricle is relaxed.

Blood Flow through the Heart

As blood courses through the body it alternates between the systemic circuit and the pulmonary circuit. The heart is the intersection between these two circuits. If you were to ride upon an erythrocyte on its journey, its passage from one circuit to the other would go as follows:

> Blood completes the systemic circuit upon entering the heart via a large vein called the vena cava (1). The first heart chamber encountered by our erythrocyte is the right atrium (2). The blood then passes through the tricuspid valve (3) to enter the right ventricle (4). Upon contraction of the right ventricle blood is expelled through the pulmonary semilunar valve (5) into the pulmonary artery (6), which directs the blood to the lungs to pick up oxygen. Oxygenated blood returns from the lungs through the pulmonary veins (7) to enter the left atrium (8). The blood then passes through the bicuspid valve (9) into the large left ventricle (10). Upon contraction of the left ventricle blood is expelled through the aortic semilunar valve (11) into the aorta (12) to be delivered to all the body. After passing through the systemic circuit, deoxygenated blood returns to the right atrium of the heart via the vena cava (1) to repeat the cycle.

This pathway is also summarized in figure 22-4.

The Cardiac Cycle

The familiar "lubb dupp" sound associated with the heart is caused by violent closing of the heart valves. The first and louder sound ("lubb") is caused by the closing of the two large AV valves at the start of *ventricular systole*[1]. The second, softer sound ("dupp") is produced by the closing of the two semilunar valves at the end of systole.

The rhythmic beating of the heart is coordinated by the *intrinsic conducting system*. This electrical system grants the heart *automaticity*, or the ability to contract independently of the nervous system. The **sinoatrial node**, or *pacemaker*, is a mass of cells in the wall of the right atrium that begins heart contraction. Electrical signals radiate from this node in all directions and stimulate contraction of both atria. The ventricles are electrically isolated from the atria by a tough band of connective tissue called the **fibrous skeleton**, so they do not contract with the atria. After a pause of about 100 milliseconds, the **atrioventricular node** passes the electrical signal through the fibrous skeleton to the ventricles. Conducting fibers – the **AV bundle** and **bundle branches** – travel through the atrioventricular septum toward the apex of the heart, sending fibers to the papillary muscles and up the outer walls of the ventricles. The fibers stimulate the myocytes of the ventricles causing them to contract simultaneously. Contraction of the ventricles is a rather tumultuous event; in addition to electrically

---

[1] *Systole* describes chamber contraction; *diastole* describes chamber relaxation

isolating the atria and ventricles, the fibrous skeleton also serves to hold the four chambers of the heart together despite the massive contractile forces they experience.

An **electrocardiogram (ECG)** is a tracing of the electrical events of the heartbeat (Figures 22-5 & 22-6). The events are detected by strategically placing probes on the chest and limbs. There are three peaks and two valleys of electrical activity found in a normal heartbeat. These peaks and valleys have been designated P, Q, R, S and T. The **P wave** is associated with depolarization of the two atria; the **QRS complex** is associated with depolarization of the ventricles and simultaneous repolarization of the atria; the **T wave** is associated with repolarization of the ventricles.

Fibrillation is a cardiac arrhythmia, or irregular heartbeat. Over 2 million Americans have chronic atrial fibrillation, which is normally treated with anticoagulants. Ventricular fibrillation is fatal unless immediately reversed by *defibrillation*.

The volume of blood and blood pressure in the heart changes throughout the cardiac cycle (Figure 22-6). Blood pressure in the atria is always low, increasing only slightly during atrial systole. In the ventricles, the pressure fluctuates from about 10 mm Hg during diastole to 120 mm Hg during systole. At the end of diastole the filled left ventricle holds about 120 mL of blood (the *end diastolic volume*, EDV); at the end of systole the

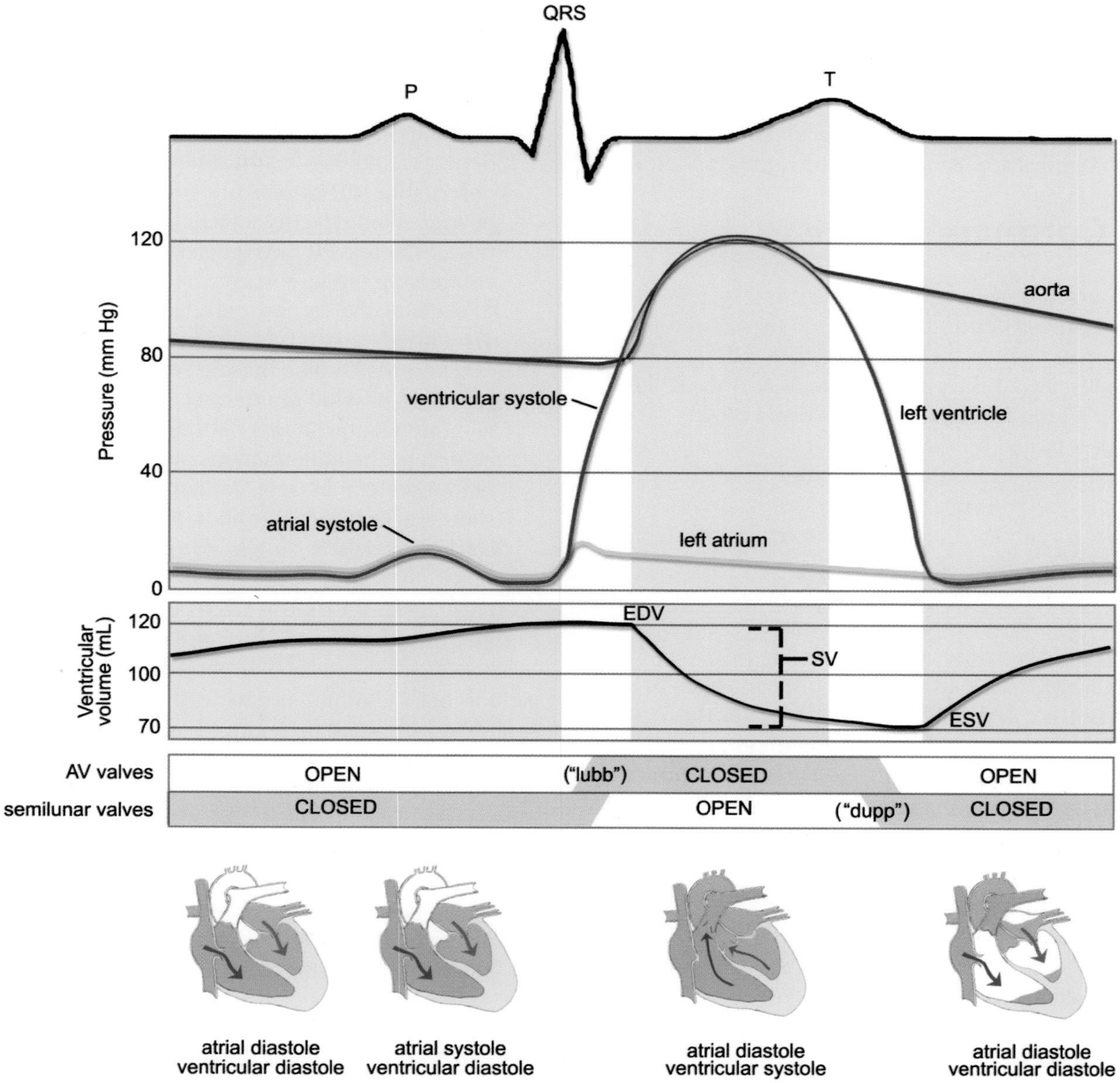

Figure 22-6: The Cardiac Cycle

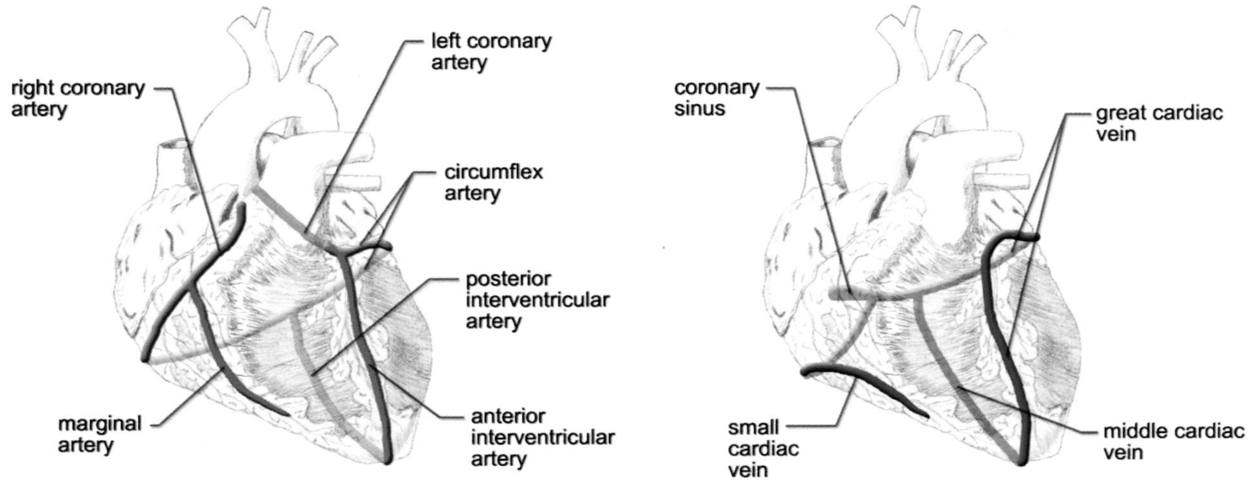

Figure 22-7: Coronary Circuit

emptied left ventricle still has about 50 mL of blood (the *end systolic volume*, ESV). Thus, the stroke volume (SV) of the left ventricle is about 70 mL. (These volumes are identical for the right ventricle).

The Coronary Circuit

We discussed already the pulmonary and systemic blood circuits. Blood passes through those circuits to pick up oxygen in the lungs and then deliver it to all body tissues. Like all other tissues & organs, the heart itself requires oxygen, glucose and other nutrients supplied by the blood. These are delivered to the heart tissues through a third circuit, which is actually a subset of the systemic circuit. This third circuit is called the **coronary circuit** (Figure 22-7).

The **left coronary artery** and **right coronary artery** emerge from the aorta immediately above the aortic semilunar valve (Figure 22-8). These arteries are both connected to the **circumflex artery** that circumnavigates the heart in the coronary sulcus (the depression between the atria and ventricles). **Interventricular arteries** are found in the interventricular sulci on both the anterior and posterior sides of the heart.

Blood is drained from heart tissues by the coronary veins. The **small cardiac vein**, **middle cardiac vein** and **great cardiac vein** all drain into the right atrium at the **coronary sinus**.

Activity 1: Microscopic Examination of Cardiac Muscle

1. Obtain a microscope and a prepared slide of cardiac muscle. Examine the tissue at high magnification (400x). Note the size of the cells, the number of nuclei, the striations, branches and intercalated discs.
2. Several features of cardiac tissue should be observable. *Striations*, or parallel stripes, can be seen inside the myocytes. These striations reflect the regular arrangement of proteins comprising the sarcomeres, the contractile units of skeletal and cardiac muscle. *Intercalated discs* are dark bands at the juction between neighboring cardiac muscle cells. These junctions provide rapid intercellular communication among cells and help coordinate cell contractions. Also notice that, unlike skeletal muscle, cardiac muscle cells are short and branched. A photomicrograph of cardiac muscle is shown in figure 4-22..

Activity 2: Auscultating Heart Sounds

In this exercise you will listen to (auscultate) the heart sounds of your lab partner using a stethoscope. Clothing dramatically obscures heart sounds, so it should be removed as much as possible. At the very least, heavy outer clothing should be removed or the stethoscope should be placed under the clothing. In addition, talking and other loud noises should be kept at a minimum during this exercise.

1. Obtain a stethoscope, cotton swabs and rubbing alcohol. Use the cotton swabs and rubbing alcohol to clean the earpieces of the stethoscope. Notice that the earpieces do not point directly to each other but are angled outward. Best results are obtained if you wear

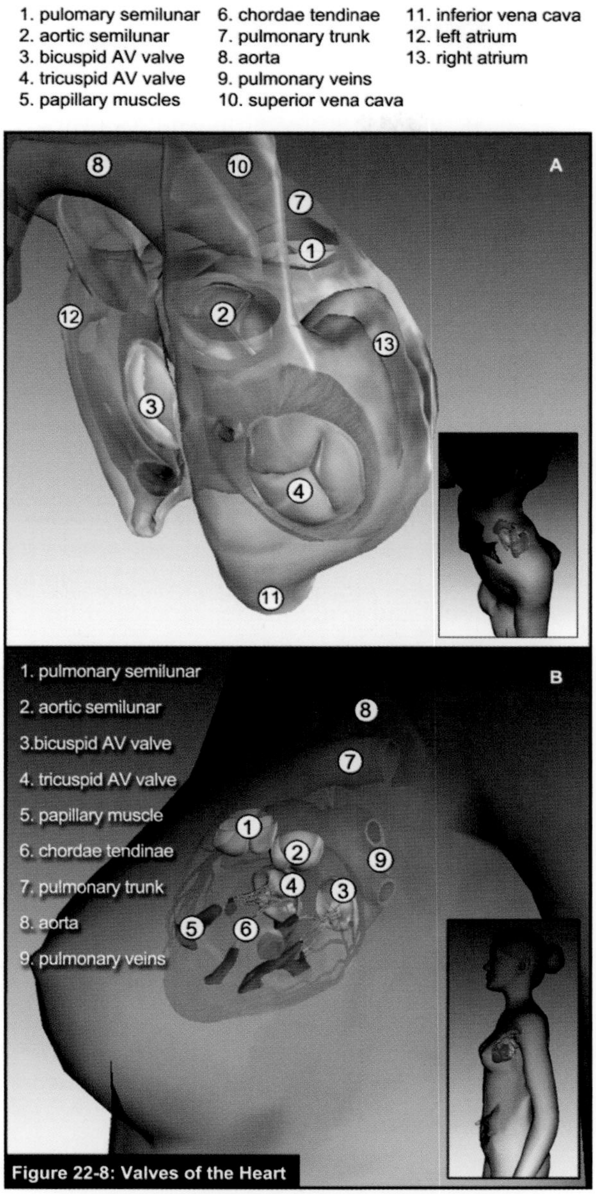

Figure 22-8: Valves of the Heart

A. The atria and great vessels have been rendered transparent to make the valves visible. B. The entire heart is transparent except the valves, chordae tendinae, and papilary muscles.

the stethoscope with the earpieces pointing *forward*.

2. Place the diaphragm of the stethoscope on your partner's thorax. Using figure 22-9 as a guide, try to hear the closing of the four heart valves. With the stethoscope placed at location "1" (to the left of the sternum between ribs 5 and 6) you should hear the bicuspid AV valve the loudest. At location "2" the tricuspid AV valve should be heard loudest; at location "3", the pulmonary semilunar valve, and at location "4", the aortic semilunar valve.
3. Focusing on the individual heart valves can often be difficult. You might want to simply

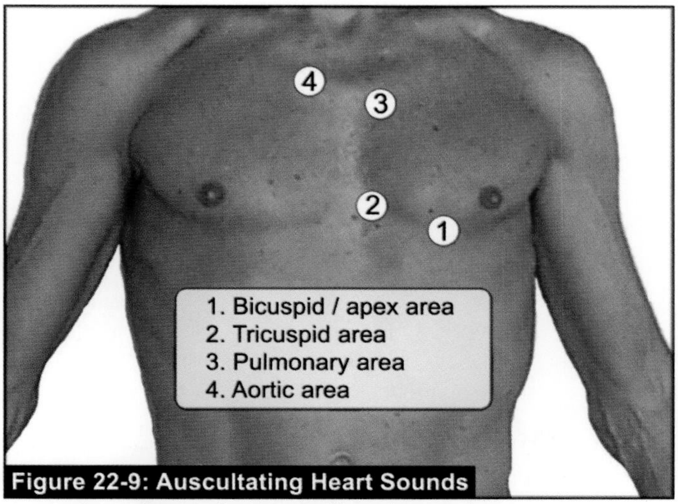

Figure 22-9: Auscultating Heart Sounds

place the stethoscope directly on the sternum. Low on the sternum near the xiphoid process, you should hear only the loud AV valves. High on the sternum near the manubrium, you may hear both the AV valves and the semilunar valves.

4. Generally, the biscupid (a.k.a., *mitral*) valve closes slightly before the tricuspid valve. A significant portion of the population (perhaps as much as 10%) display irregular heart sounds often associated with the mitral valve. These heart "murmurs" usually arise from incomplete closure of the valve during ventricular systole, allowing some blood to inappropriately "swish" through the valve. Try to locate a student with such an abnormal heart murmur.

Activity 3: Gross Dissection of Sheep Heart

1. Obtain a preserved sheep heart, a dissecting tray, a scalpel and a blunt probe. Wash the heart under water to rinse off excess preservative and rinse out the inner chambers.
2. Observe the surface features of the heart (the ventral surface is shown in figure 22-10). Locate the **base** and **apex** of the heart. Note that all of the vessels entering and leaving the heart do so at the base. Also at the base of the heart are two wrinkled, ear-like flaps called **auricles**, which are actually inflatable portions of the atria.
3. Notice the accumulation of adipose around the heart, especially in the grooves separating the chambers. These grooves are called the **coronary sulcus** around the **base** of the heart, and the **anterior / posterior interventricular sulci** traveling from the base to the **apex** on the front and back of the heart.

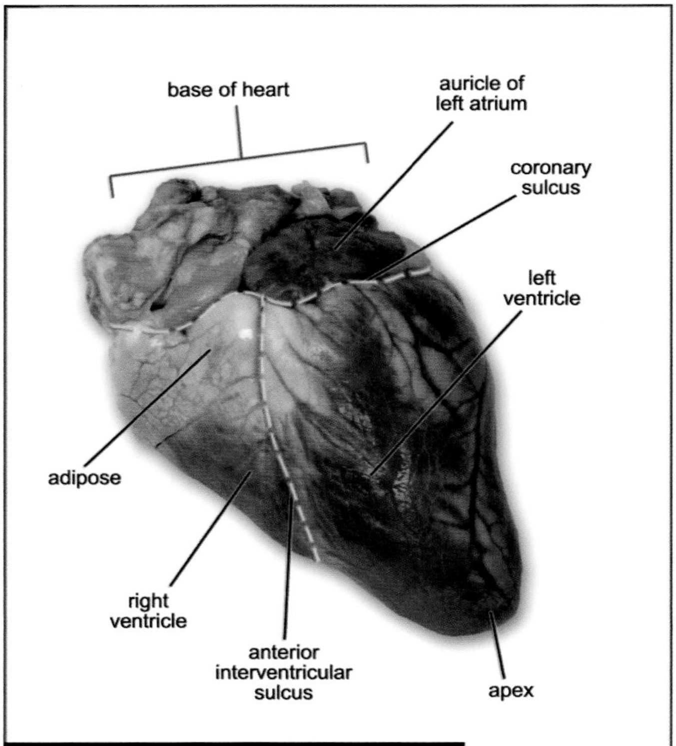

Figure 22-10: Ventral Surface of Sheep Heart

4. Carefully remove the adipose tissue in these sulci to expose blood vessels of the **coronary circuit** which supplies the heart itself with blood. Try to identify the **circumflex artery,** the **anterior interventricular artery,** the **right coronary artery** and the **marginal artery**, as well as the **cardiac veins**.
5. Identify the chambers of the heart. The two atria can be easily located by their auricles. The two ventricles are demarcated by the interventricular sulci; the left ventricle can be identified as part of the apex of the heart.
6. Identify the blood vessels protruding from the heart. Often, the vessels themselves have been completely removed from the heart, but the openings to the heart can be identified. The **aorta** is the most centrally located on the superior aspect of the heart. (If the aorta has been kept attached to the heart, you may also observe its first branch – the **brachiocephalic artery**). The **pulmonary trunk** is immediately anterior to the aorta; you may see where it divides to form the **left** and **right pulmonary arteries**. The **vena cava** is usually not left on the preserved hearts, but its large opening into the right atrium is easily seen. The opening of the **pulmonary veins** can be seen on the left atrium.
7. Four valves are found in the heart: two semilunar valves that prevent blood from back-flowing into the ventricles when the heart is relaxed, and two atrioventricular (AV) valves that prevent blood from being pushed back up into the atria when the ventricles contract. Pour some water into the right atrium and allow it to flow into the ventricle. *Slowly* squeeze the right ventricle and observe the closing of the right AV valve (i.e., the tricuspid valve). Drain the water from the heart.
8. Beginning with the superior vena cava, cut through the wall of the right atrium and continue along the interventricular sulcus beyond the apex of the heart. You can now reflect the right ventricle and right atrium and observe the interior of the heart (sectional views are shown in figures 22-11 and 22-12). Notice the smooth and white-ish appearance of the atrial wall as compared to the ventricle, whose wall appears darker and rougher. Note the chordae tendinae, or heart-strings, that connect the right AV valve to the **papillary muscles** projecting from the walls of the ventricle. A large band of tissue, the **moderator band**, may be seen stretching from the wall of the right atrium to the **interventricular septum**. This band is part of the conducting system of the heart.

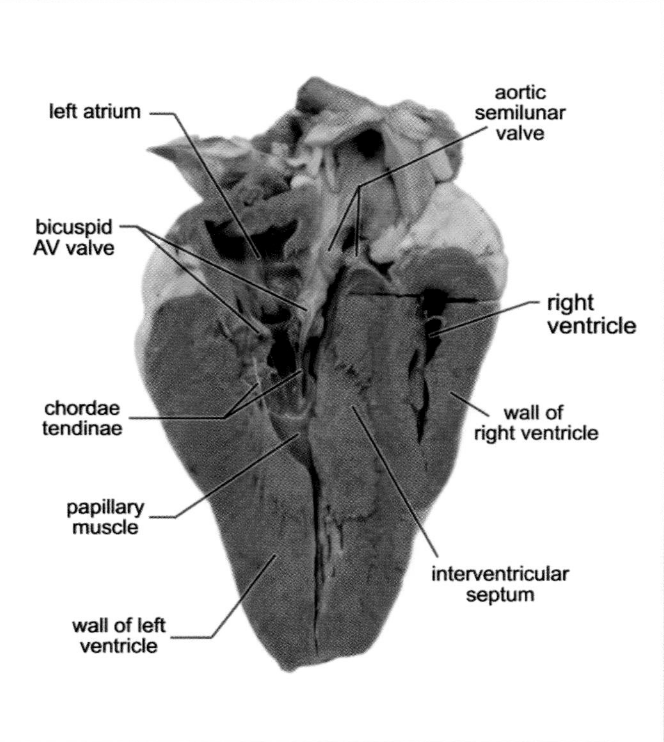

Figure 22-11: Frontal Section of Sheep Heart (posterior view)

9. Make a longitudinal incision through the left atrium and continue into the left ventricle almost to the apex. You may now reflect the left ventricle and left atrium. Notice the left AV valve (i.e., bicuspid or mitral valve) and papillary muscles. Also notice the thickness of the left ventricular wall as compared to the wall of the right ventricle.
10. Cut through the aorta and pulmonary trunk in order to see the **aortic semilunar** and **pulmonary semilunar valves**.
11. Using your blunt probe, try to trace the pathway of blood through the dissected sheep heart.

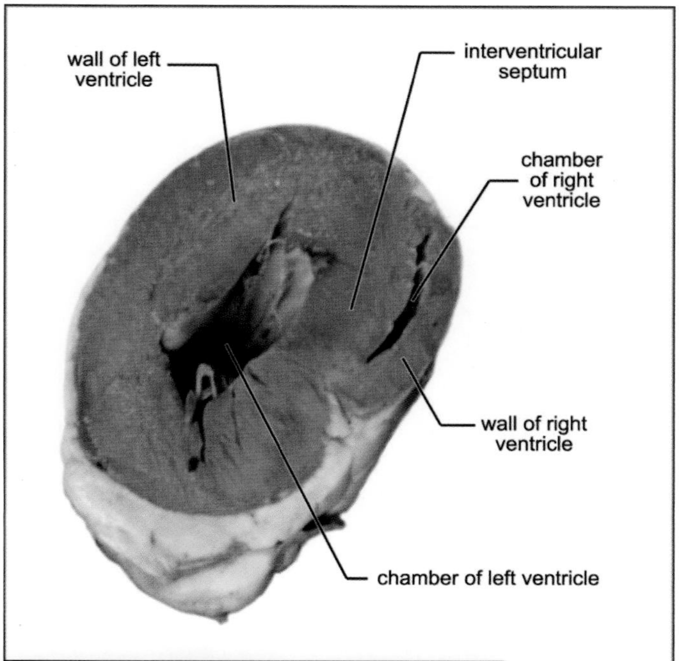

Figure 22-12: Transverse Section of Sheep Heart

1-17. Label the figure below.

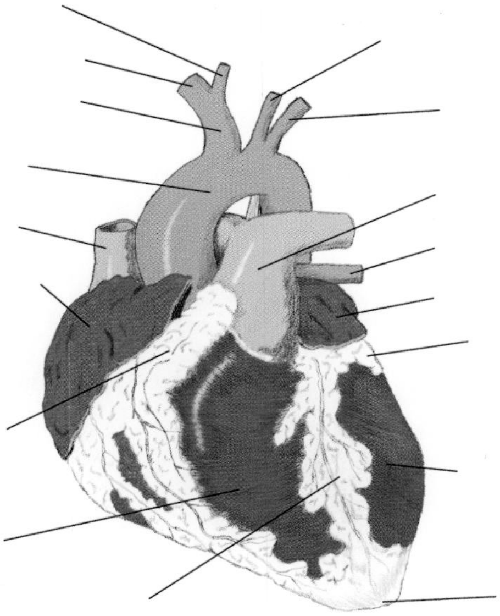

18-27. Complete the following list to describe the flow of blood through the heart.

_____Vena cava___________

____

____

____

____

____

_____Lungs________________

____

____

____

____

____

_____Aorta_______________

28. What is the function of the papillary muscle?

29. Why is the left ventricle larger than the right ventricle?

30. The heart possesses four valves. What are the names of the valves and what function do they serve?

31. Use the space below to draw a normal electrocardiogram. Label the peaks, troughs and intervals.

32. What are two primary functions of the fibrous skeleton?

33-45. Match the following terms with the correct definitions.

Ventricles	Prevent the backflow of blood into the ventricles
Chordae tendinae	The time period when the heart in contracting
Semilunar valves	Also known as "heart-strings"
Trabeculae	The largest chambers of the heart
Interventricular septum	Rough projections on the interior walls of the ventricles
Pulmonary circuit	The wall separating the two ventricles
Atria	The pathway that delivers deoxygenated blood to the lungs
Sinoatrial node	The pathway that delivers blood to cardiac tissue
Systemic circuit	The depression on the surface of the heart between the ventricles
Systole	Blood-collecting chambers of the heart
Coronary circuit	The time period when the heart is relaxed
Diastole	Also known as the "pacemaker" of the heart
Interventricular sulcus	The pathway that delivers oxygenated blood to body tissues

exercise 23

the CARDIOVASCULAR system

- BLOOD VESSELS -

*The righteous chews on wisdom like a dog on a bone,
rolls virtue around on his tongue. His heart pumps
God's Word like blood through his veins.*
Psalm 37:30 (The Message)

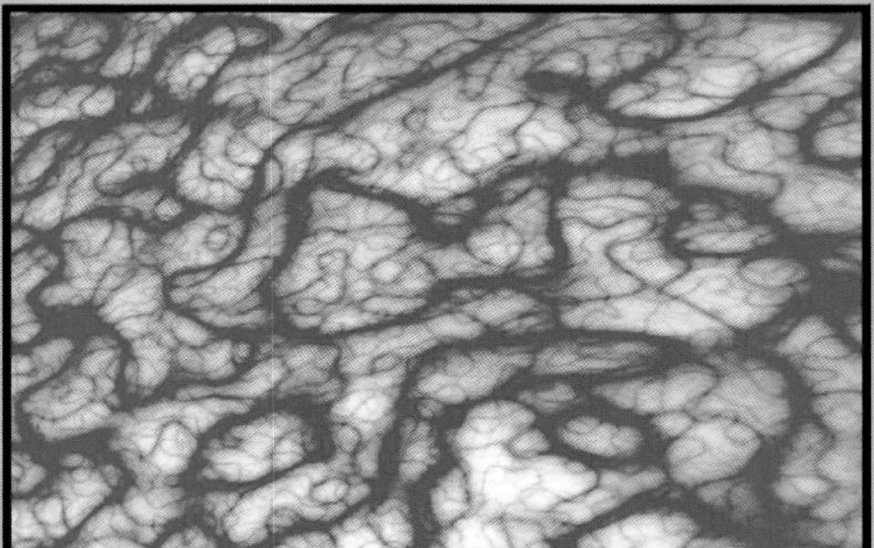

You have a total of about 60,000 miles of blood vessels in your body.

Blood vessels form the "tubing" through which blood is propelled by the heart. In this lab exercise we'll examine the anatomy of blood vessels and how they assist transporting blood and its cargo throughout the body. Much more than simple plumbing, blood vessels *i*) assist the heart in unidirectionally moving blood throughout the body, *ii*) selectively permit exchange of nutrients within tissues, *iii*) assist the formation of blood clots at sites of injury, *iv*) help regulate systemic blood pressure, and *v*) play an important role in regulating body temperature.

Structural & Functional Features of Blood Vessels

There are five types of blood vessels we will consider: Arteries, arterioles, capillaries, venules and veins. Arteries, arterioles, venules and veins are *conducting vessels*; no exchange between blood and tissue occurs in those vessels. By contrast, capillaries do allow exchange of nutrients and wastes between the blood and the extracellular fluid (i.e., interstitial fluid) of tissues.

Arteries & Arterioles

Arteries and arterioles are conducting vessels that carry blood *away* from the heart; **veins** are conducting vessels that carry blood *toward* the heart. Cross-sectional views of an artery and vein are shown in figure 23-1. Arteries are composed of three layers, or *tunics*: The outer **tunica externa** is composed primarily of connective tissue, the middle **tunica media** is mostly smooth muscle, and the inner **tunica interna** (a.k.a., *tunica intima*) is an endothelial membrane composed of epithelial and connective tissues. Arterioles are composed of only two layers: The tunica media and the tunica interna.

The arteries closest to the heart are called *elastic arteries* because of the elastic nature of the vessel walls. Those arteries expand and recoil with each heartbeat, generating a pressure pulse. The recoiling action of these vessels actually helps propel blood through the arterial system. As vessels extend farther from the heart, however, they become less elastic and more muscular and are appropriately named *muscular arteries*. The blood pressure in both elastic and muscular arteries is quite high, generally 80-120 mm Hg. A high pressure is absolutely necessary in order to force blood through tiny capillaries within tissues.

Muscular arteries may help propel blood, but they also regulate blood pressure. The muscles of these arteries may constrict the vessel lumen to increase blood pressure or dilate the lumen to decrease blood pressure. The pressure of any fluid flowing through a pipe can be described by the equation, $p = 1/r^4$ (where r refers to the radius of the pipe). Since r is raised to the 4th power in this equation, you can see that just a small change in the radius of a blood vessel can have dramatic effects

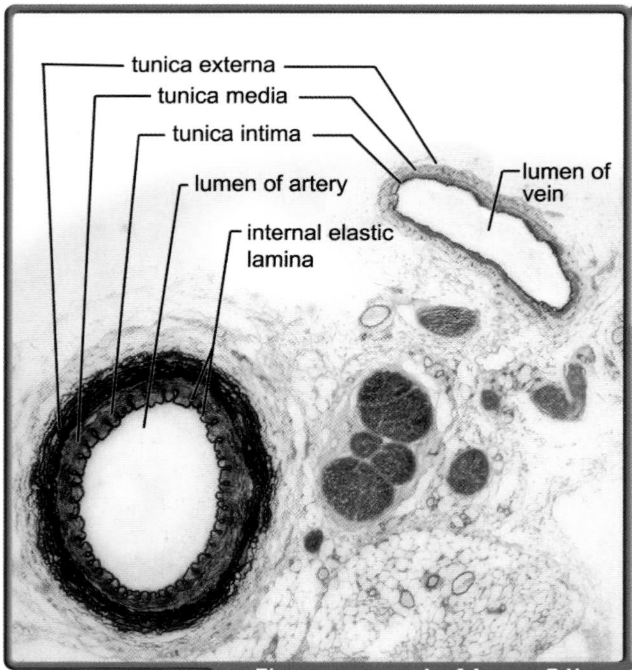

Photomicrograph of Artery & Vein

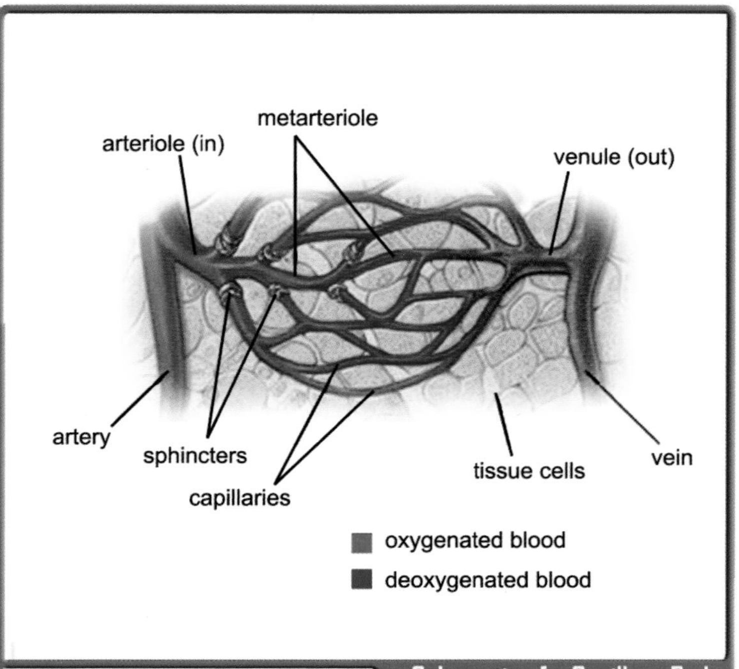

Schematic of a Capillary Bed

Figure 23-1

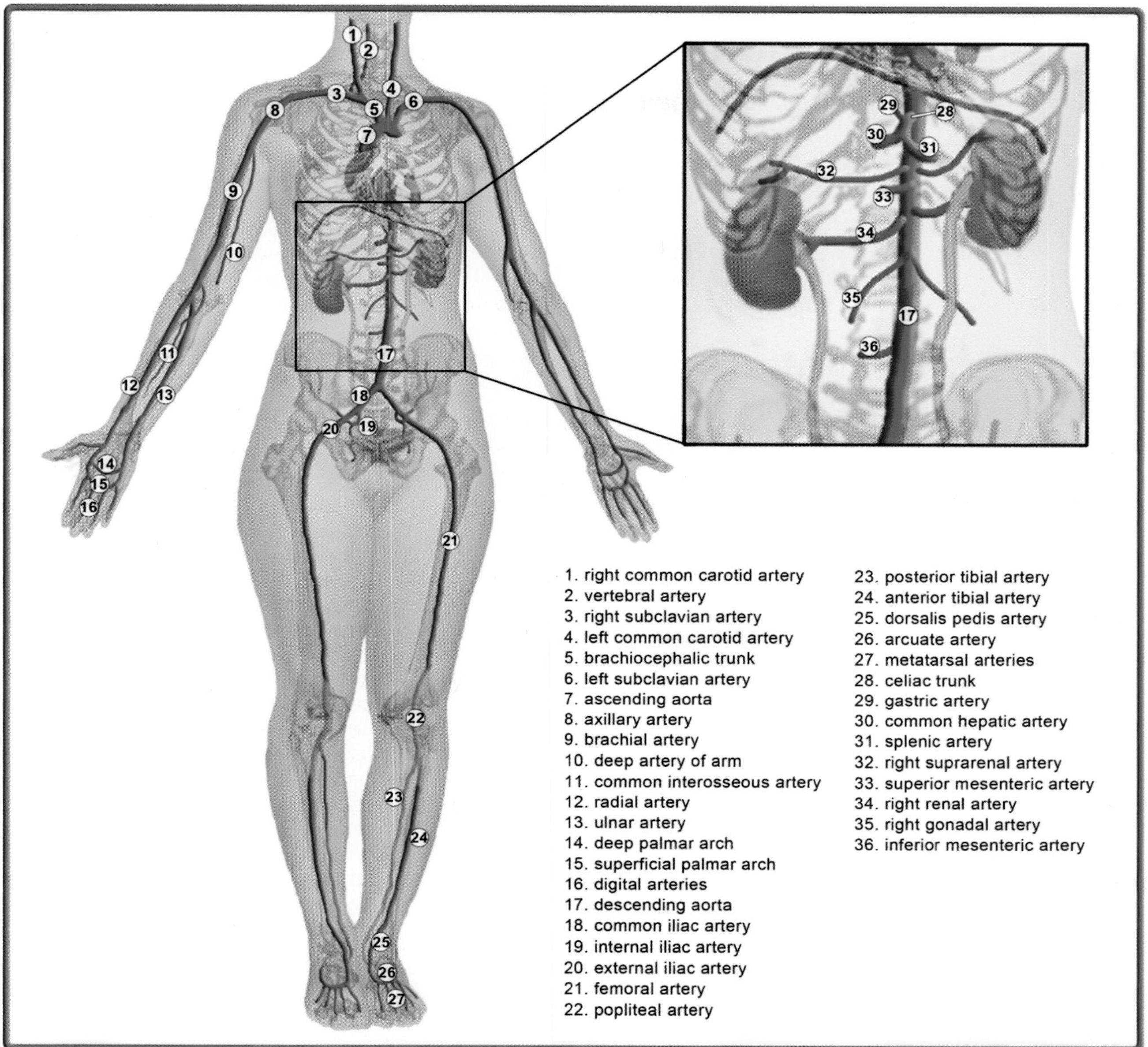

Figure 23-2 Major Systemic Arteries of the Body

on blood pressure. In fact, excessive body-wide dilation of blood vessels can be quickly fatal because of the dramatic drop in blood pressure. Such a condition is called *circulatory shock.*

As arteries penetrate into various tissues they branch and become smaller, eventually becoming **arterioles** which lack the tunica externa. Arterioles continue to branch out into capillary beds (which also lack the tunica media) where exchange of nutrients and wastes between blood and cells of the tissues takes place. Due to their vast numbers, arterioles are the most important vessels regulating arterial blood pressure.

The major arteries of the body are shown in figure 23-2.

Capillaries

Capillaries possess only one tunic, the tunica interna. The walls of these one-layer vessels are extremely thin, allowing for rapid exchange between the blood and interstitial fluids. Most capillaries have smooth, continuous walls and are thus called *smooth capillaries*. By contrast, the *fenestrated capillaries* of certain tissues (such as adipose, liver and some endocrine glands) contain large pores in their vessel walls. These pores allow large molecules, such as protein hormones, to enter or leave the bloodstream.

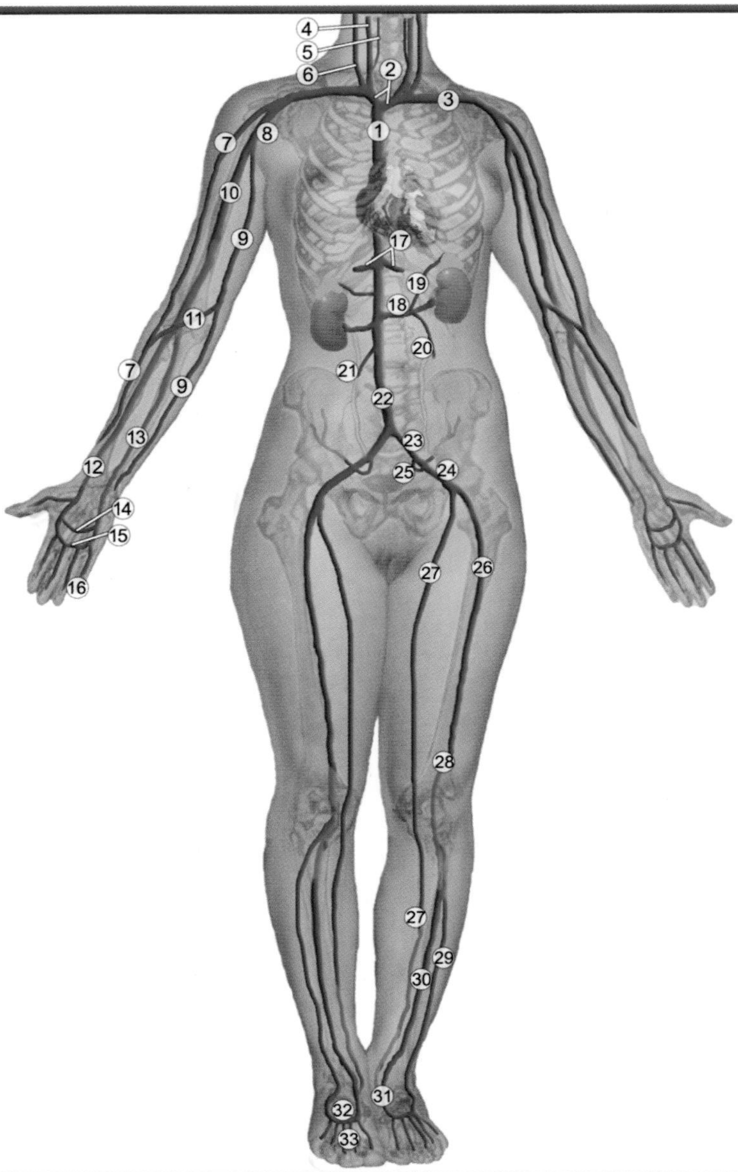

1. superior vena cava
2. brachiocephalic veins
3. left subclavian vein
4. internal jugular vein
5. vertebral vein
6. external jugular vein
7. cephalic vein
8. axillary vein
9. basilic vein
10. brachial vein
11. median cubital vein
12. radial vein
13. ulnar vein
14. deep palmer arch
15. superficial palmer arch
16. digital veins
17. hepatic veins
18. left renal vein
19. left suprarenal vein
20. left gonadal vein
21. right gonadal vein
22. inferior vena cava
23. common iliac vein
24. external iliac vein
25. internal iliac vein
26. femoral vein
27. great saphenous vein
28. popliteal vein
29. small saphenous vein
30. anterior tibial vein
31. dorsalis pedis vein
32. dorsal venous arch
33. metatarsal veins

Major Systemic Veins of the Body

Figure 23-3

Capillary vessels do not exist in isolation; rather, they form large networks called *capillary beds* (Figure 23-1). Each capillary bed may contain hundreds of individual capillaries. The bed is supplied by a single arteriole and drains into a single venule. The arterial side of most capillaries within a bed contain a small sphincter muscle which constricts to close the vessel and dilates to open the vessel. Interestingly, there's not enough blood in your body to bath all tissues at once. Consequently, tissues must share the blood by "taking turns." This is achieved by the capillary sphincter muscles: Some capillaries are closed (temporarily depriving their tissues of blood) while others are open. After a few seconds, the open capillaries will close and the closed capillaries will open. Within a capillary bed, probably just 1/3 of the capillaries are open at any given time. This sharing of the blood within a capillary bed by the continuous action of capillary sphincters is called *vasomotion*.

Veins & Venules

Capillary beds drain into small vessels called **venules**. Venules possess two tunics, the tunica externa and the tunica interna. Numerous venules converge and gain muscle to give rise to 3-layered veins.

In general, veins possess larger lumens than arteries (see Figure 23-1). Because of this, and because they are on the distal sides of capillaries from the heart, they are under very low pressures, typically less than 18 mm Hg. Venous blood pressure so low, in fact, that blood will not be returned to the heart without assistance, especially from the feet and legs when standing. Thankfully, assistance is obtained in two ways. First, medium and large-sized veins possess *valves* which allow the blood to flow toward the heart but not away from it. Second, contracting skeletal muscles (such as from walking and breathing) squeeze veins and literally massage the blood into motion. This blood can only move toward the heart because of the valves.

Besides having larger lumens, veins are also more numerous than arteries since blood may return to the heart in either deep veins or superficial veins. For these reasons considerably more blood is found in veins than arteries at any given moment. This excess blood is called the *venous reserve* and is essentially spare blood on-hand in case of moderately severe blood loss. If, for example, you lose a liter of blood through an injury blood from the venous reserve will be shunted to the arteries in order to maintain adequate arterial blood pressures.

As stated above, blood may return to the heart through either deep veins or superficial veins. The route selected is determined by body temperature. If the body becomes too hot, blood will be diverted from deep veins to more superficial veins. Heat will thereby be directed to the skin surface where, in concert with sweat gland activity, it will be radiated from the body. When the body is cold, sweat glands are inactivated and blood is returned to the heart through deep veins, conserving and distributing the heat acquired principally from working skeletal muscles.

The major veins of the body are shown in figure 23-3.

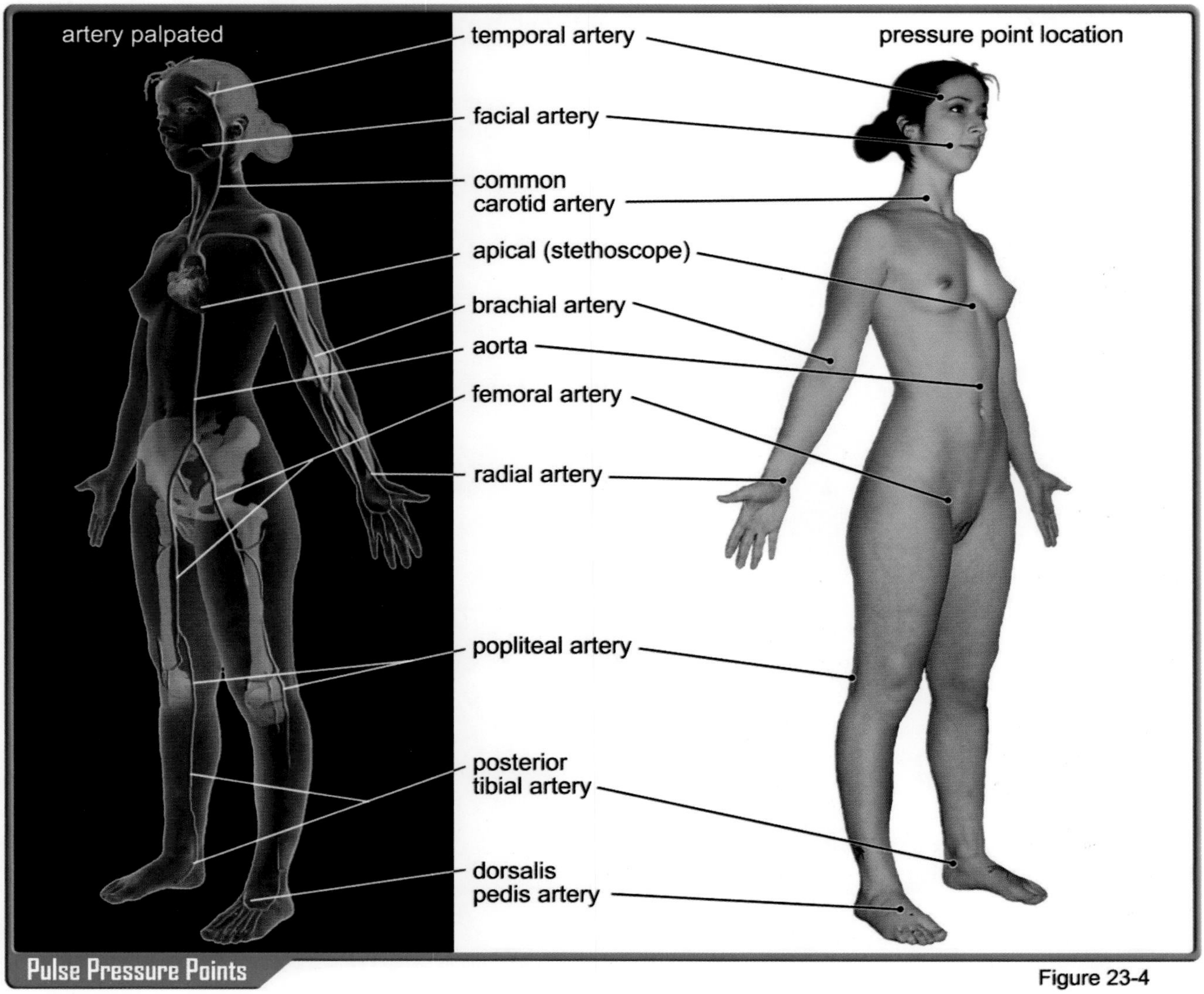

Figure 23-4

Figure 23-5

The Pulse

The alternating contraction / relaxation cycle of the beating heart produces pressure waves called *pulse pressures* that can be palpated (i.e., felt) in a number of superficial blood vessels. Interestingly, there is no correlation between the strength of the pulse and the distance from the heart; an easily palpable (and often visible) pulse can be felt (seen) even in the ankle and foot.

There are relatively few "pressure points" on the body because *i*) only arteries exhibit a pulse, and *ii*) most arteries are deep under muscle and thick fasciae. Only in a few places on the body are portions of arteries close enough to the surface to detect a pulse. Clinically, the pulse is taken as a "vital sign" to quickly assess the condition of a patient. The strength of the pulse and the regularity of the pulse can provide clues regarding blood pressure and volume and / or the condition of the heart.

Pulse points are named according to the artery being palpated. The locations of the major pulse points on the body are shown in figure 23-4.

Activity 1: Palpating Superficial Pulse Points

1. On yourself or a lab partner, locate the following pressure points and palpate a pulse. The pulse may be felt when applying firm pressure over the artery, pressing it against bone or other firm underlying structures. When taking a pulse use your index and middle fingers – do not use your thumb, as you may accidently detect your own pulse (in the thumb)

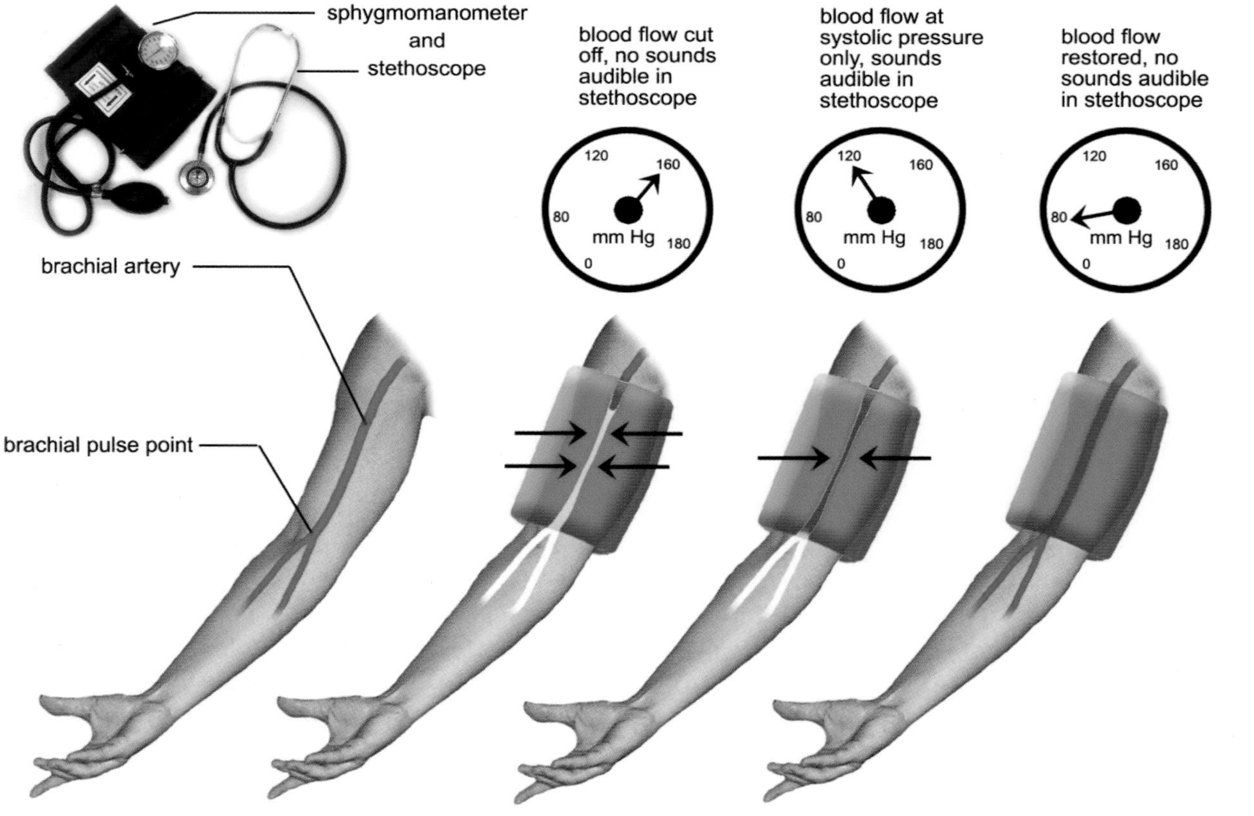

Figure 23-6

Measuring Blood Pressure with a Sphygmomanometer

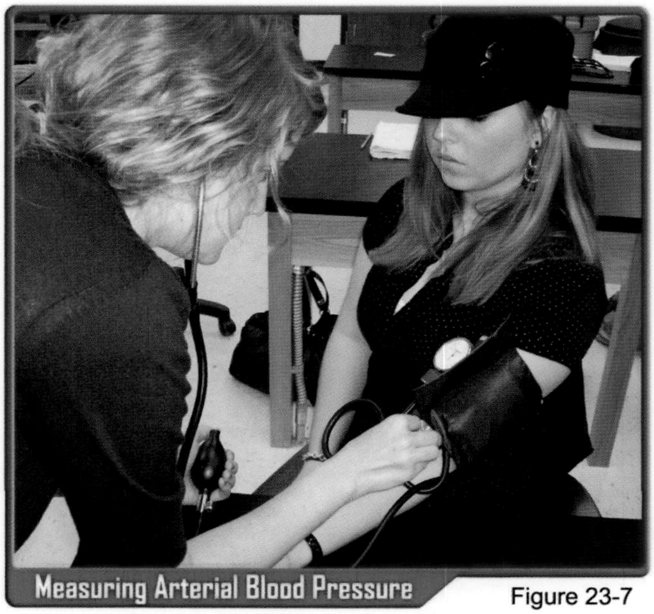

Figure 23-7

rather than a pulse in your partner.

- **Temporal artery** – on the sides of the head over the temporal bone.
- **Facial artery** – clench the teeth and press firmly on the cheeks, just behind the corners of the mouth.
- **Common carotid artery** – anterior portion of the neck between the sternocleidomastoid muscle and the trachea.
- **Brachial artery** – on the inside of the elbow (antecubital fossa). This pulse point is used when determining blood pressure with a sphygmomanometer and stethoscope.
- **Radial artery** – the anterolateral aspect of the wrist, proximal to the thenar eminence.
- **Femoral artery** – the medial aspect of the thigh, near the pubic region.
- **Popliteal artery** – behind the knee in the popliteal fossa
- **Posterior tibial artery** – on the medial side of the foot, located between the heel and the medial malleolus.[1]
- **Dorsalis pedis artery** – the dorsum of the foot.

Activity 2: Apical vs Radial Pulse

The apical pulse is taken by auscultating the apex of the heart with a stethoscope (Figures 22-9 & 23-5). Medical personnel may compare the *apical* pulse rate with the *radial* pulse rate to diagnose certain heart conditions, such as cardiac decompensation. In healthy individuals the two pulse rates should be the same; any differences between them is referred to as a "*pulse deficit.*"

1. The subject should sit comfortably while two students obtain his/her pulse rate: One student palpating the radial pulse rate and one student auscultating the apical pulse rate.
2. Count the apical and radial pulses for one minute and record your observations below. Was there a significant difference between the two pulse rates?

apical count ______________________ per minute

radial count ______________________ per minute

pulse deficit = ____________________ per minute

Activity 3: Measuring Arterial Blood Pressure

The blood within our blood vessels is under pressure. This pressure is greatest near the pump at the beginning of the circuit (i.e., the ventricles of the heart) and lowest at the end of the circuit (i.e., the atria of the heart). Blood pressure inside blood vessels is not like water pressure in household water pipes, however. In your house, a water pump keeps your water under constant and continuous pressure so it flows steadily when you open a tap. Your heart, however, pumps rhythmically via cycles of muscle contraction and relaxation. This means the blood pressure fluctuates up and down during the contraction / relaxation cycle, at least within the arteries. The capillaries dissipate the fluctuations making the pressure in the veins low and constant. When an artery is cut, blood will squirt out of the body in pulses, but it oozes slowly and continuously when a vein is cut.

A **sphygmomanometer** (or, *blood pressure cuff*) is a device used to measure arterial blood pressure – the force of blood against the walls of an artery. The device consists of an inflatable cuff that wraps around the subject's arm (Figures 23-6 & 23-7). The cuff is placed around the arm and inflated with a simple hand-operated bulb pump and the air pressure within the cuff is measured by an attached pressure gauge. The cuff is inflated tight enough to interupt blood flow through the brachial artery. As the pressure in the cuff is slowly lowered, blood first begins to enter the artery under high (systolic) pressure and this can be heard using a stethoscope. When the pressure in the cuff drops low enough to allow blood to flow unimpeded (i.e., below diastolic

[1] This particular pulse may be seen as well as felt. Simultaneously observe the posterior tibial artery pulse and the carotid artery pulse. What do you notice?

Table I Responses to Noxious Stimuli	Subject #1		Subject #2		Subject #3	
	BP	pulse	BP	pulse	BP	pulse
Baseline						
1 minute						
2 minute						
3 minute (optional)						

pressure), blood sounds are no longer detectable. Follow the steps below to obtain the blood pressure of your lab partner.

Do not leave the cuff inflated for more than 1 minute. If you have trouble obtaining a blood pressure, deflate the cuff, wait a few minutes and try again. Prolonged inflation of the cuff may cause fainting.

1. Be sure the cuff is completely deflated and the pressure gauge indicates zero pressure ("0 mm Hg").
2. With the subject sitting in a comfortable position, wrap the blood pressure cuff around the subject's arm just above the elbow. Many cuffs have an arrow which should point to the antecubital region and be positioned over the brachial artery. Secure the cuff using velcro.
3. Palpate the brachial pulse and mark its position with a lab marker or pen. Place the diaphragm of the stethoscope over the brachial pulse point.
4. Make sure the pressure valve is closed and inflate the cuff by repeatedly squeezing the bulb. Inflate the cuff to a pressure of about 160 mm Hg. At this point all blood flow to the arm is interrupted.
5. Slightly open the pressure valve so that the pressure in the cuff drops slowly. Watch the pressure gauge as you listen through the stethoscope for blood to begin entering the artery. Note the pressure (systolic pressure) reported on the gauge when you first begin hearing pulsing sounds (the "sounds of Korotkoff").
6. Continue watching the pressure gauge. The sound of blood pulsing into the artery should get louder, then softer. Note the pressure (diastolic pressure) at which you can longer hear the pulsing.
7. Fully open the pressure valve and deflate the cuff.
8. Wait a few minutes, then repeat the procedure to obtain a second blood pressure reading.

First trial: systolic pressure ______________

diastolic pressure ______________

Second trial: systolic pressure ______________

diastolic pressure ______________

The *pulse pressure* is the pressure difference between the systolic and diastolic pressures. Compute the pulse pressures determined from each trial.

Pulse pressure: First trial ____________________

Second trial __________________

Rather than reporting the two (systolic & diastolic) pressures, a mean of the two values is sometimes provided. The *mean arterial pressure* (MAP) is computed as follows:

MAP = diastolic pressure + (pulse pressure/3)

MAP: First trial ________________________

Second trial _____________________

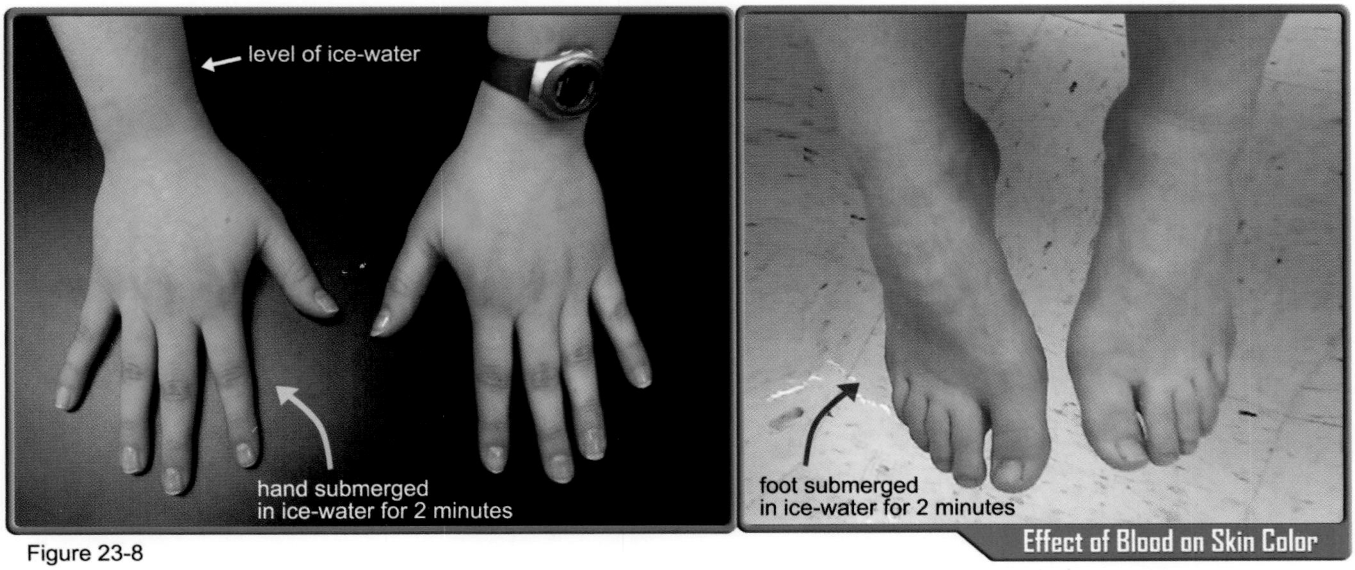

Figure 23-8

Activity 4: Noxious Stimuli & Blood Pressure

*This exercise should **not** be performed on a person with Raynaud's syndrome or other cardiovascular conditions!*

A number of factors can impact one's blood pressure. Diet and exercise are commonly known to affect long-term blood pressures, but blood pressure can fluctuate quickly and dramatically because of stress, strong emotions or pain.

In this activity we'll examine the effect of pain on arterial blood pressure and heart rate. Cold water will be used as the noxious (i.e., painful) stimulus.

1. Have a volunteer sit in a relaxed position and obtain a "baseline" measurement of heart rate and blood pressure on the volunteer. Record your observations in the table provided.
2. After the baseline values have been determined, have the subject submerge his or her hand or foot in a bucket of ice-cold water (about 50% ice, 50% water).
3. After 1 minute obtain heart rate and blood pressure measurements.
4. After 2 minutes obtain additional heart rate and blood pressure measurements.
5. Did the heart rate and / or blood pressure change after experiencing the painful stimulus? People respond to pain differently. The BP and pulse of some will not change from a noxious stimulus; however, it will for most subjects (especially the BP). If the systolic and/or diastolic blood pressure rises more than 23 mm Hg, the person is a *hyperreactor*. If the pressure rises less than 22 mm Hg, or decreases, the person is a *hyporeactor*. Repeat the procedure on at least two more volunteers.

Activity 5: Blood & Skin Color

In Exercise 5 we discussed some things that affect skin color. The main effector of skin color is the pigment melanin; however, blood can also affect skin color, especially in fair-skinned people with little melanin.

1. Observe the hand or foot of the person who performed Activity 4 above and compare it to the other hand/foot. Very likely, the skin of the extremity submerged in ice-water is considerably redder than the other extremity (Figure 23-8). Why is this?

Activity 6: Wire Blood Vessels to a Skeleton

Use red and blue pipe cleaner to "wire" a skeleton with the major blood vessels.

Activity 7: Schneider Physical Fitness Test

1. Measure the **reclining pulse rate** on your seated, relaxed partner by taking pulse for 30 seconds and multiplying by 2. Determine their score using the chart below:

1-minute pulse rate	*Points*
50-70	3
71-80	2
81-90	1
91-100	0
101+	-1

Score _______

2. Have your partner stand up and measure their **standing pulse rate**. Determine their score from the chart below:

1-minute pulse rate	*Points*
60-80	3
81-90	2
91-110	1
110-130	0
131+	-1

Score _______

3. Determine their **pulse rate increase** by subtracting the reclining pulse rate from the standing pulse rate. Determine their score from reclining pulse rate and pulse rate increase using the chart below.

Reclining pulse rate	*Pulse rate increase* 0-10	11-18	19-26	27-34	35+
50-60	3	3	2	1	1
61-70	3	2	1	0	-1
71-80	3	2	0	-1	-2
81-90	2	1	-1	-2	-3
91-100	1	0	-2	-3	-3
101+	0	-1	-3	-3	-3

Score _______

4. Have your partner step and then down from an 18-inch platform. Repeat this exercise 5 times allowing about 3 seconds for each step. Immediately measure your partner's pulse for 15 seconds and multiply by 4. Measure their pulse again at 30, 60, 90, and 120 second intervals. Record the time it takes for the pulse to return to normal standing pulse rate and determine their score from the chart below:

Pulse Rate Return After Exercise

Time (seconds)	*Points*
0-30	4
31-60	3
61-90	2
91-120	1
120+ (still 2-10 above normal)	0
120+ (still 11-30 above normal)	-1

Score _______

5. Subtract normal standing pulse rate (step 2) from pulse rate immediately after exercise (step 4). Choose the correct score from the chart below:

Standing Rate	*Rate immediately after exercise* 0-10	11-20	21-30	31-40	41+
60-70	3	3	2	1	0
71-80	3	2	1	0	-1
81-90	3	2	1	-1	-2
91-100	2	1	0	-2	-3
101-110	1	0	-1	-3	-3
111-120	1	-1	-2	-3	-3
121-130	0	-2	-3	-3	-3
131+	0	-3	-3	-3	-3

Score _______

6. Take your partner's **reclining blood pressure** (seated) and **standing blood pressure.** Determine the difference in systolic pressure (standing vs seated) and choose the correct score from the table below:

Chang in systolic BP	*Points*
Rise of more than 8 mm Hg	3
Rise of 2-7 mm Hg	2
No rise	1
Fall of 2-5 mm Hg	0
Fall of more than 6 mm Hg	-1

Score _______

7. Add up all scores from the previous tests. Determine fitness from the chart below:

Score	*Fitness Rating*
18-17	Excellent
16-14	Good
13-8	Fair
7 or less	Poor

Conclusions: What does your partner's score tell you about their physical fitness? What factors (in their case) contributed to their rating?

Schneider test adapted from Schneider, E.D., *A cardiovascular Rating as a Measure of Physical Fatigue and Efficiency*. JAMA 74:1507 (1920)

1. Label the figure below.

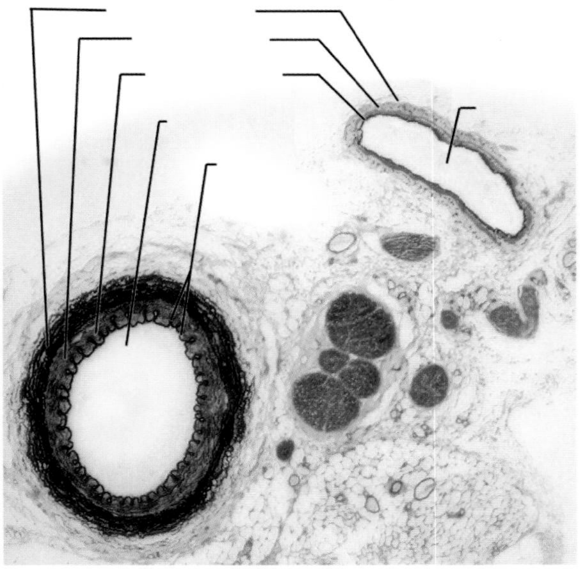

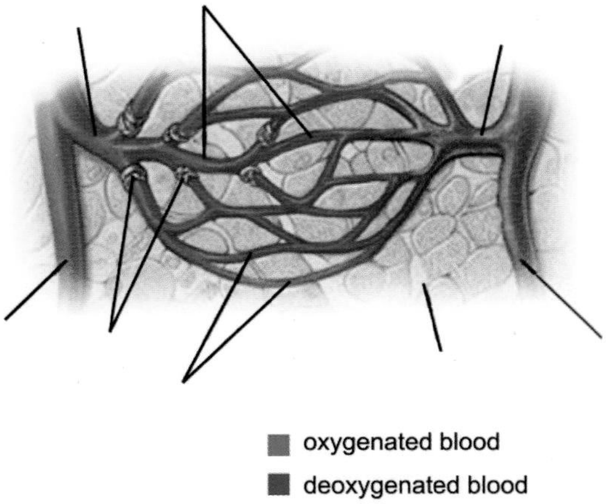

2. List the types of *conducting vessels*. Why are they called this?

3. How do capillaries differ from other blood vessels?

4. True or False: Arteries *always* carry oxygenated blood.

5. True or False: Muscular arteries assist the heart in pumping blood through vessels.

6. True or False: Vasomotion is the involuntary movement of blood vessels.

7. True or False: The pressure of blood in a vessel is a function of vessel diameter.

8. True or False: There's not enough blood in your body to bath all tissues at once.

9. Label the vessels in the figure below.

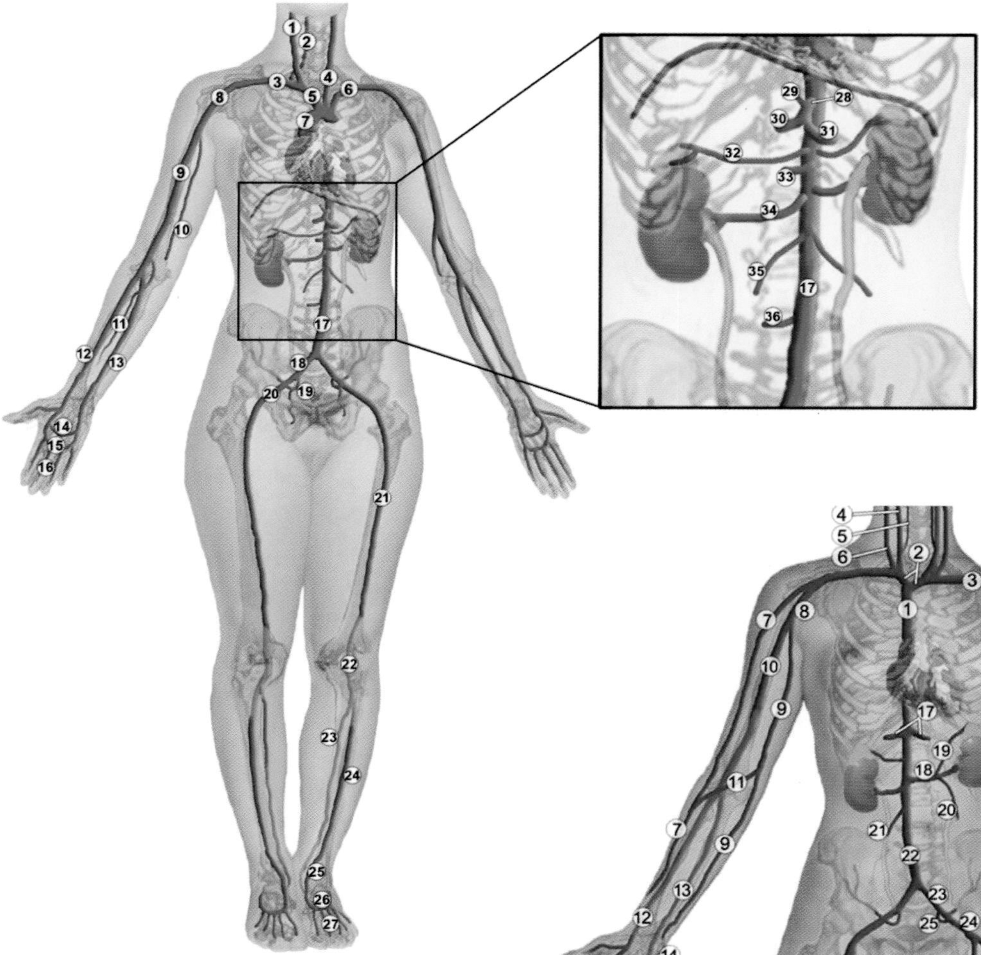

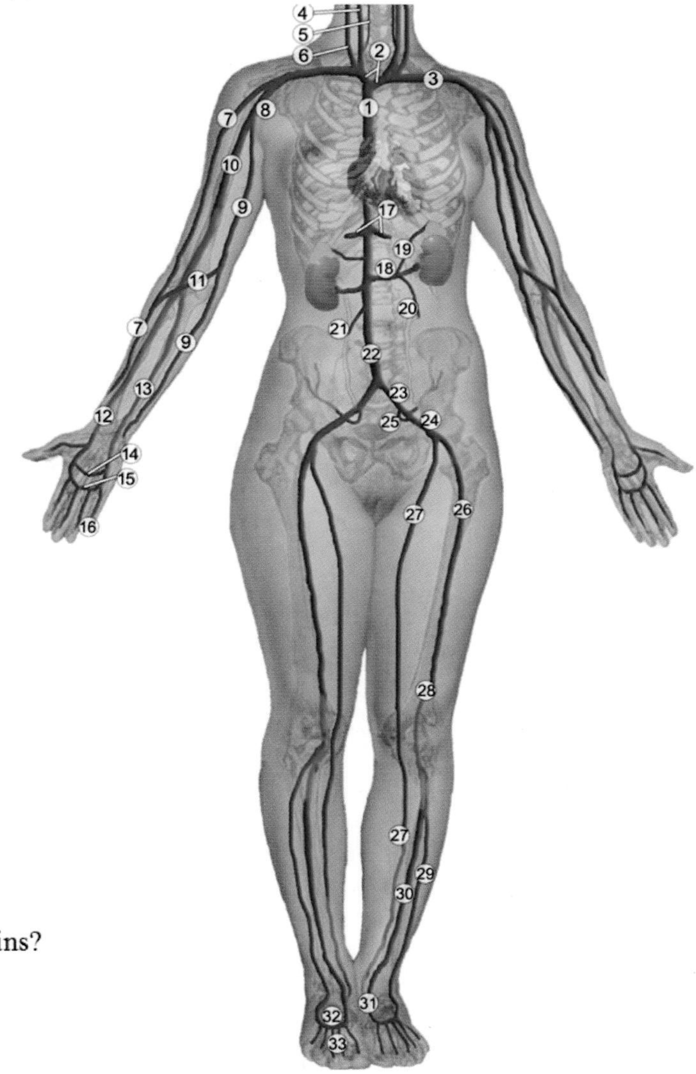

10. In which arteries can a pulse be palpated?

11. Why is a pulse only felt in arteries and not veins?

Special Focus

Special Circulation

Portal Systems

A **portal system** is a special type of circulation that incorporates two capillary beds. Normally, blood passes from the heart through arteries to a single capillary bed and then back to the heart through veins. In a portal system, blood first travels to one capillary bed and then to a second capillary bed before entering the venous system. The two capillary beds are connected by a portal vein (Figure SF-1).

Two important portal systems are found in the body: The *hepatic portal system* and the *hypophyseal portal system*. These portal systems are described in detail in the chapters on the endocrine system (hypophyseal portal), digestive system (hepatic portal) and urinary systems.

Fetal Circulation

Blood circulation in the fetus is very different than in the newborn or adult (Figure SF-2). Before birth, the fetus in the womb does not breath air, but instead obtains oxygen from the mother's blood via the placenta. Indeed, the lungs of the fetus are collapsed and will not inflate until birth. As a result, the pulmonary circuit in the fetus is nearly completely shut down. Two detours redirect the blood in the fetus away from the pulmonary circuit. First, a hole called the **foramen ovale** penetrates the wall separating the left and right atria. As a consequence, blood returning from the systemic circuit and collecting in the right atrium can flow freely into the left atrium. From there, the blood enters the left ventricle and enters again into the systemic circuit. Second, a small artery called the **ductus arteriosus** connects the pulmonary trunk to the aorta. As a result, blood pumped from the right ventricle enters the aorta (and the systemic circuit) rather than the pulmonary circuit.

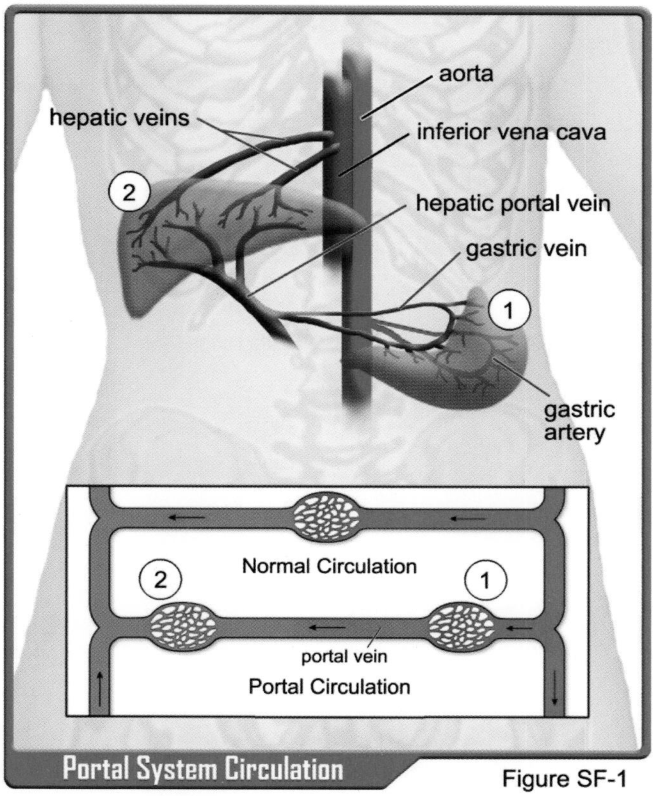

Figure SF-1

Immediately upon birth a newborn must inflate his lungs and obtain oxygen on his own. Thus, the pulmonary circuit must quickly become functional. Within minutes of birth the foramen ovale will begin closing and the ductus arteriosus begins to shrivel. A thin connective tissue "scar" called the **ligamentum arteriosum** is all that remains of this artery in the adult. Likewise, a thin membranous remnant of the foramen ovale called the **fossa ovalis** is sometimes present in the adult.

The foramen ovale and the ductus arteriosus shunt blood away from the the lungs in the fetus. How then does the baby receive oxygen? Two small arteries carry deoxygented blood from the common iliac arteries through the umbilical cord to the placenta. At the placenta, capillary exchange of oxygen moves the gas from the mother's blood to the baby's blood. One large umbilical vein conveys the oxygenated blood to the inferior vena cava, where it again enters systemic circulation.

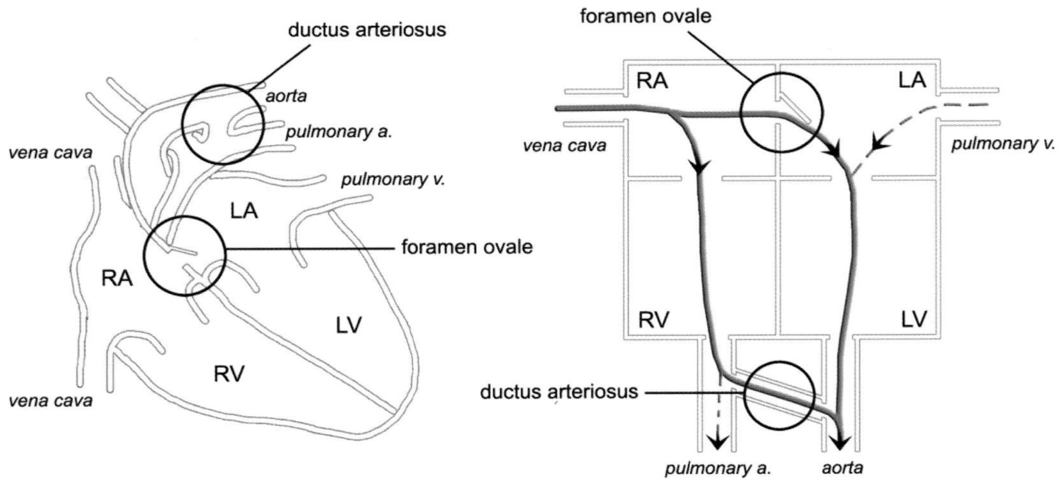

Fetal Apparatus for Bypassing the Lungs

Figure SF-2

exercise 24

the LYMPHATIC system

He will wipe every tear from their eyes. There will be no more death or mourning or crying or pain, for the old order of things has passed away.

Revelation 21:4

When the immune system mistakenly reacts to harmless antigens in the environment, the result is allergies.

The lymphatic system serves two important functions for the body: *i*) it circulates interstitial fluids and *ii*) it cleanses those fluids of debris and wastes and – importantly – invading organisms like bacteria.

Tissue Fluid Circulation

All cells are bathed in extracellular fluid, also called interstitial fluid. This fluid is derived from blood plasma that exits the arterial side of capillaries but does not re-enter the venous side. Interstitial fluid must not be allowed to remain stagnant if the cells are to stay healthy, and it must be returned to the bloodstream to prevent fluid from accumulating in body tissues (a condition called *edema*). The lymphatic system returns this fluid to the bloodstream. Once collected into the lymphatic vessels, the interstitial fluid is called ***lymph***. On its journey, it passes through a series of **lymph nodes** where it is filtered and cleansed.

The return of interstitial fluid to the blood begins as tissue fluids slowly drain into blunt-ended **lymphatic capillaries** (Figure 24-1). Lymphatic capillaries exit body tissues as small **lymphatic collecting vessels**, or simply *lymphatics*, which converge to form ever larger vessels. Eventually, these vessels drain into one of just a few large **lymphatic ducts** that empty into large veins (Figure 24-2). The **right lymphatic duct** drains lymph from the right side of the thorax, the right side of the head and the right arm into the right subclavian vein. Lymph from the rest of the body drains into the left subclavian vein via the **thoracic duct** (sometimes called the *left lymphatic duct*). Lymph from the legs and abdomen collects in the large **cisterna chyli** at the beginning of the thoracic duct. The cisterna chyli also receives fatty chyle from the intestines and its lymph is therefore rich in lipids.

Lymphatic vessels contain numerous valves that keep the lymph flowing in the proper direction (i.e., toward the heart). Note that there is no pump for lymph as there is for blood. Rather, lymph is propelled through lymphatic vessels primarily by the massaging action of working skeletal muscles while the valves insure a one-way flow of the fluid.

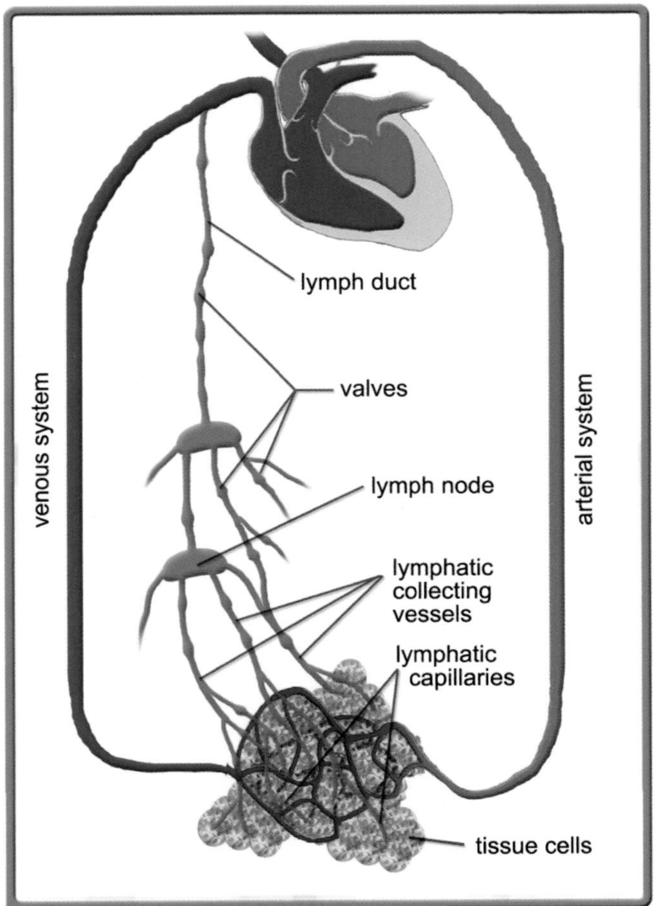

Schematic of Lymphatic System

Figure 24-1

Lymph Nodes

There are thousands of lymph nodes scattered throughout the body. Most of the nodes are nearly microscopic in size and are embedded within body tissues. However, several regions of the body contain large nodes 1 – 5 mm in diameter. Specifically, the inguinal, axillary and cervical regions possess large lymph nodes (Figure 24-2). In women, an extensive network of mammary lymphatics and prominent **mammary lymph node chains** are present (Figure 24-3). In each case, these regions are near most, warm areas of the body that are exposed to the environment and subject to invasion by pathogens. The primary function of lymph nodes is to destroy invading organisms and clean interstitial fluids of waste products and debris before being returned to the blood. During an active infection, the glands may become swollen due to increased filtering activity.

Structurally, lymph nodes are often shaped like small kidney beans (Figure 24-4). Typically, multiple **afferent ducts** will drain into a node but only one **efferent duct** will empty the node. Each node consists of a superficial **cortex** and a deep **medulla** divided into **follicles**. The nodes are rich in lymphocytes, a type of white blood cell involved in immunity.

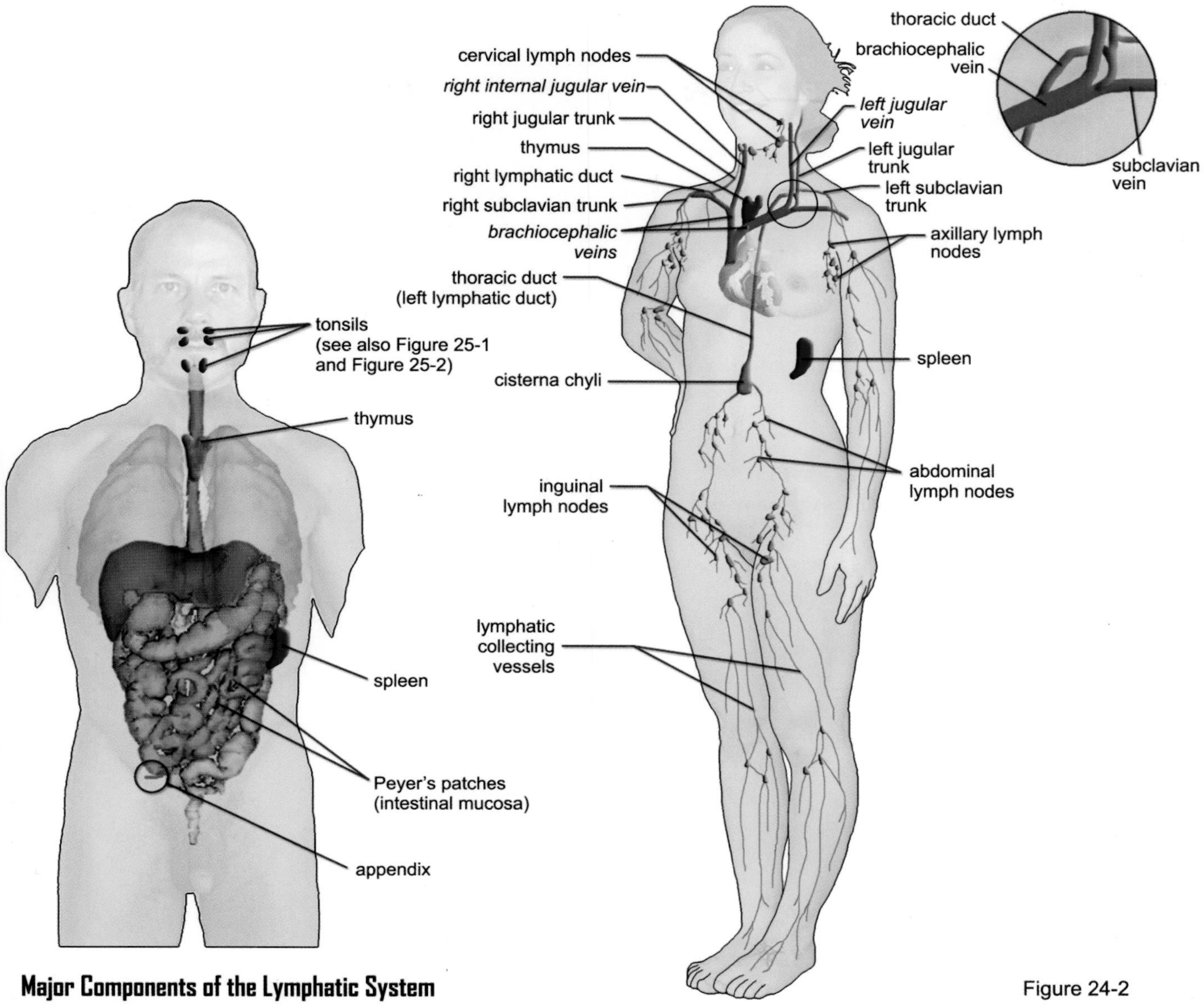

Major Components of the Lymphatic System

Figure 24-2

Other Lymphatic Organs

Besides the lymphatic vessels and lymph nodes, other lymphatic system organs and tissues are scattered throughout the body that contribute to immunity (Figure 24-2). The largest lymphatic system organ is the **spleen**, located in the abdomen and protected by the ribcage. The spleen filters blood in much the same way the lymph nodes filter lymph. It is similar to a lymph node, but much larger and darker in appearance. The spleen also stores significant amounts of iron.

The **tonsils** are pairs of lymphatic structures located in the head and neck region. The three pairs of tonsils are the palatine tonsils, the lingual tonsils and the pharyngeal tonsils (Figure 24-2; also see Figures 25-1 and 25-2). These organs protect the body from infection by microorganisms entering the oral and nasal cavities.

The **thymus** is located in the thoracic region. The primary role of the thymus is the development of specialized lymphocytes (T cells) that ward of infections. The thymus is an endocrine organ that produces several closely related hormones collectively called *thymosins*. Interestingly, the thymus undergoes atrophy with age; by the age of 50 the organ is nearly functionless and largely replaced with connective tissue.

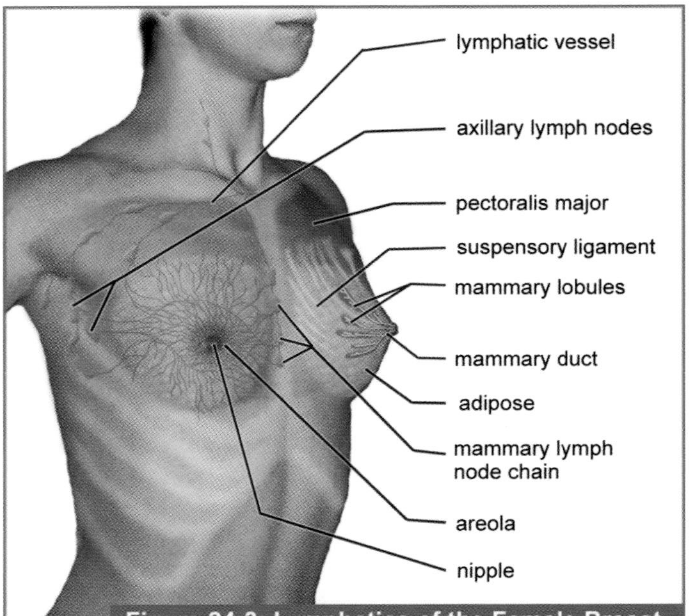

Figure 24-3: Lymphatics of the Female Breast

Peyer's patches are lymphoid tissues distributed along the gastrointestinal tract (Figure 24-2). The density of Peyer's patches increases towards the distal end of the tract where *E. coli* grows abundantly (see also figure 27-14).

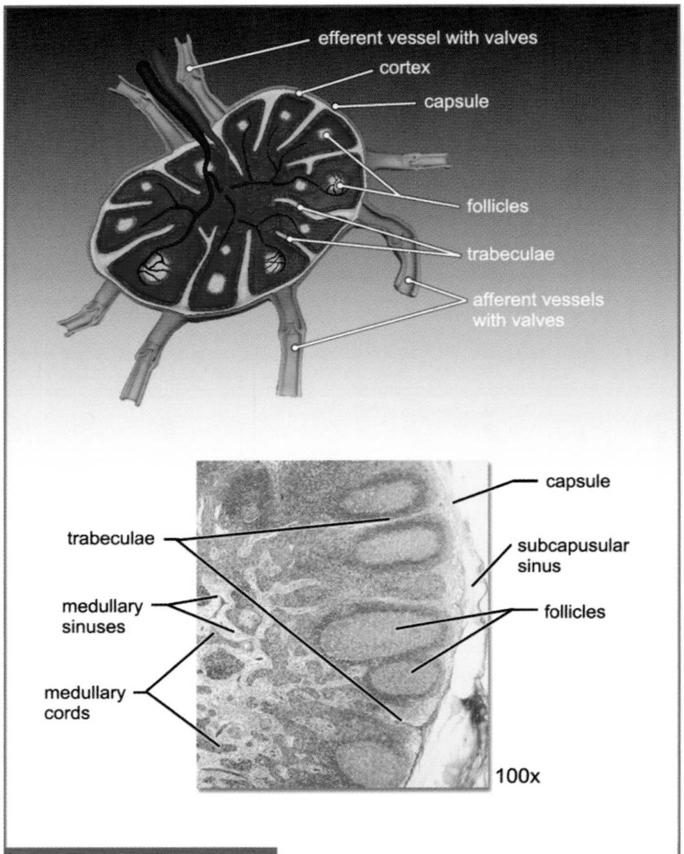

Figure 24-4: Lymph Node

Activity 1: Identify Organs of the Lymphatic System

1. Study Figure 24-2 to familiarize yourself with the organs of the lymphatic system.

Activity 2: Microscopic Examination of Lymphoid Tissue

1. Obtain a microscope and a prepared slide of a lymph node.
2. Examine the node under high power and identify as many of the structures as you can on figure 24-4.

Activity 3: Microscopic Examination of Lymphoid Tissue

1. Obtain a microscope and a prepared slide of the ileum or large intestine of the GI tract.
2. Observe the numerous Peyer's patches scattered throughout the intestinal mucosa.

Match the terms below with the correct letters on the diagram.

_______ 1. Cisterna chyli

_______ 2. Inguinal lymph nodes

_______ 3. Left internal jugular vein

_______ 4. Brachiocephalic veins

_______ 5. Axillary lymph nodes

_______ 6. Thymus

_______ 7. Thoracic duct

_______ 8. Collecting vessels

_______ 9. Abdominal lymph nodes

_______ 10. Right jugular trunk

_______ 11. Cervical lymph nodes

_______ 12. Left subclavian trunk

_______ 13. Right lymphatic duct

_______ 14. Right internal jugular vein

_______ 15. Spleen

_______ 16. Right subclavian trunk

_______ 17. Left jugular trunk

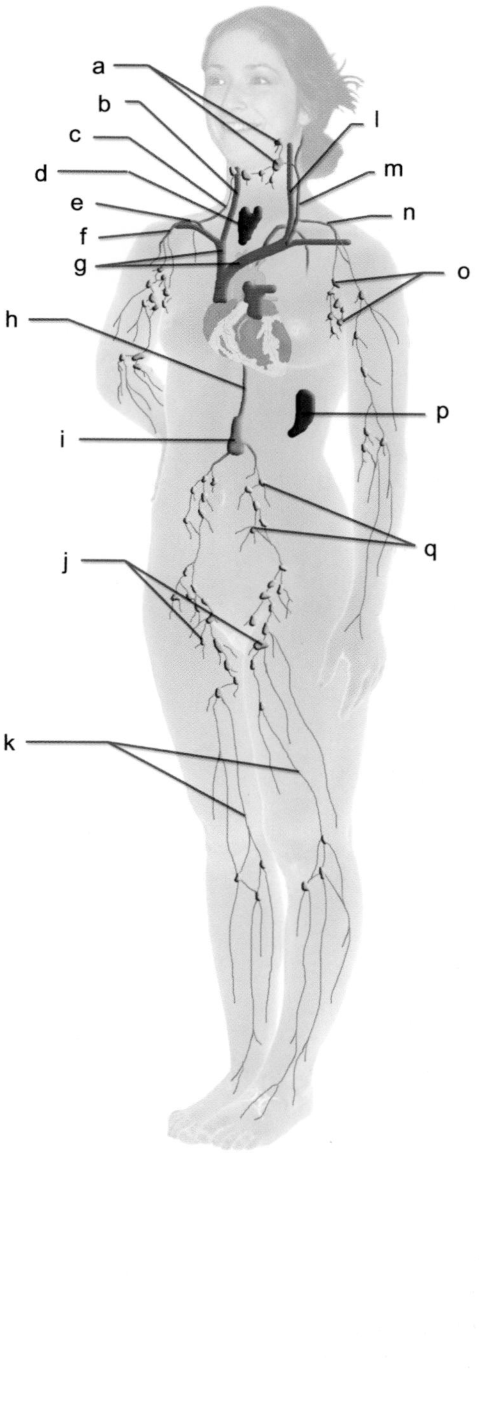

18. How is lymph propelled through the lymphatic system?

19. What are Peyer's patches? Where are they found and what is their function?

20. How does lymph from the cisterna chyli differ from lymph elsewhere in the lymphatic system?

21. What is the major function of lymph nodes?

22. Why are clusters of large lymph nodes found in the axillary, inguinal, cervical and mammary areas?

23. How are lymphatic vessels similar to veins?

24. How do lymphatic capillaries differ from cardiovascular capillaries of the bloodstream?

25. What is the role of the thymus? How does the thymus differ from many other organs of the body?

exercise 25

the RESPIRATORY system

The Lord God formed the man from the dust of the ground and breathed into his nostrils the breath of life, and the man became a living being.

Genesis 2:7

Living body cells require a continuous supply of oxygen in order to survive. If the supply is interrupted for even a few minutes death of cells – and the organism – will quickly ensue. Thankfully, oxygen is readily available, we are literally bathed in it every day of our lives. Like the regular contractions of the heart which pump blood throughout our blood vessels, regular contractions of the diaphragm "pump" gases – oxygen and carbon dioxide – into and out of our bodies. These contractions occur tirelessly, day and night, throughout our entire lives.

The diaphragm is just one part of the *Respiratory System*, the organ system dedicated to the exchange of gases between our body cells and the outside environment. Other major organs of the system include the lungs, airway conducting passages, and the nasal and oral cavities. The respiratory system relies on the cardiovascular system to transport dissolved gases to all of the body's cells. The system is divided into the upper and lower respiratory regions, each of which are discussed below.

The Upper Respiratory System Structures

Air initially enters the body through the upper respiratory structures (Figure 25-1). Although air may enter through either the **oral cavity** or the **nasal cavity**, the nasal cavity is usually the preferred route because 1) the nasal cavity contains hairs in the **external nares** which filter relatively large particles from the air, and 2) the nasal cavity contains spiral passageways (**superior, middle and inferior meatuses**) that help warm and humidify cold, dry in-coming air. These measures help protect the delicate tissues in the lower respiratory structures.

The nasal cavity is surrounded by the *paranasal sinuses*, which are hollowed out chambers in the ethmoid, sphenoid, maxillary and frontal bones. The sinuses are lined with mucosal membranes; the mucus secreted by the membranes drain into the nasal cavity. Sinus infections, colds, allergies or the flu (among other maladies) can cause inflammation of the mucous membrane and the production of excessive, abnormally thick

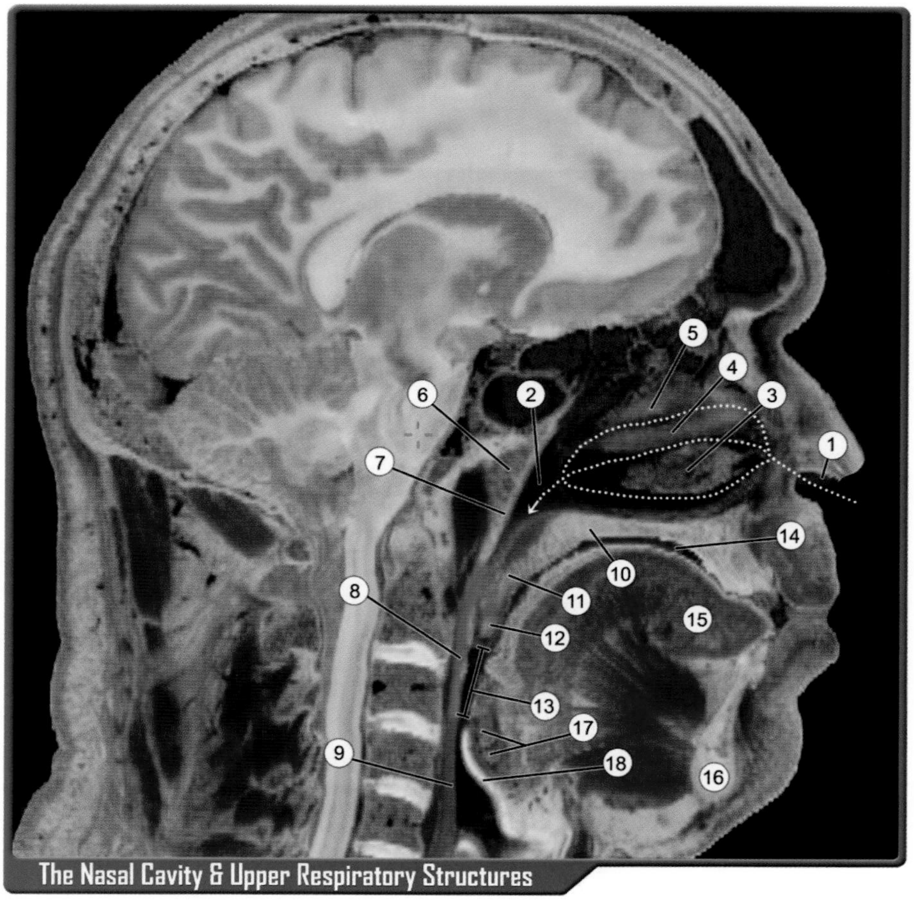

1. external nares
2. internal nares
3. inferior concha
4. middle concha
5. superior concha
6. pharyngeal tonsil
7. nasopharynx
8. oropharynx
9. laryngopharynx
10. hard palate
11. soft palate
12. uvula
13. fauces
14. oral cavity
15. tongue
16. mandible
17. lingual tonsil
18. epiglottis

········ airflow through superior, middle, and inferior meatuses

Figure 25-1

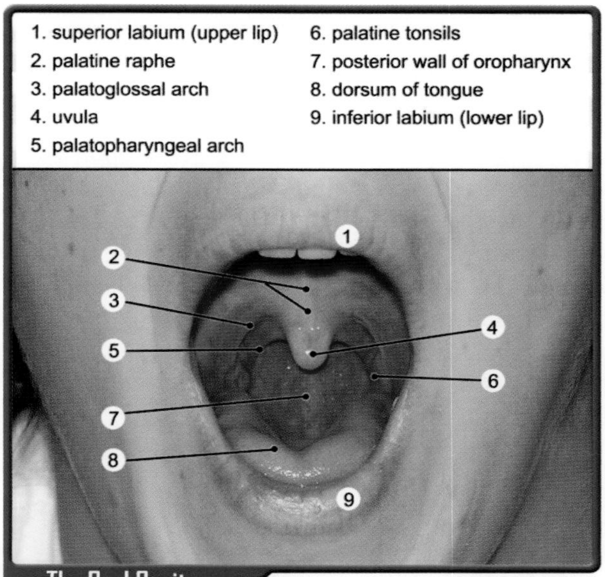

The Oral Cavity

Figure 25-2

secretions that may impede the flow of mucus. These events often lead to "sinus pressure" and / or "sinus headaches."

The oral cavity is separated from the nasal cavity by the hard and soft palates. The **hard palate** is formed by the maxillary bone; posterior to the hard palate, the **soft palate** is made of cartilage. A skin-like flap, called the **uvula** hangs from the soft palate (Figure 25-2). The exact function of this organ is a mystery, but there are several hypotheses. When swallowing food or drink, the uvula may rise and close off the nasal cavity, thus preventing materials from accidently entering the nasal passages. Because the uvula is unique to humans, Finkelstein et al. have suggested that it may be an accessory organ of speech.[1]

The tongue forms the floor of the oral cavity, while the cheeks form the walls of the cavity. Unlike the nasal cavity, the oral cavity can be closed off from the environment by the **labia**, or *lips*. The space between the lips & cheeks and the teeth & gums is called the **vestibule** of the oral cavity. Posteriorly, the **palatoglossal** and **palatopharyngeal arches** are visible behind the uvula. Between these arches are a pair of lymphoid structures called the palatine tonsils. These tonsils, along with the lingual tonsils at the root of the tongue and the pharyngeal tonsils in the nasopharynx, help protect us from airborne pathogens that enter the body through the respiratory system.

Once air has passed through the nasal cavity or oral cavity it enters the **pharynx**, commonly called the *throat*. The pharynx is divided into three regions: the **nasopharynx** behind the nasal cavity, the **oropharynx** behind the oral cavity and the **laryngopharynx** behind the larynx (Figure 25-1).

Gases, liquids and solids all enter the oral cavity. At some point, these substances must be segregated because only air enters the lungs while foods and drinks are directed to the stomach. The **larynx** is the structure responsible for separating these substances. The larynx is also called the *voice box* because it houses the **vocal cords**.

The larynx is composed of ten cartilages (Figure 25-3). The largest is the **thyroid cartilage**

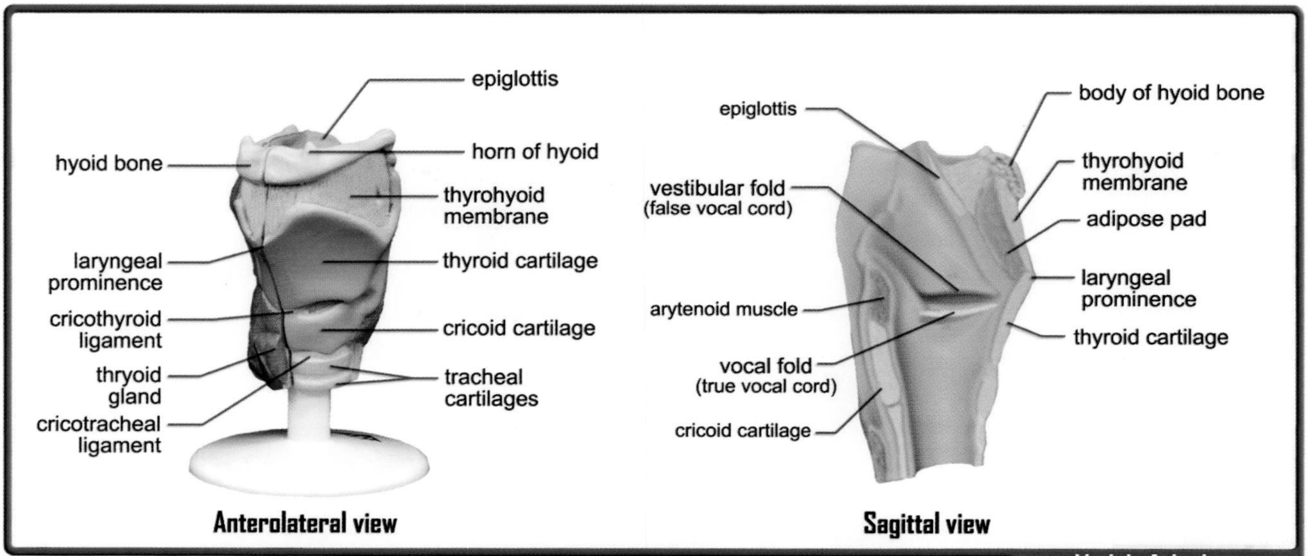

Figure 25-3

Model of the Larynx

[1] Finkelstein, Y. et al. 1992. The riddle of the uvula. *Otolaryngol Head Neck Surg*. 107(3):444-450.

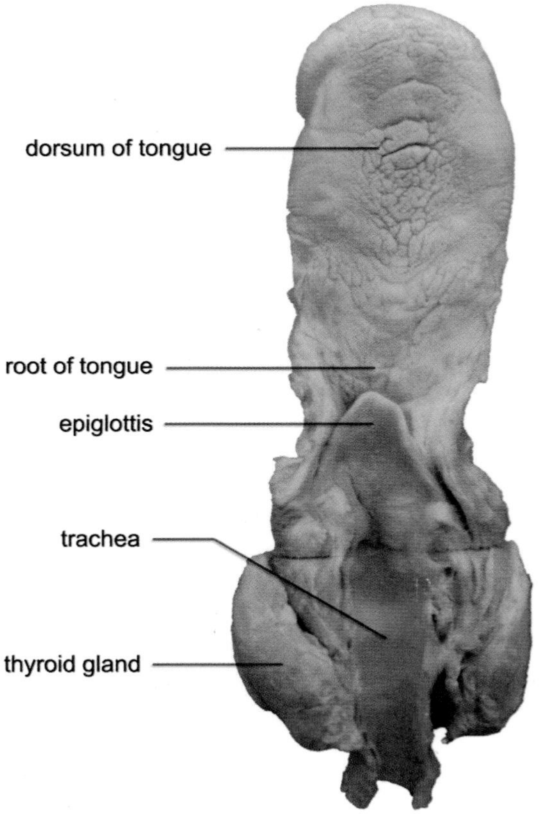

Figure 25-4 **Human Tongue & Larynx**

which forms a large shield-like structure anteriorly that guards the vocal cords. A sharp point is often visible (especially on men) called the **laryngeal prominence**, or *Adam's apple*. The **cricoid cartilage** encircles the larynx beneath the thyroid cartilage. The larynx directs air to the trachea, a "pipe" that conducts air to the lungs. Throughout its length the trachea is surrounded by cartilaginous C-shaped rings called the **tracheal cartilages**. By definition, the superior four tracheal cartilages are part of the larynx. Internally, the **cuneiform**, **corniculate** and **arytenoid cartilages** support the vocal system. Finally, at the base of the tongue is the **epiglottis** – a flap-like structure that closes off the trachea when we swallow food or drink (Figures 25-3 & 25-4). The epiglottis is made of elastic cartilage rather than hyaline cartilage like the other laryngeal cartilages. It functions to direct food and drink toward the stomach, thus preventing them from entering the lungs.

The larynx is a hollow passageway that conducts air to the trachea and lungs. Tight bands of connective tissue stretch across the inside of the larynx constricting the flow of air. These bands, called the **vocal folds**, or *vocal cords*, vibrate when air squeezes through them producing sound. These sounds allow us to speak and sing. The small opening between the cords is the **glottis**. The vocal folds can be willfully opened or closed to change the pitch of the sound produced: The tighter the cords are closed, the higher the pitch.

The Lower Respiratory System Structures

The respiratory structures beneath the larynx are considered the lower respiratory structures (Figure 25-5). The **trachea**, or *windpipe*, conducts air from the larynx superiorly and divides inferiorly to form the left and right primary bronchi. The lumen of the trachea is always held open by the **tracheal**

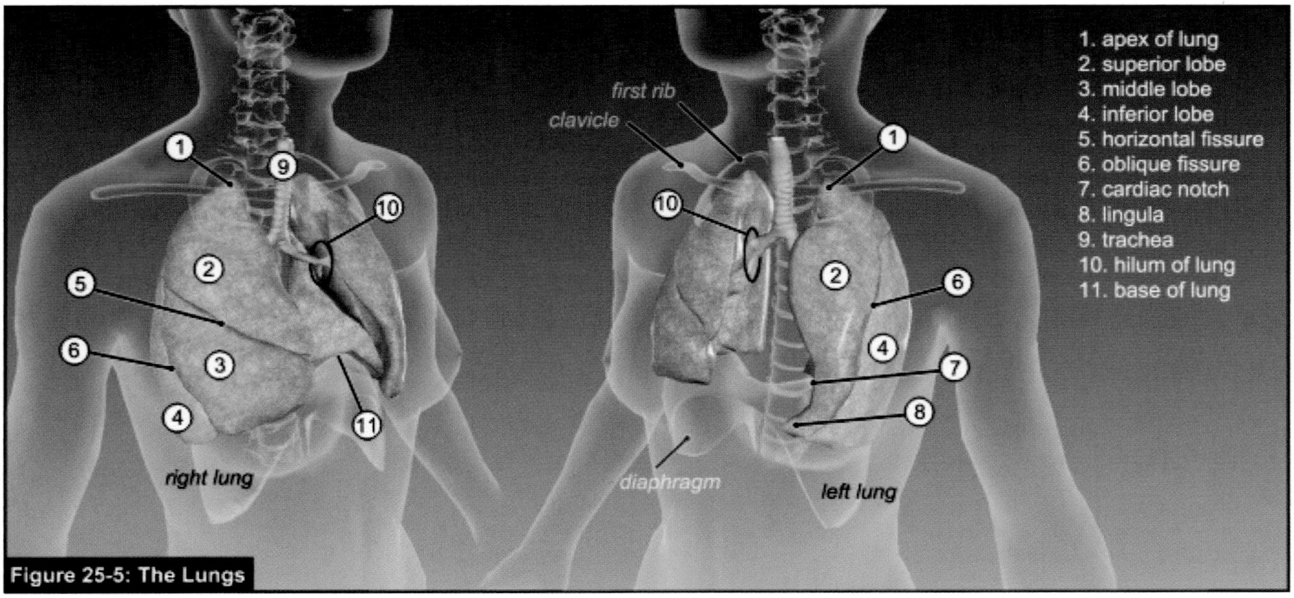

Figure 25-5: The Lungs

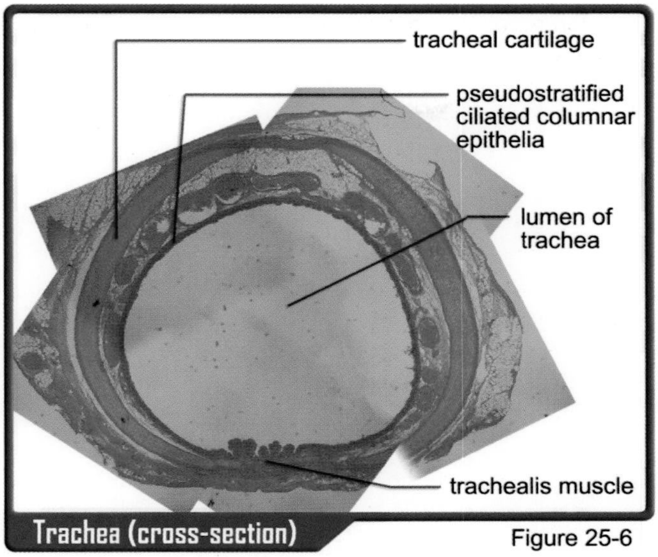

Figure 25-6

cartilages, C-shaped rings of cartilage along the length of the organ (Figure 25-6). These rings prevent the trachea from collapsing and cutting off airflow. The rings are incomplete on the posterior face of the trachea (thus the C-shape), but are connected by the **trachealis muscle**. When this muscle is relaxed the trachea is completely open, but contraction of the trachealis muscle constricts the trachea, reducing airflow.

Details of the lower respiratory passages are shown in figure 25-7. As stated above, the trachea divides into the left and right **primary bronchi** which enter the left and right lung, respectively. The bronchi, along with nerves and blood vessels of the pulmonary and systemic circuits, enter each lung at the **hilum**. Inside the lung, the primary bronchus branches out into **secondary bronchi** and then **tertiary bronchi**. (The secondary and tertiary bronchi are also called the *lobar* and *segmental* bronchi, respectively). The tertiary bronchi divide further into microscopic **bronchioles** which terminate in **alveolar sacs.** Alveolar sacs resemble clusters of grapes on a vine. The individual "grapes" are **alveoli** – the site of gas exchange between blood and air. Each alveolus is an air-filled chamber surrounded by capillary blood vessels; it may be visualized as a balloon wrapped tightly with yarn. Because oxygen levels are higher in the air than the blood, oxygen diffuses from the air in the alveoli into the blood of the capillaries where it is whisked away to the systemic circuit for delivery to body cells. By contrast, carbon dioxide is higher in the blood than the air in the alveoli, so it diffuses out of the blood into the alveolar air to be expelled into the atmosphere.

Alveoli make up the bulk of the lung. Consequently, lyophilized (i.e., freeze-dried) lungs are extremely light and "airy." Each lung is similar in overall size and appearance with the following exceptions: 1) The left lung possesses a large indentation called the **cardiac notch**, to accommodate the heart and 2) the left lung is divided into two lobes whereas the right lung is divided into three lobes. The **oblique fissure** divides the left lung into **superior** and **inferior lobes**; it divides the right lung into **inferior** and **middle lobes** while the **horizontal fissure** separates the **middle** and **superior lobes**.

Preserved sheep lungs are shown in figure 25-8. The pointed top of the lung is called the **apex** and in humans it extends to the clavicle. The **base of the lung** is deeply concave and rests securely upon the diaphragm. When the diaphragm contracts the lungs are expanded as the base is pulled downward. When the diaphragm relaxes

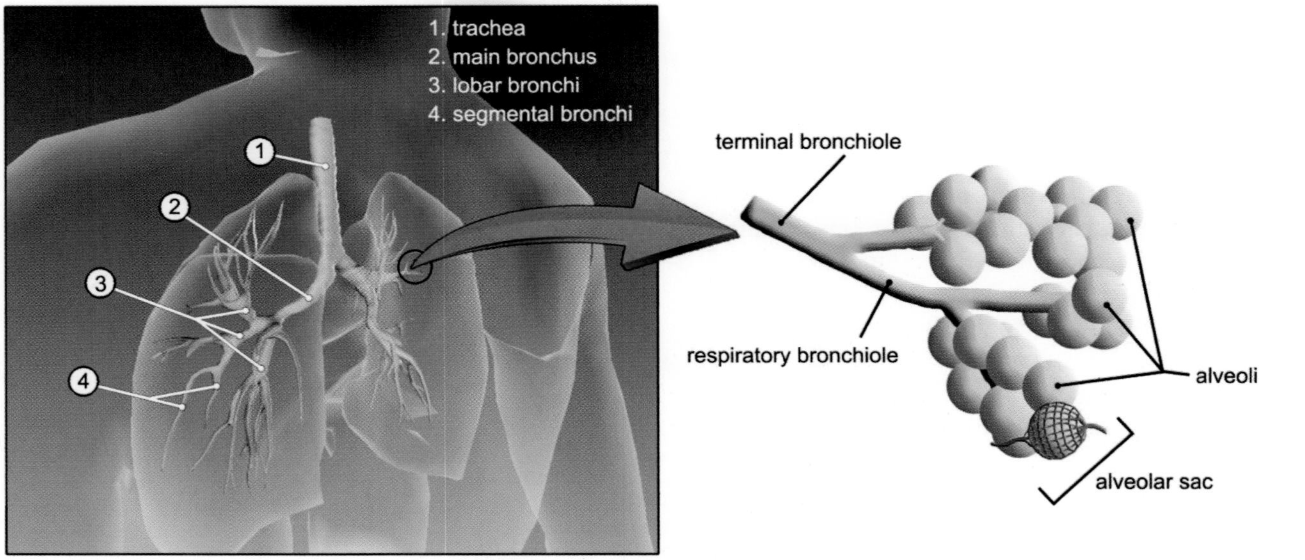

Figure 25-7: Structures of the Lower Respiratory Passageways

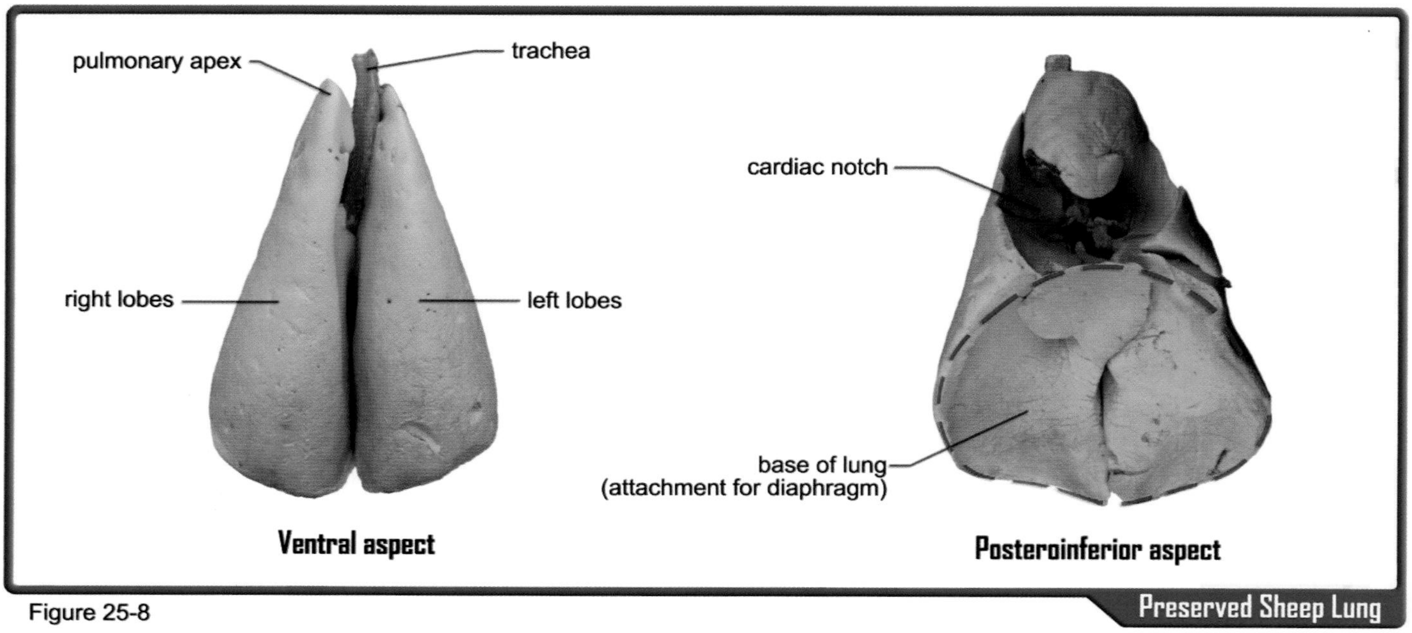

Figure 25-8

elastic fibers within the lung tissue cause the expanded lung to passively recoil.

Respiratory Histology

Microscopic examination of the lung tissue reveals how spacious and airy the alveoli are. An alveolar duct and several alveolar sacs are shaded blue for clarity in figure 25-9. The walls of the alveoli are composed of simple squamous epithelial tissue to facilitate the movement of gases between the air and red blood cells. Scattered among the alveolar sacs are fibroblasts, septal cells and macrophages. **Fibroblasts** build and maintain the elastic fibers of the lung that make it recoil when the diaphragm contracts. The recoiling action expels CO_2-rich air and "resets" the lung for the next inhalation. **Septal cells** produce *surfactant*, a soapy substance that keeps the alveoli from collapsing. At these microscopic sizes, the cohesive and adhesive forces of water molecules would cause the walls of the alveoli to stick together without a surfactant to disrupt those forces.[2] **Macrophages** engulf foreign particles that have been inhaled, especially airborne pathogens. Thus, they live deep in the lungs and assist the tonsils to protect us from sickness.

We all know that smoking cigarettes is bad for you. The effects of smoking on lung tissue is evident by microscopic examination (Figure 25-10). The lungs of smokers is filled with small carbon particles (i.e., soot) that blackens the appearance of the tissue. Many of the macrophages that usually engulf such particles are killed by the toxic compounds in cigarette smoke. With prolonged exposure, the septal cells die and the alveoli collapse. The collapsed alveoli are eventually replaced with scar tissue. Obviously, the smoker's lung is far less effective than a healthy lung at gas exchange.

We are constantly breathing in small particles like pollen, dust and floating pathogens. The tonsils and macrophages capture many of the

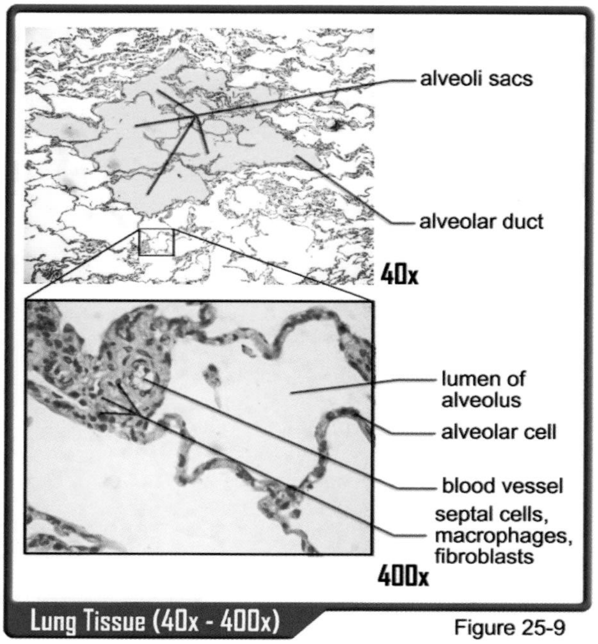

Figure 25-9

[2] Probably because fetuses don't breath, surfactant production in their lungs begins late in pregnancy. The introduction of surfactant into the lungs of premature babies dramatically improves their survival rates.

Structure = Function

The types of tissue found along the respiratory tract vary as the function of the tract varies.

Lining the oral cavity and the pharynx we find **stratified squamous epithelia**. These parts of the respiratory tract are exposed not only to air but liquids and solids, also. Consequently, these surfaces experience abrasive forces that constantly strip away the top layers of cells, which are being constantly replaced by new cells from beneath.

The trachea and bronchi are not exposed to food or drink, only air. These structures are lined by a simple layer of columnar cells that sometimes appear stratified. These **pseudostratified ciliated columnar epithelia** possess cilia that move the mucus escalator.

Deep in the lung the alveoli permit gas exchange between the blood and air. Consequently, the walls of alveoli are made of exceptionally thin **simple squamous epithelia.**

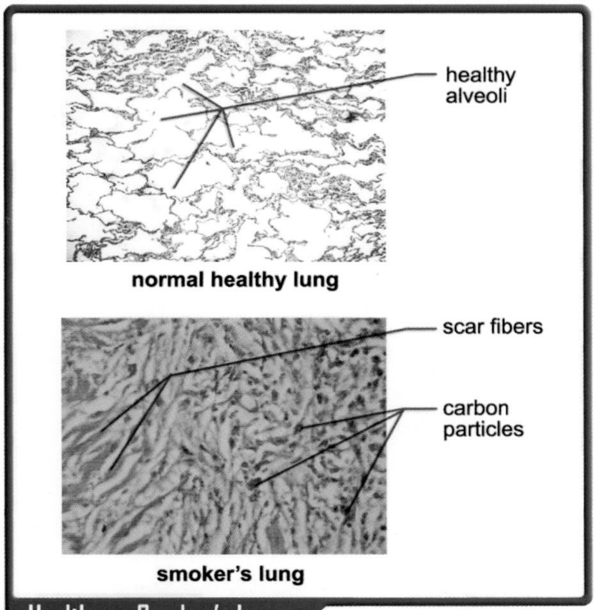

Healthy vs Smoker's Lung

Figure 25-10

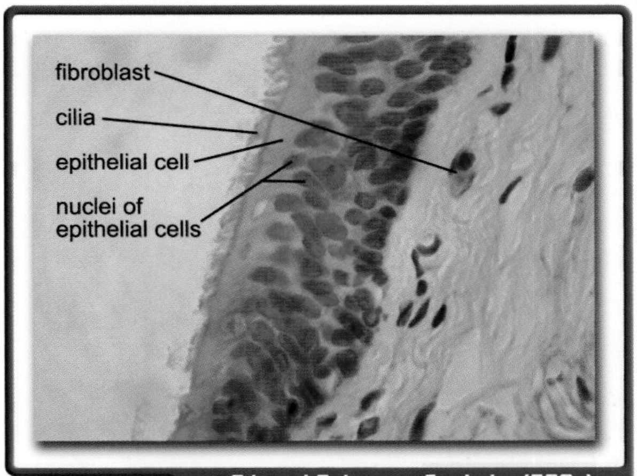

Figure 25-11 Ciliated Columnar Epithelia (800x)

pathogens and remove them from the body. Pollen, dust and other debris are cleaned up by the *mucus escalator*. Mucosal cells in the lungs, bronchi and trachea (e.g., goblet cells) produce mucus and deposit the mucus onto the surface of the epithelium lining those structures. The epithelia lining the bronchii and trachea are pseudostratified ciliated columnar cells (Figure 25-11). The cilia on these cells beat rhythmically to slowly move the mucus upward. Inhaled particles are captured in this mucus and are carried upward by the current. Eventually, the mucus rises to the larynx where it is transferred by swallowing to the esophagus and then to the "trash can" of our guts. Without thinking about it (or even being aware of it), we take a swallow about every 30-60 seconds throughout the day and night. All total, we swallow about 1.5 liters of mucus per day cleaning our lungs with the mucus escalator.

Activity 1: Examine Preserved Sheep Lung

1. Obtain a preserved sheep lung. How would you describe this organ? Is it heavy, dense, light, etc? Why do you suppose it has such unique properties?

Activity 2: Histological Examination of Respiratory Tissues

1. Obtain prepared slides of the trachea (cross-section and longitudinal section showing pseudostratified ciliated columnar epithelial cells), tongue and lung (healthy and smoker's).
2. Notice the different types of tissues (simple squamous, stratified squamous, etc) in the different locations of the respiratory tract.
3. Compare the healthy lung tissue from that taken from a smoker. What are some of the differences you notice?

1-25. Label the figure below of the upper respiratory structures.

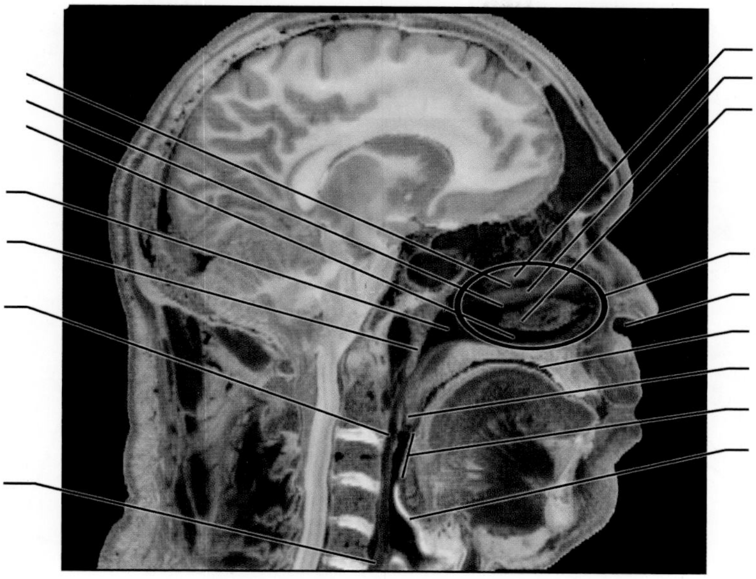

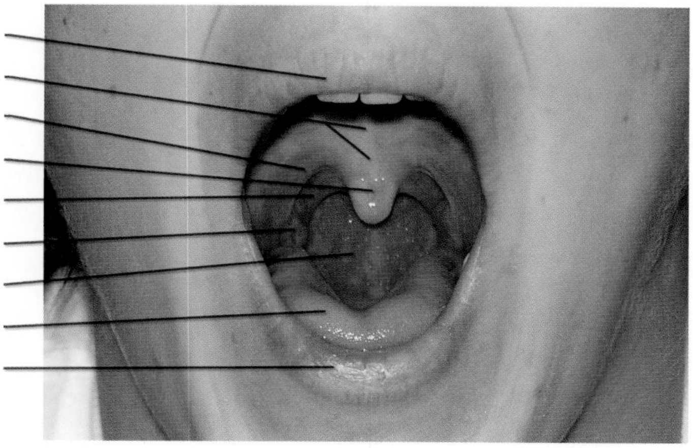

26. Why is breathing through the nose better than breathing through the mouth?

27. What are the functions of the uvula and epiglottis?

28-46. Label the figure below of the lower respiratory structures.

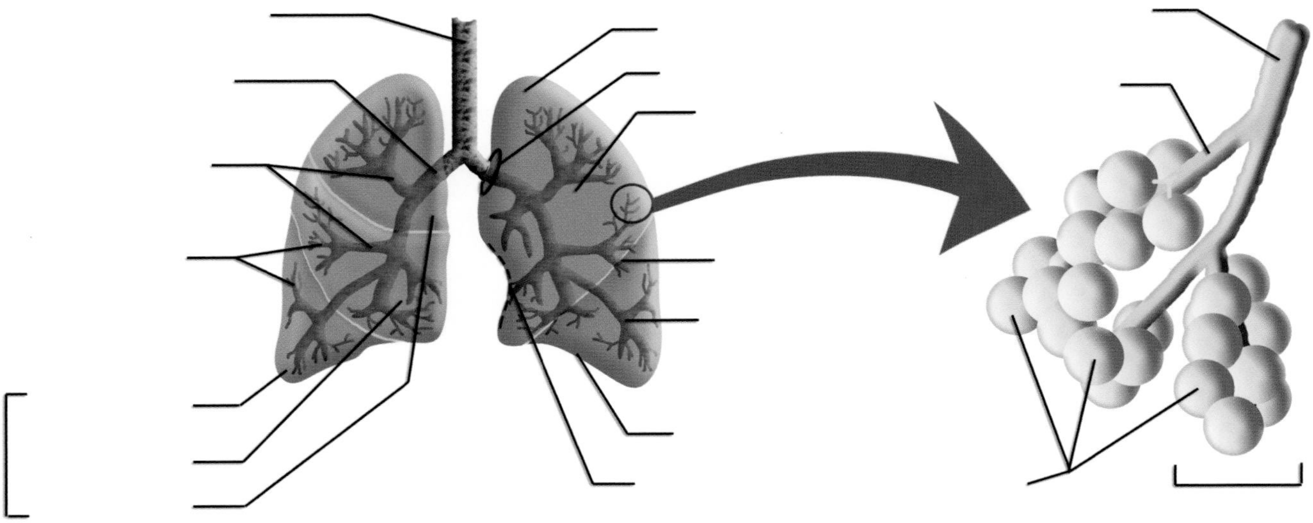

47. The oropharynx is lined with stratified epithelial cells; the trachea is lined with the pseudostratified ciliated columnar cells and the alveoli are composed of simple squamous epithelia. Explain why the cell types vary from the mouth to the lungs.

48. Describe how smoking cigarettes affects the respiratory system.

Match the following terms with their definitions.

_______	49. Sac-like structures in the lung	a. simple squamous epithelia
_______	50. Pipe that conducts air from the oral/nasal cavities to the lungs	b. epiglottis
_______	51. Cells that propel mucus through the mucus escalator	c. alveoli
_______	52. Muscle that constricts the trachea	d. larynx
_______	53. Flap-like structure that guards the trachea from food & drink	e. pharynx
_______	54. Conducting passageway that enters the lung at the hilus	f. ciliated epithelia
_______	55. Slit-like opening in the larynx	g. uvula
_______	56. Flap-like structure that guards the nasal cavity from food & drink	h.concha
_______	57. Contains the vocal cords	i. trachea
_______	58. Cells that form the alveoli	j. trachealis
_______	59. The back of the throat	k. bronchus
_______	60. Increases air turbulance in the nasal cavity	l. glottis

exercise 26

respiratory PHYSIOLOGY

Remember, O God, that my life is but a breath.
Job 7:7

The anatomy of the respiratory system was discussed in the previous exercise. Here, we'll examine functional aspects of the respiratory system. In particular, we'll examine the mechanics of breathing and the various lung capacities of clinical importance.

Mechanics of Respiration

The movement of air into and out of the lungs is called *pulmonary ventilation*, or breathing. It consists of *inspiration* (a.k.a., inhalation) and *expiration* (a.k.a., exhalation). Inspiration is an active process that requires muscular contraction of the diaphragm. By contrast, restful expiration is passive and depends upon the elasticity of the lungs: Like tiny rubber bands, extensive elastic fibers cause the lungs to spontaneously recoil when the diaphragm relaxes.

With each breath the air pressure in the lungs (i.e., intrapulmonary pressure) fluctuates between positive and negative relative to atmospheric pressure (Figure 26-1). When the diaphragm contracts the lungs are pulled open causing the air pressure within them to drop. At negative pressures air from the atmosphere rushes into the lungs to "fill the void." During that time oxygen from the atmospheric air in the alveoli diffuses into the red blood cells of the blood while carbon dioxide diffuses in the opposite direction. When the diaphragm relaxes, the lungs recoil and the air pressure inside them builds up. When the pressure becomes positive air rushes out of the lungs into the atmosphere. The entire process is complete in 4 seconds, and freshly oxygenated blood returns to the systemic circuit.

Pleural fluid plays a crucial role in lung expansion (and thoracic cage compression). In fact, without this fluid the lungs would not expand and we couldn't breathe. Lung expansion depends on the cohesive and adhesive properties of the water in the pleural fluid[1]. With each cycle of inhalation and exhalation, the hydrogen bonds in water pull the lungs open as the ribcage expands (and likewise pull the ribcage closed as the lungs recoil).

[1] Water is highly cohesive and adhesive – i.e., sticky – because of its numerous hydrogen bonds. Cohesion describes water molecules sticking to each other; adhesion describes water sticking to other things, such as containers (or in this case, the surface of the lungs and the body wall).

Emphysema and asthma are two common respiratory maladies in the United States. Emphysema is a condition in which the elasticity and recoiling ability of the lungs is compromised. Although there are genetic causes to emphysema, the most common cause of emphysema in the U.S. is cigarette smoking. Since the stretched lungs fail to recoil when the diaphragm relaxes, air gets trapped in the alveoli and gas exchange is dramatically reduced.

Some people have hyper-sensitive respiratory passages. This condition, called asthma, causes the airways to become inflamed, leading to constriction of the passageway (Figure 26-2). Constriction is often caused by certain environmental triggers called *inducers*. Alternatively, inducers may cause muscular contraction of the smooth muscle lining the bronchioles. Whether the respiratory tissues become inflamed or whether the bronchioles become constricted by muscular spasms, the result is reduced airflow to the alveoli and difficulty breathing.

Lung Volumes & Capacities

Several measurements can be taken to assess the health of a patient's lungs and respiratory system. These measurements may be taken with a **spirometer** (Figure 26-3) and the results recorded on a **spirograph** (Figure 26-4). Measuring how much air a person's lungs can hold, how much they can inhale or exhale and other parameters can provide clues to respiratory pathologies. Emphysema, for example, often has a greater effect on one's expiratory reserve volume than their inspiratory reserve volume. The various clinical measurements taken include

- **Tidal volume** = the amount of air moved in and out of the lungs with each normal breath (at rest)
- **Inspiratory reserve volume** = the amount of air that can be inhaled above and beyond the tidal volume.
- **Expiratory reserve volume** = the amount of air that can be expelled from the lungs beyond the normal tidal volume.
- **Vital capacity** = the amount of air that can forcefully expelled from the lungs after a complete inhalation.
- **Inspiratory capacity** = the maximum amount of air that can be inhaled.

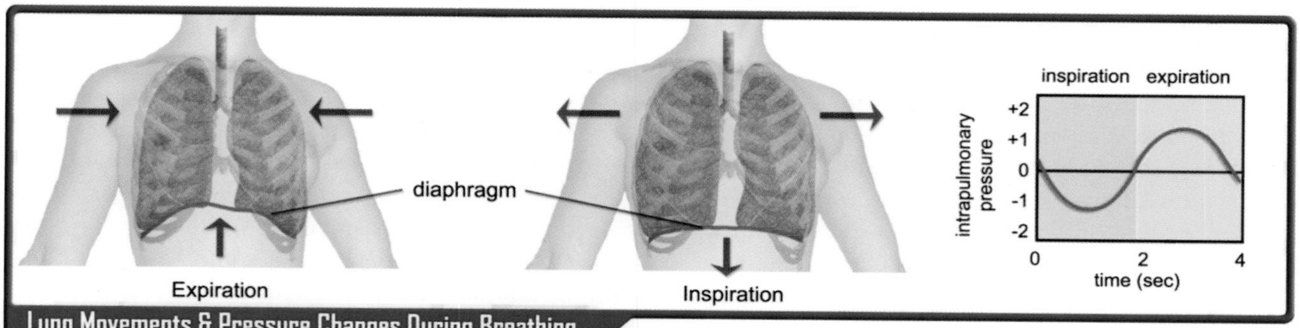

Lung Movements & Pressure Changes During Breathing

Figure 26-1

- **Residual volume** = the amount of air remaining in the lungs following a forceful expiration.
- **Total lung capacity** = the total amount of air that can be contained within the lung.

Activity 1: Examine A Model Lung

1. Obtain a model lung, or Bell Jar, from your instructor (shown in figure 26-5). Within the jar are two balloons that represent the lungs connected to the atmosphere via a pipe-like "trachea." The bottom of the jar is made of stretchy rubber with a handle attached. The rubber mimics the muscular diaphragm.
2. Pull the handle on the rubber "diaphragm" and notice what happens to the balloon "lungs."
3. Push the handle of the rubber diaphragm and again observe the effects of this action on the balloon lungs.

Activity 2: The Role of Pleural Fluid in Lung Physiology

1. The cohesive property of water and the role of cohesion in lung physiology can be easily demonstrated with two microscope glass slides. Obtain two microscope glass slides.
2. Place a small drop of water onto one slide and then cover the drop with the second slide to sandwich the water between the slides.
3. Slide the two glass slides back and forth or in a circular motion, like when rubbing the palms of your hands together. Do the slides move past each other easily, or only with difficulty?
4. Now align the edges of the slides. Try pulling the two slides apart without sliding the edges out of alignment. Can this be done easily or with much effort?
5. Explain the observations made above.

Activity 3: Auscultating Respiratory Sounds

1. Obtain a stethoscope and clean the ear pieces with an alcohol wipe.
2. Listen to the *bronchial sounds* by placing the diaphragm of the stethoscope on the throat beside the subject's Adam's apple. These sounds are generated by the rushing of air through the large conducting passageways.

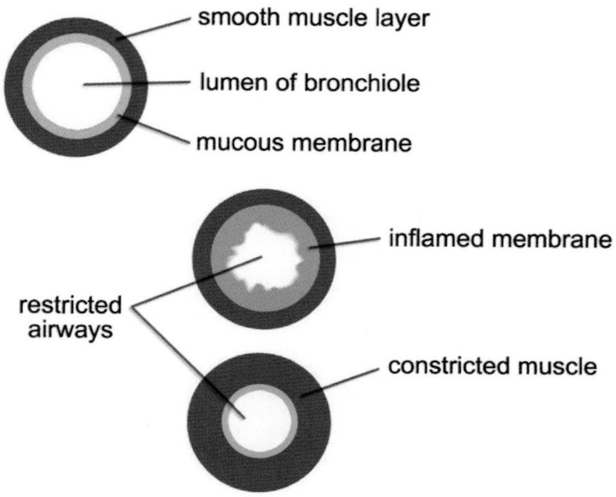

Asthmatic Restriction of Bronchioles

Figure 26-2

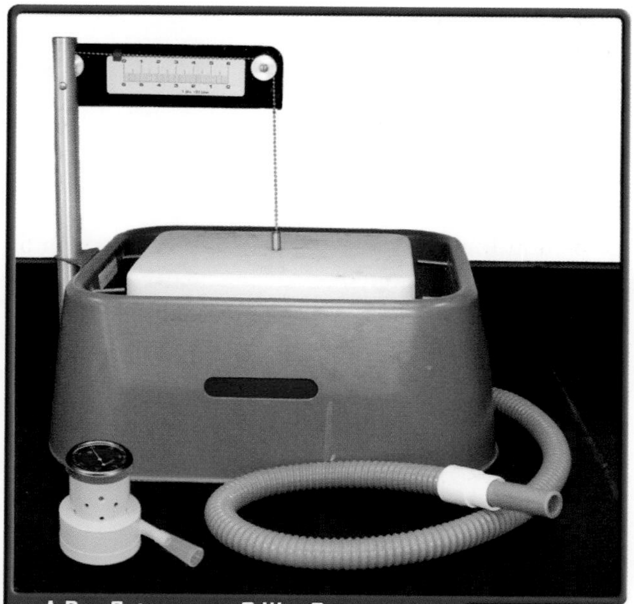

A Dry Spirometer & Wet Spirometer

Figure 26-3

3. Have the subject speak _softly_ while you listen through the stethoscope. The vocal cords produce sounds, but words are formulated by the lips, teeth and tongue in the oral cavity. Thus, you should only hear murmurings.
4. Place the stethoscope at various places on the subject's chest. Filling of the lung alveoli with air – *vesicular breathing sounds* – can often be heard just beneath the clavicles and at various intercostal spaces.
5. A good place to listen to the lungs without much interference from the heart is at the **triangle of auscultation** on the back. This triangle is a spot on the back with minimum overlap of muscles so lung sounds can be heard clearly. The triangle is bounded by the medial border of the scapula, the latissimus dorsi muscle and the trapezius muscle (Figure 26-6).

Activity 4a: Measuring Lung Volumes and Capacities Using a Wet Spirometer

Note: The wet spirometer measures expiratory volumes only, not inspiratory volumes. For best results, the subject should not watch the spirometer scale while measurements are being taken.

1. Before measuring respiratory volumes, first determine the subject's breathing rate. To do this, simply observe the subject's chest and count the number of breaths taken in one minute.

Respirations per minute (RPM) = ______________

Tidal Volume (TV)

2. Place a disposable mouthpiece on the end of the hose of the wet spirometer.
3. Have the subject breathe a few normal breaths. After several breaths, inhale normally and then exhale normally into the spirometer tube several times. Observe the volume of air exhaled; this is the subject's tidal volume (TV). Obtain three measurements and then calculate the average.

trial 1: ______________________

trial 2: ______________________

trial 3: ______________________

average: ______________________

4. Calculate the *minute respiratory volume* (MRV) as follows:

MRV = TV x RPM = _________________ mL/min

Expiratory Reserve Volume (ERV)

5. Have the subject take a few normal breaths and then, *after exhaling the normal tidal volume*, place the spirometer tube to the mouth and forcefully exhale. Attempt to completely empty the lungs of all air. The volume of air exhaled is the expiratory reserve volume. Again, take three measurements and calculate the average.

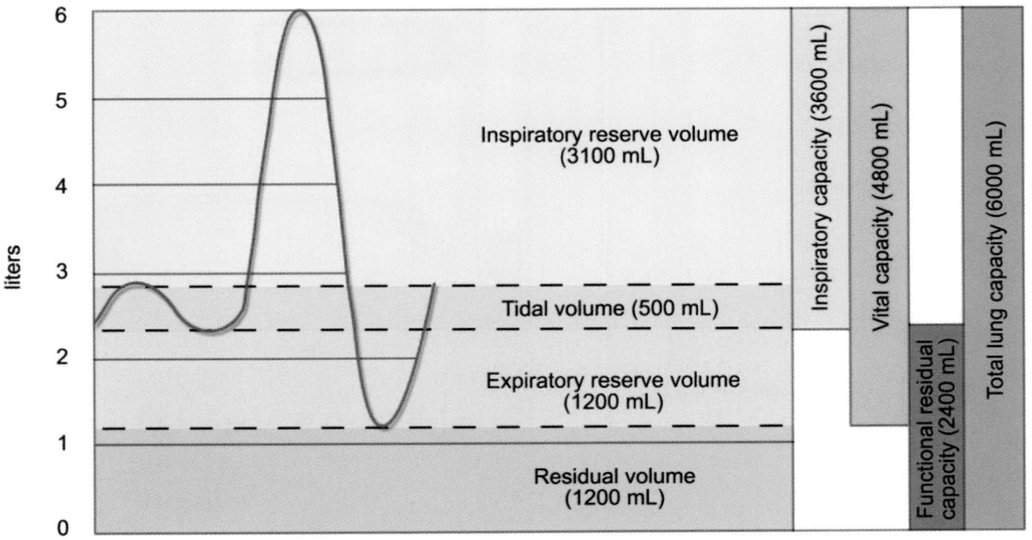

Figure 26-4

Spirographic Record

trial 1: ______________________

trial 2: ______________________

trial 3: ______________________

average: ______________________

Vital Capacity (VC)

6. Have the subject inhale as much air as possible, then exhale as much as possible into the spirometer tube. The amount of air exhaled under these conditions is the vital lung capacity, or simply, vital capacity. Take three measurements and calculate the average.

trial 1: ______________________

trial 2: ______________________

trial 3: ______________________

average: ______________________

Vital capacity is probably the most useful lung measurement clinically. Compare your vital capacity to the predicted VC for the average person of your height, age and gender. You predicted VC can be calculated from the following formulas (where H = your height in centimeters and A = your age in years). Average expected vital capacities are listed in Table 26.1

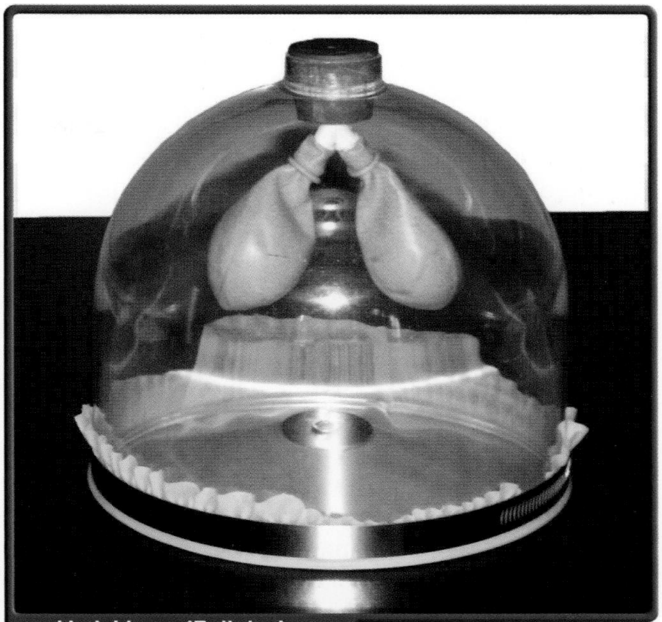

Model Lung (Bell Jar) Figure 26-5

Male: predicted VC = (0.05H) – (0.022A) – 3.5

Female: predicted VC = (0.04H) – (0.02A) – 3

Inspiratory Reserve Volume (IRV)

7. The inspiratory reserve volume cannot be directly measured using a wet spirometer; however, it can be calculated from the measurements taken above. Use the following formula to calculate the subject's IRV.

IRV = VC – (TV + ERV) = ___________________

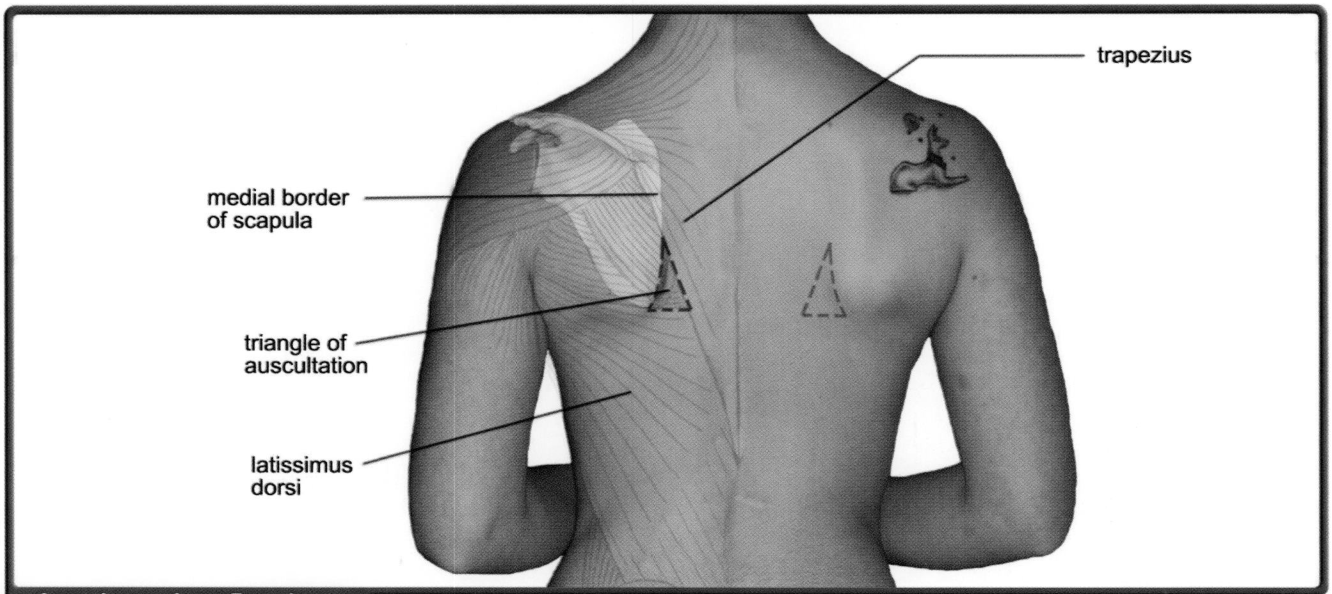

Auscultating Lung Sounds Figure 26-6

Activity 4b: Measuring Lung Volumes using a Dry Spirometer

1. You may also measure expired lung volumes using a dry spirometer.
2. Place a clean mouthpiece on the dry spirometer. Turn the dial (right or left) until the needle points to zero.
3. To measure vital capacity, inhale deeply as much as possible.
4. Exhale into the spirometer in one, strong motion. Keep the spirometer level and do not block the ventilation holes on the side of the instrument.

Activity 5: Effects of Exercise on VC

1. Exercise for 5 minutes by running in place.
2. Measure your VC immediately after exercise.
3. A decrease in vital capacity after exercise may indicate asthma or other respiratory disorder.

Activity 6: Effects of Hyperventilation

1. Have your partner inhale deeply and then hold his/her breath for as long as they can. Using a watch or timer, record how long they can hold their breath.
2. Next, have your partner hyperventilate by taking short, shallow breaths for about 1 minute. Then, have then inhale deeply and hold their breath again. Record how long they were able to hold their breath after hyperventilating.

Before hyperventilating:

__________ minutes __________ seconds

After hyperventilating:

__________ minutes __________ seconds

Table 26.1
Expected Vital Capacity Volumes

Age	Male (c.c.)	Female (c.c.)
14	3250	2480
15	3600	2700
16	3900	2700
17	4100	2750
18	4200	2800
19	4300	2800
20	4320	2800
21	4320	2800
22	4300	2800
23	4280	2790
24	4250	2780
25	4220	2770
26	4200	2760
27	4180	2740
28	4150	2720
29	4120	2710
30	4100	2700
31-35	3990	2640
36-40	3800	2520
41-45	3600	2390
46-50	3410	2250

exercise 27

the DIGESTIVE system

From the fruit of his mouth a man's stomach is filled; with the harvest from his lips he is satisfied.

Proverbs 18:20

Wiggling your fingers is a simple movement, but even that straightforward activity requires energy. Jogging five miles requires even more energy. Even sitting perfectly still requires some energy because blood must be kept coursing through your veins, nerves must constantly receive and transmit sensory information and every cell in your body must perform the myriad of chemical reactions required to maintain homeostasis. In short, living requires a lot of energy. In addition, raw materials must be obtained if growth is to occur or if worn and damaged proteins are to be repaired or replaced. It's the job of the *Digestive System* to acquire from the environment the raw materials and energy needed to maintain growth, movement and the maintenance of homeostasis at both the cellular and organismal levels. The raw materials provide the building blocks for complex biomolecules, and the energy obtained drives the construction of those molecules and anabolic processes.

Components of the Digestive System

The digestive system consists of a muscular *digestive tract* (or, *gastrointestinal [GI] tract*) and various accessory organs (Figure 27-1). As stated above, the main goal of the digestive system is to obtain raw materials and energy-rich compounds from the environment. This is achieved in four discrete steps: *Ingestion*, *mechanical digestion*, *chemical / enzymatic digestion* and *absorption*. In addition, the digestive system *excretes* unusable material back to the environment. The GI tract, which begins at the mouth (i.e., the oral cavity) and ends at the anus, plays a central role in all those steps. However, the GI tract could not complete its role in digestion without the aid of accessory organs. Accessory organs to the GI tract include the teeth, tongue, salivary glands, stomach[1], liver, gall bladder and pancreas. Each of these accessory organs plays a crucial role in the mechanical, chemical and / or enzymatic digestion of food.

The Oral Cavity

Ingestion is accomplished by the oral cavity (Figure 27-2). The roof of the oral cavity is defined by the hard and soft palates, the floor of the cavity is defined by the tongue, and the walls of the cavity are defined by the cheeks. The **hard palate** is part of the maxillary bone of the skull whereas the **soft palate** is composed of cartilage. The posterior margin of the soft palate tapers to form a flap called the **uvula**. This flap lifts upward when swallowing and prevents food or drink from entering the nasal cavity (except perhaps when laughing immediately after taking a sip of your favorite drink!). Anteriorly, the oral cavity can be opened and closed by the **labia**, or lips.

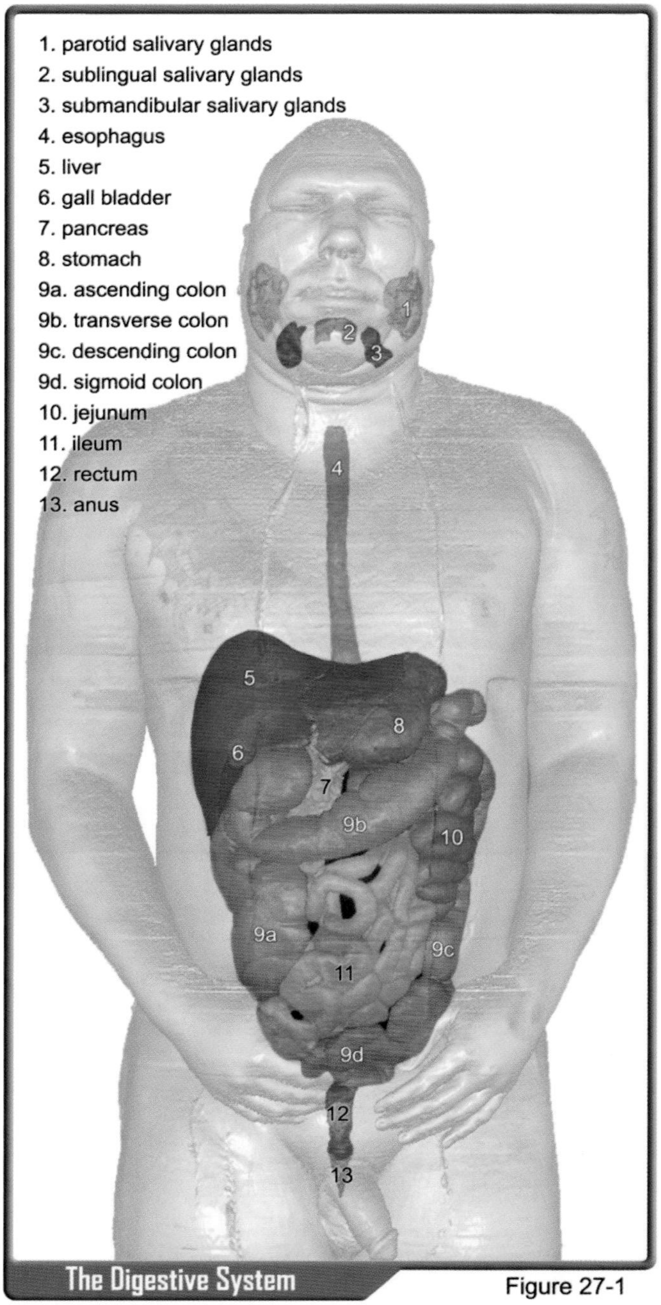

Figure 27-1

[1] Although the stomach will be discussed as an accessory organ, it's actually a part of the GI tract which runs continuously from the mouth to the anus.

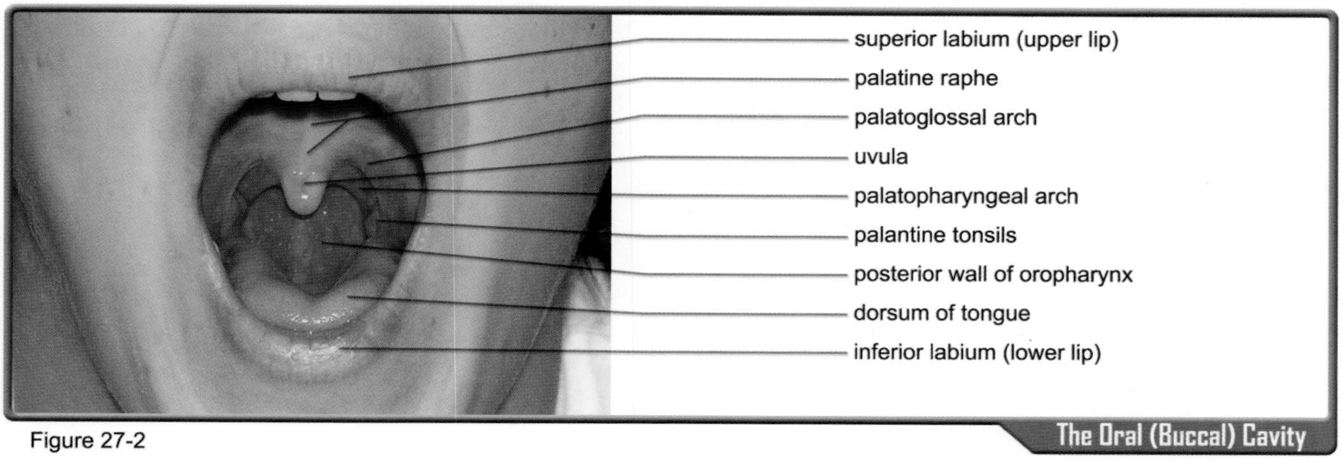

Figure 27-2

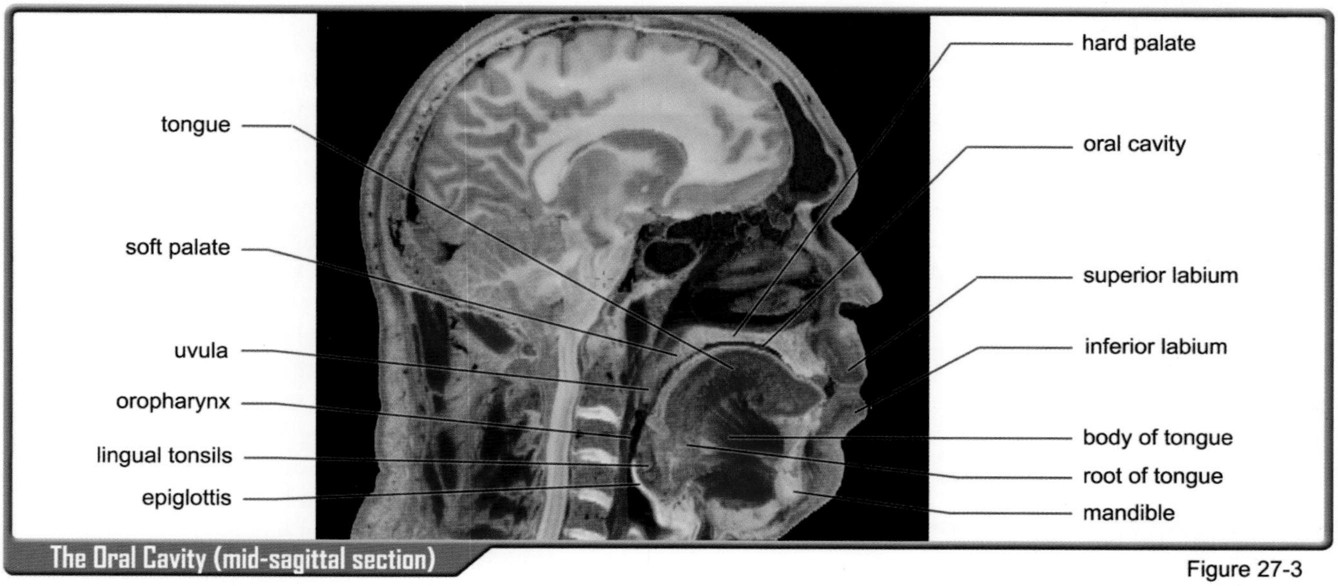

Figure 27-3

Situated snuggly between the **palatoglossal arch** and the **palatopharyngeal arch** in the back of the mouth are a pair of **palatine tonsils**. These immune structures, along with the **lingual tonsils** at the root of the tongue and the **pharyngeal tonsils** behind the nasal cavity, help protect us from airborne and ingested pathogens that enter the body through the oral and / or nasal cavities.

Posteriorly, the oral cavity opens into the pharynx, specifically the **oropharynx**, which is continuous with the esophagus (Figure 27-3). The tongue, pharanyx and esophagus carry out the swallowing reflex to move bites of food from the mouth to the stomach.

The **tongue** forms the floor of the oral cavity. The tongue is a large and unique skeletal muscle (Figure 27-3; see also Figure 25-3). It has attachments to the mandible and hyoid bones, but does not pull to move bones like other skeletal muscles. Instead, the tongue is a *muscular hydrostat*. Contractions of tongue muscle fibers, which run in numerous & complicated patterns, serve to lift, depress, protract, retract and change the shape of the tongue in a variety of ways. These movements position food in the mouth during chewing and alter sounds leaving the mouth during the formation of words while speaking or singing. Most of these movements are achieved by muscle fibers in the **body of the tongue**; swallowing is initiated by elevation of the **root of the tongue**.

The "top" of the tongue is called the *dorsum* of the tongue. The dorsum is covered with *papillae* that improve the grip of the tongue, making it easier to manipulate foods while chewing. The dorsum of the tongue is also highly innervated and supplies tactile and temperature information about substances in the oral cavity. In addition, the dorsum of the tongue possesses taste buds that provide chemical information about materials in the mouth, such as pleasurable taste sensations and

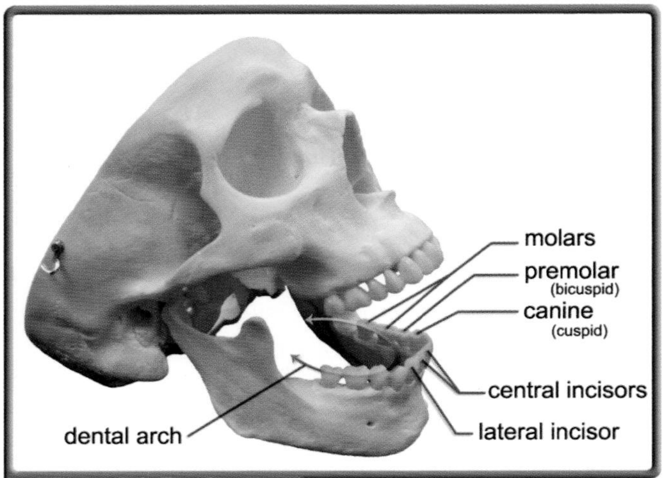

The Adult Teeth

Figure 27-4

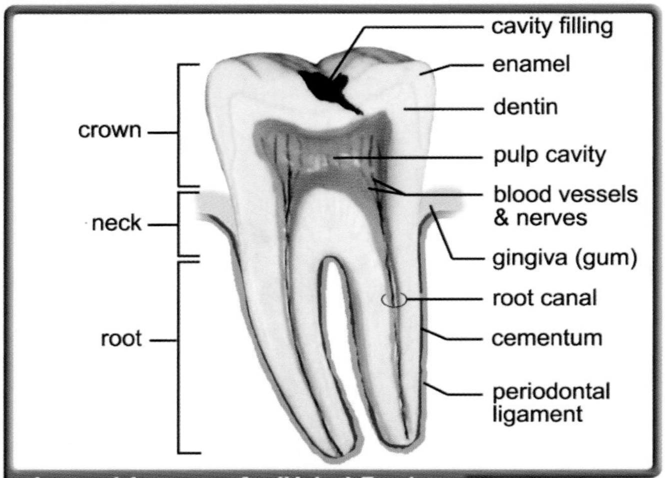

Internal Anatomy of a (Molar) Tooth

Figure 27-5

undesirable sensations from spoiled or poisonous substances. Finally, the tongue also begins enzymatic digestion of lipids by secreting the enzyme *lingual lipase.*

The **teeth** are our primary tools of mastication, or chewing, although mastication is assisted by the tongue, cheeks and roof of the mouth. Most adults have either 28 or 32 teeth that occur in pairs embedded in both the upper and lower **gingiva**, or *gums* (Figure 27-4). The teeth are laid out in a curve called the **dental arch**. The upper and lower teeth are essentially mirror-images of each other, so we will consider only the lower teeth embedded in the mandible.

The most anterior pair of teeth are the **central incisors**. On either side of the central incisors is a **lateral incisor**. The incisors have long, sharp blade-type edges that are usually serrated, or jagged. They are especially adept at slicing, such as when tearing a bite of meat. On either side of the lateral incisors is a **canine** tooth, also called the *cuspid.* The canine teeth are sharp and pointed; they are designed to puncture foods with a piercing action. (*Does it make sense that the canine teeth are posterior to the incisors?)* Posteriolateral to the canine teeth are a pair of **premolars**, also called *bicuspids.* These teeth, like the two pair of **molars** posterior to them, have flat and broad surfaces. They are best at grinding or shearing foods when chewing.

The teeth just described include the 28 pair of teeth found in most adults. Some adults grow an additional pair of molars in the upper dental arch, the lower dental arch, or both. These teeth, which usually don't erupt until the mid-to-late twenties, are called *wisdom teeth.*

Each tooth consists of a bony material called **dentin** covered with a layer of **enamel** (Figure 27-5). Enamel is the hardest biological substance on earth. Deep to the dentin is a **pulp cavity** filled with a gelatinous pulp. Living cells that maintain the tooth line the pulp cavity which also contains bloods vessels and a rich nerve supply.

Teeth are embedded in the gums (or gingiva) and bone – either the maxillary above or mandible below. The part of the tooth above the gum line is the **crown**, the part of the tooth at the gum line is the **neck**, and the part of the tooth below the gum line is the **root**. The root is held firmly in the bone by a two-layered connective tissue sheath. The inner connective tissue layer is called the **cementum**; the outer layer is called the **periodontal ligament**. The periodontal ligament allows some wiggle-room for the tooth, so it's normal for healthy teeth to be slightly movable.

Associated with the oral cavity are three pairs of salivary glands: The *parotid salivary glands* at the back of the cheeks, the *sublingual salivary glands* under the tongue and the *submandibular salivary glands* beneath the

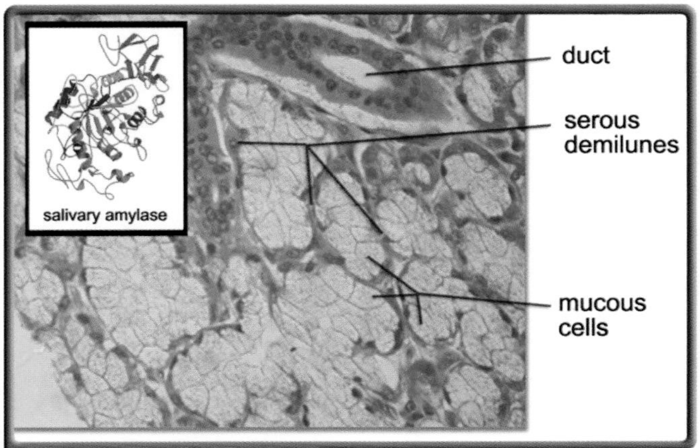

Salivary Gland (400x)

Figure 27-6

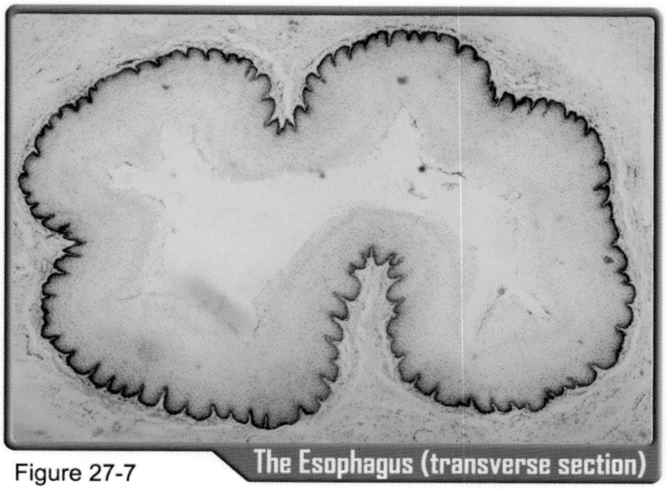

Figure 27-7

mandible. These glands produce a secretion (i.e., *saliva*) that both moistens ingested materials and begins the digestion of food. The moistening of the food helps create a packed *bolus* which is easy to swallow. The saliva from each pair of glands (but especially the parotid glands) is rich in **salivary amylase**, an enzyme that digests complex starches into smaller sugars. The structure of salivary amylase is shown in the figure 27-6.

The Pharynx & Esophagus

The pharynx forms the back of the nasal and oral cavities. It's divided into three parts: The nasopharanyx behind the nasal cavity, the oropharynx behind the oral cavity and the laryngopharynx within the larynx (Figure 27-3 and also Figure 25-1). The larynx is a cartilaginous "box" housing the epiglottis and the vocal cords and dividing the *fauces*, or posterior openings of the mouth and nose, into the esophagus and trachea. The larynx is discussed in exercise 25. The trachea directs inhaled air to the lungs, while the esophagus directs food and drink to the stomach.

The esophagus is a soft, muscular tube about 12 inches long (Figure 27-7). The lumen of the tube is collasped except when ingested materials are passing through. While swallowing, muscular contractions actively propel food or drink to the stomach; thus, it's possible to swallow even while upside-down. At the stomach, a ring of muscle – the *gastroesophageal sphincter* – closes off the esophagus from the stomach and opens only when swallowing. This sphincter protects the mucosal lining of the esophagus from the strong acids produced in the stomach. When this sphincter leaks, the stomach acids chemically burn the mucosal cells of the esophagus, giving rise to "heartburn." Severe cases are referred to as *acid reflex disease*.

The Stomach

The stomach is a distensible organ that is surprisingly small when empty but expands dramatically after eating a large meal. Thus, one role of the stomach is to temporarily store food that's just been eaten. The stomach also actively participates in digesting food in three ways: *i*) chemical digestion through the production of strong acids that break down foods, *ii*) enzymatic digestion of proteins by the stomach enzyme *pepsin* and *iii*) mechanical digestion of food by powerful muscular contractions of the stomach wall. A cat stomach is shown in figure 27-8 and the human stomach in figure 27-9.

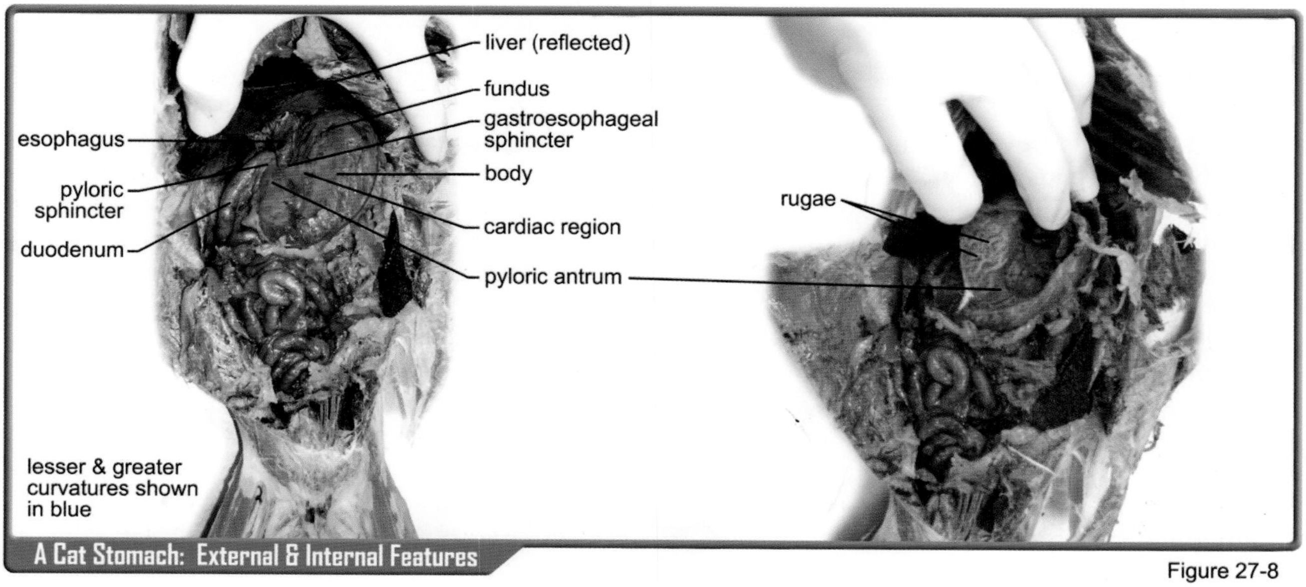

Figure 27-8

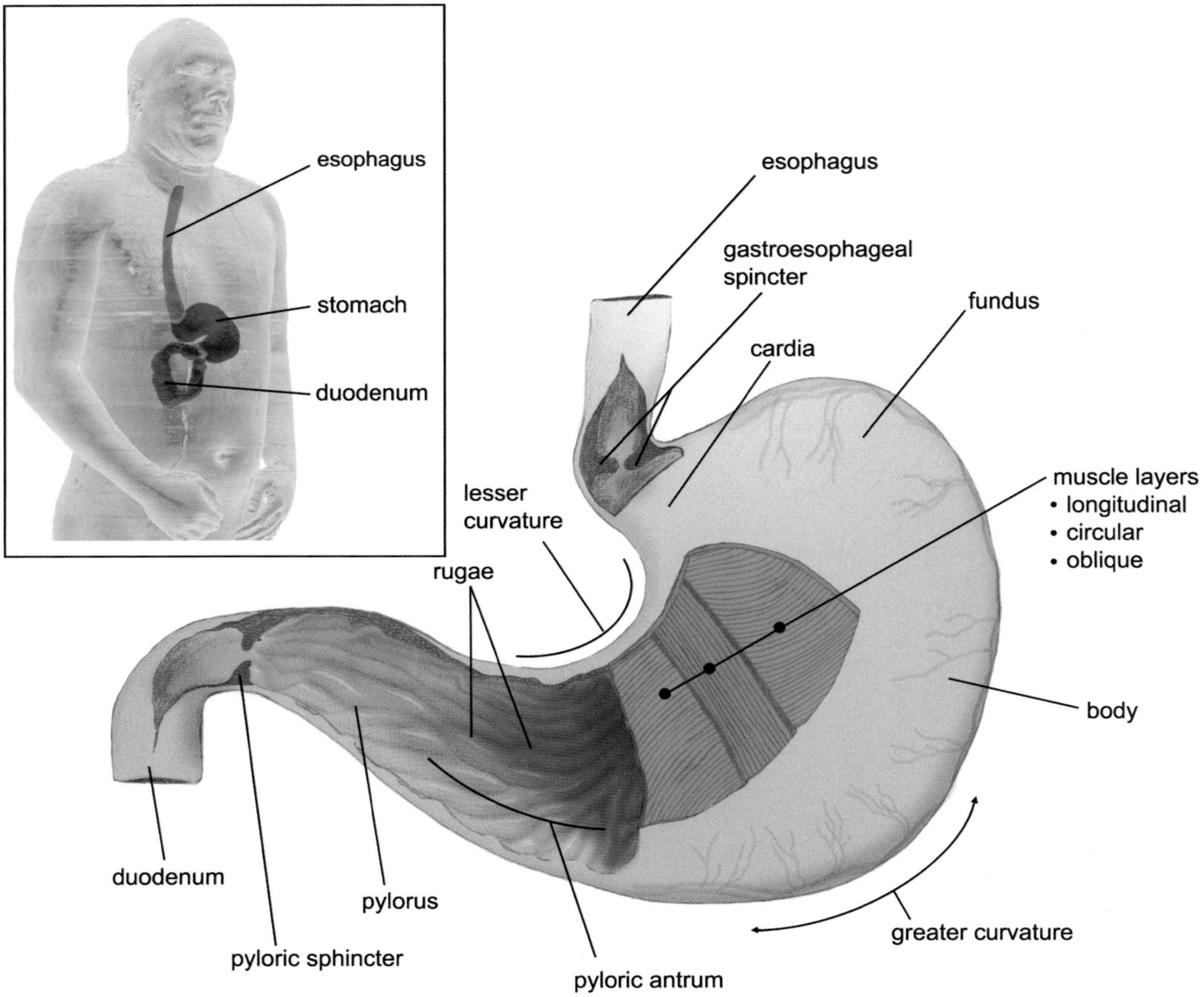

The Stomach

Figure 27-9

The mucosa of the stomach possesses deep folds called **rugae** when the stomach is empty. The rugae are not present, however, when the stomach is stretched. By contrast, microscopic folds called **gastric pits** are permanent invaginations of the mucosal lining of the stomach (Figure 27-10). The **gastric glands** within these pits contain *i*) parietal cells that produce hydrochloric acid (HCl), *ii*) mucous cells that produce large quantities of thick mucus that protects the delicate mucosa from HCl chemical burns and *iii*) chief cells that produce the digestive enzyme pepsin. Deep to the submucosa, the muscularis externa of the stomach is composed of three layers of muscle – the **oblique**, **circular** and **longitudinal muscles**.

In general, the stomach is shaped like an old wineskin. The stomach begins at the **gastroesophogeal sphincter**, a ring of muscle that closes off the stomach from the esophagus. The stomach then quickly enlarges into a rounded portion called the **fundus**. The **body** of the stomach then tapers off into a smaller portion called the **pyloric antrum**. The pyloric region of the stomach is separated from the duodenum by another sphincter – the **pyloric sphincter**. The stomach has an overall curvature to it and the gastroesophageal and pyloric sphincters are physically close to each other. The inside curve is called the **lesser curvature** and the outside curve is called the **greater curvature**. The *lesser omentum* attaches

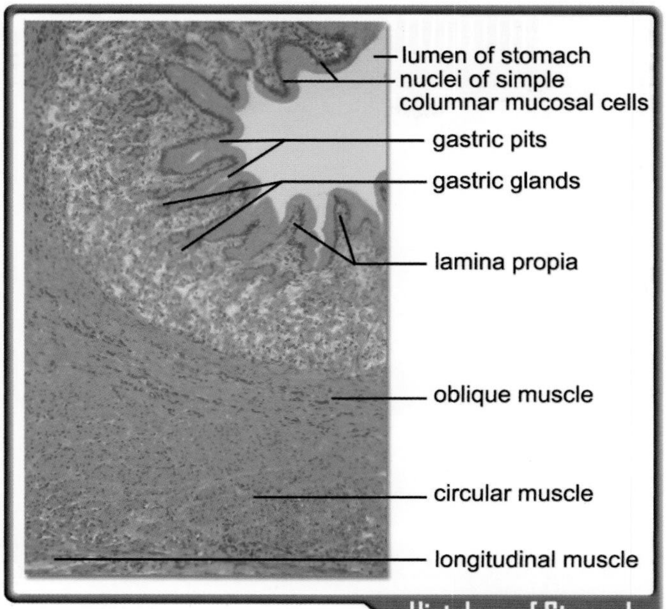

Figure 27-10 Histology of Stomach

the stomach to the liver at the lesser curvature, while the *greater omentum* hangs from the greater curvature.

The Small Intestine

Although the tongue and stomach participate in digestion and absorption, most digestion and absorption of nutrients takes place in the **small intestine** (Figure 27-11). The small intestine is a tubular structure about 20 feet in length and 1 inch in diameter. It begins at the pyloric sphincter at the stomach and ends at the ileocecal valve at the large intestine. It's the small intestine that occupies most of the abdomen, casually referred to as the belly. The small intestine is divided into three regions: The **duodenum**, **jejunum** and **ileum** (Figures 27-10 & 27-11).

Throughout the length of the small intestine are permanent folds of the mucosa called *plicae*. These folds often follow a spiralling pattern down the intestinal tract and assist peristaltic smooth muscle contractions to move food through the system. Smaller, hair-like structures, called *villi*, greatly increase the surface area of the mucosa and improve absorption of nutrients across the mucosal wall. In addition to these are *microvilli* projecting from the apical surfaces of the mucosal cells which again increase absorption surface area. The microvilli have digestive enzymes attached to them (called *brush border enzymes*) that digest foods as they pass by.

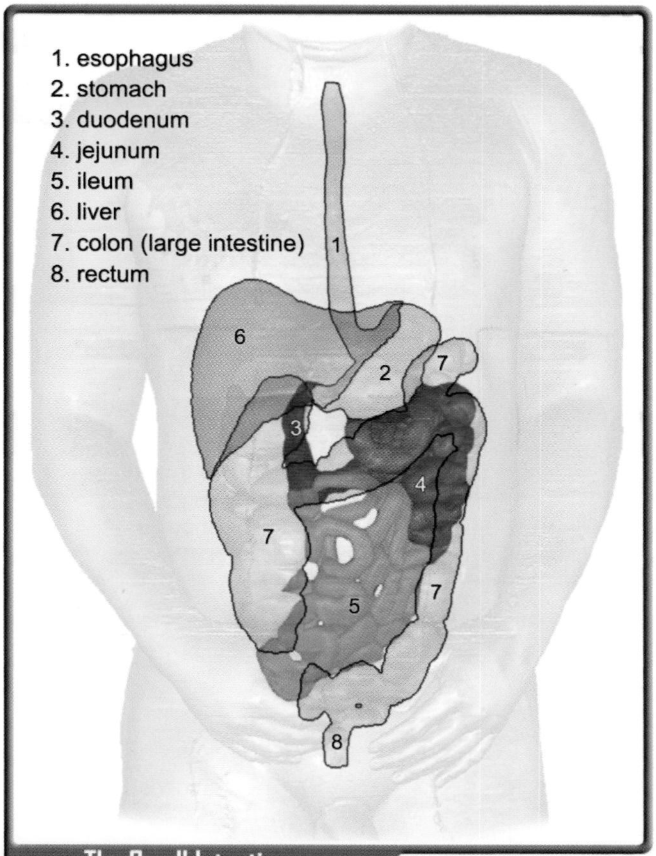

The Small Intestines Figure 27-11

The **duodenum** is the shortest of the three regions at just 10 inches (Figures 27-10 & 27-12). However, the duodenum is arguably the most important part of the small intestine. Over a period of hours following a meal, the duodenum receives bite-sized portions of partially-digested material (called *chyme*) from the stomach. This material is extremely acidic. Consequently, specialized duodenal glands secrete a thick, alkaline mucus that protects the delicate cells of the duodenal mucosa[2]. The duodenum also receives secretions from the pancreas and gall bladder.

The **jejunum** and **ileum** are quite similar anatomically and physiologically; however, there are some differences. The jejunum immediately follows the duodenum and contains numerous villi, microvilli and brush border enzymes (Figures 27-11 & 27-13). Most absorption of nutrients occurs in

[2] Duodenal gland secretion is inhibited by the sympathetic division of the autonomic nervous system. People constantly under stress have chronic inhibition of these glands leading to increased exposure of the small intestine to stomach acids. Those acids sometimes burn through the intestinal mucosa creating an *ulcer*.

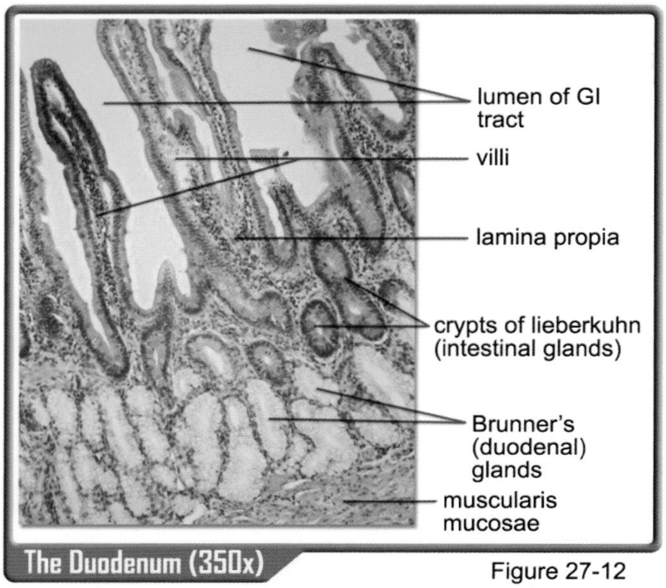

Figure 27-12

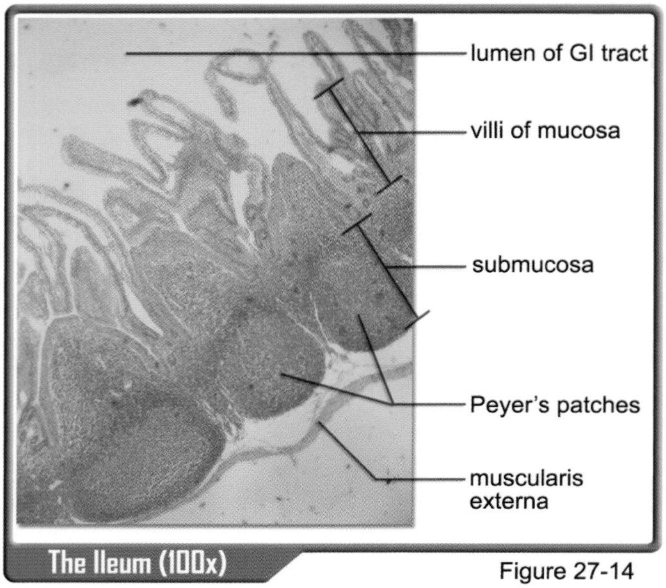

Figure 27-14

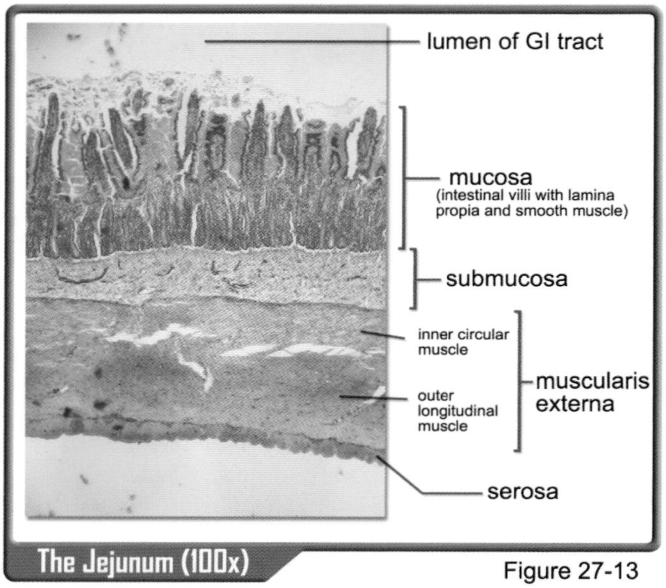

Figure 27-13

the jejunum. To facilitate absorption of nutrients into the bloodstream, the villi are highly vascular and contain special blunt-ended vessels of the lymphatic system called **lacteals**. The lacteals possess large pores that allow the absorption of lipid vesicles too big to enter the capillaries of the blood vessels. The ileum contains fewer villi but more immune structures than the jejunum (Figure 27-14). This is because the ileum is continuous with the large intestine which houses a great number of bacteria. The immune structures, called **Peyer's patches** help keep the bacteria from spreading up the small intestine or entering the bloodstream.

The Pancreas

The **pancreas** secretes an alkaline solution into the duodenum called *pancreatic juice*. The organ is located beneath the liver and secretes its juice into the duodenum (Figures 27-11, 27-15 & 27-16). The alkaline nature of this secretion neutralizes the acidic chyme. Additionally, pancreatic juice contains trypsin, chymotrypsin and dozens of digestive enzymes (including proteases, nucleases, carbohydrases and lipases) that are largely responsible for the enzymatic digestion of the foods we eat.[3] These enzymes travel with the chyme as it passes through the rest of the small intestine, breaking down the ingested proteins, lipids, DNA and sugars along the way.

The pancreas is an extremely soft organ, making it almost impossible to suture when it gets damaged or torn. It's composed of numerous lobules filled with enzyme-producing **acinar cells** (Figure 27-15). Those cells empty their secretions into small ducts that merge to form larger-and-larger ducts. Eventually, all of the smaller ducts empty into the large, central **pancreatic duct** which leaves the pancreas and empties pancreatic juice into the duodenum.

[3] Babies born with the genetic disease cystic fibrosis do not have a functional pancreas. As a result, those babies are unable to digest the foods they eat and, without treatment, usually die within 1 year of birth.

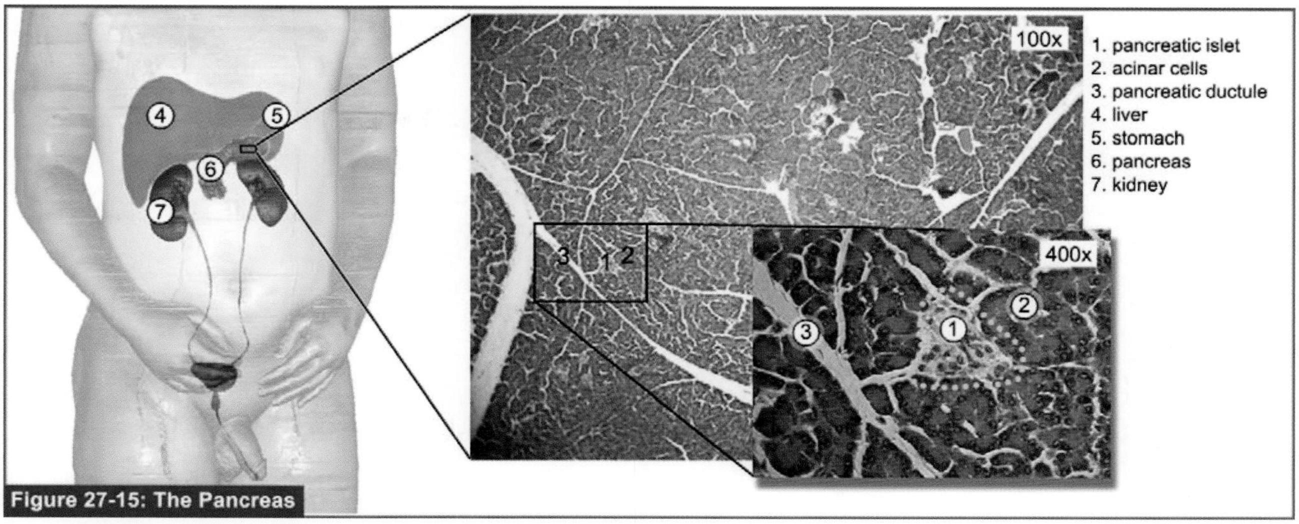

Figure 27-15: The Pancreas

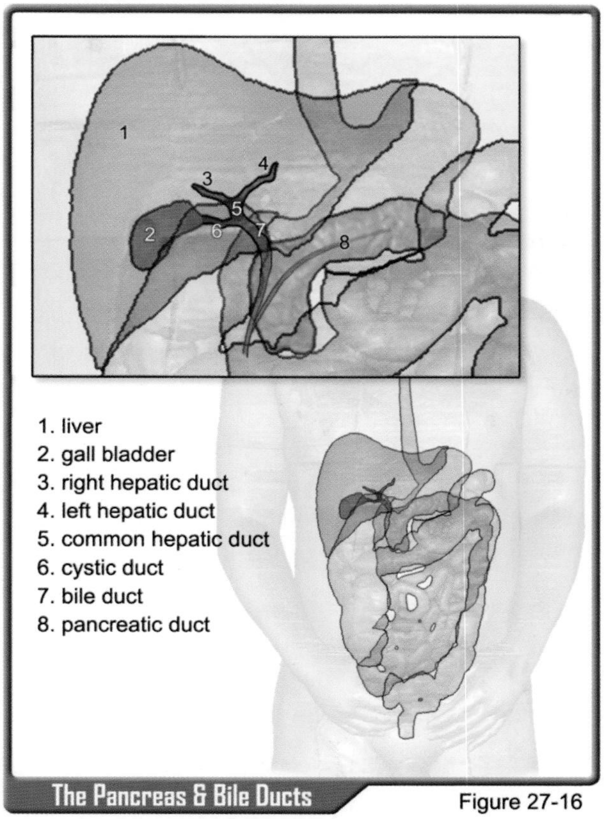

The Pancreas & Bile Ducts

Figure 27-16

Although bile is produced by the liver, it's stored in the **gall bladder** and released into the duodenum after eating a meal (Figure 27-16). The bile exits the liver though the **hepatic duct**, then "backs up" into the gall bladder via the **cystic duct**. After eating a meal, the gall bladder contracts and squeezes the bile back down the cystic duct and into the **bile duc**t, which empties into the duodenum.

The Liver & Gall Bladder

The liver produces an emulsifier called *bile* that aids lipid digestion. By their very nature, lipids do not dissolve readily in water (you have probably heard the adage, "oils and water don't mix"). An emulsifier is a compound that binds both oils and water and makes the oils more accessible to the water-based enzymes that digest them. The lipid-digesting enzymes (called *lipases)* come mostly from the pancreas.

The Large Intestine

The large intestine begins at the **ileocecal valve** and terminates at the anus (Figure 27-17). The ileocecal

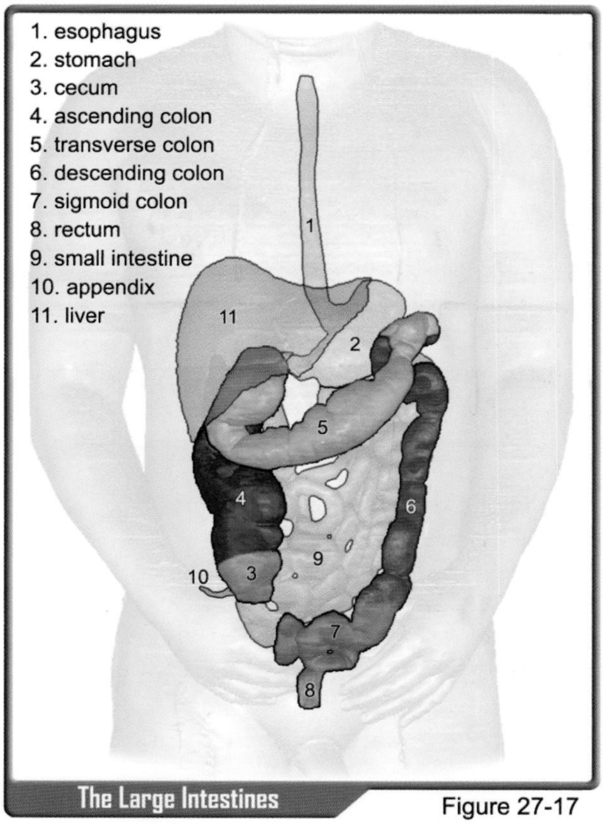

The Large Intestines

Figure 27-17

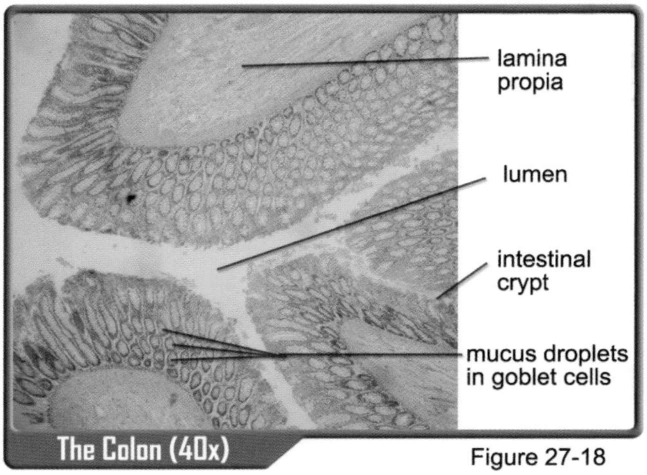

Figure 27-18

valve is a small flap that loosely separates the small intestine from the large intestine. At the beginning of the large intestine is pouch-like structure called the **cecum**. The cecum is home to about 1000 trillion bacterial cells, mostly *Escherichia coli (E. coli)*. Attached to the large intestine near the cecum is a finger-like projection called the **vermiform appendix**. This lymphatic system structure is rich with lymphocytes that help keep the intestinal microbes under control. In the large intestine, those microbes produce essential vitamins for us and aid digestion; however, it could be fatal to us if those bacterial cells leave the intestines. *E. coli* in the blood, for example, is nearly always deadly without quick treatment. In addition to the appendix, the mucosa of the large intestine contains lymphatic structures called **Peyer's patches** which also keep the bacterial cells in check.

The large intestine, or colon, is divided into regions along its length. The proximal end is called the **ascending colon** because it ascends the abdominal cavity. Likewise, the **transverse colon**

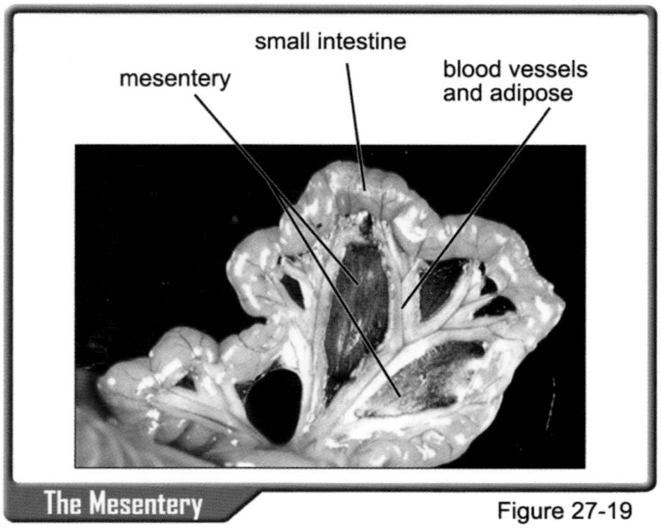

Figure 27-19

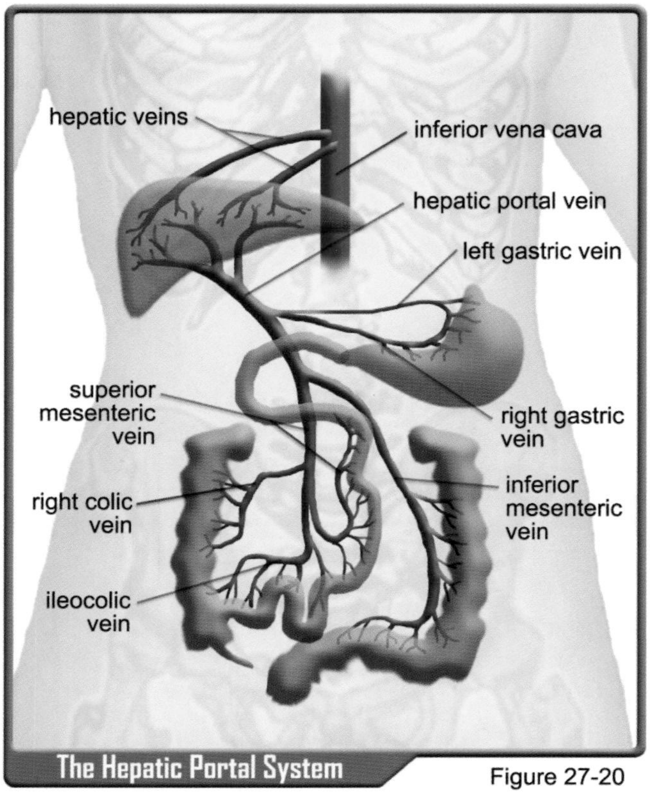

Figure 27-20

and **descending colon** are named for the directions they traverse. Distal to the descending colon the **sigmoid colon**, so named because of its S-shape, terminates at the rectum (Figure 27-17). The colon is rich in goblet cells that coat the walls with thick mucus (Figure 27-18). The mucus protects the cells from damage as the waste material hardens to become feces.

The large and small intestines are both held in position by mesentery (Figure 27-19). These sheets of connective tissue allow movement of the organs without allowing their displacement. They also provide support for blood vessels and nerves passing to and from the intestines.

The Hepatic Portal System

It's critically important that the composition of blood remain constant at all times; however, an important job of the cardiovascular system is to absorb nutrients from the GI tract. How can blood perform this function without experiencing major fluctuations in nutrient levels between and during meals? The answer lies in the **hepatic portal system** – a special blood circulatory pathway through the GI tract (Figure 27-20).

Normally, blood enters a capillary bed from the arterial system and exits the capillary bed into the venous system. A portal system, by definition, is a cardiovascular system in which blood travels from one capillary to a *second* capillary bed before returning to the veins (See Figure 27-19 and also Figure 23-8). Capillaries associated with the gastric and intestinal mucosae absorb ingested nutrients in the first capillary bed. Before returning to the veins and general circulation, however, the blood is immediately taken to a second capillary bed in the liver. There, the nutrients are removed and processed by the liver. The blood leaving the liver and returning to general circulation is similar in composition to the blood originally entering the intestines.

Activity 1: Identify Components of the GI Tract

1. Using the figures in this chapter and / or 3D anatomical models, locate the oral cavity (including teeth & tongue), esophagus, stomach, liver, gall bladder, pancreas, duodenum, jejunum, ileum, ascending colon, transverse colon, descending color, sigmoid colon, rectum and anus. Note the relationships between those organs.

Activity 2: Histological Examination of Digestive Organs

1. Obtain prepared slides of the esophagus, stomach, liver, pancreas, duodenum, jejunum, ileum, colon and rectum. Note the various histological structures discussed in this chapter.

Activity 3: Ausultating Digestive Sounds

1. Obtain a stethoscope and listen to sounds of the GI tract by placing the diaphragm of the stethoscope at various places on the abdomen.
2. Listen to the gastroesphogeal sphincter by placing the stethoscope just below the xiphoid process. Have your partner swallow a sip of water. You should hear the water splash onto the closed sphincter and then trickle down into the stomach a moment later when the sphincter opens.

Arrange the components of the gastrointestinal tract in the order in which food passes through them, beginning with where food enters the mouth and ending where waste products are excreted from the body.

_______	1.	a. stomach
_______	2.	b. oral cavity
_______	3.	c. pharynx
_______	4.	d. ileum
_______	5.	e. duodenum
_______	6.	f. anus
_______	7.	g. esophagus
_______	8.	h. jejunum
_______	9.	i. ascending colon
_______	10.	j. descending colon
_______	11.	k. cecum
_______	12.	l. rectum
_______	13.	m. transverse colon
_______	14.	n. sigmoid colon

15-23. Label the figure of the oral cavity below.

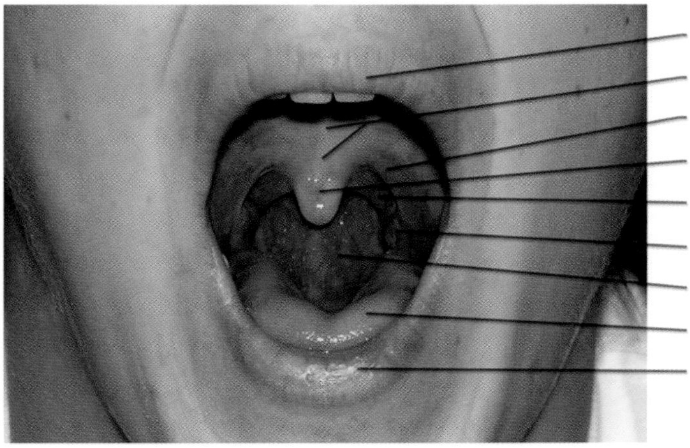

24. What digestive functions are achieved by the tongue?

25-36. Label the figure of the tooth below.

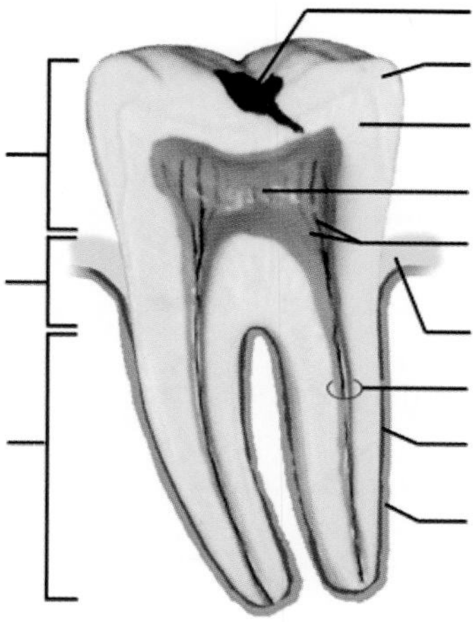

37. What digestive enzymes are produced by the following structures?

a) Tongue –

b) Salivary glands –

c) Stomach –

d) Pancreas –

e) Small intestine –

38. The duodenum is a short but important part of the GI tract. What functions are accomplished by the duodenum?

Match the following terms with their definitions.

_______	39. An emulsifier produced by the liver	a. ileocecal valve
_______	40. Temporary folds in the stomach	b. enamel
_______	41. Flap-like structure between the cecum & ileum	c. appendix
_______	42. The main food-processing organ of the body	d. pancreas
_______	43. A muscle that controls when chyme leaves the stomach	e. gall bladder
_______	44. The hardest biological substance	f. rugae
_______	45. Sac-like organ that stores bile	g. liver
_______	46. Storage depot for feces leaving the colon	h. cecum
_______	47. Finger-like lymphoid organ attached to large intestine	i. plicae
_______	48. Main enzyme-producing organ of the digestive system	j. rectum
_______	49. Large sac-like structure housing *E. coli* in the colon	k. pyloric sphincter
_______	50. Permanent folds in the walls of the small intestine	l. bile

51-64. Label the figure below.

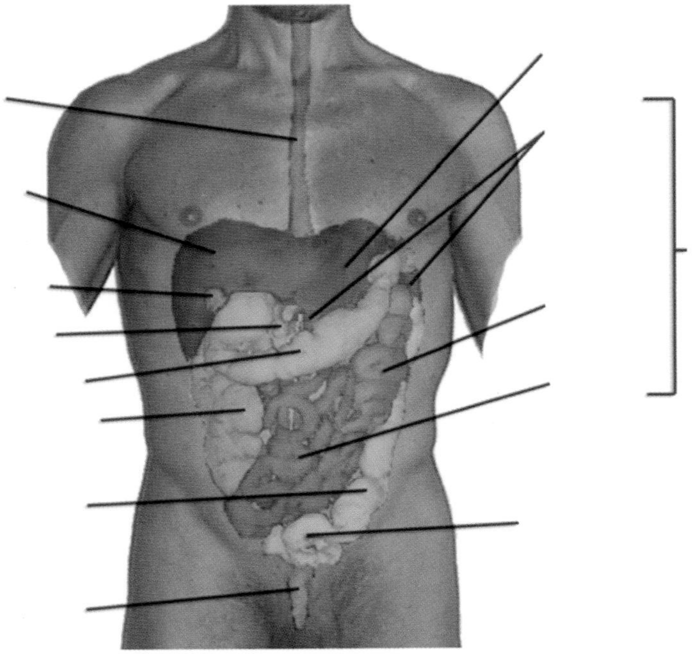

exercise 28

digestive PHYSIOLOGY

All the days of the oppressed are wretched, but the cheerful heart has a continual feast.

Proverbs 15:15

The process of digestion begins as soon as you put food into your mouth. Mechanical breakdown of food starts with the tearing, crushing and shearing action of the teeth, aided significantly by the tongue. The enzymatic breakdown of lipids and complex sugars also begins in the mouth. The tongue produces *lingual lipase* which begins the breakdown of lipids and the salivary glands produce *salivary amylase* which begins the breakdown starch, a complex sugar. As part of this laboratory exercise, we'll examine the activity of salivary amylase from saliva.

Although digestion begins in the mouth, it's completed by the stomach and small intestines. There's actually three ways in which food is digested: *i*) mechanical digestion, *ii*) chemical digestion and *iii*) enzymatic digestion. Most of the digestive tract will utilize one or more types of digestion while also absorbing the nutrients released by each process.

Once a bite of food has been mechanically crushed into small pieces by the teeth and partially degraded by lingual lipase and salivary amylase, the chewed mass (called a *bolus*) is swallowed. This action, initiated voluntarily by the tongue, carries the bolus through the esophagus to the stomach. In the stomach, the food is further degraded using all three digestion mechanisms. The food is broken down mechanically by powerful muscular contractions of the stomach wall. Chemical digestion is achieved by soaking the food in concentrated hydrochloric acid (HCl), which denatures most proteins. Finally, acid denatured proteins are enzymatically degraded into small peptides by the stomach enzyme *pepsin*, a rather exceptional protein in that it is active at extremely low pH values such as those encountered in the stomach (stomach acid is typically pH 1-2). The result of muscular churning, HCl and pepsin activity is the conversion of the bolus to a creamy-white liquid called *chyme*. Between meals, small portions of chyme periodically exit the stomach until the stomach is empty.

Chyme leaving the stomach enters the duodenum, the first 10 inches of the small intestine. There, chyme is mixed with bile from the gall bladder and a variety of digestive enzymes from the pancreas. The pancreas produces dozens of enzymes that further digest chyme as it passes through the 20-25 feet of small intestine. Brush-border enzymes attached to the intestinal wall aid the pancreatic enzymes. The released nutrients are absorbed across the wall of the GI tract into the blood.

Biomolecule type	Enzyme(s)	Source	Site of Action
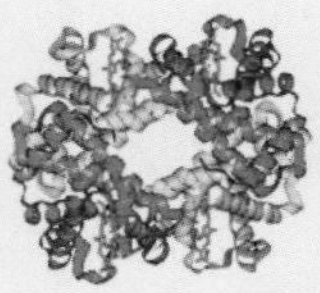 **protein**	pepsin	stomach	stomach
	trypsin, chymotrypsin carboxypeptidase	pancreas	small intestine
	aminopeptidase, carboxypeptidase, dipeptidase	brush border	small intestine
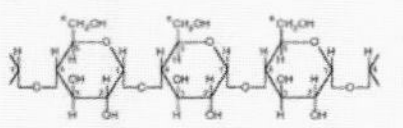 **carbohydrate**	salivary amylase	salivary glands	mouth
	pancreatic amylase	pancreas	small intestine
	dextrinase, lactase, maltase, sucrase	brush border	small intestine
 **fats (lipid)**	pancreatic lipase	pancreas	small intestine
	lingual lipase	tongue	mouth
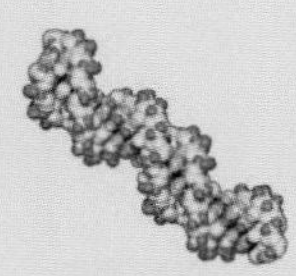 **nucleic acids**	pancreatic ribonuclease, pancreatic deoxyribonuclease	pancreas	small intestine
	nucleosidases, phosphatases	brush border	small intestine

Digestive Enzymes

Table 28.1

Undigested and unabsorbed material leaving the small intestine enter the large intestine. There, water is removed and the material, now called *feces*, becomes increasingly thicker. At the end of the large intestine, feces is held in the rectum until it's voluntarily expelled from the body through the anus in a process called *defecation*.

Enzymatic Digestion

Enzymes are proteins that are designed to convert one type of molecule (the substrate) into another type of molecule (the product). They are *catalysts* because they speed up chemical reactions (up to 1 million-fold).

There are four classes of biological molecules: proteins, nucleic acids (e.g, DNA and RNA), carbohydrates (i.e., sugars) and lipids (i.e., fats). The digestive system, particularly the pancreas, produces enzymes that act specifically on each class. Enzyme names typically end with the letters *–ase*. Thus, enzymes that digest proteins are called *proteases*, those that digest nucleic acids are called *nucleases*, those that digest sugars are called *carbohydrases* and those that digest fats are called *lipases*. Examples from each class are shown in table 28-1.

Control of Digestion

Digestion and nutrient absorption is a surprisingly complex task. A significant portion of nervous tissue is devoted to digestion. This nervous tissue, collectively called the *enteric nervous system*, contains as many neurons as the spinal cord and utilizes all the neurotransmitters found in the brain. In addition, at least 18 hormones have been identified that function primarily to control digestion. The following five hormones have been well characterized with respect to their digestive functions (See also Table 28-2):

- **Gastrin** – Gastrin is both produced by the stomach and targets the stomach, so it's name is especially appropriate. The hormone is released when the stomach wall is distended by an ingested meal and possibly by the CNS (via the vagus nerve). Gastrin stimulates acid production by the stomach and increases muscular contractions (i.e., motility) of the stomach
- **Gastric inhibitory peptide (GIP)** – GIP is released by the duodenum when acidic chyme rich in sugars and lipids leaves the stomach. The peptide hormone stimulates the release of insulin from the pancreas and lipid utilization in adipose tissue. As its name implies, the

Hormone	Stimulus	Origin	Target	Effects
gastrin	stomach stretch receptors; vagus nerve	stomach	stomach	stimulates stomach motility and HCl production
gastric inhibitory peptide (GIP)	acidid chyme containing high amounts of glucose and lipids	duodenum	pancreas stomach adipose skeletal muscle	stimulates release of insulin, lipid biosynthesis and glucose utilization; inhibits gastric activity
cholecystokinin (CCK)	acidic chyme containing high amounts of lipids and proteins	duodenum	pancreas stomach gall bladder duodenum brain	stimulates pancreas exocrine activity, contraction of gall bladder and relaxation of hepatopancreatic sphincter; inhibits gastric activity and hunger
secretin	acidic chyme in duodenum	duodenum	pancreas stomach liver	stimulates production of alkaline mucus and bile secretion; inhibits gastric secretion and motility
vasoactive intestinal peptide (VIP)	acidic chyme in duodenum	duodenum	duodenal glands stomach intestinal capillaries	stimulates buffer secretion; inhibits stomach acid (HCl) production; dilates intestinal capillaries

Table 28.2 Digestive Hormones

hormone also inhibits gastric activity of the stomach.

- **Cholecystokinin (CCK)** – CCK is released from the duodenum in response to acidic chyme rich in lipids and proteins. The hormone stimulates the secretion of digestive enzymes from the pancreas and bile from the gall bladder. CCK also inhibits gastric activity, relaxes the ileocecal valve and reduces hunger sensations.
- **Secretin** – Secretin is also released from the duodenum in response to acidic chyme leaving the stomach. It stimulates the secretion of alkaline mucus from duodenal glands and the pancreas, stimulates release of bile from the gall bladder, and inhibits gastric secretion and motility.
- **Vasoactive intestinal peptide (VIP)** – VIP is released from the duodenum in response to acidic chyme. The hormone stimulates alkaline buffer secretion from the small intestine, inhibits acid production in the stomach and causes vasodilation of intestinal blood vessels.

Glycolysis & TCA Cycle

The goal of digestion is to obtain nutrients and energy from the environment. These are used to drive *metabolism* in the body's cells. Metabolism is the sum total of all chemical reactions occuring in a cell at any given moment. Metabolic reactions are classified as either *catabolic* or *anabolic*. Catabolic reactions – like digestion itself – start with large biomolecules and break them down to simpler, smaller molecules, often with the liberation (and capture) of energy. Anabolism takes the small molecules and captured energy and uses them to build the many large biomolecules required by the cell, or to maintain concentration gradients, or to cause movements (such as muscular contractions).

There are literally thousands of anabolic reactions that occur in the cell, but comparatively few catabolic reactions. Two important catabolic pathways are **glycolysis** and the **TCA cycle**. Glycolysis is the pathway that breaks down glucose to pyruvate. The TCA cycle consumes pyruvate to generate energy.

The wide variety of sugars and related compounds absorbed by the intestines are converted to glucose by the liver. One role of the liver is to maintain a constant glucose concentration in the blood so that somatic cells throughout the body can

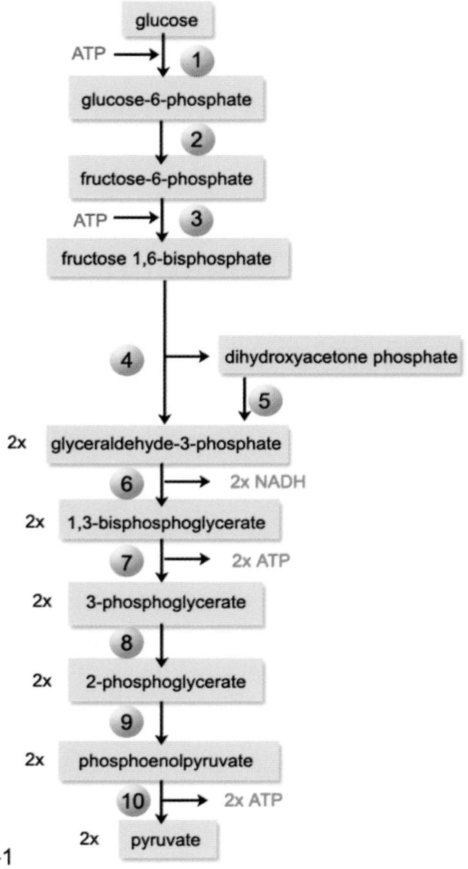

Figure 28-1

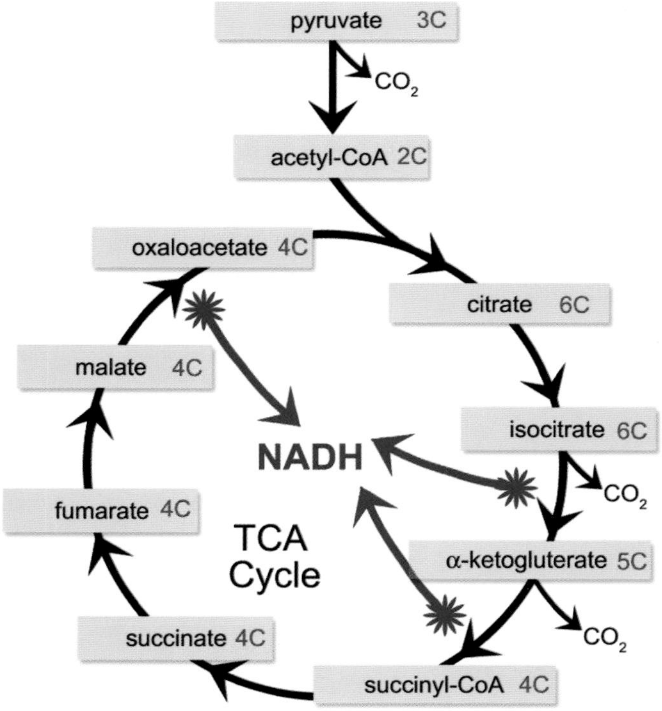

Figure 28-2

remove that glucose from the blood for energy production. The catabolic pathway they use to decompose glucose for energy capture is glycolysis (literally, "glucose-splitting"). The end product of glycolysis is two molecules of pyruvate (Figure 28-1). During the conversion of glucose to pyruvate two molecules of ATP are generated as well as two molecules of NADH. The ATP is used to drive anabolic processes in the cell. The pyruvate molecules are fed into the TCA cycle to generate more NADH (Figure 28-2). The NADH from glycolysis and the TCA cycle are fed into a third pathway called the *electron transport system* for conversion of NADH to ATP. From these three pathways, approximately 38 molecules of ATP are generated from a single molecule of glucose.

Control of Glucose Utilization

The concentration of glucose in the blood is tightly regulated, primarily by the hormones *insulin* and *glucagon*. After eating a meal, blood glucose levels rise due to absorption of sugars. In response, the pancreas releases insulin which informs cells throughout the body to absorb and metabolize glucose, thus causing a fall in blood glucose concentration (Figure 28-3). Between meals blood glucose levels fall too low. The pancreas then releases glucagon which stimulates the liver to synthesize glucose from other raw materials and excrete it into the bloodstream.

Salivary Amylase

Salivary amylase (shown in Figure 27-6) is a digestive enzyme that breaks down the complex sugar starch into simple sugars. Starch is a complex sugar found in all plants and is the primary form in which plants store energy (animals store energy as glycogen). Plants make starch by stringing together many thousands of glucose molecules. Salivary amylase breaks off two glucose units at a time, releasing a disaccharide called maltose. The maltose is then broken down to glucose by brush border enzymes in the small intestine. The structures of starch, maltose and glucose are shown in figure 28-4.

Salivary amylase is an enzyme. All enzymes convert substrates to products and as long as you can detect either the substrate or product you can determine the presence (or absence) of an enzyme activity. The substrate for salivary amylase is starch and the product is maltose. Maltose is a *reducing sugar* because one end of the sugar can undergo redox reactions. By contrast, starch is a long chain of thousands of maltose units strung together so it has no free ends for redox reactions. (Actually, starch has one free end per chain, but that

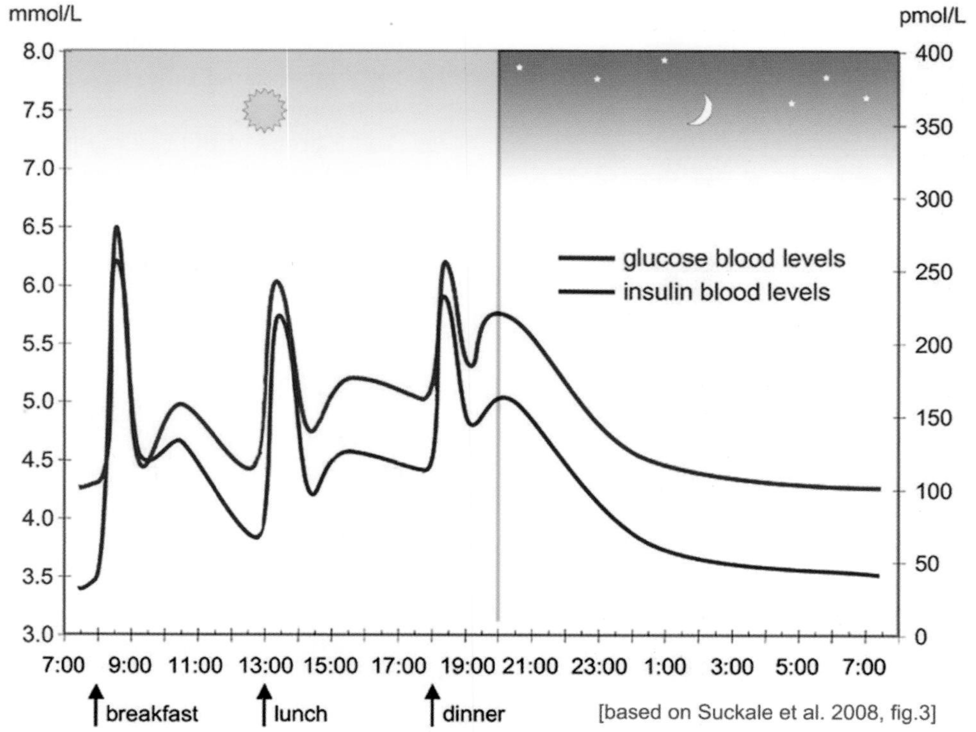

Figure 28-3 **Control of Blood Glucose Concentration by Insulin**

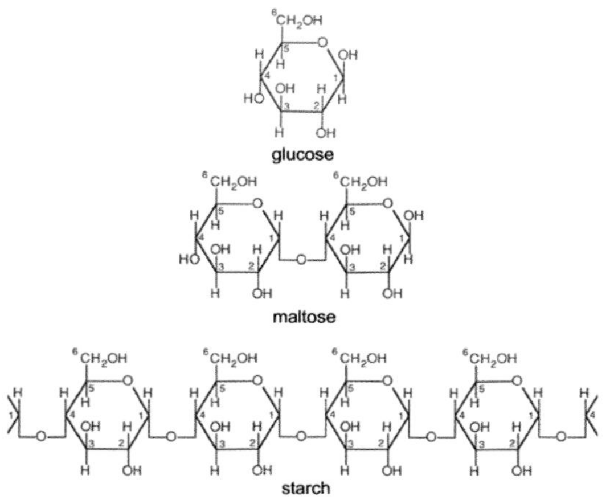

Figure 28-4 **The Structures of Glucose, Maltose & Starch**

is far fewer than the thousands of free ends available from individual maltose molecules). We can take advantage of these differences to track the activity of salivary amylase.

Benedict's reagent can be used to detect maltose generated by the enzymatic breakdown of starch. Benedict's reagent contains oxidized Cu^{2+} ions that are reduced by maltose to elemental Cu. This causes the blue Benedict's solution to turn green and (if enough maltose is present) to form an orange precipitate. Since starch is not a reducing sugar no such reaction occurs with Benedict's solution. However, starch can be detected using iodine-potassium iodide (IKI). The iodide reacts with starch to produce a dark blue-black color. In the activities that follow, we'll use Benedict's solution and IKI to follow the conversion of starch to maltose by salivary amylase (Figure 28-5).

Activity 1: The IKI Test for Complex Sugars

1. Obtain three clean test tubes (13 mm). Label the tubes #1 – #3.
2. Place 1 mL of distilled water into all test tubes.
3. Place 1 drop of 1mM maltose into tube #1.
4. Place 1 drop of 1mM starch into tube #2.
5. Place 5 drops of IKI solution into all three tubes. A dark blue or black color in any of the tubes indicates the presence of starch, a complex sugar.

Activity 2: The Benedict's Test for Simple Sugars

1. Obtain three clean test tubes (13 mm). Label the tubes #1 – #3.
2. Place 1 mL of distilled water into all test tubes.
3. Place 1 drop of 1mM maltose into tube #1.

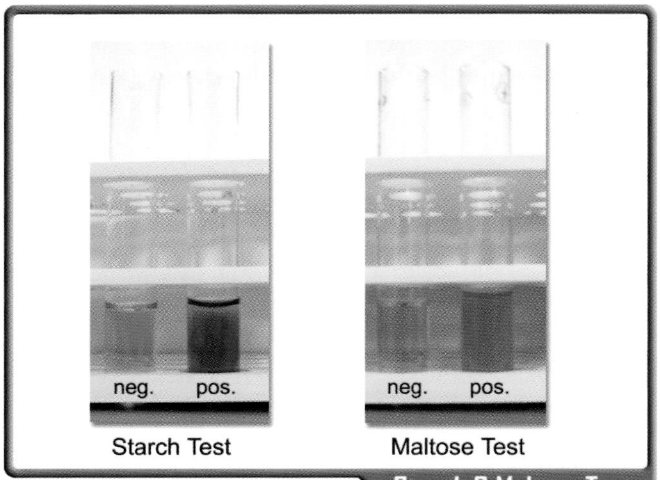

Figure 28-5 **Starch & Maltose Tests**

4. Place 1 drop of 1mM starch into tube #2.
5. Place 8-10 drops of Benedict's solution into all three tubes.
6. Place the tubes in a boiling water bath for about 5 minutes.
7. A dark orange or green precipitate indicates the presence of maltose, a simple sugar.

Activy 3: Detecting Salivary Amylase Activity

1. Collect 5 – 10 mL of saliva into a test tube[1]. If the saliva is not to be used within 5 minutes, then place the sample on ice.
2. Place 1 mL of 1mM starch into 4 test tubes, labeled #1 – #4.
3. Place 1 mL of saliva into tubes 1 and 2 only; place 1 mL of water into tubes 3 and 4.
4. Incubate the four tubes in a 37°C water bath for 5-10 minutes.
5. Add 5 drops of IKI (iodine-potassium iodide) to tubes 1 and 3. A blue-black color indicates the presence of starch and is called a *positive starch test*. If the mixture does not turn blue-black, no starch is present and this is a *negative starch test*.
6. Add 8 – 10 drops of Benedict's solution to tubes 2 and 4. Place tubes 2 and 4 into boiling water for 5 minutes. If an orange precipitate forms or the solution turns green, maltose is present and this is a *positive sugar test*. If no colored precipitate forms, no maltose is present and this is a *negative sugar test*.

---

[1] The parotid salivary glands produce more amylase than the submandibular or sublingual glands; press firmly against the parotid glands (forcing saliva from them) before expectorating (i.e., *spitting*) into the test tube.

Activity 4: Determine Your BMI

Body Mass Index (BMI) is one measure of your physical fitness. It is an indicator of body fat determined by taking a ratio of your weight-to-height. Calculate your BMI as follows:

1. Multiply your body weight (in pounds) by 703.
2. Divide #1 by your height in inches.
3. Divide #2 by your height in inches again.

Your BMI ___________________

<17.5	Seriously underweight
17.5 – 20	Underweight
20 – 25	Normal weight
25 – 30	Mildly overweight
30 – 40	Moderately overweight
40+	Morbidly overweight

Activity 5: Determine Your BMR

1. Divide your weight in pounds by 2.2 to obtain your weight in kilograms.
2. Multiply #1 by 0.9 if you are female, or by 1.0 if your are male.
3. Multiply #2 by 24 = ______________ kcal/day = basal metabolic rate (BMR)

Use the following table to approximate the amount of energy actually expended during an average day (24 hours):

Sedentary activity: add 45% of BMR to #3
Light activity: add 60%
Moderate activity: add 75%
Strenuous activity: add 100%

Approximately 35000 kcal must be expended to lose one pound of weight. The following is the approximate calorie expenditure in 10 minutes for a 150-pound person:

Walking slowly: 30 calories
Walking briskly: 45
Walking up stairs: 170
Dancing (slow): 40
Dancing (fast): 65
Running (8mph): 120
Cycling (10mph): 70
Cycling (15mph): 115
Swimming: 100

exercise 29

the URINARY system

I will cleanse them from all the sin they have committed against me and I will forgive all their sins of rebellion against me.

Jeremiah 33:8

About 180 liters of blood is filtered by the kidneys each day, cleansing the blood of waste products and making urine.

The composition of blood and interstitial fluids must remain constant if the body's 100 trillion cells are to survive. Each cell consumes nutrients and produces waste products which are toxic enough to be deadly if allowed to accumulate. Just as cities have waste management systems to dispose of public wastes, so the body has a waste management system to dispose of cellular wastes: *The Urinary System*. Without the urinary system the ability to maintain homeostasis would quickly be lost, followed by death.

Components of the Urinary System

The urinary system contains relatively few components, namely the two **kidneys**, the two **ureters**, the **urinary bladder** and the **urethra** (Figure 29-1). A waste-filled solution called *urine* is produced by the kidneys, conveyed by the ureters to the urinary bladder for storage and expelled from the body through the urethra.

The Kidneys

The **kidneys** are in effect filters for the blood. Your entire blood volume (~5 liters) filters through your kidneys about 20 times each day. In the process, toxic cellular waste products that were released into the blood are removed while useful nutrients are retained. The wastes are collected as urine and held temporarily in the bladder until willfully expelled from the body at a convenient time.

Each kidney is about 3 inches high, 2 inches wide and 1 inch deep. They are located posteriorly in the abdominal cavity adjacent to the 12th rib. Due to the large amount of space taken up by the liver, the right kidney is usually a bit lower than the left kidney. They are both held in place by fat deposits and the fibrous connective tissues surrounding them. One or both kidneys may "drop" in people having extremely low levels of body fat; a painful and potential deadly condition called *ptosis*.

The Ureters, Bladder and Urethra

The **ureters** are tubules that conduct urine from the kidneys to the urinary bladder. Each ureter is ~25 cm (~10 inches) long and gets progressively smaller in diameter toward the bladder. The walls of the ureter are lined with smooth muscle that contract in a peristaltic wave about twice each minute, assisting the flow of urine to the urinary bladder.

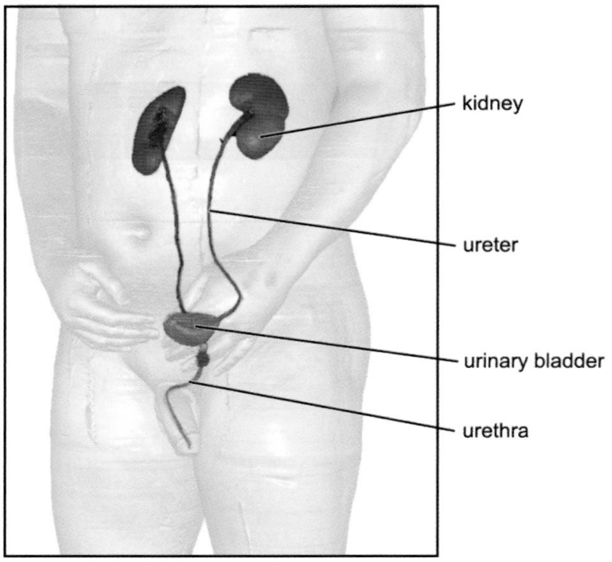

Figure 29-1 **The Urinary System**

Although urine is slowly and continuously produced by the kidneys, most of us would agree that it'd be terribly inconvenient to slowly and continuously relieve urine from the body. Thankfully, God has provided an internal holding tank for urine allowing us to store it inside our bodies until a convenient time arrives for disposal. This holding tank is the **urinary bladder**, or simply the bladder (Figure 29-2).

The urinary bladder is a flattened sac when empty and expands upward as it fills with urine. A typical bladder holds 600-800 mL of urine; men tend to have slightly larger bladders than women. Both ureters enter the bladder near its base and the urethra (discussed below) also drains the bladder from its base. The two ureters and the urethra mark the points of a triangle called the **trigone**, a relatively tough and inflexible part of the bladder.

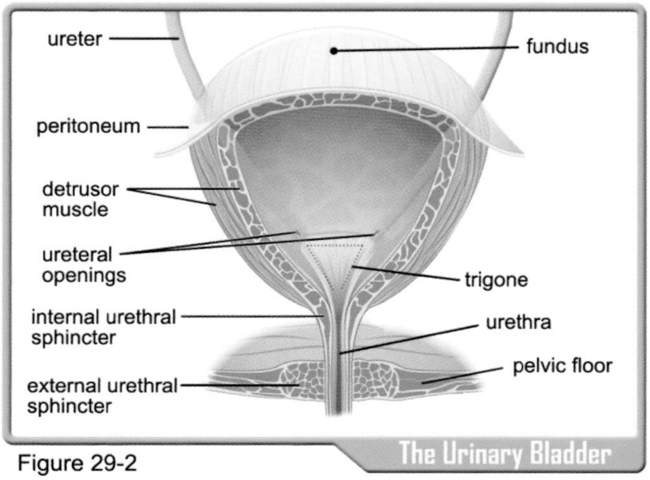

Figure 29-2 **The Urinary Bladder**

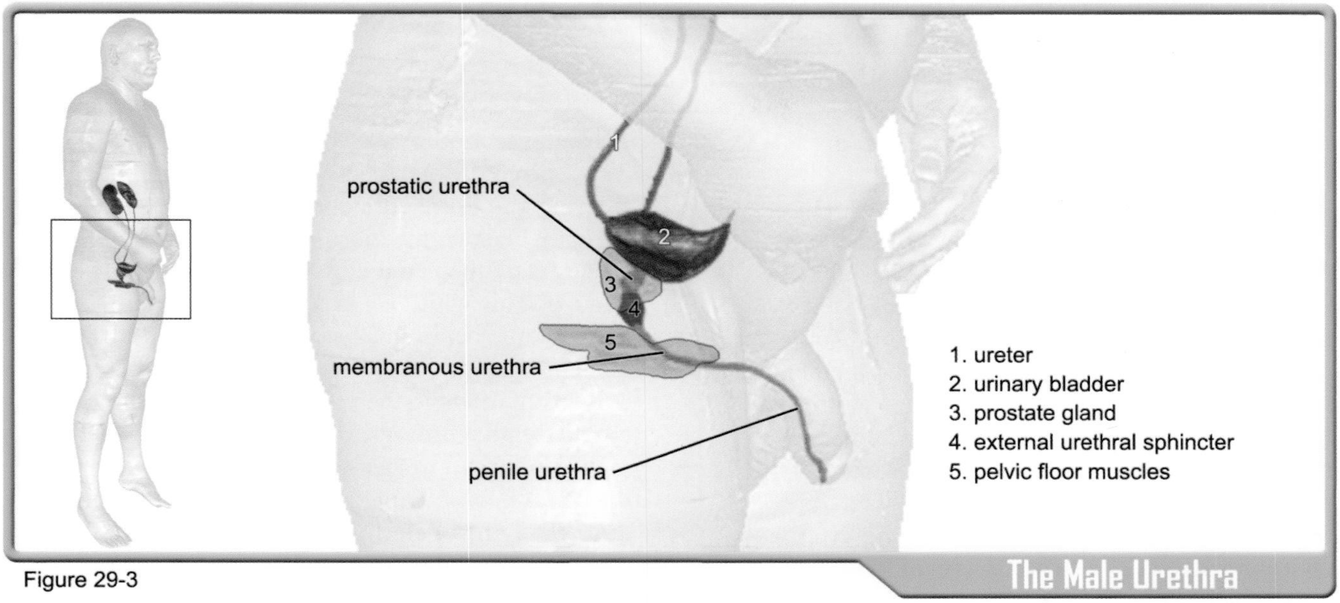

Figure 29-3

By contrast, the remainder of the bladder is quite flexible and highly muscular. The smooth muscle in the bladder walls (collectively called the **detrusor muscle**) contract to expel urine from the bladder. During micturition small flap-like projections over the ureteral openings prevent urine from being pushed back up to the kidneys.

As the urinary bladder fills with urine stretch receptors in the walls of the bladder monitor its state of distension. When roughly 250 mL of urine have been collected in the bladder these stretch receptors send a signal to the brain. At this juncture, we can consciously decide to empty the bladder or not. If the bladder is not emptied the signals from the stretch receptors will be ignored and we once again become unaware of the bladder's condition, until about 500 mL have been collected. The receptors will send increasingly stronger

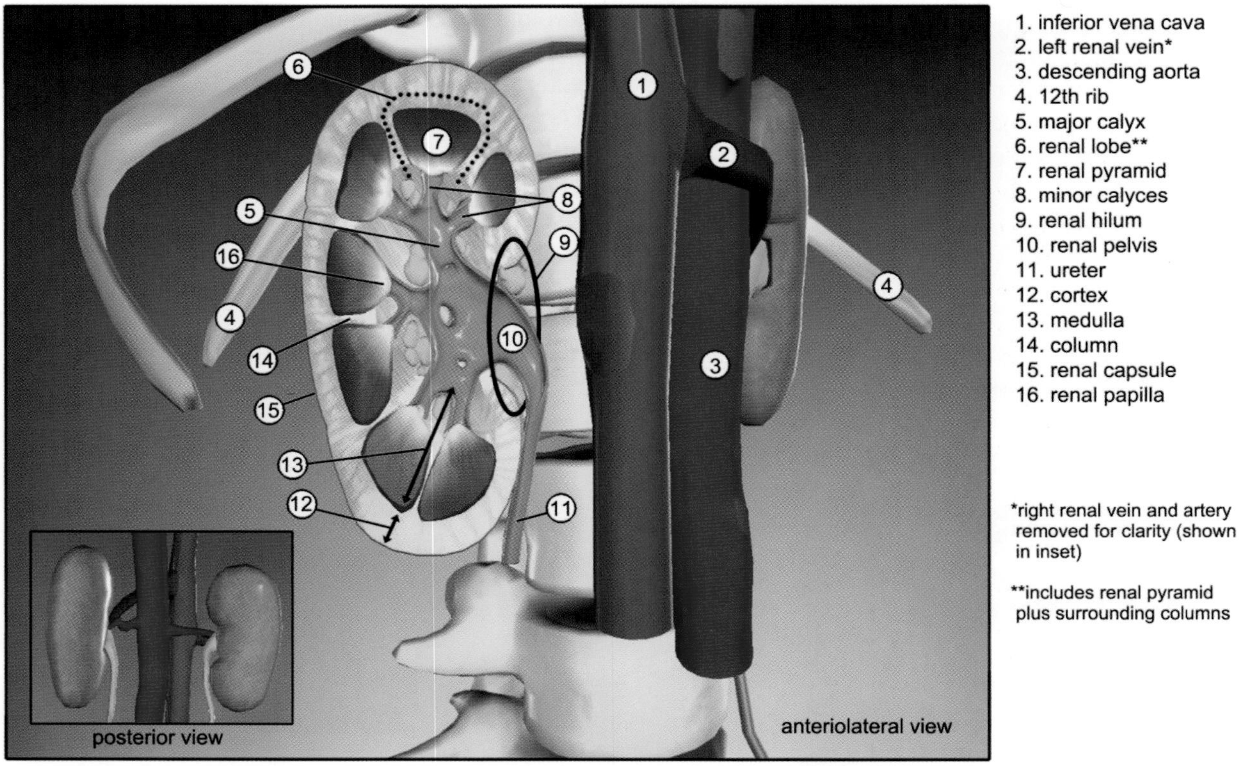

Figure 29-4: Internal Anatomy of the Kidney

signals to the brain rekindling the desire to micturate (i.e., urinate). Again, the desire can be willfully overcome and the signals ignored until the bladder reaches full capacity, roughly 700-800 mL of urine. Beyond that point urine will be uncontrollably expelled from the body.

During expulsion urine passes from the bladder to the outside world via the **urethra**. In the male, two sphincters control micturition: The **internal urethral sphincter** and the **external urethral sphincter**. The internal urethral sphincter opens reflexively (unconsciously) when the bladder is full; the external urethral sphincter is willfully opened to urinate. Contraction of the detrusor muscle expels urine. Females have no internal sphincter.

Distally, the urethra opens to the external environment at the **external urethral orifice**. In females, the urethra is short (~4 cm, or 1.5 inches) and is used exclusively by the urinary system. The external urethral orifice lies superior to the vaginal opening. In males, the urethra is considerably longer (~20 cm, or 8 inches) because it passes through the penis (Figure 29-3). It is divided into three sections: 1/ the **prostatic urethra** which passes through the prostate gland, 2/ the **membranous urethra** which passes through the muscles of the pelvic floor, and 3/ the **penile urethra** which passes through the penis. The penile urethra is also called the *spongy urethra* because it passes through the corpus spongiosum of the penis. The male urethra allows passage of urine and also the passage of sperm during the process of *ejaculation*. Thus, the male urethra is shared between the urinary and reproductive systems.

Internal Anatomy of the Kidneys

A frontal section of a kidney is shown in the figure 29-4. From this perspective many of the blood-filtering and urine-collecting structures can be seen. Directly beneath the most superficial layer of the kidney (i.e., the **renal capsule**) lies the **renal cortex**. This white-ish layer contains numerous microscopic nephrons that filter the blood. Urine generated by this filtration process passes through **collecting ducts** in the **renal pyramids** until it is emptied into a **minor calyx**. Several minor calyces merge to form a **major calyx** which empties into the **renal pelvis**. Finally, urine in the renal pelvis drains into the **ureter** and is carried by peristaltic contractions of the ureter to the bladder.

Blood Flow through the Kidneys

Each minute about ¼ of the body's total blood volume passes through the kidneys for filtration. The blood enters the kidney via the **renal artery** which divides at the hilus into **segmental arteries**. Segmental arteries divide into **lobar arteries** which supply blood to individual renal lobes. The lobar arteries divide into **interlobar arteries** that rise through the renal columns surrounding the pyramids. Interlobar arteries join via **arcuate arteries** that curve over the base of each pyramid. The arcuate arteries branch into numerous **interlobular arteries** which rise into the cortex and

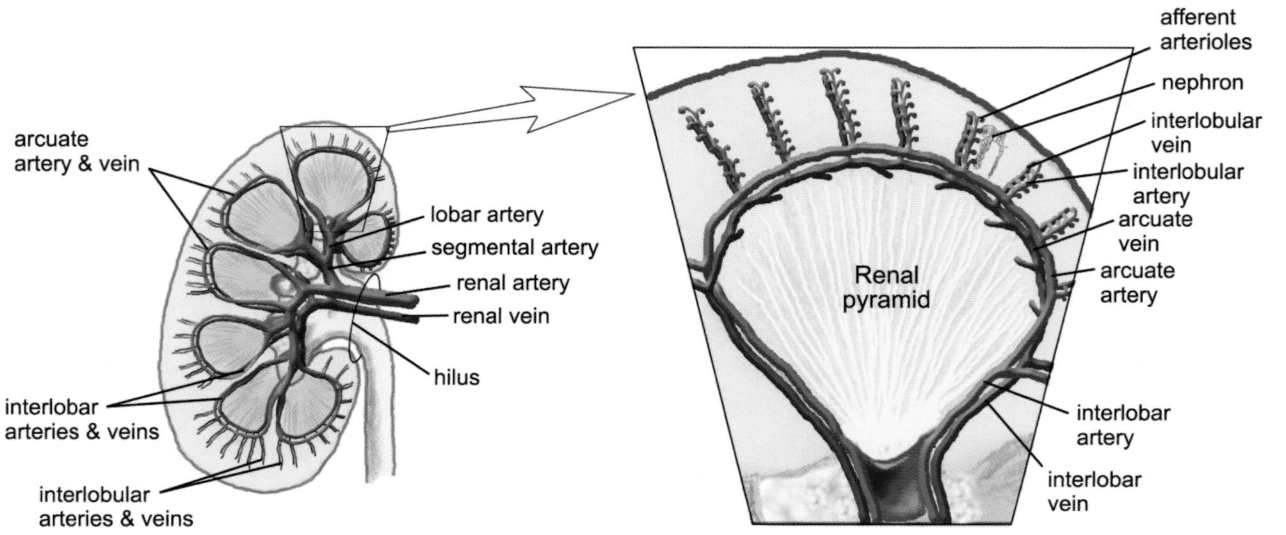

Figure 29-5 **Blood Flow through the Kidney**

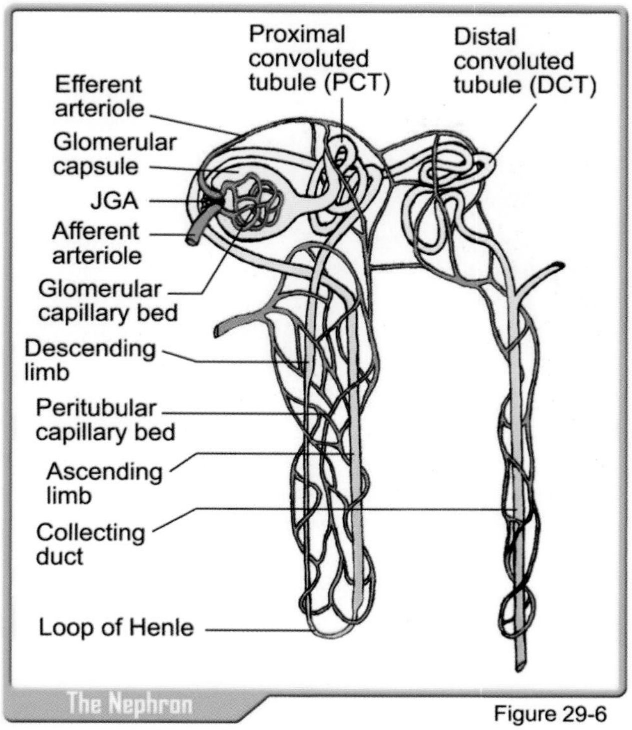

Figure 29-6

branch into **afferent arterioles**, which supply the capillary networks (glomerular and peritubular) that filter the blood. Blood drains from these capillary beds through **interlobular veins** to the **arcuate veins** to the **interlobar veins** and finally into the **renal vein** that leaves the kidney. The arrangement of these vessels is illustrated in figure 29-5.

Renal Physiology

The **nephron** is the basic functional unit of the kidney and is responsible for filtering and processing blood and producing urine (Figure 29-6). Each kidney contains over 1 million nephrons.

The production of urine is a 3-step process. First, the blood is *filtered*. Second, useful components removed by filtration are put back into the blood by *reabsorption*. Finally, toxic components not effectively removed by filtration are actively *secreted* from the blood.

Blood is filtered in the **glomerulus**, a capillary bed fed by the afferent arteriole and enclosed within a capsule called the **glomerular (or Bowman's) capsule** (Figure 29-7). About 10-15% of the blood passing through the glomerular capillary bed is squeezed through the filtration slits of podocytes, specialized cells that wrap around the glomerular capillaries. The blood passing through these slits is called *filtrate* and contains all the

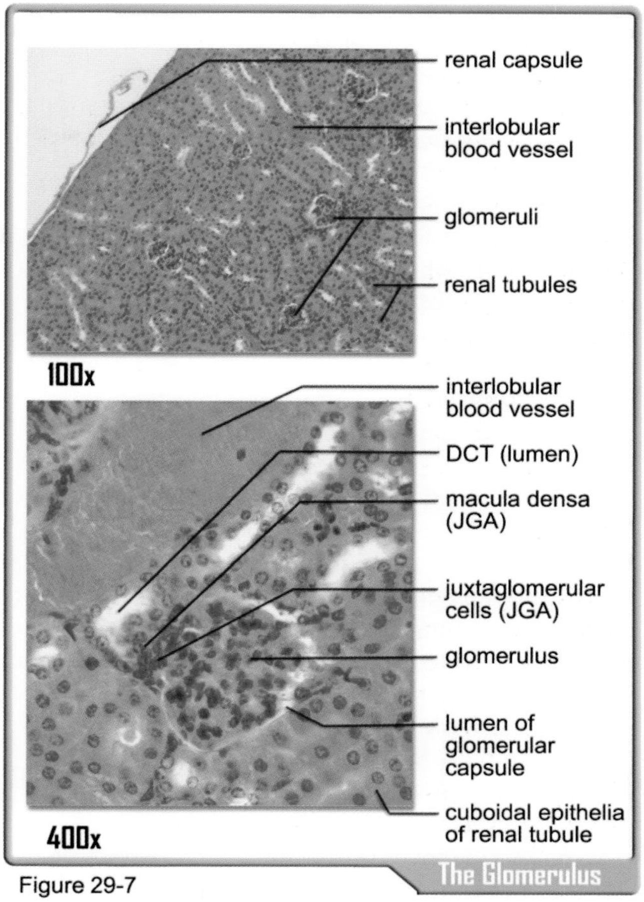

Figure 29-7

components of blood plasma smaller than proteins (proteins and larger entities are too large to pass through the filtration slits). The 85-90% of the blood which is not filtered leaves the glomerulus via the **efferent arteriole**.

The newly formed filtrate leaves the glomerulus via the **proximal convoluted tubule** (PCT) where useful components – like glucose – are selectively reabsorbed back into blood. These components re-enter the bloodstream in capillaries surrounding the tubule called the **peritubular capillary bed**, which is fed by the efferent arteriole. Once inside the tubules the filtrate is called *tubular fluid*.

Tubular fluid leaves the PCT and travels down the descending limb and up the ascending limb of the **loop of Henle**. The loop of Henle absorbs more or less water and NaCl depending on the needs of the body. Thus, this structure plays an important role in regulating the final volume and concentration of urine.

Upon leaving the loop of Henle the tubular fluid enters the **distal convoluted tubule** (DCT) where further absorption of water, salts and other nutrients takes place. The DCT is also a major site of secretion – the third step in blood processing. Ions, drugs, acids and toxins which escaped filtration in the glomerulus are actively transported (i.e., secreted) from the blood of the peritubular capillaries into the tubular fluid. Tubular fluid leaving the DCT, now called urine, drains into a **collecting duct** for eventual transport to the bladder. As in the loop of Henle, variable reabsorption of water and ions can be achieved at the collecting ducts to control urine volume and concentration.

Adjustments to urine volume and concentration are achieved by the convoluted tubules, loop of Henle and collecting ducts, but is largely regulated by specialized cells adjacent to the glomeruli. **Juxtaglomerular (JG) cells**, found within the walls of the arterioles feeding the glomerulus, detect blood pressure. If blood volume is too high, blood pressure increases and these cells cause more water to be moved from the blood to the urine. The **macula densa**, a specialized group of DCT cells located near the JG cells, contain chemoreceptors that monitor the concentration of ions and nutrients. Together, the macula densa and JG cells form the **juxtaglomerular apparatus (JGA)**, which is largely responsible for regulating urine volume and concentration (Figure 29-7).

Activity 1: Histological Examination of the Urinary System

1. Obtain a prepared slide of kidney tissue. Before placing the slide on the microscope, hold it up to the light and observe the cortex, renal lobe and pyramid.
2. Place the slide on a microscope and scan the tissue under low power. You should be able to identify the cortical and medullary areas. Individual glomeruli will be visible as tightly wound tubules – similar to a ball of rubber bands.
3. Observe a glomerulus under high magnification. You should be able to easily identify the lumen of the glomerular capsule and the contained glomerular capillaries.
4. JG cells and macula densa cells should be visible where the afferent arteriole feeds the glomerulus.
5. Tubules belonging to the DCT can be distinguished from those of the PCT by observing the lumen. The lumen of the PCT appears "fuzzy" because PCT epithelial cells project long microvilli into the lumen. These microvilli increase surface area and improve reabsorption efficiency. By contrast, the lumen of the DCT appears clear because those cells do not have microvilli.

Urinalysis Using a "Chemstrip"

Figure 29-8

6. Examine prepared slides of the ureter, bladder and urethra. Transitional epithelia should be especially apparent in the urethra sample.

Activity 2: Urinalysis

A *urinalysis* is a set of tests performed on a urine sample to assess the overall properties of the urine. A typical urinalysis includes assessment of pH, glucose concentration, protein concentration and the presence or absence of blood cells and/or hemoglobin among other things. Observation of the color and smell of the urine may also be included in a urinalysis. Abnormal urine can provide a wealth of information to doctors about the kidneys, liver, blood and many other organs and help diagnose a host of pathologies and illnesses. Specific urine tests can be applied to screen for drugs, e.g., illegal performance-enhancing drugs taken by some athletes, or even pregnancy.

Performing a urinalysis these days is much easier than it used to be. In fact, a complete battery of tests can be performed in a single step in just seconds using Chemstrips® (Figure 29-8). Complete a urinalysis as follows:

1. Obtain a urine sample from yourself or a lab partner. A small beaker or Dixie cup can be used to collect the urine. At least 50 mL of urine should be collected. Collect the urine "mid-stream" to reduce contamination.
2. Observe the color and odor of the urine. The color of urine can vary dramatically from clear to dark amber. In general, the more

concentrated the urine the darker its color and more pronounced its odor.

3. Briefly dip a Chemstrip® into the urine. Completely submerge all of the squares on the strip, but only for a few seconds.
4. Wipe off excess urine from the Chemsrip® and allow 60 seconds for the chemical reactions to occur. Each square on the strip specifically tests for one component or property.
5. After 1 minute, hold the strip next to the label on the Chemstrip® container. Compare the color of each square with the "decoder" on the label. Record your observations.

Do not allow the reaction to proceed more than 2 minutes. Prolonged reactions will generate false positives.

Urinalysis Results

Color ____________________

Odor ____________________

pH ____________________

Glucose ____________________

Ketones ____________________

Leukocytes ____________________

Nitrites ____________________

Protein ____________________

RBC/Hb ____________________

Abnormal Urine Conditions

- **Glycosuria** – Glucose levels in the urine are normally very low. Elevated levels of glucose in urine is suggestive of diabetes mellitus.
- **Ketonuria** – Ketones may be found in the urine of healthy individuals in the post-absorptive state (i.e., mild starvation). Elevated ketones in the urine may also result from diabetic ketoacidosis.
- **Leukocytes** – Leukocytes, or white blood cells, are usually not found in urine. The presence of leukocytes may indicate a urinary tract infection (UTI).
- **Nitrites** – Most common urinary pathogens are nitrite-producing gram-negative bacteria. The presence of nitrite in the urine is strongly suggestive of UTI.
- **Proteinuria** – The protein concentration in normal urine is low, usually less than 30 mg/dL. Elevated urine protein concentration is sometimes observed in pregnant women. High protein levels indicate damage to the gluomerular filtration apparatus of the kidneys.
- **Hematuria** – Blood is normally not found in urine. The presence of blood may indicate serious glomerular damage in the kidneys, or may originate from scratches along the urinary tract (e.g., by a passing kidney stone). In healthy females, blood contamination may be observed if the urine sample is collected during menstruation.

Activity 3: Specific Gravity Determination
Urine specific gravity is a measure of the density of urine as compared to water. By adding solutes to water you create a solution and the more solutes you add the denser the solution will be. The

Figure 29-9

specific gravity (*g*) of pure water is 1.000 by definition.

Urine contains a number of different types of solutes including urea, sodium, potassium, uric acid, creatine, ammonia, etc. The density of urine is often reflected in its color: the denser the urine the darker its color (Figure 29-9). The specific gravity of human urine varies in density from approximately 1.003 when very dilute to 1.030 when very concentrated. Measure the density of your urine sample as follows:

1. Pour urine into the provided glass cylinder until it's about ¾ full.
2. Carefully place the urinometer into the urine sample with the weighted bulb down. The urinometer will sink and then float with the calibrated scale emerging from the sample surface. After the urinometer has stopped "bobbing" up and down, carefully read the calibrated scale at the lowest part of the meniscus of the urine sample.
3. Dispose of the urine down the drain and rinse all glassware. Be careful not to break the fragile urinometer.

specific gravity ___________________________

Activity 4: Urine Output

Urine production can vary tremendously depending on the needs of the body. Under sympathetic stimulation ("flight or fight"), urine production may stop completely. Conversely, urine can be produced rapidly when the body is overhydrated. In this exercise we will demonstrate how rapidly urine can be produced.

It is possible to overdose on water with fatal results (a condition called hyponatremia). The amounts of water consumed in this exercise are safe for healthy students of average body weight, but students with low body weight or known medical conditions should not volunteer for this exercise. In addition, students who will be engaging in physical activity (e.g., sporting exercises) following lab should not volunteer.

1. Select a volunteer. It is often fun to select one male and one female volunteer to "compete" for most urine output. If using multiple volunteers, they should all be about the size body size and weight.
2. Have the volunteer empty their bladder early in the lab period. (One hour will be needed to complete this test).
3. After voiding their bladder, the volunteer should consume approximately 1.5 liters of water quickly, in about 10 minutes. If the volunteer is small or petite, reduce water intake to 1 liter.
4. After one hour, the volunteer should void their bladder and collect *all* of the urine in a 1-liter beaker.

Results

1. How much urine did the male volunteer produce in one hour?

2. How much urine did the female volunteer produce in one hour?

3. Divide the volume of urine produced (in mL) by the elapsed time (60 minutes) to obtain urine output rate (mL/min). What is the urine output for the male and female volunteers?

1. List the four major components of the urinary system and describe their functions.

________________ -

________________ -

________________ -

________________ -

2. Describe two ways the urethra of the male differs from the urethra of the female.

3. What is the function of the adipose tissue surrounding each kidney?

4. Arrange the vessels below in the order in which blood passes through the kidney.

_____ a. interlobar artery

_____ b. renal artery

_____ c. arcuate vein

_____ d. renal vein

_____ e. interlobular vein

_____ f. segmental artery

_____ g. interlobular artery

_____ h. interlobar vein

_____ i. arcuate artery

5. Label the figure of the kidney below.

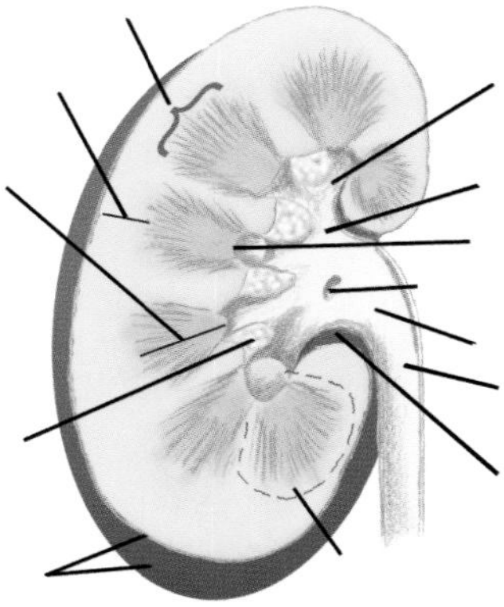

6. Label the figure of the nephron below.

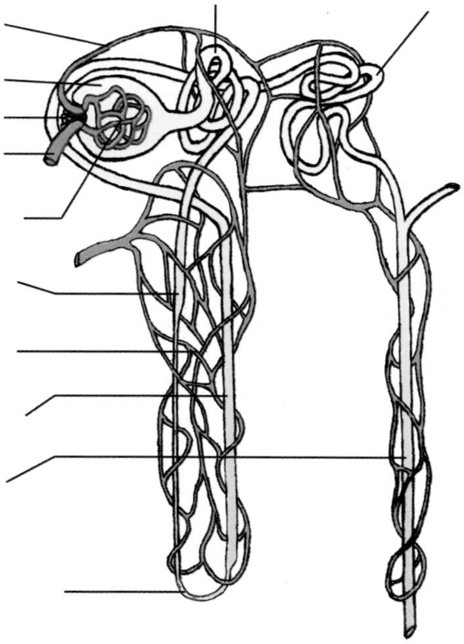

Match the following words with their correct definitions.

______	7. Houses the glomerulus, also called glomerular capsule	a. nephron
______	8. Funnel-shaped collector of urine from the renal pyramids	b. PCT
______	9. Dark, triangular-shaped structure in the renal medulla	c. glomerulus
______	10. The basic filtering unit of the kidney	d. DCT
______	11. Tough, triangular-shaped base of the bladder	e. peritubular capillaries
______	12. Convoluted tubules near the glomerulus	f. Bowman's capsule
______	13. Muscular tube that conducts urine from the kidney to the bladder	g. JGA
______	14. Capillary bed where blood filtration occurs	h. renal cortex
______	15. Muscle that forces urine out of the bladder	i. calyx
______	16. Thin connective tissue covering around the kidney	j. renal pyramid
______	17. Capillary bed where reabsorption occurs	k. trigone
______	18. Cells near the glomerulus that regulate urine concentration	l. detrusor
______	19. The superficial urine-forming part of the kidney	l. renal capsule
______	20. Convoluted tubules far from the glomerulus	l. ureter

21. Why do you suppose epithelial cells lining the PCT have microvilli projecting into the lumen, but the cells of the DCT do not?

22. Define the following urine abnormalities.

a. Ketonuria =

b. Glycosuria =

c. Proteinuria =

d. Hematuria =

exercise 30

the REPRODUCTIVE system

So God created man in his own image, in the image of God
he created him; male and female he created them.
Genesis 1:27

The reproductive system is without doubt the most unique of the eleven organ systems. It's the only system, for example, that comes in two varieties – male and female. In addition, it's the only system you can live without. All other systems are vital to your survival – consider living without your cardiovascular, respiratory or digestive systems, for example. The reproductive system, however, need not be functional for you to live. Indeed, a good argument can be made that the reproductive system does more to disturb homeostasis than maintain it. However, the system is required (in at least some members of the population) in order for the species to propogate from one generation to the next. Thus, the role of the reproductive system is continuance of the species over time.

Our discussion of the reproductive system will begin with the male because his system is far less complex than hers. The difference in complexity stems from the fact that the female must provide an environment for the developing fetus during gestation, and continue to provide life-sustaining nutrients to the post-partum infant until the baby can eat on his or her own. By contrast, the man needs only to produce and deliver his germ cells to the woman's body.

Male External Genitalia

The external genitalia of the male is depicted in figure 30-1. The most notable feature of the male external genitalia is the **penis**, which consists of a **shaft** (or *body*) that terminates with the **glans** (or *head*) of the penis. The anterior portion of the glans possesses an opening, the **external urethral meatus**, that allows expulsion of both urine and semen.

Figure 30-1 shows both a **circumcised** penis and an **uncircumcised** penis. Of course, uncircumcised is the natural state of the penis. Circumcision is a rather peculiar practice that began in Israel roughly 4,000 years ago but still persists in our culture even today. It's a medical procedure in which the **prepuce**, or *foreskin*, of the penis is surgically removed. The prepuce is a covering of skin that envelops the glans of the penis. Circumcision orginated from God himself when he commanded the Israelites to be circumcised to physically mark them as belonging to Him (Genesis 17). Circumcision remains a requirement for the Jew, but is not for the Christian. Nonetheless, the tradition has continued among Christians since the founding of Christianity 2,000 years ago. Many people would like to see the practice discontinued, but recent scientific studies suggest that circumcision actually protects men (and consequently women) from sexually-transmitted diseases, including HIV/AIDS[1].

The second notable feature of the male external genitalia is the **scrotum**. The scrotum is a sac-like structure that houses the **testes** (or *testicles*). The testes produce sperm – the male germ cell – and testosterone, a hormone that produces masculine characteristics (e.g., facial hair, low voices, etc.). The testes (singular = testis) derive their name from the fact that they provide testimony to one's manhood.

Male Internal Genitalia

The internal structure of the penis consists of three regions of erectile tissue – the two **corpora cavernosa** and the single **corpus spongiosum** (Figure 30-2). In cross-section, these three regions form a roughly triangular shape with the two larger

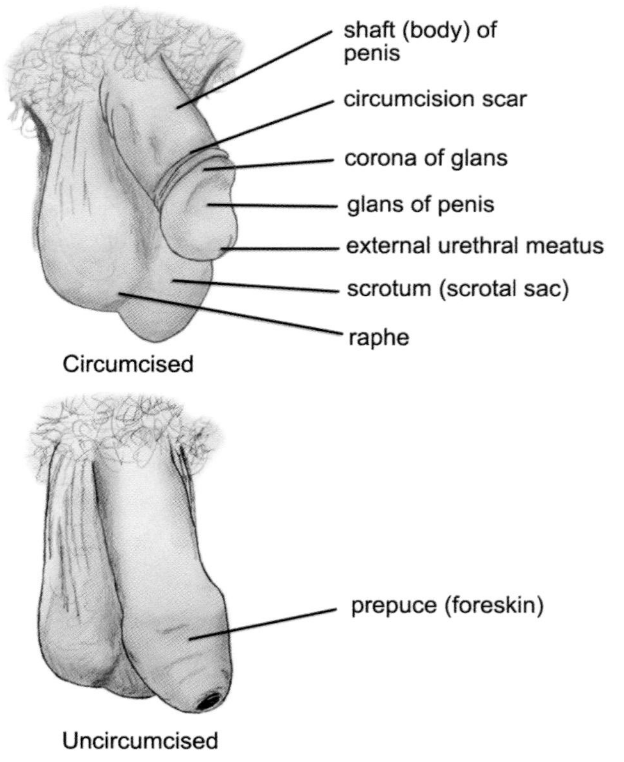

Figure 30-1: Male External Genitalia

[1] Science News (2005) vol. 168, pg. 275.

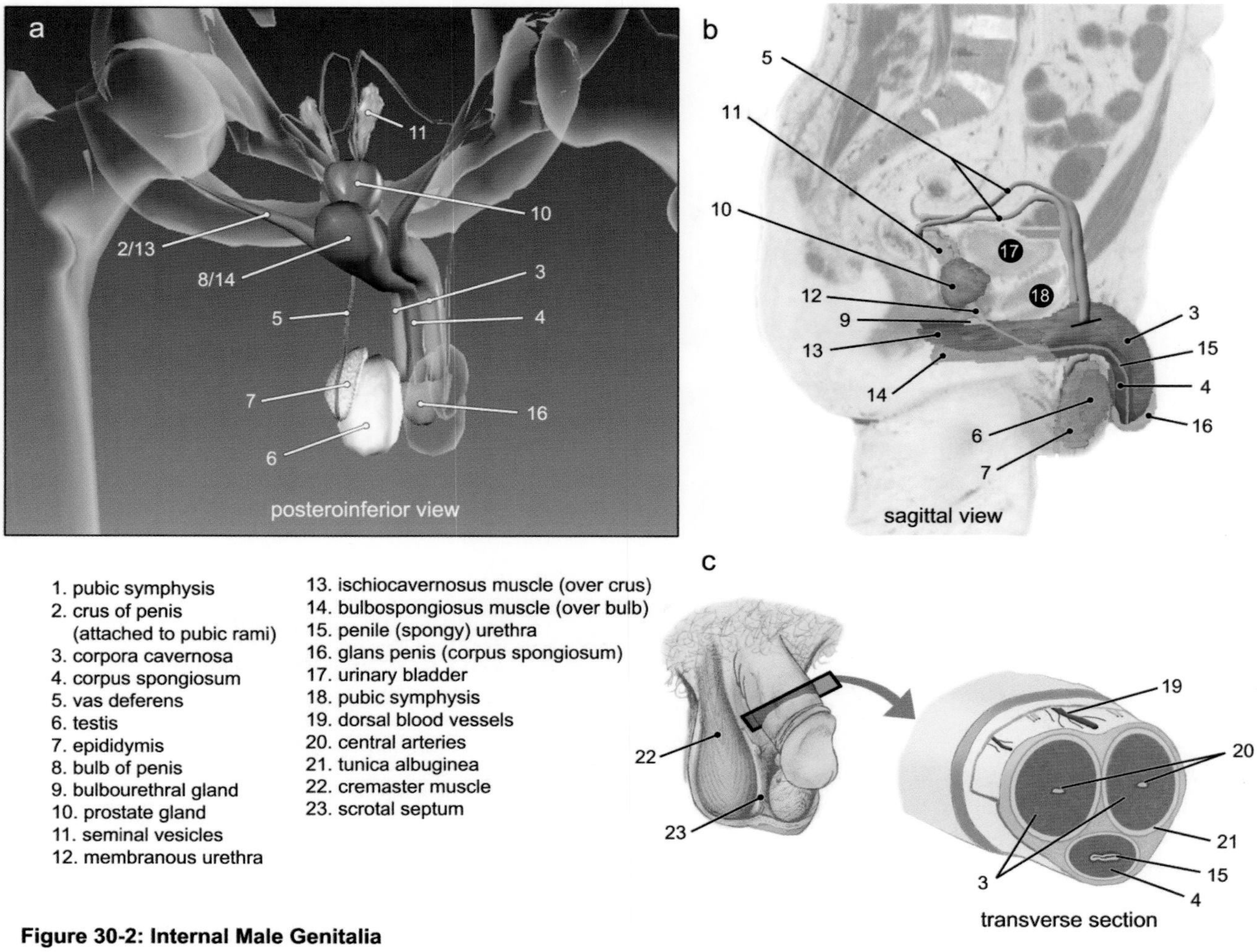

Figure 30-2: Internal Male Genitalia

corpora cavernosa superior to the smaller corpus spongiosum. The urethra passes through the corpus spongiosum, which enlarges distally to fill the glans penis. Only about ⅓ to ½ of the penis is outside of the body; the remainder penetrates deep into the body where the two corpora cavernosa attach firmly to the rami of the ischial bones. These attachments form the **crura** (singular = crus) of the penis. The corpus spongiosum attaches to the perineal membrane to form the **bulb** of the penis, which is wrapped by the **bulbospongiosus muscle**. The corpora cavernosa are enveloped by the **ischiocavernosus muscles**. These muscles contract intensely and rhythmically during orgasm and help propel semen from the male reproductive tract.

The penis may exist in one of two states – *flaccid* (as shown in figures 30-1 and 30-2) or *erect*. Normally flaccid, the penis only becomes erect when the male is stimulated sexually. Erection is achieved by engorging the erectile tissues of the penis with blood. The two larger erectile tissues possess deep arteries thar supply blood for this purpose. Interestingly, the process requires simultaneous activation of both the sympathetic and parasympathetic divisions of the autonomic nervous system.

Male Reproductive Tract

The male reproductive tract consists of the tubes that transport sperm and their accessory structures. The tract begins with the testes where sperm is produced and ends at the external urethral meatus. A convenient way to study these structures is to follow the course of the sperm.

Sperm produced in the testes are immature and cannot swim. They are transported through the reproductive tract by ciliated cells lining the ducts of the reproductive tract. From the testes, sperm are carried through the coiled tubules of the **epididymis** and then out of the scrotum through the **ductus**

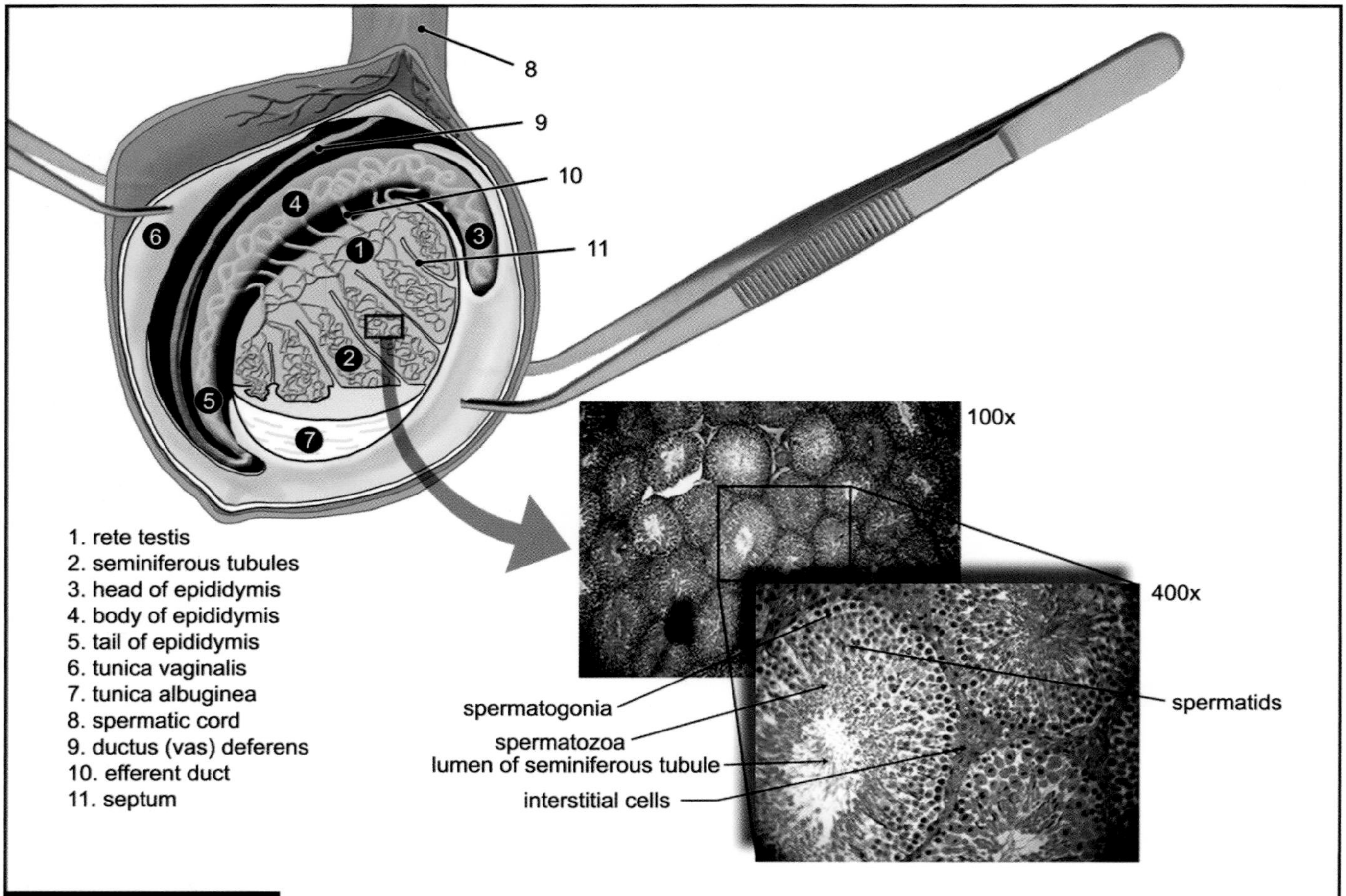

Figure 30-3: The Testes

deferens (or, *vas deferens*). Upon passing through the body wall, the ductus deferens loops up over the pubic symphysis, then above, behind and below the urinary bladder (Figure 30-2 & 20-4). Beneath the bladder the two vas deferens (one from each testis) merge to form the short **ejaculatory duct** which empties into the **urethra**. In the male, the urethra is described in three sections: the **prostatic urethra** – which passes through the prostate gland, the **membranous urethra** – which passes through muscles of the pelvic floor and the **penile** (or *spongy*) **urethra** – which passes through the penis (see also Figure 29-3).

Three glands are associated with the male reproductive tract: the seminal vesicles, the prostate gland and the bulbourethral glands. Each contributes a component to *semen* – a mixture of buffers, sugars, sperm and chemicals (such as prostaglandins) that activate sperm and/or assist fertilization.

The **seminal vesicles** are found at the posteroinferior aspect of the urinary bladder (Figure 30-4). About 70% of seminal fluid is produced by the seminal vesicles. This fluid is rich in fructose and prostaglandins. The fructose is used by sperm to produce ATP, which is used to drive their flagella. Prostaglandins stimulate smooth muscle contraction. In this case, they stimulate the uterus of the female; uterine contractions assist sperm in their journey to the egg. Also, prostaglandins in semen can induce labor in late-term pregnant women.

The **prostate gland** is a walnut-sized organ beneath the bladder (Figure 30-4). The gland produces an alkaline secretion that constitutes ~25% of seminal fluid. This alkaline solution protects sperm by neutralizing the acidic environment of the vagina.

The **bulbourethral glands** (a.k.a., *Cowper's glands*) are small, pea-sized glands located at the base of the penis. During male sexual arousal they secrete a clear, viscous solution called *pre-ejaculate*. This fluid, representing just 5% of total seminal fluid, lubricates the urethra and washes it of residual urine in preparation for ejaculation. The bulbourethral glands are

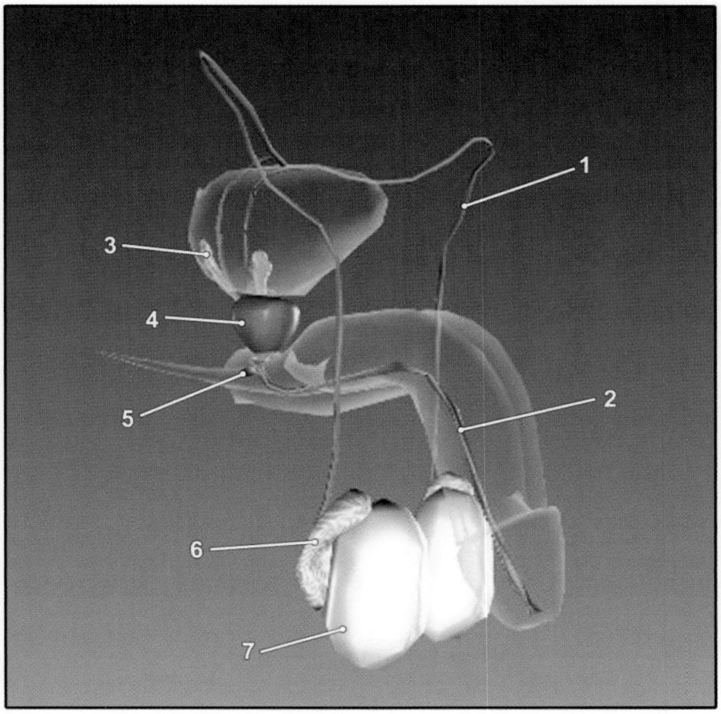

(a) anteriolateral view

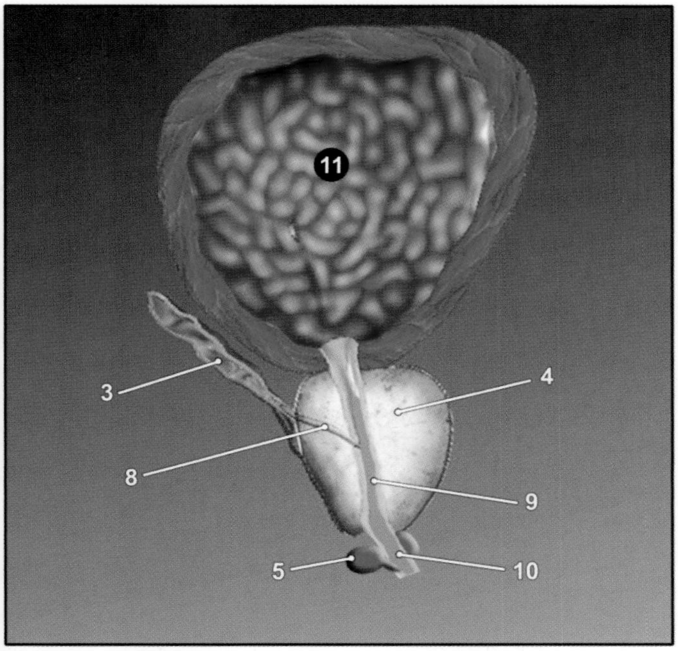

(b) sectional view of prostate

1. ductus (vas) deferens
2. penile (spongy) urethra
3. seminal vesicle
4. prostate gland
5. bulbourethral gland
6. epididymis
7. testis
8. ejaculatory duct
9. prostatic urethra
10. membranous urethra
11. urinary bladder

Figure 30-4: Semen-Producing Glands & Conducting Tubes

homologous to the greater vestibular glands in the female.

The Testes

The two testes (or, *testicles*) are the organs that make sperm cells and the hormone testosterone (Figures 30-2 & 30-3). They are found in the **scrotum** (i.e., *scrotal sac*) outside the body wall because sperm will not develop properly at normal body temperature. The temperature of the testes is carefully regulated by the cremaster and dartos muscles. The **cremaster muscle** surrounds each testis and has its origin and insertion at the inguinal ligament. When these skeletal muscles contracts the testes are lifted closer to the body where they are warmed. When the cremaster muscles relax the testes fall farther from the body where they can be cooled. The **dartos muscle** is an extremely thin layer of smooth muscle in the skin of the scrotal sac. When the dartos contracts the scrotal skin is wrinkled; the extent of wrinkling regulates how much heat is radiated from the skin surface.

The testes develop embryologically inside the male baby's body below the kidneys. Near birth the testes descend into the scrotum in a process called *descent of the testes*. As the organs pass through the body wall a portion of the peritoneal membrane is pinched off around each testis. This membrane remains around the testis throughout life as the **tunica vaginalis** and possesses both a parietal and visceral layer. A deeper connective tissue covering forms the surface of the testicle. This tough, white layer is called the **tunica albuginea**.

Sperm production begins in the tightly coiled **seminiferous tubules** within the testes (Figure 30-3). The seminiferous tubules are partitioned into 10-15 **lobules** separated by **septa**. Sperm development begins near the walls of the tubules by the division of mitotically-active stem

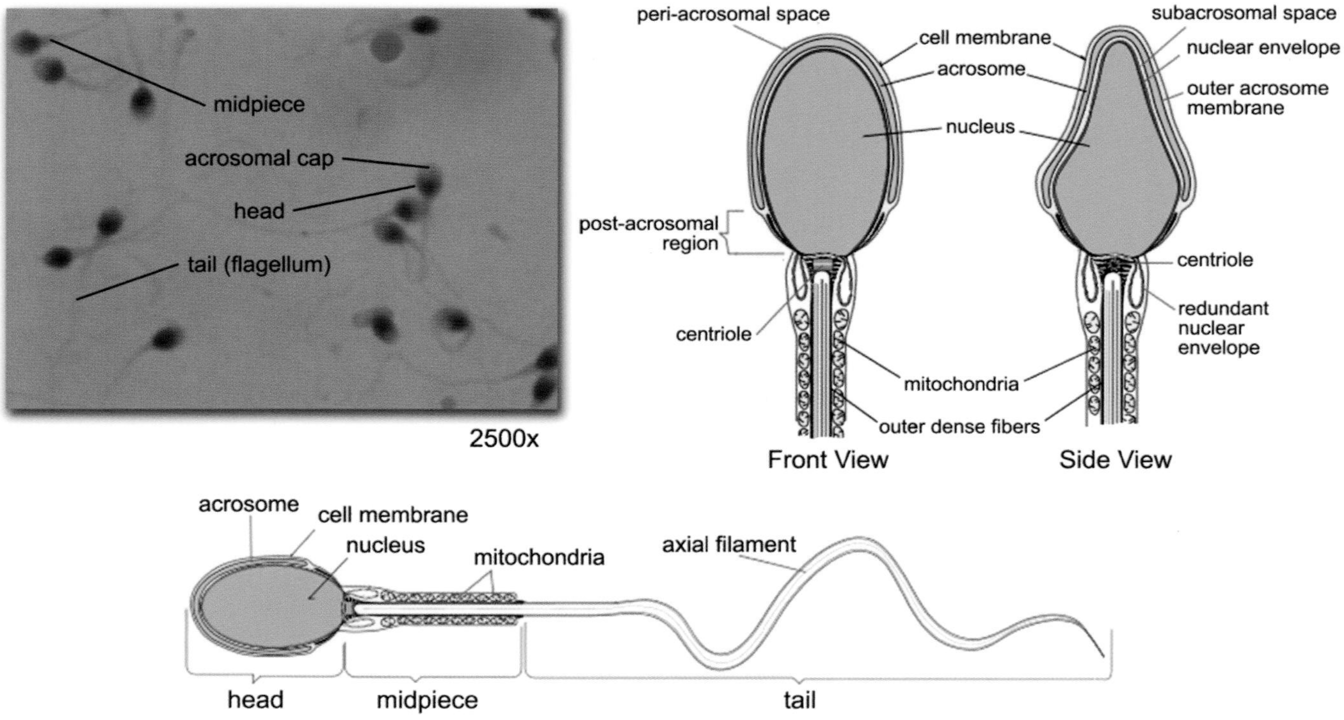

Figure 30-5: Human Spermatozoa

cells called **spermatogonia**. As the stem cells divide, the daughter cells are pushed toward the lumen of the tubule. The cells develop first into **spermatids** and then into physically mature **spermatozoa** (or, *sperm*). The spermatazoa have all the anatomical features of sperm, but they are still functionally immature and cannot swim. As stated earlier, they are swept along the reproductive tract by coordinated action of the ciliated cells lining the tract.

Spermatozoa exit the seminiferous tubules as they enter the **rete testis**, a complex network of tubules. From there, they pass through the 10-15 **efferent ductules** into the **head of the epididymis**, located on the superior aspect of the testis. The sperm continue down a coiled duct through the **body of the epididymis** which then turns abruptly at the **tail of the epididymis**. The duct travels back up along the body of the epididymis and leaves the scrotum with blood vessels and nerves in a bundle collectively called the **spermatic cord**. The total length of the duct in the epididymis is about 21 feet!

The testes also make the hormone testosterone. The hormone is produced in the testes by **interstitial cells** crowded between the seminiferous tubules (Figure 30-3).

Sperm

Sperm are among the most highly differentiated cells in the human body (Figure 30-5). For example, sperm are the only human cells with a **flagellum** (or, *tail*). The long, whip-like flagellum helps the cell swim to the egg once inside the female reproductive tract. Sperm are also among the smallest cells in the body – the head of a human spermatozoan is only 3-5 μm (but the flagellum is some 50 μm long). The **head** of the sperm contains the tightly packed DNA that will be the father's contribution to the traits of the child (among which will be the child's gender). The tip of the head contains powerful enzymes enclosed in the **acrosomal cap**; the enzymes are required for fertilization as they allow the sperm to penetrate the outer coating of the egg cell. Behind the head of the sperm is the **midpiece**. The midpiece is filled with mitochondria that provide ATP for the violent thrashing of the flagellum.

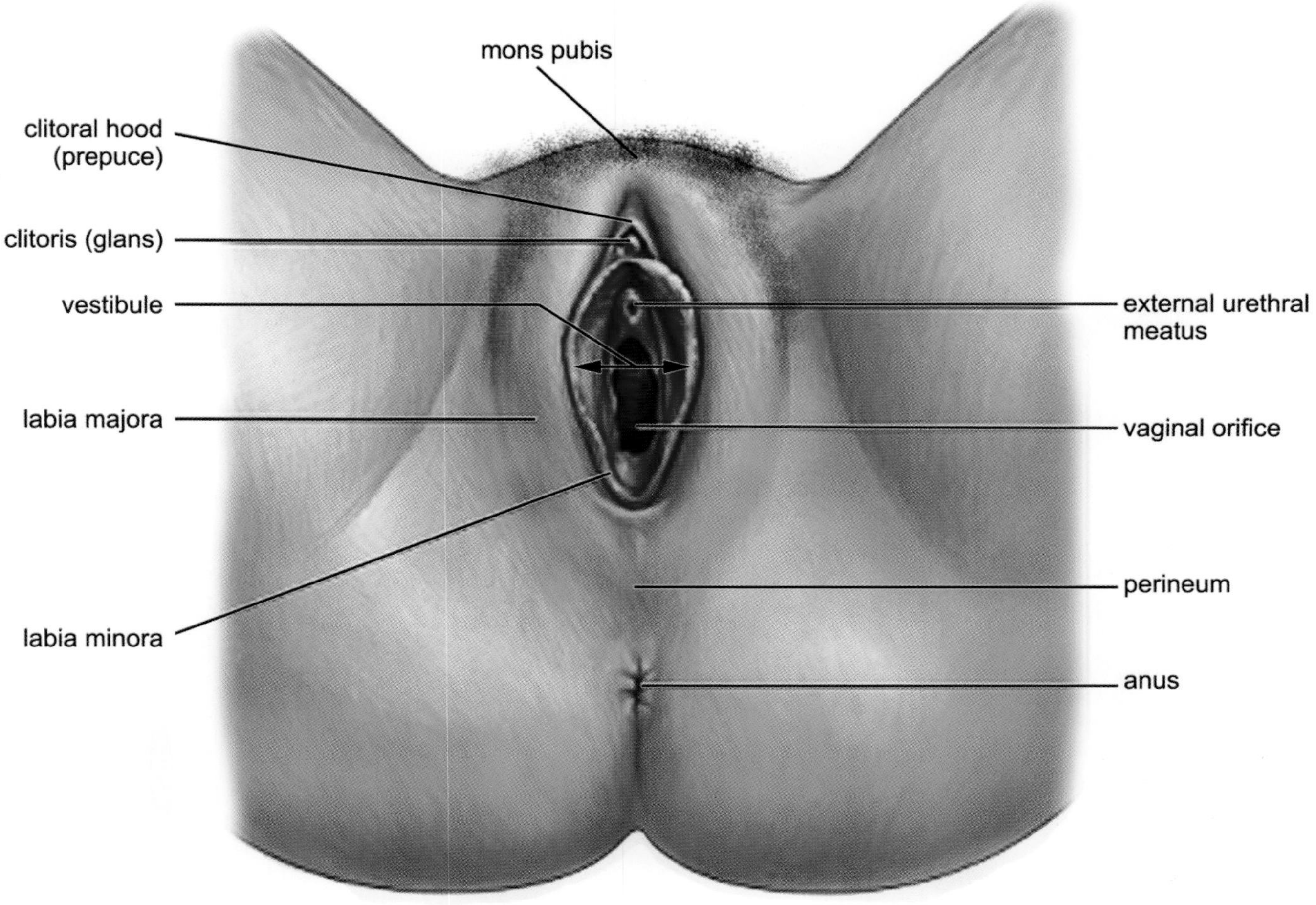

Figure 30-6: Female External Genitalia (Vulva)

Female Reproductive System

As stated earlier, the female reproductive system is more complex than the male reproductive system, primarily because the woman nurtures both the developing fetus before birth and, for a time, the newborn baby after birth. Let us now examine the structures of the female reproductive system, beginning with the external genitalia, followed by the internal reproductive organs and the breasts.

Female External Genitalia

The external genitalia (i.e., *vulva*) of the female is shown in figure 30-6. Two folds of skin – the hairless **labia minora** and the hair-covered **labia majora** – surround and guard the entrance to female internal genitalia. Opening the labia reveals the vestibule and structures housed within the vestibular area. The **clitoris** is found at the most superior aspect of the vestibule. It is sheltered by a fold of skin called the **clitoral hood**, or *prepuce,* of the clitoris. The anterior tip of the clitoris (i.e., the **glans clitoris**) contains twice as many nerve endings as the penis. Stimulation of this extremely sensitive organ is primarily responsible for the female orgasm. Although the clitoris appears small it is actually quite large; much of the organ is located deep to the body surface (Figure 30-7). Immediately behind the glans clitoris the body of the clitoris makes a 90° turn and courses inferiorly about 1 inch before bisecting into the two **corpora cavernosa**. Each corpus terminates at the **crus clitoris**. The entire organ is composed mainly of erectile tissue and, like the penis, becomes engorged with blood during sexual excitement.

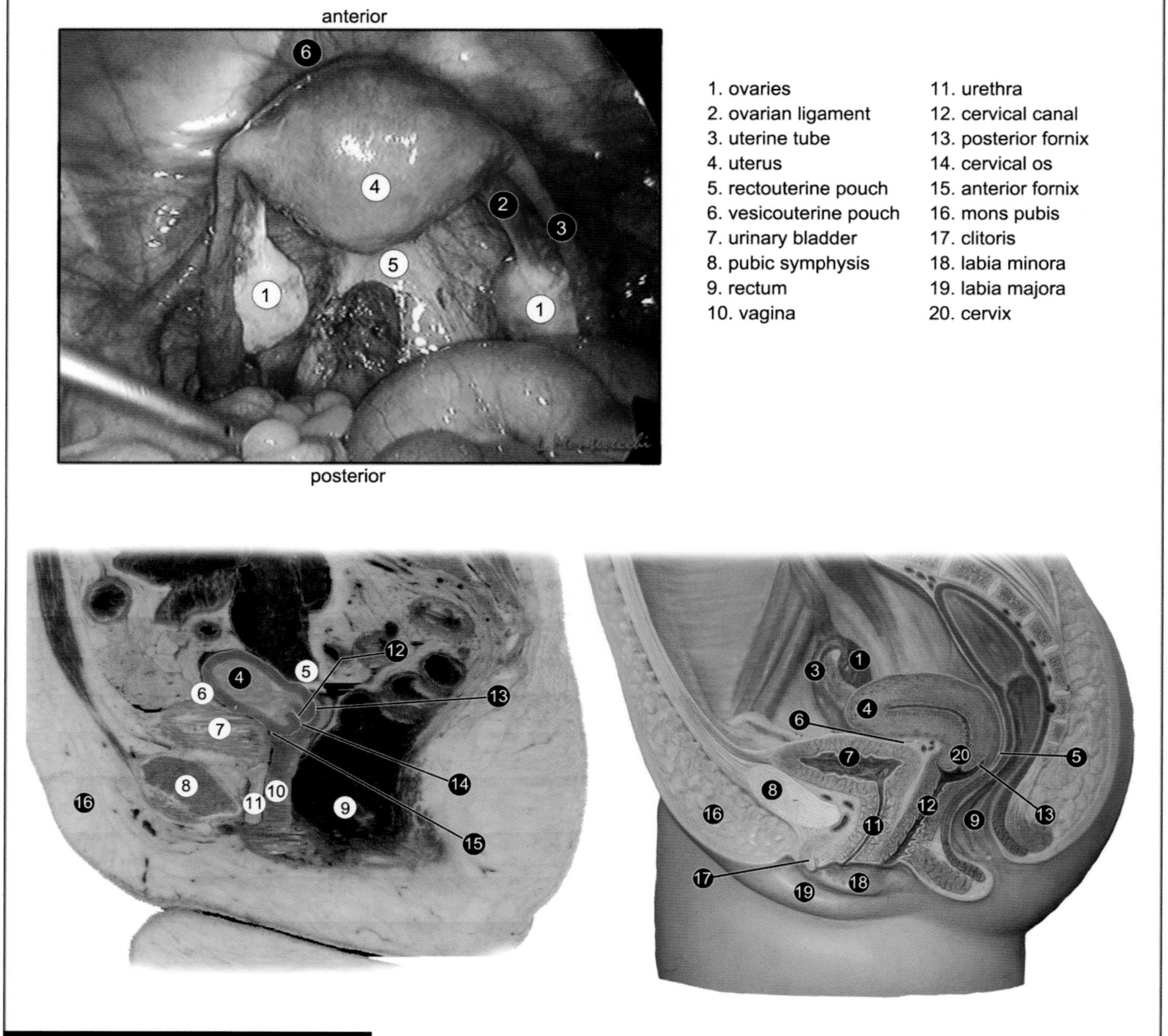

Figure 30-7: Female Internal Genitalia

The area between the labia minora is the **vestibule** (Figure 30-6). Within the vestibule are several orifices, the largest being the **vaginal orifice** which leads to the vagina. Superior to the vaginal orifice is the smaller **urethral orifice** which passes urine from the urinary bladder. (Recall that the urethra of the female functions solely for the urinary system while the urethra of the male functions for both the urinary and reproductive systems). Careful inspection of the vulva will reveal extremely small openings for the **greater** and **lesser vestibular glands**. Secretions from these glands lubricate the vestibule and distal portion of the vagina during sexual intercourse.

Superior to the labial folds is the **mons pubis** (or, *mons venus*) – a rounded eminence of adipose tissue overlaying the pubic symphysis and covered with pubic hair. The function of the mons pubis is to act as a cushion during coitis, or intercourse. Inferior to the labial folds, the **perineum** describes the region between the vulva and the anus.

Female Internal Genitalia

As with the male, a convenient way to study the female internal reproductive organs is to follow the sperm.

The **vagina** is a tube that extends 3-4 inches from the vestibule to the uterus (Figures 30-7 and 30-8). It serves as both the receptacle for the penis during intercourse and as the birth canal during childbirth. Sperm is deposited in the vagina near the uterus in an area called the **fornix**, a fold of skin created by the insertion of the pear-shaped uterus into the vaginal canal. The portion of the uterus found within the vagina is called the **cervix**; the remainder of the uterus is called the **body**. The enlarged superior region of the uterine body is the **fundus**. Near the fundus the two **uterine tubes** (a.k.a., *fallopian tubes* or *ovarian tubes*) extend from the uterus toward the **ovaries**. The ovaries release a female gamete (i.e., an oocyte) each month as part of the female reproductive cycle (discussed in detail in the next chapter).

The goal of reproduction is to have a male gamete successfully fuse with a female gamete in a process called fertilization. Fertilization typically occurs in the uterine tubes; sperm deposited in the fornix must therefore gain entry into the uterus first. Of the roughly 200 million sperm deposited in the fornix from an ejaculation, only about 10,000 will find their way through the **external cervical os** of the cervix, swim through the **cervical canal** and enter the lumen of the uterus. Only about 100 sperm will make it to the **isthmus** of the uterine tube and just 2-3 dozen will reach the oocyte near the **infundibulum**. Only 1 sperm will penetrate the protective "shell" surrounding the egg, resulting in fertilization.

Each month, only one egg is released by an ovary in a process called *ovulation*. Upon release the egg is swept up by the finger-like **fimbriae** of the uterine tube and then propelled by ciliated cells down the tube toward the uterus. Although the journey to the uterus takes 2-3 days, the egg is only viable for 24 hours following expulsion from the ovary; thus, pregnancy is most likely to occur within one day of ovulation.

Interestingly, there is no direct connection between the uterine tubes and the ovaries. Thus, in rare cases, an egg released from the ovary may not enter the uterine tube and fertilization can occur

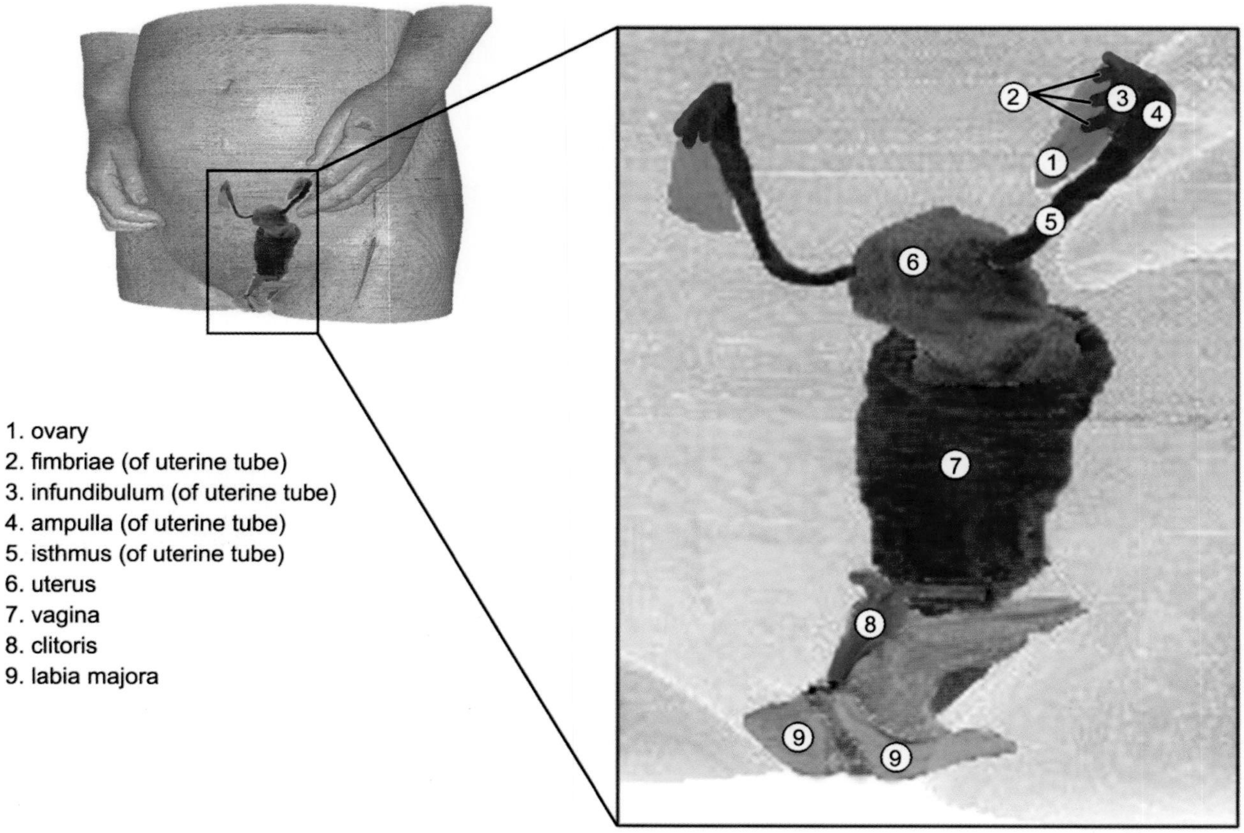

Figure 30-8: Female Internal Reproductive Organs

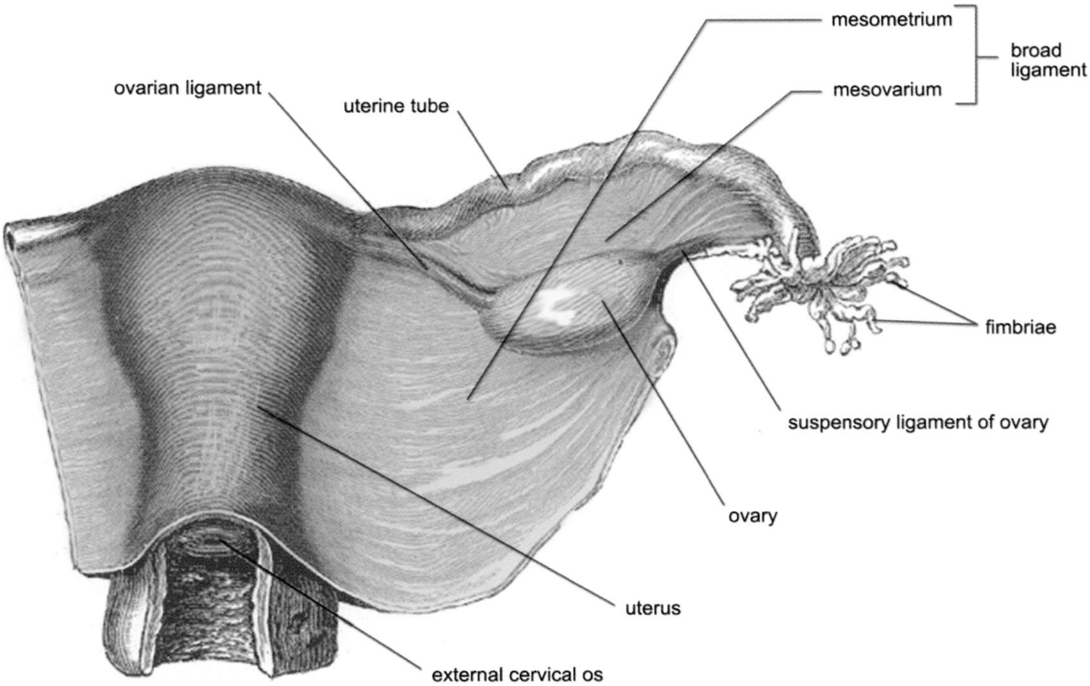

Figure 30-9: Supporting Ligaments of Female Reproductive Organs

outside the uterine tube. The fertilized egg may subsequently implant in the abdominal cavity resulting in an *ectopic pregnancy*. Also, because of the open passageway between the ovaries and the uterine tubes, reproductive system infections can rather easily spread to the pelvic viscera leading to *pelvic inflammatory disease (PID)*. During menses, sloughed off cells of the endometrium can also exit the uterus via the uterine tubes rather than the vagina. Those cells may continue to grow outside the uterus in a condition called *endometriosis*.

Supporting Ligaments

The internal reproductive organs of the female are stabilized by a number of supporting ligaments (Figure 30-9). The cord-like **ovarian ligament** supports the position of the ovary relative to the uterus. Another cord-like ligament (**suspensory ligament of ovary**) attaches the ovary to the body wall. A sheet-like band of connective tissue called the **broad ligament** connects the uterus, ovaries and uterine tubes. The **mesovarium** is a thin portion supporting the ovaries, and the **mesometrium** is a wide portion supporting the uterus. In addition to these, two more cord-like ligaments support the uterus: the *round ligament* attaches the uterus to the anterior body wall and the *uterosacral ligament* attaches the uterus to the posterior body wall.

Female Breasts

In addition to receiving the male gamete and providing the fertilized egg with a suitable place to develop, the female body also sustains the life of the postpartum baby for a year or more. This is achieved by producing and supplying the newborn with milk from the mother's mammary glands.

The **mammary glands**, or *breasts*, are present on both men and women; however, the glands are undeveloped in the male. Indeed, the milk-producing lobes of the glands are small and undeveloped in the female as well until pregnancy occurs. During pregnancy, and as long as the mother breast-feeds, the mammary glands will produce a protein- and lactose-rich solution called *milk*. The solution will nourish the newborn infant until he/she can eat solid food.

The breasts of the female are generally filled with adipose tissue giving them a rounded, soft appearance and making the **nipple** more

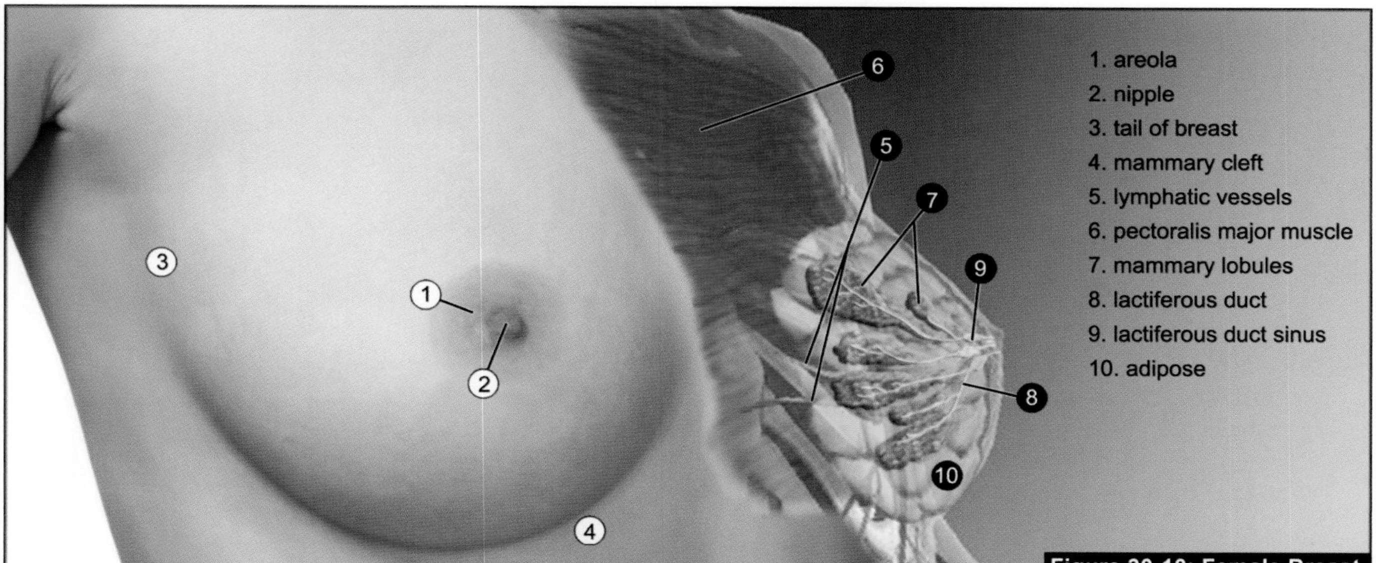

Figure 30-10: Female Breast

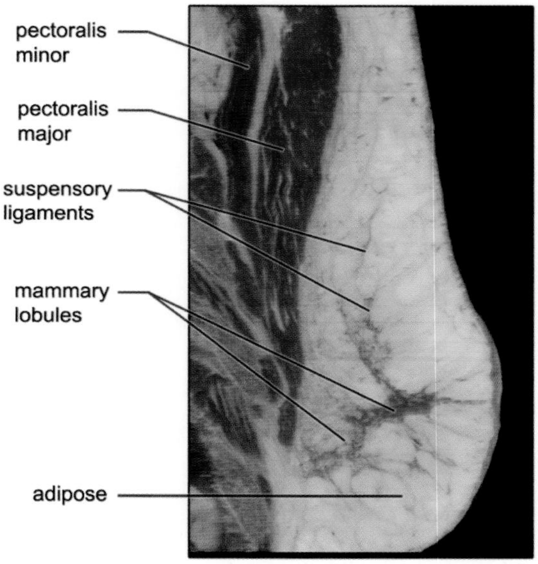

Figure 30-11: Female Breast (Cadaver)

accessible to the baby (Figure 30-10). The nipple is a small protrusion through which the mammary glands secrete their milk. It is surrounded by a pigmented area called the **areola** which increases in pigmentation upon pregnancy. The darkened areola presumably makes the nipple more visible to the newborn.

Internally, each mammary gland consists of 15-25 lobes filled with lobules of **alveoli**. Each breast produces about 1.5 mL of milk per gram of tissue per day. The milk produced by each lobe is drained via a **lactiferous duct** toward the nipple. Just beneath the nipple, each duct enlarges into a **lactiferous sinus** before reaching the body surface.

The breasts are supported by **suspensory ligaments** intertwined between the lobules. These connective tissue ligaments are continuous with the perimysium of the pectoralis major muscle.

Urogenital Homologues

The urogenital homologues are the male and female structures that form from indifferent embryonic structures.

Indifferent	Male	Female
Gonad	Testis	Ovary
Paramesonephric duct	Prostatic utricle (in male urethra)	Uterus, proximal vagina
Mesonephric duct	Epididymis, vas deferens, seminal vesicle, prostate	Periurethral gland, lesser vestibular glands
Urogenital sinus	Bladder, urethra, bulbourethral glands	Bladder, urethra, distal vagina, greater vestibular glands
Genital swelling	Scrotum	Labia majora
Urogenital folds	Distal urethra	Labia minora
Genital tubercle	Penis	Clitoris
Prepuce	Foreskin, bulb of penis, glans penis, crus of penis	Clitoral hood, vestibular bulbs, clitoral glans, clitoral crura

Activity 1: Identify Male Reproductive Structures

1. Using the figures in this exercise and models of the male genitalia, memorize the gross anatomical features of the male reproductive system.

Activity 2: Histology of the Penis

1. Obtain a prepared slide of a cross section of the penis. Under low power, observe the erectile tissues (corpus spongiosum and corpora cavernosa), the urethra, the dorsal blood vessels and the central arteries.
2. Under high power, observe the lumen of the urethra. What type of epithelium is present?

Activity 3: Histology of the Testes

1. Obtain a prepared slide of a cross section of a testis. Observe the seminiferous tubules, interstitial cells between the tubules and developing spermatozoa inside the tubules.

Activity 4: Identify Female Reproductive Structures

1. Using the figures in this exercise and models of the female genitalia, memorize the gross anatomical features of the female reproductive system.

Activity 5: Female Reproductive System Histology

1. Obtain a prepared slide of the ovaries, vagina, uterus and breast tissue.
2. In the uterus, identify the layers of the uterine wall – the endometrium, myometrium and epimetrium (a.k.a., perimetrium or serosa).
3. In the ovary, identify the large follicle that contains the developing egg.

1-7. Label the figure below of male external genitalia.

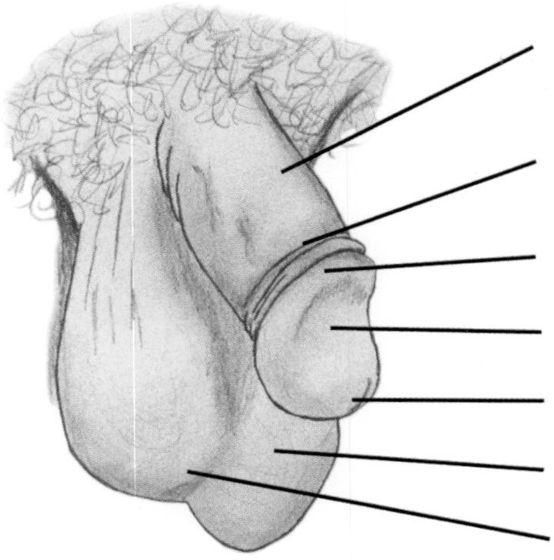

8-19. Label the figure below of male internal genitalia.

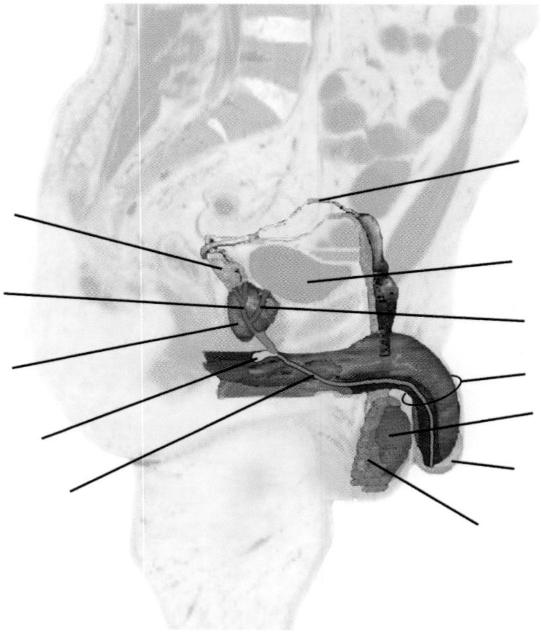

20. What are the two major functions of the testicles?

21. Why are the testes located outside the major body cavities?

22. Surgical removal of the foreskin is called ________________________________.

23. A routine physical examination includes palpation of the prostate gland. How might this be accomplished?

24. A common symptom of an enlarged prostate is difficulty urinating. Why do you think this is so?

25. Which accessory organs are responsible for the production of semen?

26. What structures are found within the spermatic cord?

27. Two muscles in particular contract intensely during ejaculation and contribute to the sensations of male orgasm. Identify these muscles.

28-38. Label the figure below of the female external genitalia.

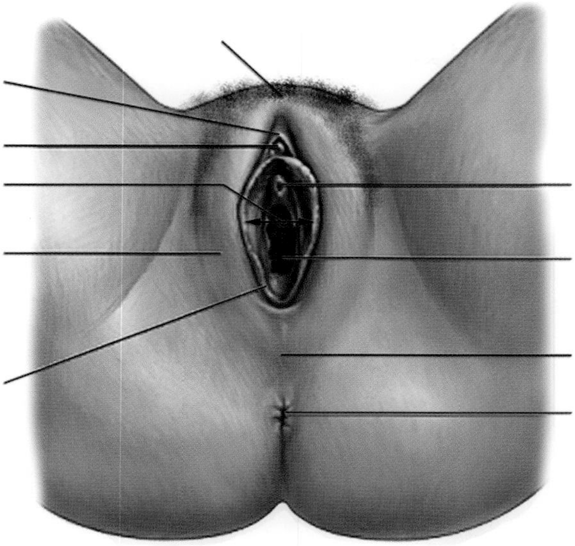

39-48. Label the figure below of the female internal genitalia.

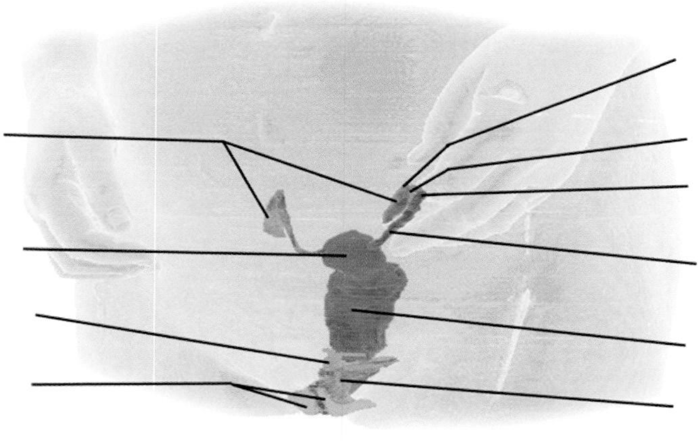

49. Collectively, the external genitalia of the female is called the ____________________________.

50. Where in the female reproductive system does fertilization usually take place?

51. Where does development of the baby occur?

52. Where in the vagina is sperm deposited during intercourse?

53. Which female organ becomes erect during sexual excitement?

54. What are the finger-like projections at the distal ends of the uterine tubes?

55. Is it possible for sperm to enter the abdominopelvic cavity? Why or why not?

56. What is an ectopic pregnancy? How does it occur?

57. Trace the pathway of sperm from their production in the testicles to the fertilized egg.

exercise 31

reproductive PHYSIOLOGY

God blessed them and said to them, "Be fruitful and increase in number; fill the earth and subdue it."

Genesis 1:28

The goal of the reproductive system is to propagate the species. For humans and other sexually reproducing organisms, this is achieved by the joining together of **gametes** (i.e., sperm & egg) during fertilization followed by the nurturing of the baby to adulthood. In both men and women, gametes are produced by a special type of cell division called *meiosis* (recall from Exercise 3 that most cells divide by *mitosis*).

Somatic cells of the body contain two copies of each gene and are said to be *diploid.* Because of meiosis, gametes contain only one copy of each gene and are called *haploid.* When two haploid gametes join at fertilization, a cell with the diploid number of genes is regenerated. This new diploid cell (called a **zygote**) will divide by mitosis many trillions of times to eventually produce a mature human being. Let's begin our discussion of sexual physiology by looking closely at meiosis.

Meiosis

The key differences between mitosis and meiosis are *DNA cross-over* and a *second* round of cell division following the first. DNA is not replicated prior to the second division, so the four daughter cells that result from meiosis are haploid; that is, they possess only one copy of each gene and thus half the DNA content of the parent diploid cell.

Recall that mitosis consists of prophase, anaphase, metaphase and telophase (you should review these events in Exercise 3). Prior to mitosis, the mother cell replicates its DNA. During mitosis, the replicated chromosomes separate and migrate to opposite poles of the cell so that when the mother cell divides the two daughter cells will possess a normal (i.e., diploid) complement of DNA. Thus, one round of DNA replication followed by one round of cell division maintains the normal diploid amount of DNA from mother cell to daughter cells.

Meiosis is similar to mitosis in that one round of DNA replication occurs in the mother cell; it differs in that DNA replication is followed by two rounds of cell division (called meiosis I & meiosis II). During meiosis I, homologous chromosomes are separated and so the daughter cells are *haploid.* During meiosis II, the sister chromatids are separated. Meiosis thus produces *four* daughter cells, each with *half* the normal complement of DNA. Also unique to meiosis, DNA cross-over events occur prior to chromosome separation and first cell division. During DNA cross-over,

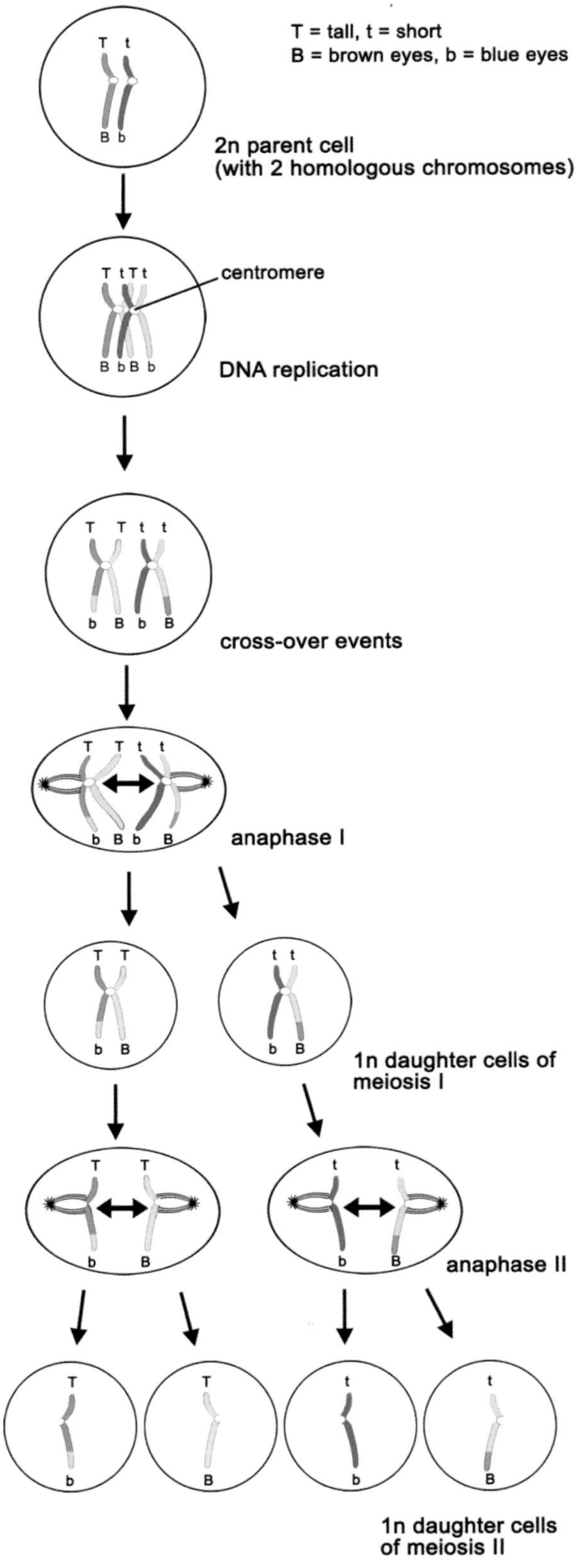

Genetic Events of Meiosis Figure 31-1

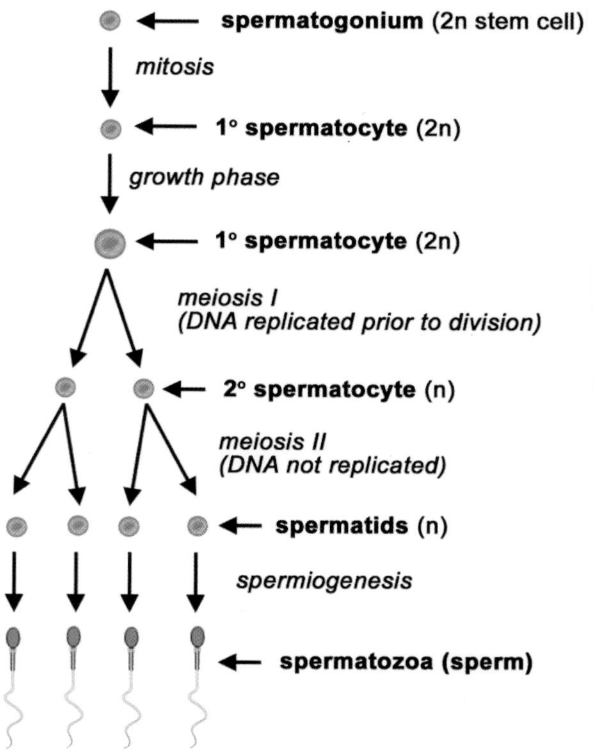

Figure 31-2 **Spermatogenesis**

portions of DNA are swapped between homologous chromosome pairs. Because of this DNA swapping, all of the daughters cells are genetically unique. (In mitosis, the daughter cells are genetic clones of the mother cell). The basic events of meiosis are depicted in Figure 31-1. In the figure, two hypothetical traits (tall/short and brown eyes/blue eyes) are followed through the process. T, t, B, and b represent gene alleles and the expression of certain traits is called *phenotype*. The details of inheritance are discussed in exercise 32.

The haploid cell produced by meiosis is called a *gamete*. Once formed, gametes remain in a form of animated suspension unless two of them (one from the mother, one from the father) are joined during fertilization. Fertilization by the joining of two haploid gametes creates a diploid *zygote*, and a new individual.

Spermatogenesis

The process of sperm development in males is called ***spermatogenesis*** (Figure 31-2). Spermatogenesis occurs prolifically and continuously in each testicle throughout the man's life, producing up to 500 million mature sperm per day.

Spermatogenesis takes place in the seminiferous tubules within the testicles (see Figure 30-3). The process begins when special stem cells called **spermatogonia** divide by mitosis. One daughter cell of this division is called the **primary (1°) spermatocyte**; the other daughter cell replaces the parent stem cell. Following a short growth phase, the 1° spermatocyte undergoes meiosis with its two rounds of cell division. DNA is replicated before the first cell division (meiosis I), but the homologous chromosomes are separated, leaving the two daughter cells of meiosis I haploid (and genetically unique due to DNA cross-over). The daughter cells of meiosis I are called **secondary (2°) spermatocytes**. Each 2° spermatocyte undergoes another round of cell division (meiosis II). The four resulting daughter cells are called **spermatids**. The undifferentiated spermatids then undergo a process called ***spermiogenesis*** in which they are physically modified into the shape of

Sperm Production	Egg Production
begins at puberty	begins before birth
continuous (500 million/day)	cyclic (1/month)
meiosis I & II unterrupted	both meiosis I & II interrupted
complete before fertilization	completed only after fertilization
four haploid spermatozoa per stem cell	one haploid ovum per stem cell
sperm cell physically small with a tail, but virtually no cytoplasm, organelles or nutrients	egg cell physically enormous with vast stores of nutrients, organelles, and cytoplasm

Table 31.1 **Spermatogenesis vs Oogenesis**

mature sperm cells, or **spermatozoa** (see Figure 30-5). Although physically mature, spermatozoa are still incapable of swimming and will be unable to do so until mixed with semen during ejaculation. Physically mature sperm may be stored in the body for months. If not ejaculated, they are destroyed and their components are absorbed and recycled.

Oogenesis

The production of the female gamete is called ***oogenesis***. The process takes place in the ovaries and differs dramatically compared to spermatogenesis. The major differences are discussed below and summarized in Table 31.1.

Sperm production in the man doesn't begin until puberty. By contrast, egg production in women begins before birth in the female infant! Division of sperm stem cells happens continuously throughout a man's life, producing up to 500 million sperm per day. Divisions of egg stem cells (**oogonia**) occur before birth to produce just 2 million **primary (1°) oocytes**. Division of oogonia does not occur after birth and only about 100,000 primary oocytes will remain in the ovaries by the onset of puberty. Meiosis I and II occur quickly in the male (usually less than 3 months); all of the 1° oocytes in the female are arrested in prophase of meiosis I for many years, even decades. Millions of secondary spermatocytes complete meiosis II daily to become fully mature sperm; each month only one (or a few) **secondary oocyte** enters meiosis II in the ovary, and meiosis II will only be completed *if* fertilization occurs. In spermatogenesis four haploid sperm are produced from a single primary spermatocyte; only one haploid egg cell is produced from a primary oocyte. The other three daughter cells (called **polar bodies**) spontaneously decompose. Finally, the physical differences between a mature sperm cell and a mature egg cell (i.e., the **ovum**) couldn't be more different. Sperm are extremely small, lack most organelles, contain virtually no cytoplasm and possess a long, whip-like flagellum for swimming. Egg cells are extremely large (the only human cells visible to the naked eye), contain an enormous volume of cytoplasm with numerous organelles and a large store of nutrients, but they cannot swim.

The events of oogenesis are shown in figure 31-3.

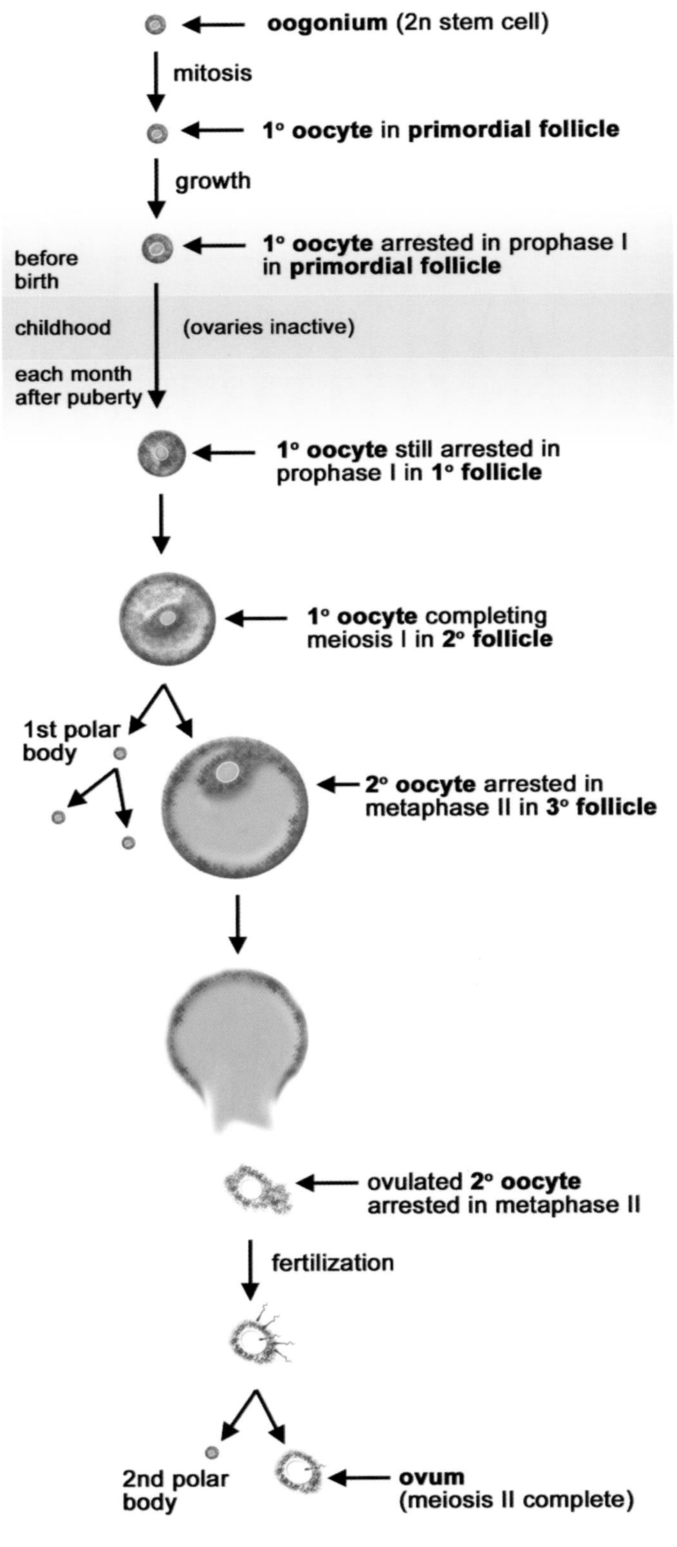

Oogenesis Figure 31-3

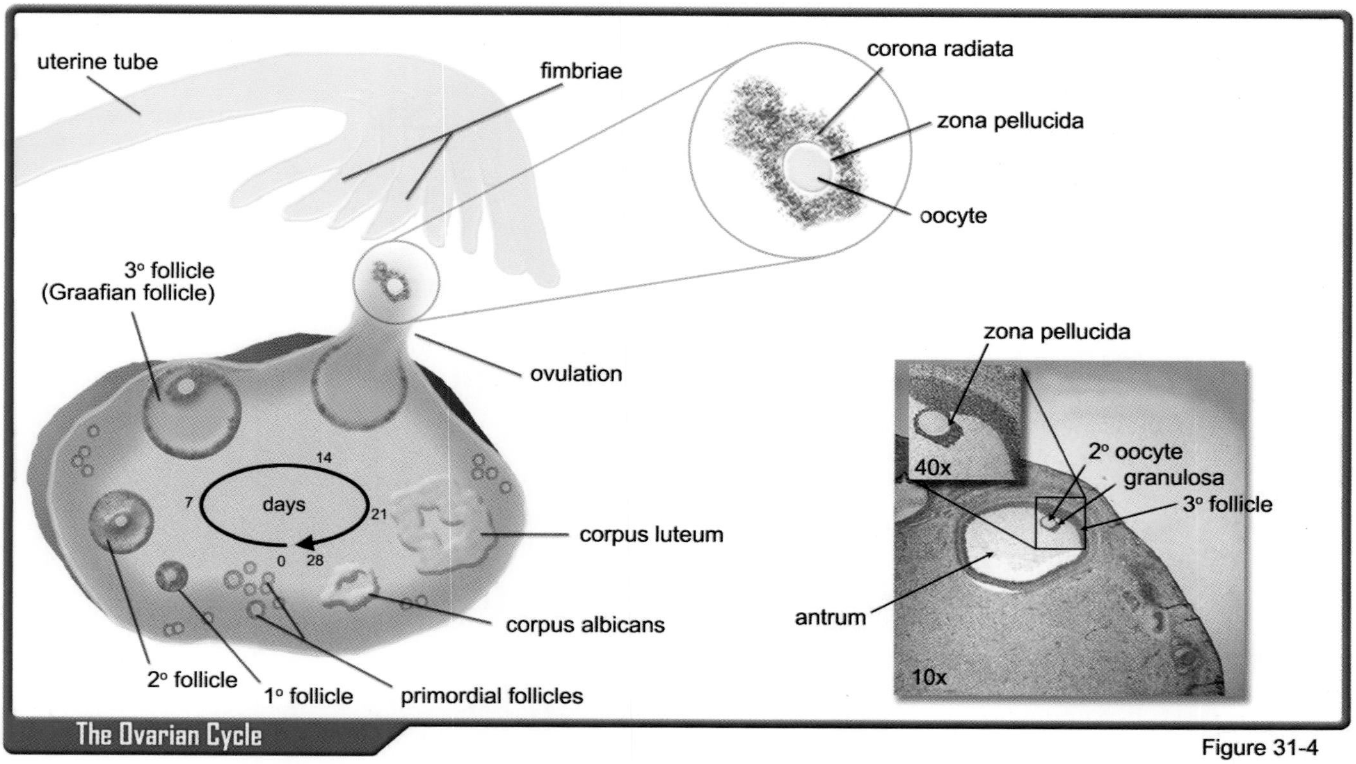

Figure 31-4

The Female Reproductive Cycle

The maturation of one egg cell per month is regulated by a complex cycle of biochemical events called the ***female reproductive cycle***, or ***menstrual cycle***. The menstrual cycle is actually the coordination of two interdependent cycles: the ***ovarian cycle*** and the ***uterine cycle***. The goal of the menstrual cycle is to produce a mature egg and deliver it to a prepared uterus. Timing is crucial; if the uterus is not prepared for implantation[1] a successful pregnancy cannot occur. Alternatively, if the uterus is prepared for implantation at a time when the ovaries are not releasing eggs, then no pregnancy can occur. A successful pregnancy can only happen when the uterus is prepared for implantation at the same time the egg is released from the ovary.

[1] Implantation only occurs when an egg is fertilized, which normally occurs as the egg is traveling from the ovary through the uterine tube toward the uterus.

The Ovarian Cycle

The ovarian cycle concerns the cyclic events occuring in the ovaries each month as part of the 28-day menstrual cycle. These events are depicted in figure 31-4.

At puberty, each ovary contains about 100,000 **primordial follicles**, each of which contains a **primary oocyte** suspended in prophase of meiosis I. Each month, at day 0 of the cycle, about one dozen primordial follicles are randomly selected to continue meiosis I and develop into **primary follicles**. Only a few of those will become **secondary follicles** and only one will become a **tertiary follicle** (or, *Graafian follicle*). The tertiary follicle contains a **secondary oocyte** arrested in metaphase of meiosis II and produces the sex hormone estrogen. This oocyte is released from the ovary at about day 14 of the cycle in a process called ***ovulation***. Upon release from the ovary, the secondary oocyte is momentarily free in the abdominopelvic cavity but is quickly swept into the uterine tube. The remains of the tertiary follicle transform into a **corpus luteum** under the influence of luteinizing hormone from the pituitary gland. The corpus luteum produces the hormone progesterone for about 10 days until it spontaneously decomposes into a small white scar called the **corpus albicans**. By day 28, this cycle is complete and ready to start again.

The Uterine Cycle

While the ovary produces and releases the oocyte, the uterus simultaneously prepares for the arriving egg via the uterine cycle. Under the influence of estrogen (produced by the developing follicle in the ovary), the endometrium of the uterus thickens during the **proliferative phase** of the uterine cycle (corresponding to the second week of the menstrual cycle). During this time the **functional layer** of the endometrium also becomes highly vascular. During the last two weeks of the menstrual cycle the endometrium develops numerous glands that increase in activity. These events of the **secretory phase** are triggered primarily by progesterone from the corpus luteum. If fertilization occurs the developing fetus produces progesterone and other hormones that sustain the corpus luteum and maintain the endometrium. If fertilization does not occur, the decline in progesterone and estrogen triggers **menses**, or shedding of the endometrium. Menses, occuring during the first week of the menstrual cycle, is characterized by bleeding because of the rich vascular supply developed in the endometrium during the proliferative phase. By the end of the first week of the menstrual cycle, estrogen from the next developing follicle rises to high enough levels to switch the uterus from menses to the next proliferative phase. Histological examination of the endometrium at each phase is shown in figure 31-5.

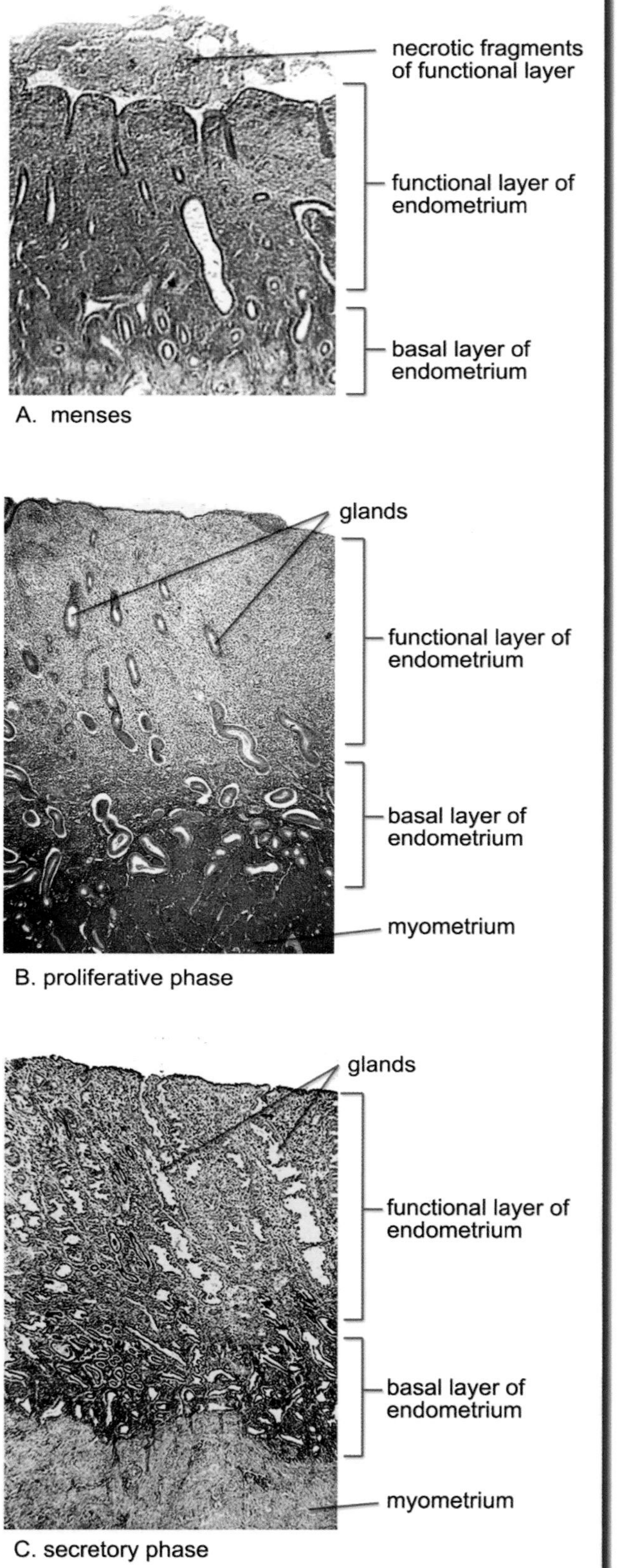

Figure 31-5

The Menstrual Cycle

As stated before, the menstrual cycle is actually the coordination of the ovarian cycle in the ovaries and the uterine cycle in the uterus. These complex events are regulated by hormones produced by the ovaries, the pituitary gland and the hypothalamus. The interdependency of these organs on their production and response to hormones makes a straightforward analysis of the menstrual cycle difficult (unlike, for example, the TCA cylce). To fully understand the cycle, pay close attention to the cause-and-effect relationships between these endocrine organs and their hormones as discussed below and shown in figure 31-6.

The menstrual cycle is a 28-day event. Figure 31-6 is a type of graph in which the 28 days

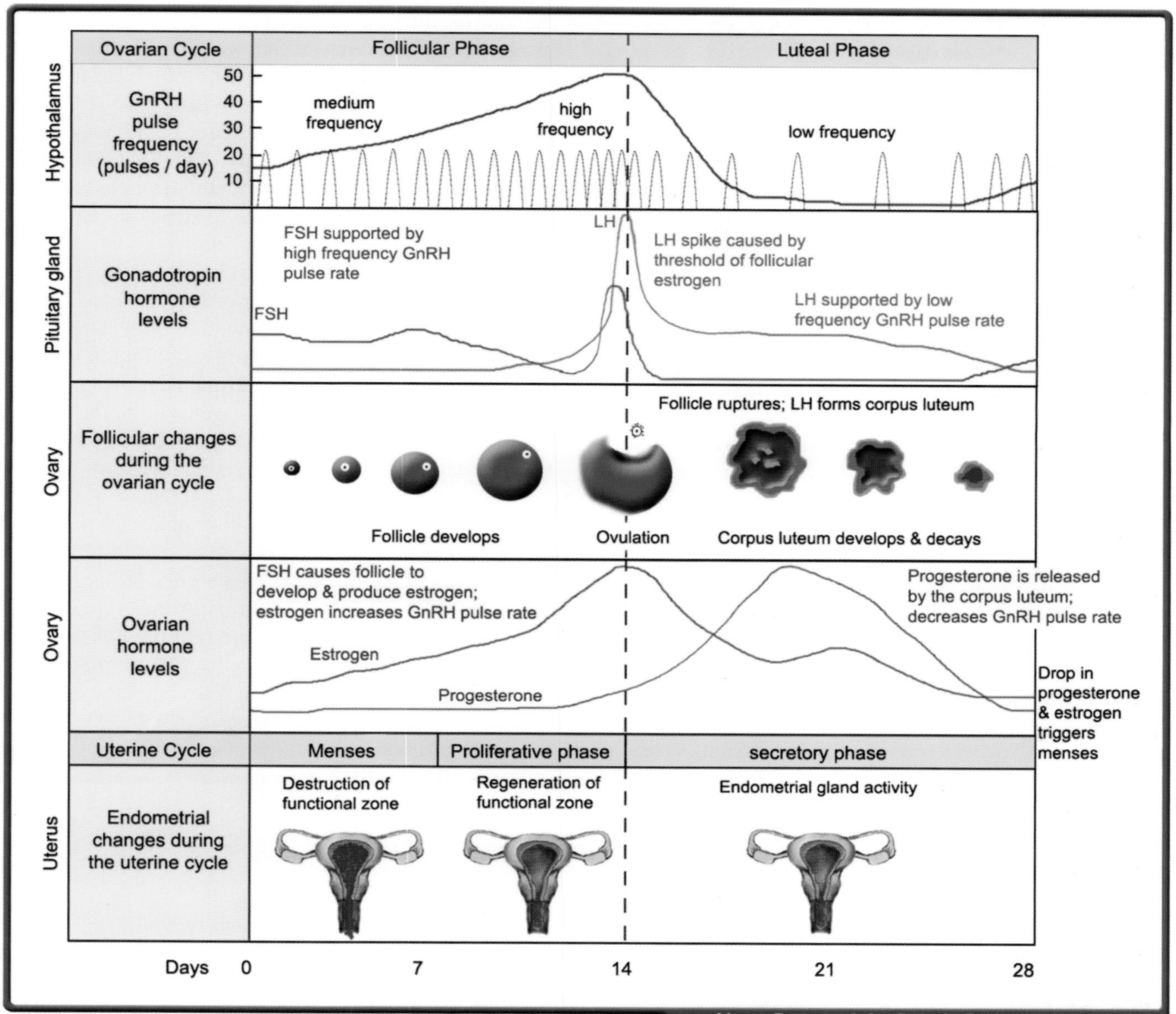

Figure 31-6

Major Events of the Female Reproductive Cycle

of the menstrual cycle are depicted on the x-axis and the organs involved are depicted on the y-axis. The graph illustrates what is happening in each of these organs throughout the 28-day cycle.

The hypothalamus secretes *gonadotropin releasing hormone* (GnRH) which ultimately regulates the whole cycle. Secretion of GnRH is never continuous but comes in pulses, ranging from as little as 2 pulses per day to as many as 50 pulses per day. The target of GnRH is the pituitary gland, which monitors the pulse rate of incoming GnRH. Just as a radio emits different music when tuned to different frequencies, the pituitary gland responds uniquely to different frequencies of GnRH. At medium to high frequences of GnRH the pituitary gland releases *follicle stimulating hormone* (FSH). In response to FSH, primordial follicles in the ovary develop into 1°, 2° and finally a 3° follicle. During the two weeks the follicle develops in the ovary it releases increasing amounts of *estrogen*. The hypothalamus responds to estrogen by increasing the pulse frequency of GnRH release (note how the lines for estrogen and GnRH pulse rate increase together during the first two weeks of the cycle). When the GnRH pulse rate reaches a high threshold frequency around day 14, the pituitary gland responds by releasing a surge of *luteinizing hormone* (LH). The ovary responds to the sudden high dose of LH by rupturing the 3° follicle and ejecting the oocyte (i.e., ovulation). Following

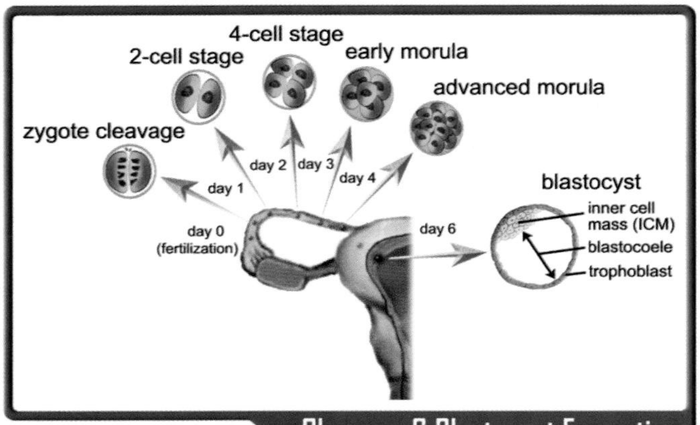

Figure 31-7 **Cleavage & Blastocyst Formation**

rupture, the follicle quits producing estrogen and transforms (under the enfluence of LH) into the corpus luteum, which begins making the hormone *progesterone*. With the loss of estrogen the pulse frequency of GnRH declines. Additionally, progesterone has the opposite effect of estrogen on GnRH release, so increasing levels of progesterone dramatically inhibit the frequency of GnRH. The pituitary gland responds to low GnRH frequency by producing more LH than FSH, which maintains the corpus luteum in the ovary. Despite this, over the course of the last two weeks of the menstrual cycle the corpus luteum decays. The resultant decline in progesterone removes inhibition of GnRH pulse frequency, which then begins to climb. Near the end of the cycle the pulses climb from low to medium frequency and the pituitary gland responds by releasing FSH instead of LH. The FSH begins the development of the next month's follicle with its rise in estrogen and positive feedback on GnRH release.

Throughout the above discussion we neglected the uterus. The uterus does not produce any hormones, but it does respond to both estrogen and progesterone. Menses is triggered by the low levels of estrogen and progesterone near the end of the cycle. Rising levels of estrogen switch the uterus from menses to the proliferative phase around day 7 of the cycle and rising levels of progesterone switch the uterus from the proliferative phase to the secretory phase after ovulation.

Each month every female goes through the above cycle of events. Most months these events continue unabated in a rhythmic fashion, but the cycle will halt if pregnancy occurs. Throughout pregnancy the ovaries suspend releasing new eggs and the uterus never enters menses. Not surprisingly, however, a host of other changes occur

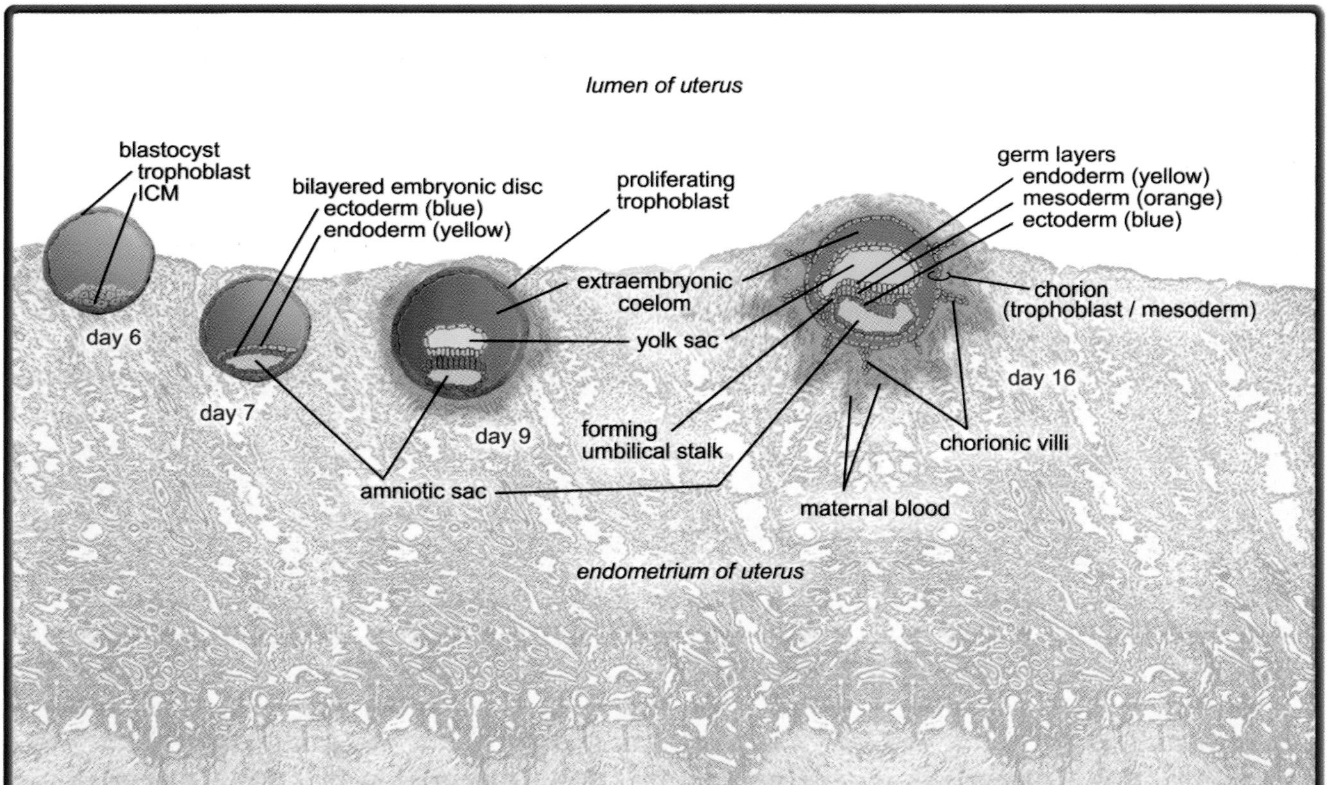

Figure 31-8 **Early Embryonic Development**

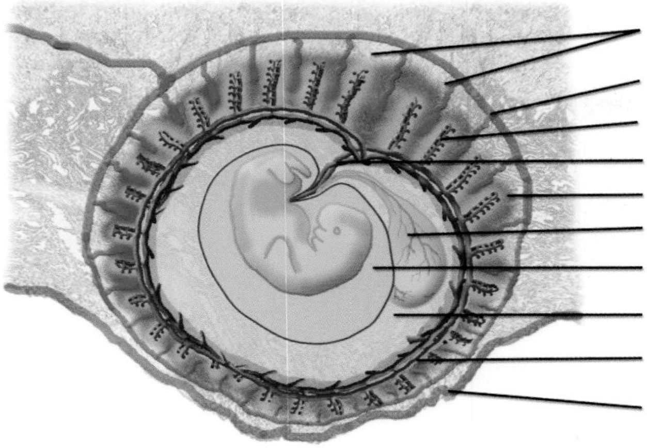

Figure 31-9

Embryo at 4½ Weeks

in the uterus as the fertilized egg implants and the baby begins development.

Early Embryology

Fertilization usually occurs within 24 hours after ovulation, about mid-way through the uterine tube. Although roughly 200 million sperm are released into the vagina during a single ejaculation, only about 10,000 will enter the uterus, just 1 or 2 dozen will reach the oocyte and only 1 will penetrate the oocyte's protective covering to fertilize it. Once the sperm has entered the oocyte, it is stimulated to complete meiosis II and become a mature ovum. The 23 chromosomes of the ovum then pair up with the 23 chromosomes from the sperm (a process called *amphimixis*) and a new individual is created. The single-cell fertilized egg, now called a **zygote**, continues its journey to the uterus; it will take about 6 days to complete the journey.

During the 6-day voyage to the uterus the zygote divides several times and begins development (Figure 31-7). The first cell division is called ***cleavage*** and results in the zygote entering the **2-cell stage**. Another round of cell division leads to the **4-cell stage** and additional divisions over the next few days produce a **morulla** consisting of 8, 16, 32, 64, 128 and then 256 cells. The morulla is a solid ball of cells that – by all appearances – are identical. However, over the next few hours those cells will migrate and form a **blastocyst** with a distinct anatomy.

The blastocyst is a hollow sphere of cells with a clump of cells attached to one point of the inner wall of the sphere. The sphere of cells is called a **trophoblast** and the clump inside is called the **inner cell mass (ICM)**. The open space inside the trophoblast is the **blastocoele**. By the time this structure has formed the blastocyst has reached the uterus. Over the next few days the blastocyst will gently bounce down the wall of the uterine cavity until it decides to implant.

Implantation usually occurs around day 7 after fertilization (Figure 31-8). During this process the blastocyst will stop rolling down the uterine wall with its ICM facing the endometrium. It will then release enzymes that digest a hole in the endometrium and allow the blastocyst to completely bury itself in the uterine wall. Bathed in maternal blood, the blastocyst can now accelerate growth and development utilizing the constant flow of oxygen and nutrients from the mother.

The blastocyst consists of about 1000 cells by the time implantation occurs. By day 7, the ICM has reorganized itself into a bilayer of cells and lifted from the trophoblast creating a cavity called the **amniotic sac**. The embryo will develop inside the protective amniotic sac. The superficial layer of cells (forming the amniotic cavity) are called the **ectoderm**; the deep layer is called the **endoderm**. By day 9, the endodermal cells have created another cavity called the **yolk sac**. By this time there are several thousand cells and soon they will need a circulatory system to supply them with oxygen and nutrients. Consequently, the heart and open blood vessels will develop in the near future (the heart will be beating by day 21). The yolk sac is the initial site of blood formation for the embryo.

After the formation of the yolk sac and amniotic sac, cells from the ectoderm migrate between the ectodermal and endodermal layers creating a third, middle layer called the **mesoderm**. The formation of these three *germ layers* is called

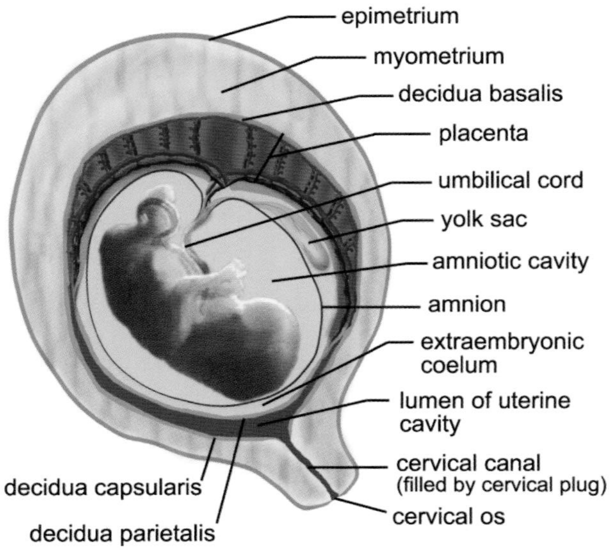

Fetus at 13 Weeks Figure 31-10

gastrulation. Mesodermal cells migrate around the inner wall of the trophoblast and form the **chorion**. Projections of mesodermal cells into the endometrium (called **chorionic villi)** will form the capillary exchange surfaces in the **placenta**.

By 4½ weeks the embryo is large enough to begin bulging out into the lumen of the uterus. Still housed within the amniotic sac, the embryo is now connected to the chorionic villi in the placenta by an umbilical cord. Many body systems, including the cardiovascular, nervous, muscular and integumentary systems are well under development. For more than a week now a heart has been pumping blood produced in the yolk sac through vessels permeating the embryo. By week 9 all body systems are in place and the embryo takes on a more human appearance. From this time until birth it is called a fetus and will rapidly grow in size as the body systems become functional.

Figure 31-10 illustrates a fetus at 13 weeks. By this time the fetus completely fills the uterine cavity and the uterus will expand dramatically throughout the rest of the pregnancy. The endometrium now consists of three divisions: the **decidua basalis** interacts with the chorion and forms part of the placenta, the **decidua capsularis** does not form part of the placenta but covers over the amniotic cavity, and the **decidua parietalis** has no contact with the developing baby (it is essentially the opposing wall across the lumen of the uterus from the fetus).

Explosive growth occurs during the first nine months of your life (Figure 31-11). A baby is born with about 5 trillion cells. The creation of 5 trillion cells over a 9-month period means that 90 billion new cells must be birthed each day, or 750 million per hour, or more than 200,000 new cells per second! Beginning with the single-celled zygote, each cell division doubles the number of cells. Eight cell doublings have occurred by implantation, thirty cell doublings have occurred by week 8 (embryo → fetus), forty-one cell doublings have occurred by birth. After birth, just three more cell doublings will occur by age 5 and a mere one more cell doubling will occur by age 20.

Activity 1: Examine Events of Spermatogenesis

1. Using histology slides of the testes, microscopically examine the development of sperm inside the seminiferous tubules. Note the spermatogonia and sustenacular cells along the inner wall of each tubule.
2. As spermatogonia divide, their daughter cells are pushed toward the lumen of the tubule. Note the layers of cells undergoing meiosis. The innermost layer of undifferentiated cells

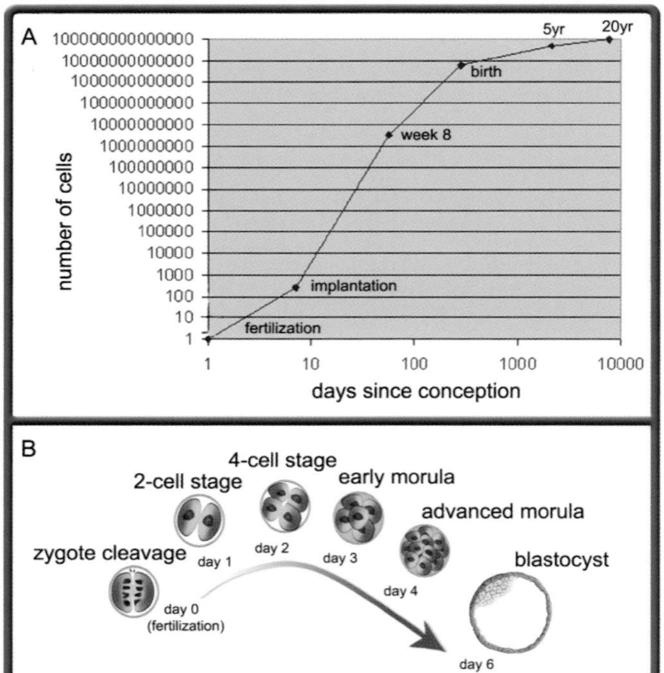

# of cell doublings	by
8	implantation
30	8 weeks
41	birth
44	kindergarten (age 5)
45	college (age 20)

Figure 31-11 **Human Growth Rate**

are the spermatids. Deep to the spermatids you should see flagella emerging from maturing sperm undergoing spermiogenesis.

Activity 2: Examine Events of Oogenesis

It is possible to examine follicles at different stages of development within a single ovary.

1. Obtain a prepared microscope slide of ovary tissue and scan the organ for primary follicles – usually a simple layer of cuboidal cells surrounding a single developing oocyte.
2. Secondary follicles are a little bigger than primary follicles. They consists of several layers of cells (granulosa) surrounding the oocyte. Signs of the antrum – a fluid-filled cavity – should be evident.
3. The tertiary follicle is large and prominent. It consists of an oocyte surrounded by granular cells called the corona radiata. Between the corona radiata and the oocyte is a clear layer called the zona pellucida. The antrum is quite large.

Activity 3: Histological Examination of the Uterus

1. Obtain prepared slides of the uterus from various phases of the uterine cycle. Observe the relatively thickness of the functional layer of the endometrium to the basalar layer and myometrium. Also note the many blood vessels and glands that develop during the proliferative and secretory phases.

Activity 4: Examine a Preserved Fetus

1. Examine the preserved human fetus supplied by the lab instructor. Note the placenta, umbilical cord and highly developed anatomy of the fetus. Compare the fetal side vs. the maternal side of the placenta.

1. Mitosis and meiosis are two different types of cell divisions; however, they share certain features. Determine whether the descriptions below describe (a) only mitosis, (b) only meiosis, or (c) both mitosis and meiosis.

a. ________ Produces two genetically-identical diploid daughter cells

b. ________ Produces two genetically-unique diploid daughter cells

c. ________ Produces four haploid daughter cells

d. ________ Consists of prophase, metaphase, anaphase and telophase

e. ________ Occurs throughout the body

f. ________ DNA is replicated prior to cell division

g. ________ Occurs only in germ cells

2. How is genetic diversity assured in meiosis?

3. In what ways do spermatogenesis and oogenesis differ?

4. The ovarian cycle takes 28 days (i.e., 4 weeks) to complete.

a. Describe the major event(s) of the 1st week of the ovarian cycle.

b. Describe the major event(s) of the 2nd week of the ovarian cycle.

c. Describe the major event(s) of the 3rd week of the ovarian cycle.

d. Describe the major event(s) of the 4th week of the ovarian cycle.

5. Describe the appearance of the uterine endometrium during

   a. the proliferative phase

   b. the secretory phase

   c. menses

6. What role do the following hormones play in the menstrual cycle?

   a. GnRH

   b. FSH

   c. LH

   d. Estrogen

   e. Progesterone

   f. Testosterone

7. In the space below draw and label a blastocyst.

8. Match the terms with their correct definitions or descriptors.

a. Gastrulation	ectoderm, mesoderm & endoderm
b. Morulla	protective sac in which the embryo develops
c. Yolk sac	formation of the germ layers
d. Germ layers	site of nutrient exchange between mother and baby
e. Amnionic sac	initial site of blood formation
f. Placenta	a solid ball of cells formed shortly after fertilization

9. What are the differences between the (a) decidual capsularis, (b) decidua basalis and (c) decidua parietalis?

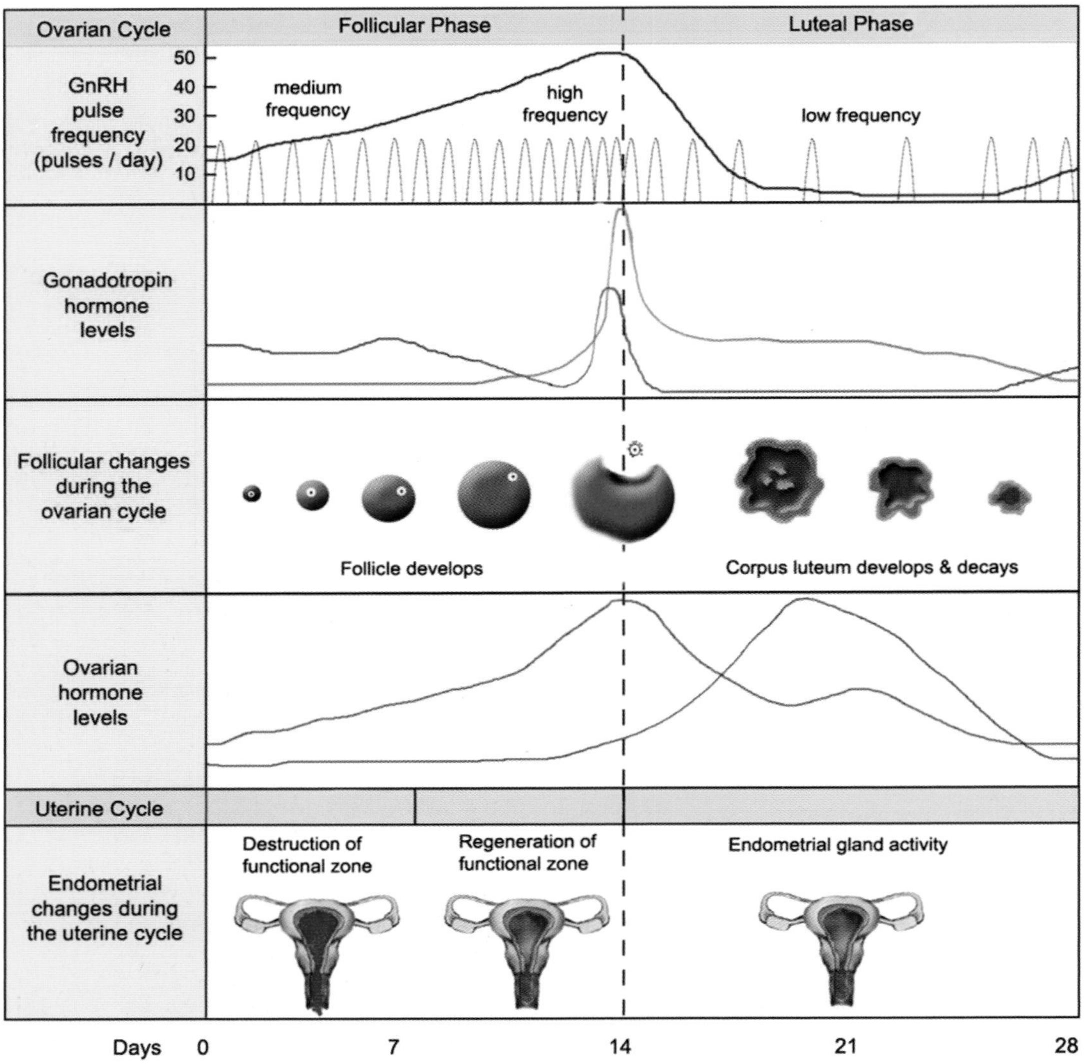
Ovarian Cycle
Follicular Phase
Luteal Phase
GnRH pulse frequency (pulses / day)
50
40
30
20
10
medium frequency
high frequency
low frequency
Gonadotropin hormone levels
Follicular changes during the ovarian cycle
Follicle develops
Corpus luteum develops & decays
Ovarian hormone levels
Uterine Cycle
Endometrial changes during the uterine cycle
Destruction of functional zone
Regeneration of functional zone
Endometrial gland activity
Days
0
7
14
21
28

exercise 32

principles of HEREDITY

The days of the blameless are known to the LORD, and their inheritance will endure forever.

Psalm 37:18

The basic principles of heredity were worked out by Gregor Johann Mendel in the mid-1800's (Figure 32-1). Mendel, now known as the father of genetics, was an Austrian monk who performed his historic experiments in the abbey's garden. Using the pea plant, he examined 17 distinct traits in some 29,000 peas, closely following the expression of those traits from parent to offspring. His observations led him to deduce two laws governing inheritance: the *law of segregation* and the *law of independent assortment*. Keep in mind that during Mendel's studies the cell had just recently been discovered and the structure and role of DNA would not be appreciated for nearly 100 more years!

Figure 32-1 **Gregor Mendel (1822-1884)**

Law of Segregation

The Law of Segregation (a.k.a., Mendel's First Law) makes three assertions:

1. Multiple versions of **genes**[1] produce the observed variations in inherited traits. This introduced the concept of **alleles**, or different versions of the same gene. For example, Mendel observed two alleles for a gene for surface texture in peas: wrinkled and smooth.
2. For each trait, an organism inherits two alleles (i.e., two copies of each gene which may or may not be the same), one from each parent. If the two alleles are the same, the individual is **homozygous**; if the two alleles are different, the individual is **heterozygous**.
3. The two alleles for each trait segregate during gamete formation. Thus, each gamete contains only one allele for a given gene (i.e., they are haploid). When two gametes join during fertilization, the diploid state is restored (i.e., two alleles for each gene) in the zygote.

Law of Independent Assortment

The Law of Independent Assortment (a.k.a., Mendel's Second Law) states that the inheritance pattern of one trait is independent of the inheritance pattern of another trait. For example, Mendel observed that the inheritance pattern of wrinkled vs smooth surface texture for peas was independent of the trait for pea color (green vs yellow).

Mendel's second law is technically only true for genes that are not *linked*, or found on the same chromosome. Often, different traits whose genes are located on the same chromosome are, in fact, inherited together (not always, however, due to DNA cross-over events, discussed in the previous exercise). A chromosome is shown in figure 32-2, depicting linked heterozygous and homozygous alleles.

Phenotype, Genotype – Dominant, Recessive

A **monohybrid cross** is one in which a single trait is followed from parent to offspring. Figure 32-3 illustrates a monohybrid cross involving dominant & recessive alleles; a cross actually performed by Gregor Mendel.

In Mendel's experiments, a trait he examined was the surface texture of peas. Two varieties of peas were observed: wrinkled and smooth. Mendel noted that when purebred[2]

[1] See Table 32.2 for a list of defined terms.

[2] A purebred always produces the same trait in all offspring. Purebred wrinkled peas always produce

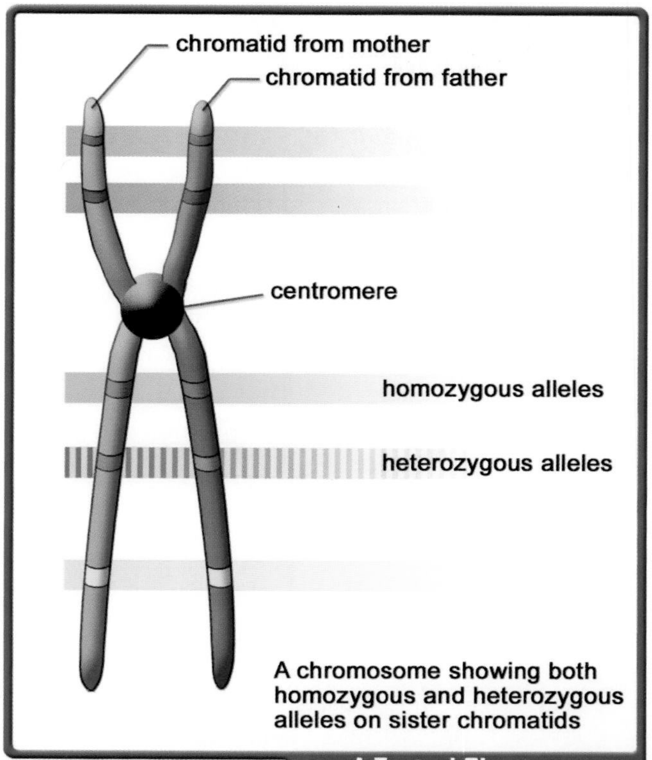

Figure 32-2 A Typical Chromosome

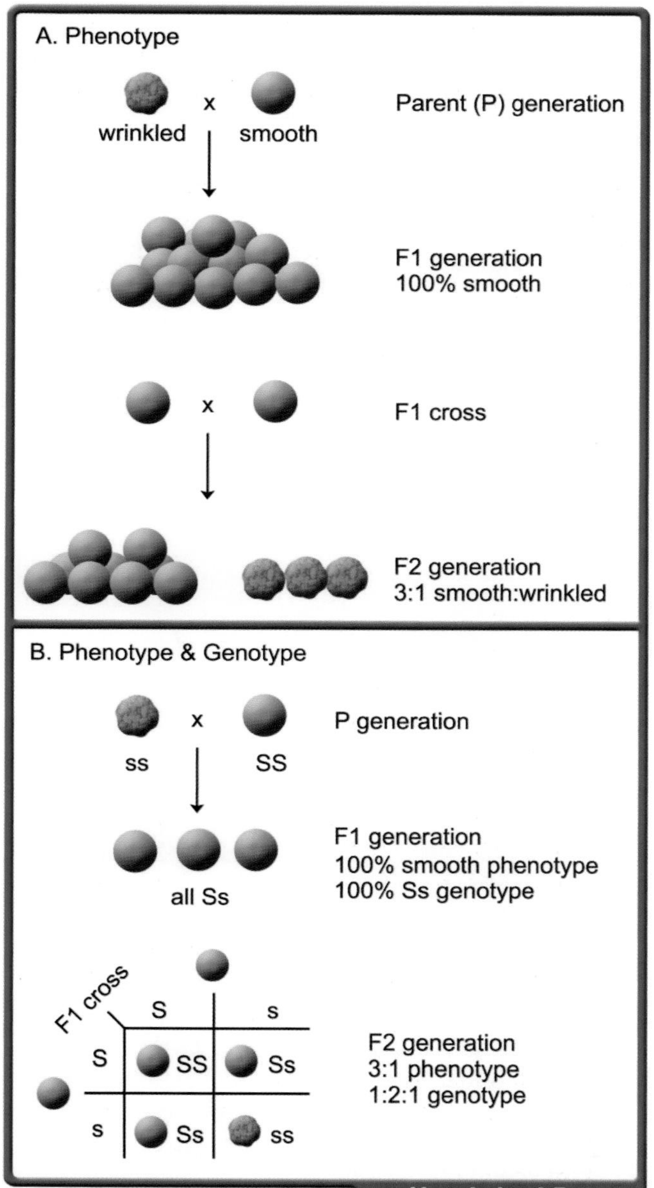

Figure 32-3 Monohybrid Cross

wrinkled plants and purebred smooth plants were crossed, only smooth offspring were produced in the next generation (called the F1 generation). He deduced that the F1 offspring possessed two alleles – one from each parent – but that expression of the smooth allele was dominant over that of the wrinkled allele. When peas of the F1 generation were crossed, he observed both smooth and wrinkled offspring always in a 3:1 ratio.

Using a Punnett square we can see why these results were obtained by Mendel. If we denote "S" as the allele for smooth surface and "s" as the allele for wrinkled surface, then every plant in the F1 generation must have the **genotype** Ss. Their **phenotype** is "smooth surface" because expression of S is dominant to s. When two F1 plants are crossed (Ss x Ss) we determine the following possible genotypes using the Punnett square: SS, Ss, Ss, ss. This explains the 3:1 ratio because any plant with the S allele will have smooth peas and only one of the four possibilities has no S allele.

Gregor Mendel also examine two traits simultaneously: wrinkled vs smooth surface and yellow vs green color (Figure 32-4). Crossing purebreds of two traits is called a **dihybrid cross**. When Mendel crossed purebred yellow-smooth with purebred green-wrinkled, he again observed a single phenotype in the F1 generation (yellow-smooth). He concluded that the genotype of this generation was YySs. When he crossed F1 plants Mendel observed offspring of every possible combination of color and texture, but always with the fixed ratio 9:3:3:1 as indicated in figure 32-4. According to the rules of probability, this is exactly what you would expect to see if each trait was inherited independently of the other. (In both cases, a monohybrid cross yields F2 offspring of 3:1 ratios).

wrinkled offspring; purebred smooth peas always produce smooth offspring.

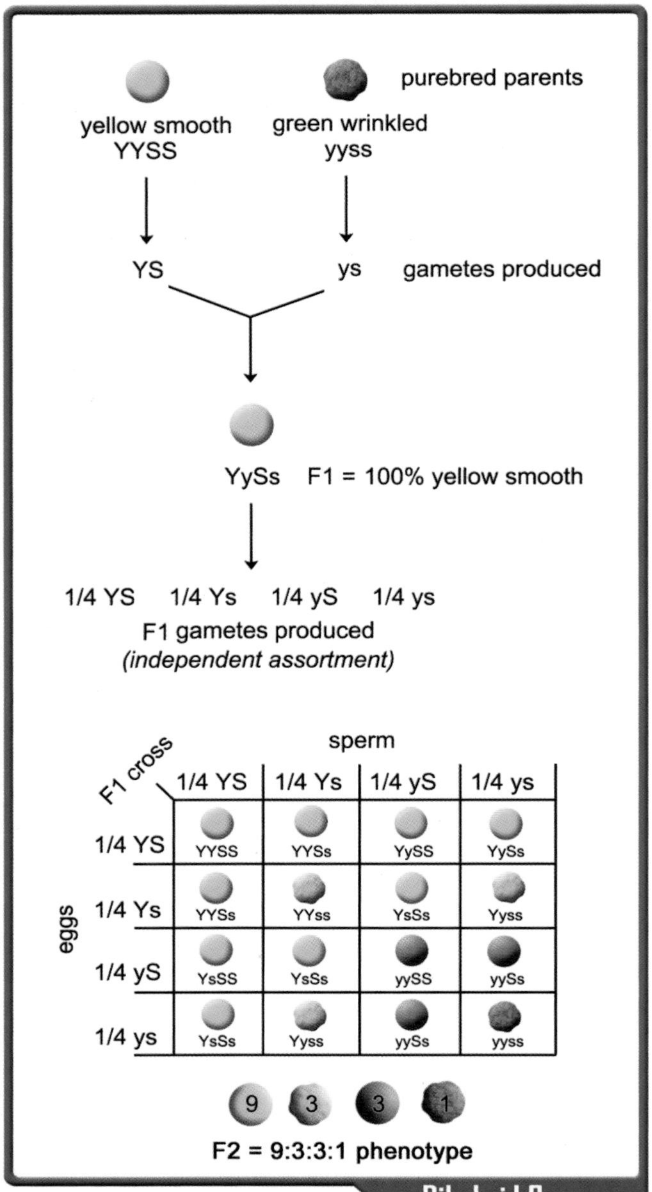

Figure 32-4 **Dihybrid Cross**

Mendel's laws of segregation and independent assortment can also be seen on Figure 31-1 as they occur during the events of meiosis.

Incomplete Dominance & Codominance

The examples above illustrate the principle of dominant-recessive alleles; however, not all alleles display such a dominant-recessive relationship. For example, flower color in some plants exhibits **incomplete dominance**. In such cases heterozygotes express both alleles, usually with a

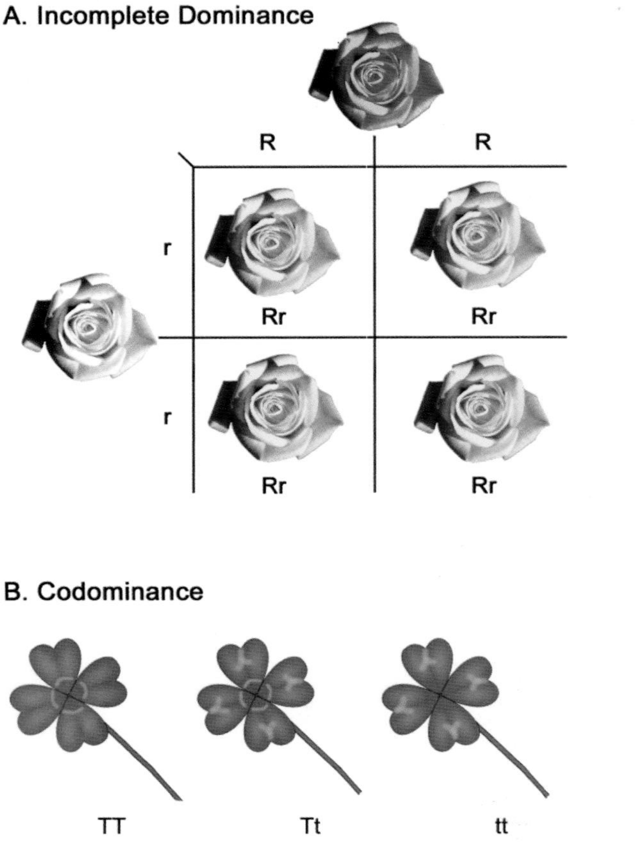

Figure 32-5 **Incomplete & Codominance**

blended phenotype. In the example in figure 32-5A, a plant with red flowers is crossed with a plant with white flowers and all the F1 plants display pink flowers. In other cases, the two alleles may both be expressed producing their own distinct phenotypes as shown in figure 32-5B. This is called **codominance**.

DNA: The Agent of Heredity

The results obtained by Mendel can now be easily understood with our modern knowledge of **DNA** (deoxyribonucleic acid). The traits we observe are due to the expression of proteins and the instructions to make proteins are encoded within DNA. A gene can thus be understood as the region of DNA encoding a specific protein product. DNA itself is an extremely long molecule composed of repeating units of four unique *bases* (called A, T, G and C). The arrangement of the bases is used to encode information, similar to the way we arrange letters of the alphabet to make a sentence (or binary

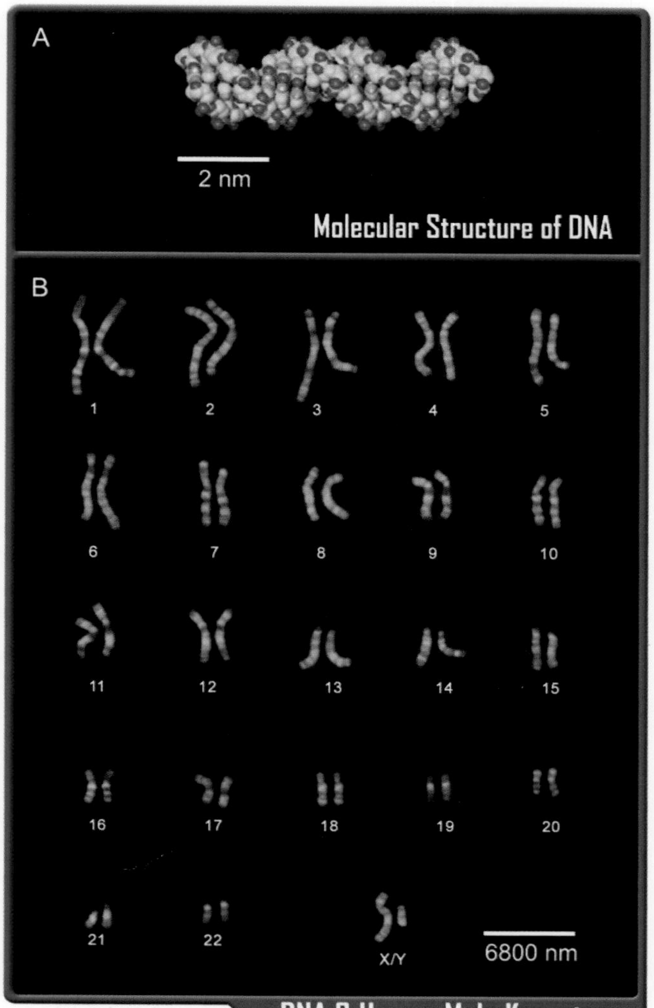

Figure 32-6 DNA & Human Male Karyotype

digits are arranged to encode a computer program). DNA represents the most densly-packed store of information in the known universe: Within the nucleus of every human cell is the information to construct an entire person. The human nucleus contains 46 strands of DNA coiled into super-structures called chromosomes (actually, there are 23 chromosomes pairs). Each generation, those chromosomes are replicated and segregated to the daughter cells – amazingly – without any apparent tangling. Try doing that with 46 extension cords!

Figure 32-6 shows a small portion of a DNA molecule and a **karyotype**, or the full complement of chromosomes from a human (in this case, a human male). Twenty-two of the chromosomes contain homologous chromatids; the twenty-third pair consists of the sex chromosomes. The female chromosome is designated X, the male chromosome is Y. Thus, a woman has the genotype XX and a man the genotype XY.

Sex-Linked Inheritance

As stated above, 22 of the 23 chromosomes are identical in both men and women. These are called the *autosomes*. The 23rd pair consists of the *sex chromosomes* which determine the gender of the individual. The Y chromosome, which confers maleness, is considerably smaller than the X chromosome and only contains genes specific for the male phenotype; there are a considerable number of genes on the larger X chromosome that are not found on the Y chromosome. Woman – genotype XX – have two copies of the X genes just as they have two copies of every gene on the autosomes. Men, however – genotype XY – have only one copy of the X genes. For this reason, genes on the X chromosome (called *sex-linked genes*) are not inherited according to the rules worked out by Mendel. For example, a woman (XX) will display the phenotype of a recessive sex-linked trait only if she has two recessive alleles, but a male (XY) will display the recessive phenotype with just one recessive allele. For this reason, males are more likely to express recessive sex-linked traits than females.

The genes for color interpretation are on the X chromosome and are thus sex-linked. Certain recessive alleles cause color-blindness. The recessive allele on the X chromosome also causes hemophilia. Thus, men are more likely to suffer from color-blindness and hemophilia than are women.

Men cannot pass on sex-linked genes to their sons, but always will to their daughters. Conversely, boys do not receive their sex-linked traits from their fathers but always from their mothers.

Activity 1: Practice with the Punnett Square

1. Figure 32-5A depicts flowers exhibiting incomplete dominance. Using a Punnett square, predict the genotypes and phenotypes of the offspring when two F1 (pink) plants are crossed.

Activity 2: Using Phenotype to Determine Genotype

Determine your phenotype and genotype for the traits listed in Table 32.1. It is impossible to determine whether you're homozygous or heterozygous if you display the dominant phenotype, therefore, list your genotype as *A-* (where "A" represents the symbol for that trait).

1. **PTC taste:** Obtain a PTC taste test strip from your instructor. Chew on the strip. PTC (phenylthiocarbamide) is a harmless chemical that some people can taste and others cannot. If the strip tastes bitter, you are positive for this test and possess at least one dominant allele (*P*) for this trait. If you do not taste the PTC, you are homozygous recessive (*pp*). About 70% of the population has the dominant allele.
2. **Sodium benzoate taste:** Obtain a sodium benzoate taste test strip from your instructor and chew on it. Sodium benzoate is used as a preservative in many foods. If the strip tastes bitter, salty or sweet, then you possess at least one dominant allele (*S*). If you cannot taste the sodium benzoate, you are homozygous recessive (*ss*).
3. **Interlocking fingers:** Clasp your hands together and interlock your fingers. Keeping your hands clasped together, observe your fingers. If your left thumb is uppermost, you possess a dominant allele (*I*). If your right thumb is uppermost, you are homozygous recessive (*ii*).
4. **Sex:** Gender is determined by the X and Y chromosomes. The genotype XX confers the female phenotype; the genotype XY confers the male phenotype.
5. **Dimples:** Dimpled cheeks are associated with the spacing between the zygomaticus major and minor muscles. The occurrence of dimples in one or both cheeks indicates the presence of the dominant allele (*D*). Absence of dimples indicates the homozygous recessive condition (*dd*).
6. **Freckles:** Freckles are clusters of concentrated melanin in the skin. Freckles are the result of a dominant allele (*F*). Absence of freckles indicates the homozygous recessive condition (*ff*).
7. **Blaze:** A blaze is a lock of hair with a different color than the rest of the head. A blaze results from a dominant allele (*B*).
8. **Widow's peak:** A distinct V-shaped hairline on the forehead is described as a widow's peak. It is determined by a dominant allele (*W*). A straight hairline indicates the homozygous recessive condition (*ww*).
9. **Tongue curl:** The ability to curl your tongue longitudinally is a genetic trait. Those with the ability to curl their tongue have the dominant allele (*T*). If you cannot curl your tongue you are homozygous recessive (*tt*).
10. **Attached earlobes:** Have your lab partner examine your earlobes. If your lobes hang free from the side of your head, they are said to be *detached.* If they instead appear to merge seamlessly into the side of your head, they are called *attached.* The detached condition is determined by a dominant allele (*E*); those with attached earlobes are homozygous recessive (*ee*).
11. **Bent pinky finger:** Examine the "pinky" finger on both of your hands. If the terminal phalynx angles towards the ring finger on either hand, you possess the dominant allele (*L*). If your pinky fingers are straight, you are homozygous recessive (*ll*).

Trait	Phenotype	Genotype
PTC taste (P,p)		
sodium benzoate taste (S,s)		
internlocking fingers (I,i)		
sex (X,Y)		
dimples (D,d)		
freckles (F,f)		
blaze (B,b)		
widow's peak (W,w)		
tongue curl (T,t)		
attached earlobe (E,e)		
bent pinky (L,l)		
finger hair (H,h)		
double-jointed thumb (J,j)		

Table 32.1 **Genotype / Phenotype**

Examples of Human Phenotypes Figure 32-7

12. **Finger hair:** The presence of hair on the proximal part of your fingers results from a dominant allele (*H*). If no hair is present on the proximal portions of your fingers, you are homozygous recessive (*hh*).
13. **Double-jointed thumb:** The flexibility of a joint is in part determined by how tight or loose its supporting ligaments are. Relatively loose ligaments in the thumb joint result from a dominant allele (*J*). Tight joints result from the homozygous recessive condition (*jj*).

Term	Definition
gene	A hereditary unit that determines a particular characteristic (trait) in an organism.
allele	One member of a pair of genes that occupy a specific location on a specific chromosome.
chromosome	In eukaryote, a threadlike linear strand of DNA with associated proteins in the nucleus that carries the genes and functions in the transmission of hereditary information.
genotype	The combination of alleles located on homologous chromosomes responsible for a particular characteristic or trait.
phenotype	The observable characteristics of an organism; the expression of a specific trait.
linked genes	Two or more genes located on the same chromosome and usually inherited together.
homozygous	Having the same alleles for a particular gene.
heterozygous	Having different alleles for a particular gene.
dominant trait	A trait that will appear in the offspring if one parent contributes the allele for that trait.
recessive trait	A trait that will appear in the offspring only if both parents contribute the allele for that trait.
incomplete dominance	A heterozygous condition in which both alleles for a given trait are expressed producing an intermediate phenotype.
codominance	A heterozygous condition in which both alleles for a given trait are expressed and distinctly observed.
chromatid	One of two identical strands of DNA making up a chromosome.

Table 32.2

Definitions of Genetic Terms

1. Match the terms with their correct definitions.

allele	a heredity unit that determines a particular trait in an organism
genotype	a trait that will appear in the offspring only if both parents contribute the allele from that trait
dominant trait	one member of a pair of genes that occupy a specific location on a specific chromosome
sex-linked genes	having different alleles for a particular trait
phenotype	the combination of alleles located on homologous chromosomes resposible for a particular trait
gene	the observable characteristics of an organism
recessive trait	genes on the X chromosome
homozygous	a trait that appears if only one parent contributes the allele for that trait
incomplete dominance	having the same alleles for a particular trait
heterozygous	a heterozygous condition in which both alleles for a given trait are expressed producing an intermediate phenotype

2. A heterozygous woman carrying the recessive allele for color-blindness (X^CX^c) marries a color-blind man (X^cY). Using a Punnett square determine the probability of

a) the number of sons likely to be color-blind
b) the number of daughters likely to be color-blind
c) the number of daughters who will be carriers of this trait.

3. A heterozygous woman carrying the recessive allele for hemophilia (X^HX^h) marries a hemophiliac (X^hY). Using a Punnett square determine the probability of

a) the number of sons likely to have hemophilia
b) the number of daughters likely to have hemophilia
c) the number of daughters who will be carriers of this trait.

4. A man (XY) marries a woman (XX). What is the probability that they will conceive a boy? A girl?

Parental genotypes: XX x XY

Probability of a boy: __________ %

Probability of having a girl: __________ %

5. Assume that the gene for eye color has two alleles: a dominant brown allele (B) and a recessive blue allele (b). A blue-eyed man marries a brown-eyed woman. They have four brown-eyed children and one blue-eyed child. What is the genotype of the man and woman?

Genotype of mother: ______________

Genotype of father: ______________

6. Assume the parents in the above question had eight brown-eyed children and no blue-eyed children. What would be the likely genotype of the mother?

Genotype of mother: ______________

7. Hair curl is determined by incomplete dominance. Genotypically, curly hair is CC, wavy hair is Cc and straight hair is cc. What percentage of the various phenotypes would be expected from a cross between a Cc woman and Cc man?

__________ % curly

__________ % wavy

__________ % straight

8. Why do you think consanguineous marriages (marriages between blood relatives) are prohibited in most cultures?

9. What is the probability of a couple having five sons in a row?

10. You have a bent pinky finger and would like to know if your homozygous or heterozygous for this dominant trait.

a) How might you determine this?

b) If you are homozygous, what is the probability that your children will show this trait?

INDEX